THE LOEB CLASSICAL LIBRARY
FOUNDED BY JAMES LOEB 1911

EDITED BY
JEFFREY HENDERSON

EDITOR EMERITUS
G. P. GOOLD

JOSEPHUS
V

LCL 242

JOSEPHUS

JEWISH ANTIQUITIES

BOOKS I–III

WITH AN ENGLISH TRANSLATION BY

H. ST. J. THACKERAY

HARVARD UNIVERSITY PRESS
CAMBRIDGE, MASSACHUSETTS
LONDON, ENGLAND

First published 1930
Reprinted 1957, 1961, 1967, 1978, 1991, 1995
Jewish Antiquities bound in nine volumes beginning 1998
Reprinted 1998, 2001

LOEB CLASSICAL LIBRARY® is a registered trademark
of the President and Fellows of Harvard College

ISBN 0-674-99575-9

*Printed in Great Britain by St Edmundsbury Press Ltd,
Bury St Edmunds, Suffolk, on acid-free paper.
Bound by Hunter & Foulis Ltd, Edinburgh, Scotland.*

CONTENTS

INTRODUCTION vii

THE JEWISH ANTIQUITIES
  BOOK I 2
  BOOK II 168
  BOOK III 320

APPENDIX. ANCIENT TABLE OF CONTENTS 476

INTRODUCTION

THE *Jewish Archaeology*,[a] or, as it is commonly called, the *Jewish Antiquities*, the *magnum opus* of Josephus, presents in many respects a marked contrast to his earlier and finer work, the *Jewish War*. The *War*, written in the prime of life, with surprising rapidity and with all the advantages of imperial patronage, was designed to deter the author's countrymen from further revolt by portraying the invincible might of Rome. The *Archaeology* was the laboured work of middle life; compiled under the oppressive reign of Domitian, the enemy of all literature and of historical writing in particular, it was often apparently laid aside in weariness and only carried to completion through the instigation of others, and with large assistance towards the close; its design was to magnify the Jewish race in the eyes of the Graeco-Roman world by a record of its ancient and glorious history.

The author thus severs his connexion with Roman political propaganda and henceforth figures solely as Jewish historian and apologist. But this severance of Roman ties and adoption of a more patriotic theme

Proem: motives and models. The LXX.

---

[a] For this brief Introduction—limited by considerations of space—I have made use of my Lectures (iii-v) on *Josephus the Man and the Historian* (New York, 1929).

… hardly warrant the suggestion[a] that he was prompted by self-interested motives, hoping thereby to rehabilitate himself with his offended countrymen. The project of writing his nation's history was no new one, having been already conceived when he wrote the *Jewish War*.[b] In an interesting proem he tells us something of the genesis, motives, and difficulties of the task. He had not lightly embarked upon it, and two questions had given him cause for serious reflection, concerning the propriety of the work and the demand for it. Was such a publication consonant with piety and authorized by precedent? Was there a Greek reading public anxious for the information? He found both questions satisfactorily answered in the traditional story of the origin of the Alexandrian version of the Law under king Ptolemy Philadelphus. He, Josephus, would imitate the high priest Eleazar's example in popularizing his nation's antiquities, confident of finding many lovers of learning like-minded with the king; while he would extend the narrative to the long and glorious later history. In this allusion to the legitimacy of paraphrasing the inspired Scriptures, the author is doubtless controverting the views of the contemporary rabbinical schools of Palestine, where the Septuagint version was now in disrepute and men like R. Johanan ben Zakkai and R. Akiba were engaged in building up a fence about the Law. As regards a reading public, he might justly count on a curiosity concerning his nation having been awakened in Rome and elsewhere by the recent war, by the sculptures on the Arch of Titus, and by that religious influence of

[a] Laqueur, *Der jüd. Historiker Flav. Josephus*, p. 260.
[b] *Ant.* i. 6.

INTRODUCTION

the race which was now permeating every household.[a]

Besides the Greek Bible, which Josephus names as in part a precursor of his own work, there was another unacknowledged model, which would have found still less favour in Palestinian circles. In the year 7 B.C. Dionysius of Halicarnassus, like Josephus a migrant from the east to the western capital, had produced in Greek his great Roman history, comprised in twenty books and entitled Ῥωμαϊκὴ Ἀρχαιολογία (*Roman Antiquities*). Exactly a century later Josephus produced his *magnum opus*, also in twenty books and entitled Ἰουδαϊκὴ Ἀρχαιολογία (*Jewish Antiquities*). There can be no doubt that this second work was designed as a counterpart to the first. If, in his *Jewish War*, the author had counselled submission to the conqueror, he would now show that his race had a history comparable, nay in antiquity far superior, to that of Rome. Dionysius had devoted the larger part of his *Archaeology* to the earlier and mythical history of the Roman race: Josephus, on the basis of the Hebrew Scriptures, which were " pure of that unseemly mythology current among others," [b] would carry his history right back to the creation. The influence of the older work may also be traced in a few details. The account of the end of Moses seems to be reminiscent of the record of the " passing " of the two founders of the Roman race, Aeneas and Romulus.[c] From Dionysius, too, probably comes a recurrent formula, relating to incidents of a miraculous or quasi-mythical character, on which the reader is left to form his own opinion.[d] Dionysius

Dionysius of Halicarnassus.

[a] *C. Ap.* ii. 284. [b] *Ant.* i. 15.
[c] *ib.* iv. 326 note. [d] *ib.* i. 108 note.

ix

INTRODUCTION

has also clearly been consulted as a model of style.

Date. In the final paragraph of his work [a] the author tells us that it was completed in the thirteenth year of the reign of Domitian and in the fifty-sixth of his own life, *i.e.* in A.D. 93-94. If it was taken in hand immediately after the publication of the Greek edition of the *Jewish War*, the larger work was some eighteen years in the making. From the concluding paragraphs the further inference may be drawn that the author issued a later edition, to which the *Autobiography* was added as an appendix. For the *Antiquities* contains two perorations, the original conclusion having (like the original preface to a modern work) been relegated to the end, while to this has been prefixed another peroration, mentioning the proposal to append the *Life*.[b] The *Life* alludes [c] to the death of Agrippa II., an event which, according to Photius, occurred in A.D. 100. We may therefore infer that this later and enlarged edition of the *Antiquities* appeared early in the second century.

Patron. The work, like the *Life* and the *Contra Apionem* which followed it, is dedicated to a certain Epaphroditus,[d] the Maecenas whom Josephus found when bereft of his earlier royal patrons, Vespasian and Titus. The name Epaphroditus was not uncommon; but of those who bore it and of whom we have any record, two only come under consideration. Niese [e] and others have identified the patron of Josephus with the freedman and secretary of Nero, who remained with that emperor to the last and assisted

[a] *Ant.* xx. 267.   [b] *ib.* xx. 259-266.   [c] *Vita* 359.
[d] *Ant.* i. 8 f., *Vita* 430, *Ap.* i. 1, ii. 1, 296.
[e] Vol. v. p. iii.

INTRODUCTION

him to put an end to himself—an act for which he was afterwards banished and slain by Domitian, when in terror of designs upon his own life.[a] The philosopher Epictetus was the freedman of this Epaphroditus; and, when Josephus describes his patron as "conversant with large affairs and varying turns of fortune" ($\tau\acute{\upsilon}\chi\alpha\iota\varsigma$ $\pi o\lambda\upsilon\tau\rho\acute{o}\pi o\iota\varsigma$),[b] it is tempting to see an allusion to the part which he had played in the death of Nero. But chronology refutes this identification:

93–94. First edition of the *Antiquities*.

c. 95–96. Banishment and death of Epaphroditus.

Yet the dedication to Epaphroditus reappears both in the *Life* (after 100) and in the *C. Apionem*, which also followed the *Antiquities* and hardly so soon as the year 94–95, as Niese supposes. With far more reason may we identify this new patron with Marcus Mettius Epaphroditus, a grammarian—mentioned by Suidas—who had been trained in Alexandria and spent the latter part of his life, from the reign of Nero to that of Nerva, in Rome, where he amassed a library of 30,000 books and enjoyed a high reputation for learning, especially as a writer on Homer and the Greek poets.[c] To him and to his large library Josephus may well owe some of his learning, in particular that intimate acquaintance with Homeric problems and Greek mythology displayed in the *Contra Apionem*.

The work naturally falls into two nearly equal parts, the dividing-line being the close of the exile reached at the end of Book X. A consideration of

Sources: Scripture.

[a] Dio Cassius, lxvii. 14.
[b] *Ant.* i. 8.   [c] Schürer, *G.J.V.* (ed. 4) i. p. 80 note.

xi

INTRODUCTION

the sources employed for the second half may be reserved for a later volume. For the first half the author is mainly dependent on Scripture and traditional interpretation of Scripture. As a rule he closely follows the order of the Biblical narrative, but he has, with apologies to his countrymen,[a] rearranged and given a condensed digest of the Mosaic code, reserving further details for a later treatise. In the history of the monarchy he has amalgamated the two accounts in *Kings* and *Chronicles*. In general he is faithful to his promise [b] to omit nothing, even the less creditable incidents in his nation's race; the most glaring omission is that of the story of the golden calf and the breaking of the first tables of the Law.[c] Here, as elsewhere,[d] he is concerned, as apologist, to give no handle to current slanders about the Jewish worship of animals. He has employed at least two forms of Biblical text, one Semitic—whether the original Hebrew or Aramaic, for there are indications in places that he is dependent on an early Targum—the other Greek. Throughout the Octateuch his main authority seems to be the Hebrew (or Aramaic) text; the use of the Greek Bible is here slight, and the translation is for the most part his own. For the later historical books the position is reversed: from 1 Samuel to 1 Maccabees the basis of his text is a Greek Bible, and the Semitic text becomes a subsidiary source.

Jewish tradition.

Notwithstanding his repeated assertion [e] that he has added nothing to the Biblical narrative, the historian has in fact incorporated a miscellaneous mass of

[a] *Ant.* iv. 196 ff. [b] *ib.* i. 17, x. 218.
[c] *ib.* iii. 99 note. [d] iii. 126 note.
[e] *ib.* i. 17, x. 218.

INTRODUCTION

traditional lore, forming a collection of first century *Midrash* of considerable value. In the realm of *Haggadah* or legendary amplification of Scripture, we have, for instance, tales of the birth and infancy of Moses [a] and of the Egyptian campaign against Ethiopia under his leadership,[b] which find partial parallels in Rabbinical and Alexandrian writings; other additions of this nature may be illustrated from the *Book of Jubilees* (c. 100 B.C.).[c] In the sphere of *Halakah*—the practical interpretation of the laws according to certain traditional rules, τὰ νόμιμα as Josephus would call them—the detailed exposition of the Mosaic regulations in the present volume [d] affords ample scope for exegesis of this nature. Where the traditions differed, the author naturally, as a rule, inclines to the Pharisaic interpretation. For the full Rabbinical parallels the reader must consult the invaluable commentary of M. Julien Weill in the French translation of Josephus edited by the late Dr. Théodore Reinach and special treatises on the subject; the principal points are mentioned in the notes to the present volume.

The account of the creation with the encomium on Moses prefixed to it [e] betrays clear dependence on the *De opificio mundi* of Philo; acquaintance with a few other works of the Alexandrian writer is shown elsewhere.[f]

Philo.

Besides the Bible, the historian quotes, wherever possible, external authority in support of it. Berosus

---

[a] *Ant.* ii. 205 ff.   [b] ii. 238 ff.
[c] i. 41, 52, 70 f., ii. 224 (with notes).
[d] iii. 224 ff., iv. 196 ff.
[e] i. 18-33 (notes).
[f] *De Abrahamo*, i. 177, 225, and perhaps *De migratione Abrahami*, i. 157 : *De Iosepho*, ii. 41 f., 72.

INTRODUCTION

Non-Jewish authorities. the Babylonian, Manetho the Egyptian, Dius the Phoenician, Menander of Ephesus, the Sibylline oracles, the Tyrian records, and other writers, supply evidence on the flood, the longevity of the patriarchs, the tower of Babel, and, for the later Biblical history, on the correspondence of Solomon and Hiram, on Sennacherib and Nebuchadnezzar. But the author's repertory is here limited, and the fact that more than once an array of such names ends with that of Nicolas of Damascus [a] suggests that he perhaps knows of the other sources mentioned only through Nicolas, whose *Universal History* was later to serve as one of his main authorities for the post-Biblical period.

The historian, or his assistant, has not scrupled, on occasion, to enliven the narrative by details derived from pagan models. A battle scene is taken over from Thucydides [b]; another episode owes touches to Herodotus.[c]

Greek assistants. Reference has been made elsewhere [d] to the aid which the historian received from Greek assistants (συνεργοί). His indebtedness to them in the *Jewish War* is acknowledged [e] and apparent in the uniformly excellent style of that earlier work. In the *Antiquities* there is no similar acknowledgement, and the style is much more uneven; but here too the collaborators have left their own impress. Two of these—the principal assistants—betray themselves in the later books, where the author, wearying of his *magnum opus*, seems to have entrusted the com-

---

[a] *Ant.* i. 94, 107 f., 158 f.; *cf.* vii. 101.
[b] iv. 92.   [c] iv. 134 note.
[d] Vol. ii. p. xv; a fuller statement in *Josephus the Man and the Historian* (New York, 1929), Lecture v.
[e] *Ap.* i. 50.

INTRODUCTION

position in the main to other hands. Books xv-xvi are the work of one of the able assistants already employed in the *War*, a cultured writer with a love of the Greek poets and of Sophocles in particular (I call him the "Sophoclean" assistant); xvii-xix show the marked mannerisms of a hack, a slavish imitator of Thucydides (I call him the "Thucydidean"). In these five books (xv-xix) these two assistants have, it seems, practically taken over the entire task. In the earlier books (i-xiv) they have lent occasional aid—the Thucydidean rarely, the poet-lover more frequently.

(i) The neat style of the "Sophoclean" assistant is traceable in many passages in Books i-iv, *e.g.* the proem, the wooing of Rebecca (i. 242 ff.) and of Rachel (i. 285 ff.), the temptation of Joseph by Potiphar's wife (ii. 39 ff.), the exodus and passage of the Red Sea, the rebellion of Korah, the story of Balaam, the passing of Moses. Elsewhere he would appear to have revised and edited the author's work, indications of his hand appearing at the end of a paragraph.

Echoes of Sophocles, not so prominent as in *A.* xv-xvi, appear in ii. 254 ἄπτεσθαι βουλευμάτων (Soph. *Ant.* 179), 300 κακοὶ κακῶς ἀπόλλυσθαι (*Phil.* 1369), iii. 15 τὰ ἐν ποσὶ κακά (cp. 12 : *Ant.* 1327), 99 πρόνοιαν ἔχειν περί τινος (*Ant.* 283), 141 and 165 περονίς (else only *Trach.* 925), 264 ἐξικετεύειν (*O.T.* 760), iv. 15 θηρᾶσθαι c. inf. (*Ai.* 2), iv. 265 ἄμοιρος γῆς (cp. *Ai.* 1326 f.). Euripides (*Herc. Fur.* 323 f.) is clearly the model in the story of Hagar's expulsion (i. 218). From Homer we have ἐπὶ γήρως οὐδῷ (i. 222 : cp. *Il.* xxii. 60 etc.), πίδακιν ὀλίγαις (iii. 33 : *Il.* xvi. 825), ἤχλυσεν (iii. 203 : *Od.* xii. 406), ὥστε παῖδας εὐφρᾶναι καὶ γυναῖκας (iv. 117 : after *Il.* v. 688). The narrative of the seduction of the Hebrew youth by the Midianite women (iv. 131 ff.) is modelled on the story of the Scythians and Amazons in Herodotus (iv. 111 ff.). From Herodotus (iii. 98) comes also the phrase πρὸς ἥλιον ἀνίσχοντα (iv. 305).

Beside this dependence on classical authors, another marked feature of this assistant, which he shares with his

INTRODUCTION

favourite poet [a] and perhaps took over from him, is his fondness for trichotomy. Three reasons, three parties, the triple group in various forms—such modes of expression are a sure index of the work of this assistant and sharply distinguish him from an inferior συνεργός who appears later on (*A.* vi) and is characterized by his love of *hendiadys* and the double group. Three reasons are given for the longevity of the patriarchs (*A.* i. 106), for narrating the plagues of Egypt in full (ii. 293), for the route of the exodus (ii. 322 f.), for the three annual feasts of the Hebrews (iv. 203). Three parties hold contrary opinions concerning the lawgiver (iii. 96 f., iv. 36 f. τῶν μὲν ... τῶν δὲ φρονίμων ... ὁ δὲ πᾶς ὅμιλος ...). Three alternative methods of delivering the Israelites at the Red Sea are open to the Deity (ii. 337). Instances of similar grouping are to be found in ii. 189, 275 (φωνή, ὄψις, προσηγορία), 283, 326, iii. 22, 45 *bis* (ὅπλων χρημάτων τροφῆς: ὀλίγον ἄνοπλον ἀσθενές), 80 (ἄνεμοι ... ἀστραπαί ... κεραυνοί), 319 (οἱ μὲν ... οἱ δὲ ... πολλοὶ δὲ ...), iv. 26 (οὐκ ἐπειδὴ ... οὐ μὴν οὐδ' εὐγενείᾳ ... οὐδὲ διὰ φιλαδελφίαν), 40 (δέσποτα τῶν ἐπ' οὐρανοῦ τε καὶ γῆς καὶ θαλάσσης, *cf.* 45), 48 (αὐτοὺς ἅμα τῇ γενεᾷ καὶ τοῖς ὑπάρχουσιν), etc.

(ii) The "Thucydidean" assistant, who towards the close of the *Antiquities* (xvii-xix) was to lend liberal aid, in the earlier books plays but a small part. His plagiarism from Thucydides and a few mannerisms betray his hand in some five passages. Here he has been employed as a sort of "war-correspondent" for battle scenes and military matters. He it is who describes the battles with the Amalekites (iii. 53 ff.) and the Amorites (iv. 87 ff.); twice his hand appears at a point where there is a transition from civil to military regulations (iii. 287 ff., iv. 292 ff.); and he has also supplied the picture of the burning of the company of Korah (iv. 54 ff.).

After elimination of the work of these two assistants, whose large aid in the later books enables us in some measure to identify their style elsewhere, it is difficult to say how much of the composition is left to the author himself. But there are cruder passages in

[a] See the writer's paper on *Sophocles and the Perfect Number* (Proceedings of the British Academy, vol. xvi).

INTRODUCTION

A. i-xiv, xx and the *Life*, which it is not unreasonable to refer to him ; and it may even be possible to detect an occasional trace of the influence of his native Aramaic speech, as in the colloquial use of ἄρχεσθαι with infinitive, familiar in the New Testament.[a]

As in previous volumes, the Greek text here printed is based on that of Niese, but is of an eclectic nature, the readings quoted in his *apparatus criticus* being occasionally adopted. The original text is to be looked for in no single group of MSS. As a rule the group followed by Niese—RO(M)—is superior[b] ; at the other extreme stands a pair of MSS—SP—which, when unsupported, are seldom trustworthy ; the remaining authorities are of a mixed character, the old Latin version being specially important.

The length of the *Jewish Antiquities* led at an early date to its bisection in the MSS,[c] and our authorities for the text of the first half of the work differ from those in the second half. The ancient authorities for *A.* i-x used by Niese and quoted in the present volume are as follows :

R Codex Regius Parisinus, cent. xiv.
O Codex Oxoniensis (Bodleianus), miscell. graec. 186, cent. xv.
M Codex Marcianus (Venetus) Gr. 381, cent. xiii.

---

[a] See an article in the *Journal of Theological Studies*, vol. xxx (1929) p. 361, on " An unrecorded ' Aramaism ' in Josephus."

[b] *e.g.* in i. 82, 148, where (R)O alone have preserved the correct figure, while the other authorities conform to the Hebrew text of Genesis.

[c] There are indications of a division at one time into *four* parts (Niese, vol. i. p. viii).

INTRODUCTION

S	Codex Vindobonensis II. A 19, historicus Graecus 2, cent. xi.
P	Codex Parisinus Gr. 1419, cent. xi.
L	Codex Laurentianus, plut. lxix. 20, cent. xiv.
Lat.	Latin version made by order of Cassiodorus, cent. v or vi.
Exc.	Excerpts made by order of Constantine VII Porphyrogenitus, cent. x.
E	Epitome, used by Zonaras, and conjectured by Niese to have been made in cent. x or xi.
Zon.	The *Chronicon* of J. Zonaras, cent. xii.
ed. pr.	The *editio princeps* of the Greek text (Basel, 1544) seems to be derived in part from some unknown MS and is occasionally an important authority.

If the author of the *Jewish Antiquities* received much assistance from others in the composition of his work, so also has his translator. In particular he must here gratefully acknowledge his constant indebtedness, both in the translation and more especially in the notes, to the invaluable work of Monsieur Julien Weill, the translator of Books i-x of the *Antiquities* in the *Œuvres complètes de Flavius Josèphe* edited by the late Dr. Théodore Reinach (Paris, 1900 etc.); M. Weill's collection of Rabbinical parallels to the historian's exposition of the Mosaic code is an indispensable companion to all students of this portion of Josephus. For the Greek text, besides the great work of Benedict Niese (Berlin, 1887), that of Naber (Leipzig, Teubner, 1888) has been consulted throughout. Among previous translations, after that of M. Weill the most helpful has been the Latin version

INTRODUCTION

of John Hudson in the edition of **Havercamp** (Amsterdam, 1726); the translation of William Whiston, revised by the Rev. A. R. Shilleto (London, 1889), has furnished occasional aid. On two special points the translator has to express his thanks to experts for assistance received: to Professor A. E. Housman and to Mrs. Maunder on an astronomical point (*A.* iii. 182); while Mr. F. Howarth, Lecturer in Botany in the Imperial College of Science and Technology, has kindly supplied a note, with illustration, on the description of the plant henbane (iii. 172). Thanks are also due to the press reader for his vigilance and acute suggestions.

ABBREVIATIONS

A. = (*Ant.*) = *Antiquitates Judaicae.*
Ap. = *Contra Apionem.*
B. (*B.J.*) = *Bellum Judaicum.*
codd. = *codices* (all MSS quoted by Niese).
conj. = conjectural emendation.
ed. pr. = *editio princeps* of Greek text (Basel, 1544).
ins. = inserted by.
om. = omit.
rell. = *codices reliqui* (the rest of the MSS quoted by Niese).

Conjectural insertions in the Greek text are indicated by angular brackets, ⟨ ⟩; doubtful MS readings by square brackets, [ ].

The smaller sections introduced by Niese are shown in the left margin of the Greek text. References throughout are to these sections. The chapter-division of earlier editions is indicated on both pages (Greek and English).

JEWISH ANTIQUITIES

ΙΟΥΔΑΪΚΗΣ ΑΡΧΑΙΟΛΟΓΙΑΣ

ΒΙΒΛΙΟΝ Α

(Proem 1) Τοῖς τὰς ἱστορίας συγγράφειν βουλομένοις οὐ μίαν οὐδὲ τὴν αὐτὴν ὁρῶ τῆς σπουδῆς γινομένην αἰτίαν, ἀλλὰ πολλὰς καὶ πλεῖστον 2 ἀλλήλων διαφερούσας. τινὲς μὲν γὰρ ἐπιδεικνύμενοι λόγων δεινότητα καὶ τὴν ἀπ' αὐτῆς θηρευόμενοι[1] δόξαν ἐπὶ τοῦτο τῆς παιδείας τὸ μέρος ὁρμῶσιν, ἄλλοι δὲ χάριν ἐκείνοις φέροντες, περὶ ὧν τὴν ἀναγραφὴν εἶναι συμβέβηκε, τὸν εἰς αὐτὴν 3 πόνον καὶ παρὰ δύναμιν ὑπέστησαν· εἰσὶ δ' οἵτινες ἐβιάσθησαν ὑπ' αὐτῆς τῆς τῶν πραγμάτων ἀνάγκης οἷς πραττομένοις παρέτυχον ταῦτα γραφῇ δηλούσῃ περιλαβεῖν· πολλοὺς δὲ χρησίμων μέγεθος πραγμάτων ἐν ἀγνοίᾳ κειμένων προὔτρεψε τὴν περὶ αὐτῶν ἱστορίαν εἰς κοινὴν ὠφέλειαν ἐξενεγ- 4 κεῖν. τούτων δὴ τῶν προειρημένων αἰτίων αἱ τελευταῖαι δύο κἀμοὶ συμβεβήκασι· τὸν μὲν γὰρ πρὸς τοὺς Ῥωμαίους πόλεμον ἡμῖν τοῖς Ἰουδαίοις γενόμενον καὶ τὰς ἐν αὐτῷ πράξεις καὶ τὸ τέλος οἷον ἀπέβη πείρᾳ μαθὼν ἐβιάσθην ἐκδιηγήσασθαι διὰ τοὺς ἐν τῷ γράφειν λυμαινομένους τὴν

[1] Ο: θηρώμενοι rell.

[a] The *Bellum Judaicum*, published some twenty years before the present work.

JEWISH ANTIQUITIES

BOOK I

(Proem 1) Those who essay to write histories are actuated, I observe, not by one and the same aim, but by many widely different motives. Some, eager to display their literary skill and to win the fame therefrom expected, rush into this department of letters; others, to gratify the persons to whom the record happens to relate, have undertaken the requisite labour even though beyond their power; others again have been constrained by the mere stress of events in which they themselves took part to set these out in a comprehensive narrative; while many have been induced by prevailing ignorance of important affairs of general utility to publish a history of them for the public benefit. Of the aforesaid motives the two last apply to myself. For, having known by experience the war which we Jews waged against the Romans, the incidents in its course and its issue, I was constrained to narrate it in detail[a] in order to refute those who in their writings were doing outrage to the truth.[b]

---

[b] *Cf. B.J.* i. 2 and 6 for these earlier histories of the war; and for the later work of the historian's main rival, Justus of Tiberias, *Vita* 336 ff.

JOSEPHUS

5 ἀλήθειαν, (2) ταύτην δὲ τὴν ἐνεστῶσαν ἐγκεχείρισμαι[1] πραγματείαν νομίζων ἅπασι φανεῖσθαι τοῖς Ἕλλησιν ἀξίαν σπουδῆς· μέλλει γὰρ περιέξειν ἅπασαν τὴν παρ' ἡμῖν ἀρχαιολογίαν καὶ [τὴν][2] διάταξιν τοῦ πολιτεύματος ἐκ τῶν Ἑβραϊκῶν μεθηρμηνευ-
6 μένην γραμμάτων. ἤδη μὲν οὖν καὶ πρότερον διενοήθην, ὅτε τὸν πόλεμον συνέγραφον, δηλῶσαι τίνες ὄντες ἐξ ἀρχῆς Ἰουδαῖοι καὶ τίσι χρησάμενοι τύχαις, ὑφ' οἵῳ τε παιδευθέντες νομοθέτῃ τὰ πρὸς εὐσέβειαν καὶ τὴν ἄλλην ἄσκησιν ἀρετῆς, πόσους τε πολέμους ἐν μακροῖς πολεμήσαντες χρόνοις εἰς τὸν τελευταῖον ἄκοντες πρὸς Ῥωμαίους κατέστη-
7 σαν. ἀλλ' ἐπειδὴ μείζων ἦν ἡ τοῦδε τοῦ λόγου περιβολή, καθ' αὑτὸν[3] ἐκεῖνον χωρίσας ταῖς ἰδίαις ἀρχαῖς αὐτοῦ καὶ τῷ τέλει τὴν γραφὴν συνεμέτρησα· χρόνου δὲ προϊόντος, ὅπερ φιλεῖ τοῖς μεγάλων ἅπτεσθαι διανοουμένοις, ὄκνος μοι καὶ μέλλησις ἐγίνετο τηλικαύτην μετενεγκεῖν ὑπόθεσιν εἰς ἀλλοδαπὴν ἡμῖν καὶ ξένην διαλέκτου
8 συνήθειαν. ἦσαν δέ τινες οἳ πόθῳ τῆς ἱστορίας ἐπ' αὐτήν με προὔτρεπον, καὶ μάλιστα δὴ πάντων Ἐπαφρόδιτος ἀνὴρ ἅπασαν μὲν ἰδέαν παιδείας ἠγαπηκώς, διαφερόντως δὲ χαίρων ἐμπειρίαις πραγμάτων, ἅτε δὴ μεγάλοις μὲν αὐτὸς ὁμιλήσας πράγμασι καὶ τύχαις πολυτρόποις, ἐν ἅπασι δὲ θαυμαστὴν φύσεως ἐπιδειξάμενος ἰσχὺν καὶ προαί-
9 ρεσιν ἀρετῆς ἀμετακίνητον. τούτῳ δὴ πειθόμενος ὡς αἰεὶ[4] τοῖς χρήσιμον ἢ καλόν τι πράττειν δυνα-

---

[1] προεγκεχείρισμαι SPL.   [2] om. O.
[3] κατ' αὐτὸν OE.   [4] ὡς αἰεὶ O: ἀεὶ rell.

[a] Josephus bases the first part of his narrative on the Biblical story; but his rôle as " translator " is limited.

JEWISH ANTIQUITIES, I. 5–9

(2) And now I have undertaken this present work in the belief that the whole Greek-speaking world will find it worthy of attention; for it will embrace our entire ancient history and political constitution, translated from the Hebrew records.[a] I had indeed ere now, when writing the history of the war, already contemplated describing the origin of the Jews, the fortunes that befell them, the great lawgiver under whom they were trained in piety and the exercise of the other virtues, and all those wars waged by them through long ages before this last in which they were involuntarily engaged against the Romans. However, since the compass of such a theme was excessive, I made the *War* into a separate volume, with its own beginning and end, thus duly proportioning my work. Nevertheless, as time went on, as is wont to happen to those who design to attack large tasks, there was hesitation and delay on my part in rendering so vast a subject into a foreign and unfamiliar tongue. However, there were certain persons curious about the history who urged me to pursue it, and above all Epaphroditus,[b] a man devoted to every form of learning, but specially interested in the experiences of history, conversant as he himself has been with large affairs and varying turns of fortune, through all which he has displayed a wonderful force of character and an attachment to virtue that nothing could deflect. Yielding, then, to the persuasions of one who is ever

Origin of present work.

The historian's patron.

For the later historical books (1 Samuel to 1 Maccabees), and to a less extent for the Pentateuch, he is largely dependent on the Alexandrian Greek Bible, which he merely paraphrases.

[b] See Introduction. The historian's later works, the *Antiquities*, its appendix the *Life* (§ 430), and the *Contra Apionem*, are all dedicated to this patron.

JOSEPHUS

μένοις συμφιλοκαλοῦντι καὶ ἐμαυτὸν αἰσχυνόμενος, εἰ δόξαιμι ῥαθυμίᾳ πλέον ἢ τῷ περὶ τὰ κάλλιστα χαίρειν πόνῳ, προθυμότερον ἐπερρώσθην, ἔτι κἀκεῖνα¹ πρὸς τοῖς εἰρημένοις λογισάμενος οὐ παρέργως, περί τε τῶν ἡμετέρων προγόνων εἰ μεταδιδόναι τῶν τοιούτων ἤθελον, καὶ περὶ τῶν Ἑλλήνων εἴ τινες αὐτῶν γνῶναι τὰ παρ' ἡμῖν ἐσπούδασαν.

10 (3) Εὗρον τοίνυν ὅτι Πτολεμαίων μὲν ὁ δεύτερος, μάλιστα δὴ βασιλεὺς περὶ παιδείαν καὶ βιβλίων συναγωγὴν σπουδάσας, ἐξαιρέτως ἐφιλοτιμήθη τὸν ἡμέτερον νόμον καὶ τὴν κατ' αὐτὸν διάταξιν τῆς 11 πολιτείας εἰς τὴν Ἑλλάδα φωνὴν μεταβαλεῖν, ὁ δὲ τῶν παρ' ἡμῖν ἀρχιερέων οὐδενὸς ἀρετῇ δεύτερος Ἐλεάζαρος τῷ προειρημένῳ βασιλεῖ ταύτης ἀπολαῦσαι τῆς ὠφελείας οὐκ ἐφθόνησε, πάντως ἀντειπὼν ἄν, εἰ μὴ πάτριον ἦν ἡμῖν τὸ μηδὲν ἔχειν 12 τῶν καλῶν ἀπόρρητον. κἀμαυτῷ δὴ πρέπειν ἐνόμισα τὸ μὲν τοῦ ἀρχιερέως μιμήσασθαι μεγαλόψυχον, τῷ βασιλεῖ δὲ πολλοὺς ὁμοίως ὑπολαβεῖν καὶ νῦν εἶναι φιλομαθεῖς· οὐδὲ γὰρ πᾶσαν ἐκεῖνος ἔφθη λαβεῖν τὴν ἀναγραφήν, ἀλλ' αὐτὰ² μόνα τὰ τοῦ νόμου παρέδοσαν οἱ πεμφθέντες ἐπὶ τὴν 13 ἐξήγησιν εἰς τὴν Ἀλεξάνδρειαν· μυρία δ' ἐστὶ τὰ δηλούμενα διὰ τῶν ἱερῶν γραμμάτων, ἅτε δὴ πεντακισχιλίων ἐτῶν ἱστορίας ἐν αὐτοῖς ἐμ-

¹ O: κἀκεῖνο rell. Lat.   ² ἀλλὰ (om. αὐτὰ) O.

---

[a] Ptolemy II. " Philadelphus " (283–245 b.c., E. Bevan).
[b] The reputed high priest in the Aristeas story.
[c] The traditional story of the origin of the Greek version

an enthusiastic supporter of persons with ability to produce some useful or beautiful work, and ashamed of myself that I should be thought to prefer sloth to the effort of this noblest of enterprises, I was encouraged to greater ardour. Besides these motives, there were two further considerations to which I had given serious thought, namely, whether our ancestors, on the one hand, were willing to communicate such information, and whether any of the Greeks, on the other, had been curious to learn our history.

(3) I found then that the second of the Ptolemies,[a] that king who was so deeply interested in learning and such a collector of books, was particularly anxious to have our Law and the political constitution based thereon translated into Greek; while, on the other side, Eleazar,[b] who yielded in virtue to none of our high priests, did not scruple to grant the monarch the enjoyment of a benefit, which he would certainly have refused had it not been our traditional custom to make nothing of what is good into a secret.[c] Accordingly, I thought that it became me also both to imitate the high priest's magnanimity and to assume that there are still to-day many lovers of learning like the king. For even he failed to obtain [d] all our records : it was only the portion containing the Law which was delivered to him by those who were sent to Alexandria to interpret it. The things narrated in the sacred Scriptures are, however, innumerable, seeing that they embrace the history of

An earlier model: the Greek version of the Law.

of the Pentateuch is told in the so-called Letter of Aristeas and repeated by Josephus in *A*. xii. 11-118.

[d] Or " to forestall me by obtaining." Josephus does not mention that the version of the Law was followed up by translations, which he has freely used, of the rest of the Hebrew Scriptures.

περιειλημμένης, καὶ παντοῖαι μέν εἰσι παράλογοι περιπέτειαι, πολλαὶ δὲ τύχαι πολέμων καὶ στρατηγῶν ἀνδραγαθίαι καὶ πολιτευμάτων μεταβολαί.
14 τὸ σύνολον δὲ μάλιστά τις ἂν ἐκ ταύτης μάθοι τῆς ἱστορίας ἐθελήσας αὐτὴν διελθεῖν, ὅτι τοῖς μὲν θεοῦ γνώμῃ κατακολουθοῦσι καὶ τὰ καλῶς νομοθετηθέντα μὴ τολμῶσι παραβαίνειν[1] πάντα κατορθοῦται πέρα πίστεως καὶ γέρας εὐδαιμονία πρόκειται παρὰ θεοῦ· καθ' ὅσον δ' ἂν ἀποστῶσι τῆς τούτων ἀκριβοῦς ἐπιμελείας, ἄπορα μὲν γίνεται τὰ πόριμα, τρέπεται δὲ εἰς συμφορὰς ἀνηκέστους
15 ὅ τι ποτ' ἂν ὡς ἀγαθὸν δρᾶν σπουδάσωσιν. ἤδη τοίνυν τοὺς ἐντευξομένους τοῖς βιβλίοις παρακαλῶ τὴν γνώμην θεῷ προσανέχειν καὶ δοκιμάζειν τὸν ἡμέτερον νομοθέτην, εἰ τήν τε φύσιν ἀξίως αὐτοῦ κατενόησε καὶ τῇ δυνάμει πρεπούσας ἀεὶ τὰς πράξεις ἀνατέθεικε πάσης καθαρὸν τὸν περὶ αὐτοῦ φυλάξας λόγον τῆς παρ' ἄλλοις ἀσχήμονος μυθο-
16 λογίας· καίτοι γε ὅσον ἐπὶ μήκει χρόνου καὶ παλαιότητι πολλὴν εἶχεν[2] ἄδειαν ψευδῶν πλασμάτων· γέγονε γὰρ πρὸ ἐτῶν δισχιλίων, ἐφ' ὅσον πλῆθος αἰῶνος οὐδ' αὐτῶν οἱ ποιηταὶ τὰς γενέσεις τῶν θεῶν, μήτι γε τὰς τῶν ἀνθρώπων πράξεις ἢ τοὺς
17 νόμους ἀνενεγκεῖν ἐτόλμησαν. τὰ μὲν οὖν ἀκριβῆ τῶν ἐν ταῖς ἀναγραφαῖς προϊὼν ὁ λόγος κατὰ τὴν οἰκείαν τάξιν σημανεῖ· τοῦτο γὰρ διὰ ταύτης ποιήσειν τῆς πραγματείας ἐπηγγειλάμην οὐδὲν προσθεὶς οὐδ' αὖ παραλιπών.

[1] παραλαβεῖν R : παριδεῖν O.   [2] potuisset (ἂν εἶχεν?) Lat.

---

[a] ἄπορα γίνεται τὰ πόριμα, the reverse of the phrase of Aeschylus (*P.V.* 904), ἄπορα πόριμος " making impossibilities

five thousand years and recount all sorts of surprising reverses, many fortunes of war, heroic exploits of generals, and political revolutions. But, speaking generally, the main lesson to be learnt from this history by any who care to peruse it is that men who conform to the will of God, and do not venture to transgress laws that have been excellently laid down, prosper in all things beyond belief, and for their reward are offered by God felicity; whereas, in proportion as they depart from the strict observance of these laws, things (else) practicable become impracticable,[a] and whatever imaginary good thing they strive to do ends in irretrievable disasters. At the outset, then, I entreat those who will read these volumes to fix their thoughts on God, and to test whether our lawgiver has had a worthy conception of His nature and has always assigned to Him such actions as befit His power, keeping his words concerning Him pure of that unseemly mythology current among others; albeit that, in dealing with ages so long and so remote, he would have had ample licence to invent fictions. For he was born two thousand years ago, to which ancient date the poets never ventured to refer even the birth of their gods, much less the actions or the laws of mortals. The precise details of our Scripture records will, then, be set forth, each in its place, as my narrative proceeds, that being the procedure that I have promised to follow throughout this work, neither adding nor omitting anything.[b]

Moral lesson of present work.

possible," which is perhaps in the mind of the historian's cultured assistant, notwithstanding its association with the "unseemly mythology" denounced below.

[b] § 5. In fact he "adds" some curious legends, on Moses in particular, and there are some few pardonable omissions.

18 (4) Ἐπειδὴ δὲ [τὰ]¹ πάντα σχεδὸν ἐκ τῆς τοῦ νομοθέτου σοφίας ἡμῖν ἀνήρτηται Μωυσέος, ἀνάγκη μοι βραχέα περὶ ἐκείνου προειπεῖν, ὅπως μή τινες τῶν ἀναγνωσομένων διαπορῶσι, πόθεν ἡμῖν ὁ λόγος περὶ νόμων² καὶ πράξεων ἔχων τὴν ἀναγραφὴν ἐπὶ τοσοῦτον φυσιολογίας κεκοινώνηκεν.
19 ἰστέον οὖν, ὅτι πάντων ἐκεῖνος ἀναγκαιότατον ἡγήσατο τῷ καὶ τὸν ἑαυτοῦ μέλλοντι βίον οἰκονομήσειν καλῶς καὶ τοῖς ἄλλοις νομοθετεῖν θεοῦ πρῶτον φύσιν κατανοῆσαι καὶ τῶν ἔργων τῶν ἐκείνου θεατὴν τῷ νῷ γενόμενον οὕτως παράδειγμα τὸ πάντων ἄριστον μιμεῖσθαι, καθ' ὅσον
20 οἷόν τε, καὶ πειρᾶσθαι κατακολουθεῖν. οὔτε γὰρ αὐτῷ ποτ' ἂν γενέσθαι νοῦν ἀγαθὸν τῷ νομοθέτῃ ταύτης ἀπολειπομένῳ τῆς θέας, οὔτε τῶν γραφησομένων εἰς ἀρετῆς λόγον οὐδὲν ἀποβήσεσθαι τοῖς λαβοῦσιν, εἰ μὴ πρὸ παντὸς ἄλλου διδαχθεῖεν, ὅτι πάντων πατήρ τε καὶ δεσπότης ὁ θεὸς ὢν καὶ πάντα ἐπιβλέπων τοῖς μὲν ἑπομένοις αὐτῷ δίδωσιν εὐδαίμονα βίον, τοὺς ἔξω δὲ βαίνοντας ἀρετῆς
21 μεγάλαις περιβάλλει συμφοραῖς. τοῦτο δὴ παιδεῦσαι βουληθεὶς Μωυσῆς τὸ παίδευμα τοὺς ἑαυτοῦ πολίτας τῆς τῶν νόμων θέσεως οὐκ ἀπὸ συμβολαίων καὶ τῶν πρὸς ἀλλήλους δικαίων ἤρξατο τοῖς ἄλλοις παραπλησίως, ἀλλ' ἐπὶ τὸν θεὸν καὶ τὴν τοῦ κόσμου κατασκευὴν τὰς γνώμας αὐτῶν ἀναγαγὼν καὶ πείσας, ὅτι τῶν ἐπὶ γῆς ἔργων τοῦ

¹ om. O. ² περὶ λόγων RE Lat.: παραλόγων O.

a Greek "physiology," *i.e.* the investigation of the origin of existence in the account of creation. He uses the cognate verb with reference to Gen. ii. 7 in particular (§ 34).

JEWISH ANTIQUITIES, I. 18-21

(4) But, since well-nigh everything herein related is dependent on the wisdom of our lawgiver Moses, I must first speak briefly of him, lest any of my readers should ask how it is that so much of my work, which professes to treat of laws and historical facts, is devoted to natural philosophy.[a] Be it known, then, that that sage deemed it above all necessary, for one who would order his own life aright and also legislate for others, first to study the nature of God, and then, having contemplated his works with the eye of reason, to imitate so far as possible that best of all models and endeavour to follow it. For neither could the lawgiver himself, without this vision, ever attain to a right mind, nor would anything that he should write in regard to virtue avail with his readers, unless before all else they were taught that God, as the universal Father and Lord who beholds all things, grants to such as follow Him a life of bliss, but involves in dire calamities those who step outside the path of virtue. Such, then, being the lesson which Moses desired to instil into his fellow-citizens, he did not, when framing his laws, begin with contracts and the mutual rights of man, as others have done [b]; no, he led their thoughts up to God and the construction of the world; he convinced them that of all God's works upon earth

Moses contrasted with other legislators.

[b] Here and in the sequel the writer has before him Philo's *De opificio mundi*, a work which he has used again in the *Contra Apionem*. Philo's work begins with a similar contrast between Moses and other legislators. Of these some have set out their codes bare and unadorned, others have deluded the multitude by prefixing to them mythical inventions. Moses did neither, but, in order to mould ($προτυπῶσαι$) the minds of those who were to use his laws, did not at once prescribe what they should do or not do ($μήτ'\ εὐθὺς\ ἃ\ χρὴ\ πράττειν\ ἢ\ τοὐναντίον\ ὑπειπών$), but began with a marvellous account of creation (§§ 1-3 Cohn-Wendland).

θεοῦ κάλλιστόν ἐσμεν ἄνθρωποι, ὅτε πρὸς τὴν εὐσέβειαν ἔσχεν ὑπακούοντας, ῥᾳδίως ἤδη περὶ 22 πάντων ἔπειθεν. οἱ μὲν γὰρ ἄλλοι νομοθέται τοῖς μύθοις ἐξακολουθήσαντες τῶν ἀνθρωπίνων ἁμαρτημάτων εἰς τοὺς θεοὺς τῷ λόγῳ τὴν αἰσχύνην μετέθεσαν καὶ πολλὴν ὑποτίμησιν τοῖς πονηροῖς 23 ἔδωκαν· ὁ δ' ἡμέτερος νομοθέτης ἀκραιφνῆ τὴν ἀρετὴν ἔχοντα τὸν θεὸν ἀποφήνας ᾠήθη δεῖν τοὺς ἀνθρώπους ἐκείνης πειρᾶσθαι μεταλαμβάνειν καὶ τοὺς μὴ ταῦτα φρονοῦντας μηδὲ μὴν πιστεύοντας 24 ἀπαραιτήτως ἐκόλασε. πρὸς ταύτην οὖν τὴν ὑπόθεσιν ποιεῖσθαι τὴν ἐξέτασιν τοὺς ἀναγνωσομένους παρακαλῶ· φανεῖται γὰρ σκοπουμένοις οὕτως οὐδὲν οὔτ' ἄλογον αὐτοῖς οὔτε πρὸς τὴν μεγαλειότητα τοῦ θεοῦ καὶ τὴν φιλανθρωπίαν ἀνάρμοστον· πάντα γὰρ τῇ τῶν ὅλων φύσει σύμφωνον ἔχει τὴν διάθεσιν, τὰ μὲν αἰνιττομένου τοῦ νομοθέτου δεξιῶς, τὰ δ' ἀλληγοροῦντος μετὰ σεμνότητος, ὅσα δ' ἐξ εὐθείας λέγεσθαι συνέφερε 25 ταῦτα ῥητῶς ἐμφανίζοντος. τοῖς μέντοι βουλομένοις καὶ τὰς αἰτίας ἑκάστου σκοπεῖν πολλὴ γένοιτ' ἂν ἡ θεωρία καὶ λίαν φιλόσοφος, ἣν ἐγὼ νῦν μὲν ὑπερβάλλομαι, θεοῦ δὲ διδόντος ἡμῖν χρόνον πειράσομαι μετὰ ταύτην γράψαι τὴν πραγ- 26 ματείαν. τρέψομαι δὲ ἐπὶ τὴν ἀφήγησιν ἤδη τῶν πραγμάτων μνησθεὶς πρότερον ὧν περὶ τῆς τοῦ κόσμου κατασκευῆς εἶπε Μωυσῆς· ταῦτα δ' ἐν

---

[a] The idea of the Law being in harmony with the universe again comes from Philo. " The opening of the narrative is, as I said, most marvellous, comprising the creation of the world, ὡς καὶ τοῦ κόσμου τῷ νόμῳ καὶ τοῦ νόμου τῷ κόσμῳ συνᾴδοντος καὶ τοῦ νομίμου ἀνδρὸς εὐθὺς ὄντος κοσμοπολίτου πρὸς

JEWISH ANTIQUITIES, I. 21–26

we men are the fairest; and when once he had won their obedience to the dictates of piety, he had no further difficulty in persuading them of all the rest. Other legislators, in fact, following fables, have in their writings imputed to the gods the disgraceful errors of men and thus furnished the wicked with a powerful excuse; our legislator, on the contrary, having shown that God possesses the very perfection of virtue, thought that men should strive to participate in it, and inexorably punished those who did not hold with or believe in these doctrines. I therefore entreat my readers to examine my work from this point of view. For, studying it in this spirit, nothing will appear to them unreasonable, nothing incongruous with the majesty of God and His love for man; everything, indeed, is here set forth in keeping with the nature of the universe [a]; some things the lawgiver shrewdly veils in enigmas, others he sets forth in solemn allegory; but wherever straightforward speech was expedient, there he makes his meaning absolutely plain. Should any further desire to consider the reasons for every article in our creed, he would find the inquiry profound and highly philosophical; that subject for the moment I defer, but, if God grants me time, I shall endeavour to write upon it after completing the present work.[b] I shall now accordingly turn to the narrative of events, first mentioning what Moses has said concerning the creation of the world,

τὸ βούλημα τῆς φύσεως τὰς πράξεις ἀπευθύνοντος, καθ' ἣν καὶ ὁ σύμπας κόσμος διοικεῖται," *De op. mundi* 3.

[b] This projected work on " Customs and Causes " (*A.* iv. 198) was apparently never completed, but the mention of its " four books " (*A.* xx. 268) and scattered allusions in the *Antiquities* to its intended contents suggest that it had taken shape in the author's mind and was actually begun.

13

ταῖς ἱεραῖς βίβλοις εὗρον ἀναγεγραμμένα. ἔχει δὲ οὕτως·

27 (i. 1) Ἐν ἀρχῇ ἔκτισεν ὁ θεὸς τὸν οὐρανὸν καὶ τὴν γῆν. ταύτης δ' ὑπ' ὄψιν οὐκ ἐρχομένης, ἀλλὰ βαθεῖ μὲν κρυπτομένης σκότει, πνεύματος δ' αὐτὴν ἄνωθεν ἐπιθέοντος, γενέσθαι φῶς ἐκέλευσεν ὁ
28 θεός. καὶ γενομένου τούτου κατανοήσας τὴν ὅλην ὕλην διεχώρισε τό τε φῶς καὶ τὸ σκότος καὶ τῷ μὲν ὄνομα ἔθετο νύκτα, τὸ δὲ ἡμέραν ἐκάλεσεν, ἑσπέραν τε καὶ ὄρθρον τὴν ἀρχὴν τοῦ φωτὸς καὶ
29 τὴν ἀνάπαυσιν προσαγορεύσας. καὶ αὕτη μὲν ἂν εἴη πρώτη ἡμέρα, Μωυσῆς δ' αὐτὴν μίαν εἶπε· τὴν δὲ αἰτίαν ἱκανὸς μέν εἰμι ἀποδοῦναι καὶ νῦν, ἐπεὶ δ' ὑπέσχημαι τὴν αἰτιολογίαν πάντων ἰδίᾳ συγγραψάμενος παραδώσειν, εἰς τότε καὶ τὴν περὶ
30 αὐτῆς ἑρμηνείαν ἀναβάλλομαι. μετὰ δὴ τοῦτο τῇ δευτέρᾳ τῶν ἡμερῶν τὸν οὐρανὸν τοῖς ὅλοις ἐπιτίθησιν, ὅτ' αὐτὸν ἀπὸ τῶν ἄλλων διακρίνας καθ' αὑτὸν ἠξίωσε τετάχθαι, κρύσταλλόν τε περιπήξας αὐτῷ καὶ νότιον αὐτὸν καὶ ὑετώδη πρὸς τὴν ἀπὸ τῶν δρόσων ὠφέλειαν ἁρμοδίως[1] τῇ
31 γῇ μηχανησάμενος. τῇ δὲ τρίτῃ ἵστησι τὴν γῆν ἀναχέας περὶ αὐτὴν τὴν θάλασσαν· κατ' αὐτὴν δὲ ταύτην τὴν ἡμέραν εὐθὺς φυτά τε καὶ σπέρματα γῆθεν ἀνέτειλε. τῇ τετάρτῃ δὲ διακοσμεῖ τὸν οὐρανὸν ἡλίῳ καὶ σελήνῃ καὶ τοῖς ἄλλοις ἄστροις κινήσεις αὐτοῖς ἐπιστείλας καὶ δρόμους, οἷς ἂν

---

[1] LE: ἁρμονίως rell.

[a] Or "founded": Josephus, in common with the later translator of Scripture, Aquila (2nd cent. A.D.), writes ἔκτισεν, not ἐποίησεν of the earlier Alexandrian translators.

[b] Gen. i. 5 "There was evening and there was morning,

as I find it recorded in the sacred books. His account is as follows:

(i. 1) In the beginning God created^a the heaven and the earth. The earth had not come into sight, but was hidden in thick darkness, and a breath from above sped over it, when God commanded that there should be light. It came, and, surveying the whole of matter, He divided the light from the darkness, calling the latter night and the former day, and naming morning and evening the dawn of the light and its cessation. This then should be the first day, but Moses spoke of it as "one" day^b; I could explain why he did so now, but, having promised to render an account of the causes of everything in a special work,^c I defer till then the explanation of this point also. After this, on the second day, He set the heaven above the universe, when He was pleased to sever this from the rest and to assign it a place apart, congealing ice about it and withal rendering it moist and rainy to give the benefit of the dews in a manner congenial to the earth. On the third day he established the earth, pouring around it the sea; and on the self-same day plants and seeds sprang forthwith^d from the soil. On the fourth he adorned the heaven with sun and moon and the other stars, prescribing their motions and courses

The creation. Genesis i. 1

one day." Jewish Rabbis sought to explain the use of the cardinal number here, rather than the ordinal "first." Philo, whose work is in the writer's mind, has a mystical interpretation of his own: ἡμέραν ὁ ποιῶν ἐκάλεσε, καὶ ἡμέραν οὐχὶ πρώτην, ἀλλὰ μίαν, ἢ λέλεκται διὰ τὴν τοῦ νοητοῦ κόσμου μόνωσιν μοναδικὴν ἔχοντος φύσιν, *De opif.* (9) § 35.

^c § 25 note.

^d So Philo, *op. cit.* (12) § 40 (quoted by Weill): ἐβεβρίθει δὲ πάντα καρποῖς εὐθὺς ἅμα τῇ πρώτῃ γενέσει κατὰ τὸν ἐναντίον τρόπον ἢ τὸν νυνὶ καθεστῶτα.

15

32 αἱ τῶν ὡρῶν περιφοραὶ σημαίνοιντο. πέμπτῃ δ᾽ ἡμέρᾳ ζῷά τε κατ᾽ αὐτὴν νηκτὰ καὶ μετάρσια τὰ μὲν κατὰ βάθους¹ τὰ δὲ δι᾽ ἀέρος ἀνῆκε συνδησάμενος αὐτὰ κοινωνίᾳ καὶ μίξει γονῆς ἕνεκα καὶ τοῦ συναύξεσθαι καὶ πλεονάζειν αὐτῶν τὴν φύσιν. τῇ δὲ ἕκτῃ ἡμέρᾳ δημιουργεῖ τὸ τῶν τετραπόδων γένος ἄρρεν τε καὶ θῆλυ ποιήσας· ἐν ταύτῃ δὲ καὶ
33 τὸν ἄνθρωπον ἔπλασε. καὶ τὸν κόσμον ἓξ ταῖς πάσαις ἡμέραις Μωυσῆς καὶ πάντα τὰ ἐν αὐτῷ φησι γενέσθαι, τῇ δὲ ἑβδόμῃ ἀναπαύσασθαι καὶ λαβεῖν ἀπὸ τῶν ἔργων ἐκεχειρίαν, ὅθεν καὶ ἡμεῖς σχολὴν ἀπὸ τῶν πόνων κατὰ ταύτην ἄγομεν τὴν ἡμέραν προσαγορεύοντες αὐτὴν σάββατα· δηλοῖ δὲ ἀνάπαυσιν κατὰ τὴν Ἑβραίων διάλεκτον τοὔνομα.

34 (2) Καὶ δὴ καὶ φυσιολογεῖν Μωυσῆς μετὰ τὴν ἑβδόμην ἤρξατο περὶ τῆς τἀνθρώπου κατασκευῆς λέγων οὕτως· ἔπλασεν ὁ θεὸς τὸν ἄνθρωπον χοῦν ἀπὸ τῆς γῆς λαβών, καὶ πνεῦμα ἐνῆκεν αὐτῷ καὶ ψυχήν. ὁ δ᾽ ἄνθρωπος οὗτος Ἄδαμος ἐκλήθη· σημαίνει δὲ τοῦτο κατὰ γλῶτταν τὴν Ἑβραίων πυρρόν,² ἐπειδήπερ ἀπὸ τῆς πυρρᾶς γῆς φυραθείσης ἐγεγόνει· τοιαύτη γάρ ἐστιν ἡ παρθένος γῆ
35 καὶ ἀληθινή. παρίστησι δὲ ὁ θεὸς τῷ Ἀδάμῳ κατὰ γένη τὰ ζῷα θῆλύ τε καὶ ἄρρεν ἀποδειξάμενος, καὶ τούτοις ὀνόματα τίθησιν οἷς ἔτι καὶ νῦν καλοῦνται. βλέπων δὲ τὸν Ἄδαμον οὐκ ἔχοντα κοινωνίαν πρὸς τὸ θῆλυ καὶ συνδιαίτησιν,

¹ βυθοῦ SPL. ² πυρρός SPL Lat.

---

[a] *i.e.*, as modern critics recognize, near the point of transition from one document ("P") to another ("J").

to indicate the revolutions of the seasons. The fifth day He let loose in the deep and in the air the creatures that swim or fly, linking them in partnership and union to generate and to increase and multiply their kind. The sixth day He created the race of four-footed creatures, making them male and female: on this day also He formed man. Thus, so Moses tells us, the world and everything in it was made in six days in all; and on the seventh day God rested and had respite from His labours, for which reason we also pass this day in repose from toil and call it the sabbath, a word which in the Hebrew language means "rest."

(2) And here, after the seventh day,[a] Moses begins to interpret nature,[b] writing on the formation of man in these terms: "God fashioned man by taking dust from the earth and instilled into him spirit and soul." (Gen. ii. 7.) Now this man was called Adam, which in Hebrew signifies "red," because he was made from the red earth kneaded together; for such is the colour of the true virgin soil.[c] And God brought before Adam the living creatures after their kinds, exhibiting both male and female, and gave[d] them the names by which they are still called to this day. Then seeing Adam to be without female partner and consort (for indeed there was none), and looking with astonishment at the

---

[b] Greek "physiologize"; *cf.* § 18.

[c] *Adâmah* = "ground," from which Adam or man was formed (Gen. ii. 7): *Adôm* = "red" (*cf.* Edom). "The old derivation [of Adam and *Adamah*] from the verb 'be red' is generally abandoned, but none better has been found to replace it" (Skinner, *Genesis*).

[d] In Gen. ii. 20 Adam names the animals: in Josephus there is no indication of a change of subject to justify the rendering "and he (Adam) gave," etc.

JOSEPHUS

οὐδὲ γὰρ ἦν, ξενιζόμενον δ' ἐπὶ τοῖς ἄλλοις ζῴοις οὕτως ἔχουσι, μίαν αὐτοῦ κοιμωμένου πλευρὰν 36 ἐξελὼν ἐξ αὐτῆς ἔπλασε γυναῖκα.[1] καὶ ὁ Ἄδαμος προσαχθεῖσαν αὐτὴν ἐγνώρισεν ἐξ αὐτοῦ γενομένην. ἔσσα δὲ καθ' Ἑβραίων διάλεκτον καλεῖται γυνή, τὸ δ' ἐκείνης ὄνομα τῆς γυναικὸς Εὔα ἦν· σημαίνει δὲ τοῦτο πάντων [τῶν ζώντων][2] μητέρα.

37 (3) Φησὶ δὲ τὸν θεὸν καὶ παράδεισον πρὸς τὴν ἀνατολὴν καταφυτεῦσαι παντοίῳ τεθηλότα φυτῷ· ἐν τούτοις δ' εἶναι καὶ τῆς ζωῆς τὸ φυτὸν καὶ ἄλλο τὸ τῆς φρονήσεως, ᾗ[3] διεγινώσκετο τί [τε] 38 εἴη τὸ ἀγαθὸν καὶ τί τὸ κακόν. εἰς τοῦτον δὲ τὸν κῆπον εἰσαγαγόντα τόν τε Ἄδαμον καὶ τὴν γυναῖκα κελεῦσαι τῶν φυτῶν ἐπιμελεῖσθαι. ἄρδεται δ' οὗτος ὁ κῆπος ὑπὸ ἑνὸς ποταμοῦ πᾶσαν ἐν κύκλῳ τὴν γῆν περιρρέοντος, ὃς εἰς τέσσαρα μέρη σχίζεται. καὶ Φεισῶν μέν, σημαίνει δὲ πληθὺν τοὔνομα, ἐπὶ τὴν Ἰνδικὴν φερόμενος ἐκδίδωσιν εἰς τὸ πέλαγος 39 ὑφ' Ἑλλήνων Γάγγης λεγόμενος, Εὐφράτης δὲ καὶ Τίγρις ἐπὶ τὴν Ἐρυθρὰν ἀπίασι θάλασσαν· καλεῖται δὲ ὁ μὲν Εὐφράτης Φοράς,[4] σημαίνει δὲ ἤτοι σκεδασμὸν ἢ ἄνθος, Τίγρις δὲ Διγλάθ, ἐξ οὗ φράζεται τὸ μετὰ στενότητος ὀξύ· Γηὼν δὲ διὰ

[1] RO: τὴν γυναῖκα rell.
[2] om. RO.   [3] RO: ᾧ rell.   [4] RO Lat.: Φορά rell.

[a] *Isshah* in modern transcription (Gen. ii. 23 R.V. margin).
[b] Strictly *Ḥavvah* (Eve) = "living" or "life": Josephus, constantly loose in his etymology, following the Biblical "because she was the mother of all living," implies that that is the actual meaning of the word.
[c] Heb. Pishon, river and etymology unknown (by some connected with Heb. *push* = "spring up"); Josephus

other creatures who had their mates, He extracted one of his ribs while he slept and from it formed woman; and when she was brought to him Adam recognized that she was made from himself. In the Hebrew tongue woman is called *essa* [a]; but the name of that first woman was Eve, which signifies "mother of all (living)." [b]

Gen. ii. 23, iii. 20.

(3) Moses further states that God planted eastward a park, abounding in all manner of plants, among them being the tree of life and another of the wisdom by which might be distinguished what was good and what evil; and into this garden he brought Adam and his wife and bade them tend the plants. Now this garden is watered by a single river whose stream encircles all the earth and is parted into four branches. Of these Phison [c] (a name meaning "multitude") runs towards India and falls into the sea, being called by the Greeks Ganges; Euphrates and Tigris end in the Erythraean [d] Sea: the Euphrates is called Phoras,[e] signifying either "dispersion" or "flower," and the Tigris Diglath,[f] expressing at once "narrowness" and "rapidity";

Paradise.

Gen. ii. 10 ff.

identifies "the land of Havilah where there is gold" with India.

[d] Greek "Red Sea," in the wider meaning, found in Herodotus, of the Indian Ocean, including its two gulfs, the Red Sea and the Persian Gulf.

[e] Heb. Perâth: derived by Josephus from either (?) √*Pâras* "divide" or √*Pârâh* "be fruitful." Philo adopts the second interpretation, rendering by καρποφορία (*Leg. Alleg.* i. 23, § 72). These etymologies are probably taken over from others.

[f] Diglath is the *Aramaic* equivalent of Heb. Ḥiddeḳel; Josephus quotes the Aramaic form but translates the Hebrew! *Ḥad* = "sharp" (ὀξύ), *daḳ* = "thin" (στενόν); this, though it leaves out the last syllable *el*, seems the most satisfactory explanation.

τῆς Αἰγύπτου ῥέων δηλοῖ τὸν ἀπὸ τῆς ἐναντίας[1]
ἀναδιδόμενον ἡμῖν, ὃν δὴ Νεῖλον Ἕλληνες προσ-
αγορεύουσιν·

40 (4) Ὁ δὴ τοίνυν θεὸς τὸν Ἄδαμον καὶ τὴν
γυναῖκα τῶν μὲν ἄλλων φυτῶν ἐκέλευε, γεύεσθαι,
τοῦ δὲ τῆς φρονήσεως ἀπέχεσθαι, προειπὼν ἁψα-
41 μένοις ἀπ' αὐτοῦ ὄλεθρον γενησόμενον. ὁμο-
φωνούντων δὲ κατ' ἐκεῖνο καιροῦ τῶν ζῴων
ἁπάντων ὄφις συνδιαιτώμενος τῷ τε Ἀδάμῳ καὶ
τῇ γυναικὶ φθονερῶς μὲν εἶχεν ἐφ' οἷς αὐτοὺς
εὐδαιμονήσειν ᾤετο πεπεισμένους τοῖς τοῦ θεοῦ
42 παραγγέλμασιν, οἰόμενος δὲ συμφορᾷ περιπεσεῖσθαι
παρακούσαντας ἀναπείθει κακοήθως τὴν γυναῖκα
γεύσασθαι τοῦ φυτοῦ τῆς φρονήσεως ἐν αὐτῷ
λέγων εἶναι τήν τε τἀγαθοῦ καὶ τοῦ κακοῦ διάγνωσιν, ἧς γενομένης αὐτοῖς μακάριον καὶ μηδὲν
43 ἀπολείποντα τοῦ θείου διάξειν βίον. καὶ παρα-
κρούεται μὲν οὕτω τὴν γυναῖκα τῆς ἐντολῆς τοῦ
θεοῦ καταφρονῆσαι· γευσαμένη δὲ τοῦ φυτοῦ καὶ
ἡσθεῖσα τῷ ἐδέσματι καὶ τὸν Ἄδαμον ἀνέπεισεν
44 αὐτῷ χρήσασθαι. καὶ συνίεσάν τε αὐτῶν ἤδη
γεγυμνωμένων καὶ τὴν αἰσχύνην ὕπαιθρον ἔχοντες
σκέπην αὑτοῖς ἐπενόουν· τὸ γὰρ φυτὸν ὀξύτητος
καὶ διανοίας ὑπῆρχε. φύλλοις οὖν ἑαυτοὺς συκῆς
ἐσκέπασαν καὶ ταῦτα πρὸ τῆς αἰδοῦς προβαλλό-
μενοι[2] μᾶλλον ἐδόκουν εὐδαιμονεῖν ὡς ἃν πρότερον

[1] RO: ἀνατολῆς rell. [2] προβαλόμενοι Niese with S².

---

[a] Heb. Gihon; derived by Josephus, as by modern critics, from *giaḥ* "burst forth." The reading "from the opposite (world)" is preferable to the other "from the east." Ancient writers rather looked to the west for the source of the Nile;

JEWISH ANTIQUITIES, I. 39-44

lastly Geon,^a which flows through Egypt, means "that which wells up to us from the opposite world," and by Greeks is called the Nile.

(4) Now God bade Adam and his wife partake of the rest of the plants, but to abstain from the tree of wisdom, forewarning them that, if they touched it, it would prove their destruction. At that epoch all the creatures spoke a common tongue,^b and the serpent, living in the company of Adam and his wife, grew jealous of the blessings which he supposed were destined for them if they obeyed God's behests, and, believing that disobedience would bring trouble upon them, he maliciously persuaded the woman to taste of the tree of wisdom, telling her that in it resided the power of distinguishing good and evil, possessing which they would lead a blissful existence no whit behind that of a god. By these means he misled the woman to scorn the commandment of God: she tasted of the tree, was pleased with the food, and persuaded Adam also to partake of it. And now they became aware that they were naked and, ashamed of such exposure to the light of day, bethought them of a covering; for the tree served to quicken their intelligence. So they covered themselves with fig-leaves, and, thus screening their persons, believed themselves the happier for having

The fall and expulsion from Paradise.

Gen. iii. 1

thus Dio Cassius, using the same verb as Josephus, writes ἐκ τοῦ Ἄτλαντος τοῦ ὄρους σαφῶς ἀναδίδοται (lxxv. 13).

^b This legend appears in the *Book of Jubilees* (c. 100 B.C.): "On that day [of Adam's exit from Paradise] was closed the mouth of all beasts ... so that they could no longer speak: for they had all spoken one with another with one lip and with one tongue" (iii. 28 trans. Charles). *Cf.* also Philo, *De opif. mundi* 55, § 156 λέγεται τὸ παλαιὸν τὸ ἰοβόλον καὶ γηγενὲς ἑρπετὸν [ὄφις] ἀνθρώπου φωνὴν προΐεσθαι (quoted by Weill).

45 ἐσπάνιζον εὑρόντες. τοῦ θεοῦ δ' εἰς τὸν κῆπον ἐλθόντος ὁ μὲν Ἄδαμος, πρότερον εἰς ὁμιλίαν αὐτῷ φοιτῶν, συνειδὼς αὑτῷ τὴν ἀδικίαν ὑπεχώρει, τὸν δὲ θεὸν ἐξένιζε τὸ πραττόμενον καὶ τὴν αἰτίαν ἐπυνθάνετο, δι' ἣν πρότερον ἡδόμενος τῇ πρὸς αὐτὸν ὁμιλίᾳ νῦν φεύγει ταύτην καὶ περιΐσταται.
46 τοῦ δὲ μηδὲν φθεγγομένου διὰ τὸ συγγινώσκειν ἑαυτῷ παραβάντι τὴν τοῦ θεοῦ πρόσταξιν " ἀλλ' ἐμοὶ μέν," εἶπεν ὁ θεός, " ἔγνωστο περὶ ὑμῶν, ὅπως βίον εὐδαίμονα καὶ κακοῦ παντὸς ἀπαθῆ βιώσετε μηδεμιᾷ ξαινόμενοι τὴν ψυχὴν φροντίδι, πάντων δ' ὑμῖν αὐτομάτων ὅσα πρὸς ἀπόλαυσιν καὶ ἡδονὴν συντελεῖ κατὰ τὴν ἐμὴν ἀνιόντων πρόνοιαν χωρὶς ὑμετέρου πόνου καὶ ταλαιπωρίας, ὧν παρόντων γῆράς τε θᾶττον οὐκ ἂν ἐπέλθοι καὶ
47 τὸ ζῆν ὑμῖν μακρὸν γένοιτο. νῦν δ' εἰς ταύτην μου τὴν γνώμην ἐνύβρισας παρακούσας τῶν ἐμῶν ἐντολῶν· οὐ γὰρ ἐπ' ἀρετῇ τὴν σιωπὴν ἄγεις, ἀλλ'
48 ἐπὶ συνειδότι πονηρῷ." Ἄδαμος δὲ παρῃτεῖτο τῆς ἁμαρτίας αὑτὸν καὶ παρεκάλει τὸν θεὸν μὴ χαλεπαίνειν αὐτῷ, τὴν γυναῖκα τοῦ γεγονότος αἰτιώμενος καὶ λέγων ὑπ' αὐτῆς ἐξαπατηθεὶς
49 ἁμαρτεῖν, ἡ δ' αὖ κατηγόρει τοῦ ὄφεως. ὁ δὲ θεὸς ἥττονα γυναικείας συμβουλίας αὐτὸν γενόμενον ὑπετίθει τιμωρίᾳ, τὴν γῆν οὐκέτι μὲν οὐδὲν αὐτοῖς ἀναδώσειν αὐτομάτως εἰπών, πονοῦσι δὲ καὶ τοῖς ἔργοις τριβομένοις τὰ μὲν παρέξειν, τῶν δ' οὐκ ἀξιώσειν. Εὔαν δὲ τοκετοῖς καὶ ταῖς ἐξ ὠδίνων ἀλγηδόσιν ἐκόλαζεν, ὅτι τὸν Ἄδαμον οἷς αὐτὴν ὁ ὄφις ἐξηπάτησε τούτοις παρακρουσαμένη
50 συμφοραῖς περιέβαλεν. ἀφείλετο δὲ καὶ τὸν ὄφιν τὴν φωνὴν ὀργισθεὶς ἐπὶ τῇ κακοηθείᾳ τῇ πρὸς

found what they lacked before. But, when God entered the garden, Adam, who ere then was wont to resort to His company, conscious of his crime withdrew; and God, met by action so strange, asked for what reason he who once took delight in His company now shunned and avoided it. But when he spoke not a word, conscious of having transgressed the divine command, God said, " Nay, I had decreed for you to live a life of bliss, unmolested by all ill, with no care to fret your souls; all things that contribute to enjoyment and pleasure were, through my providence, to spring up for you spontaneously, without toil or distress of yours; blessed with these gifts, old age would not soon have overtaken you and your life would have been long. But now thou hast flouted this my purpose by disobeying my commands; for it is through no virtue that thou keepest silence but through an evil conscience." Adam then began to make excuse for his sin and besought God not to be wroth with him, laying the blame for the deed upon the woman and saying that it was her deception that had caused him to sin; while she, in her turn, accused the serpent. Thereupon God imposed punishment on Adam for yielding to a woman's counsel, telling him that the earth would no more produce anything of herself, but, in return for toil and grinding labour, would but afford some of her fruits and refuse others. Eve He punished by child-birth and its attendant pains, because she had deluded Adam, even as the serpent had beguiled her, and so brought calamity upon him. He moreover deprived the serpent of speech,[a] indignant at his

[a] See § 41 (note).

JOSEPHUS

τὸν Ἄδαμον καὶ ἰὸν ἐντίθησιν ὑπὸ τὴν γλῶτταν αὐτῷ πολέμιον ἀποδείξας ἀνθρώποις καὶ ὑποθέμενος κατὰ τῆς κεφαλῆς φέρειν τὰς πληγάς, ὡς ἐν ἐκείνῃ τοῦ τε κακοῦ τοῦ πρὸς ἀνθρώπους κειμένου καὶ τῆς τελευτῆς ῥᾴστης τοῖς ἀμυνομένοις ἐσομένης, ποδῶν τε αὐτὸν ἀποστερήσας σύρεσθαι 51 κατὰ τῆς γῆς ἰλυσπώμενον ἐποίησε. καὶ ὁ μὲν θεὸς ταῦτα προστάξας αὐτοῖς πάσχειν μετοικίζει τὸν Ἄδαμον καὶ τὴν Εὔαν ἐκ τοῦ κήπου εἰς ἕτερον χωρίον.

52 (ii. 1) Γίνονται δὲ αὐτοῖς παῖδες ἄρρενες δύο· προσηγορεύετο δὲ αὐτῶν ὁ μὲν πρῶτος Κάϊς, κτῆσιν δὲ σημαίνει τοῦτο μεθερμηνευόμενον τοὔνομα, Ἄβελος δὲ ὁ δεύτερος, σημαίνει δὲ οὐθὲν[1] 53 τοῦτο· γίνονται δὲ αὐτοῖς καὶ θυγατέρες. οἱ μὲν οὖν ἀδελφοὶ διαφόροις ἔχαιρον ἐπιτηδεύμασιν· Ἄβελος μὲν γὰρ ὁ νεώτερος δικαιοσύνης ἐπεμελεῖτο καὶ πᾶσι τοῖς ὑπ' αὐτοῦ πραττομένοις παρεῖναι τὸν θεὸν νομίζων ἀρετῆς προενόει,[2] ποιμενικὸς δ' ἦν ὁ βίος αὐτῷ· Κάϊς δὲ τά τε ἄλλα πονηρότατος ἦν καὶ πρὸς τὸ κερδαίνειν μόνον ἀποβλέπων γῆν τε ἀροῦν ἐπενόησε πρῶτος καὶ κτείνει δὲ τὸν 54 ἀδελφὸν ἐκ τοιαύτης αἰτίας· θῦσαι τῷ θεῷ δόξαν αὐτοῖς ὁ μὲν Κάϊς τοὺς ἀπὸ τῆς γεωργίας καὶ φυτῶν καρποὺς ἐπήνεγκεν, Ἄβελος δὲ γάλα καὶ τὰ πρωτότοκα τῶν βοσκημάτων. ὁ δὲ θεὸς ταύτῃ

[1] R^{vid} O Lat.: πένθος rell. [2] προέβη RO.

[a] Greek "Kais"; Josephus, for the sake of his readers, hellenizes Hebrew proper names, as he explains below (§ 129). For a like reason the familiar forms are generally retained in this translation.

[b] So the Biblical etymology "I have gotten a man" (LXX ἐκτησάμην), from Heb. *ḳanah* "acquire."

malignity to Adam; He also put poison beneath his tongue, destining him to be the enemy of men, and admonishing them to strike their blows upon his head, because it was therein that man's danger lay and there too that his adversaries could most easily inflict a mortal blow; He further bereft him of feet and made him crawl and wriggle along the ground. Having imposed these penalties upon them, God removed Adam and Eve from the garden to another place.

The serpent deprived of speech. Gen. iii. 15.

(ii. 1) Two male children were born to them; the first was called Cain,[a] whose name being interpreted means "acquisition,"[b] and the second Abel, meaning "nothing."[c] They also had daughters.[d] Now the brothers took pleasure in different pursuits. Abel, the younger, had respect for justice[e] and, believing that God was with him in all his actions, paid heed to virtue; he led the life of a shepherd. Cain, on the contrary, was thoroughly depraved and had an eye only to gain: he was the first to think of ploughing the soil, and he slew his brother for the following reason. The brothers having decided to sacrifice to God, Cain brought the fruits of the tilled earth and of the trees, Abel came with milk[f] and the firstlings of his flocks. This was the offering which found more

Cain and Abel. Gen. iv. 1.

---

[c] Abel, Heb. *Hebel* = "vapour" or "vanity": the noun is translated, as here, by οὐθέν in Is. xlix. 4. The reading πένθος (= Heb. *'ébel*) presents another etymology found also in Philo, *De migr. Abr.* 13, § 74 ὄνομα δ' ἐστι τὰ θνητὰ πενθοῦντος (quoted by Weill).

[d] Legendary addition: *Jubilees* iv. 1, 8 names them 'Awan and 'Azura.

[e] Or "righteousness."

[f] Heb. "fat" and so LXX (στεάτων): Josephus, with a different vocalization of the Heb. *ḥlb*, reads "milk," showing independence of the Greek Bible.

μᾶλλον ἥδεται τῇ θυσίᾳ, τοῖς αὐτομάτοις καὶ κατὰ
φύσιν γεγονόσι τιμώμενος, ἀλλ' οὐχὶ τοῖς κατ'
ἐπίνοιαν ἀνθρώπου πλεονέκτου [καὶ] βίᾳ πεφυκόσιν.
55 ἔνθεν ὁ Κάις παροξυνθεὶς ἐπὶ τῷ προτετιμῆσθαι
τὸν Ἄβελον ὑπὸ τοῦ θεοῦ κτείνει τὸν ἀδελφὸν καὶ
τὸν νεκρὸν αὐτοῦ ποιήσας ἀφανῆ λήσειν ὑπέλαβεν.
ὁ δὲ θεὸς συνεὶς τὸ ἔργον ἧκε πρὸς τὸν Κάιν περὶ
τἀδελφοῦ πυνθανόμενος, ποῖ ποτ' εἴη· πολλῶν γὰρ
αὐτὸν οὐκ ἰδεῖν ἡμερῶν τὸν ἄλλον χρόνον πάντα
56 μετ' αὐτοῦ βλέπων αὐτὸν ἀναστρεφόμενον. ὁ δὲ
Κάις ἀπορούμενος καὶ οὐκ ἔχων ὅ τι λέγοι πρὸς
τὸν θεὸν ἀμηχανεῖν μὲν καὶ αὐτὸς ἔφασκε τὸ
πρῶτον ἐπὶ τἀδελφῷ μὴ βλεπομένῳ, παροξυνθεὶς
δὲ τοῦ θεοῦ λιπαρῶς ἐγκειμένου καὶ πολυπραγμο-
νοῦντος οὐκ εἶναι παιδαγωγὸς καὶ φύλαξ αὐτοῦ
57 καὶ τῶν ὑπ' αὐτοῦ πραττομένων ἔλεγεν. ὁ δὲ
θεὸς τοὐντεῦθεν ἤλεγχεν ἤδη τὸν Κάιν φονέα
τἀδελφοῦ γενόμενον καὶ " θαυμάζω," φησίν, " εἰ
περὶ ἀνδρὸς ἀγνοεῖς εἰπεῖν τί γέγονεν, ὃν αὐτὸς
58 ἀπολώλεκας." τῆς μὲν οὖν ἐπὶ τῷ φόνῳ τιμωρίας
αὐτὸν ἠφίει, θυσίαν τε ἐπιτελέσαντα καὶ δι' αὐτῆς
ἱκετεύσαντα μὴ λαβεῖν ὀργὴν [ἐπ'] αὐτῷ χαλεπωτέραν, ἐπάρατον δ' αὐτὸν ἐτίθει καὶ τοὺς
ἐγγόνους αὐτοῦ τιμωρήσεσθαι κατὰ τὴν ἑβδόμην
ἠπείλησε γενεάν, καὶ τῆς γῆς αὐτὸν ἐκείνης
59 ἐκβάλλει σὺν τῇ γυναικί. τοῦ δὲ μὴ θηρίοις ἁλώ-

---

[a] Weill quotes *Pirkê R. Eliezer* xxi " He took the corpse of his brother Abel and hid it in the field."

[b] Cain's words " My punishment is greater than I can bear " (Gen. iv. 13) were, in Rabbinical opinion, " reckoned

JEWISH ANTIQUITIES, I. 54–59

favour with God, who is honoured by things that grow spontaneously and in accordance with natural laws, and not by the products forced from nature by the ingenuity of grasping man. Thereupon Cain, incensed at God's preference for Abel, slew his brother and hid his corpse,[a] thinking to escape detection. But God, aware of the deed, came to Cain, and asked him whither his brother had gone, since for many days He had not seen him, whom he had constantly before beheld in Cain's company. Cain, in embarrassment, having nothing to reply to God, at first declared that he too was perplexed at not seeing his brother, and then, enraged at the insistent pressure and strict inquiries of God, said that he was not his brother's guardian to keep watch over his person and his actions. Upon that word God now accused Cain of being his brother's murderer, saying, "I marvel that thou canst not tell what has become of a man whom thou thyself hast destroyed." God, however, exempted him from the penalty merited by the murder, Cain having offered a sacrifice and therewith supplicated Him not to visit him too severely in His wrath[b]; but He made him accursed and threatened to punish his posterity in [c] the seventh generation, and expelled him from that land with his wife. But, when Cain feared that in his wanderings

Cf. Gen. iv. 13-15.

to him as repentance " (*Pirķê R. Eliezer*, xxi, quoted with other passages by Weill).

[c] The rendering of κατά by "until" seems unwarranted. Josephus apparently, in common with the Targum (Weill), means that Cain's penalty is suspended until the seventh generation, cf. § 65. Gen. iv. 15, however, on which this interpretation is based, as interpreted by modern critics states something quite different, viz. that seven lives, that of the slayer and six of his family, would be exacted for the slaughter of Cain.

μενος περιπέσῃ δεδιότος καὶ τοῦτον ἀπόληται τὸν
τρόπον, ἐκέλευε μηδὲν ὑφορᾶσθαι σκυθρωπὸν ἀπὸ
τοιαύτης αἰτίας, ἀλλ' ἕνεκα τοῦ μηδὲν αὐτῷ ἐκ
θηρίων γενέσθαι δεινὸν διὰ πάσης ἀδεῶς χωρεῖν
γῆς· καὶ σημεῖον ἐπιβαλών, ᾧ γνώριμος ἂν εἴη,
προσέταξεν ἀπιέναι.

60 (2) Πολλὴν δ' ἐπελθὼν γῆν ἱδρύεται μετὰ τῆς
γυναικὸς Κάις[1] Ναΐδα τόπον οὕτω καλούμενον καὶ
αὐτόθι ποιεῖται τὴν κατοίκησιν, ἔνθ' αὐτῷ καὶ
παῖδες ἐγένοντο. οὐκ ἐπὶ νουθεσίᾳ δὲ τὴν κόλασιν
ἔλαβεν, ἀλλ' ἐπ' αὐξήσει τῆς κακίας, ἡδονὴν μὲν
πᾶσαν ἐκπορίζων αὐτοῦ τῷ σώματι, κἂν μεθ'
61 ὕβρεως τῶν συνόντων δέῃ ταύτην ἔχειν· αὔξων
δὲ τὸν οἶκον πλήθει χρημάτων ἐξ ἁρπαγῆς καὶ
βίας πρὸς ἡδονὴν καὶ λῃστείαν τοὺς ἐντυγχάνοντας
παρακαλῶν διδάσκαλος αὐτοῖς ὑπῆρχε πονηρῶν
ἐπιτηδευμάτων, καὶ τὴν ἀπραγμοσύνην, ᾗ πρότερον
συνέζων οἱ ἄνθρωποι, μέτρων ἐπινοίᾳ καὶ
σταθμῶν μετεστήσατο ἀκέραιον αὐτοῖς ὄντα τὸν
βίον ἐκ τῆς τούτων ἀμαθίας καὶ μεγαλόψυχον εἰς
62 πανουργίαν περιαγαγών, ὅρους τε γῆς πρῶτος
ἔθετο καὶ πόλιν ἐδείματο καὶ τείχεσιν ὠχύρωσεν
εἰς ταὐτὸν συνελθεῖν τοὺς οἰκείους καταναγκάσας.
καὶ τὴν πόλιν δὲ ταύτην ἀπὸ Ἀνώχου τοῦ πρε-
63 σβυτάτου παιδὸς Ἄνωχαν ἐκάλεσεν. Ἀνώχου δὲ
Ἰαράδης υἱὸς ἦν, ἐκ δὲ τούτου Μαρούηλος, οὗ
γίνεται παῖς Μαθουσάλας, τοῦ δὲ Λάμεχος, ᾧ
παῖδες ὑπῆρξαν ἑπτὰ καὶ ἑβδομήκοντα ἐκ δύο
64 γυναικῶν αὐτῷ φύντες Σελλᾶς καὶ Ἄδας. τούτων

[1] +εἰς E (Lat. in loco).

---

[a] Mentioned in a Rabbinical commentary *in loc.* (" who-

JEWISH ANTIQUITIES, I. 59-64

he would fall a prey to wild beasts *a* and perish thus, God bade him have no melancholy foreboding from such cause : he would be in no danger from beasts, and might fare unafraid through every land. He then set a mark upon him, by which he should be recognized, and bade him depart.

(2) After long travels Cain settled with his wife in a place called Nais,*b* where he made his abode and children were born to him. His punishment, however, far from being taken as a warning, only served to increase his vice. He indulged in every bodily pleasure, even if it entailed outraging his companions ; he increased his substance with wealth amassed by rapine and violence ; he incited to luxury and pillage all whom he met, and became their instructor in wicked practices. He put an end to that simplicity in which men lived before by the invention of weights and measures : the guileless and generous existence which they had enjoyed in ignorance of these things he converted into a life of craftiness. He was the first to fix boundaries of land and to build a city, fortifying it with walls and constraining his clan to congregate in one place. This city he called Anocha after his eldest son Anoch.*c* Anoch had a son Jarad,*d* of whom came Maruel,*e* who begat Mathousalas, the father of Lamech, who had seventy-seven *f* children by his two wives, Sella and

Descendants of Cain. Gen. iv. 16.

---

soever slayeth ") as assembling to avenge the blood of Abel (Weill). *b* Heb. Nod, LXX Ναίδ.

c Heb. and LXX Enoch (city and son).
d Heb. Irad, LXX Γαιδάδ.   *e* Heb. Mehujael.
f As suggested by Weill, these seventy-seven children, not mentioned in Scripture, have probably been extracted, through some misreading of the text, out of the allusion to "Lamech" being avenged "seventy and sevenfold" (Gen. iv. 24, LXX ἐκ δὲ Λάμεχ ἑβδομηκοντάκις ἑπτά).

JOSEPHUS

Ἰώβηλος μὲν ἐξ Ἄδας γεγονὼς σκηνὰς ἐπήξατο
καὶ προβατείαν ἠγάπησεν, Ἰούβαλος δέ, ὁμομήτριος
δ' ἦν αὐτῷ, μουσικὴν ἤσκησε καὶ ψαλτήρια καὶ
κιθάρας ἐπενόησεν, Ἰουβῆλος[1] δὲ τῶν ἐκ τῆς
ἑτέρας γεγονότων ἰσχύι πάντας ὑπερβαλὼν τὰ
πολεμικὰ διαπρεπῶς μετῆλθεν, ἐκ τούτων καὶ τὰ
πρὸς ἡδονὴν τοῦ σώματος ἐκπορίζων, χαλκείαν
65 τε πρῶτος ἐπενόησεν. πατὴρ δὲ θυγατρὸς γενόμενος ὁ Λάμεχος Νοεμᾶς ὄνομα, ἐπεὶ τὰ θεῖα
σαφῶς ἐξεπιστάμενος ἑώρα δίκην αὐτὸν ὑφέξοντα
τῆς Κάιος ἀδελφοκτονίας [μείζονα],[2] τοῦτο ταῖς
66 ἑαυτοῦ γυναιξὶν ἐποίησε φανερόν. ἔτι δὲ ζῶντος
Ἀδάμου Κάιος τοὺς ἐγγόνους πονηροτάτους συνέβη
γενέσθαι κατὰ διαδοχὴν καὶ μίμησιν ἄλλον ἄλλου
χείρονα τελευτῶντα· πρός τε γὰρ πολέμους εἶχον
ἀκράτως καὶ πρὸς λῃστείαν ὡρμήκεσαν· ἄλλως[3]
δ' εἴ τις ὀκνηρὸς ἦν πρὸς τὸ φονεύειν, ἄλλην[4]
ἀπόνοιαν ἦν θράσους ὑβρίζων καὶ πλεονεκτῶν.
67 (3) Ἄδαμος δὲ ὁ πρῶτος ἐκ γῆς γενόμενος,
ἀπαιτεῖ γὰρ ἡ διήγησις τὸν περὶ αὐτοῦ λόγον,
Ἀβέλου μὲν ἐσφαγμένου, Κάιος δὲ διὰ τὸν ἐκείνου
φόνον πεφευγότος, παιδοποιίας ἐφρόντιζε, καὶ
δεινὸς εἶχεν αὐτὸν γενέσεως ἔρως ἔτη τριάκοντ' ἤδη
καὶ διακόσια ἠνυκότα τοῦ βίου, πρὸς οἷς ἕτερα

RO (Lat.): Θόβελος (Θεόβ.) rell.   [2] om. SPL Exc.
[3] conj. Niese: ἄλλος or ὅλως codd.
[4] ἀλλ' οὖν SP Exc.

---

[a] So LXX: Heb. Jabal.
[b] Heb. Tubal-cain, LXX Θοβέλ (see other reading in Josephus).
[c] So LXX: Heb. Naamah.

30

Ada. Of these children, Jobêl,[a] son of Ada, erected tents and devoted himself to a pastoral life; Jubal, born of the same mother, studied music and invented harps and lutes; Jubêl,[b] one of the sons of the other wife, surpassing all men in strength, distinguished himself in the art of war, procuring also thereby the means for satisfying the pleasures of the body, and first invented the forging of metal. Lamech was also the father of a daughter named Noema[c]; and because through his clear knowledge of divine things he saw that he was to pay the penalty[d] for Cain's murder of his brother, he made this known to his wives. Thus, within Adam's lifetime, the descendants of Cain went to depths of depravity, and, inheriting and imitating one another's vices, each ended worse than the last. They rushed incontinently into battle and plunged into brigandage; or if anyone was too timid for slaughter, he would display other forms of mad recklessness by insolence and greed.[e]

(3) Meanwhile Adam, the man first formed out of earth—for my narrative requires me to revert to him—after the slaughter of Abel and the consequent flight of his murderer Cain, longed for children, and was seized with a passionate desire to beget a family, when he had now completed 230[f] years of his life;

Descendants of Seth.

Gen. v. 3 f.

---

[d] Or, with the other reading, "a greater penalty." See § 58 note: Lamech was but five generations from Cain, but in his address to his wives (obviously misunderstood by Josephus) the allusions to "a man" and "a young man" may have been taken to refer to a son and grandson, thus completing the predicted seven generations.

[e] Text a little doubtful.

[f] So LXX: in the Heb. Bible Adam was 130 years old when he begat Seth and lived for 800 years more after that date. Similar numerical divergences will be met with later, §§ 83 ff.

JOSEPHUS

68 ζήσας ἑπτακόσια τελευτᾷ. γίνονται μὲν οὖν αὐτῷ παῖδες ἄλλοι τε πλείους καὶ Σῆθος· ἀλλὰ περὶ μὲν τῶν ἄλλων μακρὸν ἂν εἴη λέγειν, πειράσομαι δὲ μόνα τὰ τῶν ἀπὸ Σήθου διελθεῖν. τραφεὶς γὰρ οὗτος καὶ παρελθὼν εἰς ἡλικίαν ἤδη [τὰ] καλὰ κρίνειν δυναμένην [ἀρετὴν ἐπετήδευσε][1] καὶ γενόμενος αὐτὸς ἄριστος μιμητὰς τῶν αὐτῶν τοὺς ἀπο-
69 γόνους κατέλιπεν. οἱ δὲ πάντες ἀγαθοὶ φύντες γῆν τε τὴν αὐτὴν ἀστασίαστοι κατῴκησαν εὐδαιμονήσαντες, μηδενὸς αὐτοῖς ἄχρι καὶ τελευτῆς δυσκόλου προσπεσόντος, σοφίαν τε τὴν περὶ τὰ οὐράνια καὶ
70 τὴν τούτων διακόσμησιν ἐπενόησαν. ὑπὲρ δὲ τοῦ μὴ διαφυγεῖν τοὺς ἀνθρώπους τὰ εὑρημένα μηδὲ πρὶν εἰς γνῶσιν ἐλθεῖν φθαρῆναι, προειρηκότος ἀφανισμὸν Ἀδάμου τῶν ὅλων ἔσεσθαι, τὸν μὲν κατ' ἰσχὺν πυρὸς τὸν ἕτερον δὲ κατὰ βίαν καὶ πλῆθος ὕδατος, στήλας δύο ποιησάμενοι τὴν μὲν ἐκ πλίνθου τὴν ἑτέραν δὲ ἐκ λίθων ἀμφοτέραις
71 ἐνέγραψαν τὰ εὑρημένα, ἵνα καὶ τῆς πλινθίνης ἀφανισθείσης ὑπὸ τῆς ἐπομβρίας ἡ λιθίνη μείνασα παράσχῃ μαθεῖν τοῖς ἀνθρώποις τὰ ἐγγεγραμμένα δηλοῦσα καὶ πλινθίνην ὑπ' αὐτῶν ἀνατεθῆναι. μένει δ' ἄχρι δεῦρο κατὰ γῆν τὴν Σειρίδα.[2]
72 (iii. 1) Καὶ οὗτοι μὲν ἑπτὰ γενεὰς διέμειναν θεὸν ἡγούμενοι δεσπότην εἶναι τῶν ὅλων καὶ πάντα πρὸς ἀρετὴν ἀποβλέποντες, εἶτα προϊόντος χρόνου

[1] om. RO. [2] Σιριάδα SPF Exc.

[a] See preceding note.
[b] The Bible mentions "sons and daughters," but names none except Seth: *Jubilees* iv. 10 specifies "yet nine sons."
[c] Rabbinical amplification; Enoch in particular was credited with these discoveries (*Jubilees* iv. 17 and the book that bears his name).

he lived for 700 ᵃ years more before he died. Many other children ᵇ were born to him, and among them Seth; it would take me too long to speak of the rest, and I will only endeavour to narrate the story of the progeny of Seth. He, after being brought up and attaining to years of discretion, cultivated virtue, excelled in it himself, and left descendants who imitated his ways. These, being all of virtuous character, inhabited the same country without dissension and in prosperity, meeting with no untoward incident to the day of their death; they also discovered the science of the heavenly bodies and their orderly array.ᶜ Moreover, to prevent their discoveries from being lost to mankind and perishing before they became known—Adam having predicted a destruction of the universe, at one time by a violent fire and at another by a mighty deluge of water—they erected two pillars, one of brick and the other of stone, and inscribed these discoveries on both; so that, if the pillar of brick disappeared in the deluge, that of stone would remain to teach men what was graven thereon and to inform them that they had also erected one of brick.ᵈ It exists to this day in the land of Seiris.ᵉ

Their astronomical discoveries

(iii. 1) For seven generations these people continued to believe in God as Lord of the universe and in everything to take virtue for their guide; then,

and later degeneration.

ᵈ Another version of this story appears in *Jubilees* viii. 3 (discovery of a writing carved on the rock recording the teaching of the watchers or angels concerning the heavenly bodies).

ᵉ Unidentified: Seirah, mentioned in connexion with "sculptured stones" in the story of Ehud (Jud. iii. 26), has been suggested. The tradition, as Reinach writes, doubtless arose from some ancient monument with an inscription in unknown (? Hittite) characters.

JOSEPHUS

μεταβάλλονται πρὸς τὸ χεῖρον ἐκ τῶν πατρίων
ἐθισμῶν μήτε τὰς νενομισμένας τιμὰς ἔτι τῷ θεῷ
παρέχοντες μήτε τοῦ πρὸς ἀνθρώπους δικαίου
ποιούμενοι λόγον, ἀλλ' ἣν πρότερον εἶχον τῆς
ἀρετῆς ζήλωσιν διπλασίονα τῆς κακίας τότ' ἐπιδεικνύμενοι δι' ὧν ἔπραττον· ἔνθεν ἑαυτοῖς τὸν
73 θεὸν ἐξεπολέμωσαν. πολλοὶ γὰρ ἄγγελοι θεοῦ
γυναιξὶ συνιόντες ὑβριστὰς ἐγέννησαν παῖδας καὶ
παντὸς ὑπερόπτας καλοῦ διὰ τὴν ἐπὶ τῇ δυνάμει
πεποίθησιν· ὅμοια γὰρ τοῖς ὑπὸ γιγάντων τε-
τολμῆσθαι λεγομένοις ὑφ' Ἑλλήνων καὶ οὗτοι
74 δρᾶσαι παραδίδονται. Νῶχος δὲ τοῖς πραττομένοις ὑπ' αὐτῶν δυσχεραίνων καὶ τοῖς βουλεύμασιν ἀηδῶς ἔχων ἔπειθεν ἐπὶ τὸ κρεῖττον τὴν
διάνοιαν αὐτοὺς καὶ τὰς πράξεις μεταφέρειν,
ὁρῶν δ' οὐκ ἐνδιδόντας, ἀλλ' ἰσχυρῶς ὑπὸ τῆς
ἡδονῆς τῶν κακῶν κεκρατημένους, δείσας μὴ καὶ
φονεύσωσιν αὐτὸν μετὰ γυναικῶν[1] καὶ τέκνων
καὶ τῶν τούτοις συνοικουσῶν ἐξεχώρησε τῆς γῆς.
75 (2) Ὁ δὲ θεὸς τοῦτον μὲν τῆς δικαιοσύνης
ἠγάπησε, κατεδίκαζε δ' οὐκ ἐκείνων μόνων τῆς
κακίας, ἀλλὰ καὶ πᾶν ὅσον ἦν ἀνθρώπινον τότε
δόξαν αὐτῷ διαφθεῖραι καὶ ποιῆσαι γένος ἕτερον
πονηρίας καθαρόν, ἐπιτεμόμενος αὐτῶν τὸν βίον
καὶ ποιήσας ἐτῶν οὐχ ὅσα πρότερον ἔζων, ἀλλ'
ἑκατὸν εἴκοσιν, εἰς θάλασσαν τὴν ἤπειρον μετέβαλε.
76 καὶ οἱ μὲν οὕτως ἀφανίζονται πάντες, Νῶχος δὲ
σῴζεται μόνος, ὑποθεμένου μηχανὴν αὐτῷ καὶ

---

[1] γυναικὸς Bekker with Lat.

---

[a] So the LXX renders the Heb. "sons of God"; from the 2nd cent. A.D. Jewish Rabbis, to avoid this "unseemly

in course of time, they abandoned the customs of their fathers for a life of depravity. They no longer rendered to God His due honours, nor took account of justice towards men, but displayed by their actions a zeal for vice twofold greater than they had formerly shown for virtue, and thereby drew upon themselves the enmity of God. For many angels [a] of God now consorted with women and begat sons who were overbearing and disdainful of every virtue, such confidence had they in their strength; in fact the deeds that tradition ascribes to them resemble the audacious exploits told by the Greeks of the giants. But Noah,[b] indignant at their conduct and viewing their counsels with displeasure, urged them to come to a better frame of mind and amend their ways [c]; but seeing that, far from yielding, they were completely enslaved to the pleasure of sin, he feared that they would murder him and, with his wives and sons and his sons' wives, quitted the country.

Gen. vi. 1.

Noah's preaching.

(2) God loved Noah for his righteousness, but, as for those men, He condemned not them alone for their wickedness, but resolved to destroy all mankind then existing and to create another race pure of vice, abridging their term of life from its former longevity to one hundred and twenty years; he therefore converted the dry land into sea. Thus were they all obliterated, while Noah alone was saved, God having

The flood.

Gen. vi. 3.

mythology " (§ 15), interpreted the phrase to mean members of aristocratic families.

[b] " Nôchos."

[c] For Noah as " preacher of righteousness " *cf.* 2 Peter ii. 5 (1 Peter iii. 20); Book I. of the *Sibylline Oracles* (a work of mixed Jewish and Christian origin) devotes some 50 lines to two of his addresses. Genesis knows nothing of this or of Noah's migration mentioned below.

JOSEPHUS

77 πόρον πρὸς σωτηρίαν τοῦ θεοῦ τοιαύτην· λάρνακα τετράστεγον κατασκευάσας πηχῶν τὸ μῆκος τριακοσίων πεντήκοντα δὲ τὸ πλάτος καὶ τριάκοντα τὸ βάθος, εἰς ταύτην σὺν τῇ μητρὶ τῶν παίδων καὶ ταῖς τούτων γυναιξὶν ἀνέβη,[1] τά τε ἄλλα ὅσα πρὸς τὰς χρείας ἐπικουρήσειν αὐτοῖς ἔμελλεν ἐνθέμενος, ζῷά τε παντοῖα πρὸς διατήρησιν τοῦ γένους αὐτῶν ἄρρενάς τε καὶ θηλείας συνεισβαλόμενος ἄλλα τε τούτων ἑπταπλασίονα τὸν ἀριθμόν.

78 ἦν δ' ἡ λάρναξ τούς τε τοίχους καρτερὰ καὶ τὸν ὄροφον, ὡς μηδαμόθεν ἐπικλύζεσθαι μηδ' ἡττᾶσθαι τῆς τοῦ ὕδατος βίας. καὶ Νῶχος μὲν οὕτως μετὰ

79 τῶν οἰκείων διασώζεται. ἦν δ' αὐτὸς μὲν ἀπὸ Ἀδάμου δέκατος· Λαμέχου γάρ ἐστιν υἱός, οὗ πατὴρ ἦν Μαθουσάλας, οὗτος δὲ ἦν τοῦ Ἀνώχου τοῦ Ἰαρέδου, Μαλαήλου δὲ Ἰάρεδος ἐγεγόνει, ὃς ἐκ Καϊνᾶ τεκνοῦται τοῦ Ἀνώσου σὺν ἀδελφαῖς πλείοσιν, Ἄνωσος δὲ Σήθου υἱὸς ἦν τοῦ Ἀδάμου.

80 (3) Συνέβη δὲ τοῦτο τὸ πάθος κατὰ τὸ ἑξακοσιοστὸν ἔτος ἤδη Νώχου τῆς ἀρχῆς, ἐν μηνὶ δευτέρῳ Δίῳ μὲν ὑπὸ Μακεδόνων λεγομένῳ, Μαρσουάνῃ δ' ὑπὸ Ἑβραίων· οὕτω γὰρ ἐν Αἰγύπτῳ

81 τὸν ἐνιαυτὸν ἦσαν διατεταχότες. Μωυσῆς δὲ τὸν Νισᾶν, ὅς ἐστι Ξανθικός, μῆνα πρῶτον ἐπὶ ταῖς

[1] OL: ἐνέβη rell.

---

[a] Josephus employs the word used by classical writers of Deucalion's ark (λάρναξ), not κιβωτός of the LXX.

[b] Three only in Scripture.

[c] These words must have accidentally dropped out of the Greek text.

[d] Viz. the "clean" beasts, the "unclean" being limited to pairs (Gen. vii. 2 "J"): the Priestly narrator ("P") makes no such distinction and speaks only of pairs (Gen. vi. 19).

JEWISH ANTIQUITIES, I. 77–81

put into his mind a device and means of salvation on this wise. He constructed an ark[a] of four[b] stories, three hundred cubits in length, fifty in breadth and thirty in depth, on which he embarked with [his children,][c] the mother of his children and his sons' wives, not only furnishing it with all things requisite to supply their needs, but also taking with him creatures of every kind, male and female, to preserve their species, some among them being numbered by sevens.[d] This ark had stout sides and roof so as not to be overwhelmed from any quarter and to defy the violence of the waters. Thus was Noah saved with his family. He was the tenth descendant of Adam, being son of Lamech, whose father was Mathusalas,[e] the son of Anoch,[f] the son of Jared, the son of Malael,[g] who with many sisters[h] was begotten by Cainas,[i] son of Anos,[j] the son of Seth, the son of Adam.

(3) This catastrophe happened in the six hundredth year of Noah's rulership,[k] in what was once the second month, called by the Macedonians Dius and by the Hebrews Marsuan,[l] according to the arrangement of the calendar which they followed in Egypt. Moses, however, appointed Nisan, that is to say Xanthicus,

Gen. vi. 15 f.

Date of the flood.
Gen. vii. 11.

---

[e] Heb. Methuselah.
[f] Heb. Enoch.
[g] Heb. Mahalalel.
[h] Read perhaps ἀδελφοῖς = " brothers and sisters."
[i] Heb. Kenan.
[j] Heb. Enosh.
[k] " Life " must be meant (Gen. vii. 6, 11) : the first-born is regarded as becoming head of the clan at his birth. *Cf.* §§ 86 f.
[l] Heb. *Marḥeshwan* (=October-November). Josephus commonly takes the names of the months from the Macedonian calendar, appending the Hebrew post-exilic equivalents.

JOSEPHUS

ἑορταῖς ὥρισε κατὰ τοῦτον ἐξ Αἰγύπτου τοὺς
Ἑβραίους προαγαγών· οὗτος δ' αὐτῷ καὶ πρὸς
ἁπάσας τὰς εἰς τὸ θεῖον τιμὰς ἦρχεν, ἐπὶ μέντοι
γε πράσεις καὶ ὠνὰς καὶ τὴν ἄλλην διοίκησιν
τὸν πρῶτον κόσμον διεφύλαξε· τὴν δ' ἐπομβρίαν
ἄρξασθαί φησιν ἑβδόμῃ τοῦ προειρημένου μηνὸς
82 καὶ εἰκάδι. χρόνος δὲ οὗτος ἀπὸ Ἀδάμου τοῦ
πρώτου γεγονότος ἐτῶν ὑπῆρχε δισχιλίων δια-
κοσίων ἑξηκονταδύο.¹ ἀναγέγραπται δὲ ὁ χρόνος
ἐν ταῖς ἱεραῖς βίβλοις σημειουμένων μετὰ πολλῆς

---

¹ δισχιλίων ἑξακοσίων πεντηκονταέξ SPL Lat.

---

^a *Cf.* Exod. xii. 2.

^b The old Hebrew year began in autumn ; later custom transferred the opening, for certain purposes, to the spring. The Babylonian year began in spring, and the completion of the change in Hebrew practice doubtless dates from the exile, though there are indications before that date of the alternative custom. In attributing an innovation to Moses Josephus is merely following the Priestly (exilic) editor of Exodus xii. : in referring to him a distinction between an ecclesiastical and a civil year the historian seems to impute to earlier ages the custom of his own day. For this there is a classical passage in the Mishnah, *Rosh Hashanah*, i. 1, distinguishing four New Years' Days for various purposes. (Driver on Exodus *loc. cit.*; I. Abrahams in Hastings' *B.D.*, art. " Time " supports the accuracy of Josephus.)

^c So LXX : Heb. " on the seventeenth day."

^d So Niese, with the best MS. of Josephus here extant, cod. O ; there is a lacuna at this point in its usual companion, cod. R. The figure 2262 is the correct total of the items which follow and is doubtless original (Niese, Preface p. xxxv). The figures in the other authorities (2656 SPL Lat., 1656 Zonaras, 1056 Epitome) are due to conformation, partial or complete, to the Hebrew text of Genesis. For the Hebrew and the Greek texts of that book here diverge, representing two different schemes of antediluvian chronology ; and Josephus follows the LXX or an allied text. The lifetime of each patriarch remains constant in both schemes. The main

38

as the first month for the festivals, because it was in this month that he brought the Hebrews out of Egypt[a]; he also reckoned this month as the commencement of the year for everything relating to divine worship, but for selling and buying and other ordinary affairs he preserved the ancient order.[b] It was, he tells us, on the seven and twentieth [c] day of the said month that the deluge began. The time of this event was 2262 [d] years after the birth of Adam, the first man; the date is recorded in the sacred books, it being the custom of that age to note with

Moses alteration of the calendar.

The year of the flood anno mundi

difference between the totals of the first and third columns below arises from the repeated transference of a century from one portion of the life to the other; clearly a deliberate and arbitrary alteration made in one or other of the texts in the interest of some scheme of world chronology.

HEBREW TEXT (Gen. v. 3-31).			GREEK TEXT (LXX and Josephus).		Both Texts.
	Age at birth of first-born.	After life.	Age at birth of first-born.	After life (LXX).	Total.
Adam	130	800	230	700	930
Seth	105	807	205	707	912
Enosh	90	815	190	715	905
Kenan	70	840	170	740	910
Mahalalel	65	830	165	730	895
Jared	162	800	162	800	962
Enoch	65	300	165	200	365
Methuselah	187	782	187	782	969
Lamech	182	595	188	565	{ Heb. 777 LXX 753 Jos. 707
	Age at Flood (Gen. vii. 6, 11)		Age at Flood (*Ant.* i. 80).		
Noah	600	..	600	..	..
Total = date of Flood *anno mundi*	1656	..	2262	..	..

ἀκριβείας τῶν τότε καὶ τὰς γενέσεις τῶν ἐπιφανῶν ἀνδρῶν καὶ τὰς τελευτάς.

83 (4) Ἀδάμῳ μὲν [οὖν] τριακοστῷ ἤδη καὶ διακοσιοστῷ ἔτει γεγονότι παῖς Σῆθος γίνεται, ὃς ἐνακόσια καὶ τριάκοντα ἔτη ἐβίωσε. Σῆθος δὲ κατὰ πέμπτον καὶ διακοσιοστὸν ἔτος ἐγέννησεν Ἄνωσον, ὃς πέντε ζήσας ἔτη καὶ ἐνακόσια Καϊνᾷ τῷ παιδὶ τὴν τῶν πραγμάτων ἐπιμέλειαν δίδωσι τεκνώσας αὐτὸν περὶ ἐνενηκοστὸν καὶ ἑκατοστὸν ἔτος· οὗτος ἐβίωσεν ἔτη δώδεκα πρὸς τοῖς ἐνα-
84 κοσίοις. Καϊνᾶς δὲ βιοὺς δέκα καὶ ἐνακόσια Μαλάηλον υἱὸν ἔσχεν ἔτει γενόμενον ἑβδομηκοστῷ καὶ ἑκατοστῷ. οὗτος ὁ Μαλάηλος ζήσας πέντε καὶ ἐνενήκοντα καὶ ὀκτακόσια ἔτη ἐτελεύτησεν Ἰάρεδον καταλιπὼν υἱόν, ὃν ἔτος πέμπτον ἑξηκοστὸν καὶ ἑκατοστὸν γενόμενος ἐγέννησε.
85 τοῦτον εἰς δύο¹ καὶ ἑξήκοντα πρὸς τοῖς ἐνακοσίοις βιώσαντα Ἄνωχος υἱὸς διαδέχεται γεννηθεὶς περὶ ἔτη δύο καὶ ἑξήκοντα καὶ ἑκατὸν τοῦ πατρὸς αὐτῷ τυγχάνοντος. οὗτος ζήσας πέντε καὶ ἑξήκοντα πρὸς τοῖς τριακοσίοις ἀνεχώρησε πρὸς τὸ θεῖον,
86 ὅθεν οὐδὲ τελευτὴν αὐτοῦ ἀναγεγράφασι. Μαθουσάλας δὲ Ἀνώχου παῖς κατὰ ἔτος αὐτῷ γεγονὼς πέμπτον καὶ ἑξηκοστὸν καὶ ἑκατοστὸν Λάμεχον υἱὸν ἔσχε περὶ ἔτη γεγονὼς ἑπτὰ καὶ ὀγδοήκοντα καὶ ἑκατόν, ᾧ τὴν ἀρχὴν παρέδωκεν αὐτὸς αὐτὴν κατασχὼν ἐννέα καὶ ἑξήκοντα καὶ ἐνακοσίοις.
87 Λάμεχος δὲ ἄρξας ἑπτὰ καὶ ἑπτακοσίοις ἔτεσι Νῶχον τῶν πραγμάτων ἀποδείκνυσι προστάτην υἱόν, ὃς Λαμέχῳ γενόμενος ὄγδοον καὶ ὀγδοηκοστὸν καὶ ἑκατοστὸν ἔτος ἠνυκότι πεντήκοντα
88 καὶ ἐνακοσίοις ἔτεσιν ἦρξε τῶν πραγμάτων. ταῦτα

JEWISH ANTIQUITIES, I. 82–88

minute care the birth and death of the illustrious men.

(4) For Adam was 230 years old when his son Seth was born and [a] lived (in all) 930 years. Seth at the age of 205 begat Anos,[b] who when aged 905 years delivered the care of affairs to his son Cainas,[c] whom he had begotten when he was about 190 years old; Seth[d] lived in all 912 years. Cainas lived 910 years and in his 170th year had a son Malael.[e] This Malael died aged 895 years, leaving a son Jared, whom he begat at the age of 165. Jared lived 969 years and was succeeded by his son Anoch,[f] born when his father was in his 162nd year; Anoch lived 365 years and then returned to the divinity,[g] whence it comes that there is no record in the chronicles of his death. Mathusalas[h] the son of Anoch was born when his father was 165, and at the age of 187 had a son Lamech, to whom he transmitted the rulership which he had held for 969 years. Lamech bare rule for 707 years and put at the head of affairs his son Noah, who was born when his father was 188, and for 950 years held the reins of power. These years,

fixed by the genealogy of the patriarchs.
Gen. v. 3-3L

Ib. ix. 29.

---

[a] Gr. "who," apparently referring to Seth. But Adam must be intended (see table): Seth's age at death is mentioned below. Josephus is not concerned with the ages at death which do not help to fix the date of the flood (§ 88); and the two clauses in § 83 ὅς ... ἐβίωσε, οὗτος ἐβίωσεν κτλ. may be later marginal insertions which have become misplaced in the text.

[b] Enosh. [c] Kenan. [d] Gr. "he": see note a.
[e] Mahalalel. [f] Enoch.
[g] "God took him" or in LXX "transported him" (μετέθηκεν), Gen. v. 24; Josephus uses the same phrase "return to the divinity" of the passing of Moses, A. iv. 326 (iii. 96). [h] Methuselah.

---

[1] ἐννέα O Lat.

συναγόμενα τὰ ἔτη τὸν προαναγεγραμμένον πληροῖ[1] χρόνον. ἐξεταζέτω δὲ μηδεὶς τὰς τελευτὰς τῶν ἀνδρῶν, τοῖς γὰρ αὐτῶν παισὶ καὶ τοῖς ἐκείνων ἀπογόνοις παρεξέτεινον[2] τὸν βίον, ἀλλὰ τὰς γενέσεις αὐτῶν μόνον ὁράτω.

89 (5) Ἐπισημήναντος δὲ τοῦ θεοῦ καὶ ὕειν ἀρξαμένου τὸ ὕδωρ ἡμέραις τεσσαράκοντα ὅλαις κατεφέρετο, ὡς ἐπὶ πήχεις πεντεκαίδεκα τὴν γῆν ὑπερέχειν. καὶ τοῦτο ἦν τὸ αἴτιον τοῦ μὴ διασωθῆναι πλείονας φυγῆς ἀφορμὴν οὐκ ἔχοντας. 90 παυσαμένου δὲ τοῦ ὑετοῦ μόλις ἤρξατο ὑποβαίνειν τὸ ὕδωρ ἐφ' ἡμέρας ἑκατὸν καὶ πεντήκοντα, ὡς μηνὶ ἑβδόμῳ, ἱσταμένου δὲ ἦν ἑβδόμη, κατ' ὀλίγον ὑπονοστεῖν ἀπολήγοντος. ἔπειτα τῆς λάρνακος περὶ ἄκραν τινὰ ὄρους σταθείσης κατὰ τὴν Ἀρμενίαν συνεὶς ὁ Νῶχος ἀνοίγει τ' αὐτὴν[3] καὶ θεασάμενος γῆν βραχεῖαν περὶ αὐτὴν ἐπὶ χρηστο- 91 τέρας ἤδη γεγονὼς ἐλπίδος ἠρέμει. ὀλίγαις δ' ὕστερον ἡμέραις μᾶλλον ὑποχωροῦντος τοῦ ὕδατος μεθήῃσι κόρακα, βουλόμενος μαθεῖν εἴ τι καὶ ἄλλο τῆς γῆς ἐκλελειμμένον ὑπὸ τοῦ ὕδατος ἀσφαλὲς

---

[1] συμπληροῖ SPL.
[2] συμπαρεξέτεινον SPL.
[3] τ' αὐτὴν Niese: ταύτην codd.

---

[a] Greek ὡς " so that " : possibly ἕως should be read.
[b] Gr. "in the seventh month, and it was the seventh (day) of its first decade."
[c] Such I take to be the meaning: ἀπολήγοντος (sc. τοῦ μηνός) is the converse of ἱσταμένου and a variant for the normal ἀπιόντος or φθίνοντος, the technical term for the last decade of the month. The Scriptural account, composed of two sources, "J" and "P," is different: "(J) And the waters returned from off the earth continually: (P) and *after the end of*

JEWISH ANTIQUITIES, I. 88–91

added together, give the total above mentioned. The reader should not examine the ages of the individuals at death, for their life-times extended into those of their sons and of their sons' descendants, but should confine his attention to their dates of birth.

(5) When God gave the signal and caused the rain- Subsidence of the flood. fall to begin, the water poured down for forty entire Gen. vii. days, insomuch that it rose to fifteen cubits above 17, 20. the surface of the earth. That was the reason why no more escaped, since they had no place of refuge. When the rain at length ceased, for 150 days the *Ib.* viii. 3 f. water scarcely began to sink, until *a* at the opening of the seventh month, from the seventh day,*b* it little by little subsided as the month drew to a close.*c* Then the ark settled on a mountain-top in Armenia: observing this, Noah opened the ark and, seeing a little land surrounding it, with hopes now revived, remained where he was. But a few days later,*d* the water continuing to sink, he let loose a raven, to *Ib.* 7 learn whether any other portion of the earth had emerged from the flood and would now make it safe

---

150 days the waters decreased. And the ark rested in the 7th month, on the 17th (LXX 27th) day of the month, upon the mountains of Ararat." Josephus indicates three dates. a period of 150 days, not of stagnation but of slight, almost imperceptible, subsidence (this he apparently gets from " J "), a more pronounced fall at the opening of the 7th month, increasing towards its close. The distinct mention of the opening and closing decades of the month may have arisen from conflicting readings in his Scriptural MSS., one of which named the 7th day as the turning-point, the other (like the LXX) the 27th. On the further stages in the subsidence (Gen. viii. 5, 14) he is silent.

d Gen. viii. 6 (J) Noah sends out the raven " at the end of " the " forty days " of the flood.

ἐστιν ἤδη πρὸς ἔκβασιν· ὁ δὲ πᾶσαν εὑρὼν ἔτι
λιμναζομένην πρὸς Νῶχον ἐπανῆλθε. μετὰ δὲ
ἡμέρας ἑπτὰ περιστερὰν ἐπὶ τῷ γνῶναι τὰ περὶ
92 τὴν γῆν προὔπεμψεν· ἐπανελθούσης δὲ πεπηλωμένης ἅμα καὶ θαλλὸν ἐλαίας κομιζούσης, μαθὼν
τὴν γῆν ἀπηλλαγμένην τοῦ κατακλυσμοῦ μείνας
ἄλλας ἑπτὰ ἡμέρας τά τε ζῷα τῆς λάρνακος
ἐξαφίησιν αὐτός τε μετὰ τῆς γενεᾶς προελθὼν
καὶ θύσας τῷ θεῷ συνευωχεῖτο τοῖς οἰκείοις.
ἀποβατήριον μέντοι τὸν τόπον τοῦτον Ἀρμένιοι
καλοῦσιν· ἐκεῖ γὰρ ἀνασωθείσης τῆς λάρνακος ἔτι
νῦν αὐτῆς¹ τὰ λείψανα ἐπιδεικνύουσι.

93 (6) Τοῦ δὲ κατακλυσμοῦ τούτου καὶ τῆς λάρνακος μέμνηνται πάντες οἱ τὰς βαρβαρικὰς ἱστορίας ἀναγεγραφότες, ὧν ἐστι Βηρωσὸς ὁ Χαλδαῖος·
διηγούμενος γὰρ τὰ περὶ τὸν κατακλυσμὸν οὕτως
που διέξεισι· " λέγεται δὲ καὶ τοῦ πλοίου ἐν τῇ
Ἀρμενίᾳ πρὸς τῷ ὄρει τῶν Κορδυαίων ἔτι μέρος
τι εἶναι καὶ κομίζειν τινὰς τῆς ἀσφάλτου ἀφαιροῦν-
τας· χρῶνται δ' οἱ ἄνθρωποι τῷ κομιζομένῳ πρὸς
94 τοὺς ἀποτροπιασμούς." μέμνηται δὲ τούτων καὶ
Ἱερώνυμος ὁ Αἰγύπτιος ὁ τὴν ἀρχαιολογίαν τὴν
Φοινικικὴν συγγραψάμενος καὶ Μνασέας δὲ καὶ

¹ αὐτῆς RO: οἱ ἐπιχώριοι M Lat.: the rest, including
Euseb., present a conflate text.

---

[a] Condensation of the Scriptural account in which the
dove is sent out three times at intervals of seven days (Gen.
viii. 8, 10, 12).

[b] πεπηλωμένης: this detail comes apparently from Berosus
(mentioned below), who writes in his account of the flood

to disembark; but the bird found the whole land inundated and returned to Noah. Seven days after he sent forth a dove [a] to explore the condition of the earth; it returned bearing the marks of clay [b] and an olive-branch in its mouth. Noah, thus learning that the earth was delivered from the flood, waited yet seven days, and then let the animals out of the ark, went forth himself with his family, sacrificed to God and feasted with his household. The Armenians call that spot the Landing-place, for it was there that the ark came safe to land, and they show the relics of it to this day.

(6) This flood and the ark are mentioned by all who have written histories of the barbarians. Among these is Berosus the Chaldaean,[c] who in his description of the events of the flood writes somewhere [d] as follows: "It is said, moreover, that a portion of the vessel still survives in Armenia on the mountain of the Cordyaeans,[e] and that persons carry off pieces of the bitumen, which they use as talismans." These matters are also mentioned by Hieronymus the Egyptian,[f] author of the ancient history of Phoenicia,

Gen. viii. 8.
Ib. 11.

External witnesses to the flood.

ταῦτα (τὰ ὄρνεα) δὲ πάλιν εἰς τὴν ναῦν ἐλθεῖν τοὺς πόδας πεπηλωμένους ἔχοντα, C. Müller, *Frag. Hist. Graec.* ii. 501.

[c] A Hellenized Babylonian priest, c. 330–250 B.C., who wrote a history of Babylon in three books (*Ap.* i. 129 ff.). His account of the Chaldaean flood and the salvation of the hero Xisouthros (the equivalent of Noah) has been preserved by Alexander Polyhistor, through Syncellus, and is printed in Müller, *loc. cit.* (last note).

[d] Or "somewhat." The text quoted by Syncellus differs slightly from that below.

[e] *Alias* Gordyaeans or Carduchi, occupying approximately the modern Kurdistan.

[f] Otherwise unknown (to be distinguished from Hieronymus of Cardia, historian of the Diadochi, mentioned elsewhere, *Ap.* i. 213).

JOSEPHUS

ἄλλοι πλείους, καὶ Νικόλαος δὲ ὁ Δαμασκηνὸς ἐν τῇ ἐνενηκοστῇ καὶ ἕκτῃ βίβλῳ ἱστορεῖ περὶ αὐτῶν 95 λέγων οὕτως· " ἔστιν ὑπὲρ τὴν Μινυάδα μέγα ὄρος κατὰ τὴν Ἀρμενίαν Βάρις λεγόμενον, εἰς ὃ πολλοὺς συμφυγόντας ἐπὶ τοῦ κατακλυσμοῦ λόγος ἔχει περισωθῆναι καί τινα ἐπὶ λάρνακος ὀχούμενον ἐπὶ τὴν ἀκρώρειαν ὀκεῖλαι καὶ τὰ λείψανα τῶν ξύλων ἐπὶ πολὺ σωθῆναι. γένοιτο δ' ἂν οὗτος, ὅντινα καὶ Μωυσῆς ἀνέγραψεν ὁ Ἰουδαίων νομοθέτης."

96 (7) Νῶχος δὲ φοβούμενος, μὴ καθ' ἕκαστον ἔτος ἐπικλύζῃ τὴν γῆν ὁ θεὸς φθορὰν ἀνθρώπων καταψηφισάμενος, ἱερὰ[1] καύσας ἐδεῖτο τὸν θεὸν τοῦ λοιποῦ ἐπὶ τῆς πρώτης μένειν εὐταξίας καὶ μηδὲν ἔτι τοιοῦτον ἐπενεγκεῖν πάθος, ὑφ' οὗ κινδυνεύσει πᾶν ἀπολέσθαι τὸ τῶν ζῴων γένος, ἀλλὰ τετιμωρημένον τοὺς πονηροὺς φειδὼ ποιεῖσθαι τῶν διὰ χρηστότητα περιλειφθέντων καὶ τὸ δεινὸν 97 διαφυγεῖν κεκριμένων· κακοδαιμονεστέρους γὰρ ἐκείνων ἔσεσθαι καὶ χείρω κακίαν καταδικασθέντας, εἰ μὴ πρὸς τὸ παντελὲς εἶεν σεσωσμένοι, τηρηθεῖεν δ' ἑτέρῳ κατακλυσμῷ, τοῦ μὲν πρώτου τὸν φόβον καὶ τὴν ἱστορίαν μαθόντες,[2] τοῦ δευ98τέρου δὲ τὴν ἀπώλειαν. εὐμενῶς τε οὖν αὐτὸν προσδέχεσθαι τὴν θυσίαν παρεκάλει καὶ μηδεμίαν

[1] RO Lat. (*fana*!): ἱερεία rell.
[2] *v.l.* παθόντες, which should probably be inserted after ἀπώλειαν.

---

[a] Of Patara in Lycia, antiquary and disciple of Eratosthenes, end of third cent. B.C.: there are passing allusions to him in *Ap.* i. 216, ii. 112.

[b] Friend and biographer of Herod the Great and author of a Universal History which was one of the main sources

JEWISH ANTIQUITIES, I. 94–98

by Mnaseas[a] and by many others. Nicolas of Damascus[b] in his ninety-sixth book relates the story as follows: "There is above the country of Minyas[c] in Armenia a great mountain called Baris, where, as the story goes, many refugees found safety at the time of the flood, and one man, transported upon an ark, grounded upon the summit, and relics of the timber were for long preserved; this might well be the same man of whom Moses, the Jewish legislator, wrote."

(7) Noah, fearing that God, having sentenced mankind to annihilation, might annually inundate the earth, offered burnt-sacrifices and besought Him to maintain for the future the primitive order (of nature) and to inflict no more such calamity as would bring the whole race of living creatures into danger of destruction, but, having now punished the wicked, to spare those who for their rectitude had survived and been judged fit to escape the peril. For their lot would be more miserable than that of those miscreants, and they would be condemned to a yet worse evil, were they now not absolutely secure but reserved for another deluge, and after learning the terrible reality and tale of the first, they were to be the victims of the second. He therefore entreated Him graciously to accept his sacrifice and to be moved

Noah's fear of a second flood.

of Josephus. Here, as in § 108, Nicolas is the last name in a list of authorities; and Josephus perhaps takes over the other names from him and has no first-hand knowledge of Hieronymus, etc.

[c] The Minni of the O.T. (Jer. li. 27), like the *Mannu* of Assyrian inscriptions, are mentioned in close connexion with Ararat. Another tradition, mentioned elsewhere by Josephus (*A.* xx. 24 f.), places the relics of the ark in a region remote from Ararat, viz. at Carrhae, S.E. of Edessa.

ὀργὴν ἐπὶ τὴν γῆν ὁμοίαν λαβεῖν,[1] ὅπως ἔργοις τε τοῖς ταύτης προσλιπαροῦντες καὶ πόλεις ἀναστήσαντες εὐδαιμόνως ζῆν ἔχοιεν καὶ μηδενὸς ὧν καὶ πρὸ τῆς ἐπομβρίας ἀπέλαυον ὑστερῶσιν ἀγαθῶν, εἰς μακρὸν αὐτῶν γῆρας καὶ βίου μῆκος ὅμοιον τοῖς τάχιον ἐπερχομένων.

99 (8) Νώχου δὲ ταύτας ποιησαμένου τὰς ἱκετείας ὁ θεὸς ἐπὶ δικαιοσύνῃ τὸν ἄνδρα ἀγαπῶν ἐπένευεν αὐτῷ τὰς εὐχὰς εἰς τέλος ἄξειν, οὔτε τοὺς διεφθαρμένους λέγων αὐτὸς ἀπολέσαι, κακίᾳ δὲ τῇ οἰκείᾳ ταύτην αὐτοὺς ὑποσχεῖν τὴν δίκην, οὔτ᾽ ἄν, εἰ γενομένους ἀνθρώπους ἀφανίσαι διεγνώκει, 100 παραγαγεῖν αὐτοὺς εἰς τὸν βίον, σῶφρον γὰρ εἶναι τὴν ἀρχὴν αὐτοῖς μηδὲ χαρίσασθαι τὸ ζῆν ἢ δόντα τοῦτο διαφθείρειν· "ἀλλ᾽ οἷς ἐξύβριζον εἰς τὴν ἐμὴν εὐσέβειαν καὶ ἀρετήν, τούτοις ἐξεβιάσαντό με ταύτην αὐτοῖς ἐπιθεῖναι τὴν δίκην. 101 παύσομαι δὲ τοῦ λοιποῦ μετὰ τοσαύτης ὀργῆς τὰς τιμωρίας ἐπὶ τοῖς ἀδικήμασιν εἰσπραττόμενος καὶ πολὺ μᾶλλον σοῦ παρακαλοῦντος. εἰ δ᾽ ἐπὶ πλέον ποτὲ χειμάσαιμι, μὴ δείσητε τῶν ὄμβρων τὸ μέγεθος· οὐ γὰρ ἔτι τὴν γῆν ἐπικλύσει τὸ ὕδωρ. 102 παραινῶ μέντοι σφαγῆς ἀνθρωπίνης ἀπέχεσθαι καὶ καθαρεύειν φόνου τοὺς δράσαντάς τι τοιοῦτον κολάζοντας, χρῆσθαι δὲ τοῖς ἄλλοις ζῴοις ἅπασι πρὸς ἃ βούλεσθε καὶ τὰς ὀρέξεις ἔχετε· δεσπότας γὰρ ἁπάντων ὑμᾶς εἶναι πεποίηκα τῶν τε χερσαίων

---

[1] So most mss. (*cf.* i. 58): βαλεῖν RO.

---

[a] τάχιον is occasionally used in Josephus as equivalent to πρότερον, *e.g.* *A.* xvi. 179, *B.* i. 284 (= τὸ πρῶτον in the parallel

JEWISH ANTIQUITIES, I. 98–102

no more to such wrath against the earth, that so they might assiduously devote themselves to its cultivation, erect cities, live in happiness, lacking none of the blessings which they enjoyed before the deluge, and attain to a ripe old age and a length of days like that of the men of yore.[a]

(8) Noah having ended his supplications, God, who loved this man for his righteousness, signified to him that He would grant his prayers. Those who had perished, He said, had not been destroyed by Him, but through their own wickedness had incurred this punishment; had He determined to annihilate mankind when made, He would not have called them into existence, for it were reasonable not to have bestowed the boon of life at all rather than having given to destroy it. "No, it was the outrages with which they met my reverent regard[b] and goodness that constrained me to impose this penalty upon them. Howbeit from henceforth I will cease to exact punishment for crimes with such wrathful indignation; I will cease above all at thy petition. And if ever I send tempests of exceeding fury, fear ye not the violence of the rainfall; for never more shall the water overwhelm the earth. Yet I exhort you to refrain from shedding human blood, to keep yourselves pure from murder and to punish those guilty of such crime. The other living creatures ye may use as may meet your desires and appetites, for I have made you lords of all, creatures both of the land and of the deep, and such

God's covenant with Noah. Cf. Gen. viii. 21 ff.

---

passage in *A.* xiv. 384), 432 καὶ τάχιον μὲν μάλιστα δὲ μετὰ τὴν .. ἄφιξιν. There is no need, as Weill thinks, to alter the text to τοῖς πάλαι.

[b] εὐσέβεια, *pietas*, rather strangely placed in the mouth of the Deity, seems to denote His *respect* for His creatures, unless it is a synonym for "holiness."

καὶ νηκτῶν καὶ ὅσα τὴν μετάρσιον αἰώραν ἔχει καὶ φοράν, χωρὶς αἵματος· ἐν τούτῳ γὰρ ἐστιν ἡ 103 ψυχή. σημανῶ¹ δὲ ὑμῖν παῦλαν ἐσομένην τοξείᾳ τῇ ἐμῇ,'' τὴν ἶριν ἀποσημαίνων· τόξον γὰρ εἶναι τοῦ θεοῦ παρὰ τοῖς ἐκεῖ νενόμισται. καὶ ὁ μὲν θεὸς ταῦτ' εἰπὼν καὶ ὑποσχόμενος ἀπαλλάσσεται.

104 (9) Νῶχος δὲ βιοὺς μετὰ τὴν ἐπομβρίαν πεντήκοντα καὶ τριακόσια ἔτη καὶ πάντα τὸν χρόνον τοῦτον εὐδαιμόνως διαγαγὼν τελευτᾷ ζήσας ἐτῶν 105 ἀριθμὸν ἐνακοσίων καὶ πεντήκοντα. μηδεὶς δὲ πρὸς τὸν νῦν βίον καὶ τὴν βραχύτητα τῶν ἐτῶν ἃ ζῶμεν συμβαλὼν τὸν τῶν παλαιῶν ψευδῆ νομιζέτω τὰ περὶ ἐκείνων λεγόμενα τῷ μηδένα νῦν τοσοῦτον ἐν τῷ βίῳ παρατείνειν χρόνον τεκμαιρόμενος μηδ' ἐκείνους εἰς ἐκεῖνο τὸ μῆκος τῆς ζωῆς 106 ἀφῖχθαι. οἱ μὲν γὰρ θεοφιλεῖς ὄντες καὶ ὑπ' αὐτοῦ τοῦ θεοῦ γενόμενοι καὶ διὰ τὰς τροφὰς ἐπιτηδειοτέρας πρὸς πλείονα χρόνον οὔσας εἰκότως ἔζων πλῆθος τοσοῦτον ἐτῶν· ἔπειτα καὶ δι' ἀρετὴν καὶ τὴν εὐχρηστίαν ὧν ἐπενόουν, ἀστρονομίας² καὶ γεωμετρίας, πλεῖον ζῆν τὸν θεὸν αὐτοῖς παρασχεῖν, ἅπερ οὐκ ἦν ἀσφαλῶς αὐτοῖς προειπεῖν μὴ ζήσασιν ἑξακοσίους ἐνιαυτούς· διὰ τοσούτων γὰρ ὁ μέγας 107 ἐνιαυτὸς πληροῦται. μαρτυροῦσι δέ μου τῷ λόγῳ πάντες οἱ παρ' Ἕλλησι καὶ βαρβάροις συγγραψάμενοι τὰς ἀρχαιολογίας· καὶ γὰρ καὶ Μανέθων ὁ τὴν Αἰγυπτίων ποιησάμενος ἀναγραφὴν καὶ Βηρωσὸς ὁ τὰ Χαλδαϊκὰ συναγαγὼν καὶ Μῶχός τε καὶ Ἑστιαῖος καὶ πρὸς τούτοις ὁ Αἰγύπτιος Ἱερώνυμος, οἱ τὰ Φοινικικὰ συγγραψάμενοι,³ συμ-

¹ SPL : σημαίνω rell. Lat.
² ἀστρολογίας SP Lat. Eus. ³ ROE : συνταξάμενοι rell.

as hover aloft or wing the air—yet without the blood, for therein is the soul. Moreover I will manifest the truce that ye shall have by displaying my bow." He meant the rainbow, which in those countries was believed to be God's bow. Having spoken these words and promises God left him.

(9) Noah lived after the deluge for 350 years, all happily passed, and died at the age of 950. Nor let the reader, comparing the life of the ancients with our own and the brevity of its years, imagine that what is recorded of them is false; let him not infer that, because no life is so prolonged to-day, they too never reached such a span of existence. For, in the first place, they were beloved of God and the creatures of God Himself; their diet too was more conducive to longevity: it was then natural that they should live so long. Again, alike for their merits and to promote the utility of their discoveries in astronomy and geometry, God would accord them a longer life; for they could have predicted nothing with certainty had they not lived for 600 years, that being the complete period of the great year.[a] Moreover, my words are attested by all historians of antiquity, whether Greeks or barbarians: Manetho the annalist of the Egyptians, Berosus the compiler of the Chaldaean traditions; Mochus, Hestiaeus, along with the Egyptian Hieronymus, authors of Phoenician his-

Gen. ix. 28. The longevity of the patriarchs, three reasons for it.

---

[a] As suggested by Weill, Josephus appears here to be ultimately dependent on Berosus (possibly through the medium of Nicolas or other later writer). Berosus (Frag 4 in Müller, *F.H.G.* ii. 498) reckoned world history by cycles of 60, 600 and 3600 years: the "great year" of Josephus is the middle cycle called by Berosus νῆρος.

JOSEPHUS

108 φωνοῦσι τοῖς ὑπ' ἐμοῦ λεγομένοις, Ἡσίοδός τε καὶ Ἑκαταῖος καὶ Ἑλλάνικος καὶ Ἀκουσίλαος καὶ πρὸς τούτοις Ἔφορος καὶ Νικόλαος ἱστοροῦσι τοὺς ἀρχαίους ζήσαντας ἔτη χίλια. περὶ μὲν [οὖν]¹ τούτων, ὡς ἂν ἑκάστοις ᾖ φίλον, οὕτω σκοπείτωσαν.

109 (iv. 1) Οἱ δὲ Νώχου παῖδες τρεῖς ὄντες, Σήμας καὶ Ἰάφθας καὶ Χάμας, ἔτεσιν ἑκατὸν ἔμπροσθεν τῆς ἐπομβρίας γεγονότες, πρῶτοι κατελθόντες ἀπὸ τῶν ὀρῶν εἰς τὰ πεδία τὴν ἐν τούτοις οἴκησιν ἐποιήσαντο καὶ τοὺς ἄλλους σφόδρα δεδιότας διὰ τὸν κατακλυσμὸν τὰ πεδία καὶ ὀκνηρῶς ἔχοντας πρὸς τὴν ἀπὸ τῶν ὑψηλῶν τόπων κατάβασιν ἔπει-
110 σαν θαρσήσαντας μιμητὰς αὐτῶν γενέσθαι. καὶ τὸ μὲν πεδίον, εἰς ὃ πρῶτον αὐτοὶ κατῴκησαν,² καλεῖται Σεναάρ³· τοῦ δὲ θεοῦ κελεύσαντος αὐτοὺς διὰ πολυανθρωπίαν στέλλειν ἀποικίας, ἵνα μὴ στασιάζοιεν πρὸς ἀλλήλους, ἀλλὰ γῆν πολλὴν γεωργοῦντες ἀφθονίας ἀπολαύοιεν τῶν καρπῶν, ὑπὸ ἀμαθίας παρήκουσαν τοῦ θεοῦ καὶ διὰ τοῦτο συμφοραῖς περιπεσόντες ᾔσθοντο τῆς ἁμαρτίας.
111 ἐπεὶ γὰρ ἤνθουν νεότητος πλήθει, πάλιν ὁ θεὸς

¹ om. ROE.
² So most mss. (supported by LXX): Niese αὐτοὺς κατῴκισαν.
³ Σέναρον L.

---

[a] For Nicolas as last of the list see note on § 94.

[b] The first occurrence of a formula which, with variations, recurs repeatedly where anything of a miraculous nature is in question (ii. 348, iii. 81, etc.). Dionysius of Halicarnassus in his *Roman Antiquities* (the unnamed model for our author's *Jewish Antiquities*) had already used similar formulas in the same connexion, *e.g.* i. 48. 1 κρινέτω δὲ ὡς ἕκαστος τῶν ἀκουόντων βούλεται; and by the 2nd century A.D. this non-committal attitude to the marvellous had become

tories, concur in my statements; while Hesiod, Hecataeus, Hellanicus, Acusilaus, as well as Ephorus and Nicolas,[a] report that the ancients lived for a thousand years. But on these matters let everyone decide according to his fancy.[b]

(iv. 1) The three sons of Noah—Shem, Japhet and Ham—born a hundred years[c] before the deluge, were the first to descend from the mountains to the plains and to make their abode there; the rest,[d] who by reason of the flood were sore afraid of the plains and loath to descend from the heights,[e] they persuaded to take courage and follow their example. The plain where they first settled is called Senaar.[f] God bade them, owing to increasing population, to send out colonies, that they might not quarrel with each other but cultivate much of the earth and enjoy an abundance of its fruits; but in their blindness they did not hearken to Him, and in consequence were plunged into calamities which made them sensible of their error. For when they had a flourishing youthful popu-

The descent to the plain and refusal to colonize. Gen. ix. 18

Ib. xi. 2.

---

a rule for historians. "And should any myth come into question, it should be related but not wholly credited: rather it should be left open (ἐν μέσῳ θετέος) for readers to conjecture about it as they will, but do you take no risks and incline neither to one opinion nor to the other," Lucian, *Quomodo hist. sit conscribenda* 60 (67).

[c] Noah was 500 years of age when he begat them (Gen. v. 32) and 600 at the date of the flood (vii. 6).

[d] Presumably the grandsons and later descendants, unless this is a relic of some version of the story in which others beside the family of Noah survived the flood.

[e] Non-Biblical, like most of this paragraph. Weill quotes a partial parallel from the *Pirke Rabbi Eliezer*, cap. xi. (tr. Friedlander, p. 80), "All the creatures were dwelling in one place and they were afraid of the waters of the flood, and Nimrod was king over them."

[f] LXX form of the Heb. Shinar.

αὐτοῖς συνεβούλευσε ποιεῖσθαι τὴν ἀποικίαν· οἱ
δὲ οὐ κατὰ τὴν εὐμένειαν τὴν ἐκείνου νομίζοντες
ἔχειν τὰ ἀγαθά, τὴν δ' ἰσχὺν αὐτοῖς τὴν οἰκείαν
αἰτίαν τῆς εὐπορίας ὑπολαμβάνοντες οὐκ ἐπεί-
112 θοντο. προσετίθεσαν δὲ τῷ παρακούειν τῆς τοῦ
θεοῦ γνώμης καὶ τὸ κατ' ἐπιβουλὴν ὑπονοεῖν εἰς
ἀποικίαν αὐτοὺς παρορμᾶν, ἵνα διαιρεθέντες εὐ-
επιχειρητότεροι γένωνται.
113 (2) Ἐξῆρέ τε αὐτοὺς πρός τε ὕβριν τοῦ θεοῦ
καὶ καταφρόνησιν Νεβρώδης,[1] ὃς υἱωνὸς μὲν ἦν
Χάμου τοῦ Νώχου, τολμηρὸς δὲ καὶ κατὰ χεῖρα
γενναῖος· ἔπειθεν οὖν αὐτοὺς μὴ τῷ θεῷ διδόναι
τὸ δι' ἐκεῖνον εὐδαιμονεῖν, ἀλλὰ τὴν ἰδίαν ἀρετὴν
114 ταῦτα παρέχειν αὐτοῖς ἡγεῖσθαι, καὶ περιίστα δὲ
κατ' ὀλίγον εἰς τυραννίδα τὰ πράγματα, μόνως
οὕτως νομίζων ἀποστήσειν τοὺς ἀνθρώπους τοῦ
φόβου τοῦ παρὰ τοῦ θεοῦ, εἰ χρώμενοι τῇ αὐτοῦ
δυνάμει διατελοῖεν, ἀμυνεῖσθαί τε τὸν θεὸν πάλιν
ἠπείλει τὴν γῆν ἐπικλύσαι θελήσαντα· πύργον γὰρ
οἰκοδομήσειν ὑψηλότερον ἢ τὸ ὕδωρ ἀναβῆναι
δυνηθείη, μετελεύσεσθαι δὲ καὶ τῆς τῶν προγόνων
ἀπωλείας.
115 (3) Τὸ δὲ πλῆθος πρόθυμον ἦν τοῖς Νεβρώδου
ἕπεσθαι δόγμασι δουλείαν ἡγούμενοι[2] τὸ εἴκειν τῷ
θεῷ, καὶ τὸν πύργον ᾠκοδόμουν οὐδὲν ἀπο-
λείποντες σπουδῆς οὐδὲ πρὸς τὸ ἔργον ὀκνηρῶς
ἔχοντες· ἐλάμβανε δε θᾶττον ὕψος ἢ προσεδό-
116 κησεν ἄν τις ὑπὸ πολυχειρίας. τὸ μέντοι πάχος

[1] So most (with LXX): Niese with other mss. Ναβρώδης.
[2] M: ἡγούμενον rell.

[a] Nimrod, LXX Νεβρώδ. His connexion with the tower

lation, God again counselled them to colonize; but they, never thinking that they owed their blessings to His benevolence and regarding their own might as the cause of their felicity, refused to obey. Nay, to this disobedience to God's will they even added the suspicion that God was plotting against them in urging them to emigrate, in order that, being divided, they might be more open to attack.

(2) They were incited to this insolent contempt of God by Nebrodes,[a] grandson of Ham the son of Noah, an audacious man of doughty vigour. He persuaded them to attribute their prosperity not to God but to their own valour, and little by little transformed the state of affairs into a tyranny, holding that the only way to detach men from the fear of God[b] was by making them continuously dependent upon his own power. He threatened to have his revenge on God if He wished to inundate the earth again; for he would build a tower higher than the water could reach and avenge the destruction of their forefathers.

The rebel Nimrod builds the tower of Babel.

(3) The people were eager to follow this advice of Nebrodes, deeming it slavery to submit to God; so they set out to build the tower with indefatigable ardour and no slackening in the task; and it rose with a speed beyond all expectation, thanks to the multitude of hands. Its thickness, however, was so

---

of Babel is unbiblical and inferred from his activity as city-builder (Gen. x. 11 f.); such identification of names and deductions from Scripture are in Rabbinic vein and recur in Josephus. The same identification appears in the *Pirke R. Eliezer*, cap. xxiv. (Weill).

[b] A saying attributed in the Talmud to Johanan ben Zakkai (a contemporary of Josephus) speaks of "Nimrod the wicked who led all the world to rebel against (God)," *Chagigah* 13a, i. (Streane); again I owe the reference to M. Weill.

ἦν ἰσχυρὸν τοσοῦτον, ὥσθ' ὑπ' αὐτοῦ μειοῦσθαι
τοῖς ὁρῶσι τὸ μῆκος. ᾠκοδομεῖτο δὲ ἐκ πλίνθου
ὀπτῆς ἀσφάλτῳ συνδεδεμένης, ὡς ἂν μὴ περιρρέοι.
οὕτως δὲ μεμηνότας αὐτοὺς ὁρῶν ὁ θεὸς ἀφανίσαι
μὲν ἐκ παντὸς οὐκ ἔκρινεν, ὅτι μηδ' ὑπὸ τῶν
117 πρώτων ἀπολωλότων σωφρονισθεῖεν, εἰς στάσιν
δὲ αὐτοὺς ἐνέβαλεν ἀλλογλώσσους ἀπεργασάμενος
καὶ ὑπὸ πολυφωνίας ποιήσας ἑαυτῶν ἀσυνέτους
εἶναι. ὁ δὲ τόπος ἐν ᾧ τὸν πύργον ᾠκοδόμησαν
νῦν Βαβυλὼν καλεῖται διὰ τὴν σύγχυσιν τοῦ περὶ
τὴν διάλεκτον πρῶτον ἐναργοῦς· Ἑβραῖοι γὰρ τὴν
118 σύγχυσιν βαβὲλ καλοῦσι. περὶ δὲ τοῦ πύργου τούτου καὶ τῆς ἀλλοφωνίας τῶν ἀνθρώπων μέμνηται
καὶ Σίβυλλα λέγουσα οὕτως· '' πάντων ὁμοφώνων
ὄντων τῶν ἀνθρώπων πύργον ᾠκοδόμησάν τινες
ὑψηλότατον ὡς ἐπὶ τὸν οὐρανὸν ἀναβησόμενοι δι'
αὐτοῦ. οἱ δὲ θεοὶ ἀνέμους ἐπιπέμψαντες ἀν-
έτρεψαν τὸν πύργον καὶ ἰδίαν ἑκάστῳ φωνὴν ἔδω-
καν· καὶ διὰ τοῦτο Βαβυλῶνα συνέβη κληθῆναι τὴν
119 πόλιν.'' περὶ δὲ τοῦ πεδίου τοῦ λεγομένου Σεναὰρ
ἐν τῇ Βαβυλωνίᾳ χώρᾳ μνημονεύει Ἑστιαῖος λέγων
οὕτως· '' τῶν δὲ ἱερέων τοὺς διασωθέντας τὰ τοῦ
Ἐνναλίου Διὸς ἱερώματα λαβόντας εἰς Σεναὰρ τῆς
Βαβυλωνίας ἐλθεῖν.''

---

[a] So the Heb. and LXX (using the same Greek word σύγχυσις).

[b] There follows a prose paraphrase, loosely taken over from Alexander Polyhistor, of *Oracula Sibyllina* iii. 97 ff., a Jewish work of about the 2nd cent. B.C. (ed. Rzach, 1891). The original runs:

ἀλλ' ὁπότ' ἂν μεγάλοιο θεοῦ τελέωνται ἀπειλαί,
ἅς ποτ' ἐπηπείλησε βροτοῖς, ὅτε πύργον ἔτευξαν
χώρῃ ἐν Ἀσσυρίῃ· ὁμόφωνοι δ' ἦσαν ἅπαντες

stout as to dwarf its apparent height. It was built Gen. xi. 3. of baked bricks cemented with bitumen to prevent them from being washed away. Seeing their mad enterprise, God was not minded to exterminate them utterly, because even the destruction of the first victims had not taught their descendants wisdom; but He created discord among them by making them speak different languages, through the variety of which they could not understand one another. The place where they built the tower is now called Babylon from the confusion of that primitive speech once intelligible to all, for the Hebrews call confusion "Babel.*a*" This tower and the confusion of the *Ib.* 9. tongues of men are mentioned also by the Sibyl in the following terms *b*: "When all men spoke a common language, certain of them built an exceeding high tower, thinking thereby to mount to heaven. But the gods *c* sent winds against it and overturned the tower and gave to every man a peculiar language; whence it comes that the city was called Babylon." And as concerning the plain called Senaar in the region of Babylon, Hestiaeus *d* speaks as follows: "Now the priests who escaped took the sacred vessels of Zeus Enyalius *e* and came to Senaar in Babylonia."

καὶ βούλοντ' ἀναβῆναι ἐς οὐρανὸν ἀστερόεντα·
αὐτίκα δ' ἀθάνατος μεγάλην ἐπέθηκεν ἀνάγκην
πνεύμασιν· αὐτὰρ ἔπειτ' ἄνεμοι μέγαν ὑψόθι πύργον
ῥίψαν καὶ θνητοῖσιν ἐπ' ἀλλήλους ἔριν ὦρσαν·
τοὔνεκά τοι Βαβυλῶνα βροτοὶ πόλει οὔνομ' ἔθεντο.

c The plural comes from Alexander's paraphrase (*ap.* Rzach), τοὺς δὲ θεοὺς ἀνέμους ἐμφυσήσαντας ἀνατρέψαι.

d Already mentioned (§ 107) as author of a Phoenician history; his date is unknown.

e "The Warlike" (Enyo = Lat. Bellona), in Homer epithet of Ares, here only applied to Zeus: Gutschmid proposed to read Z. Ἐνάλιος, *i.e.* Poseidon (T. Reinach).

JOSEPHUS

120 (v.) Σκίδνανται δὴ τὸ λοιπὸν ἐντεῦθεν ὑπὸ τῆς ἀλλογλωσσίας τὰς ἀποικίας ποιησάμενοι πανταχοῦ, καὶ γῆν ἕκαστοι κατελάμβανον τὴν ἐντυχοῦσαν καὶ εἰς ἣν αὐτοὺς ἦγεν ὁ θεός, ὡς πληρωθῆναι πᾶσαν αὐτῶν ἤπειρον μεσόγεών τε καὶ παράλιον· εἰσὶ δ' οἳ καὶ περαιωσάμενοι ναυσὶ τὰς νήσους κατῴκησαν.

121 καὶ τῶν ἐθνῶν ἔνια μὲν διασῴζει τὰς ὑπὸ τῶν κτισάντων κειμένας προσηγορίας, ἔνια δὲ καὶ μετέβαλεν,[1] οἱ δὲ καὶ πρὸς τὸ σαφέστερον εἶναι δοκοῦν τοῖς παροικοῦσι τροπὴν ἔλαβον. Ἕλληνες δ' εἰσὶν οἱ τούτου καταστάντες αἴτιοι· ἰσχύσαντες γὰρ ἐν τοῖς ὕστερον ἰδίαν ἐποιήσαντο καὶ τὴν πάλαι δόξαν, καλλωπίσαντες τὰ ἔθνη τοῖς ὀνόμασι πρὸς τὸ συνετὸν αὐτοῖς καὶ κόσμον θέμενοι πολιτείας ὡς ἀφ' αὐτῶν γεγονόσιν.

122 (vi. 1) Ἦσαν δὲ τῶν Νώχου παίδων υἱοί, ὧν ἐπὶ τιμῇ τοῖς ἔθνεσι τὰ ὀνόματα ἐπετίθεσαν οἱ γῆν τινα καταλαβόντες. Ἰάφθα μὲν οὖν τοῦ Νώχου παιδὸς ἦσαν ἑπτὰ υἱοί. κατοικοῦσι δὲ οὗτοι ἀπὸ Ταύρου καὶ Ἀμάνου τῶν ὀρῶν ἀρξάμενοι καὶ προῆλθον ἐπὶ μὲν τῆς Ἀσίας ἄχρι ποταμοῦ Ταναΐδος, ἐπὶ δὲ τῆς Εὐρώπης ἕως Γαδείρων[2] γῆν ἣν ἔτυχον καταλαμβάνοντες, καὶ μηδενὸς προκατῳκηκότος τὰ ἔθνη τοῖς αὐτῶν ἐκάλουν ὀνό-

123 μασιν. τοὺς [μὲν] γὰρ νῦν ὑφ' Ἑλλήνων Γαλάτας καλουμένους, Γομαρεῖς δὲ λεγομένους, Γόμαρος ἔκτισε. Μαγώγης δὲ τοὺς ἀπ' αὐτοῦ Μαγώγας

[1] μετέβαλον codd.   [2] Γαζήρων RO (Gazirorum Lat.).

[a] Or " to sojourners among them."   [b] Greek " Japhtha."
[c] The Don, regarded in antiquity as the boundary between Asia and Europe.   [d] Cadiz.   [e] Or " provinces."
[f] Biblical Gomer: in reality " the *Gamir* of the Assyrian

JEWISH ANTIQUITIES, I. 120–123

(v.) From that hour, therefore, they were dispersed through their diversity of languages and founded colonies everywhere, each group occupying the country that they lit upon and to which God led them, so that every continent was peopled by them, the interior and the seaboard alike; while some crossed the sea on shipboard and settled in the islands. Of the nations some still preserve the names which were given them by their founders, some have changed them, while yet others have modified them to make them more intelligible to their neighbours.[a] It is the Greeks who are responsible for this change of nomenclature; for when in after ages they rose to power, they appropriated even the glories of the past, embellishing the nations with names which they could understand and imposing on them forms of government, as though they were descended from themselves.

The dispersion and founding of colonies. Gen. x. 32.

(vi. 1) Noah's children had sons, who were honoured by having their names conferred upon the nations by the first occupants of the several countries. Japheth,[b] son of Noah, had seven sons. These, beginning by inhabiting the mountains of Taurus and Amanus, advanced in Asia up to the river Tanais[c] and in Europe as far as Gadeira,[d] occupying the territory upon which they lit, and, as no inhabitant had preceded them, giving their own names to the nations.[e] Thus those whom to-day the Greeks call Galatians were named Gomarites, having been founded by Gomar.[f] Magog founded the Magogians, thus

Nations descended from Japheth. Cf. Gen. x. 1 ff.

inscriptions, the Cimmerians of the Greeks," Skinner, *Genesis*. Here and in the sequel the alleged ancient eponymous names of the nations are generally fictitious. The Greek terminations as in Gomar(os), Magog(es), etc., are as a rule not reproduced in translation.

ὀνομασθέντας ᾤκισεν, Σκύθας δὲ ὑπ᾽ αὐτῶν
προσαγορευομένους. τῶν δὲ Ἰάφθα παίδων Ἰαυά-
νου¹ καὶ Μάδου ἀπὸ μὲν τούτου Μαδαῖοι γίνονται
ἔθνος, οἳ πρὸς Ἑλλήνων Μῆδοι κέκληνται, ἀπὸ δὲ
Ἰαυάνου Ἰωνία καὶ πάντες Ἕλληνες γεγόνασι.
κατοικίζει δὲ καὶ Θεοβήλους Θεόβηλος, οἵτινες ἐν
τοῖς νῦν Ἴβηρες καλοῦνται. καὶ Μεσχῆνοι δὲ ὑπὸ
Μέσχου κτισθέντες Καππάδοκες μὲν ἄρτι κέκληνται, τῆς δὲ ἀρχαίας αὐτῶν προσηγορίας σημεῖον
δείκνυται· πόλις γάρ ἐστι παρ᾽ αὐτοῖς ἔτι καὶ νῦν
Μάζακα, δηλοῦσα τοῖς συνιέναι δυναμένοις οὕτως
ποτὲ προσαγορευθὲν πᾶν τὸ ἔθνος. Θείρης δὲ
Θείρας μὲν ἐκάλεσεν ὧν ἦρξεν, Ἕλληνες δὲ Θρᾷ-
κας αὐτοὺς μετωνόμασαν. καὶ τοσαῦτα μὲν ἔθνη
ὑπὸ τῶν Ἰάφθου παίδων κατοικεῖται· Γομάρου δὲ
τριῶν υἱῶν γενομένων Ἀσχανάξης μὲν Ἀσχα-
νάξους ᾤκισεν, οἳ νῦν Ῥήγινες ὑπὸ τῶν Ἑλλήνων
καλοῦνται, Ῥιφάθης δὲ Ῥιφαθαίους τοὺς Παφλα-
γόνας λεγομένους, Θυγράμης δὲ Θυγραμαίους, οἳ
δόξαν Ἕλλησι Φρύγες ὠνομάσθησαν. Ἰαυάνου δὲ
τοῦ Ἰάφθου τριῶν καὶ αὐτοῦ παίδων γενομένων

¹ Ἰαυγάνου RO: Ἰωνάνου SPL (similar variants below).

^a Bibl. Madai (the common Heb. name for Media and the Medes).
^b Bibl. Tubal (LXX Θοβέλ).
^c Bibl. Meshech (Μοσόχ). Josephus's identification of Meshech and Tubal, who are mentioned together elsewhere in Scripture, with Iberians and Cappadocians respectively is "arbitrary." "Since Bochart no one has questioned their identity with the Τιβαρηνοί and Μόσχοι" of Herodotus (iii. 94, vii. 78); they appear in Assyrian monuments as *Tabali* and *Muski* and are regarded by modern writers as **remnants of the Hittites** (Skinner).

named after him, but who by the Greeks are called Scythians. Two other sons of Japheth, Javan and Mados,*a* gave birth, the latter to the Madaeans—the race called by the Greeks Medes—the former to Ionia and all the Greeks. Theobel *b* founded the Theobelians, nowadays called Iberians. The Meschenians, founded by Meschos,*c* are to-day called Cappadocians, but a clear trace of their ancient designation survives; for they still have a city of the name of Mazaca,*d* indicating to the expert that such was formerly the name of the whole race. Theires *e* called his subjects Theirians, whom the Greeks have converted into Thracians. So numerous are the nations founded by the sons of Japheth. Gomar had three sons, of whom Aschanaxes *f* founded the Aschanaxians, whom the Greeks now call Reginians,*g* Riphathes*h* the Riphataeans—the modern Paphlagonians—and Thugrames *i* the Thugramaeans, whom the Greeks thought good to call Phrygians. Javan, son of Japhet, also had three sons: of these

---

d The name had in fact been changed to Caesarea when Cappadocia became a Roman province under Tiberius.

e Bibl. Tiras: now conjectured to be identical with the Τυρσηνοί, Mediterranean pirates who gave their name to the Etruscans (Skinner; his valuable edition of Genesis in the *Int. Crit. Comm.* has been consulted throughout this passage).

f Bibl. Ashkenaz, often connected with the Homeric Ascania (in Asia Minor), now thought to be Scythians; the name survives to-day in the *Ashkenazim*, one of the two main classes of Jews, those of German and Slavonic-speaking countries, as opposed to *Sephardim* (Spanish and Portuguese).

g Name unknown, perhaps corrupt.

h Bibl. Riphath; otherwise unknown.

i Bibl. Togarmah (LXX Θεργαμά, Θοργαμά); "traditionally associated with Armenia" (Skinner).

JOSEPHUS

Ἁλισᾶς μὲν Ἁλισαίους ἐκάλεσεν ὧν ἦρχεν, Αἰολεῖς δὲ νῦν εἰσι, Θάρσος δὲ Θαρσεῖς· οὕτως γὰρ ἐκαλεῖτο τὸ παλαιὸν ἡ Κιλικία. σημεῖον δέ· Ταρσὸς γὰρ παρ᾽ αὐτοῖς τῶν πόλεων ἡ ἀξιολογωτάτη καλεῖται, μητρόπολις οὖσα, τὸ ταῦ πρὸς τὴν 128 κλῆσιν ἀντὶ τοῦ θῆτα μεταβαλόντων. Χέθιμος δὲ Χέθιμα τὴν νῆσον ἔσχε, Κύπρος αὕτη νῦν καλεῖται, καὶ ἀπ᾽ αὐτῆς νησοί τε πᾶσαι καὶ τὰ πλείω τῶν παρὰ θάλατταν Χεθὶμ[1] ὑπὸ Ἑβραίων ὀνομάζεται· μάρτυς δέ μου τῷ λόγῳ μία τῶν ἐν Κύπρῳ πόλεων ἰσχύσασα τὴν προσηγορίαν φυλάξαι· Κίτιον γὰρ ὑπὸ τῶν ἐξελληνισάντων αὐτὴν καλεῖται μηδ᾽ οὕτως διαφυγοῦσα τοῦ Χεθίμου τὸ ὄνομα. Ἰάφθα μὲν δὴ παῖδές τε καὶ υἱωνοὶ τοσαῦτα ἔσχον ἔθνη.
129 ὃ δ᾽ ἴσως ὑφ᾽ Ἑλλήνων ἀγνοεῖται, τοῦτο προειπὼν τρέψομαι πρὸς τὴν ἀφήγησιν ὧν κατέλιπον. τὰ γὰρ ὀνόματα διὰ τὸ τῆς γραφῆς εὐπρεπὲς ἡλλήνισται πρὸς ἡδονὴν τῶν ἐντευξομένων· οὐ γὰρ ἐπιχώριος ἡμῖν ὁ τοιοῦτος αὐτῶν τύπος, ἀλλ᾽ ἕν τε αὐτῶν σχῆμα καὶ τελευτὴ μία· Νῶχός γέ τοι Νῶε καλεῖται καὶ τοῦτον τὸν τύπον ἐπὶ παντὸς τηρεῖ σχήματος.
130 (2) Οἱ δὲ Χάμου παῖδες τὴν ἀπὸ Συρίας καὶ Ἀμάνου καὶ Λιβάνου τῶν ὀρῶν γῆν κατέσχον, ὅσα

[1] Lat. (*Cethim*): Χέθη (·ημ) etc. codd.

---

[a] Bibl. Elishah (Ἐλισά), else only known as the name of " isles " supplying Tyre with purple (Ezek. xxvii. 7); Conder's identification with *Alasia* of the Tel-Amarna Tablets (probably = Cyprus) is now widely accepted.

[b] Bibl. Tarshish (Θαρσείς), doubtless = Ταρτησσός in the south of Spain; Tarsus in Semitic has no *s* but a *z* (*Tarzi*).

[c] Bibl. Kittim (Κήτιοι); the view here given and still prevalent that Cyprus is primarily intended has recently been questioned, a site farther west being desiderated.

Halisas *a* gave his name to his subjects the Halisaeans — the modern Aeolians — and Tharsos *b* to the Tharsians; the latter was the ancient name of Cilicia, as is proved by the fact that its principal and capital city is called Tarsus, the *Th* having been converted into *T*. Chethimos *c* held the island of Chethima — the modern Cyprus — whence the name *Chethim* given by the Hebrews to all islands and to most maritime countries *d*; here I call to witness one of the cities of Cyprus which has succeeded in preserving the old appellation, for even in its Hellenized form Cition *e* is not far removed from the name of Chethimos.*f* So many were the countries possessed by the sons and grandsons of Japheth. I have one thing to add, of which Greeks are perhaps unaware, before reverting to the narrative where I left it. With a view to euphony and my readers' pleasure these names have been Hellenized.*g* The form in which they here appear is not that used in our country, where their structure and termination remain always the same; thus Nochos (Noah) in Hebrew is Noe,*h* and the name retains this form in all the cases.

(2) The children of Ham held the countries branching from Syria and the mountain-ranges of Amanus and Libanus, occupying all the district in the direction

Descendants of Ham. *Cf.* Gen. x. 6 ff.

d In the phrase "ships of Kittim" it denotes the coastlands of the Mediterranean generally, including in one instance (Dan. xi. 30) Greece.   *e* Mod. Larnaka.
f Josephus omits one name, Dodanim (LXX Ῥόδιοι), also omitted in one group of MSS. of the Greek Bible.
g This is why he elsewhere omits lists of strange names as unnecessary (vii. 369, xi. 68, 152, xii. 57): an exception is made for a special reason in ii. 176. Other writers, such as Strabo, did the same. (Cadbury, *Making of Luke-Acts*, p. 124.)
h The usual LXX transliteration of the Hebrew NḤ (in the vocalized Masoretic form Noaḥ).

πρὸς θάλασσαν αὐτῆς ἐτέτραπτο καταλαβόντες
καὶ τὰ μέχρι τοῦ ὠκεανοῦ ἐξιδιωσάμενοι· αἱ μέντοι
προσηγορίαι τῶν μὲν καὶ παντελῶς ἐξίτηλοι
γεγόνασιν, ἐνίων δὲ μεταβαλοῦσαι καὶ μεταρρυθ-
μισθεῖσαι πρὸς ἑτέρας δύσγνωστοι τυγχάνουσιν,
ὀλίγοι δὲ οἱ φυλάξαντες ἀκεραίους τὰς προσ-
131 ηγορίας ὑπάρχουσι. τεσσάρων γὰρ Χάμου παίδων
γενομένων Χουσαῖον μὲν οὐδὲν ἔβλαψεν ὁ χρόνος·
Αἰθίοπες γὰρ ὧν ἦρξεν ἔτι καὶ νῦν ὑπὸ ἑαυτῶν τε
καὶ τῶν ἐν τῇ Ἀσίᾳ πάντων Χουσαῖοι καλοῦνται.
132 ἐτηρήθη δὲ καὶ Μερσαίοις[1] ἡ κατὰ τὴν προσηγορίαν
μνήμη· τὴν γὰρ Αἴγυπτον Μέρσην καὶ Μερσαίους
τοὺς Αἰγυπτίους ἅπαντες οἱ ταύτῃ καλοῦμεν. ἔκτισε δὲ καὶ Φούτης τὴν Λιβύην Φούτους ἀφ' αὑτοῦ
133 καλέσας τοὺς ἐπιχωρίους. ἔστι δὲ καὶ ποταμὸς
ἐν τῇ Μαύρων χώρᾳ τοῦτο ἔχων τὸ ὄνομα, ὅθεν
καὶ τοὺς πλείστους τῶν Ἑλληνικῶν ἱστοριογράφων
ἔστιν ἰδεῖν μεμνημένους τοῦ ποταμοῦ καὶ τῆς
παρακειμένης αὐτῷ χώρας Φούτης λεγομένης.
μετέβαλε δὲ ὃ νῦν αὐτῇ ἐστιν ὄνομα ἀπὸ τῶν
Μερσαίου[2] υἱῶν Λίβυος λεγομένου· μετ' οὐ πολὺ
δ' ἐροῦμεν τὴν αἰτίαν, δι' ἣν αὐτὴν καὶ Ἀφρικαν
134 προσαγορεύεσθαι συμβέβηκε. Χαναναῖος δὲ τέταρτος ὢν Χάμου παῖς τὴν νῦν Ἰουδαίαν καλουμένην οἰκίσας ἀφ' αὑτοῦ Χαναναίαν προσηγόρευσεν.
γίνονται δὲ παῖδες ἐξ αὐτῶν Χούσου μὲν ἕξ, ὧν
Σάβας μὲν Σαβαίους, Εὐίλας δὲ Εὐιλαίους ἔκτισεν,

---

[1] Μεστραίοις SPE and so (with Μέστρην) below.
[2] Niese (cf. § 132): Μεσ(τ)ράμου codd.

[a] The Mediterranean.   [b] The Indian Ocean.
[c] Bibl. Cush (LXX Χούς).
[d] Or (with v.l.) "Mestraeans": Bibl. Mizraim (LXX, some MSS., Μεστραείμ).

JEWISH ANTIQUITIES, I. 130–134

of the sea *a* and appropriating the regions reaching to the ocean.*b* Of the names of these countries, however, some have altogether disappeared, others have been altered and remodelled beyond recognition, few have been preserved unimpaired. Thus, of the four sons of Ham, the name of one, Chusaeus,*c* has escaped the ravages of time: the Ethiopians, his subjects, are to this day called by themselves and by all in Asia Chusaeans. The Mersaeans *d* also have kept their memory alive in their name, for we in these parts *e* all call Egypt Merse *f* and the Egyptians Mersaeans.*d* Phut *g* colonized Libya and called the inhabitants after his name Phutians. There is moreover a river in Mauretania which bears this name: mention of the river and of the adjacent region, called Phute, is to be found in most Greek historians.*h* But this country has changed its name into that which it now bears, taken from one of the sons of Mersaeus *i* named Libys; I shall state shortly why it also came to be called Africa.*j* Chananaeus,*k* the fourth son of Ham, settled in the country now called Judaea and named it after himself Chananaea. The sons of Ham had sons in their turn. Chus *l* had six, of whom Sabas *m* founded the Sa- Gen. x. 7 baeans,*n* Evilas *o* the Evilaeans, the Gaetulians of

---

e The author, writing in Rome, adopts the standpoint of his native Palestine.   *f* Or "Mestre."
g Bibl. Put (Φούθ or Φούδ).   *h* Unverifiable.
i Or "Mestramus."   *j* §§ 239-241.
k Bibl. Canaan (LXX Χαναάν).
l Bibl. Cush, called Chusaeus above.   *m* Bibl. Seba.
n There were Sabaeans on either side of the Red Sea and elsewhere; as the Ethiopian branch seems to be alluded to below, this may mean the Arabian clan.
o Bibl. Havilah, probably to be located in N. Arabia, not in N.W. Africa, as here.

οἳ νῦν Γαιτοῦλοι λέγονται, Σαβάθης δὲ Σαβαθη-
νούς, ὀνομάζονται δὲ Ἀστάβαροι παρ' Ἕλλησιν·
135 οἰκίζει δὲ καὶ Σαβάκτας Σαβακτηνούς· Ῥάμος
δὲ Ῥαμαίους ᾤκισε καὶ δύο παῖδας ἔσχεν, ὧν
Ἰουδάδας μὲν Ἰουδαδαίους Αἰθιοπικὸν ἔθνος τῶν
ἑσπερίων οἰκίσας ἐπώνυμον αὑτοῦ κατέλιπε, Σαβαίους δὲ Σαβαῖος· Ναβρώδης δὲ Χούσου υἱὸς
ὑπομείνας παρὰ Βαβυλωνίοις ἐτυράννησεν, ὡς καὶ
136 πρότερόν μοι δεδήλωται. τῶν δὲ Μερσαίου[1]
παίδων ὀκτὼ γενομένων οἱ πάντες τὴν ἀπὸ Γάζης
ἕως Αἰγύπτου γῆν κατέσχον, μόνου δὲ Φυλιστίνου
τὴν ἐπωνυμίαν ἡ χώρα διεφύλαξε· Παλαιστίνην
137 γὰρ οἱ Ἕλληνες αὐτοῦ τὴν μοῖραν καλοῦσι. τῶν
δὲ ἄλλων, Λουμαίου καὶ Ἀναμία καὶ Λαβίμου τοῦ
μόνου κατοικήσαντος ἐν Λιβύῃ καὶ ὧδε τὴν χώραν
ἀφ' αὑτοῦ καλέσαντος, Νεδέμου τε καὶ Πεθρωσίμου
καὶ Χεσλοίμου καὶ Χεφθώμου πέρα τῶν ὀνομάτων
οὐδὲν ἴσμεν· ὁ γὰρ Αἰθιοπικὸς πόλεμος, περὶ οὗ
δηλώσομεν ὕστερον, ἀναστάτους αὐτῶν τὰς πόλεις
138 ἐποίησεν. ἐγένοντο δὲ καὶ Χαναναίου παῖδες,
Σιδώνιος ὃς καὶ πόλιν ἐπώνυμον ἔκτισεν ἐν τῇ
Φοινίκῃ, Σιδὼν δ' ὑφ' Ἑλλήνων καλεῖται, Ἀμα-

[1] *v.l.* Μεστραίου.

---

[a] Bibl. Sabtah.
[b] Astaboras appears elsewhere as a tributary of the upper Nile, which it joined at the city of Saba, the later Meroe, capital of the Ethiopian realm of the Queen of Sheba (*A.* ii. 249).
[c] Bibl. Sabteca. [d] Bibl. Raamah (LXX Ῥεγμά).
[e] Heb. Dedan (a merchant tribe of N. Arabia); but the form in Josephus has the support of one group of LXX MSS. and—a constant ally—the Armenian version.

JEWISH ANTIQUITIES, I. 134-138

to-day, Sabathes[a] the Sabathenians, whom the Greeks call Astabarians,[b] Sabactas[c] the Sabactenians, and Ramus[d] the Ramaeans; the last-named had two sons, Judadas,[e] founder of the Judadaeans, a people of western Aethiopia to whom he bequeathed his name, and Sabaeus,[f] who stood in the same relation to the Sabaeans.[g] Nabrodes,[h] [the sixth] son of Chus, remained in Babylonia, where he held sway, as I have previously related.[i]

Mersaeus[j] had eight sons, all of whom occupied the territory extending from Gaza to Egypt; but Phylistinus is the only one whose country has preserved the founder's name, for the Greeks call his portion Palestine. Of the rest, Lumaeus, Anamias, Labimus[k]—who alone settled in Libya and thus gave his name[l] to the country,—Nedemus, Pethrosimus, Chesloimus and Cephthomus,[m] we know nothing beyond their names; for the Ethiopian war, of which we shall speak later,[n] reduced their cities to ruins.

Chananaeus also had sons, of whom Sidonius built in Phoenicia a city named after him, still called Sidon by the Greeks, and Amathus[o] founded Amathus,[p]

Gen. x. 13.

Ib. 15.

---

[f] Bibl. Sheba.

[g] Another mention of this ubiquitous name: the Heb. refers to the great state in S.W. Arabia.

[h] Nimrod. [i] § 113. [j] i.e. Mizraim.

[k] Bibl. Ludim, Anamim, Lehabim.

[l] Given differently as Libys in § 133.

[m] Bibl. " Naphtuhim, Pathrusim, Casluhim (whence went forth the Philistines) and Caphtorim." Pathros = Upper Egypt; Caphtor = Crete.

[n] A. ii. 238 ff.

[o] Bibl. " the Hamathite " (LXX Ἀμαθί). Josephus here deserts the Biblical order of names.

[p] Hamath on the Orontes, modern Hamah: the " Macedonian " or Seleucid name was short-lived.

θοῦς δὲ Ἀμάθουν κατῴκισεν, ἥτις ἔστι καὶ νῦν ὑπὸ μὲν τῶν ἐπιχωρίων Ἀμάθη καλουμένη, Μακεδόνες δ' αὐτὴν Ἐπιφάνειαν ἀφ' ἑνὸς τῶν ἐπιγόνων ἐπωνόμασαν, Ἀρουδαῖος δὲ Ἄραδον τὴν νῆσον ἔσχεν, Ἀρουκαῖος δὲ Ἄρκην τὴν ἐν τῷ 139 Λιβάνῳ. τῶν δὲ ἄλλων ἑπτά, Εὐαίου Χετταίου Ἰεβουσαίου Ἀμορραίου Γεργεσαίου Σειναίου Σαμαραίου, πλὴν τῶν ὀνομάτων ἐν ταῖς ἱεραῖς βίβλοις οὐδὲν ἔχομεν· Ἑβραῖοι γὰρ αὐτῶν ἀνέστησαν τὰς πόλεις ἐκ τοιαύτης αἰτίας ἐν συμφορᾷ γενομένας·

140 (3) Νῶχος μετὰ τὴν ἐπομβρίαν τῆς γῆς κατασταθείσης εἰς τὴν αὑτῆς φύσιν ἐπ' ἔργα χωρεῖ καὶ καταφυτεύσας αὐτὴν ἀμπέλοις, ἡνίκα τοῦ καρποῦ τελεσφορηθέντος καθ' ὥραν ἐτρύγησε καὶ παρῆν εἰς χρῆσιν ὁ οἶνος, θύσας ἐν εὐωχίαις ἦν. 141 μεθυσθεὶς δὲ εἰς ὕπνον καταφέρεται καὶ γεγυμνωμένος παρακόσμως ἔκειτο. θεασάμενος δὲ αὐτὸν ὁ νεώτατος τῶν παίδων τοῖς ἀδελφοῖς ἐπιγελῶν 142 δείκνυσιν· οἱ δὲ περιστέλλουσι τὸν πατέρα. καὶ Νῶχος αἰσθόμενος τοῖς μὲν ἄλλοις παισὶν εὐδαιμονίαν εὔχεται, τῷ δὲ Χάμᾳ διὰ τὴν συγγένειαν αὐτῷ μὲν οὐ κατηράσατο, τοῖς δ' ἐγγόνοις αὐτοῦ· καὶ τῶν ἄλλων διαπεφευγότων τὴν ἀρὰν τοὺς Χαναναίου παῖδας μέτεισιν ὁ θεός· καὶ περὶ μὲν τούτων ἐν τοῖς ἑξῆς ἐροῦμεν.

---

[a] Bibl. "the Arvadite" (LXX τὸν Ἀράδιον): Arvad (Ezek. xxvii. 8), or Aradus, an island off the north coast of Phoenicia, founded, according to Strabo (xvi. 2. 13), by exiles from Sidon.

[b] So LXX, Heb. "the Arkite": Arca at the N.W. foot of Lebanon, near Tripolis, was a seat of the worship of Astarte

which the inhabitants to this day call Amathe, though the Macedonians renamed it Epiphaneia after one of Alexander's successors. Arudaeus[a] occupied the island of Aradus, and Arucaeus[b] Arce in Lebanon. Of the seven others—Euaeus,[c] Chettaeus,[d] Jebuseus, Amorreus, Gergesaeus, Seinaeus, Samaraeus[e]—we have no record in the sacred Scriptures beyond their names; for the Hebrews destroyed their cities, which owed this calamity to the following cause.

(3) After the flood, when the earth was restored to its natural state, Noah set to work and planted vines upon it; and when the fruit ripened in due season he gathered the vintage and, the wine being ready, he held a sacrifice and gave himself up to festivity. Drunken, he fell asleep and lay in an indecent state of nudity. His youngest son[f] saw him and with mockery showed the sight to his brethren, but they wrapped a covering about their father. Noah, on learning what had passed, invoked a blessing on his other sons, but cursed—not Ham himself, because of his nearness of kin, but his posterity. The other descendants of Ham escaped the curse, but divine vengeance pursued the children of Chananaeus. But of this I shall speak hereafter.

The curse upon the Canaanites. Gen. ix. 20.

and the birthplace of the Roman emperor, Alexander Severus.

[c] So LXX, Heb. "Hiv(v)ite."

[d] So LXX, Heb. "Heth": the wide range of the Hittite empire has been revealed by modern exploration.

[e] Bibl. Jebusite, Amorite, Girgashite, Sinite (LXX Ἀσενναῖος), Zemarite (LXX as in Josephus).

[f] Ham elsewhere in Genesis is the second son, yet in this incident is called "the youngest son" (ix. 24). The Bibl. writer apparently follows a distinct tradition in which Canaan was the youngest son, the actual sinner, and Ham disappears.

143 (4) Σῆμα δὲ τῷ τρίτῳ τῶν Νώχου υἱῶν πέντε γίνονται παῖδες, οἳ τὴν μέχρι τοῦ κατ' Ἰνδίαν ὠκεανοῦ κατοικοῦσιν Ἀσίαν ἀπ' Εὐφράτου τὴν ἀρχὴν πεποιημένοι. Ἔλυμος μὲν γὰρ Ἐλυμαίους Περσῶν ὄντας ἀρχηγέτας κατέλιπεν· Ἀσσούρας δὲ Νίνον οἰκίζει πόλιν καὶ τοὺς ὑπηκόους Ἀσσυρίους ἐπωνόμασεν, οἳ μάλιστα εὐδαιμόνησαν·
144 Ἀρφαξάδης δὲ τοὺς νῦν Χαλδαίους καλουμένους Ἀρφαξαδαίους ὠνόμασεν ἄρξας αὐτῶν· Ἀραμαίους δὲ Ἄραμος ἔσχεν, οὓς Ἕλληνες Σύρους προσαγορεύουσιν· οὓς δὲ Λυδοὺς νῦν καλοῦσι, Λούδους
145 δὲ τότε, Λούδας ἔκτισε. τῶν δὲ Ἀράμου παίδων τεσσάρων ὄντων Οὔσης μὲν κτίζει τὴν Τραχωνῖτιν καὶ Δαμασκόν, μέση δ' ἐστὶ τῆς Παλαιστίνης καὶ κοίλης Συρίας, Ἀρμενίαν δὲ Οὖρος,[1] καὶ Γεθέρης Βακτριανούς, Μήσας δὲ Μησαναίους, Σπασίνου
146 Χάραξ ἐν τοῖς νῦν καλεῖται. Ἀρφαξάδου δὲ παῖς γίνεται Σέλης, τοῦ δὲ Ἔβερος, ἀφ' οὗ τοὺς Ἰουδαίους Ἑβραίους ἀρχῆθεν ἐκάλουν· Ἔβερος δὲ Ἰούκταν καὶ Φάλεγον ἐγέννησεν· ἐκλήθη δὲ Φάλεγος, ἐπειδὴ κατὰ τὸν ἀποδασμὸν[2] τῶν οἰκήσεων τίκτεται· φαλὲκ γὰρ τὸν μερισμὸν Ἑβραῖοι

[1] Niese: Ὄτρος most mss.: Οὖλος (after lxx) SP.
[2] LM: τὸν ἀπόστολον (τὴν ἀποστολήν E) the rest.

[a] First in age, but Josephus follows Scripture in naming his descendants, the progenitors of the Hebrews, last.
[b] Bibl. Elam (Αἰλάμ), a non-Semitic people.
[c] Bibl. Asshur.
[d] Bibl. Arpachshad: Josephus, in common with many modern commentators, recognized in the last part of the word the name Chesed (Gen. xxii. 22), whence Chasdim, the Biblical name for the Chaldaeans.
[e] Bibl. Lud: the equation with Lydia in Asia Minor presents difficulties.

(4) Shem, the third *a* of Noah's sons, had five sons, Descendants who inhabited Asia as far as the Indian Ocean, of Shem. beginning at the Euphrates. Elymus *b* had for his Gen. x. 21. descendants the Elymaeans, ancestors of the Persians. Assyras *c* founded the city of Ninus, and gave his name to his subjects, the Assyrians, who rose to the height of prosperity. Arphaxades named those under his rule Arphaxadaeans, the Chaldaeans of to-day.*d* Aramus ruled the Aramaeans, whom the Greeks term Syrians ; while those whom they now call Lydians were then Ludians, founded by Ludas.*e* Of the four sons of Aramus, Uses *f* founded Trachonitis and Damascus, situated between Palestine and Coele Syria, Urus *g* founded Armenia, Getheres the Bactrians, and Mesas *h* the Mesanaeans in the region to-day called Spasini Charax. Arphaxades was the father of Seles *i* and he of Heber, after whom the Jews were originally called Hebrews. Heber begat Juctas *j* and Phaleg, who was thus called because he was born at the time of the partition of territories, *Phalek* being the Hebrew for " division." *k* Juctas,

f Bibl. Uz (Ὠς), probably identical with the first-born of Nahor (Gen. xxii. 21) and therefore pointing to a region north-east of Palestine, near Haran, distinct from Uz the home of Job in the south. *g* Bibl. Hul (Οὐλ).

h Bibl. Mash (Μοσόχ), " perhaps connected with Mons Masius " (Skinner), the mountain-chain forming the north boundary of Mesopotamia ; this would suit J.'s identification with " Spasini Charax," which he elsewhere locates in the neighbourhood of Adiabene, in the upper Tigris region (*A.* xx. 22, 34). *i* Bibl. Shelah (Σαλά).

j Bibl. Joktan (Ἰεκτάν), representing the southern (Arabian) branch, as Peleg the northern (Aramaean) branch of the Semites.

k A popular etymology repeated from Scripture and referring either to the dispersion at the time of the Tower of Babel or to the severance of the northern and southern Semites.

JOSEPHUS

147 καλοῦσιν. Ἰούκτᾳ δὲ τῶν Ἑβέρου παίδων ἦσαν υἱοὶ Ἐλμόδαδος Σάλεφος Ἀζερμώθης Εἰράης Ἐδώραμος Οὐζάλης Δάκλης Ἤβαλος Ἀβιμάηλος Σάφας Ὀφίρης Εὐίλης Ἰόβηλος. οὗτοι ἀπὸ Κωφῆνος ποταμοῦ τῆς Ἰνδικῆς καὶ τῆς πρὸς αὐτῇ Σηρίας¹ τινὰ κατοικοῦσι. ταῦτα μὲν περὶ τῶν Σήμα παίδων ἱστορήσθω.²

148 (5) Ποιήσομαι δὲ³ περὶ Ἑβραίων τὸν λόγον· Φαλέγου γὰρ τοῦ Ἑβέρου γίνεται παῖς Ῥεούς· τούτου δὲ Σεροῦγος, ᾧ Ναχώρης υἱὸς τίκτεται· τούτου δὲ Θέρρος· πατὴρ δὲ οὗτος Ἀβράμου γίνεται, ὃς δέκατος μέν ἐστιν ἀπὸ Νώχου, δευτέρῳ δ' ἔτει καὶ ἐνενηκοστῷ πρὸς ἐνακοσίοις μετὰ
149 τὴν ἐπομβρίαν ἐγένετο. Θέρρος μὲν γὰρ ἑβδομη-

---

¹ M : Συρίας the rest.   ² Bekker : ἱστορείσθω codd.
³ δὴ RSP : read perhaps δ' ἤδη.

---

a So LXX : Heb. Almodad.
b Bibl. Sheba (LXX Σαβεῦ or the like).
c Bibl. Havilah (Εὐειλά).
d Bibl. Jobab, and so (Ἰώβαβος or the like) some MSS. of Josephus.   *e* Tributary of the Indus.
f Probably N.W. China. The corresponding Biblical verse (Gen. x. 30) runs: " And their dwelling was from Mesha, as thou goest toward Sephar (LXX Σωφηρά), the mountain of the east." The names are probably Arabian: but the LXX, in which Σωφείρ elsewhere = Ophir, seemed to point to the far east. Ophir has been identified by some modern commentators with Abhira near the mouths of the Indus. *Cf. A.* viii. 164 of Solomon's sending for gold εἰς τὴν πάλαι μὲν Σώφειραν νῦν δὲ χρυσῆν γῆν καλουμένην, τῆς Ἰνδικῆς ἐστιν αὕτη.   *g* Bibl. Terah (Θαρά).
h So Niese's two principal MSS., R and O : the figure here given is approximately the total of the figures that follow (993) and is doubtless original. The reading of the other MSS. (292) has been taken over from the Hebrew Bible. For, as before in the case of the date of the flood (§ 82), we have to

72

JEWISH ANTIQUITIES, I. 147-149

Heber's other son, was the father of Elmodad,[a] Saleph, Azermoth, Ira, Edoram, Uzal, Dacles, Ebal, Abimael, Saphas,[b] Ophir, Evil,[c] Jobel.[d] These, proceeding from the river Cophen,[e] inhabited parts of India and of the adjacent country of Seria.[f] That is all that I have to tell of the children of Shem.

(5) I shall now speak of the Hebrews. Phaleg, son of Heber, had a son Reus; of Reus was born Serug, of Serug Nachor(es), of Nachor Therrus[g]; he was the father of Abraham, who was tenth in descent from Noah, and was born in the nine-hundred-and-ninety-second year after the flood.[h] For Therrus

Origin of the Hebrews. Gen. xi. 18.

do with two (or three) different schemes of world chronology. The interval from the flood to the birth of Abraham has, in the scheme followed by Josephus, apparently been increased by 700 years by the simple process of adding a century to the age of most of the parents at the date of birth of their first-born. The scheme of Josephus approximates to that of the LXX, but in the latter the total has been further increased by the insertion of another name (Καινάν). The three schemes run thus:

		HEBREW TEXT (Gen. xi. 10-26).	LXX.	Josephus.
Shem	Years after flood at birth of first-born	2	2	12
Arpachshad	Age at birth of first-born	35	135	135
Καινάν	,, ,,	..	130	..
Shelah	,, ,,	30	130	130
Eber	,, ,,	34	134	134
Peleg	,, ,,	30	130	130
Reu	,, ,,	32	132	130
Serug	,, ,,	30	130	132
Nahor	,, ,,	29	79	120
Terah	,, ,,	70	70	70
TOTAL =	Years from flood to birth of Abraham	292	1072	993

73

κοστῷ ποιεῖται τὸν Ἄβραμον· Ναχώρης δὲ
Θέρρον εἰκοστὸν αὐτὸς καὶ ἑκατοστὸν ἤδη γεγονὼς ἐγέννησε· Σερούγῳ δὲ Ναχώρης τίκτεται
περὶ ἔτος δεύτερον καὶ τριακοστὸν καὶ ἑκατοστόν·
Ῥοῦμος δὲ Σεροῦγον [ἔσχεν] ἔτη τριάκοντα γεγονὼς πρὸς τοῖς ἑκατόν· ἐν δὲ τοῖς αὐτοῖς ἔτεσι
150 καὶ Ῥοῦμον Φάλεγος ἔσχεν· Ἕβερος δὲ τετάρτῳ
καὶ τριακοστῷ πρὸς τοῖς ἑκατὸν γεννᾷ Φάλεγον
γεννηθεὶς αὐτὸς ὑπὸ Σέλου τριακοστὸν ἔτος ἔχοντος καὶ ἑκατοστόν, ὃν Ἀρφάξαδος ἐτέκνωσε κατὰ
πέμπτον καὶ τριακοστὸν ἔτος πρὸς τοῖς ἑκατόν·
Σῆμα δὲ υἱὸς Ἀρφαξάδης ἦν μετὰ ἔτη δώδεκα τῆς
151 ἐπομβρίας γενόμενος. Ἄβραμος δὲ εἶχεν ἀδελφοὺς
Ναχώρην καὶ Ἀράνην· τούτων Ἀράνης μὲν υἱὸν
καταλιπὼν Λῶτον καὶ Σάρραν καὶ Μελχὰν
θυγατέρας ἐν Χαλδαίοις ἀπέθανεν ἐν πόλει Οὐρῇ
λεγομένῃ τῶν Χαλδαίων, καὶ τάφος αὐτοῦ μέχρι
νῦν δείκνυται. γαμοῦσι δὲ τὰς ἀδελφιδᾶς Μελχὰν
152 μὲν Ναχώρης Σάρραν δὲ Ἄβραμος. Θέρρου δὲ
μισήσαντος τὴν Χαλδαίαν διὰ τὸ Ἀράνου πένθος
μετοικίζονται πάντες εἰς Χαρρὰν τῆς Μεσοποταμίας, ὅπου καὶ Θέρρον τελευτήσαντα θάπ-
τουσιν ἔτη βιώσαντα πέντε καὶ διακόσια· συν-
ετέμνετο γὰρ ἤδη τοῖς ἀνθρώποις τὸ ζῆν καὶ
βραχύτερον ἐγίνετο μέχρι τῆς Μωυσέος γενέσεως,
μεθ' ὃν ὅρος ἦν τοῦ ζῆν ἑκατὸν ἔτη πρὸς τοῖς
εἴκοσι τοσαῦθ'[1] ὁρίσαντος τοῦ θεοῦ, ὅσα καὶ
153 Μωυσεῖ συνέβη βιῶναι. Ναχώρῃ μὲν οὖν ἐκ τῆς
Μελχᾶς ὀκτὼ παῖδες ἐγένοντο, Οὖξος Βαοῦξος

[1] Dindorf: ταῦθ' MSS.

[a] Called Reus above (Heb. Reu): Ῥάγανος, the reading of other MSS. of Josephus, is doubtless derived from the LXX (Ῥαγαύ).

begat Abraham at the age of 70; Nachor was 120 when he begat Therrus, and Serug about 132 when Nachor was born; Rumus *a* was 130 when he begat Serug, and Phaleg the same age at the birth of Rumus; Heber was 134 when he begat Phaleg, having been begotten himself by Seles when the latter was 130; Seles was born when Arphaxad was in his 135th year, while Arphaxad was son of Shem, and was born 12 years after the flood.

Abraham had brothers, Nachor and Aran.*b* Aran left a son, Lot, and daughters, Sarra*c* and Melcha: he died in Chaldaea in a city called Ur of the Chaldees, and his sepulchre is shown to this day. Nachor married his niece Melcha, and Abraham his niece Sarra. Therrus having come to hate Chaldaea because of the loss of his lamented Aran, they all migrated to Charran*d* in Mesopotamia, where Therrus also died and was buried, after a life of 205 years. For the duration of human life was already being curtailed and continued to diminish until the birth of Moses, after whom the limit of age was fixed by God at 120 years—the length of the life of Moses.*e* Nachor had eight children by Melcha, namely, Ux, Baux,*f*

Abraham and his family.
Gen. xi. 27.

Ib. 32.
Abbreviation of human life.

Gen. xxii. 20.

---

b Bibl. Haran.
c Bibl. Sarai, later in the narrative Sarah: the spelling Σάρρα of Josephus (for Σάρα) has the support of one important group of LXX MSS. According to Gen. xi. 29 Haran's two daughters were Milcah and *Iscah*: the latter, otherwise unknown, is identified with Sarah by Josephus, following Rabbinical tradition. In Josephus Sarah is Abraham's niece, in Scripture (Gen. xx. 12) his half-sister, daughter of Terah by another wife.
d Bibl. Haran (Ḥarran), the Latin Carrhae.
e A combination of Gen. vi. 3 with Deut. xxxiv. 7.
f Bibl. Uz and Buz (Ὤξ, Βαύξ).

Μαθούηλος[1] Χάζαμος Ἀζαοῦος Ἰαδελφᾶς Ἰαδαφᾶς Βαθούηλος· οὗτοι μὲν Ναχώρου παῖδες γνήσιοι· Ταβαῖος γὰρ καὶ Γάδαμος καὶ Ταανος καὶ Μαχᾶς ἐκ Ῥούμας παλλακῆς αὐτῷ γεγόνασι. Βαθουήλῳ δὲ τῶν Ναχώρου γνησίων παίδων γίνεται Ῥεβέκκα θυγάτηρ καὶ Λάβανος υἱός.

154 (vii. 1) Ἄβραμος δὲ Λῶτον τὸν Ἀράνου τοῦ ἀδελφοῦ υἱὸν τῆς δὲ γυναικὸς αὐτοῦ Σάρρας ἀδελφὸν εἰσεποιήσατο γνησίου παιδὸς ἀπορῶν, καὶ καταλείπει τὴν Χαλδαίαν ἑβδομήκοντα καὶ πέντε γεγονὼς ἔτη τοῦ θεοῦ κελεύσαντος εἰς τὴν Χαναναίαν μετελθεῖν, ἐν ᾗ [καὶ] κατῴκησε καὶ τοῖς ἀπογόνοις κατέλιπε, δεινὸς ὢν συνιέναι τε περὶ πάντων καὶ πιθανὸς τοῖς ἀκροωμένοις περί τε ὧν 155 εἰκάσειεν οὐ διαμαρτάνων. διὰ τοῦτο καὶ φρονεῖν μεῖζον ἐπ' ἀρετῇ τῶν ἄλλων ἠργμένος καὶ τὴν περὶ τοῦ θεοῦ δόξαν, ἣν ἅπασι συνέβαινεν εἶναι, καινίσαι καὶ μεταβαλεῖν ἔγνω. πρῶτος οὖν τολμᾷ θεὸν ἀποφήνασθαι δημιουργὸν τῶν ὅλων ἕνα, τῶν δὲ λοιπῶν εἰ καί τι πρὸς εὐδαιμονίαν συντελεῖ κατὰ προσταγὴν τὴν τούτου παρέχειν ἕκαστον 156 καὶ οὐ κατ' οἰκείαν ἰσχύν. εἴκαζε[2] δὲ ταῦτα τοῖς γῆς καὶ θαλάσσης παθήμασι τοῖς τε περὶ τὸν ἥλιον καὶ τὴν σελήνην καὶ πᾶσι τοῖς κατ' οὐρανὸν συμβαίνουσι· δυνάμεως γὰρ αὐτοῖς παρούσης κἂν[3] προνοῆσαι τῆς καθ' αὑτοὺς εὐταξίας, ταύτης δ'

---

[1] So or Μαούηλος mss.: Camuel (with LXX) Lat.
[2] εἰκάζεται RO. [3] Niese: καὶ codd.

---

[a] Bibl. Kemuel. [b] Bibl. Chesed.
[c] So LXX: Heb. Hazo.
[d] Bibl. Pildash and Jidlaph.
[e] So LXX: Heb. Bethuel. [f] Bibl. Tebah (Ταβέκ).

JEWISH ANTIQUITIES, I. 153–156

Mathuel,[a] Chazam,[b] Azau,[c] Iadelphas, Iadaphas,[d] Bathuel.[e] These were Nachor's legitimate children; his other sons, Tabai,[f] Gadam, Taau, and Machas,[g] were born of his concubine Ruma. Bathuel, one of the legitimate children, had a daughter Rebecca and a son Laban.

(vii. 1) Now Abraham, having no legitimate son, adopted Lot, his brother Aran's son and the brother of his wife Sarra; and at the age of seventy-five he left Chaldaea, God having bidden him to remove to Canaan, and there he settled, and left the country to his descendants. He was a man of ready intelligence on all matters, persuasive with his hearers, and not mistaken in his inferences. Hence he began to have more lofty conceptions of virtue than the rest of mankind, and determined to reform and change the ideas universally current concerning God. He was thus the first boldly to declare that God, the creator of the universe, is one, and that, if any other being contributed aught to man's welfare, each did so by His command and not in virtue of its own inherent power. This he inferred from the changes to which land and sea are subject, from the course of sun and moon, and from all the celestial phenomena; for, he argued, were these bodies endowed with power, they would have provided for their own regularity,[h] but, since they lacked this last, it was

Abraham's migration to Canaan. His revolutionary monotheistic doctrine. Gen. xii. 1

---

[g] Bibl. Gaham, Tahash, Maacah.
[h] Or "uniformity": Greek "good order." The heavenly bodies betray irregularity, *e.g.* in the varying hours of sunrise and sunset, the phases of the moon, etc. Had they been their own masters they would have behaved in more regular fashion. But since, notwithstanding these irregularities, they work together for man's good, there must clearly be some controlling Power behind them.

ὑστεροῦντας φανεροὺς γίνεσθαι μηδ' ὅσα πρὸς τὸ χρησιμώτερον ἡμῖν συνεργοῦσι κατὰ τὴν αὑτῶν ἐξουσίαν, ἀλλὰ κατὰ τὴν τοῦ κελεύοντος ἰσχὺν ὑπουργεῖν, ᾧ καλῶς ἔχει μόνῳ τὴν τιμὴν καὶ 157 τὴν εὐχαριστίαν ἀπονέμειν. δι' ἅπερ Χαλδαίων τε καὶ τῶν ἄλλων Μεσοποταμιτῶν στασιασάντων πρὸς αὐτὸν μετοικεῖν δοκιμάσας κατὰ βούλησιν καὶ βοήθειαν τοῦ θεοῦ τὴν Χαναναίαν ἔσχε γῆν, ἱδρυθείς τε αὐτόθι βωμὸν ᾠκοδόμησε καὶ θυσίαν ἐτέλεσε τῷ θεῷ.

158 (2) Μνημονεύει δὲ τοῦ πατρὸς ἡμῶν Ἀβράμου Βηρωσός, οὐκ ὀνομάζων λέγων δ' οὕτως· "μετὰ δὲ τὸν κατακλυσμὸν δεκάτῃ γενεᾷ παρὰ Χαλδαίοις τις ἦν δίκαιος ἀνὴρ καὶ μέγας καὶ τὰ οὐράνια 159 ἔμπειρος." Ἑκαταῖος δὲ καὶ τοῦ μνησθῆναι πλεῖόν τι πεποίηκε· βιβλίον γὰρ περὶ αὐτοῦ συνταξάμενος κατέλιπε. Νικόλαος δὲ ὁ Δαμασκηνὸς ἐν τῇ τετάρτῃ τῶν ἱστοριῶν λέγει οὕτως· "Ἀβράμης ἐβασίλευσεν¹ ἔπηλυς σὺν στρατῷ ἀφιγμένος ἐκ τῆς γῆς τῆς ὑπὲρ Βαβυλῶνος Χαλδαίων λεγο- 160 μένης. μετ' οὐ πολὺν δὲ χρόνον μεταναστὰς καὶ ἀπὸ ταύτης τῆς χώρας σὺν τῷ σφετέρῳ λαῷ εἰς τὴν τότε μὲν Χαναναίαν λεγομένην νῦν δὲ Ἰουδαίαν μετῴκησε καὶ οἱ ἀπ' ἐκείνου πληθύσαντες,

---

¹ RO: ἐβασίλευσε Δαμασκοῦ rell.

---

[a] Philo in several passages (cited by Weill) refers to the motives for Abraham's migration and to the tenets of his opponents, the Chaldaean astronomers and astrologers, who taught ὡς δίχα τῶν φαινομένων οὐδενός ἐστιν οὐδὲν αἴτιον τὸ παράπαν, ἀλλ' ἡλίου καὶ σελήνης καὶ τῶν ἄλλων ἀστέρων αἱ περίοδοι τά τε ἀγαθὰ καὶ τὰ ἐναντία ἑκάστῳ τῶν ὄντων ἀπονέμουσι

JEWISH ANTIQUITIES, I. 156–160

manifest that even those services in which they co-operate for our greater benefit they render not in virtue of their own authority, but through the might of their commanding sovereign, to whom alone it is right to render our homage and thanksgiving. It was in fact owing to these opinions that the Chaldaeans and the other peoples of Mesopotamia rose against him,[a] and he, thinking fit to emigrate, at the will and with the aid of God, settled in the land of Canaan. Established there, he built an altar and offered a sacrifice to God.

Gen. xii. 7.

(2) Berosus mentions our father Abraham, without naming him, in these terms: "In the tenth generation after the flood there lived among the Chaldaeans a just man and great and versed in celestial lore." Hecataeus has done more than mention him: he has left us a book which he composed about him.[b] Nicolas of Damascus, again, in the fourth book of his *Histories* makes the following statement: "Abram(es) reigned (in Damascus), an invader who had come with an army from the country beyond Babylon called the land of the Chaldees. But, not long after, he left this country also with his people for the land then called Canaan but now Judaea, where he settled, he and his

External allusions to Abraham.

(*De migrat. Abr.* § 32, i. 464 M.). This is the argument combated in the text above.

[b] *Cf. Ap.* i. 183 "Hecataeus ... makes no mere passing allusion to us, but wrote a book entirely about the Jews." Hecataeus of Abdera lived in Egypt *c.* 300 B.C. That he wrote *inter alia* on the Jews appears certain, and the extracts which follow the above words in the *Contra Apionem* are probably genuine. But apocryphal Jewish productions were fathered upon him, and the work "on Abraham and the Egyptians" from which Clement of Alexandria (*Strom.* v. 14. 113) quotes spurious verses of Sophocles must be rejected as a forgery.

περὶ ὧν ἐν ἑτέρῳ λόγῳ διέξειμι τὰ ἱστορούμενα. τοῦ δὲ Ἀβράμου ἔτι καὶ νῦν ἐν τῇ Δαμασκηνῇ τὸ ὄνομα δοξάζεται καὶ κώμη δείκνυται ἀπ' αὐτοῦ Ἀβράμου οἴκησις λεγομένη."

161 (viii. 1) Λιμοῦ δὲ χρόνοις ὕστερον τὴν Χαναναίαν[1] καταλαβόντος Ἄβραμος Αἰγυπτίους εὐδαιμονεῖν πυθόμενος μεταίρειν προς αὐτοὺς ἦν πρόθυμος τῆς τε ἀφθονίας τῆς ἐκείνων μεθέξων καὶ τῶν ἱερέων ἀκροατὴς ἐσόμενος ὧν λέγοιεν περὶ θεῶν· ἢ γὰρ κρείσσοσιν εὑρεθεῖσι κατακολουθήσειν ἢ μετακοσμήσειν αὐτοὺς ἐπὶ τὸ βέλτιον αὐτὸς ἄμεινον

162 φρονῶν. ἐπαγόμενος δὲ καὶ τὴν Σάρραν καὶ φοβούμενος τὸ πρὸς τὰς γυναῖκας τῶν Αἰγυπτίων ἐπιμανές, μὴ διὰ τὴν εὐμορφίαν τῆς γυναικὸς ὁ βασιλεὺς αὐτὸν ἀνέλῃ, τέχνην ἐπενόησε τοιαύτην· ἀδελφὸς αὐτῆς εἶναι προσεποιήσατο κἀκείνην τοῦθ'

163 ὑποκρίνασθαι, συμφέρειν γὰρ αὐτοῖς, ἐδίδαξεν. ὡς δ' ἧκον εἰς τὴν Αἴγυπτον, ἀπέβαινε τῷ Ἀβράμῳ καθὼς ὑπενόησε· τὸ γὰρ κάλλος ἐξεβοήθη τῆς γυναικὸς αὐτοῦ, διὸ καὶ Φαραώθης ὁ βασιλεὺς τῶν Αἰγυπτίων οὐ τοῖς περὶ αὐτῆς λεγομένοις ἀρκεσθεὶς ἀλλὰ καὶ θεάσασθαι σπουδάσας οἷός τ'

164 ἦν ἅψασθαι τῆς Σάρρας. ἐμποδίζει δὲ αὐτοῦ ὁ θεὸς τὴν ἄδικον ἐπιθυμίαν νόσῳ τε καὶ στάσει τῶν πραγμάτων· καὶ θυομένῳ περὶ ἀπαλλαγῆς κατὰ μῆνιν θεοῦ τὸ δεινὸν αὐτῷ παρεῖναι ἀπεσήμαινον

---

[1] Ἰουδαίαν RO.

---

[a] Nicolas (i. 94) is good authority for the traditions of his native place. A rather earlier Latin writer, Trogus Pompeius (c. 20 B.C.), likewise mentions Abraham among the kings of Damascus: " Post Damascum (the eponymous king) Azelus, mox Adores et Abrahames et Israhel reges

JEWISH ANTIQUITIES, I. 160–164

numerous descendants, whose history I shall recount in another book. The name of Abram is still celebrated in the region of Damascus, and a village is shown that is called after him 'Abram's abode.'"[a]

(viii. 1) Some time later, Canaan being in the grip of a famine, Abraham, hearing of the prosperity of the Egyptians, was of a mind to visit them, alike to profit by their abundance and to hear what their priests said about the gods; intending, if he found their doctrine more excellent than his own, to conform to it, or else to convert them to a better mind should his own beliefs prove superior. He took Sarra with him and, fearing the Egyptians' frenzy for women, lest the king should slay him because of his wife's beauty, he devised the following scheme: he pretended to be her brother and, telling her that their interest required it, instructed her to play her part accordingly. On their arrival in Egypt all fell out as Abraham had suspected: his wife's beauty was noised abroad, insomuch that Pharaothes,[b] the king of the Egyptians, not content with the reports of her, was fired with a desire to see her and on the point of laying hands on her. But God thwarted his criminal passion by an outbreak of disease and political disturbance; and when he had sacrifices offered to discover a remedy, the priests declared that his calamity was due to

Abraham in Egypt. Gen. xii. 10.

---

fuere " (Justin's *Epitome* xxxvi. 2). T. Reinach, to whom I owe this reference, adds that these traditions must have arisen at the time when Damascus and Israel were on intimate terms.

[b] The Hellenized form of Pharaoh normally employed by Josephus: once (*A.* viii. 151) he writes Φαραώνης, once (*B.* v. 379) Φαραώ. In the last-mentioned passage he gives a strange version of the present story, in which Φ., surnamed Νεχαώς, is represented as invading Palestine and carrying off Sarra.

οἱ ἱερεῖς, ἐφ' οἷς ἠθέλησεν ὑβρίσαι τοῦ ξένου τὴν
165 γυναῖκα. ὁ δὲ φοβηθεὶς ἠρώτα τὴν Σάρραν, τίς
τε εἴη καὶ τίνα τοῦτον ἐπάγοιτο, πυθόμενός τε
τὴν ἀλήθειαν Ἅβραμον παρῃτεῖτο· νομίζων γὰρ
ἀδελφὴν ἀλλ' οὐ γυναῖκα αὐτοῦ σπουδάσαι περὶ
αὐτὴν συγγένειαν ποιήσασθαι βουλόμενος, ἀλλ' οὐκ
ἐνυβρίσαι κατ' ἐπιθυμίαν ὡρμημένος· δωρεῖταί
τε αὐτὸν πολλοῖς χρήμασι, καὶ συνῆν[1] Αἰγυπτίων
τοῖς λογιωτάτοις, τήν τε ἀρετὴν αὐτῷ καὶ τὴν
ἐπ' αὐτῇ δόξαν ἐντεῦθεν ἐπιφανεστέραν συνέβη
γενέσθαι.

166 (2) Τῶν γὰρ Αἰγυπτίων διαφόροις ἀρεσκομένων
ἔθεσι καὶ τὰ παρ' ἀλλήλοις ἐκφαυλιζόντων νόμιμα
καὶ διὰ τοῦτο δυσμενῶς ἐχόντων πρὸς ἀλλήλους,
συμβαλὼν αὐτῶν ἑκάστοις καὶ διαπτύων τοὺς
λόγους οὓς ἐποιοῦντο περὶ τῶν ἰδίων κενοὺς καὶ
167 μηδὲν ἔχοντας ἀληθὲς ἀπέφαινε. θαυμασθεὶς οὖν
ὑπ' αὐτῶν ἐν ταῖς συνουσίαις ὡς συνετώτατος
καὶ δεινὸς ἀνὴρ οὐ νοῆσαι μόνον ἀλλὰ καὶ πεῖσαι
λέγων περὶ ὧν ἂν ἐπιχειρήσειε διδάσκειν, τήν τε
ἀριθμητικὴν αὐτοῖς χαρίζεται καὶ τὰ περὶ ἀστρο-
168 νομίαν[2] παραδίδωσι. πρὸ γὰρ τῆς Ἀβράμου
παρουσίας Αἰγύπτιοι[3] τούτων εἶχον ἀμαθῶς· ἐκ
Χαλδαίων γὰρ ταῦτ' ἐφοίτησεν εἰς Αἴγυπτον, ὅθεν
ἦλθε καὶ εἰς τοὺς Ἕλληνας.

169 (3) Ὡς δ' εἰς τὴν Χαναναίαν ἀφίκετο, μερίζεται

[1] συνεῖναι RO.   [2] ἀστρολογίαν L Lat. Eus.
[3] Euseb., Eustath.: εἰς Αἴγυπτον RO: the rest have a conflate text.

[a] Amplification of Scripture; cf. Eupolemus (c. 150 B.C., ap. Euseb. Praep. Ev. ix. 17, quoted by Weill) μάντεις δὲ αὐτοῦ καλέσαντος τοῦτο φάναι, μὴ εἶναι χήραν τὴν γυναῖκα.

[b] Or perhaps with the other reading " permission to

the wrath of God, because he had wished to outrage the stranger's wife.[a] Terrified, he asked Sarra who she was and who was this man she had brought with her. On learning the truth he made his excuses to Abraham : it was, he said, in the belief that she was his sister, not his wife, that he had set his affections on her ; he had wished to contract a marriage alliance and not to outrage her in a transport of passion. He further gave him abundant riches, and Abraham consorted [b] with the most learned of the Egyptians, whence his virtue and reputation became still more conspicuous.

(2) For, seeing that the Egyptians were addicted to a variety of different customs and disparaged one another's practices and were consequently at enmity with one another, Abraham conferred with each party and, exposing the arguments which they adduced in favour of their particular views, demonstrated that they were idle and contained nothing true. Thus gaining their admiration at these meetings as a man of extreme sagacity, gifted not only with high intelligence but with power to convince his hearers on any subject which he undertook to teach, he introduced them to arithmetic and transmitted to them the laws of astronomy.[c] For before the coming of Abraham the Egyptians were ignorant of these sciences, which thus travelled from the Chaldaeans into Egypt, whence they passed to the Greeks.

(3) On his return to Canaan, he divided the land

Abraham instructs the Egyptians.

Division of Canaan with Lot. Gen. xiii. 6.

consort." In Scripture the presents are given before the discovery, after which Abraham and his wife are dismissed forthwith.

[c] So Artapanus (c. 2nd cent. B.C.) states that Abraham migrated with his household to Egypt and taught Pharethones astrology (ap. Eus. *Praep. Ev.* ix. 18).

JOSEPHUS

πρὸς Λῶτον τὴν γῆν τῶν ποιμένων αὐτοῖς στασιαζόντων περὶ τῆς χώρας ἐν ᾗ νέμοιεν· τὴν ἐκλογὴν
170 μέντοι καὶ τὴν αἴρεσιν ἐπιτρέπει τῷ Λώτῳ, λαβὼν δ' αὐτὸς τὴν ὑπ' ἐκείνου καταλελειμμένην ὑπώρειαν ᾤκει ἐν τῇ Ναβρῷ πόλει· παλαιοτέρα δέ ἐστιν ἔτεσιν ἑπτὰ πρὸ Τάνιδος τῆς Αἰγύπτου. Λῶτος δὲ τὴν πρὸς τὸ πεδίον κειμένην καὶ ποταμὸν Ἰόρδανον εἶχεν οὐκ ἄπωθεν τῆς Σοδομιτῶν πόλεως, ἣ τότε μὲν ἦν ἀγαθή, νῦν δὲ ἠφάνισται κατὰ βούλησιν θεοῦ. τὴν δὲ αἰτίαν κατὰ χώραν σημανῶ.

171 (ix.) Κατ' ἐκεῖνον δὲ τὸν καιρὸν Ἀσσυρίων κρατούντων τῆς Ἀσίας Σοδομίταις ᾔνθει τὰ πράγματα εἴς τε πλοῦτον αὐτῶν ἐπιδεδωκότων καὶ νεότητα πολλήν· βασιλεῖς δὲ αὐτοῖς πέντε διεῖπον τὴν χώραν, Βάλας Βαλαίας Συναβάνης καὶ Συμμόβορος ὅ τε Βαλήνων βασιλεύς· μοίρας δ' ἦρχον
172 ἕκαστος ἰδίας. ἐπὶ τούτους στρατεύσαντες Ἀσσύριοι καὶ μέρη τέσσαρα ποιήσαντες τῆς στρατιᾶς ἐπολιόρκουν αὐτούς· στρατηγὸς δ' ἑκάστοις ἦν εἷς ἐπιτεταγμένος. γενομένης δὲ μάχης νικήσαντες οἱ Ἀσσύριοι φόρον ἐπιτάσσουσι τοῖς Σοδομιτῶν
173 βασιλεῦσι. δώδεκα μὲν οὖν ἔτη δουλεύοντες καὶ τοὺς ἐπιταχθέντας αὐτοῖς φόρους τελοῦντες ὑπέμειναν, τῷ δὲ τρισκαιδεκάτῳ ἀπέστησαν, καὶ διαβαίνει στρατὸς Ἀσσυρίων ἐπ' αὐτοὺς στρατη-

---

[a] Bibl. Hebron. This name takes a variety of forms in different parts of Josephus: Ναβρῶ (or Ναβρών), Νεβρών, Γιβρών, Ἑβρών and Χεβρών.

[b] Cf. Numb. xiii. 22, "Hebron was built seven years before Zoan in Egypt." Zoan, or Tanis, lay in the E. part of the Delta; its foundation is dated by modern scholars

JEWISH ANTIQUITIES, I. 169-173

with Lot, since their shepherds quarrelled about grazing ground; but he left Lot to select what he chose. Taking for himself the lowland that the other left him, he dwelt in Nabro,*a* a city that is more ancient by seven years than Tanis in Egypt.*b* Lot for his part occupied the district in the direction of the plain and the river Jordan,*c* not far from the city of Sodom, which was then prosperous but has now by God's will been obliterated; the cause of its fate I shall indicate in its place.*d* Gen. xiii. 18.

(ix.) At that time, however, when the Assyrians were masters of Asia, the people of Sodom were in a flourishing condition; their wealth had grown and their youth were numerous; and five kings governed their country—Balas, Balaias, Synabanes, Symmobor, and the king of the Baleni *e* — each ruler having his own province. Against these kings the Assyrians marched out and, dividing their army into four bodies, with one general in command of each, besieged them. A battle took place, and the victorious Assyrians imposed tribute on the kings of the Sodomites. For twelve years, then, the latter submitted to serve and to pay the appointed tribute; but in the thirteenth year they rebelled and an army of Assyrians strode off*f* against them, under the command War of Sodomites and Assyrians. Lot taken prisoner. Gen. xiv. 1.

" before 2000 B.C." (G. B. Gray, *Int. Crit. Comm.* on Numbers *loc. cit.*). Elsewhere (*B.J.* iv. 530) we read that local tradition in the time of Titus regarded Hebron (Χεβρών) as 2300 years old, and " more ancient than Egyptian *Memphis*."

c Gen. xiii. 10, " the Plain of Jordan," or rather " the Circle (or " Oval," Heb. *kikkar*) of J.," the broader portion of the Jordan valley at its southern end.

d § 194.

e Biblical names Bera (LXX Βαλά), Birsha (Βαρσά), Shinab, Shemeber, Bela (Βαλάκ).

f Or " crossed over " (*sc.* the Euphrates).

γούντων Ἀμαραψίδου Ἀριόχου Χοδολαμόρου Θα-
174 δάλου. οὗτοι τήν τε Συρίαν ἅπασαν διηρπάσαντο
καὶ τοὺς τῶν γιγάντων ἀπογόνους κατεστρέψαντο,
γενόμενοι δὲ κατὰ τὰ Σόδομα στρατοπεδεύουσι
κατὰ τὴν κοιλάδα τὴν λεγομένην φρέατα ἀσφάλτου·
κατ' ἐκεῖνον γὰρ τὸν καιρὸν φρέατα ἦν ἐν τῷ τόπῳ,
νῦν μέντοι τῆς Σοδομιτῶν πόλεως ἀφανισθείσης
ἡ κοιλὰς ἐκείνη λίμνη γέγονεν ἡ Ἀσφαλτῖτις
175 λεγομένη. περὶ μὲν οὖν τῆς λίμνης ταύτης αὖθις
μετ' οὐ πολὺ δηλώσομεν, τῶν δὲ Σοδομιτῶν συμ-
βαλόντων τοῖς Ἀσσυρίοις καὶ καρτερᾶς τῆς μάχης
γενομένης, πολλοὶ μὲν αὐτῶν ἀπέθανον, οἱ λοιποὶ
δὲ ἠχμαλωτίσθησαν, σὺν οἷς καὶ Λῶτος ἤγετο τοῖς
Σοδομίταις σύμμαχος ἐληλυθώς.

176 (x. 1) Ἀβράμῳ δὲ ἀκούσαντι τὴν συμφορὰν
αὐτῶν φόβος τε ἅμα περὶ Λώτου τοῦ συγγενοῦς
εἰσῆλθε καὶ οἶκτος περὶ τῶν Σοδομιτῶν φίλων
177 ὄντων καὶ γειτνιώντων. καὶ βοηθεῖν αὐτοῖς δοκιμάσας οὐκ ἀνέμεινεν, ἀλλ' ἐπειχθεὶς καὶ κατὰ
πέμπτην ἐπιπεσὼν νύκτα τοῖς Ἀσσυρίοις περὶ
Δάνον, οὕτως γὰρ ἡ ἑτέρα τοῦ Ἰορδάνου προσαγορεύεται πηγή, καὶ φθάσας πρὶν ἐν ὅπλοις
γενέσθαι τοὺς μὲν ἐν ταῖς κοίταις ὄντας ἀπέκτεινε
μηδ' ἐπίνοιαν τῆς συμφορᾶς ἔχοντας, οἱ δὲ μήπω
πρὸς ὕπνον τετραμμένοι μάχεσθαι δ' ὑπὸ μέθης

---

[a] Bibl. Amraphel (Ἀμαρφάλ).
[b] Bibl. Chedorlaomer (Χοδολλογομόρ).
[c] Bibl. Tidal (Θαλγά or the like).

of Amarapsides,[a] Arioch, Chodolamor[b] and Thadal.[c] These ravaged the whole of Syria and subdued the descendants of the giants[d]; then, on reaching the region of Sodom, they encamped in the valley called "Bitumen pits." For at that time there were pits in that district, but now that the city of Sodom has disappeared the valley has become a lake, the so-called Asphaltitis[e]; to that lake, however, I shall shortly revert.[f] The Sodomites, then, joined battle with the Assyrians and there was a stubborn contest: many of their number perished, and the rest were taken prisoners. Among the latter was Lot, who had come to fight as an ally of the Sodomites.

Gen. xiv. 10 LXX.

(x. 1) Abraham, hearing of their disaster, was moved alike with fear for his kinsman Lot and with compassion for his friends and neighbours, the Sodomites. Determining to succour them, without loss of time he set out in haste and on the fifth night[g] fell upon the Assyrians in the neighbourhood of Dan[h] (such is the name of one of the two sources of the Jordan),[i] surprising them before they had time to arm: some, unconscious of their fate, he slew in their beds; while those who were not yet plunged in sleep but through drunkenness were incapable of fighting

Abraham defeats the Assyrians. Gen. xiv. 13.

[d] Gen. xiv. 5. "the Rephaim" (LXX τοὺς γίγαντας).

[e] "Bituminous" (lake), the Dead Sea. Josephus, in common perhaps with the Biblical narrative (Gen. xiii. 10), conceives it to have been non-existent at this time.

[f] § 203, describing the fate of Sodom, does not mention the lake; a description is given in *B.J.* iv. 476 ff.

[g] These details of time and circumstances are legendary.

[h] So Gen. xiv. 14: the older Laish, renamed Dan in the period of the Judges.

[i] Josephus appears to countenance the popular etymology, which saw in the name a compound of two alleged sources of the river, Jor and Dan!

178 ἀδύνατοι ἔφυγον. Ἄβραμος δὲ διώκων εἵπετο μέχρι καὶ δευτεραίους συνήλασεν αὐτοὺς εἰς Ὠβὰ τῆς Δαμασκηνῶν γῆς, ἐπιδείξας ὅτι τὸ νικᾶν οὐκ ἐν τῷ πλήθει καὶ τῇ πολυχειρίᾳ κεῖσθαι συμβέβηκεν, ἀλλὰ προθυμία τῶν μαχομένων καὶ τὸ γενναῖον κρατεῖ παντὸς ἀριθμοῦ, τριακοσίοις καὶ δεκαοκτὼ οἰκέταις αὐτοῦ καὶ τρισὶ φίλοις τοσούτου στρατοῦ περιγενόμενος. ὁπόσοι δὲ αὐτῶν καὶ διέφυγον ἀδόξως ἀνέστρεψαν.

179 (2) Ἄβραμος δὲ τοὺς τῶν Σοδομιτῶν σώσας αἰχμαλώτους, οἳ ληφθέντες ἔφθησαν ὑπὸ τῶν Ἀσσυρίων, καὶ τὸν συγγενῆ Λῶτον ἀνέζευξεν μετὰ εἰρήνης. ἀπήντησε δὲ αὐτῷ ὁ τῶν Σοδομιτῶν βασιλεὺς εἰς τόπον τινὰ ὃν καλοῦσι πεδίον
180 βασιλικόν. ἔνθα ὁ τῆς Σολυμᾶ ὑποδέχεται βασιλεὺς αὐτὸν Μελχισεδέκ· σημαίνει δὲ τοῦτο βασιλεὺς δίκαιος· καὶ ἦν δὲ τοιοῦτος ὁμολογουμένως, ὡς διὰ ταύτην αὐτὸν τὴν αἰτίαν καὶ ἱερέα γενέσθαι τοῦ θεοῦ· τὴν μέντοι Σολυμᾶ ὕστερον ἐκάλεσαν[1]
181 Ἱεροσόλυμα. ἐχορήγησε δὲ οὗτος ὁ Μελχισεδὲκ τῷ Ἀβράμου στρατῷ ξένια καὶ πολλὴν ἀφθονίαν τῶν ἐπιτηδείων παρέσχε καὶ παρὰ τὴν εὐωχίαν αὐτόν τε ἐπαινεῖν ἤρξατο καὶ τὸν θεὸν εὐλογεῖν

---

[1] ἐκάλεσεν ROP.

[a] Weill quotes a striking parallel from Philo, *De Abr.* (40) § 233 Cohn: ἐπιπίπτει τοῖς πολεμίοις δεδειπνοποιημένοις ἤδη καὶ πρὸς ὕπνον μέλλουσι τρέπεσθαι· καὶ τοὺς μὲν ἐν εὐναῖς ἱέρευε, τοὺς δ' ἀντιταχθέντας ἄρδην ἀνῄρει, πάντων δ' ἐρρωμένως ἐπεκράτει τῷ θαρραλέῳ τῆς ψυχῆς μᾶλλον ἢ ταῖς παρασκευαῖς.
[b] Bibl. Hobah (Χωβάλ), Gen. xiv. 15.
[c] Gen. xiv. 14.   [d] Gen. xiv. 24 (*cf.* 13).
[e] "The King's Vale," mentioned in the story of Absalom

JEWISH ANTIQUITIES, I. 178-181

took to their heels.[a] Abraham followed hotly in pursuit until on the following day he had driven them all into Oba[b] in the country of the Damascenes; thereby proving that victory does not depend on numbers and a multitude of hands, but that the ardour and mettle of the combatants overcome all odds, seeing that with three hundred and eighteen of his servants[c] and three friends[d] he had defeated so great a host. And all those who succeeded in escaping returned ingloriously home.

(2) So Abraham, having rescued the Sodomite prisoners, previously captured by the Assyrians, including his kinsman Lot, returned in peace. The king of the Sodomites met him at a place which they call the "royal plain.[e]" There he was received by the king of Solyma,[f] Melchisedek; this name means "righteous king,[g]" and such was he by common consent, insomuch that for this reason he was moreover made priest of God; Solyma was in fact the place afterwards called Hierosolyma.[h] Now this Melchisedek hospitably entertained Abraham's army, providing abundantly for all their needs, and in the course of the feast he began to extol Abraham and to

His meeting with Melchisedek. Gen. xiv. 16.

(2 Sam. xviii. 18), and located by Josephus two "stadia" from Jerusalem (*A*. vii. 243).

[f] Bibl. Salem (Σαλήμ).

[g] The usual Jewish interpretation—"king of righteousness" (*zedek*)—repeated in *B.J.* vi. 438 (βασιλεὺς δίκαιος, ἦν γὰρ δὴ τοιοῦτος) and found in the N.T. (Hebr. vii. 2) and elsewhere; probable meaning "my king is Zedek," Z. being the name of a Canaanite deity.

[h] The Hellenized form of Jerusalem (LXX Ἱερουσαλήμ) used throughout Josephus, who here and elsewhere (*A*. vii. 67, *B*. vi. 438, *cf. Ap.* i. 174) takes over, besides the name, the popular fantastic etymology of it, "the holy Solyma" (or Salem).

ὑποχειρίους αὐτῷ ποιήσαντα τοὺς ἐχθρούς. Ἀβράμου δὲ διδόντος καὶ τὴν δεκάτην τῆς λείας αὐτῷ
182 προσδέχεται τὴν δόσιν. ὁ δὲ τῶν Σοδομιτῶν βασιλεὺς τὴν μὲν λείαν ἔχειν Ἄβραμον παρεκάλει, τοὺς δ' ἀνθρώπους ἀπολαβεῖν ἠξίου, οὓς παρὰ τῶν Ἀσσυρίων ἔσωσεν οἰκείους ὄντας. Ἄβραμος δὲ οὐκ ἔφη τοῦτο ποιήσειν, οὐδ' ἂν ἄλλην ὠφέλειαν ἐκ τῆς λείας ἐκείνης εἰς αὐτὸν ἥξειν πλὴν ὅσα τροφὴ τοῖς οἰκέταις αὐτοῦ γένοιτο· μοῖραν μέντοι τινὰ τοῖς φίλοις αὐτοῦ παρέσχε[1] τοῖς συστρατευομένοις. Ἔσχων δ' ὁ πρῶτος ἐκαλεῖτο [καὶ] Ἔννηρος καὶ Μαμβρῆς.

183 (3) Ἐπαινέσας δὲ αὐτοῦ τὴν ἀρετὴν ὁ θεός, "ἀλλ' οὐκ ἀπολεῖς," φησί, "μισθοὺς οὓς ἄξιόν ἐστίν σε ἐπὶ τοιαύταις εὐπραγίαις κομίζεσθαι." τοῦ δ' ὑπολαβόντος καὶ τίς ἂν εἴη χάρις τούτων τῶν μισθῶν, οὐκ ὄντων οἳ διαδέξονται μετ' αὐτόν, ἔτι γὰρ ἦν ἄπαις, ὁ θεὸς καὶ παῖδα αὐτῷ γενήσεσθαι καταγγέλλει καὶ πολλὴν ἐξ ἐκείνου γενεάν, ὡς παραπλησίως αὐτὴν τοῖς ἄστροις ἔσεσθαι τὸν
184 ἀριθμόν. καὶ ὁ μὲν ταῦτ' ἀκούσας θυσίαν προσφέρει τῷ θεῷ κελευσθεὶς ὑπ' αὐτοῦ. ἦν δὲ ὁ τρόπος τῆς θυσίας τοιοῦτος· δάμαλιν τριετίζουσαν καὶ αἶγα τριετίζουσαν καὶ κριὸν ὁμοίως τριετῆ καὶ τρυγόνα καὶ περιστερὰν κελεύσαντος διεῖλε,
185 τῶν ὀρνέων οὐδὲν διελών. εἶτα πρὶν στῆναι τὸν βωμὸν οἰωνῶν ἐφιπταμένων ἐπιθυμίᾳ τοῦ αἵματος φωνὴ θεία παρῆν ἀποσημαίνουσα πονηροὺς αὐτοῦ τοῖς ἐγγόνοις γείτονας ἐπὶ ἔτη τετρακόσια[2] γενησομένους κατὰ τὴν Αἴγυπτον, ἐν οἷς κακοπαθήσαντας

[1] ROM: παρασχεῖν rell.
[2] τριακόσια RO.

bless God for having delivered his enemies into his hand. Abraham then offered him the tithe of the spoil, and he accepted the gift. As for the king of Sodom, he entreated Abraham to keep the spoil, and desired only to recover those of his subjects whom he had rescued from the Assyrians. But Abraham replied that he could not do this and that no further profit should accrue to him from those spoils beyond what would meet his servants' maintenance. However, he offered a portion to his comrades in arms : of these the first was named Eschon,[a] the others Ennêr[b] and Mambres.[c]

(3) God commended his virtue and said, " Nay, thou shalt not lose the rewards that are thy due for such good deeds." And when he replied, " What pleasure can those rewards afford, when there is none to succeed to them after me ? " (for he was still childless), God announced that a son would be born to him, whose posterity would be so great as to be comparable in number to the stars. On hearing these words Abraham offered a sacrifice to God as bidden by Him. And the sacrifice was on this wise : he took a heifer of three years old, a she-goat of three years old and a ram of the same age, with a turtle-dove and a pigeon, and, at God's bidding, divided them in twain, save the birds which he divided not. Then, before the altar was erected, while birds of prey were flying to the scene lusting for the blood, there came a voice divine announcing that his posterity would for four hundred years find evil neighbours in Egypt, but that after affliction among them they would overcome their

Gen. xiv. 24. God's promises to Abraham. Gen. xv. 1.

[a] Bibl. Eshcol : Josephus agrees with LXX in placing this name " first," not second.
[b] Bibl. Aner (LXX Αὐνάν).
[c] Bibl. Mamre.

JOSEPHUS

περιέσεσθαι τῶν ἐχθρῶν καὶ κρατήσαντας πολέμῳ Χαναναίων ἕξειν αὐτῶν τὴν γῆν καὶ τὰς πόλεις.

186 (4) Ἅβραμος δὲ κατῴκει μὲν περὶ τὴν Ὠγύγην καλουμένην δρῦν, ἔστι δὲ τῆς Χαναναίας τὸ χωρίον οὐ πόρρω τῆς Ἑβρωνίων πόλεως, δυσφορῶν δὲ ἐπὶ γυναικὶ μὴ κυούσῃ ἱκετεύει τὸν θεὸν γονὴν 187 αὐτῷ παιδὸς ἄρσενος παρασχεῖν. τοῦ δὲ θεοῦ θαρσεῖν αὐτὸν παρακελευομένου τοῖς τε ἄλλοις ἅπασιν ὡς ἐπ' ἀγαθοῖς αὐτὸν ἀπὸ τῆς Μεσοποταμίας ἠγμένον καὶ παίδων ἐσομένων, Σάρρα τοῦ θεοῦ κελεύσαντος ἐπικλίνει μίαν τῶν θεραπαινίδων Ἀγάρην ὄνομα, γένος οὖσαν Αἰγυπτίαν, 188 ὡς ἐξ αὐτῆς παιδοποιησομένῳ. καὶ γενομένη ἐγκύμων ἡ θεραπαινὶς ἐξυβρίζειν εἰς τὴν Σάρραν ἐτόλμησε βασιλίζουσα, ὡς τῆς ἡγεμονίας περιστησομένης εἰς τὸν ὑπ' αὐτῆς τεχθησόμενον. Ἁβράμου δὲ αὐτὴν πρὸς αἰκίαν παραδιδόντος τῇ Σάρρᾳ δρασμὸν ἐπεβούλευσεν οὐχ ὑπομένουσα τὰς ταλαιπωρίας καὶ τὸν θεὸν ἱκέτευεν οἶκτον αὐτῆς 189 λαβεῖν. ὑπαντιάζει δὲ διὰ τῆς ἐρήμου προϊοῦσαν αὐτὴν ἄγγελος θεῖος κελεύων πρὸς τοὺς δεσπότας ἐπανιέναι· βίου γὰρ μείζονος τεύξεσθαι σωφρονοῦσαν· καὶ γὰρ νῦν εἰς τὴν δέσποιναν ἀγνώμονα καὶ αὐθάδη γενομένην ἐν τούτοις εἶναι τοῖς κακοῖς· 190 παρακούουσαν μὲν τοῦ θεοῦ καὶ προσωτέρω χωροῦσαν ἔλεγεν ἀπολεῖσθαι, νοστήσασαν δὲ αὐτὴν ὀπίσω γενήσεσθαι μητέρα παιδὸς τῆς γῆς ἐκείνης βασιλεύσοντος. τούτοις πείθεται καὶ ἐπανελθοῦσα

---

[a] Bibl. " the oaks (or " terebinths ") of Mamre," and so Josephus, following the LXX, writes below, § 196 πρὸς τῇ δρυῒ τῇ Μαμβρῇ; in B. iv. 533 he speaks of " a huge tere-

foes, vanquish the Canaanites in battle, and take possession of their land and cities.

(4) Abraham was living near the oak called Ogyges,[a] a place in Canaan not far from the city of the Hebronites, when, distressed at his wife's sterility, he besought God to grant him the birth of a male child. Thereon God bade him be assured that, as in all else he had been led out of Mesopotamia for his welfare, so children would come to him; and by God's command Sarra brought to his bed one of her handmaidens, an Egyptian named Agar,[b] that he might have children by her. Becoming pregnant, this servant had the insolence to abuse Sarra, assuming queenly airs as though the dominion were to pass to her unborn son. Abraham having thereupon consigned her to Sarra for chastisement, she, unable to endure her humiliations, resolved to fly and entreated God to take pity on her. But as she went on her way through the wilderness an angel of God met her and bade her return to her master and mistress, assuring her that she would attain a happier lot through self-control, for her present plight was but due to her arrogance and presumption towards her mistress; and that if she disobeyed God and pursued her way she would perish, but if she returned home she would become the mother of a son hereafter to reign over that country. Obedient to this behest she returned

Hagar and Ishmael. Gen. xiii. 18, xvi. 1.

---

binth " six *stadia* from Hebron, " which is said to have stood there ever since the creation." Here for his Greek readers he appears to give this famous tree the name of a primaeval Greek hero associated in Attic and Boeotian legend with stories of a flood. But the adjective " Ogygian " was used in Greek for " primaeval," " antediluvian," and was perhaps what he wrote.

[b] Greek Agare: Bibl. Hagar.

πρὸς τοὺς δεσπότας συγγνώμης ἔτυχε· τίκτει δὲ
μετ' οὐ πολὺ Ἰσμάηλον, θεόκλυτον ἄν τις εἴποι,
διὰ τὸ εἰσακοῦσαι τὸν θεὸν τῆς ἱκεσίας.

191 (5) Ἀβράμῳ μὲν οὖν ἕκτον ἤδη καὶ ὀγδοηκοστὸν
ἔτος γεγονότι ὁ προειρημένος ἐγεννήθη, εἰς ἔνατον
δ' αὐτῷ καὶ ἐνενηκοστὸν παρελθόντι ἐπιφανεὶς ὁ
θεὸς ἀπήγγειλεν ὡς παῖς αὐτῷ ἐκ Σάρρας ἔσοιτο·
κελεύει δ' αὐτὸν καλέσαι Ἴσακον δηλῶν ἐσόμενα
ἔθνη μεγάλα ἀπ' αὐτοῦ καὶ βασιλεῖς, καὶ ὅτι
πολεμήσαντες καθέξουσι τὴν Χαναναίαν ἅπασαν
192 ἀπὸ Σιδῶνος μέχρι Αἰγύπτου, προσέταξέ τε βουλόμενος τὸ ἀπ' αὐτοῦ γένος μένειν τοῖς ἄλλοις οὐ
συμφυρόμενον περιτέμνεσθαι τὰ αἰδοῖα καὶ τοῦτο
ποιεῖν ὀγδόῃ ἡμέρᾳ μετὰ τὸ γεννηθῆναι. τὴν
αἰτίαν δὲ τῆς περιτομῆς ἡμῶν ἐν ἄλλοις δηλώσω.
193 πυθομένῳ δὲ Ἀβράμῳ καὶ περὶ τοῦ Ἰσμαήλου,
εἰ ζήσεται, πολυχρόνιόν τε ἀπεσήμαινεν ὁ θεὸς καὶ
μεγάλων ἐθνῶν πατέρα. καὶ Ἄβραμος μὲν ἐπὶ
τούτοις εὐχαριστήσας τῷ θεῷ περιτέμνεται παραχρῆμα καὶ πάντες οἱ παρ' αὐτοῦ καὶ ὁ παῖς Ἰσμάηλος, οὗ κατ' ἐκείνην τὴν ἡμέραν τρισκαιδέκατον
ἔτος ἔχοντος αὐτὸς ἐνενηκοστὸν πρὸς τοῖς ἐννέα
διῆγεν.
194 (xi. 1) Ὑπὸ δὴ τοῦτον τὸν καιρὸν οἱ Σοδομῖται
πλήθει[1] καὶ μεγέθει χρημάτων ὑπερφρονοῦντες εἴς
τε ἀνθρώπους ἦσαν ὑβρισταὶ καὶ πρὸς τὸ θεῖον

[1] ROE : πλούτῳ rell.

---

[a] Or possibly, in the classical active sense of the word,
"calling upon God"; the name can mean either "May
God hear" or "God hears." Philo translates ἀκοὴ θεοῦ (*De
mut. nom.* 37 § 202).

JEWISH ANTIQUITIES, I. 190–194

to her master and mistress, was forgiven, and not long after gave birth to Is(h)mael, a name which may be rendered "Heard of God,"*a* because God had hearkened to her petition.

Cf. Gen. xvi. 11.

(5) Abraham was already eighty-six years of age when this son was born to him. He had attained his ninety-ninth year when God appeared to him and announced that he should have a son by Sarra, bidding him call him Isa(a)c, and revealing how great nations and kings would spring from him, and how they would win possession, by war, of all Canaan from Sidon to Egypt. Furthermore, to the intent that his posterity should be kept from mixing with others,*b* God charged him to have them circumcised and to perform the rite on the eighth day after birth. The reason for our practice of circumcision I shall expound elsewhere.*c* Abraham then inquiring concerning Ishmael also, whether he was to live,*d* God made known to him that he would live to an advanced age and become the father of great nations. So Abraham rendered thanks to God for these blessings and was circumcised forthwith, he and all his household and his son Ishmael, who on that day was in his thirteenth year, his father's age being ninety-nine.

Birth of Isaac. Institution of circumcision.
Gen. xvii. 1.

Ib. 1.

(xi. 1) Now about this time the Sodomites, overweeningly proud of their numbers and the extent of their wealth, showed themselves insolent to men and impious to the Divinity, insomuch that they no

Impiety of the arrogant Sodomites.

---

b Motive not mentioned in Scripture.

c In the projected work on "Customs and Causes," often alluded to elsewhere (§ 25 note).

d Josephus seems to have read Gen. xvii. 18 as a question. Ἰσμαὴλ οὗτος ζήσεται (so one ms. of LXX for ζήτω) ἐναντίον σου Heb. "Oh that I. might live before thee!"

95

ἀσεβεῖς, ὡς μηκέτι μεμνῆσθαι τῶν παρ' αὐτοῦ γενομένων ὠφελειῶν, εἶναί τε μισόξενοι καὶ τὰς
195 πρὸς ἄλλους[1] ὁμιλίας ἐκτρέπεσθαι. χαλεπήνας οὖν ἐπὶ τούτοις ὁ θεὸς ἔγνω τιμωρήσασθαι τῆς ὑπερηφανίας αὐτοὺς καὶ τήν τε πόλιν αὐτῶν[a] κατασκάψασθαι καὶ τὴν χώραν οὕτως ἀφανίσαι, ὡς μήτε φυτὸν ἔτι μήτε καρπὸν ἕτερον ἐξ αὐτῆς ἀναδοθῆναι.

196 (2) Ταῦτα τοῦ θεοῦ κρίναντος περὶ τῶν Σοδομιτῶν Ἅβραμος θεασάμενος τρεῖς ἀγγέλους, ἐκαθέζετο δὲ πρὸς τῇ δρυῒ τῇ Μαμβρῇ παρὰ τῇ θύρᾳ τῆς αὐτοῦ αὐλῆς, καὶ νομίσας εἶναι ξένους ἀναστὰς ἠσπάσατό τε καὶ παρ' αὐτῷ καταχθέντας παρεκάλει
197 ξενίων μεταλαβεῖν. ἐπινευσάντων δὲ ἄρτους τε προσέταξεν εὐθὺς ἐκ σεμιδάλεως γενέσθαι καὶ μόσχον θύσας καὶ ὀπτήσας ἐκόμισεν αὐτοῖς ὑπὸ τῇ δρυῒ κατακειμένοις· οἱ δὲ δόξαν αὐτῷ παρέσχον ἐσθιόντων, ἔτι δὲ καὶ περὶ τῆς γυναικὸς ἐπυνθάνοντο, ποῖ ποτ' [ἂν][3] εἴη Σάρρα. τοῦ δ' εἰπόντος ἔνδον εἶναι, ἥξειν ἔφασαν εἰς τὸ μέλλον καὶ εὑρήσειν
198 αὐτὴν ἤδη μητέρα γεγενημένην. τῆς δὲ γυναικὸς ἐπὶ τούτῳ μειδιασάσης καὶ ἀδύνατον εἶναι τὴν τεκνοποιίαν εἰπούσης, αὐτῆς μὲν ἐνενήκοντα ἔτη

[1] SP: ἀλλήλους rell.   [2] αὐτὴν ROE.
[3] ins. RO: om. most MSS., reading ποῖ ποτ' εἴη τυγχάνουσα ἡ Σ.

---

[a] The μισοξενία of the Sodomites is mentioned in Wisdom xix. 13 f., and emphasized in Rabbinical writings, *e.g.* Pirkè R. Eliezer c. xxv. " The men of Sodom showed no consideration for the honour of their Owner by distributing food to the wayfarer and the stranger, but they even fenced in all the trees," etc.

more remembered the benefits that they had received from Him, hated foreigners and declined all intercourse with others.[a] Indignant at this conduct, God accordingly resolved to chastise them for their arrogance, and not only to uproot their city, but to blast their land so completely that it should yield neither plant nor fruit whatsoever from that time forward.

Cf. Gen. xviii. 20.

(2) After God had pronounced this doom upon the Sodomites, Abraham, while sitting beside the oak of Mambre before the door of his court-yard,[b] espied three angels, and, taking them for strangers, arose and saluted them and invited them to lodge with him and partake of his hospitality. On their assenting, he ordered loaves of fine flour to be made forthwith and killed a calf and cooked it and brought it to them as they reclined under the oak; and they gave him to believe that they did eat.[c] They inquired, moreover, about his wife, what might have become of Sarra; and when he replied that she was within, they declared that they would return one day[d] and find that she had become a mother. Threat the woman smiled[e] and said that child-bearing was impossible, seeing that she was ninety years old and

Abraham's angel visitors.
Gen. xvii[i]. 1.

[b] In Genesis "tent": Josephus introduces the idea of a Greek house.

[c] Gen. xviii. 8, "they did eat." The "Docetic" paraphrase of Josephus reappears almost verbatim in Philo: τεράστιον δὲ . . . τὸ μὴ ἐσθίοντας ἐσθιόντων παρέχειν φαντασίαν, *De Abrahamo*, 23 § 118 (*cf.* § 116 παρέσχον ὑπόληψιν). *Cf.* also the Palestinian Targum, "He (Abraham) quieted himself (to see) whether they would eat." Such avoidance of anthropomorphism is characteristically Rabbinic.

[d] εἰς τὸ μέλλον (*cf.* Lk. xiii. 9): the Heb. is taken to mean "a year hence."

[e] Gen. "laughed within herself."

97

ἐχούσης τοῦ δ' ἀνδρὸς ἑκατόν, οὐκέτι κατέσχον
λανθάνοντες ἀλλ' ἐμήνυσαν ἑαυτοὺς ὄντας ἀγγέλους
τοῦ θεοῦ, καὶ ὅτι πεμφθείη μὲν ὁ εἷς σημανῶν
περὶ τοῦ παιδός, οἱ δύο δὲ Σοδομίτας καταστρεψό-
μενοι.

199 (3) Ταῦτ' ἀκούσας Ἄβραμος ἤλγησεν ἐπὶ τοῖς
Σοδομίταις καὶ τὸν θεὸν ἀναστὰς ἱκέτευσε παρακαλῶν, μὴ τοὺς δικαίους καὶ ἀγαθοὺς συναπ-
ολλύναι τοῖς πονηροῖς. τοῦ δὲ θεοῦ φήσαντος μηδένα εἶναι τῶν Σοδομιτῶν ἀγαθόν, εἰ γὰρ ἐν αὐτοῖς
δέκα εἶεν συγχωρεῖν ἅπασι τὴν ἐπὶ τοῖς ἁμαρ-
200 τήμασι τιμωρίαν, ὁ μὲν Ἄβραμος ἡσύχαζεν[1]· οἱ
δὲ ἄγγελοι παρεγένοντο εἰς τὴν τῶν Σοδομιτῶν
πόλιν, καὶ ὁ Λῶτος αὐτοὺς ἐπὶ ξενίαν παρεκάλει·
λίαν γὰρ ἦν περὶ τοὺς ξένους φιλάνθρωπος καὶ
μαθητὴς τῆς Ἀβράμου χρηστότητος. οἱ δὲ Σοδομῖται θεασάμενοι τοὺς νεανίσκους εὐπρεπείᾳ τῆς
ὄψεως διαφέροντας καὶ παρὰ Λώτῳ καταχθέντας
201 ἐπὶ βίαν καὶ ὕβριν αὐτῶν τῆς ὥρας ἐτράπησαν. τοῦ
δὲ Λώτου παραινοῦντος σωφρονεῖν καὶ μὴ χωρεῖν
ἐπ' αἰσχύνῃ τῶν ξένων, ἀλλ' ἔχειν αἰδῶ τῆς παρ'
αὐτῷ καταγωγῆς, εἰ δὲ ἔχουσιν ἀκρατῶς, τὰς
θυγατέρας αὐτοῦ ὑπὲρ ἐκείνων ταῖς ἐπιθυμίαις
αὐτῶν λέγοντος παρέξειν, οὐδ' οὕτως ἐπείσθησαν.
202 (4) Ὁ θεὸς οὖν ἀγανακτήσας αὐτῶν ἐπὶ τοῖς
τολμήμασι τοὺς μὲν ἠμαύρωσεν, ὡς μὴ δυνηθῆναι
τὴν εἴσοδον τὴν εἰς τὴν οἰκίαν εὑρεῖν, Σοδομιτῶν
δὲ κατέκρινε πάνδημον ὄλεθρον. Λῶτος δὲ τοῦ

[1] ἡσύχασεν RO.

[a] This difference of functions was inferred in Rabbinical tradition (cited by Weill) from Gen. xix. 1, where two angels only are mentioned as visiting Sodom. The text of that verse

her husband an hundred; whereupon they could maintain dissimulation no longer but confessed themselves messengers of God, of whom one had been sent to announce the news of the child and the other two to destroy the Sodomites.[a]

(3) On hearing this Abraham was grieved for the men of Sodom and arose and made supplication to God, imploring him not to destroy the just and good along with the wicked. To this God answered that not one of the Sodomites was good, for were there but ten such he would remit to all the chastisement for their crimes; so Abraham held his peace. But the angels came to the city of the Sodomites and Lot invited them to be his guests, for he was very kindly to strangers and had learnt the lesson of Abraham's liberality.[b] But the Sodomites, on seeing these young men of remarkably fair appearance whom Lot had taken under his roof, were bent only on violence and outrage to their youthful beauty. Lot adjured them to restrain their passions and not to proceed to dishonour his guests, but to respect their having lodged with him, offering in their stead, if his neighbours were so licentious, his own daughters to gratify their lust. But not even this would content them.

The angels at Sodom.
Gen. xviii. 23.
Ib. xix. 1.

(4) God, therefore, indignant at their atrocities, blinded the criminals so that they could not find the entrance to the house, and condemned the whole people of the Sodomites to destruction. Lot, being

Destruction of Sodom.
Gen. xix. 11.

has itself perhaps been affected by motives of reverence: Jehovah must be kept from direct contact with the wicked Sodomites (so Philo, *De Abr.* 28).

[b] Weill quotes Rabbinical parallels. Prov. xiii. 20, "He who walks with the wise shall be wise," was interpreted of "Lot, who walked with our father Abraham and learned of his good deeds and ways" (Pirķê R. Eliezer, xxv.).

JOSEPHUS

θεοῦ τὴν μέλλουσαν ἀπώλειαν τῶν Σοδομιτῶν αὐτῷ φράσαντος ἀπαλλάσσεται τήν τε γυναῖκα καὶ τὰς θυγατέρας, δύο δὲ ἦσαν ἔτι παρθένοι, ἀναλαβών· οἱ γὰρ μνηστῆρες περιεφρόνησαν[1] τῆς ἐξόδου εὐήθειαν ἐπικαλοῦντες τοῖς ὑπὸ τοῦ Λώτου 203 λεγομένοις. καὶ ὁ θεὸς ἐνσκήπτει βέλος εἰς τὴν πόλιν καὶ σὺν τοῖς οἰκήτορσιν κατεπίμπρα τὴν γῆν ὁμοίᾳ πυρώσει ἀφανίζων, ὥς μοι καὶ πρότερον λέλεκται τὸν Ἰουδαϊκὸν ἀναγράφοντι πόλεμον. ἡ δὲ Λώτου γυνὴ παρὰ τὴν ἀναχώρησιν συνεχῶς εἰς τὴν πόλιν ἀναστρεφομένη καὶ πολυπραγμονοῦσα τὰ περὶ αὐτήν, ἀπηγορευκότος τοῦ θεοῦ τοῦτο μὴ ποιεῖν, εἰς στήλην ἁλῶν μετέβαλεν· ἱστόρησα δ'
204 αὐτήν, ἔτι γὰρ καὶ νῦν διαμένει. διαφεύγει δ' αὐτὸς μετὰ τῶν θυγατέρων εἰς βραχύ τι χωρίον κατασχὼν περιγραφὲν ὑπὸ τοῦ πυρός· Ζωὼρ ἔτι καὶ νῦν λέγεται· καλοῦσι γὰρ οὕτως Ἑβραῖοι τὸ ὀλίγον. ἐνταῦθα τοίνυν ὑπό τε ἀνθρώπων ἐρημίας καὶ τροφῆς ἀπορίας ταλαιπώρως διῆγεν.

205 (5) Αἱ δὲ παρθένοι πᾶν ἠφανίσθαι τὸ ἀνθρώπινον ὑπολαβοῦσαι τῷ πατρὶ πλησιάζουσι προνοήσασαι λαθεῖν· ἐποίουν δὲ τοῦτο ὑπὲρ τοῦ μὴ τὸ γένος ἐκλιπεῖν. γίνονται δὲ παῖδες ὑπὸ μὲν τῆς πρεσβυτέρας Μώαβος· εἴποι δ' ἄν τις ἀπὸ πατρός. Ἄμμανον δ' ἡ νεωτέρα ποιεῖται· γένους υἱὸν

[1] RO: ὑπερεφρόνησαν rell.

---

[a] The phrase recalls Hdt. iv. 79 ἐς ταύτην (τὴν οἰκίην) ὁ θεὸς ἐνέσκηψε βέλος· καὶ ἡ μὲν κατεκάη πᾶσα.
[b] B.J. iv. 483-485.
[c] Describing the range of salt hills, *Jebel Usdum*, at the S.W. end of the Dead Sea, Dr. C. Geikie writes (*Holy Land and the Bible*, ii. 121), " Here and there, harder portions of

JEWISH ANTIQUITIES, I. 202–205

forewarned by God of the ruin impending over the Sodomites, then departed, taking with him only his wife and his two daughters, who were still virgins; for their suitors scorned this exodus, ridiculing as an absurdity what they were told by Lot. God then hurled his bolt upon the city[a] and along with its inhabitants burnt it to the ground, obliterating the land with a similar conflagration, as I have previously related in my account of the Jewish War.[b] But Lot's wife, who during the flight was continually turning round towards the city, curious to observe its fate, notwithstanding God's prohibition of such action, was changed into a pillar of salt: I have seen this pillar which remains to this day.[c] Lot himself escaped with his daughters, finding refuge in a tiny spot forming an oasis in the flames: it is still called Zoar,[d] that being the Hebrew word for "little." Gen. xix. 22. There, isolated from mankind and in lack of food, he passed a miserable existence.

(5) His maiden daughters, in the belief that the whole of humanity had perished, had intercourse with their father, taking care to elude detection; they acted thus to prevent the extinction of the race. And of these unions children were born: the elder daughter gave birth to Moab, as much as to say "of the father," the younger to Amman,[e] the name

Origin of Moab and Ammon.
Gen. xix. 30.

the salt . . . rise up as isolated pillars, one of which bears, among the Arabs, the name of Lot's wife." A "salt pillar" is shown here in the *Atlas of the Holy Land* (Smith and Bartholomew, Map 30).

[d] Bibl. Zoar (LXX Σήγωρ), usually located to the S.E. of the Dead Sea, some five miles from the present shore. Heb. *za'ir* = "little," "insignificant."

[e] So LXX (Heb. Ben-ammi). From the LXX also Josephus takes over the interpretation of both names.

101

206 ἀποσημαίνει τὸ ὄνομα. καὶ κτίζει δ' αὐτῶν ὁ μὲν Μωαβίτας μέγιστον ὄντας καὶ νῦν ἔθνος, Ἀμμανίτας δὲ ὁ ἕτερος· Συρίας τῆς κοίλης ἐστὶν ἀμφότερα. καὶ Λώτῳ μὲν τοιαύτην συνέβη τὴν ἐκ Σοδομιτῶν ἀναχώρησιν γενέσθαι.

207 (xii. 1) Ἄβραμος δὲ μετῴκησεν εἰς Γέραρα τῆς Παλαιστίνης ἐν ἀδελφῆς ἐπαγόμενος σχήματι τὴν Σάρραν, ὅμοια τοῖς πρὶν ὑποκρινάμενος διὰ τὸν φόβον· ἐδεδίει γὰρ Ἀβιμέλεχον τὸν βασιλέα τῶν ἐπιχωρίων, ὃς καὶ αὐτὸς ἐρασθεὶς τῆς Σάρρας
208 φθείρειν οἷός τε ἦν. εἴργεται δὲ τῆς ἐπιθυμίας ὑπὸ νόσου χαλεπῆς αὐτῷ προσπεσούσης ἐκ θεοῦ, καὶ τῶν ἰατρῶν αὐτὸν ἀπεγνωκότων ὑπνώσας ὄναρ ὁρᾷ μηδὲν ὑβρίζειν τὴν τοῦ ξένου γυναῖκα, καὶ ῥᾷον διατεθεὶς φράζει πρὸς τοὺς φίλους, ὡς ὁ θεὸς αὐτῷ ταύτην ἐπαγάγοι[1] τὴν νόσον ὑπὲρ ἐκδικίας τοῦ ξένου φυλάσσων ἀνύβριστον αὐτῷ τὴν γυναῖκα, μὴ γὰρ ἀδελφὴν οὖσαν ἐπάγεσθαι νόμῳ δ' αὐτῷ συνοικοῦσαν, ἐπαγγέλλεταί τε παρέξειν αὐτὸν εὐμενῆ τὸ λοιπὸν ἀδεοῦς ἐκείνου περὶ τὴν γυναῖκα γενο-
209 μένου. ταῦτα εἰπὼν μεταπέμπεται τὸν Ἄβραμον συμβουλευσάντων τῶν φίλων καὶ μηδὲν ἔτι περὶ τῆς γυναικὸς αὐτὸν ὡς πεισομένης τι τῶν αἰσχρῶν ἐκέλευσε δεδιέναι, θεὸν γὰρ αὐτοῦ κήδεσθαι, καὶ κατὰ τὴν συμμαχίαν τὴν ἐκείνου μεμενηκυῖαν ἀνύβριστον κομίζεσθαι τοῦ τε[2] θεοῦ μάρτυρος ὄντος καὶ τοῦ τῆς γυναικὸς συνειδότος· ἔλεγέ ⟨τε⟩[3] μηδ' ἂν ὀρεχθῆναι τὴν ἀρχήν, εἰ γαμετὴν

[1] ἐπάγει ROE. [2] conj. Niese: δὲ codd.
[3] ins. Niese.

signifying "son of the race." The former was the progenitor of the Moabites, still to-day a mighty nation, the latter of the Ammanites,[a] both being peoples of Coele-Syria.[b] Such then was the manner of Lot's escape from the Sodomites.

(xii. 1) Abraham now migrated to Gerara in Philistia, accompanied by Sarra, whom he passed off as his sister, practising the same dissimulation as before[c] from fear; for he dreaded Abimelech, the king of that district, who too being enamoured of Sarra was prepared to seduce her. But he was restrained from his lustful intent by a grievous disease inflicted upon him by God; the physicians had already despaired of his life,[d] when he saw in his sleep a vision (admonishing him) to do no outrage to the stranger's wife; and, beginning to recover, he told his friends that it was God who had brought this malady upon him to vindicate the rights of his guest and to preserve his wife from violence, since it was not his sister that accompanied him but his lawful wife, and that God promised to show himself gracious hereafter, were Abraham reassured concerning his wife. Having said this he sent for Abraham, on the advice of his friends, and bade him have no further fear of any indignity to his wife, for God was watching over him, and through His help and protection he would receive her back inviolate, as God and the woman's conscience would testify. He added that he would never have yearned for her at

Abraham and Abimelech. Gen. xx. 1.

[a] So LXX (Heb. "children of Ammon").
[b] "To Josephus Coele-Syria is all Eastern Palestine," G. A. Smith, *Hist. Geography of the Holy Land*, 538 (on the varying meanings of the name, originally given to the hollow between the Lebanons).
[c] In Egypt, § 162. [d] Amplification of Scripture.

οὖσαν ἠπίστατο, ὡς ἀδελφὴν δὲ ἀγόμενον[1] οὐκ
210 ἠδίκουν. παρακαλεῖ τε πρᾴως ἔχειν πρὸς αὐτὸν
καὶ τὸν θεὸν εὐμενῆ ποιεῖν, παρ' αὐτῷ τε μένειν
βουλομένῳ πᾶσαν ἀφθονίαν ὑπάρξειν, ἀπιέναι τε
προαιρούμενον τεύξεσθαι πομπῆς καὶ πάντων
211 ὅσων καὶ χρῄζων πρὸς αὐτὸν ἀφίκοιτο. ταῦτ'
εἰπόντος Ἅβραμος οὔτε τὴν συγγένειαν τῆς γυναικὸς ἐψεῦσθαι ἔλεγεν, ἀδελφοῦ γὰρ αὐτὴν εἶναι
παῖδα, καὶ δίχα τοιαύτης ὑποκρίσεως οὐκ ἀσφαλῆ
τὴν ἐπιδημίαν ὑπολαβεῖν. ὅσα τε ἐπὶ τῷ μηδὲν
αἴτιος τῆς νόσου γεγονέναι προθυμηθῆναι δ' αὐτοῦ
περὶ τὴν σωτηρίαν, ἑτοίμως ἔφασκεν ἔχειν παρ'
212 αὐτῷ μένειν. καὶ Ἀβιμέλεχος τήν τε γῆν πρὸς
αὐτὸν νέμεται καὶ τὰ χρήματα, καὶ συντίθενται
ἀδόλως πολιτεύσεσθαι[2] ὑπέρ τινος φρέατος ποιούμενοι τὸν ὅρκον, ὃ Βηρσουβαὶ καλοῦσιν· ὅρκιον δὲ
φρέαρ λέγοιτ' ἄν. οὕτω δ' ἔτι καὶ νῦν ὑπὸ τῶν
ἐπιχωρίων ὠνόμασται.

213 (2) Γίνεται δὲ Ἀβράμῳ μετ' οὐ πολὺ καὶ παῖς ἐκ
Σάρρας, ὡς αὐτῷ ὑπὸ τοῦ θεοῦ προείρητο, ὃν
Ἴσακον ὠνόμασε· τοῦτο γέλωτα σημαίνει· διὰ
μέντοι τὸ τὴν Σάρραν μειδιᾶσαι τέξεσθαι φήσαντος
αὐτὴν τοῦ θεοῦ μὴ προσδοκῶσαν ἤδη τοκετοῦ
πρεσβυτέραν οὖσαν τὸν υἱὸν οὕτως ἐκάλεσεν· αὐτὴ
μὲν γὰρ ἐνενήκοντα εἶχεν ἔτη ἑκατὸν δὲ Ἅβραμος.

[1] MP²L: +ἦν rell.
[2] Niese: πολιτεύσασθαι or -εύεσθαι codd.

---

[a] According to Josephus, she was the daughter of Haran, Abraham's brother, and therefore Abraham's *niece* (§ 151),

all, had he known her to be married, but as Abraham had brought her as his sister he had done him no wrong. He begged him moreover to be indulgent to him and to conciliate God's favour : if he wished to remain with him, he should have abundance of everything ; if he preferred to depart, he should be given an escort and all that he had sought in coming to his country. To this Abraham replied that he had not belied his relationship to his wife, for she was his brother's child,[a] and that without such dissimulation he would have felt it unsafe to sojourn in the country ; and to show that he was in no way responsible for the king's illness but anxious for his recovery, he declared that he would gladly remain with him. So Abimelech assigned to him land and riches and they covenanted to deal honestly with each other, swearing an oath over a well which they call Bêrsubai,[b] that is to say " well of the oath " : it is still so named by the inhabitants of the country.

Cf. Gen. xx. 12.

Ib. 14.

Ib. xxi. 31.

(2) Not long after, Abraham, as God had foretold him, had a son by Sarra, whom he called Isaac ; the name means " laughter " and was given him by his father because Sarra had smiled[c] when God said that she would give birth, child-bearing at her advanced age being beyond her expectations ; for she was then ninety years old and Abraham a hundred. Their

Birth of Isaac. Gen. xxi. 1.

Ib. xvii. 17 ; xxi. 5.

---

[a] ἀδελφιδῆ not ἀδελφή; but the latter can be used loosely = "kinswoman." According to Genesis she was Abraham's half-sister.

[b] Heb. Beer-sheba, strictly = " well of seven " (or "seven wells "). Josephus takes over the Biblical etymology : LXX translates by Φρέαρ ὁρκισμοῦ (or τοῦ ὅρκου), vv. 31, 33. The two words were probably not unallied, if, as is thought, the Heb. verb " to swear " originally meant " to bind oneself by pledging seven things."   [c] § 198.

JOSEPHUS

214 τίκτεται δὲ παῖς ἑκατέρων τῷ ὑστάτῳ ἔτει, ὃν εὐθὺς μετ' ὀγδόην ἡμέραν περιτέμνουσι, κἀξ ἐκείνου μετὰ τοσαύτας ἔθος ἔχουσιν οἱ Ἰουδαῖοι ποιεῖσθαι τὰς περιτομάς, Ἄραβες δὲ μετὰ ἔτος τρισκαιδέκατον· Ἰσμάηλος γὰρ ὁ κτίστης αὐτῶν τοῦ ἔθνους Ἀβράμῳ γενόμενος ἐκ τῆς παλλακῆς ἐν τούτῳ περιτέμνεται τῷ χρόνῳ· περὶ οὗ τὸν πάντα λόγον ἐκθήσομαι μετὰ πολλῆς ἀκριβείας.

215 (3) Σάρρα δὲ γεννηθέντα τὸν Ἰσμάηλον ἐκ τῆς δούλης αὐτῆς Ἀγάρης τὸ μὲν πρῶτον ἔστεργεν οὐδὲν ἀπολείπουσα τῆς [ὡς]¹ πρὸς ἴδιον υἱὸν εὐνοίας, ἐτρέφετο γὰρ ἐπὶ τῇ τῆς ἡγεμονίας διαδοχῇ, τεκοῦσα δ' αὐτὴ τὸν Ἴσακον οὐκ ἠξίου παρατρέφεσθαι τούτῳ τὸν Ἰσμάηλον ὄντα πρεσβύτερον καὶ κακουργεῖν δυνάμενον τοῦ πατρὸς αὐτοῖς ἀπο-

216 θανόντος. ἔπειθεν οὖν τὸν Ἀβραμον εἰς ἀποικίαν ἐκπέμπειν αὐτὸν μετὰ τῆς μητρός. ὁ δὲ κατὰ μὲν ἀρχὰς οὐ προσετίθετο τὴν αὐτοῦ γνώμην οἷς ἡ Σάρρα ἐσπουδάκει πάντων ὠμότατον ἡγούμενος εἶναι παῖδα νήπιον καὶ γυναῖκα ἄπορον τῶν ἀναγ-

217 καίων ἐκπέμπειν. ὕστερον δέ, καὶ γὰρ ὁ θεὸς ἠρέσκετο τοῖς ὑπὸ τῆς Σάρρας προσταττομένοις, πεισθεὶς παρεδίδου τὸν Ἰσμάηλον τῇ μητρὶ μήπω δι' αὐτοῦ χωρεῖν δυνάμενον, ὕδωρ τε ἐν ἀσκῷ καὶ ἄρτον φερομένην ἐκέλευεν ἀπιέναι ὁδηγῷ τῇ ἀνάγκῃ

218 χρωμένην. ὡς δ' ἀπιοῦσαν ἐπιλελοίπει τὰ ἀναγκαῖα, ἐν κακοῖς ἦν, ὕδατος δὲ σπανίζοντος ὑπ' ἐλάτῃ τινὶ θεῖσα τὸ παιδίον ψυχορραγοῦν, ὡς μὴ

¹ om. ROE.

ᵃ Literally "And a child is born of the pair in the last year." I follow Weill in the rendering of this puzzling clause, but would suggest that it is unnecessary to alter the text.

JEWISH ANTIQUITIES, I. 214–218

child was born in the year after (that prediction).[a] Eight days later they promptly circumcised him; and from that time forward the Jewish practice has been to circumcise so many days after birth. The Arabs defer the ceremony to the thirteenth year, because Ishmael, the founder of their race, born of Abraham's concubine, was circumcised at that age. I propose in future to expound this whole subject in detail.[b]

(3) Sarra at the first, when Ishmael was born of her servant Hagar, cherished him with an affection no less than if he had been her own son, seeing that he was being trained as heir to the chieftaincy; but when she herself gave birth to Isaac, she held it wrong that her boy should be brought up with Ishmael, who was the elder child and might do him an injury after their father was dead. She therefore urged Abraham to send him and his mother away to settle elsewhere. He, however, at first refused to consent to Sarra's scheme, thinking nothing could be more brutal than to send off an infant child with a woman destitute of the necessaries of life. But afterwards, seeing that Sarra's behests were sanctioned also by God, he yielded and, committing Ishmael to his mother, the child being not yet of age to go alone, bade her take a skin full of water and a loaf and be gone, with necessity to serve as her guide. She went her way, but, so soon as her provisions failed her, was in evil case; and the water being well-nigh spent, she laid the little child, expiring, under a fir-tree and went

Expulsion of Hagar.

Cf. Gen. xxi 10.

---

[a] As πρῶτος in late Greek is used for πρότερος and ἔσχατος in LXX for "latter," so Josephus may have used ὕστατος for ὕστερος. The obvious rendering, "in the last year of both," is impossible; the parents, we are told, lived for many more years.

[b] See § 192 note.

παρούσης τὴν ψυχὴν ἀφῇ, προῄει πορρωτέρω.
219 συντυχὼν δ' αὐτῇ θεῖος ἄγγελος πηγήν τε φράζει
παρακειμένην καὶ κελεύει προνοεῖν τῆς ἀνατροφῆς
τοῦ παιδίου· μεγάλα γὰρ αὐτὴν ἀγαθὰ περιμένειν
ἐκ τῆς Ἰσμαήλου σωτηρίας. ἡ δ' ἐθάρσησε τοῖς
προκατηγγελμένοις καὶ συμβαλοῦσα ποιμέσι διὰ
τὴν ἐξ αὐτῶν ἐπιμέλειαν διαφεύγει τὰς ταλαιπωρίας.

220 (4) Ἀνδρωθέντι δὲ τῷ παιδὶ γύναιον ἄγεται τὸ
γένος Αἰγύπτιον, ἐνθένδε ἦν καὶ αὐτὴ τὸ ἀρχαῖον,
ἐξ οὗ παῖδες Ἰσμαήλῳ γίνονται δώδεκα πάντες,
Ναβαιώθης Κήδαρος Ἀβδέηλος Μάσσαμος Μάσμασος Ἰδουμᾶς Μάσμησος Χόδαμος Θαίμανος Ἰετού-
221 ρος Νάφαισος Κάδμασος. οὗτοι πᾶσαν τὴν ἀπ'
Εὐφράτου καθήκουσαν πρὸς τὴν Ἐρυθρὰν θάλασσαν
κατοικοῦσι Ναβατηνὴν τὴν χώραν ὀνομάσαντες.
εἰσὶ δὲ οὗτοι, οἳ τὸ τῶν Ἀράβων ἔθνος καὶ τὰς[1]
φυλὰς ἀφ' αὐτῶν[2] καλοῦσι διά τε τὴν ἀρετὴν αὐτῶν
καὶ τὸ Ἀβράμου ἀξίωμα.

222 (xiii. 1) Ἴσακον δὲ ὁ πατὴρ Ἅβραμος ὑπερηγάπα
μονογενῆ ὄντα καὶ ἐπὶ γήρως οὐδῷ κατὰ δωρεὰν
αὐτῷ τοῦ θεοῦ γενόμενον. προεκαλεῖτο δὲ εἰς
εὔνοιαν καὶ τὸ φιλεῖσθαι μᾶλλον ὑπὸ τῶν γονέων

[1] καὶ τὰς] κατὰ Lat. (secundum tribus).
[2] Bekker: ἀπ' αὐτῶν codd.

---

[a] Modelled on Eurip. *Hercules Furens*, 323 f. ὡς μὴ τέκν' εἰσίδωμεν, ἀνόσιον θέαν, | ψυχορραγοῦντα καὶ καλοῦντα μητέρα. That play seems to have been a favourite of the author, or rather of his assistant. [b] Amplification of Scripture.
[c] So one group of LXX MSS.: Heb. Adbeel.
[d] So LXX: Heb. Mibsam.
[e] After LXX: Heb. Mishma.

JEWISH ANTIQUITIES, I. 218–222

farther on, that she might not be there when he gave up his spirit.[a] But she was met by an angel of God, who told her of a spring hard by and bade her look to the nurture of the young child, for great blessings awaited her through the preservation of Ishmael. These promises gave her new courage, and, meeting some shepherds,[b] she through their care escaped her miseries.

(4) When the child reached manhood, his mother found him a wife of that Egyptian race whence she herself had originally sprung; and by her twelve sons in all were born to Ishmael, Nabaioth(es), Kedar, Abdeêl,[c] Massam,[d] Masmas,[e] Idum(as),[f] Masmes,[g] Chodam,[h] Thaiman,[i] Jetur, Naphais,[j] Kadmas.[k] These occupied the whole country extending from the Euphrates to the Red Sea and called it Nabatene[l]; and it is these who conferred their names on the Arabian nation and its tribes[m] in honour both of their own prowess and of the fame of Abraham.

Descendants of Ishmael. Gen. xxv. 12.

Cf. ib. 18.

(xiii. 1) Now Isaac was passionately beloved of his father Abraham, being his only son and born to him "on the threshold of old age"[n] through the bounty of God. On his side, the child called out the affection of his parents and endeared himself to them yet more by

The trial of Abraham. Gen. xxii. 1.

---

[f] After LXX : Heb. Dumah. [g] Bibl. Massa (Μασσή).
[h] After LXX (Χοδδάν) : Heb. Hadad.
[i] With LXX : Heb. Tema.
[j] Bibl. Naphish (Ναφές). [k] Bibl. Kedemah (Κεδμά).
[l] The Nabataeans were a flourishing kingdom in Graeco-Roman times : Josephus derives the name from Ishmael's eldest son Nabaioth.
[m] Or (with the other reading) "on the various tribes of the Arabian nation." One cannot resist the suspicion of a preposterous connexion of the name Arab with the first two letters of ἀρ-ετή and of Ἄβ-ραμος !
[n] Homeric phrase.

καὶ αὐτὸς ὁ παῖς ἐπιτηδεύων πᾶσαν ἀρετὴν καὶ τῆς
τε τῶν πατέρων θεραπείας ἐχόμενος καὶ περὶ τὴν
223 τοῦ θεοῦ θρησκείαν ἐσπουδακώς. Ἅβραμος δὲ
τὴν ἰδίαν εὐδαιμονίαν ἐν μόνῳ τῷ τὸν υἱὸν ἀπαθῆ
καταλιπὼν ἐξελθεῖν τοῦ ζῆν ἐτίθετο. τούτου μέντοι
κατὰ τὴν τοῦ θεοῦ βούλησιν ἔτυχεν, ὃς διάπειραν
αὐτοῦ βουλόμενος λαβεῖν τῆς περὶ αὐτὸν θρησκείας
ἐμφανισθεὶς αὐτῷ καὶ πάντα ὅσα εἴη παρεσχημένος
224 καταριθμησάμενος, ὡς πολεμίων τε κρείττονα
ποιήσειε καὶ τὴν παροῦσαν εὐδαιμονίαν ἐκ τῆς
αὐτοῦ σπουδῆς ἔχοι καὶ τὸν υἱὸν Ἴσακον, ᾔτει τοῦτον αὐτῷ θῦμα καὶ ἱερεῖον [αὐτὸν] παρασχεῖν,
ἐκέλευέ τε εἰς τὸ Μώριον ὄρος ἀναγαγόντα ὁλοκαυ-
τῶσαι βωμὸν ἱδρυσάμενον· οὕτως γὰρ ἐμφανίσειν
τὴν περὶ αὐτὸν θρησκείαν, εἰ καὶ τῆς τοῦ τέκνου
σωτηρίας προτιμήσειε τὸ τῷ θεῷ κεχαρισμένον.
225 (2) Ἅβραμος δὲ ἐπὶ μηδενὶ κρίνων παρακούειν
τοῦ θεοῦ δίκαιον ἅπαντα δ'[1] ὑπουργεῖν, ὡς ἐκ τῆς
ἐκείνου προνοίας ἀπαντώντων[2] οἷς ἂν εὐμενὴς ᾖ,
ἐπικρυψάμενος πρὸς τὴν γυναῖκα τήν τε τοῦ θεοῦ
πρόρρησιν καὶ ἣν εἶχεν αὐτὸς γνώμην περὶ τῆς
τοῦ παιδὸς σφαγῆς, ἀλλὰ μηδὲ τῶν οἰκετῶν τινι
δηλώσας, ἐκωλύετο γὰρ ἂν ὑπηρετῆσαι τῷ θεῷ,
λαβὼν τὸν Ἴσακον μετὰ δύο οἰκετῶν καὶ τὰ πρὸς
τὴν ἱερουργίαν ἐπισάξας ὄνῳ ἀπῄει πρὸς τὸ ὄρος.
226 καὶ δύο μὲν ἡμέρας αὐτῷ συνώδευσαν οἱ οἰκέται,

[1] ἅπαντά θ' ROE.
[2] ἀπάντων ζώντων ed. pr. with Lat. is attractive, but *cf.* for ἀπαντᾶν § 254: perhaps ἁπάντων has dropped out before ἀπ. (Niese).

---

[a] Genesis (xxii. 2) speaks of "one of the mountains" in "the land of Moriah" (LXX τὴν γῆν τὴν ὑψηλήν). "Mount Moriah" is named in 2 Chron. iii. 1 as the site of Solomon's

the practice of every virtue, showing a devoted filial obedience and a zeal for the worship of God. Abraham thus reposed all his own happiness on the hope of leaving his son unscathed when he departed this life. This object he indeed attained by the will of God, who, however, desiring to make trial of his piety towards Himself, appeared to him and after enumerating all the benefits that He had bestowed upon him—how He had made him stronger than his enemies, and how it was His benevolence to which he owed his present felicity and his son Isaac—required him to offer up that son by his own hand as a sacrifice and victim to Himself. He bade him take the child up to the Morian Mount,[a] erect an altar and make a holocaust of him: thus would he manifest his piety towards Himself, if he put the doing of God's good pleasure even above the life of his child.

(2) Abraham, deeming that nothing would justify disobedience to God and that in everything he must submit to His will, since all that befell His favoured ones was ordained by His providence,[b] concealed from his wife God's commandment and his own resolve concerning the immolation of the child; nay, revealing it not even to any of his household,[c] lest haply he should have been hindered from doing God's service, he took Isaac with two servants and having laden an ass with the requisites for the sacrifice departed for the mountain. For two days the

Preparations for the sacrifice of Isaac.

temple. The locality here intended is unknown; its identification by Josephus (§ 226) and by Rabbinical tradition with the temple mount cannot be sustained.

[b] Or (with the other text) "since all His favoured ones lived through His providence."

[c] Cf. Philo, De Abr. 32, § 170 μηδενὶ τῶν ἔνδον ἐξειπὼν τὸ λόγιον.

τῇ τρίτῃ δὲ ὡς κάτοπτον ἦν αὐτῷ τὸ ὄρος, καταλιπὼν ἐν τῷ πεδίῳ τοὺς συνόντας μετὰ μόνου τοῦ παιδὸς παραγίνεται εἰς τὸ ὄρος, ἐφ' οὗ τὸ ἱερὸν 227 Δαυίδης ὁ βασιλεὺς ὕστερον ἱδρύεται. ἔφερον δὲ σὺν αὑτοῖς ὅσα λοιπὰ πρὸς τὴν θυσίαν ἦν πλὴν ἱερείου. τοῦ δ' Ἰσάκου πέμπτον τε καὶ εἰκοστὸν ἔτος ἔχοντος τὸν βωμὸν κατασκευάζοντος καὶ πυθομένου, τί καὶ μέλλοιεν θύειν ἱερείου μὴ παρόντος, [ὁ δὲ]¹ τὸν θεὸν αὐτοῖς παρέξειν ἔλεγεν ὄντα ἱκανὸν καὶ τῶν οὐκ ὄντων εἰς εὐπορίαν ἀνθρώπους² παραγαγεῖν καὶ τὰ ὄντα τῶν ἐπ' αὐτοῖς θαρρούντων ἀφελέσθαι· δώσειν οὖν κἀκείνῳ ἱερεῖον, εἴπερ εὐμενὴς μέλλει τῇ θυσίᾳ παρατυγχάνειν αὐτοῦ.

228 (3) Ὡς δ' ὁ βωμὸς παρεσκεύαστο καὶ τὰς σχίζας ἐπενηνόχει καὶ ἦν εὐτρεπῆ, λέγει πρὸς τὸν υἱόν "ὦ παῖ, μυρίαις εὐχαῖς αἰτησάμενός σε γενέσθαι μοι παρὰ τοῦ θεοῦ, ἐπεὶ παρῆλθες εἰς τὸν βίον, οὐκ ἔστιν ὅ τι μὴ περὶ τὴν σὴν ἀνατροφὴν ἐφιλοτιμησάμην οὐδ' ἐφ' ᾧ μᾶλλον εὐδαιμονήσειν ᾤμην, ὡς εἰ σέ τ' ἴδοιμι ἠνδρωμένον καὶ τελευτῶν διάδοχον τῆς ἀρχῆς τῆς ἐμαυτοῦ καταλίποιμι. 229 ἀλλ' ἐπεὶ θεοῦ τε βουλομένου σὸς πατὴρ ἐγενόμην καὶ πάλιν τούτῳ δοκοῦν ἀποτίθεμαί σε, φέρε γενναίως τὴν καθιέρωσιν· τῷ θεῷ γάρ σε παραχωρῶ ταύτης ἀξιώσαντι παρ' ἡμῶν τῆς τιμῆς, ἀνθ' ὧν εὐμενὴς γέγονέ μοι παραστάτης καὶ σύμμαχος, 230 νῦν ἐπιτυχεῖν. ἐπεὶ δ' ἐγεννήθης ∗ ∗ ἄπιθι νῦν³ οὐ

¹ om. RO.   ² ed. pr.: ἀνθρώποις codd.
³ ἄπιθι νῦν SP: ἀποθάνῃς most MSS.; text doubtful and probably defective.

---

a Or rather "Solomon . . . in the place that David had appointed" (2 Chron. iii. 1). But see § 224 note.

servants accompanied him, but on the third, when the mountain was in view, he left his companions in the plain and proceeded with his son alone to that mount whereon king David [a] afterwards erected the temple. They brought with them all else needed for the sacrifice except a victim. Isaac, therefore, who was now twenty-five years of age,[b] while constructing the altar, asked what sacrifice they were about to offer, having no victim; to which his father replied that God would provide for them, seeing that He had power alike to give men abundance of what they had not and to deprive of what they had those who felt assured of their possessions: He would therefore grant him too a victim, should He vouchsafe to grace his sacrifice with His presence.

(3) But when the altar had been prepared and he had laid the cleft wood upon it and all was ready, he said to his son: "My child, myriad were the prayers in which I besought God for thy birth, and when thou camedst into the world, no pains were there that I did not lavish upon thine upbringing, no thought had I of higher happiness than to see thee grown to man's estate and to leave thee at my death heir to my dominion. But, since it was by God's will that I became thy sire and now again as pleases Him I am resigning thee, bear thou this consecration valiantly; for it is to God I yield thee, to God who now claims from us this homage in return for the gracious favour He has shown me as my supporter and ally. Aye, since thou wast born (out of the course of nature, so)[c] quit thou now this life not by the

Abraham's address to his son.

---

[b] Age unrecorded in Scripture.
[c] Apparent lacuna in the Greek

τὸν κοινὸν ἐκ τοῦ ζῆν τρόπον, ἀλλ' ὑπὸ πατρὸς ἰδίου θεῷ τῷ πάντων πατρὶ νόμῳ θυσίας προπεμπόμενος, ἄξιον οἶμαί σε κρίναντος αὐτοῦ μήτε νόσῳ μήτε πολέμῳ μήτε ἄλλῳ τινὶ τῶν παθῶν, ἃ συμπίπτειν πέφυκεν ἀνθρώποις, ἀπαλλαγῆναι
231 τοῦ βίου, μετ' εὐχῶν δὲ καὶ ἱερουργίας ἐκείνου ψυχὴν τὴν σὴν προσδεξομένου καὶ παρ' αὑτῷ καθέξοντος· ἔσῃ τ' ἐμοὶ εἰς κηδεμόνα καὶ γηροκόμον, διὸ καὶ σὲ μάλιστα ἀνετρεφόμην, τὸν θεὸν ἀντὶ σαυτοῦ παρεσχημένος.''

232 (4) Ἴσακος δέ, πατρὸς γὰρ ἦν οἵου τετυχηκότα γενναῖον ἔδει τὸ φρόνημα εἶναι, δέχεται πρὸς ἡδονὴν τοὺς λόγους καὶ φήσας, ὡς οὐδὲ γεγονέναι τὴν ἀρχὴν ἦν δίκαιος, εἰ θεοῦ καὶ πατρὸς μέλλει κρίσιν ἀπωθεῖσθαι καὶ μὴ παρέχειν αὑτὸν τοῖς ἀμφοτέρων βουλήμασιν¹ ἑτοίμως, ὅτε καὶ μόνου τοῦ πατρὸς ταῦτα προαιρουμένου μὴ ὑπακούειν ἄδικον ἦν, ὥρμησεν ἐπὶ τὸν βωμὸν καὶ τὴν σφαγήν.
233 κἂν ἐπράχθη τὸ ἔργον μὴ στάντος ἐμποδὼν τοῦ θεοῦ· βοᾷ γὰρ ὀνομαστὶ τὸν Ἅβραμον εἴργων τῆς τοῦ παιδὸς σφαγῆς. οὐ γὰρ ἐπιθυμήσας αἵματος ἀνθρωπίνου τὴν σφαγὴν αὐτῷ προστάξαι τοῦ παιδὸς ἔλεγεν, οὐδὲ οὗ πατέρα ἐποίησεν αὐτὸς ἀφελέσθαι τούτου βουλόμενος μετὰ τοιαύτης ἀσεβείας, ἀλλὰ δοκιμάσαι θέλων αὐτοῦ τὴν διάνοιαν,
234 εἰ καὶ τοιαῦτα προστασσόμενος ὑπακούοι. μαθὼν δὲ αὐτοῦ τὸ πρόθυμον καὶ τὴν ὑπερβολὴν τῆς θρησκείας ἥδεσθαι μὲν οἷς αὐτῷ παρέσχεν, οὐχ ὑστερήσειν δὲ αὐτὸν ἀεὶ πάσης ἐπιμελείας καὶ τὸ γένος ἀξιοῦντα, ἔσεσθαί τε τὸν υἱὸν αὐτοῦ πολυχρονιώτατον καὶ βιώσαντα εὐδαιμόνως παισὶν ἀγαθοῖς καὶ γνησίοις παραδώσειν μεγάλην ἡγε-

JEWISH ANTIQUITIES, I. 230–234

common road, but sped by thine own father on thy way to God, the Father of all, through the rites of sacrifice. He, I ween, accounts it not meet for thee to depart this life by sickness or war or by any of the calamities that commonly befall mankind, but amid prayers and sacrificial ceremonies would receive thy soul and keep it near to Himself; and for me thou shalt be a protector and stay of my old age—to which end above all I nurtured thee—by giving me God in the stead of thyself."

(4) The son of such a father could not but be brave-hearted, and Isaac received these words with joy. He exclaimed that he deserved never to have been born at all, were he to reject the decision of God and of his father and not readily resign himself to what was the will of both, seeing that, were this the resolution of his father alone, it would have been impious to disobey; and with that he rushed to the altar and his doom. And the deed would have been accomplished, had not God stood in the way, for He called upon Abraham by name, forbidding him to slay the lad. It was, He said, from no craving for human blood that He had given command for the slaughter of his son, nor had He made him a father only to rob him in such impious fashion of his offspring; no, He wished but to test his soul and see whether even such orders would find him obedient. Now that He knew the ardour and depth of his piety, He took pleasure in what He had given him and would never fail to regard with the tenderest care both him and his race; his son should attain to extreme old age and, after a life of felicity, bequeath to a virtuous and lawfully begotten offspring a great

The salvation of Isaac and the divine benediction.

---

[1] *v.l.* βουλεύμασιν.

235 μονίαν. προεδήλου τε τὸ γένος τὸ αὐτῶν εἰς ἔθνη πολλὰ καὶ πλοῦτον ἐπιδώσειν, καὶ μνήμην αἰώνιον αὐτῶν ἔσεσθαι τοῖς γενάρχαις, τήν τε Χαναναίαν ὅπλοις κατακτησαμένους ζηλωτοὺς
236 ἔσεσθαι πᾶσιν ἀνθρώποις. ταῦτα ὁ θεὸς εἰπὼν κριὸν ἐκ τἀφανοῦς παρήγαγεν αὐτοῖς εἰς τὴν ἱερουργίαν. οἱ δὲ παρ' ἐλπίδας αὐτοὺς κεκομισμένοι¹ καὶ τοιούτων ἀγαθῶν ἀγγελίας ἀκηκοότες ἠσπάζοντό τε ἀλλήλους καὶ θύσαντες ἀπενόστησαν πρὸς τὴν Σάρραν καὶ διῆγον εὐδαιμόνως, ἐφ' ἅπασιν οἷς ἐθελήσειαν τοῦ θεοῦ συλλαμβάνοντος αὐτοῖς.
237 (xiv.) Καὶ Σάρρα μὲν οὐ πολὺ ὕστερον ἀποθνήσκει βιώσασα ἔτη ἑπτὰ καὶ εἴκοσι πρὸς τοῖς ἑκατόν. θάπτουσι δ' αὐτὴν ἐν Νεβρῶνι συγχωρούντων μὲν τῶν Χαναναίων καὶ δημοσίᾳ χοῦν αὐτῆς τὸν τάφον, Ἀβράμου δὲ ὠνησαμένου τὸ χωρίον σίκλων τετρακοσίων παρ' Ἐφραίμου τινὸς ἐκ τῆς Νεβρῶνος. καὶ τὰ μνημεῖα Ἀβραμός τε καὶ οἱ ἀπόγονοι αὐτοῦ ταύτῃ κατεσκευάσαντο.
238 (xv.) Γαμεῖ δ' αὐτὸς Κατούραν ὕστερον, ἐξ ἧς αὐτῷ παῖδες ἓξ γίνονται πρός τε πόνους καρτεροὶ καὶ δεινοὶ συνιέναι, Ζεμβράνης Ἰαζάρης Μαδάνης Μαδιάνης Λουσούβακος Σοῦος. φύονται δὲ καὶ τούτοις παῖδες· καὶ Σούου μὲν Σαβακίνης γίνεται καὶ Δαδάνης, τούτου δὲ Λατούσιμος Ἄσσουρις Λούουρις· Μαδάνου δὲ Ἠφᾶς Ἐώφρην Ἄνωχος
239 Ἐβιδᾶς Ἐλδᾶς. τούτοις ἅπασι τοῖς παισὶ καὶ τοῖς υἱωνοῖς Ἄβραμος ἀποικιῶν στόλους μη-

¹ αὐτοῦ κεκομισμένου ROE.

---

a Greek "Nebron," see § 170 note. *b* Bibl. Ephron.
c Bibl. Keturah (Χεττουρά). *d* Bibl. Zimran.
e Bibl. Jokshan (Ἰεξάν). *f* With...

JEWISH ANTIQUITIES, I. 235-239

dominion. He moreover foretold that their race would swell into a multitude of nations, with increasing wealth, nations whose founders would be had in everlasting remembrance, that they would subdue Canaan by their arms and be envied of all men. Having spoken thus God brought from obscurity into their view a ram for the sacrifice. And they, restored to each other beyond all hope and having heard promises of such great felicity, embraced one another and, the sacrifice ended, returned home to Sarra and lived in bliss, God assisting them in all that they desired.

(xiv.) Not long after Sarra died at the age of one hundred and twenty-seven years. They buried her in Hebron,[a] where the Canaanites offered burial-ground for her at the public expense, but Abraham bought the spot for four hundred shekels of Ephraim,[b] a native of the place. Here too Abraham and his descendants built their own tombs.

Death of Sarah. Gen. xxiii. 1.

(xv.) Abraham afterwards married Katura,[c] by whom he had six sons, strong to labour and quick of understanding, viz., Zembran(es),[d] Jazar(es),[e] Madan(es),[f] Madian(es),[g] Lousoubak(os),[h] Souos.[i] These too had families: Souos begat Sabakin(es)[j] and Dadan(es),[k] from whom sprung Latousim(os), Assuris and Lououris[l]; Madan begat Êphas,[m] Eôphrên,[n] Anôch(os), Ebidas[o] and Eldas.[p] All these sons and grandsons Abraham contrived to send out

Abraham's descendants by his second wife. Gen xxv. 1.

---

[g] LXX (some MSS.): Heb. Midian.
[h] Bibl. Ishbak ('Ισβόκ).   [i] Bibl. Shuah (Σουέ).
[j] Bibl. Sheba (Σαβάκ LXX, some MSS.).
[k] With LXX (some MSS.): Heb. Dedan.
[l] Bibl. "Asshurim, Letushim (Λατουσιείμ), Leummim" (in this order).   [m] Bibl. Ephah (Γεφάρ).
[n] Bibl. Epher ('Αφέρ).   [o] Bibl. Abida.
[p] Bibl. Eldaah (LXX Θεργαμά with *v.l.*).

JOSEPHUS

χανᾶται, καὶ τήν τε Τρωγλοδῦτιν καταλαμβάνουσι καὶ τῆς εὐδαίμονος Ἀραβίας ὅσον ἐπὶ τὴν Ἐρυθρὰν καθήκει θάλασσαν. λέγεται δ᾽ ὡς οὗτος ὁ Ἐώφρην στρατεύσας ἐπὶ τὴν Λιβύην κατέσχεν αὐτὴν καὶ οἱ υἱωνοὶ αὐτοῦ κατοικήσαντες ἐν αὐτῇ τὴν γῆν ἀπὸ τοῦ ἐκείνου ὀνόματος Ἄφρικαν προσηγόρευσαν.
240 μαρτυρεῖ δέ μου τῷ λόγῳ Ἀλέξανδρος ὁ πολυίστωρ λέγων οὕτως· " Κλεόδημος δέ φησιν ὁ προφήτης, ὁ καὶ Μάλχος, ἱστορῶν τὰ περὶ Ἰουδαίων, καθὼς καὶ Μωυσῆς ἱστόρησεν ὁ νομοθέτης αὐτῶν, ὅτι ἐκ τῆς Κατούρας Ἀβράμῳ ἐγένοντο παῖδες ἱκανοί.
241 λέγει δὲ αὐτῶν καὶ τὰ ὀνόματα ὀνομάζων τρεῖς Ἀφέραν Σούρην Ἰάφραν. ἀπὸ Σούρου μὲν τὴν Ἀσσυρίαν κεκλῆσθαι, ἀπὸ δὲ τῶν δύο Ἰάφρα τε καὶ Ἀφέρου πόλιν τε Ἀφρᾶν[1] καὶ τὴν χώραν Ἄφρικαν ὀνομασθῆναι. τούτους γὰρ Ἡρακλεῖ συστρατεῦσαι ἐπὶ Λιβύην καὶ Ἀνταῖον, γήμαντά τε τὴν Ἀφράνου θυγατέρα Ἡρακλέα γεννῆσαι υἱὸν ἐξ αὐτῆς Δίδωρον· τούτου δὲ γενέσθαι Σόφωνα, ἀφ᾽ οὗ τοὺς βαρβάρους Σόφακας λέγεσθαι."
242 (xvi. 1) Ἰσάκῳ δὲ[2] περὶ τεσσαρακοστὸν ἔτος γεγονότι γυναῖκα γνοὺς ἀγαγέσθαι ὁ πατὴρ Ἄβραμος Ῥεβέκκαν, Ναχώρου παιδὸς θυγατέρα τἀδελφοῦ, τὸν πρεσβύτατον πέμπει τῶν οἰκετῶν ἐπὶ τὴν μνηστείαν ἐνδησάμενος μεγάλαις πίστεσι.

[1] Ἐφράν most MSS.   [2] δὴ ML.

[a] The Arabian shore of the Red Sea: the name may also include the opposite coast. Gen. xxv. 6 speaks of their being sent " eastward unto the east country."
[b] Cf. § 133.
[c] Alexander Cornelius, a contemporary of Sulla, wrote a treatise on the Jews containing extracts from Jewish and Samaritan writings of the second cent. B.C.; the fragments have

JEWISH ANTIQUITIES, I. 239–242

to found colonies, and they took possession of Troglodytis *a* and that part of Arabia Felix which extends to the Red Sea. It is said moreover that this Eôphrên led an expedition against Libya and occupied it and that his grandsons settled there and called the land after his name Africa.*b* I have a witness to this statement in Alexander Polyhistor,*c* whose words are as follows : " Cleodemus the prophet, also called Malchus, in his history of the Jews relates, in conformity with the narrative of their lawgiver Moses, that Abraham had several sons by Katura. He moreover gives their names, mentioning three— Apheras, Sures, Japhras—adding that Sures gave his name to Assyria, and the two others, Japhras and Apheras, gave their names to the city of Aphra and the country of Africa. In fact, he adds, these latter joined Heracles in his campaign against Libya and Antaeus ; and Heracles, marrying the daughter of Aphranes,*d* had by her a son Didorus, who begat Sophon, from whom the barbarians take their name of Sophakes."

(xvi. 1) Now when Isaac was about forty years old,*e* his father Abraham, having decided to give him to wife Rebecca, the granddaughter of his brother Nahor, sent the eldest of his servants to ask for her hand in marriage, after binding him by solemn

The wooing of Rebecca. Gen. xxiv. 1.

---

been collected by Freudenthal (*Hellenistiche Studien*). The work of Malchus (in Freudenthal's opinion a Samaritan) "seems to have been a classic example of that intermixture of Oriental and Greek traditions, which was popular" in Hellenistic times. The legends about Heracles recurred, with variations, in the Libyan history of King Juba (Plutarch *Sertor.* 9, quoted by Schürer).

d The fluctuating spelling leaves it uncertain which son is intended.   *e* Gen. xxv. 20.

243 γίνονται δὲ αὗται τοῦτον τὸν τρόπον· ὑπὸ τοὺς μηροὺς ἀλλήλοις τὰς χεῖρας ἐπαγαγόντες ἔπειτα ἐπικαλοῦνται τὸν θεὸν μάρτυρα τῶν ἐσομένων. ἔπεμπε δὲ καὶ δῶρα τοῖς ἐκεῖ διὰ τὸ σπάνιον 244 ἢ μηδ' ὅλως ἐπιχωριάζειν ἐκτετιμημένα. οὗτος ἀπερχόμενος χρόνῳ διὰ τὸ εἶναι χαλεπὴν ὁδεύεσθαι τὴν Μεσοποταμίαν, χειμῶνι μὲν ὑπὸ πηλῶν βάθους θέρους δ' ὑπὸ ἀνυδρίας, ἔτι δὲ καὶ λῃστηρίων ὄντων ἐν αὐτῇ, ἃ διαφυγεῖν οὐκ ἐνῆν μὴ προνοοῦσι τούτου τοῖς ὁδεύουσιν, εἰς πόλιν ἀφικνεῖται Χάρραν,[1] καὶ γενόμενος ἐν τοῖς προαστείοις παρθένοις ἐντυγχάνει πλείοσιν ἐφ' ὕδωρ βαδιζούσαις·
245 εὔχεται μὲν οὖν τῷ θεῷ Ῥεβέκκαν, ἣν τῷ παιδὶ Ἅβραμος μνηστευσόμενον ἐξαπέστειλαν, εἰ κατὰ νοῦν τὸν αὐτοῦ μέλλει ὁ γάμος οὗτος συντελεῖσθαι, ἐν ἐκείναις εὑρεθῆναι γνωρισθῆναί τε αὐτὴν τῶν μὲν ἄλλων αἰτοῦντι ποτὸν ἀρνουμένων ἐκείνης δὲ αὐτῷ παρασχούσης.

246 (2) Καὶ ὁ μὲν ἐπὶ ταύτης ὢν τῆς διανοίας ἐπὶ τὸ φρέαρ παραγίνεται καὶ παρακαλεῖ τὰς παρθένους ποτὸν αὐτῷ παρασχεῖν· τῶν δ' ἐκτρεπομένων ὡς[2] χρῃζουσῶν οἴκαδε κομίζειν, ἀλλ' οὐκ ἐκείνῳ παρασχεῖν, καὶ γὰρ οὐδ' εὔληπτον εἶναι τὸ ὕδωρ, μία ἐξ ἁπασῶν ἐκείναις τε τῆς πρὸς τὸν ξένον ἐπιπλήττει δυσκολίας, τίνος ἄλλου κοινωνήσειν πρὸς ἀνθρώπους αὐτάς ποτε, αἳ μηδ' ὕδατος μετέδοσαν
247 λέγουσα, καὶ παρέχει αὐτῷ φιλοφρόνως. ὁ δὲ ἐν ἐλπίδι μὲν τῶν ὅλων γενόμενος, βουλόμενος δὲ τὴν ἀλήθειαν μαθεῖν, ἐπῄνει τε τῆς εὐγενείας αὐτὴν καὶ τῆς χρηστότητος, ὅτι καὶ μετ' οἰκείου πόνου τοῖς δεομένοις ἐπαρκεῖν οὐκ ἔφυγεν, ἐπυνθάνετο

[1] Κάρραν most mss.   [2] SPE: καὶ rell.

pledges. These pledges are given on this wise : each party places his hands under the other's thigh, and they then invoke God as witness of their future actions. He also sent to his friends over there presents, which, by reason of their rarity or their being wholly unobtainable in those parts, were inestimable. The servant's journey was prolonged, because travel is rendered difficult in Mesopotamia, in winter by the depth of mud, and in summer through the drought ; moreover, the country is infested by bands of brigands whom travellers could not escape without taking necessary precautions. But at length he reached the city of Charran, in the suburbs of which he fell in with a number of maidens going to fetch water. He therefore prayed God to grant that, if it were His pleasure that this marriage should be consummated, Rebecca, for whose hand Abraham had sent him to sue on behalf of his son, might be found among these maidens and be made known to him by her proffering him drink at his request, when the rest refused it.

(2) With this purpose in mind he approached the well and asked the maidens to give him drink. But they declined, saying that they wanted the water to carry home and not for serving him, for it was no easy matter to draw it. One only of them all rebuked the rest for their churlishness to the stranger, saying " What will you ever share with anyone, who refuse even a drop of water ? ", and with that she graciously offered him some. He, now in high hopes of attaining his main object, but wishing to learn the truth, commended her for her nobility and goodness of heart in not hesitating to minister to another's need at the cost of her own toil, and inquired who

Scene at the well.

τε τίνων εἴη γονέων καὶ κατεύχεται αὐτοῖς ὄνησιν τοιαύτης παιδὸς καὶ " νυμφεύσειαν," φησίν, " ὡς αὐτοῖς ἐστι κεχαρισμένον, εἰς οἶκον ἀνδρὸς ἀγαθοῦ
248 παῖδας αὐτῷ τεξομένην γνησίους." ἡ δὲ οὐδὲ τούτων ἐφθόνησεν αὐτῷ βουλομένῳ μαθεῖν, ἀλλὰ καὶ τὸ γένος ἀπεσήμαινε καὶ " 'Ρεβέκκα μέν," φησίν, " ἐγὼ καλοῦμαι, πατὴρ δέ μοι Βαθούηλος ἦν· ἀλλ' ὁ μὲν ἤδη τέθνηκε, Λάβανος δὲ ἀδελφός ἐστιν ἡμέτερος τοῦ τε οἴκου παντὸς σὺν τῇ μητρὶ προνοούμενος καὶ τῆς ἐμῆς παρθενίας ἐπιμελό-
249 μενος." τούτων ἀκροασάμενος ἔχαιρέ τε τοῖς γεγονόσι καὶ τοῖς εἰρημένοις τὸν θεὸν οὕτως ὁρῶν αὐτῷ τῆς ὁδοῦ σαφῶς συλλαμβανόμενον,[1] καὶ προκομίσας ὁρμίσκον τε καί τινας κόσμους, οὓς εὐπρεπὲς φορεῖν παρθένοις, ἀνεδίδου τῇ κόρῃ τῆς ἐπὶ τῷ πιεῖν χάριτος ἀμοιβὴν εἶναι καὶ γέρας, δίκαιον λέγων τοιούτων αὐτὴν τυγχάνειν ἀγαθὴν
250 παρὰ τὰς τοσαύτας παρθένους γενομένην. ἠξίου τε παρ' αὐτοῖς καταχθῆναι, τοῦ προσωτέρω χωρεῖν τῆς νυκτὸς αὐτὸν ἀφαιρουμένης, κόσμον τε φέρων γυναικεῖον πολυτελῆ πιστεύειν αὐτὸν οὐκ ἀσφαλεστέροις ἔφασκεν ἢ τοιούτοις, οἵας[2] αὐτῆς ἐπειράθη. τεκμαίρεσθαι δὲ καὶ τὴν τῆς μητρὸς καὶ τἀδελφοῦ φιλανθρωπίαν αὐτῆς ἔλεγεν, ὡς οὐ δυσχερανοῦσιν, ἐκ τῆς περὶ αὐτὴν ἀρετῆς· οὐδὲ γὰρ ἔσεσθαι βαρὺς μισθόν τε τῆς φιλοξενίας τελέσας
251 καὶ δαπάναις ἰδίαις χρησάμενος. ἡ δὲ περὶ μὲν τῆς τῶν γονέων φιλανθρωπίας αὐτῆς ὀρθῶς εἰκάζειν αὐτὸν εἶπεν, ἐπεμέμφετο δὲ ὡς μικρο-

---

[1] συλλαμβάνοντα RO.
[2] Bekker: οἷς mss. Niese with some mss. reads τούτοις οἷς αὐτὸς ἐπ.

were her parents, wishing them joy of such a child and saying, " May they marry thee to their hearts' content into the house of a good man to bear him children in wedlock ! " Nor yet did she grudge him this information that he sought but told him also of her family, saying, " I am called Rebecca, and my father was Bathuel, but he is now dead,[a] and our brother Laban directs the whole household, with my mother, and is guardian of my maidenhood." On hearing this the servant rejoiced alike at the deeds done and the words spoken, seeing that God was so manifestly furthering his mission ; and, producing a necklace and some ornaments [b] becoming for maidens to wear, he offered them to the damsel as a recompense and reward for her courtesy in giving him drink, saying that it was right that she should receive such things, having outstripped so many maidens in charity. He also besought that he might lodge with them, night prohibiting him from journeying farther, and, being the bearer of women's apparel of great price, he said that he could not entrust himself to safer hosts than such as he had found her to be. He could guess from her own virtues the kindliness of her mother and brother, and that they would not take his request amiss ; nor would he be burdensome to them, but would pay a price for their gracious hospitality and live at his own expense. To this she replied that with regard to her parents' humanity he judged aright, but she upbraided him for suspecting

[a] Not stated in Genesis, but implied by xxiv. 28 (" her mother's house ").
[b] Gen. xxiv. 22, " a golden ring (LXX, 'gold earrings') ... and two bracelets."

λόγους ὑπειληφότα· πάντων γὰρ ἀμισθὶ μεθέξειν. δηλώσασα μέντοι Λαβάνῳ πρότερον τἀδελφῷ συγχωροῦντος ἄξειν αὐτὸν ἔλεγεν.

252 (3) Ὡς οὖν τούτου γενομένου παρῆγε τὸν ξένον, τὰς μὲν καμήλους αὐτοῦ παραλαμβάνοντες οἱ Λαβάνου θεράποντες ἐτημέλουν, αὐτὸς δὲ δειπνήσων εἰσήγετο σὺν αὐτῷ. καὶ μετὰ τὸ δεῖπνόν φησι πρός τε αὐτὸν καὶ τὴν μητέρα τῆς κόρης '' "Ἄβραμος Θέρρου¹ μέν ἐστιν υἱός, συγγενὴς δ' ὑμέτερος· Ναχώρης γὰρ ὁ τούτων, ὦ γύναι, τῶν παίδων πάππος ἀδελφὸς ἦν Ἀβράμου ὁμοπάτριός τε καὶ 253 ὁμομήτριος. πέμπει τοίνυν οὗτος πρὸς ὑμᾶς ἀξιῶν τὴν κόρην ταύτην παιδὶ τῷ ἑαυτοῦ λαβεῖν πρὸς γάμον, ὃς γνήσιός ἐστιν αὐτῷ καὶ μόνος ἐπὶ τοῖς πᾶσι τεθραμμένος· ᾧ τῶν μὲν ἐκεῖ γυναικῶν δυνατὸν ⟨ὂν⟩ αὐτῷ τὴν εὐδαιμονεστάτην λαβεῖν οὐκ ἠξίωσεν ἀγαγέσθαι, τιμῶν δὲ τὸ γένος τὸν γάμον πολιτεύει 254 τοῦτον. οὗ τὴν σπουδὴν καὶ τὴν προαίρεσιν μὴ ὑβρίσητε· κατὰ γὰρ θεοῦ βούλησιν τά τε ἄλλα μοι κατὰ τὴν ὁδὸν ἀπήντησε καὶ τὴν παῖδα καὶ τὸν ὑμέτερον οἶκον εὗρον. ἐπεὶ γὰρ πλησίον τῆς πόλεως ἐγενόμην, παρθένους ἰδὼν πολλὰς ἐπὶ τὸ φρέαρ παραγινομένας ηὐξάμην εἰς ταύτην ἐμπεσεῖν, 255 ὃ δὴ γέγονε. γάμον οὖν ὑπὸ θείας μνηστευόμενον ἐπιφανείας καὶ ὑμεῖς κυρώσατε καὶ Ἄβραμον τὸν μετὰ τοσαύτης ἀπεσταλκότα σπουδῆς τῷ κατανεῦσαι τὴν κόρην τιμήσατε.'' οἱ δέ, καλὰ γὰρ ἦν αὐτοῖς καὶ κεχαρισμένα, τήν τε γνώμην τοῦ θεοῦ συνῆκαν καὶ πέμπουσιν ἐφ' οἷς ἠξίου τὴν θυγατέρα. γαμεῖ δὲ ταύτην ὁ Ἴσακος τῶν πραγμάτων εἰς

them of meanness, for he should have everything free of cost; however, she would first speak to her brother Laban and with his consent would bring him in.

(3) So, this being done, she introduced the stranger, his camels were received by Laban's servants who took charge of them, and he himself was brought in to sup with the master. Supper ended, he addressed Laban and the mother of the damsel thus: "Abraham is the son of Therrus[a] and a kinsman of yours; for Nahor, the grandfather of these children, dear lady, was Abraham's brother: they had the same father and the same mother. Well, it is this Abraham who sends me to you to ask this damsel in wedlock for his son—his lawful son, who has been brought up as sole heir to his whole estate. Aye, though he might have taken for him the wealthiest of the women yonder, he scorned such a match, and in honour of his own kin now plans this marriage. Flout not his ardour and his proposal; for it was through God's will that all else befell me on my journey and that I found this child and your house. For when I drew nigh to the city I saw many maidens coming to the well and I prayed that I might light upon this one, as indeed has come to pass. Nuptials thus manifestly blessed of heaven do you then ratify, and show honour to Abraham, who with such zeal has sent me hither, by consenting to give the damsel away." And they, since the suit was honourable and to their liking, understood God's will and sent their daughter in accordance with the servant's request. And Isaac married her, being now

Marriage of Isaac.

---

[a] Or Tharrus (Bibl. Terah), § 148.

[1] *v.l.* Θάρρου, Θάρρα.

αὐτὸν ἀφικομένων· οἱ γὰρ ἐκ τῆς Κατούρας εἰς τὰς ἀποικίας ἐξεληλύθεισαν.

256 (xvii.) Τελευτᾷ δὲ καὶ Ἄβραμος μετ' ὀλίγον, ἀνὴρ πᾶσαν ἀρετὴν ἄκρος καὶ τῆς περὶ αὐτὸν σπουδῆς ἀξίως ὑπὸ τοῦ θεοῦ τετιμημένος. ἐβίωσε δὲ τὸν πάντα χρόνον ἐτῶν ἑβδομηκονταπέντε πρὸς τοῖς ἑκατὸν καὶ θάπτεται ἐν Νεβρῶνι μετὰ τῆς γυναικὸς Σάρρας ὑπὸ τῶν παίδων Ἰσάκου καὶ Ἰσμαήλου.

257 (xviii. 1) Ἰσάκῳ δὲ μετὰ τὴν Ἁβράμου τελευτὴν ἐκύει τὸ γύναιον, καὶ τῆς γαστρὸς ἐπὶ μεῖζον ὀγκουμένης ἀγωνιάσας ἀνήρετο τὸν θεόν. φράζει δ' αὐτῷ διδύμους τέξεσθαι τὴν Ῥεβέκκαν καὶ φερώνυμα ἔσεσθαι τοῖς παισὶν ἔθνη, τοῦ δὲ μείζονος

258 προτερήσειν τὸ δοκοῦν ἔλασσον εἶναι. τίκτεται δ' αὐτῷ μετ' ὀλίγον κατὰ πρόρρησιν τοῦ θεοῦ δίδυμα παιδία, ὧν τὸ μὲν πρεσβύτερον ἀπὸ κεφαλῆς ἐπὶ τοὺς πόδας περισσῶς ἦν δασύ, τὸ δὲ νεώτερον εἴχετο προϊόντος αὐτοῦ κατὰ πτέρναν. ἠγάπα δὲ ὁ μὲν πατὴρ τὸν πρεσβύτερον Ἡσαῦν λεγόμενον κατ' ἐπωνυμίαν τῆς τριχώσεως· Ἑβραῖοι γὰρ τὸ ἤσαυρον[1] τρίχωμα λέγουσιν· Ἰάκωβος δὲ ὁ νεώτερος τῇ μητρὶ προσφιλὴς ἦν.

259 (2) Λιμοῦ δὲ τὴν γῆν καταλαβόντος Ἴσακος, δόξαν αὐτῷ χωρεῖν εἰς Αἴγυπτον τῆς χώρας ἀγαθῆς ὑπαρχούσης, ἐπὶ Γεράρων ἀπῄει τοῦ θεοῦ κελεύσαντος. ὑποδέχεται δ' αὐτὸν ὁ βασιλεὺς Ἀβιμέ-

---

[1] Σήειρον MSLE, Seirion Lat.: after τριχώσεως SP ins. εἶχε δὲ καὶ ἕτερον ὄνομα Σήειρον λεγόμενον τῆς τριχώσεως (doubtless a gloss).

---

[a] A condensation of Gen. xxv. 21 f., where Isaac first

master of his father's estate; for his sons by Katura
had departed to found their colonies.   Gen. xxv. 5.

(xvii.) Not long after Abraham died, a man in
every virtue supreme, who received from God the
due meed of honour for his zeal in His service. He
lived in all one hundred and seventy-five years and
was buried at Hebron, beside his wife Sarra, by their
sons Isaac and Ishmael.   Death of Abraham. Gen. xxv. 8.

(xviii. 1) Now after Abraham's death Isaac's
young wife conceived, and seeing her inordinately
big with child her husband anxiously consulted God.[a]
And He told him that Rebecca would give birth to
twins, that nations would bear their names, and that
he that to appearance was the lesser would excel the
greater. Not long after, as God had foretold, twin
children were born to him, the elder of whom was
excessively hairy from head to foot; the younger
held his brother, issuing before him from the womb,
by the heel. The father loved the elder son, who was
called Esau after his hairiness, since the Hebrews
call shaggy hair *êsauron*[b]; but Jacob the younger
was the darling of his mother.   Birth of Esau and Jacob. Gen. xxv. 21

(2) A famine now prevailing in the land, Isaac
resolved to go into Egypt, where the country was
fruitful, but at God's bidding removed to Gerara.[c]
Here king Abimelech welcomed him in virtue of his   Isaac at Gerar(a). Gen. xxvi. 1.

entreats the Lord for his barren wife, and then she in the
pangs of childbirth goes to inquire of Him, and is the recipient
of the oracle.

[b] Esau is thought to be connected with an Arabic word
meaning "hirsute," for which there is no known Hebrew
equivalent; Gen. xxv. 25 contains plays on the names
Edom ("red") and Seir ("hairy"), but not apparently on
Esau itself. Josephus is weak in philology, and it is idle to
discuss his text and meaning.

[c] Gerar in Philistia.

JOSEPHUS

λεχος κατὰ ξενίαν καὶ φιλίαν τὴν Ἀβράμου καὶ πολλῇ πάνυ πρὸς αὐτὸν εὐνοίᾳ χρησάμενος κατ' ἀρχὰς ἐπὶ ταύτης ὑπὸ φθόνου μεῖναι πρὸς τὸ πᾶν
260 ἐκωλύθη. ὁρῶν γὰρ τὸν θεὸν τῷ Ἰσάκῳ συμπαρόντα καὶ τοσαύτῃ περὶ αὐτὸν σπουδῇ χρώμενον ἀπώσατο αὐτόν. ὁ δὲ τοιούτου πάλιν ἐκ μεταβολῆς τῆς ἀπὸ τοῦ βασκάνου πειραθεὶς Ἀβιμελέχου τότε μὲν ἀνεχώρησεν εἰς τὴν λεγομένην Φάραγγα χωρίον οὐ μακρὰν Γεράρων, ὀρύσσοντι δ' αὐτῷ φρέαρ ποιμένες ἐπιπεσόντες εἰς μάχην ἐχώρησαν κωλύοντες τὸ ἔργον, καὶ μὴ βουληθέντος φιλονικεῖν
261 ἔδοξαν κεκρατηκέναι. ὑποχωρήσας δὲ ὤρυσσεν ἕτερον, καὶ βιασαμένων ἄλλων τινῶν Ἀβιμελέχου ποιμένων καὶ τοῦτο καταλιπὼν ἀπεχώρησεν εὐγνώμονι λογισμῷ κτώμενος αὐτῷ τὴν ἄδειαν.
262 εἶτα ⟨τ⟩αὐτομάτου παρασχόντος αὐτῷ τὴν φρεωρυχίαν ἀνεπικώλυτον, Ῥοωβὼθ τὸ φρέαρ ὠνόμασεν· εὐρύχωρον ἀποσημαίνει τὸ ὄνομα. τῶν δὲ προτέρων τὸ μὲν Ἔσκον καλεῖται· μάχην ἄν τις αὐτὸ φήσειε· τὸ δ' ἕτερον Στένα[1]· ἔχθραν ἀποσημαίνει τὸ ὄνομα.
263 (3) Ἰσάκῳ μὲν οὖν ἀκμάζειν συνέβαινε τὴν ἰσχὺν ὑπὸ μεγέθους πραγμάτων, Ἀβιμέλεχος δὲ καθ' αὑτοῦ φύεσθαι νομίζων τὸν Ἴσακον, ὑπόπτου μὲν αὐτοῖς καὶ τῆς συνδιαιτήσεως γενομένης, ἐπ' οὐ φανερᾷ δὲ ἔχθρᾳ τοῦ Ἰσάκου ὑπεκστάντος, δείσας μὴ τῆς προτέρας αὐτῷ φιλίας οὐδὲν ὄφελος γένηται πρὸς ἄμυναν ὧν ἔπαθεν Ἰσάκου τραπέντος φιλίαν ἄνωθεν ποιεῖται πρὸς αὐτόν, ἕνα τῶν στρατηγῶν

---

[1] After Niese (Στέναν): Σύαιvναν or Σύεννα(ν) codd.

[a] § 212.

former friendship and hospitality to Abraham [a] and at first showed him the utmost benevolence, but was prevented by envy from maintaining these feelings to the end; for seeing that God was with Isaac and showered such favours upon him, he cast him off. Meeting with this change in the temper of Abimelech, arising from jealousy, Isaac then withdrew to a place called the Ravine [b] not far from Gerara. Here, as he was digging a well, some shepherds fell upon him and started a fight in order to stop the work; and, when Isaac declined a quarrel, they claimed a victory. He retired and began digging another, but when other shepherds of Abimelech did him violence he left this also and departed, purchasing his security by reasonable calculation. Then, when accident enabled him to dig unmolested, he called this well Roôbôth, a name which denotes "spacious.[c]" Of the former wells one was called Eskos,[d] that is to say "Combat," the other Stena,[e] signifying "Hatred."

Gen. xxvi. 20 ff.

(3) Isaac's power thus steadily mounted through increasing wealth; and Abimelech, thinking that his growing fortunes were a threat to himself (since their relations had been strained even when living together and Isaac had retired dissimulating his hatred), and fearing that his former friendship might avail him nothing when Isaac should turn to avenge himself for his injuries, made renewed overtures to him, taking with him Philoch,[f] one of his generals.

Reconciliation with Abimelech Gen. xxvi. 26.

[b] After LXX, taking Φάραγξ as a proper name: Heb. "in the vale of Gerar."
[c] After LXX (εὐρυχωρία): Heb. Rehoboth = "broad places."
[d] Heb. Esek, "contention": LXX ἀδικία.
[e] Heb. Sitnah, "enmity": LXX ἐχθρία.
[f] Heb. Phicol: the same transposition of consonants occurs in some MSS. of LXX.

JOSEPHUS

264 Φίλοχον ἐπαγόμενος. πάντων δὲ τετυχηκὼς ὧν ἠξίου διὰ τὴν Ἰσάκου χρηστότητα, ὀργῆς προσφάτου πρεσβυτέραν χάριν εἰς αὐτόν τε καὶ τὸν πατέρα γεγενημένην προτιμῶντος, ἀπῆρεν εἰς τὴν ἑαυτοῦ.

265 (4) Τῶν δὲ Ἰσάκου παίδων Ἡσαῦς, περὶ ὃν μάλιστα ὁ πατὴρ ἐσπουδάκει, τεσσαράκοντα γεγονὼς ἔτη γαμεῖ Ἄδαν τὴν Ἥλωνος καὶ Ἀλιβάμην τὴν Εὐσεβεῶνος,[1] δυναστευόντων ἐν Χαναναίοις ἀνδρῶν θυγατέρας, ἑαυτὸν ποιήσας τῆς περὶ τὸν γάμον ἐξουσίας κύριον καὶ μηδὲ τῷ πατρὶ συμ-
266 βουλευσάμενος· οὐδὲ γὰρ ἂν ἐπέτρεψεν Ἴσακος ἐπ' αὐτῷ τῆς γνώμης γενομένης· οὐ γὰρ ἦν αὐτῷ δι' ἡδονῆς συνάψασθαι συγγένειαν πρὸς τοὺς ἐπιχωρίους. οὐ βουλόμενος δὲ ἀπεχθὴς εἶναι τῷ παιδὶ κελεύων ἀφίστασθαι τῶν γυναικῶν σιγᾶν ἔκρινε.

267 (5) Γηραιὸς δὲ ὢν καὶ τὰς ὄψεις εἰς τὸ παντελὲς ἠφανισμένος προσκαλεσάμενος τὸν Ἡσαῦν καὶ τὸ γῆρας εἰπὼν ὡς καὶ δίχα τῆς πηρώσεως καὶ τοῦ κατὰ τὰς ὄψεις πάθους ἐμποδὼν ἦν αὐτῷ θερα-
268 πεύειν τὸν θεόν, ἐκέλευσεν ἐξελθεῖν ἐπὶ κυνηγέσιον καὶ θηρασάμενον ὅσα ἂν αὐτῷ δυνατὸν γίνηται παρασκευάσαι δεῖπνον, ἵνα μετὰ τοῦτο ἱκετεύσῃ τὸν θεὸν σύμμαχον αὐτῷ καὶ συνεργὸν εἰς ἅπαντα παρεῖναι τὸν βίον, ἄδηλον μὲν εἶναι λέγων, ὁπότε καὶ τελευτήσειε, πρὸ δὲ τούτου παρασχεῖν αὐτῷ

[1] Ἐσεβεῶνος Bernard.

And, having obtained complete satisfaction of his desires, thanks to the good nature of Isaac, who set more store on ancient favours bestowed on himself and his father than on recent indignation, he returned home.

(4) Of Isaac's two children, Esau, the favourite of his father, at the age of forty married[a] Ada and Alibame,[b] daughters respectively of Helon[c] and Eusebeon,[d] Canaanite chieftains; these marriages he contracted on his own responsibility without consulting his father, for Isaac would never have permitted them, had his advice been sought, having no desire to form ties of affinity with the indigenous population. However, not wishing to become at enmity with his son through ordering him to separate himself from these women, he resolved to hold his peace.

Esau's wives. Gen. xxvi. 34 with xxxvi. 2.

(5) But when he was old and had completely lost his sight, he called Esau to him and after speaking of his old age, and how, apart from his affliction in the loss of his vision, his years hindered him from ministering to[e] God, bade him go out to the chase, catch whatever he could and prepare him a supper, that so, after partaking of it, he might beseech God to support and assist his son throughout all his life; adding that it was uncertain when he might die, but he wished

Isaac's old age. Gen. xxvii. 1.

---

[a] Scripture contains three inconsistent records of Esau's marriages. Josephus, in common with a few LXX MSS., here introduces the names mentioned in Gen. xxxvi. 2: the Heb. here has the names Judith and Basemath.

[b] Bibl. Oholibamah (LXX Ἐλιβεμά or Ὀλ.).

[c] Bibl. Elon (Ἐλώμ).

[d] Bibl. Zibeon (Σεβεγών).

[e] He could not procure a sacrifice himself: such seems to be the meaning.

βούλεσθαι τὸν θεὸν ταῖς εὐχαῖς ταῖς ὑπὲρ αὐτοῦ
παρακεκλημένον.

269 (6) Καὶ Ἠσαῦς μὲν ἐπὶ τὸ κυνηγέσιον ἐξώρμησεν·
ἡ δὲ Ῥεβέκκα τὸν θεὸν εἰς τὴν εὔνοιαν ἀξιοῦσα τὴν
Ἰακώβου παρακαλεῖν καὶ παρὰ τὴν Ἰσάκου γνώμην
ἐκέλευσεν αὐτὸν ἐρίφους κατασφάξαντα δεῖπνον
παρασκευάζειν. ὁ δὲ Ἰάκωβος ὑπηρέτει τῇ μητρὶ
270 πάντα παρ' αὐτῆς πεπυσμένος· ἐπεὶ δ' εὐτρεπὲς
ἦν τὸ δεῖπνον, ἐρίφου δέρματι τὸν βραχίονα περι-
βαλών, ἵνα πιστεύοιτο παρὰ τῷ πατρὶ διὰ τὴν
δασύτητα Ἠσαῦς εἶναι, τὰ γὰρ ἄλλα πάντ' ὢν
ὅμοιος διὰ τὸ εἶναι δίδυμος τούτῳ μόνῳ διέφερε,
καὶ φοβηθεὶς μὴ πρὶν γενέσθαι τὰς εὐχὰς εὑρεθεὶς
κακουργῶν εἰς τοὐναντίον παροξύνῃ τὸν πατέρα
ποιήσασθαι ταύτας, προσέφερε τῷ πατρὶ τὸ δεῖπ-
271 νον. καὶ ὁ Ἴσακος ἐπαισθόμενος τῷ κατὰ τὴν
φωνὴν ἰδίῳ προσκαλεῖται τὸν υἱόν· τοῦ δὲ τὸν
βραχίονα προτείναντος, ᾧ τὴν αἰγέαν περιβέβλητο,
ταύτης ἐπαφώμενος " φωνεῖς μέν," εἶπεν, " Ἰακώβῳ παραπλήσιον, κατὰ δὲ τὸ τῆς τριχὸς βάθος
272 Ἠσαῦς εἶναί μοι δοκεῖς." καὶ μηδὲν ὑπολαβὼν
κακοῦργον δειπνήσας τρέπεται πρὸς εὐχὰς καὶ
παράκλησιν τοῦ θεοῦ " δέσποτα," λέγων, " παντὸς
αἰῶνος καὶ δημιουργὲ τῆς ὅλης οὐσίας· σὺ γὰρ
πατρὶ τῷ ἐμῷ μεγάλην ἰσχὺν προὔθηκας ἀγαθῶν
κἀμὲ τῶν παρόντων ἠξίωσας καὶ τοῖς ἐξ ἐμοῦ
γενομένοις ὑπέσχου βοηθὸς εὐμενὴς¹ καὶ δοτὴρ
273 ἀεὶ τῶν κρειττόνων ἔσεσθαι· ταῦτ' οὖν καὶ βε-
βαίωσον καὶ μὴ περίδῃς με διὰ τὴν παροῦσαν
ἀσθένειαν, δι' ἣν καὶ μᾶλλόν σου δεόμενος τυγχάνω,
καί μοι παῖδα τοῦτον εὐμενὴς σῷζε καὶ παντὸς
ἀπαθῆ κακοῦ διαφύλαττε δοὺς αὐτῷ βίον εὐδαίμονα

before that time to procure God's protection for him by his prayers on his behalf.

(6) So Esau sped forth to the chase; but Rebecca, being determined to invoke God's favour upon Jacob, even in defiance of Isaac's intent, bade him kill some kids and prepare a meal. And Jacob obeyed his mother, taking all his instructions from her. Accordingly, when the meal was ready, he put the skin of a kid about his arm, in order to make his father believe by reason of its hairiness that he was Esau—for being his twin he resembled his brother in all else but this—fearful lest before the benedictions his guile might be discovered and provoke his father to convert them into a curse, and so brought the supper to his father. Isaac, detecting him by the peculiarity of his voice, called his son to him, but Jacob extended the arm which he had wrapped in the goatskin, feeling which his father exclaimed, " Thy voice is like that of Jacob, but from the thickness of the hair I take thee to be Esau." So, suspecting no fraud, he supped and then turned to prayer and invocation of God, saying,[a] " Lord of all the ages and Creator of universal being, forasmuch as thou didst bestow upon my father great store of good things, and to me hast vouchsafed all that I possess, and to my descendants hast promised thy gracious aid and to grant them ever greater blessings; now therefore confirm these promises and think not scorn of me for my present infirmity, by reason of which I need thee the more; graciously protect this my son and preserve him from every touch of ill; grant him a bliss-

The blessing of Jacob.

[a] Wholly independent of Gen. xxvii. 27 ff.

---

[1] Casaubon: εὐμενῆ codd.

καὶ κτῆσιν ἀγαθῶν, ὅσων σοι δύναμις παρασχεῖν, ποιήσας δ' αὐτὸν φοβερὸν μὲν ἐχθροῖς φίλοις δὲ τίμιον καὶ κεχαρισμένον."

274 (7) Καὶ ὁ μὲν νομίζων εἰς Ἡσαῦν ποιεῖσθαι τὰς εὐχὰς παρεκάλει τὸν θεόν· ἄρτι δὲ πέπαυτο τούτων καὶ παρῆν Ἡσαῦς ἀπὸ τῆς θήρας. καὶ τῆς διαμαρτίας Ἴσακος αἰσθόμενος ἡσυχίαν ἄγει, Ἡσαῦς δὲ ἠξίου τῶν ὁμοίων τἀδελφῷ παρὰ τοῦ πατρὸς 275 τυγχάνειν· τοῦ δὲ [πατρὸς][1] ἀρνουμένου διὰ τὸ πάσας εἰς Ἰάκωβον τὰς εὐχὰς ἀνηλωκέναι πένθος ἦγεν ἐπὶ τῇ διαμαρτίᾳ. καὶ αὐτοῦ τοῖς δάκρυσιν ἀχθόμενος ὁ πατὴρ τὰ μὲν περὶ τὸ κυνηγέσιον καὶ δύναμιν σώματος ἐν ὅπλοις καὶ πᾶσιν ἔργοις εὐδοκιμήσειν αὐτὸν ἔφασκε καὶ καρπώσεσθαι[2] τὴν ἐπ' αὐτοῖς δόξαν δι' αἰῶνος καὶ τὸ ἀπ' αὐτοῦ γένος, δουλεύσειν δὲ τἀδελφῷ.

276 (8) Ἰάκωβον δὲ φοβούμενον τὸν ἀδελφὸν τιμωρίαν βουλόμενον λαβεῖν[3] τῆς ἐπὶ ταῖς εὐχαῖς[4] διαμαρτίας ἡ μήτηρ ῥύεται· πείθει γὰρ τὸν ἄνδρα Μεσοποταμίαν ἀγαγέσθαι τῷ Ἰακώβῳ γυναῖκα 277 συγγενῆ. ἤδη γὰρ τὴν Ἰσμαήλου παῖδα Ἡσαῦς παρειλήφει πρὸς γάμον Βασεμάθην· οὐ γὰρ εὐνόουν τοῖς Χαναναίοις οἱ περὶ τὸν Ἴσακον, ὥστε ἐπὶ τοῖς πρότερον αὐτοῦ γάμοις δυσχερῶς διακειμένων εἰς τὸ ἐκείνοις κεχαρισμένον τὴν Βασεμάθην παρέλαβε μάλιστα περὶ αὐτὴν σπουδάσας.

278 (xix. 1) Ἰάκωβος δὲ εἰς τὴν Μεσοποταμίαν στελλόμενος ὑπὸ τῆς μητρὸς κατὰ γάμον τῆς Λαβάνου θυγατρὸς τοῦ ἐκείνης ἀδελφοῦ, ἐπιτρέψαντος Ἰσάκου τὸν γάμον διὰ τὸ πείθεσθαι τοῖς βουλήμασι τῆς γυναικός, διὰ τῆς Χαναναίας

[1] om. O Lat.   [2] ed. pr.: καρπώσασθαι codd.

ful life and the possession of all good things that thou hast power to bestow; and make him a terror to his foes, to his friends a treasure and a delight."

(7) Thus did he invoke God, believing that he was offering these prayers for Esau; but scarce had he ended them when Esau came in from his hunting. Perceiving his error Isaac held his peace, but Esau desired to obtain from his father the same benedictions as his brother, and when his father refused because he had exhausted all his prayers on Jacob, loudly lamented his disappointment. His father, moved by his tears, then pronounced that he would be renowned in the chase and for strength of body in arms and in labours of all kinds, and that he and his posterity would thence reap an age-long reputation, but that he would serve his brother.

_{The prediction upon Esau. Gen. xxvii. 30.}

(8) Jacob being now in terror of his brother, who wished to avenge himself for being defrauded of the benedictions, was rescued by his mother, who persuaded her husband to take a wife for him from his kinsfolk in Mesopotamia. Esau, for his part, had already taken to wife Basemath,^a the daughter of Ishmael; for Isaac and his family had no love for the Canaanites, wherefore, seeing their vexation at his former marriages, to gratify them he took this Basemath, to whom he was deeply devoted.

_{Esau's third wife. Gen. xxvii. 41. Ib. xxviii. 8.}

(xix. 1) Jacob then was sent by his mother to Mesopotamia to espouse the daughter of her brother Laban, Isaac consenting to the marriage in compliance with his wife's wishes. He journeyed through

_{Jacob's journey to Mesopotamia. Gen. xxviii. 1, 11.}

---

^a Heb. Mahalath (Gen. xxviii. 9); but the small group of LXX MSS., to which the text of Josephus is most closely allied, reads Μασεμάθ.

³ ἀπολαβεῖν MSPL.   ⁴ ἀραῖς OMSP.

ἐπορεύετο καὶ διὰ τὸ πρὸς τοὺς ἐπιχωρίους μῖσος
279 παρ' οὐδενὶ[1] μὲν ἠξίου κατάγεσθαι, ὕπαιθρος[2] δὲ
ηὐλίζετο τὴν κεφαλὴν λίθοις ὑπ' αὐτοῦ συμ-
φορουμένοις ἐπιτιθείς καὶ τοιαύτην κατὰ τοὺς
ὕπνους ὄψιν ὁρᾷ παραστᾶσαν αὐτῷ· κλίμακα γῆθεν
ἔδοξεν ἐφικνουμένην τοῦ οὐρανοῦ βλέπειν καὶ δι'
αὐτῆς ὄψεις κατιούσας σεμνότερον ἢ κατὰ ἀνθρώπου
φύσιν ἐχούσας, καὶ τελευταῖον ὑπὲρ αὐτῆς τὸν
θεὸν ἐναργῶς αὐτῷ φαινόμενον ὀνομαστί τε
280 καλέσαι καὶ ποιήσασθαι τοιούτους λόγους· " Ἰά-
κωβε, πατρὸς ὄντα σε ἀγαθοῦ καὶ πάππου δόξαν
ἀρετῆς μεγάλης εὐραμένου κάμνειν ἐπὶ τοῖς
παροῦσιν οὐ προσῆκεν, ἀλλ' ἐλπίζειν τὰ κρείττονα·
281 καὶ γὰρ ἄφθονος ἐκδέξεταί σε μεγάλων ἀγαθῶν
παρουσία πρὸς τὸ πᾶν κατὰ τὴν ἐμὴν ἐπικουρίαν.
Ἀβραμόν τε γὰρ ἐγὼ [ἐκ][3] τῆς Μεσοποταμίας
δεῦρο ἤγαγον ἐλαυνόμενον ὑπὸ τῶν συγγενῶν, καὶ
πατέρα τὸν σὸν εὐδαίμονα ἀπέφηνα· ὧν οὐχ ἥττω
282 μοῖραν εἰς σὲ καταθήσομαι. θαρρῶν οὖν καὶ
ταύτην πορεύου τὴν ὁδὸν ἐμοὶ προπομπῷ[4] χρώ-
μενος· ἀνυσθήσεται γάρ σοι γάμος, ἐφ' ὃν ἐσπού-
δακας, καὶ γενήσονταί σοι παῖδες ἀγαθοί, τὸ δὲ
πλῆθος αὐτῶν ἀριθμοῦ κρεῖττον ἔσται, μείζοσιν
υἱοῖς αὐτῶν καταλιμπάνοντες· οἷς ἐγὼ τὸ ταύτης
κράτος τῆς γῆς δίδωμι καὶ παισὶ τοῖς αὐτῶν, οἳ
πληρώσουσιν ὅσην ἥλιος ὁρᾷ καὶ γῆν καὶ θάλασσαν.
283 ἀλλὰ μήτε κίνδυνον ὑφορῶ μηδένα μήτ' εὐλαβοῦ
τὸ πλῆθος τῶν πόνων, ἐμοῦ ποιουμένου τῶν σοὶ
πραχθησομένων πρόνοιαν ἔν τε τοῖς νῦν καὶ πολὺ
πλέον ἐν τοῖς ὕστερον."

284 (2) Ταῦτα μὲν οὖν ὁ θεὸς Ἰακώβῳ προαγορεύει·

[1] οὐδένα ROE.   [2] ὕπαιθριος RO.

Canaan and, because of his hatred of the inhabitants, disdained to seek lodging with any of them, but passed the night in the open air, resting his head on some stones which he had collected; and this was the vision which appeared to him in his sleep. He thought that he saw a ladder reaching from earth to heaven, down which were descending phantoms of nature more august than that of mortals, and above it last of all plainly visible to him was God, who called him by name and addressed him thus : " Jacob, offspring of a good sire and of a grandsire who won renown for exceeding virtue, it would beseem thee not to repine at thy present lot, but to hope for better things ; for indeed an abundant and abiding store of great blessings awaiteth thee through my succour. For it was I that led Abraham hither from Mesopotamia when he was driven out by his kinsfolk and that brought thy father to prosperity ; and no less than theirs shall be the portion that I shall bestow on thee. With courage, then, go thou on this journey too, with me for thine escort. For this marriage on which thine heart is set shall be consummated, and goodly children shall be born to thee, whose descendants [a] shall be beyond number and shall leave their heritage to a yet greater posterity.[b] To them do I grant dominion over this land, to them and to their children who shall fill all that the sun beholds of earth and sea. Nay, fear no danger nor be dismayed at thy multitude of toils, for it is I who am watching over all that thou shalt do both now and far more hereafter."

(2) That was what God foretold to Jacob; and he,

[a] Greek " multitude."   [b] Text doubtful.

---

[3] ed. pr., Lat.: om. codd.   [4] RO: πομπῷ rell.

ὁ δὲ περιχαρὴς γενόμενος ἐπὶ τοῖς ἑωραμένοις καὶ κατηγγελμένοις φαιδρύνει τε τοὺς λίθους ὡς τηλικούτων ἀγαθῶν ἐπ' αὐτοῖς προρρήσεως γεγενημένης καὶ εὐχὴν ποιεῖται θύσειν ἐπ' αὐτῶν, εἰ κτησάμενος βίον ἀπαθὴς ἐπανίοι, τῷ θεῷ [δὲ]¹ δεκάτην τῶν πεπορισμένων ποιεῖσθαι οὕτως [αὖθις]² ἀφικόμενος, τίμιόν τε κρίνει τὸ χωρίον ὄνομα αὐτῷ Βεθὴλ θέμενος· σημαίνει δὲ τοῦτο θείαν ἑστίαν κατὰ τὴν τῶν Ἑλλήνων γλῶτταν.

285 (3) Προϊὼν δὲ ἐπὶ τῆς Μεσοποταμίας χρόνῳ παρῆν εἰς τὴν Χαρράν, καὶ ποιμένας ἐν τοῖς προαστείοις καταλαβὼν καὶ παῖδας ἐφήβους καὶ παρθένους ὑπέρ τινος ἱδρυμένους φρέατος συνδιέτριβεν αὐτοῖς χρῄζων ποτοῦ, εἴς τε λόγους αὐτοῖς ἀφικνούμενος ἀνέκρινεν αὐτούς, εἰ τυγχάνουσι Λάβανόν τινα παρ' αὐτοῖς εἰδότες ἔτι 286 περιόντα. οἱ δὲ πάντες ἐπίστασθαί τε ἔφασαν, οὐ γὰρ εἶναι τοιοῦτον ὥστε ἀγνοεῖσθαι, καὶ συμποιμαίνειν αὐτοῖς θυγατέρα αὐτοῦ, ἣν θαυμάζειν ὅτι μήπω παρείη· "παρὰ γὰρ ταύτης μεμαθήκεις ἂν ἀκριβέστερον ὅσα περὶ αὐτῶν ἀκοῦσαι ποθεῖς." ταῦτα δ' αὐτῶν ἔτι λεγόντων παρῆν ἡ παῖς σὺν 287 τοῖς ἐπικατιοῦσι τῶν ποιμένων. καὶ δεικνύουσι τὸν Ἰάκωβον αὐτῇ λέγοντες, ὡς ξένος οὗτος ἥκοι τὰ περὶ τοῦ πατρὸς αὐτῆς ἀναπυνθανόμενος. ἡ δὲ ἡσθεῖσα ὑπὸ νηπιότητος τῇ παρουσίᾳ τοῦ Ἰακώβου ἀνέκρινεν αὐτόν, τίς τε ὢν καὶ πόθεν ἥκοι πρὸς αὐτοὺς καὶ ὑπὸ τίνος χρείας ἠγμένος, ηὔχετο δὲ δυνατὸν εἶναι αὐτοῖς παρέχειν ὧν ἀφικνεῖται δεόμενος.

288 (4) Ἰάκωβος δὲ οὐχ ὑπὸ τῆς συγγενείας οὐδὲ

¹ ins. L: om. RO: τῷ δὲ θεῷ (καὶ τῷ θεῷ) rell.

overjoyed at these visions and promises, polished [a] the stones whereon he lay when such great blessings were predicted, and made a vow to sacrifice upon them, should he, after gaining a livelihood, return unscathed, and to offer to God a tithe of all that he had acquired, should he come back in such fashion; he moreover held the spot in veneration and gave it the name of Bethel, which denotes in the Greek tongue θεία ἑστία—" God's hearth-stone.[b] "

Consecration of Bethel. Gen. xxviii. 18.

(3) Proceeding on his way to Mesopotamia, he at length reached Charran. Here meeting with shepherds in the suburbs, young men and maidens seated beside a well, he joined their company, craving for a drink, and entering into conversation with them he inquired whether they chanced to know of one of their people named Laban and if he were still alive. And they all replied that they knew him, for (they said) he was not a man who could remain unknown, and that his daughter tended the flocks along with them, and they wondered that she was not yet come; "from her," they said, "thou wouldest have learnt more fully all that thou desirest to hear of their family." And even as they said this the maiden arrived with the last of the shepherds to descend to the well. And they pointed out Jacob to her and told her that this stranger had come to ask after her father. Thereupon she, with childish delight at Jacob's coming, asked him who he was, whence had he come to them, and what business had brought him, and prayed that it might be in their power to supply his wants.

Meeting with Rachel. Gen. xxix. 1.

(4) But Jacob was not so much moved by their

---

[a] Sc. with oil: LXX ἐπέχεεν ἔλαιον.
[b] LXX οἶκος θεοῦ.

---

[2] om. RO.

τῆς διὰ ταύτην εὐνοίας, ἀλλ' ἔρωτι τῆς παιδὸς ἡττηθεὶς ἐκπέπληκτό τε τοῦ κάλλους ὁρῶν οὕτως ἔχουσαν, ὡς ὀλίγαι τῶν τότε γυναικῶν ἤνθουν, καί φησιν " ἀλλ' ἐμοὶ πρὸς σὲ καὶ πατέρα τὸν σόν, εἴπερ Λαβάνου παῖς τυγχάνεις, οἰκειότης ἐστὶ πρεσβυτέρα τῆς τε σῆς καὶ ἐμῆς γενέσεως·
289 ἐκ Θέρρου γὰρ Ἄβραμος καὶ Ἀρράνης καὶ Ναχώρης ἦσαν υἱοί, ὧν Βαθούηλος ὁ σὸς πάππος Ναχώρου γίνεται παῖς, Ἀβράμου δὲ καὶ τῆς Ἀρράνου Σάρρας Ἴσακος ὁ ἐμὸς πατήρ. ἔγγιον δὲ καὶ νεώτερον τοῦθ' ἡμεῖς τῆς συγγενείας ὁμή-
290 ρευμα πρὸς ἀλλήλους ἔχομεν· Ῥεβέκκα γὰρ μήτηρ ἐμὴ Λαβάνου πατρὸς τοῦ σοῦ ἀδελφὴ πατρός τε τοῦ αὐτοῦ καὶ μητρός, ἀνεψιοὶ δ' ἐσμὲν ἡμεῖς ἐγώ τε καὶ σύ. καὶ νῦν δεῦρο ἥκω ἀσπασόμενός τε ὑμᾶς καὶ τὴν προϋπάρχουσαν ἡμῖν συγγένειαν
291 ἀνανεωσόμενος." ἡ δὲ ὑπὸ μνήμης, ὁποῖα φιλεῖ συντυγχάνειν τοῖς νέοις, προπεπυσμένη παρὰ τοῦ πατρὸς τὰ περὶ τῆς Ῥεβέκκας καὶ τοὺς γονεῖς εἰδυῖα ποθοῦντας αὐτῆς τὸ ὄνομα, ὑπὸ τῆς περὶ τὸν πατέρα εὐνοίας ἔνδακρυς γενομένη περιβάλλει
292 τὸν Ἰάκωβον, καὶ κατασπασαμένη τὴν εὐκταιοτάτην καὶ μεγίστην ἡδονὴν αὐτὸν κομίσαι τῷ πατρὶ καὶ τοῖς ἐπὶ τῆς οἰκίας ἅπασιν ἔλεγεν ἐπὶ τῇ μνήμῃ τῆς μητρὸς αὐτοῦ κειμένῳ καὶ πρὸς μόνῃ ταύτῃ τυγχάνοντι· φανεῖσθαι δ' αὐτῷ παντὸς ἀντάξιον ἀγαθοῦ. χωρεῖν τε ἐκέλευεν ἤδη πρὸς τὸν πατέρα καὶ ἕπεσθαι πρὸς αὐτὸν ἡγουμένῃ καὶ τῆς ἡδονῆς μὴ ἀφαιρεῖσθαι τὸ πλέον αὐτὸν βραδύνοντα.
293 (5) Ταῦτ' εἰποῦσα παρῆγεν αὐτὸν πρὸς τὸν Λάβανον, καὶ γνωρισθεὶς ὑπὸ τοῦ μήτρωος αὐτός

relationship or the affection consequent thereon, as overcome with love for the maid; he was amazed at the sight of beauty such as few women of those days could show, and said: "Nay, but the kinship that unites me to thee and to thy father, seeing that thou art Laban's child, dates from before thy birth and mine. For Abraham, Arran[a] and Nahor were sons of Therrus,[b] and to Nahor was born Bathuel thy grandsire, and of Abraham and Sarra, daughter of Arran, came my father Isaac. But we have a closer and more recent pledge of kinship uniting us to each other, for Rebecca, my mother, is thy father Laban's sister: they had the same father and the same mother: so we are cousins, I and thou. And now I am come hither to salute you all and to renew that alliance that already exists between us." And she, as young people are wont to do, recalling what ere now she had heard her father tell of the story of Rebecca, and knowing that her parents were longing to have word of her, from filial affection burst into tears and flung her arms round Jacob, and after tenderly embracing him said that he had brought the most cherished and keenest of pleasures to her father and to all their household, for her father was devoted to the memory of Jacob's mother and dwelt only upon it, and his coming would appear to him worth more than every blessing in the world. And she bade him come straight to her father, following her lead, and to deprive him no longer of this pleasure by delay.

(5) Having thus spoken she conducted him to Laban[c]; and being recognized by his uncle he for his

Jacob and Laban. Gen. xxix. 13.

---

[a] Bibl. Haran.   [b] Bibl. Terah.
[c] In Genesis Laban runs to meet him, and brings him into his house.

JOSEPHUS

τε ἀδεὴς ἦν ἐν φίλοις γενόμενος κἀκείνοις πολλὴν ἡδονὴν παρεῖχεν ἀδοκήτως ἐπιφανείς. μετὰ δὲ οὐ πολλὰς ἡμέρας ὁ Λάβανος χαίρειν μὲν ἐπ' αὐτῷ παρόντι μειζόνως ἢ ὡς τῷ λόγῳ δηλώσειεν ἔλεγε, τὴν δ' αἰτίαν δι' ἣν ἀφῖκται μητέρα τε καὶ πατέρα πρεσβύτας καταλιπὼν καὶ θεραπείας τῆς παρ' αὐτοῦ δεομένους ἀνεπυνθάνετο· παρέξειν γὰρ αὐτῷ καὶ πρὸς ἅπασαν ἐπαμυνεῖν[1] χρείαν. Ἰάκωβος δὲ πᾶσαν αὐτῷ τὴν αἰτίαν διηγεῖτο λέγων Ἰσάκῳ γενέσθαι παῖδας διδύμους αὐτόν τε καὶ Ἡσαῦν, ὅν, ἐπεὶ τῶν τοῦ πατρὸς εὐχῶν διήμαρτε σοφίᾳ τῆς μητρὸς εἰς αὐτὸν γενομένων, ἀποκτεῖναι ζητεῖν αὐτὸν ὡς ἀφῃρημένον τῆς παρὰ τοῦ θεοῦ βασιλείας καὶ ἀγαθῶν ὧν ὁ πατὴρ ηὔξατο· ταύτην τε εἶναι τὴν αἰτίαν τῆς ἐνθάδε παρουσίας κατὰ τὴν τῆς μητρὸς ἐντολήν. "πάπποι[2] τε γὰρ ἡμῖν ἀδελφοὶ τυγχάνουσι καὶ πλέον τοῦ κατ' ἐκείνους συγγενοῦς ἡ μήτηρ προσλαμβάνει. ἔρυμα δὲ τῆς ἐμῆς," φησίν, "ἀποδημίας σέ τε καὶ τὸν θεὸν ποιούμενος θαρρῶ τοῖς παροῦσι."

(6) Λάβανος δὲ καὶ διὰ τοὺς προγόνους ὑπισχνεῖται πάσης αὐτῷ μεταδώσειν φιλανθρωπίας καὶ διὰ τὴν μητέρα, πρὸς ἣν τὴν εὔνοιαν διὰ τῆς περὶ αὐτὸν σπουδῆς ἐνδείξεσθαι[3] καὶ μὴ παρούσης· ποιμνίων τε γὰρ αὐτὸν ἐπιμελητὴν καταστήσειν ἔφασκε καὶ προνομίας[4] ἀντὶ τούτων ἀξιώσειν, καὶ πρὸς τοὺς ἰδίους ἀπαλλάττεσθαι γονεῖς βουλόμενον μετὰ δώρων ἐπανήξειν καὶ τιμῆς ὅσης εἰκὸς ἦν τυχεῖν τὸν οὕτω συγγενῆ. Ἰακώβου δὲ ἀσμένως ταῦτα ἀκούσαντος καὶ φήσαντος ἡδέως πάντα μένων παρ' αὐτῷ πόνον εἰς ἡδονὴν ὑπομενεῖν[5] τὴν

[1] Naber: ἐπαμύνειν codd.

JEWISH ANTIQUITIES, I. 293-298

part now felt secure among friends and withal afforded them great pleasure by his unlooked-for appearance. A few days later Laban said that his presence indeed gave him more joy than he could express, but he asked him for what reason he had come, leaving his mother and father at an age when they would need his care, and assured him of his aid and succour in his every need. Jacob then recounted the whole matter to him, saying that Isaac had twin sons, himself and Esau; and Esau, being defrauded of his father's blessings, which through his mother's artifice had been bestowed upon himself, sought to kill him for having deprived him of God's destined gift of the kingdom and of the benefits invoked by his father; that was the reason for his coming thither in compliance with his mother's behest. "For," said he, "our grandfathers were brothers, and my mother brings us into yet closer relationship than that. And so, placing myself on my sojourn here under thy protection and God's, I have confidence in my present state."

(6) Laban thereon promised to show him every kindness, both in the name of their ancestors and also for his mother's sake, his affection for whom, though absent, he would display by his solicitude for her son: he would in fact make him overseer of his flocks and accord him privileges for these services; and should he wish to depart to his parents, he should return laden with presents and all the honours befitting so near a kinsman. Jacob welcomed these words and said that he would gladly tarry with him and endure

Jacob's service and marriages.

---

² Niese: πᾶσι codd.
³ Bakker: ἐνδείξασθαι codd.   ⁴ προνομῆς ROE.
⁵ Dindorf: ὑπομένειν codd.

ἐκείνου, μισθὸν δὲ ὑπὲρ τούτου λαβεῖν ἀξιοῦντος τὸν Ῥαχήλας γάμον, διά τε τὰ ἄλλα τιμῆς ἀξίας παρ' αὐτοῦ τυγχάνειν οὔσης καὶ ὅτι διάκονος τῆς πρὸς αὐτὸν ἀφίξεως γένοιτο· ὁ γὰρ τῆς παιδὸς ἔρως αὐτὸν ἠνάγκασε ποιήσασθαι τοὺς περὶ τούτου λόγους· Λάβανος δὲ ἡσθεὶς τούτοις ἐπινεύει τὸν γάμον αὐτῷ τῆς παιδὸς οὐκ ἄλλον ἀμείνω γαμβρὸν εὐξάμενος ἐλθεῖν· εἰ μέντοι παρ' αὐτῷ μένοι τινὰ χρόνον, τοῦτο ποιήσειν· εἰς γὰρ Χαναναίους οὐκ ἂν πέμψειν[1] τὴν θυγατέρα, μεταμέλειν γὰρ αὐτῷ καὶ τοῦ τῆς ἀδελφῆς κήδους ἐκεῖ συναφθέντος. τοῦ δ' Ἰακώβου τούτοις συγχωροῦντος ἑπτὰ ἐτῶν χρόνον συντίθεται· τοσάδε γὰρ αὐτῷ κέκριται θητεῦσαι τῷ πενθερῷ, ἵνα τῆς ἀρετῆς πεῖραν δοὺς ἐπιγνωσθῇ μᾶλλον τίς εἴη. καὶ προσδεξάμενος τὸν λόγον Λάβανος τοῦ χρόνου διελθόντος προυτίθει τὴν εὐωχίαν τῶν γάμων. νυκτὸς δ' ἐπιγενομένης οὐδὲν προῃσθημένῳ τῷ Ἰακώβῳ παρακατακλίνει τὴν ἑτέραν τῶν θυγατέρων πρεσβυτέραν τε τῆς Ῥαχήλας καὶ τὴν ὄψιν οὐκ εὐπρεπῆ. συνελθὼν δ' ἐκεῖνος ὑπὸ μέθης καὶ σκότους, εἶτα μεθ' ἡμέραν γνούς, ἀδικίαν ἐπεκάλει Λαβάνῳ. ὁ δὲ συγγνώμην ᾐτεῖτο τῆς ἀνάγκης, ὑφ' ἧς ταῦτα πράξειεν· οὐ γὰρ κατὰ κακουργίαν αὐτῷ τὴν Λείαν παρασχεῖν, ἀλλ' ὑφ' ἑτέρου μείζονος νενικημένον. τοῦτο μέντοι γ' οὐδὲν ἐμποδίζειν πρὸς τὸν Ῥαχήλας γάμον, ἀλλ' ἐρῶντι δώσειν ταύτην μετ' ἄλλην ἑπταετίαν. πείθεται δ' ὁ Ἰάκωβος,

---

[1] πέμψαι Niese.

[a] Implied by Gen. xxix. 17, though only one defect is mentioned, viz. that her eyes lacked lustre.

[b] Greek, here and throughout, "Leia."

any labour to please him; but for his wages in return for this he asked the hand of Rachel, who on all grounds deserved his esteem, and not least for her ministry in bringing him to Laban—the love that he bare the maiden constraining him thus to speak. Laban, delighted at his words, consented to the marriage with his child, saying that he could not have prayed for a better son-in-law; on condition, however, that he would abide for some time with him, for he would not send his daughter among the Canaanites: indeed he regretted that his sister's marriage had been contracted over there. Jacob, approving these conditions, covenanted for a period of seven years: such was the term for which he resolved to serve his father-in-law, in order to give proof of his worth and that it might the better be seen what manner of man he was. Laban accepted this proposal and, when the time expired, prepared to celebrate the nuptial festivities. But at nightfall he brought to the chamber of the all-unconscious Jacob his other daughter, who was older than Rachel and devoid of beauty.[a] Jacob, deluded by wine and the dark, had union with her; then, when daylight came, he recognized her and accused Laban of perfidy. The other craved his pardon for the necessity which had constrained him so to act, saying that it was not out of malice that he had given him Leah [b] but from another more overpowering motive.[c] This would, however, in no way debar his marriage with Rachel: no, if he loved her, he would give her to him after another seven years. To this Jacob submitted, his love for

---

[c] Weill suspects a lacuna in the text: the motive is stated in Gen. xxix. 26, "It is not so done in our place, to give the younger before the firstborn."

JOSEPHUS

οὐδὲν γὰρ ἕτερον αὐτῷ ποιεῖν ὁ τῆς κόρης ἔρως ἐπέτρεπε, καὶ διελθούσης ἄλλης ἑπταετίας τὴν Ῥαχήλαν παρέλαβεν.

303 (7) Ἦσαν δ' ἑκατέραις θεραπαινίδες τοῦ πατρὸς δόντος, Ζέλφα μὲν Λείας Ῥαχήλας δὲ Βάλλα, δοῦλαι μὲν¹ οὐδαμῶς ὑποτεταγμέναι δέ. καὶ τῆς Λείας ἥπτετο δεινῶς ὁ πρὸς τὴν ἀδελφὴν ἔρως τἀνδρός, προσεδόκα τε παίδων γενομένων ἔσεσθαι 304 τιμία ἱκέτευέ τε τὸν θεὸν διηνεκῶς. καὶ γενομένου παιδὸς ἄρρενος καὶ διὰ τοῦτο πρὸς αὐτὴν ἐπεστραμμένου τἀνδρὸς Ῥουβῆλον ὀνομάζει τὸν υἱόν, διότι κατ' ἔλεον αὐτῇ τοῦ θεοῦ γένοιτο· τοῦτο γὰρ σημαίνει τὸ ὄνομα. τεκνοῦνται δὲ αὐτῇ καὶ τρεῖς ἕτεροι μετὰ χρόνον· Συμεών,² ἀποσημαίνει δὲ τὸ ὄνομα τὸ ἐπήκοον αὐτῇ τὸν θεὸν γεγονέναι, εἶτα Λευίς, κοινωνίας οἷον βεβαιωτής, μεθ' ὃν 305 Ἰούδας, εὐχαριστίαν τοῦτο δηλοῖ. Ῥαχήλα δὲ φοβουμένη, μὴ διὰ τὴν εὐτεκνίαν τῆς ἀδελφῆς ἥττονος παρὰ τἀνδρὸς μοίρας τυγχάνῃ, παρακατακλίνει τῷ Ἰακώβῳ τὴν αὑτῆς θεραπαινίδα Βάλλαν. γίνεται δὲ παιδίον ἐξ αὐτῆς Δάν, θεόκριτον ἄν τινες εἴποιεν κατὰ τὴν Ἑλλήνων γλῶτταν· καὶ μετ' αὐτὸν Νεφθάλεις, μηχανητὸς³ οἷον, διὰ τὸ ἀντιτεχνάσασθαι πρὸς τὴν εὐτεκνίαν τῆς ἀδελφῆς.

---

¹ + οὖν R.O.   ² Σεμεών M.
³ O Lat. (ex machinationibus): ἀμηχάνητος (εὐμηχάνητος) rell.

ᵃ So LXX (Gen. xxx. 9): Heb. Zilpah.
ᵇ So LXX (Gen. xxix. 29): Heb. Bilhah.
ᶜ Bibl. Reuben (Ῥουβήν), "because," according to Scriptural etymology, "Jehovah hath *looked upon my*

the damsel permitting of no other course, and after the lapse of seven years more he won Rachel.

(7) The two sisters had each a handmaid given them by their father—Leah had Zelphah[a] and Rachel Balla[b]—in no way slaves but subordinates. Now Leah was grievously mortified by her husband's passion for her sister, and hoping to win his esteem by bearing children she made continual supplication to God. Then a boy was born and, her husband's affection being consequently drawn towards her, she called her son Rubel,[c] because he had come to her through the mercy of God; for that is the meaning of the name. Three more sons were born to her later: Symeon, the name signifying that God had hearkened[d] to her, then Levi(s), that is to say a "surety of fellowship,"[e] and after him Judas, which denotes "thanksgiving." Rachel, fearing that her sister's fecundity would lessen her own share in her husband's affections, now gave as concubine to Jacob her handmaid Balla. By her he had an infant, Dan,[f] which might be rendered in Greek by *Theocritos* ("adjudged of God"), and after him Nephthali(s),[g] that is to say "contrived," because his mother had outmanœuvred

Jacob's children.

Gen. xxix. 32.

Ib. xxx. 1.

---

affliction (raah beonyi)." Josephus here and throughout adopts the Syriac and probably older form *Rubil*, finding in the last syllable the divine name *El*; how he extracted the sense of "mercy" from the first is obscure. Modern scholars see in the final syllable not *El* but *Baal*.

[d] Heb. *shama* "hear."

[e] In Biblical etymology (Gen. xxix. 34) connected with the root *lavah*, "join," "adhere"; now thought to be the gentilic name for the Leah tribe as a whole.

[f] Meaning in Heb. "he judged."

[g] Bibl. Naphtali (Νεφθαλεί): the verb *niphtal* (translated "wrestle"), from which Scripture derives the name, means rather "twist," suggesting tortuousness, cunning.

306 τὸ δ' αὐτὸ καὶ Λεία ποιεῖ πρὸς τὸ τῆς ἀδελφῆς ἔργον ἀντιτεχνασαμένη· παρακατακλίνει γὰρ τὴν αὐτῆς θεράπαιναν, γίνεταί τε καὶ ἐκ τῆς Ζέλφης υἱὸς Γάδας, τυχαῖον ἄν τις καλέσειεν αὐτόν, καὶ μετ' αὐτὸν Ἄσηρος, μακαριστὴς λέγοιτ' ἂν ἐξ
307 ὧν πρὸς εὔκλειαν[1] προσελάμβανε. Ῥουβήλου δὲ τοῦ πρεσβυτάτου τῶν υἱῶν Λείας μανδραγόρου μῆλα κομίζοντος τῇ μητρὶ Ῥαχήλα θεασαμένη παρακαλεῖ μεταδοῦναι δι' ἐπιθυμίας τοῦ βρώματος γενομένης. τῆς δ' οὐ πειθομένης, ἀρκεῖσθαι δ' αὐτὴν ἀξιούσης, ὅτι τῆς τιμῆς αὐτὴν ἀφέλοιτο τῆς παρὰ τοῦ ἀνδρός, Ῥαχήλα πεπαίνουσα τὸν θυμὸν τῆς ἀδελφῆς παραχωρήσειν αὐτῇ τἀνδρὸς ἔλεγε κοιμησομένου παρ' αὐτῇ κατ' ἐκείνην τὴν ἑσπέραν.
308 τῆς δὲ προσιεμένης τὴν χάριν Ἰάκωβος συγκαθεύδει τῇ Λείᾳ Ῥαχήλᾳ χαριζόμενος. πάλιν οὖν γίνονται παῖδες αὐτῇ, Ἰσσαχάρης μὲν σημαίνων τὸν ἐκ μισθοῦ γενόμενον, Ζαβουλὼν δὲ ἠνεχυρασμένον εὐνοίᾳ τῇ πρὸς αὐτήν, θυγάτηρ δὲ Δεῖνα. χρόνοις δ' ὕστερον καὶ Ῥαχήλᾳ γίνεται [ὁ] Ἰώσηπος υἱός· προσθήκην γενησομένου τινὸς δηλοῖ.

309 (8) Τοῦτον ἅπαντα τὸν χρόνον, ἔτη δ' ἐστὶν εἴκοσιν, ἐποίμαινε τῷ πενθερῷ· μετὰ τοῦτον δ'[2] ἠξίου τὰς γυναῖκας ἀναλαβὼν ἀπαλλάττεσθαι πρὸς αὑτόν· τοῦ δὲ πενθεροῦ μὴ συγχωροῦντος κρύφα
310 τοῦτο ποιεῖν ἐπενόει. τῶν γυναικῶν οὖν ἀπεπειρᾶτο, πῶς ἔχοιεν πρὸς τὴν ἀποδημίαν, τῶν

---

[1] RO: +τῇ Λείᾳ rell.
[2] μετὰ τὸν δ' RO: μετὰ τοῦτο δὲ most MSS.

---

[a] Gad, "the name of an Aramaean and Phoenician god of Luck, mentioned in Is. lxv. 11" (Skinner).

[b] Bibl. Asher (Ἀσήρ), there derived from the verb "call

her sister's fecundity. Leah responded to her sister's action by the same stratagem: she too gave her own handmaid as concubine, and of Zelpha was born a son Gad(as) *a*—" Godsend " we may call him—and after him Aser,*b* or as we may say " Beatific," because of this addition to the woman's fame. Now when Rubel, the eldest of Leah's sons, brought some apples of the mandrake to his mother, Rachel spied them and begged her to give her of them, having a longing to eat of them. Leah refusing and protesting that she ought to be content with having robbed her of her husband's esteem, Rachel to appease her sister's wrath said that she would surrender her place to her and let her husband sleep with her that evening. She accepted this favour and Jacob, to please Rachel, slept with Leah. So she again had children: Issachar,*c* meaning " one born of hire," Zabulon " pledged by affection towards her," *d* and a daughter, Dinah. Later on Rachel also bare a son, Joseph, signifying an " addition of one to come."*e*

(8) Throughout all this period of twenty years Jacob was tending the flocks of his father-in-law; but at the close of it he desired leave to take his wives and depart to his own home, and, when his father-in-law refused, he planned to do this thing secretly. He accordingly tested his wives' feelings concerning this

Flight of Jacob and his family.
Gen. xxx. 25.
Ib. xxxi. 4.

Gen. xxx. 14.

happy," but possibly " related to the Canaanite goddess Asherah."

c = either " man of hire " or " there is a reward."

d Genesis (xxx. 20) offers two derivations, from *zabad*, " endow " (*zebed*, " dowry "), or *zabal*, " dwell ": Josephus seems to connect the word with *ḥabôl*, " a pledge."

e Or " of something to come." Josephus adopts the second of the two Biblical etymologies of his own name, " May Jehovah add " (LXX προσθέτω ὁ θεός μοι ἕτερον υἱόν, Gen. xxx. 24).

JOSEPHUS

δ' ἐχουσῶν ἡδέως Ῥαχήλα καὶ τοὺς τύπους τῶν θεῶν, οὓς σέβειν πατρίους ὄντας νόμιμον ἦν, συνανελομένη συναπεδίδρασκε μετὰ τῆς ἀδελφῆς οἵ τε ἑκατέρων παῖδες καὶ αἱ θεραπαινίδες σὺν 311 τοῖς υἱοῖς εἴ τέ τις ἦν κτῆσις αὐταῖς. ἐπήγετο δὲ Ἰάκωβος καὶ τῶν βοσκημάτων τὴν ἡμίσειαν Λαβάνου μὴ προεγνωκότος. τοὺς δὲ τύπους ἐπεφέρετο τῶν θεῶν ἡ Ῥαχήλα καταφρονεῖν μὲν τῆς τοιαύτης τιμῆς τῶν θεῶν διδάξαντος αὐτὴν Ἰακώβου, ἵνα δ' εἰ καταληφθεῖεν ὑπὸ τοῦ πατρὸς αὐτῆς διωχθέντες ἔχοι τούτοις προσφυγοῦσα συγγνώμης τυγχάνειν.

312 (9) Λάβανος δὲ μεθ' ἡμέραν πρώτην γνοὺς τήν τε Ἰακώβου ἀναχώρησιν καὶ τῶν θυγατέρων δεινοπαθῶν ἤλαυνεν ἐπ' αὐτὸν μετὰ δυνάμεως ἐπειγόμενος, καὶ καθ' ἑβδόμην ἡμέραν ἐπί τινος 313 λόφου λαμβάνει προκαθιδρυμένους. καὶ τότε μέν, ἑσπέρα γὰρ ἦν, ἡσύχαζεν· ὄναρ δὲ ὁ θεὸς ἐπιστὰς αὐτῷ παρῄνεσε λαβόντι τὸν γαμβρὸν καὶ τὰς θυγατέρας ἠρεμεῖν καὶ μηδὲν εἰς αὐτοὺς ὑπὸ θυμοῦ τολμᾶν, σπονδὰς δὲ ποιεῖσθαι πρὸς Ἰάκωβον, αὐτὸς λέγων ἐκείνῳ συμμαχήσειν, εἰ καταφρονήσας αὐτοῦ τῆς ὀλιγότητος χωρήσειεν αὐτῷ διὰ μάχης. 314 Λάβανος δὲ τοιαύτης αὐτῷ προρρήσεως γεγενημένης μεθ' ἡμέραν τὸν Ἰάκωβον εἰς λόγους προκαλεσάμενος καὶ δηλώσας αὐτῷ τὸ ὄναρ, ἐπεὶ πρὸς αὐτὸν ἦλθε πεισθείς, ἤρξατο κατηγορεῖν αὐτοῦ προφέρων ὅτι καὶ πένητα αὐτὸν ἐλθόντα πρὸς αὐτὸν καὶ πάντων ἄπορον ὑπεδέξατο καὶ

---

[a] Midrashic addition. For other motives given for the theft of the Teraphim *cf. Pirkè R. Eliezer*, c. 36 (Friedlander), " Rachel stole them, so that they should not tell Laban that

migration; and, they being well content, Rachel, taking with her even the images of the gods which the religion of her fathers made it customary to venerate, escaped along with her sister and the children of both wives, the handmaids with their sons and all their possessions. Jacob, moreover, took with him one half of the cattle without the knowledge of Laban. Rachel, who carried the images of the gods, had indeed been taught by Jacob to despise such worship, but her motive was that, in case they were pursued and overtaken by her father, she might have recourse to them to obtain pardon.[a]

Gen. xxxi. 19.

(9) Laban having, a day later,[b] discovered the escape of Jacob and his daughters, indignant at such treatment, set out after him with a band of men in hot pursuit, and on the seventh day overtook them on a hill where they were encamped. It being then evening, he took his rest; and God appeared to him in a dream and warned him, now that he had overtaken his son-in-law and his daughters, to act gently and take no rash measures against them in wrath, but to make a covenant with Jacob; He would Himself, He said, come to Jacob's aid if, in contempt of his inferiority of numbers, he should proceed to attack him. Thus forewarned, Laban at break of day summoned Jacob to a parley, telling him of his dream, and when Jacob thereon confidently approached him, began to accuse him, protesting that, on his arrival at his house in poverty and utter destitution, he (Laban)

Dispute between Jacob and Laban. Gen. xxxi. 22.

Jacob had fled, and not only that, but also to remove idolatrous worship from her father's house." The Teraphim = an idol or idols in human form, used for divination (Zech. x. 2); thought to have been household gods, like the Latin *Penates*, and connected with ancestor-worship.

[b] After the lapse of a whole day = Bibl. "on the third day."

παράσχοι πᾶσαν ἀφθονίαν τῆς αὑτοῦ κτήσεως· " καὶ γὰρ καὶ θυγατέρας ἐμὰς συνέζευξα τὴν εὔνοιάν σου τὴν πρὸς ἡμᾶς τούτοις αὐξήσεσθαι
315 λογιζόμενος. σὺ δὲ οὔτε τῆς μητρὸς τῆς σαυτοῦ καὶ [κοινωνίας]¹ ἧς ἔχεις πρὸς ἐμὲ συγγενείας οὔτε γυναικῶν ἃς ἔγημας αἰδῶ ποιησάμενος οὐδὲ τέκνων ὧν εἰμι πάππος φροντίσας, ἐχρήσω μοι πολέμου νόμῳ, κτῆσιν μὲν ἄγων τὴν ἐμὴν θυγατέρας δὲ ἀναπείσας ἀποδρᾶναι τὸν γεγεννηκότα,
316 ἱερά τε πάτρια βαστάσας οἴχῃ φερόμενος ὑπό τε τῶν ἐμῶν τιμηθέντα προγόνων καὶ ὑπ' ἐμοῦ θρησκείας τῆς αὐτῆς ἐκείνοις ἀξιωθέντα· καὶ ταῦτα ἃ μηδὲ οἱ πολεμήσαντες τοὺς ἐχθροὺς ἔδρασαν ὁ συγγενὴς σὺ καὶ τῆς μὲν ἀδελφῆς τῆς ἐμῆς υἱός, θυγατέρων δὲ τῶν ἐμῶν ἀνήρ, ξένος δὲ καὶ ἐφέστιος τῆς ἐμῆς οἰκίας γεγενημένος
317 ἔδρασας." ταῦτα εἰπόντος Λαβάνου Ἰάκωβος ἀπελογεῖτο μὴ μόνῳ πατρίδος ἔρωτα τὸν θεόν, ἀλλὰ καὶ πᾶσιν ἐμφῦσαι, καὶ μετὰ τοσοῦτον χρόνον
318 καλῶς ἔχειν αὐτῷ κατελθεῖν εἰς ταύτην. " ὑπὲρ δὲ τῆς λείας ἧς ἐγκαλεῖς," φησίν, " ἀδικῶν αὐτὸς ἂν εὑρεθείης ἐπ' ἄλλῳ κριτῇ· ὑπὲρ γὰρ ἧς ἐχρῆν σε χάριν ἡμῖν ἔχειν καὶ φυλαχθείσης ὑφ' ἡμῶν καὶ πλείονος γεγενημένης, ὑπὲρ ταύτης πῶς οὐ διαμαρτάνεις τῶν δικαίων χαλεπαίνων ἐμοί, εἰ μοῖραν αὐτῆς ὀλίγην λαβόντες ἔχομεν; περὶ μέντοι γε τῶν θυγατέρων ἴσθι μὴ κατ' ἐμὴν κακουργίαν ἀπαναστήσαντος ἀκολουθεῖν, ἀλλὰ κατ' εὔνοιαν δικαίαν, ἣν γυναιξὶ γαμεταῖς πρὸς τοὺς συνοικοῦντας εἶναι συμβέβηκεν· ἕπονται τοίνυν οὐχ ὡς ἐμοὶ τοσοῦτον,
319 ὅσον τοῖς παισὶν αὐτῶν." καὶ ταῦτα μὲν ὑπὲρ

¹ om. ROE.

had entertained him and supplied him with ample abundance of his possessions. " Aye," said he, " I even gave thee my daughters in wedlock, reckoning thereby to increase thy affection towards us. But thou, without regard either for thine own mother or for the kinship which unites thee to me or for the wives whom thou hast wed, without a thought for the children of whom I am the grandsire, hast dealt with me by the laws of warfare, plundering my property, instigating my daughters to flee from their sire, and making off with the sacred objects of my family which my forefathers venerated and I have deemed worthy of the same worship as they. And these actions which even in war one would not have practised upon a foe, thou, a kinsman, the son of my own sister, the husband of my daughters, the guest and sharer of my hearth and home, hast done to me." To this speech of Laban Jacob replied in self-defence that he was not the only one in whose heart God had implanted a love of native country, that it was innate in all, and that after so long a time it was right that he should return to his own. " As for the charge of spoiling thee," he proceeded, " it is thou thyself who wouldst be found the wrongdoer before any other judge. For whereas thou oughtest to be grateful to me for having kept and multiplied thy cattle, is it not unreasonable to be wroth with me for the small portion of them that we have taken with us ? As concerning thy daughters, I would have thee know that it is no malice on my part that has forced them to accompany my flight, but that just affection which wedded wives are wont to have for their husbands ; in truth it is not so much me whom they follow as their children." Such was his

τοῦ μηδὲν ἀδικεῖν αὐτὸς ἔλεγε, προσενεκάλει δὲ καὶ κατηγορίαν ἐποιεῖτο, ὅτι μητρὸς ὢν ἀδελφὸς τῆς αὑτοῦ καὶ συζεύξας αὐτῷ τὰς θυγατέρας ἐπιτάγμασιν ἐκτρυχώσειε χαλεποῖς εἴκοσιν ἐτῶν ἀριθμὸν ἐν αὐτοῖς κατασχών. καὶ τὰ μὲν προφάσει τῶν γάμων ὑπ' αὐτοῦ γενόμενα καίπερ ὄντα χαλεπὰ κουφότερα ἔφασκε, χείρω δὲ τὰ μετὰ τοὺς 320 γάμους καὶ ἅ τις ἂν ἔπαθεν ἐχθρός.[1] καὶ γὰρ σφόδρα κακούργως ὁ Λάβανος ἐχρήσατο τῷ Ἰακώβῳ· ὁρῶν γὰρ αὐτῷ τὸν θεὸν πρὸς ὅ τι θελήσειε συλλαμβανόμενον ὑπισχνεῖτο τῶν τεχθησομένων αὐτῷ παρέξειν ἔσθ' ὅτε μὲν ὅ τι καὶ γένοιτο λευκόν, ποτὲ δ' αὖ τὰ μέλανα τῶν γεννωμένων.
321 πληθυόντων δὲ τῶν ἐπ' ὀνόματι τῷ Ἰακώβου τικτομένων, τὴν μὲν εἰς τὸ παρὸν οὐκ ἐφύλαττε πίστιν, εἰς ἔτος δὲ παρέξειν ἐπηγγέλλετο[2] διὰ τὸ ἐποφθαλμιᾶν τῷ πλήθει τῆς κτήσεως, ἐπαγγελλόμενος μὲν διὰ τὸ δυσέλπιστον γενέσθαι τοσαῦτα, ψευδόμενος δὲ ἐπὶ γενομένοις.

322 (10) Περὶ μέντοι τῶν ἱερωμάτων ἐκέλευεν ἔρευναν ποιεῖσθαι· δεξαμένου δὲ Λαβάνου τὴν ἔρευναν Ῥαχήλα πυνθανομένη κατατίθησι τοὺς τύπους εἰς τὴν σάγην τῆς φερούσης αὐτὴν καμήλου· ἐκαθέζετο δὲ φάσκουσα τὴν κατὰ φύσιν κάθαρσιν 323 αὐτῇ ἐνοχλεῖν. καὶ Λάβανος μὲν ἀφίσταται τῆς ἐπὶ πλεῖον ἐρεύνης οὐκ ἂν οἰηθεὶς τὴν θυγατέρα μετὰ τοιούτου πάθους τοῖς τύποις προσελθεῖν, ποιεῖται δ' ὅρκους πρὸς Ἰάκωβον οὐδενὸς αὐτῷ μνησικακήσειν τῶν γενομένων, ἀλλὰ κἀκεῖνος

[1] ἅ τις ἐχθρὸς ἔφυγεν ἂν SPL: ἅ τις ἂν ἔπαθεν (om. ἔπαθεν M) ἐχθρὸς ἔφυγε rell.
[2] ROE: +τὸ ἑξῆς rell.

JEWISH ANTIQUITIES, I. 319–323

defence to prove that he had done no wrong, from which he proceeded to complaint and accusation against Laban: he, though he was his mother's brother and had given him his daughters in wedlock, had worn him out by imposing grievous tasks and by detaining him there for the space of twenty years. What Laban had made him suffer, he added, on the pretext of the marriages, notwithstanding its cruelty, was indeed comparatively light; but what had followed those marriages was worse and a fate such as might have befallen an enemy.[a] And indeed Laban had used Jacob exceedingly ill; for when he saw that God assisted him in whatsoever he desired, he promised to grant him from the young of the flock at one time all that should be born white, at another all the black progeny. But when the offspring that should have been credited to Jacob proved numerous, he did not keep his word at the moment, but promised to deliver them a year later, since he looked askance at his becoming possessed of so much. He made these promises because such numbers were not to be expected, but when they came he proved faithless. Gen. xxx. 27 ff.

(10) As for the sacred objects, Jacob bade him institute a search. This offer Laban accepted, whereupon Rachel, hearing of it, deposited the images in the pack-saddle of the camel which carried her and sat upon it, professing to be incommoded by the functions natural to women. Laban then desisted from further search, never supposing that his daughter in that condition would approach the images; he moreover made an oath to Jacob that he would bear him no grudge for the past, while

[a] Or (with the other text) "such as an enemy would have refrained from inflicting."

The reconciliation. Gen. xxxi. 32.

JOSEPHUS

324 ἀγαπήσειν αὐτοῦ τὰς θυγατέρας. καὶ τὰς πίστεις τὰς ἐπὶ τούτοις ἐποιήσαντο ὑπὲρ ὁρῶν τινων, ἐφ' οἷς στήλην ἀνέθεσαν κατὰ βωμοῦ σχῆμα, ὅθεν Γαλάδης[1] λέγεται [ὁ] βουνός, ἀφ' οὗ καὶ νῦν Γαλαδηνὴν καλοῦσι τὴν γῆν. ἑστιαθέντων δὲ ἐπὶ τοῖς ὅρκοις ὁ μὲν Λάβανος ἀνέζευξεν.

325 (xx. 1) Ἰακώβῳ δὲ εἰς τὴν Χαναναίαν προϊόντι φαντάσματα συνετύγχανεν ἀγαθὰς ἐλπίδας ὑπαγορεύοντα περὶ τῶν ἐς ὕστερον· καὶ τὸν μὲν τόπον ἐκεῖνον προσαγορεύει θεοῦ στρατόπεδον, βουλόμενος δὲ εἰδέναι, τί ὁ ἀδελφὸς αὐτοῦ φρονεῖ, τοὺς γνωσομένους ἕκαστα μετὰ ἀκριβείας προύπεμψε

326 δεδιὼς αὐτὸν διὰ τὴν προτέραν ὑποψίαν. ἐνετέλλετο δὲ τοῖς πεμπομένοις λέγειν πρὸς τὸν Ἡσαῦν, ὅτι νομίσας Ἰάκωβος ἄδικον συνδιαιτᾶσθαι αὐτοῦ τῇ ὀργῇ τῆς χώρας ἑκὼν ὑπεξέλθοι, καὶ νῦν τὸν χρόνον ἱκανὸν ἡγούμενος εἶναι διαλλάκτην ἐπανήκοι γυναῖκάς τε καὶ παῖδας ἐπαγόμενος μετὰ τοῦ πορισθέντος βίου, μετὰ τῶν τιμιωτάτων ἑαυτὸν ἐκείνῳ παραδιδούς, ὅτι κρίνοι μέγιστον ἀγαθὸν τὸ τῷ ἀδελφῷ συμμεταλαμβάνειν τῶν

327 ὑπὸ τοῦ θεοῦ δεδομένων. καὶ οἱ μὲν ταῦτα ἐδήλουν, Ἡσαῦς δὲ περιχαρὴς γίνεται καὶ τῷ ἀδελφῷ ὑπήντα σὺν ὁπλίταις τετρακοσίοις. καὶ Ἰάκωβος πυνθανόμενος ἥκειν αὐτὸν ὑπαντησόμενον μετὰ τοσούτων ἦν περίφοβος, τῷ μέντοι θεῷ τὴν ἐλπίδα τῆς σωτηρίας ἐπέτρεπε καὶ πρόνοιαν εἶχεν ἐκ τῶν παρόντων, ὅπως αὐτὸς ἀπαθὴς σώζοι τοὺς σὺν αὐτῷ κρατήσας τῶν ἐχθρῶν εἰ θέλοιεν ἀδικεῖν.

---

[1] Γαλάδην M : Γαλαδηνή rell.

[a] Strictly " a slab " : Josephus takes over the Greek word *stēlē* from the LXX.

Jacob on his side swore to love his daughters. To these engagements they pledged themselves on some hills, whereon they erected a monument[a] in the form of an altar; hence comes the name Galad(es)[b] given to the hill, and hence to this day they call the district Galadene.[c] A feast having followed the oath-taking, Laban withdrew.

Gen. xxxi. 47.

(xx. 1) Jacob now pursuing his journey to Canaan had visions which inspired him with good hopes for the future; and he called that spot "God's camp.[d]" Being, however, desirous to know his brother's intentions, he sent forward a party to obtain full and precise information; for he feared him by reason of their suspicions of old. He charged these messengers to tell Esau that he, Jacob, had left the country of his own free will, thinking it wrong to live with him while his wrath persisted, and that now, deeming that the time past was sufficient to reconcile them, he was returning with wives and children and all the substance that he had procured and was entrusting himself into his hands with all that he treasured most, holding it the greatest of blessings to share with his brother what God had given him. This message they delivered, and Esau, overjoyed, went to meet his brother with four hundred men-at-arms. Jacob, on learning that he was coming to receive him with so large a force, was sore afraid, but committed to God his hopes of salvation, while he took all available precautions to secure himself, to save his companions and to master his foes should they wish to injure him.

Jacob's return to Canaan. Gen. xxxii.1.

[b] Bibl. Galeed = "cairn of witness" (LXX βουνὸς μαρτυρεῖ).
[c] The Hellenized form of Bibl. Gilead.
[d] Bibl. Mahanaim = "two hosts" (LXX παρεμβολή or παρεμβολαί).

328 νείμας οὖν τοὺς σὺν αὐτῷ τοὺς μὲν προύπεμπε, τοὺς δὲ λειπομένους ἆσσον ἐκέλευσεν ἀκολουθεῖν, ὅπως εἰ βιασθεῖεν οἱ προπεμφθέντες ἐπιθεμένου τοῦ ἀδελφοῦ, καταφυγὴν ἔχοιεν τοὺς ἑπομένους.
329 καὶ τοῦτον διατάξας τοὺς σὺν αὐτῷ τὸν τρόπον πέμπει τινὰς δῶρα κομίζοντας τἀδελφῷ· ὑποζύγια δὲ ἦν τὰ πεμπόμενα καὶ πλῆθος τετραπόδων ποικίλων, ἃ δὴ τίμια τοῖς ληψομένοις ἔμελλεν
330 ἔσεσθαι παρὰ τὸ σπανίζειν αὐτῶν. ἦσαν[1] δὲ οἱ πεμφθέντες ἐκ διαλειμμάτων, ἵνα συνεχέστερον ἐντυγχάνοντες πολλοὶ δοκῶσιν· ἀνήσειν γὰρ ὑπὸ τῶν δωρεῶν τῆς ὀργῆς, εἰ διαμένοι τεθυμωμένος· ἔτι μέντοι καὶ λόγοις χρηστοῖς ὁμιλεῖν πρὸς αὐτὸν εἴρητο τοῖς πεμπομένοις.

331 (2) Ταῦτα συνθεὶς διὰ πάσης τῆς ἡμέρας νυκτὸς ἐπιγενομένης ἐκίνει τοὺς σὺν αὐτῷ· καὶ χειμάρρουν τινὰ Ἰάβακχον λεγόμενον διαβεβηκότων Ἰάκωβος ὑπολελειμμένος φαντάσματι συντυχὼν διεπάλαιεν, ἐκείνου προκατάρχοντος τῆς μάχης, ἐκράτει τε
332 τοῦ φαντάσματος, ὃ δὴ καὶ φωνῇ χρῆται καὶ λόγοις πρὸς αὐτόν, χαίρειν τε τοῖς γεγενημένοις παραινοῦν καὶ μὴ μικρὸν[2] κρατεῖν ὑπολαμβάνειν, ἀλλὰ θεῖον ἄγγελον νενικηκέναι, καὶ σημεῖον ἡγεῖσθαι τοῦτο μεγάλων ἀγαθῶν ἐσομένων καὶ τοῦ μηδέποτε τὸ γένος ἐκλείψειν αὐτοῦ, μηδὲ ὑπέρτερον ἀνθρώπων
333 τινὰ τῆς ἰσχύος ἔσεσθαι τῆς ἐκείνου. ἐκέλευέ τε καλεῖν[3] αὐτὸν Ἰσράηλον· σημαίνει δὲ τοῦτο κατὰ τὴν Ἑβραίων γλῶτταν τὸν ἀντιστάτην[4] ἀγγέλῳ

---

[1] ἦσαν codd. [2] μικρῶν MPL.
[3] καλεῖσθαι SPL Lat.: perhaps αὐτὸν should be read for αὐτόν.
[4] RO: ἀντιστάντα rell.

JEWISH ANTIQUITIES, I. 328-333

Accordingly, dividing his company, he sent one party in advance and bade the remainder follow close behind, in order that if the advance guard were overpowered by an attack from his brother, they might have those in the rear to fall back upon. Having disposed his men after this fashion, he sent a party to carry presents to his brother: the convoy consisted of beasts of burden and a multitude of quadrupeds of divers kinds such as would be treasured by their recipients on account of their rarity. These emissaries marched with intervals between, in order to appear more numerous by arriving continuously. It was hoped that Esau would be induced by the presents to relax his wrath, were he still indignant; moreover the messengers had instructions to address him affably.

(2) Having spent the whole day in making these arrangements, at nightfall he put his company in motion; and when they had crossed a torrent called Jabacchos,[a] Jacob, being left behind, encountered a phantom, wrestled with it and overcame it. The struggle had been begun by the spectre, which now found a tongue and addressed him, bidding him rejoice in his achievement and not to imagine that it was a puny adversary whom he had mastered: he had defeated an angel of God and should deem this victory an omen of great blessings to come and an assurance that his race would never be extinguished and that no mortal man would surpass him in strength. He moreover bade him take the name of Israel,[b] which in the Hebrew tongue denotes the opponent of an angel of God. This revelation indeed

His wrestle with an angel. Gen. xxxii. 22.

---

[a] Bibl. Jabbok.
[b] = " striver with God," or " God strives."

θεοῦ. ταῦτα μέντοι προύλεγεν Ἰακώβου δεηθέντος· αἰσθόμενος γὰρ ἄγγελον εἶναι θεοῦ, τίνα μοῖραν ἕξει σημαίνειν παρεκάλει. καὶ τὸ μὲν 334 φάντασμα ταῦτ' εἰπὸν ἀφανὲς γίνεται. ἠσθεὶς δὲ τούτοις Ἰάκωβος Φανουήλον ὀνομάζει τὸν τόπον, ὃ σημαίνει θεοῦ πρόσωπον. καὶ γενομένου διὰ τὴν μάχην ἀλγήματος αὐτῷ περὶ τὸ νεῦρον τὸ πλατὺ αὐτός τε ἀπέχεται τῆς τούτου βρώσεως καὶ δι' ἐκεῖνον οὐδὲ ἡμῖν ἐστιν ἐδώδιμον.

335 (3) Πλησίον δ' ἤδη τὸν ἀδελφὸν πυνθανόμενος κελεύει προϊέναι τῶν γυναικῶν ἑκατέραν καθ' αὑτὴν μετὰ τῶν θεραπαινίδων, ἵνα πόρρωθεν ἀφορῷεν τὰ ἔργα τῶν ἀνδρῶν μαχομένων, εἰ τοῦτο θελήσειεν Ἡσαῦς· προσεκύνει δ' αὐτὸς τὸν ἀδελφὸν ἐγγὺς αὐτῷ γενόμενον οὐδὲν περὶ αὐτοῦ δόλιον 336 φρονοῦντα. καὶ ὁ Ἡσαῦς ἀσπασάμενος αὐτὸν ἀνήρετο τῶν παίδων τὸν ὄχλον καὶ τὰς γυναῖκας, ἠξίου τε μαθὼν περὶ αὐτῶν τὸ πᾶν καὶ αὐτὸς συμβαδίζειν αὐτοῖς πρὸς τὸν πατέρα, Ἰακώβου δὲ προφασιζομένου τὸν κόπον τῶν ὑποζυγίων ὑπεχώρησεν εἰς Σάειραν· ἐνταῦθα γὰρ ἐποιεῖτο τὴν δίαιταν προσαγορεύσας τὸ χωρίον ἀπὸ τῆς αὑτοῦ τριχώσεως [δασεῖαν].[1]

337 (xxi. 1) Ἰάκωβος δὲ ἀφίκετο εἰς τὰς ἔτι νῦν Σκηνὰς λεγομένας, ὅθεν εἰς Σίκιμον παρῆν· Χαναναίων δ' ἐστὶν ἡ πόλις. τῶν δὲ Σικιμιτῶν ἑορτὴν ἀγόντων Δεῖνα, θυγάτηρ ἦν Ἰακώβου

[1] Probably a gloss ("Bushy").

[a] Bibl. Peniel (LXX εἶδος θεοῦ).
[b] Commonly explained as the sciatic nerve, running from thigh to ankle. [c] Bibl. Seir (Σηείρ).
[d] So LXX renders, correctly, the Heb. Succoth, Gen. xxxiii. 17. [e] After LXX: Heb. Shechem.

he gave at the request of Jacob, who, perceiving him to be a messenger of God, besought him to declare what destiny was in store for him. The apparition, having thus spoken, vanished; and Jacob, delighted with the vision, named the place Phanuel,[a] that is to say, "the face of God." And because in the contest he had suffered injury near the broad sinew,[b] he himself abstained from eating that sinew, and for his sake we too are forbidden to eat of it.

(3) Learning that his brother was now at hand, Jacob ordered his two wives to go forward, each apart with their handmaidens, that they might view from afar the actions of the combatants, should Esau desire battle. For his part he prostrated himself before his brother, who, however, approached him with no thought of treachery. Esau embraced him, questioned him concerning this crowd of children and his womenkind, and, having learnt the whole history of them, desired to conduct them himself to their father; but, on Jacob pleading the fatigue of the beasts of burden, Esau withdrew to Saeira,[c] for it was there that he had his abode, having so named the place after his own shaggy hair.

His meeting with Esau. Gen. xxxiii. 1.

(xxi. 1) Jacob next reached the place still to this day called "Booths,[d]" whence he passed to Sikim,[e] which is a city of the Canaanites. As the Sikimites were holding a festival,[f] Dina(h), Jacob's only

Rape of Dinah: the brothers' reprisals. Gen. xxxiv. 1.

[f] Genesis merely states that Dinah "went out to see the daughters of the land." The "festival" perhaps comes from Theodotus, the (Samaritan?) author of a hexameter poem on this episode, who is mentioned elsewhere by Josephus (*Ap.* i. 216). According to the paraphrase of this poem given in Eusebius, *Praep. Ev.* ix. 22, Theodotus related that τὴν Δείναν παρθένον οὖσαν εἰς τὰ Σίκιμα ἐλθεῖν πανηγύρεως οὔσης, βουλομένην θεάσασθαι τὴν πόλιν. The passage, with Rabbinical parallels, is quoted by M. Weill.

μόνη, παρῆλθεν εἰς τὴν πόλιν ὀψομένη τὸν κόσμον τῶν ἐπιχωρίων γυναικῶν. θεασάμενος δ' αὐτὴν Συχέμμης [δ]ᵃ Ἐμμώρου τοῦ βασιλέως υἱὸς φθείρει δι' ἁρπαγῆς καὶ διατεθεὶς ἐρωτικῶς ἱκετεύει τὸν 338 πατέρα λαβεῖν αὐτῷ πρὸς γάμον τὴν κόρην. ὁ δὲ πεισθεὶς ἧκε πρὸς τὸν Ἰάκωβον δεόμενος τῷ παιδὶ αὐτοῦ Συχέμμῃ συζεῦξαι Δεῖναν κατὰ νόμον. Ἰάκωβος δὲ οὔτ' ἀντιλέγειν ἔχων διὰ τὸ ἀξίωμα τοῦ παρακαλοῦντος οὔτε νόμιμον ἡγούμενος ἀλλοφύλῳ συνοικίζειν τὴν θυγατέρα ἠξίωσεν ἐπιτρέψαι 339 αὐτῷ βουλὴν ἀγαγεῖν περὶ ὧν παρακαλεῖ. ἀπῄει μὲν οὖν ὁ βασιλεὺς ἐλπίζων Ἰάκωβον παρέξειν τὸν γάμον, Ἰάκωβος δὲ τοῖς παισὶ δηλώσας τήν τε φθορὰν τῆς ἀδελφῆς καὶ τοῦ Ἐμμώρου τὴν δέησιν ἠξίου βουλεύεσθαι τί δεῖ ποιεῖν. οἱ μὲν οὖν πλείους ἡσύχαζον γνώμης ἀποροῦντες, Συμεὼν¹ δὲ καὶ Λευὶς ὁμομήτριοι τῆς κόρης ἀδελφοὶ συν 340 τίθενται πρὸς ἀλλήλους τοιάνδε τινὰ πρᾶξιν· οὔσης ἑορτῆς καὶ τῶν Σικιμιτῶν εἰς ἄνεσιν καὶ εὐωχίαν τετραμμένων νύκτωρ πρώτοις ἐπιβαλόντες τοῖς φύλαξι κτείνουσι κοιμωμένους καὶ παρελθόντες εἰς τὴν πόλιν ἀναιροῦσι πᾶν ἄρρεν καὶ τὸν βασιλέα σὺν αὐτοῖς καὶ τὸν υἱὸν αὐτοῦ, φείδονται δὲ τῶν γυναικῶν. πράξαντες δὲ ταῦτα δίχα τῆς τοῦ πατρὸς γνώμης ἐπανάγουσι τὴν ἀδελφήν.

341 (2) Ἰακώβῳ δὲ ἐκπλαγέντι πρὸς τὸ μέγεθος τῶν γεγονότων καὶ χαλεπαίνοντι πρὸς τοὺς υἱοὺς ὁ θεὸς παραστὰς ἐκέλευσε θαρρεῖν, ἁγνίσαντι δὲ τὰς σκηνὰς θυσίας ἐπιτελεῖν, ἃς τὸ πρῶτον ἀπιὼν εἰς τὴν Μεσοποταμίαν ἐπὶ τῇ ὄψει τοῦ ὀνείρου ηὔξατο.

---
¹ Σεμεὼν RM.

ᵃ Bibl. Shechem, son of Hamor.

JEWISH ANTIQUITIES, I. 337–341

daughter, went into the city to see the finery of the women of the country. There she was perceived by Sychem,[a] son of king Emmor, who carried her off and ravished her, and being enamoured of her besought his father to procure the damsel for him in marriage. To this Emmor consented and went to Jacob to ask him to give Dinah to his son Sychem in lawful wedlock. Jacob, who could not refuse in view of the petitioner's rank and yet on the other hand deemed it unlawful to marry his daughter to a foreigner, asked permission to hold a council on the subject of his request. So the king departed, hoping that Jacob would allow the marriage, but Jacob told his sons of the seduction of their sister and of Emmor's request and asked them to deliberate what ought to be done. Most of them held their peace, not knowing what to think; but Symeon and Levi, the girl's brothers, born of the same mother, mutually agreed upon the following course. During a feast,[b] when the Sikimites were given up to indulgence and festivity, they, under cover of night, first surprised the sentries, whom they slew in their sleep, and then penetrating into the town killed all the males, the king and his son among them, sparing only the women. Having perpetrated this deed without their father's sanction, they brought their sister back.

(2) Jacob being aghast at the enormity of these acts and indignant at his sons, God appeared beside him and bade him take courage, purify his tents, and perform those sacrifices which he had vowed to offer when at the first he set out for Mesopotamia

Purification ceremonies. Gen. xxxiv. 30.

---

[b] This second feast is another importation into the Biblical narrative.

342 ἁγνίζων οὖν τοὺς ἑπομένους ἐπιτυγχάνει τοῖς
Λαβάνου θεοῖς, οὐ γὰρ ἠπίστατο ὑπὸ τῆς Ῥαχήλης
κλαπέντας, καὶ αὐτοὺς ἔκρυψεν ἐν Σικίμοις εἰς
γῆν ὑπό τινα δρῦν, ἀπάρας τε τοὐντεῦθεν ἐν
Βαιθήλοις ἔθυεν, ὅπου τὸ ὄνειρον ἐθεάσατο χωρῶν
πρότερον ἐπὶ τῆς Μεσοποταμίας.

343 (3) Ἐντεῦθεν δὲ προϊὼν ἐπεὶ κατὰ τὴν Ἐφρα-
θηνὴν γίνεται, ἐνθάδε Ῥαχήλαν ἐκ τοκετοῦ
θανοῦσαν θάπτει, μόνην τῶν συγγενῶν τῆς ἐν
Ἑβρῶνι τιμῆς οὐ τυχοῦσαν. πενθήσας δὲ μεγάλως τὸ ἐξ αὐτῆς παιδίον Βενιαμεὶν ἐκάλεσε διὰ
344 τὴν ἐπ᾽ αὐτῷ γενομένην ὀδύνην τῇ μητρί. οὗτοι
Ἰακώβου παῖδες οἱ πάντες, ἄρρενες μὲν δώδεκα
θήλεια δὲ μία. τούτων ὀκτὼ γνήσιοι, ἐκ Λείας
μὲν ἕξ, δύο δὲ ἐκ Ῥαχήλης, τέσσαρες δὲ ἐκ τῶν
θεραπαινίδων, δύο ἐξ ἑκατέρας, ὧν καὶ τὰ ὀνόματα
πάντων προεῖπον.

345 (xxii.) Παρῆν δ᾽ ἐντεῦθεν ἐπὶ Ἑβρῶνα πόλιν ἐν
Χαναναίοις κειμένην· ἐκεῖ δὲ Ἴσακος τὴν δίαιταν
εἶχε. καὶ βραχέα μὲν ἀλλήλοις συνδιατρίβουσι· τὴν
γὰρ Ῥεβέκκαν Ἰάκωβος οὐ κατέλαβε ζῶσαν,
θνήσκει δὲ καὶ Ἴσακος οὐ μετὰ πολὺ τῆς ἀφίξεως
τοῦ υἱοῦ καὶ ταφῆς ἔτυχεν ὑπὸ τῶν παίδων σὺν τῇ
γυναικὶ ἐν Ἑβρῶνι μνημείου προγονικοῦ ἐν αὐτῇ
346 τυγχάνοντος αὐτοῖς. ἐγένετο δὲ Ἴσακος ἀνὴρ
θεοφιλὴς καὶ προνοίας πολλῆς ἠξιωμένος ὑπ᾽

---

[a] § 284.
[b] Genesis mentions "strange gods" generally, without specifying the Teraphim of Laban.
[c] "The burial of idolatrous emblems under this sacred tree

and had seen the dream.*a* While he was purifying his company accordingly, he lit upon the gods of Laban,*b* being unaware that Rachel had stolen them; these he hid in the ground beneath an oak at Sikim,*c* and departing thence offered sacrifice at Bethel, where he had seen the dream when journeying of yore to Mesopotamia.

Cf. Gen. xxxv. 4; xxxi. 32.

(3) Thence he proceeded on his way, and when he was come over against Ephratene *d* Rachel died in childbirth and there he buried her, being the only one of his family who had not the honour of burial at Hebron. Deeply he mourned her and he called the child whom she bore Benjamin because of the suffering which he had caused his mother.*e* These then are all the children of Jacob, twelve sons and one daughter. Of these sons eight were born in wedlock, six by Leah and two by Rachel; four he had by the handmaidens, two by each of them; I have already given the names of all.

Death of Rachel. Gen. xxxv. 16.

(xxii.) From there he came to Hebron, a city in Canaanite territory, where Isaac had his abode. They lived but a short while together, for Jacob did not find Rebecca alive and Isaac also died not long after the coming of his son; he was buried by his children beside his wife at Hebron in their ancestral tomb. Isaac was a man beloved of God and was deemed worthy of His special providence after his

Death of Rebecca and of Isaac. Gen. xxxv. 27.

has some traditional meaning which we cannot now explain" (Skinner).

d Bibl. Ephrath ('Εφραθά); in Benjamite territory, otherwise unknown.

e A confused statement, regardless of etymology. In Genesis the dying mother calls the child Ben-oni ("son of my sorrow"); the father, to avert the omen, names him Ben-jamin ("son of the right hand").

αὐτοῦ μετ' Ἄβραμον τὸν πατέρα, πολυχρονιώτατος δέ· βιώσας γὰρ ἔτη πέντε καὶ ὀγδοήκοντα πρὸς τοῖς ἑκατὸν μετὰ ἀρετῆς οὕτως ἀπέθανεν.

---

^a Doubtless a contrast is intended between the 175 years of Abraham (§ 256) and the 185 years of Isaac, whose exceptional longevity had been predicted (§ 234, πολυχρονιώτατον as here). But it is unnecessary to alter the superlative to the comparative; the former includes the latter (see note on ὕστατος § 214, and *cf.* in N.T. Jo. i. 15 πρῶτός μου ἦν).

father Abraham; in longevity he even surpassed him,[a] having completed one hundred and eighty-five years of a virtuous life when he died.[b]

[b] Josephus breaks off the book at the end of Gen. xxxv. The recently edited 3rd cent. *Berlin Fragment of Genesis* (ed. Sanders and Schmidt, New York, 1927) breaks off in the same chapter (xxxv. 8), with the subscription γένεσις κόσμου as though at the close of a work. Was the Greek Genesis ever divided at this point? I may refer to my Schweich Lectures (1920), App. IV. " The Bisection of Old Testament books."

ΒΙΒΛΙΟΝ Β

(i. 1) Μετὰ δὲ τὴν Ἰσάκου τελευτὴν οἱ παῖδες αὐτοῦ μερισάμενοι τὴν οἴκησιν πρὸς ἀλλήλους οὐχ ἣν ἔλαβον ταύτην κατέσχον, ἀλλ' Ἡσαῦς μὲν τῆς Νεβρωνίας[1] πόλεως ἐκχωρήσας τἀδελφῷ ἐν Σαείρᾳ διῃτᾶτο καὶ τῆς Ἰδουμαίας ἦρχεν οὕτω καλέσας τὴν χώραν ἀφ' αὑτοῦ· Ἄδωμος γὰρ ἐπωνομάζετο κατὰ τοιαύτην αἰτίαν τυχὼν τῆς ἐπικλήσεως. 2 ἀπὸ θήρας ποτὲ καὶ πόνου τοῦ περὶ τὸ κυνηγέσιον[2] λιμώττων ἐπανῆκεν, ἔτι δὲ ἦν παῖς τὴν ἡλικίαν, ἐπιτυχὼν δὲ τἀδελφῷ φακῆν ἐσκευακότι πρὸς ἄριστον αὑτῷ, ξανθὴν σφόδρα τὴν χροιάν, καὶ διὰ τοῦτ' ἔτι μᾶλλον ὀρεχθεὶς ἠξίου παρασχεῖν αὐτῷ 3 πρὸς τροφήν. ὁ δὲ ἀποδόσθαι τὸ πρεσβεῖον αὑτῷ τοῦ φαγεῖν συνεργῷ χρησάμενος τῇ πείνῃ τὸν ἀδελφὸν ἠνάγκαζε,[3] κἀκεῖνος ὑπὸ τοῦ λιμοῦ προαχθεὶς παραχωρεῖ τῶν πρεσβείων αὐτῷ μεθ' ὅρκων. ἔνθεν διὰ τὴν ξανθότητα τοῦ βρώματος ὑπὸ τῶν ἡλικιωτῶν κατὰ παιδιὰν Ἄδωμος ἐπικληθείς, ἄδωμα γὰρ Ἑβραῖοι τὸ ἐρυθρὸν καλοῦσι,

---

[1] Χεβρωνίας SPE.   [2] κυνήγιον RE.
[3] SP: ἠνάγκασε rell.

---

[a] Gen. xxxvi. 7, " For their substance was too great for them to dwell together, and the land of their sojournings

BOOK II

(i. 1) After the death of Isaac his sons divided the territory between them, not retaining that which they had inherited.[a] Esau, for his part, left the city of Hebron to his brother, and taking up his abode in Saeira [b] ruled over Idumaea, calling the country thus after himself: for he bore the surname of Adom,[c] which he had obtained under the following circumstances. One day, while yet a lad, he was returning from the chase, fatigued with his hunting and famished, when, meeting his brother who had just prepared for his midday meal a dish of lentils of a rich tawny hue, which still further whetted his appetite, he asked him to give him to eat. Jacob, thereupon, taking advantage of his famished state, required his brother to sell to him in exchange for the food his rights as firstborn son; and he, instigated by hunger, surrendered to him his rights under an oath. Hence, by reason of the ruddy colour of the pottage, he was jestingly nicknamed by his youthful comrades Adom—*adoma* [d] being the Hebrews' word for "red"—and that was how he

<small>Esau sells his birthright. Gen. xxxvi. 6.</small>

<small>xxv. 27, 29.</small>

<small>xxv. 30.</small>

(LXX τῆς παροικήσεως, whence τὴν οἴκησιν of Jos.) could not bear them because of their cattle."

[b] Gen. "mount Seir." Josephus (like the narrative in Genesis, compiled from two independent sources) ignores the previous mention of Saeira as the abode of Esau, i. 336.

[c] Bibl. Edom.   [d] Heb. *âdôm* = "red."

τὴν χώραν οὕτως προσηγόρευσεν· Ἕλληνες γὰρ αὐτὴν ἐπὶ τὸ σεμνότερον Ἰδουμαίαν ὠνόμασαν.

4 (2) Γίνεται δὲ καὶ πατὴρ παίδων πέντε τὸν ἀριθμόν, ὧν Ἰάους μὲν καὶ Ἰόλαμος καὶ Κόρηος ἐκ γυναικὸς μιᾶς Ἀλιβάμης τοὔνομα, τῶν δὲ λοιπῶν Ἀλιφάζης μὲν ἐξ Ἀδάσης, Ῥαουῆλος δὲ 5 ἐκ Βασαμάθης ὑπῆρξαν αὐτῷ γεγονότες. καὶ Ἡσαῦ μὲν οὗτοι παῖδες ἦσαν· Ἀλιφάζῃ δὲ γίνονται γνήσιοι πέντε Θημανὸς Ὅμερος Σόφους¹ Ἰόθαμος Καναζός· Ἀμαλῆκος γὰρ νόθος ἦν ἐκ παλλακῆς 6 αὐτῷ γεγονὼς Θαμνάης ὄνομα. οὗτοι κατῴκησαν τῆς Ἰδουμαίας τὴν Γοβολῖτιν λεγομένην καὶ τὴν ἀπὸ Ἀμαλήκου κληθεῖσαν Ἀμαληκῖτιν· πολλὴ γὰρ γενομένη ποτὲ ἡ Ἰδουμαία τό τε πάσης αὐτῆς ἀπέσωζεν ὄνομα καὶ τοῖς μέρεσι τὰς ἀπὸ τῶν οἰκητόρων προσηγορίας διεφύλαξεν.

7 (ii. 1) Ἰακώβῳ δὲ συνέβη παρελθεῖν εἰς εὐδαιμονίας μέγεθος οἷον οὐκ ἄλλῳ τινὶ ῥᾳδίως· πλούτῳ τε γὰρ ὑπερέβαλλε τοὺς ἐπιχωρίους καὶ παίδων ἀρεταῖς ζηλωτὸς καὶ περίβλεπτος ἦν· οὐδενὸς γὰρ ὅλως ὑστέρουν, ἀλλὰ καὶ πρὸς ἔργα χειρῶν καὶ πόνων ὑπομονὴν ἦσαν εὔψυχοι καὶ δεινοὶ συνιέναι. 8 τοσαύτην δ᾽ ἄρα τὸ θεῖον αὐτοῦ πρόνοιαν ἔσχε καὶ τῆς εὐδαιμονίας ἐπιμέλειαν, ὡς κἀκ τῶν λυπηρῶν αὐτῷ δοξάντων τὴν ὑπερβολὴν τῶν ἀγαθῶν παρασχεῖν καὶ ποιῆσαι τῆς ἀπ᾽ Αἰγύπτου τῶν ἡμετέρων

¹ Niese: Ὄφους (etc.) codd.

ᵃ Bibl. Jeush (Ἰεούς). ᵇ Bibl. Jalam (Ἰεγλόμ).
ᶜ Bibl. Korah (Κορέ).
ᵈ Bibl. Oholibamah (Αἰλιβαμά, the reading of one ms. of the lxx, approximates to the Josephan form).
ᵉ Bibl. Eliphaz. ᶠ Bibl. Adah (Ἀδά).
ᵍ Bibl. Reuel (Ῥαγουήλ). ʰ Bibl. Basemath.

called the country: the more dignified name of Idumaea it owes to the Greeks.

(2) He became the father of five children: of these, Iaûs,[a] Iolam(os)[b] and Korê(os)[c] came of one wife named Alibame[d]; as for the others, Aliphaz(es)[e] was born of Adasa[f] and Raûel(os)[g] of Basamathe.[h] Such were the sons of Esau. Aliphaz had five legitimate sons—Thêman(os),[i] Omer(os),[j] Sophous,[k] Jotham(os),[l] Kanaz(os)[m]: Amalek(os) was a bastard born to him by a concubine named Thamnae.[n] These occupied the region of Idumaea termed Gobolitis[o] and that called, after Amalek, Amalekitis; for Idumaea, formerly extensive, has kept that name for the whole country and in its several provinces preserved the names that were derived from their founders.

Esau's descendants. Gen. xxxvi. 1.

xxxvi. 11.

(ii. 1) To Jacob, on the other hand, it befell to reach a degree of prosperity hardly attained by any man. In riches he surpassed the inhabitants of the country and his children's virtues made him an object of envy and admiration; for there was no quality that they lacked: courageous for manual labour and endurance of toil they were withal quick of understanding. Moreover, the Deity showed such providential care for their father and his welfare, that He made even events that seemed to him deplorable become the source of the utmost felicity and brought about the departure of our ancestors from Egypt by means

Prosperity of Jacob. Gen. xxxvii. 1.

---

[i] Bibl. Teman (Θαιμάν). [j] Bibl. Omar.
[k] Bibl. Zepho (Σωφάρ).
[l] Bibl. Gatam ('Ιοθόμ the MS. of LXX mentioned above).
[m] Bibl. Kenaz (Κενέζ). [n] Bibl. Timna (Θαμνά).
[o] Cf. A. iii. 40 "The inhabitants of G. and Petra who are called Amalekites," and ix. 188 "Gabalites" (‖ Amalekites and Idumaeans); it is the Gebal mentioned beside Amalek in Ps. lxxxiii. 7, Arabic *Jibal*, in north Edom.

προγόνων ἀναχωρήσεως αἴτιον αὐτόν τε καὶ τοὺς ἐξ αὐτοῦ γεγονότας ὑπὸ τοιαύτης αἰτίας.

9 Ἰώσηπον ἐκ Ῥαχήλας πεπαιδοποιημένος Ἰάκωβος διά τε τὴν τοῦ σώματος εὐγένειαν καὶ διὰ ψυχῆς ἀρετήν, φρονήσει γὰρ διέφερε, τῶν ἄλλων 10 πλέον υἱῶν ἠγάπα. τούτῳ παρὰ τῶν ἀδελφῶν ἥ τε τοῦ πατρὸς στοργὴ φθόνον ἐκίνησε καὶ μῖσος ἥ τε ἐκ τῶν ὀνειράτων, ἃ θεασάμενος τῷ τε πατρὶ καὶ τούτοις ἐμήνυσεν, εὐδαιμονία καταγγελλομένη, ζηλοτυπούντων ἄρα τῶν ἀνθρώπων καὶ τὰς τῶν οἰκειοτάτων εὐπραγίας. αἱ δὲ ὄψεις, ἃς κατὰ τοὺς ὕπνους εἶδεν Ἰώσηπος, τοιαίδε ἦσαν.

11 (2) Ἐκπεμφθεὶς μετὰ τῶν ἀδελφῶν παρὰ τοῦ πατρὸς ἐπὶ συλλογῇ τῶν καρπῶν θέρους ἀκμάζοντος ὁρᾷ πολὺ τῶν κατὰ συνήθειαν ἐπιφοιτώντων κατὰ τοὺς ὕπνους ὀνειράτων διαφέρουσαν ὄψιν, ἣν περιεγερθεὶς τοῖς ἀδελφοῖς ὡς κρινοῦσιν αὐτῷ τὸ σημαινόμενον ἐξέθετο, λέγων ἰδεῖν ἐπὶ τῆς παρελθούσης νυκτὸς τὸ μὲν αὐτοῦ δράγμα τῶν πυρῶν ἠρεμεῖν ἐφ' οὗ κατέθηκε τόπου, τὰ δὲ ἐκείνων προστρέχοντα προσκυνεῖν αὐτὸ καθάπερ 12 οἱ δοῦλοι τοὺς δεσπότας. οἱ δὲ συνέντες ἰσχὺν αὐτῷ καὶ μέγεθος πραγμάτων τὴν ὄψιν προλέγουσαν καὶ κατ' αὐτῶν τὴν ἐξουσίαν ἐσομένην τῷ μὲν Ἰωσήπῳ τούτων οὐδὲν ὡς οὐ γνώριμον αὐτοῖς τὸ ὄναρ ὂν διεσάφησαν, ἀρὰς δ' ἐποιήσαντο μηδὲν εἰς τέλος αὐτῷ παρελθεῖν ὧν ὑπενόουν καὶ πρὸς αὐτὸν ἔτι μᾶλλον ἀπεχθῶς ἔχοντες διετέλουν.

13 (3) Τῷ δὲ παρ' αὐτῶν φθόνῳ προσφιλονικήσαν τὸ θεῖον δευτέραν ὄψιν ἐπιπέμπει τῷ Ἰωσήπῳ

---

[a] For Rachel's exceptional beauty *cf.* i. 288.

of Jacob and his offspring under circumstances that I proceed to relate.

Joseph, whom Jacob begat by Rachel, was beloved of his father above all his sons, alike for the beauty of person that he owed to his birth[a] and for virtuous qualities of soul, for he was endowed with exceptional understanding. This tender affection of his father aroused against him the envy and hatred of his brethren, as did also the dreams, predictive of good fortune, which he saw and related both to his father and to them: so jealous are men of the successes even of their nearest relatives. Now the visions which Joseph saw were on this wise.

Joseph the favourite son. Gen. xxxvii. 3.

(2) Having been sent out with his brethren by their father to gather in the crops at midsummer, he had a vision very different from the dreams that ordinarily visit us in sleep, which on awaking he recounted to his brethren for them to interpret to him its signification. He had seen, he said, during the past night his own wheat-sheaf standing motionless on the spot where he had placed it, while their sheaves ran up and bowed down to it like slaves before their masters. But they, understanding that the vision predicted for him power and majesty and a destined supremacy over themselves, revealed nothing of this to Joseph, as though the dream were unintelligible to them; they uttered prayers, however, that nothing of what they augured might[b] ever come to pass and continued to hate him yet the more.

His first dream. Gen. xxxvii. 5.

(3) But the Deity, counteracting their jealousy, sent Joseph a second vision far more marvellous than

His second dream. Gen. xxxvii. 9.

[b] Or "vowed (or "bound themselves under a curse") that nothing . . . should" etc.

JOSEPHUS

πολὺ τῆς προτέρας θαυμασιωτέραν· τὸν ἥλιον γὰρ
ἔδοξε τὴν σελήνην παραλαβόντα καὶ τοὺς λοιποὺς
ἀστέρας ἐπὶ τὴν γῆν κατελθεῖν καὶ προσκυνεῖν
14 αὐτόν. ταύτην τὴν ὄψιν τῷ πατρὶ μηδὲν παρὰ τῶν
ἀδελφῶν κακόηθες ὑφορώμενος καὶ τούτων παρα-
τυγχανόντων διεσάφησε, τί καὶ βούλεται σημαίνειν
15 φράσαι παρακαλῶν. ὁ δὲ ἥσθη[1] τῷ ὀνείρατι, τὴν
γὰρ πρόρρησιν αὐτοῦ τῇ διανοίᾳ συλλαβὼν καὶ
μετὰ σοφίας οὐκ ἀσκόπως εἰκάσας ἔχαιρεν ἐπὶ
μεγάλοις τοῖς σημαινομένοις, ἃ εὐδαιμονίαν τῷ
παιδὶ κατήγγελλε καὶ καιρὸν ἥξειν θεοῦ δόντος,
καθ' ὃν αὐτὸν ὑπό τε τῶν γονέων καὶ τῶν ἀδελφῶν
16 ἔσεσθαι τίμιον καὶ προσκυνήσεως ἄξιον, τὴν μὲν
σελήνην καὶ τὸν ἥλιον μητρὶ καὶ πατρί, τῆς μὲν
αὐξούσης ἅπαντα καὶ τρεφούσης τοῦ δ' ἐκτυποῦν-
τος καὶ τὴν ἄλλην ἰσχὺν ἐντιθέντος εἰκάζων, τοὺς
δ' ἀστέρας τοῖς ἀδελφοῖς· καὶ γὰρ τούτους ἕνδεκα
εἶναι καθάπερ καὶ τοὺς ἀστέρας ἀπό τε ἡλίου καὶ
σελήνης τὴν ἰσχὺν λαμβάνοντας.

17 (4) Καὶ ὁ μὲν Ἰάκωβος τοιαύτην οὐκ ἀσυνέτως
ἐποιήσατο τῆς ὄψεως τὴν κρίσιν, τοὺς δ' ἀδελφοὺς
τοῦ Ἰωσήπου σφόδρα ἐλύπησε τὰ προειρημένα καὶ
διετέθησαν ὡς ἐπ' ἀλλοτρίῳ τινὶ μέλλοντι τὰ
σημαινόμενα διὰ τῶν ὀνειράτων ἀγαθὰ ἥξειν,[2] ἀλλ'
οὐκ ἀδελφῷ καὶ ᾧ συναπολαύσειν αὐτοὺς[3] εἰκὸς ἦν,
κοινωνοὺς ὡς τῆς γενέσεως οὕτως καὶ τῆς εὐ-
18 δαιμονίας ἐσομένους· ἀνελεῖν τε ὡρμήκεσαν τὸ μει-

---

[1] Hudson, Dindorf: ἡσθεὶς codd.
[2] ἕξειν OP.
[3] Niese: ὧν συναπολαύσειν αὐτῷ codd.

---

[a] Gen. xxxvii. 10 f. says that "his father rebuked him" but "kept the saying in mind." Parallels from Midrash

JEWISH ANTIQUITIES, II. 13–18

the first; for he believed that he saw the sun, attended by the moon and the other stars, descend to earth and make obeisance to him. This vision he recounted to his father in the presence of his brethren, suspecting no malice on their part, and besought him to explain what it meant. Jacob was delighted with the dream *a* : grasping in his mind what it predicted and sagely and unerringly divining its import, he rejoiced at the great things that it betokened, which promised prosperity to his son and that, by the gift of God, a time would come when he would be honoured and held worthy of veneration by his parents and his brethren : the moon and the sun he conjectured to mean mother and father, the one giving increase and nourishment to all things, the other moulding their form and implanting in them their stores of strength : the stars were his brethren, who, like them, were eleven in number *b* and borrowed, like them, their strength from sun and moon.

(4) Thus shrewdly did Jacob interpret the vision. But Joseph's brethren were sorely aggrieved by these predictions and bore themselves as though it were some stranger who was to receive the benefits indicated by these dreams, and not a brother, whose fortunes it was but natural that they should share, becoming his partners, as in parentage, so likewise in prosperity ; and they were eager to slay the lad.

His brothers plot his death.

and Philo for the interpretation put upon these last words by Josephus are quoted by Weill.

b Cf. Gen. xxxvii. 9, " eleven stars " (without definite article). The absence of the article makes it improbable that there was any allusion to the signs of the Zodiac in the mind of the Biblical writer ; but such an allusion is implied by Josephus and expressly mentioned by Philo (*De Somniis*, ii. 16, quoted by Reinach).

ράκιον, καὶ ταύτην κυρώσαντες τὴν βουλήν, ἐπεὶ τὰ τῆς συγκομιδῆς αὐτοῖς πέρας εἶχεν, ἐπὶ Σικίμων τραπέντες, χώρα δ' ἐστὶν αὕτη βόσκειν ἀγαθὴ θρέμματα καὶ νομὰς ἐκτρέφειν,[1] αὐτόθι τῶν ποιμνίων ἐπεμελοῦντο μὴ προδηλώσαντες τῷ πατρὶ
19 τὴν ἐκεῖσε ἄφιξιν. ὁ δὲ ὑπὸ τῆς ἀγνοίας καὶ τοῦ μηδὲ ἀπὸ τῶν ποιμνίων πρὸς αὐτὸν ἀφικέσθαι τινὰ τὸν περὶ τῶν παίδων αὐτῷ τἀληθὲς σημαίνειν δυνάμενον, σκυθρωπότερον τὴν περὶ αὐτῶν διάνοιαν λαμβάνων καὶ περιδεὴς ὢν πέμπει τὸν Ἰώσηπον εἰς τὰ ποίμνια μαθησόμενον τὰ περὶ τῶν ἀδελφῶν καὶ τί πράττοιεν σημανοῦντα.

20 (iii. 1) Οἱ δὲ τὸν ἀδελφὸν ὡς εἶδον πρὸς αὐτοὺς ἀφιγμένον, ἤσθησαν μέν, ἀλλ' οὐχ ὡς ἐπ' οἰκείου παρουσίᾳ καὶ πατρὸς ἀπεσταλκότος, ἀλλ' ὡς ἐπ' ἐχθροῦ καὶ ταῖς χερσὶν αὐτῶν κατὰ θείαν βούλησιν παραδοθέντος, ἀναιρεῖν τε ἤδη καὶ μὴ τὸν ἐν
21 ποσὶν ὑπερβαλέσθαι καιρὸν ὡρμήκεσαν. οὕτως δ' αὐτοὺς Ῥούβηλος ὁρῶν ἔχοντας ὁ πρεσβύτατος αὐτῶν καὶ πρὸς τὴν πρᾶξιν ὠμονοηκότας ἐπειρᾶτο κατέχειν ὑποδεικνὺς τὸ μέγεθος τοῦ τολμήματος
22 καὶ τὸ ἐπ' αὐτῷ μύσος, ὡς πονηρὸν μὲν καὶ θεῷ καὶ ἀνθρώποις ἀνόσιον δοκοῦν καὶ τὸ μὴ συγγενοῦς ἀνθρώπου χειρουργῆσαι φόνον, πολὺ μέντοι μιαρώτερον τὸ σφαγὴν ἀδελφοῦ δράσαντας ὀφθῆναι, ᾧ πατήρ τε ἀναιρουμένῳ συναδικεῖται καὶ μήτηρ εἰς πένθος καὶ παιδὸς ἀποστέρησιν οὐ κατ'
23 ἀνθρώπινον γενομένην νόμον συγκατασπᾶται. τού-

---

[1] ἐκφέρειν RO.

[a] Amplification of Scripture.   [b] Shechem.
[c] In Gen. xxxvii. 13 Jacob opines that they are in Shechem.

JEWISH ANTIQUITIES, II. 18-23

Having determined upon this scheme, they, now that their harvest labours were ended,[a] betook themselves to Sikima,[b] a district excellent for the feeding of cattle and for its crop of pasturage, and there tended their flocks, having given their father no warning of their departure thither.[c] He, in his ignorance of their movements and because no one came to him from the flocks who could give him certain news of his sons, conceived the gloomiest forebodings concerning them and, full of anxiety, sent Joseph off to the flocks to learn what had befallen his brothers and to bring him word of their doings.

Gen. xxxvii. 12.

(iii. 1) They, on seeing that their brother had come to them, were delighted, not, however, at this visit from a relative and their father's envoy, but rather as if it had been an enemy, who by the will of God had been delivered into their hands; and they were keen to kill him outright and not to let slip this opportunity that offered itself. But Rubel,[d] the eldest of them, seeing them thus minded and unanimous for the deed, endeavoured to restrain them, representing to them the enormity and abominable nature of the crime. If it were a sin before God and a sacrilege in the eyes of men to perpetrate the murder of one having no kinship with them, far fouler would appear their deed in slaughtering a brother, whose destruction would entail grievous injury to a father and plunge a mother[e] into mourning, thus unnaturally bereft of a child. He besought

Rubel's attempt to save him. Gen. xxxvii. 18.

[d] Reuben (see i. 304 note). We have here the first of many rhetorical speeches, or pairs of speeches, with which the narrative is diversified.

[e] Rachel was already dead (i. 343); but Josephus had Biblical warrant for the inconsistency (Gen. xxxvii. 10, interpretation of the second dream).

τῶν οὖν αὐτῶν αἰδῶ λαβόντας καὶ τῷ λογισμῷ τί
καὶ πείσονται τεθνηκότος αὐτοῖς παιδὸς ἀγαθοῦ
καὶ νεωτάτου παραθεμένους ἀποσχέσθαι τοῦ τολμήματος παρεκάλει, καὶ τὸν θεὸν δείσαντας, ὃς
θεατὴς ἅμα καὶ μάρτυς ἤδη καὶ τῆς βουλῆς αὐτῶν
τῆς ἐπὶ τὸν ἀδελφὸν γεγενημένος[1] ἀποστάντας μὲν
τῆς πράξεως ἀγαπήσει[2] μετανοίᾳ καὶ τῷ σωφρονεῖν
24 εἴξαντας, προελθόντας δ' ἐπὶ τοὖργον οὐκ ἔστιν ἣν
οὐκ εἰσπράξεται τῆς ἀδελφοκτονίας δίκην μιάναντας
αὐτοῦ τὴν πανταχοῦ παροῦσαν πρόνοιαν καὶ μήτε
τῶν ἐπ' ἐρημίαις[3] πραττομένων ὑστεροῦσαν μήτε
τῶν κατὰ τὰς πόλεις· ὅπου γὰρ ἂν ἄνθρωπος ᾖ
25 χρὴ δοκεῖν ἐνταῦθα παρεῖναι καὶ θεόν. τό τε
συνειδὸς αὐτοὺς τὸ ἴδιον ἕξειν ἐχθρὸν ἐπὶ τοῖς τολ-
μηθεῖσιν ἔλεγεν, ὃ μήτε τοῖς ἀγαθὸν αὐτὸ ἔχουσι
μήτε τοιοῦτον ὁποῖον αὐτοῖς συνοικήσει[4] τὸν ἀδελ-
26 φὸν ἀνελοῦσιν ἔστιν ἀποδρᾶναι. προσετίθει δὲ καὶ
ταῦτα τοῖς προειρημένοις, ὡς ἀδελφὸν οὐδὲ
ἀδικήσαντα κτείνειν ὅσιον, καλὸν δὲ καὶ τὸ μὴ
μνησικακεῖν τοῖς οὕτω φίλοις ὑπὲρ ὧν ἁμαρτεῖν
ἔδοξαν. Ἰώσηπον δὲ οὐδὲ πονηρὸν εἰς αὐτοὺς
γεγενημένον διαφθεροῦσιν, ᾧ τὸ τῆς ἡλικίας
ἀσθενὲς ἔλεον μᾶλλον καὶ τὴν παρ' ἡμῶν ἐρανί-
27 ζεται κηδεμονίαν· ἥ τε αἰτία τῆς ἀναιρέσεως πολὺ
χείρω τὴν πρᾶξιν αὐτοῖς τίθησι, διὰ φθόνον τῶν
ἐσομένων ἀγαθῶν αὐτῷ τοῦ ζῆν ἐξαγαγεῖν δι-
εγνωκότων, ὧν τὸ ἴσον ἀπολαύσουσι κοινωνοῦντες
αὐτῷ τῆς μετουσίας οὐκ ἀλλοτρίων ὄντων ἀλλ'
28 οἰκείων· ἴδια γὰρ αὐτῶν ὑπολαμβάνειν, ὅσα ὁ θεὸς
Ἰωσήπῳ δώσει· προσήκειν οὖν[5] τὴν ὀργὴν καὶ διὰ

---

[1] Bekker: γεγενημένης codd. [2] O: ἀγαπήσειν rell.
[3] ἐρημίᾳ ROE. [4] συνοικήσειν L.

them, therefore, to have consideration for their
parents, to reflect what they too would suffer through
the death of a son so virtuous and so young, and to
desist from their mad intent; to fear God, who at
that very moment was watching and witnessing their
designs upon their brother and would be well content
should they renounce the deed, yielding to penitence
and sober reflexion; whereas, should they proceed
to accomplish it, there was no chastisement which
He would not inflict for their fratricide upon those
who had profaned His providence, present in every
place and from which nothing done, whether in
desert solitude or in city, could be hid; for wheresoever man was found, there too must God be deemed
to be present. Their own conscience too, he said,
would be their enemy in their enterprise—conscience
from which, whether pure or such as would haunt
them after the murder of their brother, it was impossible to flee. To these remonstrances he added
that even though a brother had injured one it were
impious to slay him, and gracious rather to bear no
malice against persons so dear, for their seeming
errors. But now it was Joseph, who had not so much
as done them wrong, whom they would destroy,
" he whose tender age should rather elicit all our
compassion and care." And then the motive for the
murder rendered the deed far worse, seeing that it
was through envy of his future fortune that they
had resolved to take his life, although they would
each have an equal share in that fortune and partake
of it in common with him, being not strangers to
him but relatives; for they might consider all that
God gave to Joseph as their own. They ought there-

---

[b] πρὸς ἐκεῖνον οὖν Niese with cod. O: προσεκίνουν R.

JOSEPHUS

τοῦτο [καλῶς ἔχειν][1] χαλεπωτέραν ἔσεσθαι νομίζειν, εἰ τὸν ὑπ' αὐτοῦ κεκριμένον τῶν ἐλπιζομένων ἀγαθῶν ἄξιον ἀποκτείναντες ἀφαιρήσονται τὸν θεὸν ᾧ ταῦτα χαρίσεται.

29 (2) Καὶ ὁ μὲν Ῥούβηλος ταῦτα λέγων καὶ πρὸς τούτοις ἔτι πλείω καὶ δεόμενος ἐπειρᾶτο τῆς ἀδελφοκτονίας αὐτοὺς ἀποτρέπειν, ἐπεὶ δὲ οὐδὲν μετριωτέρους ὑπὸ τῶν λόγων ἑώρα γεγενημένους, ἀλλὰ σπεύδοντας ἐπὶ τὴν ἀναίρεσιν, συνεβούλευε τὸ κακὸν αὐτοὺς ἐπιεικέστερον ποιῆσαι τῷ τρόπῳ 30 τῆς ἀναιρέσεως, [καὶ γὰρ][2] ἄμεινον μὲν ⟨ἂν⟩[3] οἷς παρῄνεσε τὸ πρῶτον πεπεῖσθαι λέγων αὐτούς, ἐπεὶ δ' ἐκράτησαν ὥστε ἀνελεῖν τὸν ἀδελφόν, οὐκ ἔσεσθαι σφόδρα κακοὺς οἷς νῦν παραινεῖ πεισθέντας· ἐν γὰρ τούτοις εἶναι καὶ τὸ ἔργον, ἐφ' ᾧ σπεύδουσιν, οὐ μέντοι τοιοῦτον, ἀλλ' ὡς ἐν ἀπόροις 31 κουφότερον. ἠξίου γὰρ αὐτοὺς αὐτόχειρας μὲν μὴ γενέσθαι τἀδελφοῦ, ῥίψαντας δὲ εἰς τὸν παρακείμενον λάκκον οὕτως ἀποθανεῖν ἐᾶσαι καὶ τό γε [μὴ][4] μιανθῆναι τὰς χεῖρας αὐτῶν κερδαίνειν. συναινεσάντων δὲ τούτοις τῶν νεανίσκων παραλαβὼν ὁ Ῥούβηλος τὸ μειράκιον καὶ καλῳδίου ἐκδήσας ἠρέμα καθίησιν[5] εἰς τὸν λάκκον· καὶ γὰρ ἱκανῶς ἄνυδρος ἦν. καὶ ὁ μὲν τοῦτο ποιήσας ἀπαλλάσσεται κατὰ ζήτησιν χωρίων πρὸς νομὰς ἐπιτηδείων.

32 (3) Ἰούδας δὲ καὶ αὐτὸς ὢν τῶν Ἰακώβου παίδων ἐμπόρους ἰδὼν Ἄραβας τοῦ Ἰσμαηλιτῶν γένους ἀρώματα καὶ Σύρα φορτία κομίζοντας

---

[1] Probably a gloss on προσήκειν. [2] Bracketed by Niese.
[3] ins. edd. with Exc. [4] om. RO (Lat.?).
[5] RO: καθίμησεν rell.

JEWISH ANTIQUITIES, II. 28–32

fore to expect His wrath on this ground also to be more severe, if, in killing him whom He had adjudged worthy of these coveted blessings, they should rob God of the recipient of His favours.

(2) With these and many more such appeals and entreaties did Rubel endeavour to deter them from fratricide; but, when he saw that his words failed to moderate their passion and that they were bent on the murder, he counselled them to mitigate the iniquity of it by the manner of destruction. The better course, he said, would have been to follow his first advice, but since their determination to slay their brother had prevailed, their wickedness would be less heinous if they listened to what he would now advise; this involved, to be sure, the deed on which they had set their heart, but in a different and, where it was a choice of evils, a less aggravated form. He begged them, in fact, not to raise their own hands against their brother, but to cast him into the adjacent pit and so leave him to die: it would at least profit them not to have soiled their hands in his blood. To this the young men consented, and Rubel took the lad and, tying him to a rope, gently let him down into the pit, which was as good as [a] dry. This done, he departed in search of grounds suitable for pasturage.[b]

His second speech. Cf. Gen. xxxvii. 21.

(3) But Judas, another of the sons of Jacob, having seen some Arab traders of the race of Ishmaelites conveying spices and Syrian merchandise from Gala-

Joseph sold to the Ishmaelites. Gen. xxxvii. 25.

---

[a] Gen. xxxvii. 24, "The pit was empty, there was no water in it." The adverb ἱκανῶς ("sufficiently") in Josephus may be due to misreading of κενός ("empty") found in some MSS. of the LXX.

[b] Amplification of Scripture.

181

JOSEPHUS

Αἰγυπτίοις ἐκ τῆς Γαλαδηνῆς μετὰ τὴν ἀναχώρησιν τὴν Ῥουβήλου τοῖς ἀδελφοῖς συνεβούλευεν ἀνιμήσασι τὸν Ἰώσηπον ἀπεμπολῆσαι τοῖς Ἄραψιν·
33 ἐκεῖνόν τε γὰρ ὅτι πορρωτάτω γενόμενον καὶ τεθνήξεσθαι παρὰ τοῖς ξένοις, αὐτούς τε τοῦ μιάσματος οὕτως ἀπαλλαγήσεσθαι. δόξαν οὖν τοῦτο, τοῖς ἐμπόροις ἀποδίδονται τὸν Ἰώσηπον ἀνελκύσαντες ἐκ τοῦ λάκκου μνῶν εἴκοσιν, ἑπτα-
34 καίδεκα ἐτῶν γεγονότα. Ῥουβῆλος δὲ νύκτωρ ἐπὶ τὸν λάκκον ἐλθὼν σῶσαι τοὺς ἀδελφοὺς λαθὼν τὸν Ἰώσηπον ἐγνώκει, καὶ ὡς ἀνακαλουμένῳ μὴ ὑπήκουσε, δείσας μὴ ἐφθάρκασιν αὐτὸν μετὰ τὴν ἀναχώρησιν αὐτοῦ κατεμέμφετο τοὺς ἀδελφούς. τῶν δὲ τὸ πραχθὲν αὐτῷ φρασάντων παύεται τοῦ πένθους Ῥουβῆλος.
35 (4) Ὡς δὲ ταῦτα περὶ τὸν Ἰώσηπον τοῖς ἀδελφοῖς ἐπέπρακτο, τί ποιήσαντες ἂν ἔξω τῆς ὑπονοίας παρὰ τῷ πατρὶ γενηθεῖεν ἐζήτουν, καὶ δὴ τὸν χιτωνίσκον, ὃν ἀφῖκτο μὲν πρὸς αὐτοὺς ὁ Ἰώσηπος ἐνδεδυμένος, περιηρήκεσαν δ᾿ αὐτὸν ὅτε καθίεσαν εἰς τὸν λάκκον, ἔδοξεν αὐτοῖς διασπαράξασιν αἵματι τράγου μολῦναι καὶ τῷ πατρὶ δεῖξαι φέροντας, ὡς ἂν ὑπὸ θηρίων αὐτῷ φανείη δι-
36 εφθαρμένος. καὶ τοῦτο ποιήσαντες ἧκον πρὸς τὸν πρεσβύτην ἤδη τῶν περὶ τὸν υἱὸν εἰς γνῶσιν ἀφιγμένων, ἔλεγον δὲ τὸν μὲν Ἰώσηπον οὔτ᾿ ἰδεῖν οὔθ᾿ ᾗ κέχρηται συμφορᾷ μεμαθηκέναι, χιτῶνα δὲ τοῦτον εὑρεῖν ἡμαγμένον καὶ λελακισμένον, ὅθεν αὐτοῖς ὑπόνοιαν εἶναι περιπεσόντα θηρίοις αὐτὸν

---

[a] Bibl. Gilead.

dene *a* for the Egyptian market, after Rubel's departure advised his brethren to draw up Joseph and sell him to these Arabs; for he, banished to remotest exile, would die among strangers, while they would thus be free from the guilt of his blood. To this then they agreed, and they drew Joseph out of the pit and sold him to the merchants for twenty minas,*b* he being then seventeen years of age.*c* As for Rubel, he returned by night *d* to the pit, having resolved to rescue Joseph without the knowledge of his brethren, and when his calls met with no response, fearing that they had put an end to him after his departure, he heaped abuse upon his brethren. But they told him what had passed and Rubel ceased from lamentation.

(4) When Joseph's brethren had thus disposed of him, they considered what they should do to elude their father's suspicion. There was that tunic, which Joseph was wearing when he came to them and of which they had stripped him when they let him down into the pit: this they decided to tear in pieces, befoul with goat's blood, and take and show to their father, giving him to believe that his son had been destroyed by wild beasts. Having so done they came to the old man, who had already received news of his son's misadventure,*d* and told him that they had neither seen Joseph nor discovered what accident had befallen him, but that they had found this tunic, bloodstained and mangled, from which they surmised that he had encountered wild beasts and perished,

<small>Jacob's grief.
Gen. xxxvii. 31.</small>

---

b Heb. "20 (sc. shekels) of silver," the price of a male slave between the ages of 5 and 20 (Lev. xxvii. 5): LXX "20 (pieces) of gold." Josephus, in naming the mina, like the LXX in another fashion, greatly magnifies the sum.

c Gen. xxxvii. 2.   *d* Amplification.

ἀπολωλέναι, εἴγε τοῦτον ἐνδεδυμένος οἴκοθεν
37 ἐστάλη. Ἰάκωβος δὲ ἐπὶ κουφοτέραις ὢν ἐλπίσιν ὡς ἠνδραποδισμένου δῆθεν αὐτῷ τοῦ παιδός, τοῦτον μὲν ἀφίησι τὸν λογισμόν, πίστιν δ' αὐτοῦ τῆς τελευτῆς ἐναργῆ τὸν χιτῶνα ὑπολαβών, καὶ γὰρ ἐγνώρισεν [ὡς]¹ ἐκεῖνον αὐτὸν ὂν ἐνδεδυμένον ἐκπέμποι πρὸς τοὺς ἀδελφούς, ὡς ἐπὶ νεκρῷ τὸ λοιπὸν οὕτω διέκειτο ἐπὶ τῷ μειρακίῳ πενθῶν.
38 καὶ ὡς ἑνὸς πατὴρ ὢν καὶ τῆς ἐξ ἄλλων παραμυθίας ἐστερημένος οὕτως ἦν παρὰ τῷ κακῷ, πρὶν ἢ τοῖς ἀδελφοῖς συμβαλεῖν εἰκάζων ὑπὸ θηρίων Ἰώσηπον ἀφανῆ γεγονέναι. ἐκαθέζετο δὲ σακκίον ἐξαιψάμενος καὶ τῇ λύπῃ βαρύς, ὡς μήθ' ὑπὸ παίδων παρηγορούντων αὐτὸν ῥᾴονα γενέσθαι μήτε κάμνοντα τοῖς πόνοις ἀπαγορεύειν.

39 (iv. 1) Ἰώσηπον δὲ πωλούμενον ὑπὸ τῶν ἐμπόρων ὠνησάμενος Πεντεφρής,² ἀνὴρ Αἰγύπτιος ἐπὶ τῶν Φαραώθου μαγείρων τοῦ βασιλέως, εἶχεν ἐν ἁπάσῃ τιμῇ καὶ παιδείαν τε τὴν ἐλευθέριον ἐπαίδευε καὶ διαίτῃ χρῆσθαι κρείττονι τῆς ἐπὶ δούλῳ τύχης ἐπέτρεπεν, ἐγχειρίζει τε τὴν τῶν κατὰ τὸν οἶκον
40 αὐτῷ πρόνοιαν. ὁ δὲ τούτων τε ἀπέλαυε καὶ τὴν ἀρετήν, ἥτις ἦν περὶ αὐτόν, οὐδ' ὑπὸ τῆς μεταβολῆς ἐγκατέλιπεν, ἀλλὰ διέδειξε τὸ φρόνημα κρατεῖν τῶν ἐν τῷ βίῳ δυσκόλων δυνάμενον, οἷς ἂν παρῇ γνησίως καὶ μὴ πρὸς τὰς εὐπραγίας τὰς κατὰ καιρὸν μόνον ἡρμοσμένον.
41 (2) Τῆς γὰρ τοῦ δεσπότου γυναικὸς διά τε τὴν

¹ om. RO.
² v.l. Πετεφρής (and so below).

---

[a] Heb. Potiphar: the mss. of Josephus and of the LXX

JEWISH ANTIQUITIES, II. 36-41

at least if that was the garment he was wearing when dispatched from home. Jacob, who was cherishing the more tolerable hope that his boy had been kidnapped, now abandoned that thought and, regarding the tunic as manifest evidence of his death—for he recognized it as that which he wore when he sent him off to his brethren—thenceforward acted even as though he were dead, in his mourning for the lad. And such was his affliction that he appeared to be the father of but one son and deprived of all consolation from the rest, imagining that Joseph, or ever he joined his brethren, had been annihilated by wild beasts. There he sat with sackcloth about him and heavy with grief—grief such that neither his sons could comfort and bring him ease, nor he himself tire and weary of his woes.

(iv. 1) But Joseph had been sold by the merchants and bought by Pentephres,[a] an Egyptian and chief of the cooks[b] of king Pharaothes; this man held him in the highest esteem, gave him a liberal education,[c] accorded him better fare than falls to the lot of a slave, and committed the charge of his household into his hands. Yet, while enjoying these privileges, he even under this change of fortune abandoned not that virtue that enveloped him, but displayed how a noble spirit can surmount the trials of life, where it is genuine and does not simply accommodate itself to passing prosperity.

(2) For his master's wife, by reason both of his

Joseph and Potiphar (Pentephres). Gen. xxxix. 1.

Joseph and Potiphar's wife. Gen. xxxix. 6.

vary between Petephres and Pentephres, a slightly more Hellenized form.

[b] So LXX ἀρχιμάγειρος: the Hebrew word (literally "slaughterers") means "apparently the royal cooks or butchers, who had come to be the bodyguard" (Skinner).

[c] Amplification.

185

εὐμορφίαν καὶ τὴν περὶ τὰς πράξεις αὐτοῦ δεξιότητα
ἐρωτικῶς διατεθείσης καὶ νομιζούσης, εἰ ποιήσειεν
αὐτῷ τοῦτο φανερόν, ῥᾳδίως πείσειν αὐτὸν εἰς
ὁμιλίαν ἐλθεῖν εὐτύχημα ἡγησάμενον τὸ τὴν
42 δέσποιναν αὐτοῦ δεηθῆναι, καὶ πρὸς τὸ σχῆμα τῆς
τότε δουλείας ἀλλ' οὐ πρὸς τὸν τρόπον ἀφορώσης
τὸν καὶ παρὰ τὴν μεταβολὴν παραμένοντα, τήν
τε ἐπιθυμίαν αὐτῷ ποιησάσης καταφανῆ καὶ
λόγους προσφερούσης περὶ μίξεως, παρέπεμπε
τὴν ἀξίωσιν οὐ κρίνας ὅσιον εἶναι τοιαύτην αὐτῇ
διδόναι χάριν, ἐν ᾗ τοῦ πριαμένου καὶ τοσαύτης
ἠξιωκότος τιμῆς ἀδικίαν συνέβαινεν εἶναι καὶ
43 ὕβριν, ἀλλὰ κρατεῖν τε τοῦ πάθους κἀκείνην
παρεκάλει τὴν ἀπόγνωσιν τοῦ τεύξεσθαι τῆς
ἐπιθυμίας προβαλλόμενος, σταλήσεσθαι γὰρ [τε]
αὐτῇ τοῦτο μὴ παρούσης ἐλπίδος, αὐτός τε πάντα
μᾶλλον ὑπομενεῖν[1] ἔλεγεν ἢ πρὸς τοῦτο κατα-
πειθὴς ἔσεσθαι· καὶ γὰρ εἰ τῇ δεσποίνῃ δοῦλον
ὄντα δεῖ ποιεῖν μηδὲν ἐναντίον, ἡ πρὸς τὰ τοιαῦτα
τῶν προσταγμάτων ἀντιλογία πολλὴν ἂν ἔχοι
44 παραίτησιν. τῆς δ' ἔτι μᾶλλον ἐπέτεινε τὸν
ἔρωτα τὸ μὴ προσδοκώσῃ τὸν Ἰώσηπον ἀντισχεῖν
καὶ δεινῶς ὑπὸ τοῦ κακοῦ πολιορκουμένῃ δευτέρᾳ
πάλιν πείρᾳ προεθυμεῖτο κατεργάσασθαι.

45 (3) Δημοτελοῦς οὖν ἑορτῆς ἐπιστάσης, καθ' ἣν
εἰς τὴν πανήγυριν καὶ γυναιξὶ φοιτᾶν νόμιμον ἦν,
σκήπτεται νόσον πρὸς τὸν ἄνδρα θηρωμένη μόνωσιν
καὶ σχολὴν εἰς τὸ δεηθῆναι τοῦ Ἰωσήπου, καὶ
γενομένης αὐτῇ ταύτης λιπαρεστέρους ἔτι τῶν

[1] Bekker: ὑπομένειν codd.

comely appearance^a and his dexterity in affairs, became enamoured of him. She thought that if she disclosed this passion to him, she would easily persuade him to have intercourse with her, since he would deem it a stroke of fortune to be solicited by his mistress: she was looking but at the outward guise of his present servitude, but not at his character, which notwithstanding his change of fortune stood firm. So, when she declared her passion and proposed an illicit union,^b Joseph scouted her overtures, deeming it impious to afford her such gratification as would be an iniquity and outrage to the master who had bought him and deigned to honour him so highly. Nay, he besought her to govern her passions, representing the hopelessness of satisfying her lust, which would shrink and die when she saw no prospect of gratifying it, while for his part, he would endure anything rather than be obedient to this behest; for although as a slave he ought never to defy his mistress, contradiction to orders such as these would have abundant excuse. But the woman's love was only the more intensified by this unexpected opposition of Joseph, and being sorely beset by her wicked passion, she determined by a renewed assault to subdue him.

(3) So, on the approach of a public festival,^c when it was customary for women also to join the general assembly, she made illness an excuse to her husband, in quest of solitude and leisure to solicit Joseph; and, having obtained her opportunity, she addressed

[Her renewed solicitation of Joseph.]

---

^a εὐμορφία: Philo, *De Jos.* 9 § 40, uses the same word.

^b Phrase taken from Philo, *loc. cit.* (περὶ μίξεως λόγους προσέφερεν).

^c A legendary addition, for which there are Rabbinical parallels (quoted by Weill), invented to explain why "there was none of the men of the house within" (Gen. xxxix. 11).

46 πρώτων αὐτῷ προσηνέγκατο λόγους, ὡς καλῶς
μὲν εἶχεν αὐτὸν μετὰ τὴν ἐξ ἀρχῆς δέησιν εἶξαι
καὶ μηδὲν ἀντειρηκέναι κατά τε τὴν τῆς παρα-
καλούσης ἐντροπὴν καὶ τὴν τοῦ πάθους ὑπερβολήν,
ὑφ᾽ οὗ βιασθείη δέσποινα οὖσα τοῦ κατ᾽ αὐτὴν[1]
ἀξιώματος ταπεινοτέρα γενέσθαι, φρονήσει δὲ[2]
καὶ νῦν ἄμεινον ἐνδοὺς καὶ τὸ ἐπὶ τοῖς παρελθοῦσιν
47 ἄγνωμον διορθώσεται· εἴτε γὰρ δευτέραν δέησιν
ἐξεδέχετο, ταύτην γεγονέναι καὶ μετὰ πλείονος
σπουδῆς· νόσον τε γὰρ προφασίσασθαι καὶ τῆς
ἑορτῆς καὶ τῆς πανηγύρεως τὴν πρὸς αὐτὸν ὁμιλίαν
προτιμῆσαι· εἴτε τοῖς πρώτοις ὑπὸ ἀπιστίας
ἀντέκρουσε λογισμοῖς, τοῦ μηδεμίαν κακουργίαν
εἶναι κρίνειν σύμβολον τὸ τοῖς αὐτοῖς ἐπιμένειν.
48 προσδοκᾶν τε τῶν παρόντων ἀγαθῶν ὄνησιν, ὧν
ἤδη μετέχειν,[3] προσθέμενον αὐτῆς τῷ ἔρωτι καὶ
μειζόνων ἀπόλαυσιν[4] ὑπήκοον γενόμενον, ἄμυναν
δὲ καὶ μῖσος παρ᾽ αὐτῆς ἀποστραφέντα τὴν
ἀξίωσιν καὶ τοῦ χαρίζεσθαι τῇ δεσποίνῃ τὴν τῆς
49 σωφροσύνης δόκησιν ἐπίπροσθε θέμενον. οὐ γὰρ
αὐτὸν τοῦτο ὠφελήσειν τραπείσης εἰς κατηγορίαν
αὐτοῦ καὶ καταψευσαμένης πεῖραν ἐπὶ τἀνδρί,
προσέξειν δὲ μᾶλλον τοῖς αὐτῆς λόγοις Πεντεφρῆ
ἢ τοῖς ἐκείνου, κἂν ὅτι μάλιστα ἀπὸ τῆς ἀληθείας
φέρωνται.
50 (4) Ταῦτα λεγούσης τῆς γυναικὸς καὶ δακρυούσης
οὔτε οἶκτος αὐτὸν μὴ σωφρονεῖν ἔπεισεν οὔτ᾽
ἠνάγκασε φόβος, ἀλλὰ ταῖς δεήσεσιν ἀντέσχε καὶ
ταῖς ἀπειλαῖς οὐκ ἐνέδωκε, καὶ[5] παθεῖν ἀδίκως καὶ

[1] κατὰ ταύτην ROE.   [2] Dindorf with Lat.: τε codd.

him even more importunately than before. It had been well for him, she said, to have yielded to her first request and in no wise gainsaid her, both out of respect for his petitioner and because of the excess of the passion which constrained a mistress to abase herself beneath her dignity; but even now by a better surrender to discretion he might repair his folly in the past. Were he awaiting a second invitation, here it was, made with yet greater ardour, for she had feigned sickness and preferred to the feast and the assembly an interview with him; was it from mistrust that he had repulsed her first overtures, he should take it as a token of her lack of guile that she still persisted in them. Again, he might look not only for the enjoyment of those present privileges that were already his, by responding to her love, but for benefits yet greater, would he only submit; but for vengeance and hatred on her part, should he reject her suit and set more store on a reputation for chastity than on gratifying his mistress. For that would serve him nought, were she to turn his accuser and charge him falsely to her husband of an assault upon her; and Pentephres would listen to her words, however wide of the truth, rather than to his.[a]

(4) So spake the woman, weeping withal; yet neither pity could induce him to unchastity nor fear compel: he resisted her entreaties and yielded not to her threats, choosing to suffer unjustly and to

His chaste reply.

[a] Or perhaps "rather than to his, however truthful they might be"; so previous translators. The phrase "to be carried away (or "proceed") from the truth" is ambiguous.

³ μετέχει Niese.   ⁴ Niese: ἀπολαύσειν (-λαύειν) codd.
⁵ O: δείσας (δείσας καὶ) rell.

ὑπομένειν[1] τι τῶν χαλεπωτέρων εἵλετο μᾶλλον
ἢ τῶν παρόντων ἀπολαύειν χαρισάμενος ἐφ' οἷς
51 ἂν αὐτῷ συνειδῇ δικαίως ἀπολουμένῳ. γάμου τε
αὐτὴν ὑπεμίμνησκε καὶ τῆς πρὸς τὸν ἄνδρα συμ-
βιώσεως καὶ τούτοις τὸ πλέον νέμειν ἢ προσκαίρῳ
τῆς ἐπιθυμίας ἡδονῇ παρεκάλει, τῆς μὲν καὶ μετάνοιαν ἑξούσης αὖθις ἐπ' ὀδύνῃ γενησομένης οὐκ
ἐπὶ διορθώσει τῶν ἡμαρτημένων καὶ φόβον τοῦ
μὴ κατάφωρον γενέσθαι [καὶ[2] χάριν τοῦ λαθεῖν
52 ἀγνοουμένου τοῦ κακοῦ], τῆς δὲ πρὸς τὸν ἄνδρα
κοινωνίας ἀπόλαυσιν ἐχούσης ἀκίνδυνον καὶ προσέτι πολλὴν τὴν ἀπὸ τοῦ συνειδότος καὶ πρὸς τὸν
θεὸν παρρησίαν καὶ πρὸς ἀνθρώπους· καὶ ὡς αὐτοῦ
δεσπόσει μᾶλλον μείνασα καθαρὰ καὶ δεσποίνης
ἐξουσίᾳ χρήσεται πρὸς αὐτόν, ἀλλ' οὐ συνεξ-
αμαρτάνοντος αἰδοῖ· πολὺ δὲ κρεῖττον εἶναι θαρρεῖν
ἐπὶ γινωσκομένοις τοῖς εὖ βεβιωμένοις ἢ ἐπὶ
λανθανούσῃ κακοπραγίᾳ.
53 (5) Ταῦτα λέγων καὶ ἔτι πλείω τούτοις ὅμοια
τὴν τῆς γυναικὸς ὁρμὴν ἐπέχειν ἐπειρᾶτο καὶ τὸ
πάθος αὐτῆς εἰς λογισμὸν ἐπιστρέφειν, ἡ δὲ
βιαιότερον ἐχρῆτο τῇ σπουδῇ καὶ ἐπιβαλοῦσα τὰς
χεῖρας ἀναγκάζειν ἀπογνοῦσα τοῦ πείθειν ἤθελεν.
54 ὡς δ' ἐξέφυγεν ὑπὸ ὀργῆς ὁ Ἰώσηπος προσκατα-
λιπὼν καὶ τὸ ἱμάτιον, κατεχούσης καὶ γὰρ αὐτὸν
ἐκ τούτου μεθεὶς ἐξεπήδησε τοῦ δωματίου, περιδεὴς γενομένη, μὴ κατείπῃ πρὸς τὸν ἄνδρα αὐτῆς,
καὶ τῆς ὕβρεως περιαλγῶς ἔχουσα φθάσαι κατα-
ψεύσασθαι πρὸς τὸν Πεντεφρὴν ἔγνω τοῦ Ἰωσήπου,
καὶ τούτῳ τῷ τρόπῳ τιμωρῆσαι μὲν αὐτῇ δεινῶς

[1] κἂν (sic RO) ὑπομένῃ Niese.   [2] v.l. ἀλλά.

endure even the severest penalty, rather than take advantage of the moment[a] by an indulgence for which he was conscious that he would justly deserve to die. He recalled to her mind her marriage and wedded life with her husband and besought her to pay more regard to these than to the transient pleasure of lust: that would bring subsequent remorse, which would make her suffer for her sins without correcting them, and also fear of detection,[b] whereas union with her husband afforded enjoyment without danger, and moreover that perfect confidence before God and man arising from a good conscience. He added that by remaining chaste she would have more command over him and exercise authority as his mistress, as she could not with the guilty feeling of being his partner in sin; and it was far better to put faith in a known reputation for a well-spent life than in the secrecy of crime.

(5) By these words and yet more to like effect he endeavoured to curb the woman's impulse and to turn her passion into the path of reason; but she displayed only a more violent ardour and, flinging her arms about him, despairing of persuasion she would have had resort to force. Joseph fled from her in indignation, leaving with her his cloak, by which she had held him and which he abandoned when he leapt from the chamber; then, terrified lest he should inform her husband, and smarting under this affront, she resolved to forestall Joseph by falsely accusing him to Pentephres: this method of avenging

The woman's vengeance. Gen. xxxix. 12.

---

[a] *Cf.* Heb. xi. 25, " choosing rather to be evil entreated . . . than to enjoy the pleasures of sin for a season " (of Moses).
[b] I follow Reinach in rejecting the obscure words in brackets as a gloss.

ὑπερηφανημένῃ, προλαβεῖν δὲ τὴν διαβολὴν σοφὸν
55 ἅμα καὶ γυναικεῖον ἡγήσατο. καὶ καθῆστο μὲν
κατηφὴς καὶ συγκεχυμένη τὴν ἐπὶ τῷ διαμαρτεῖν
τῆς ἐπιθυμίας λύπην ὡς ἐπὶ πείρᾳ διαφθορᾶς
πλασαμένη μετ' ὀργῆς, ἐλθόντι δὲ τἀνδρὶ καὶ πρὸς
τὴν ὄψιν ταραχθέντι καὶ πυνθανομένῳ τὴν αἰτίαν
τῆς κατηγορίας τῆς Ἰωσήπου κατήρξατο καὶ
" τεθναίης," εἶπεν, " ἄνερ, ἢ πονηρὸν δοῦλον
56 κοίτην μιᾶναι τὴν σὴν ἐθελήσαντα κόλασον, ὃς
οὔθ' οἷος ὢν εἰς τὸν ἡμέτερον οἶκον ἀφῖκται
μνησθεὶς ἐσωφρόνησεν οὔθ' ὧν ἐκ τῆς σῆς χρηστότητος ἔτυχεν, ἀλλ' ἀχάριστος ὢν ἄν, εἰ μὴ
πάντα παρεῖχεν αὐτὸν ἀγαθὸν εἰς ἡμᾶς, ἐπεβούλευσεν ὑβρίσαι γάμον τὸν σὸν καὶ ταῦτ' ἐν ἑορτῇ
τὴν σὴν ἀπουσίαν παραφυλάξας· ὡς ὅσα καὶ
μέτριος ἐδόκει πρότερον διὰ τὸν ἐκ σοῦ φόβον
57 ἠρέμει καὶ οὐχὶ φύσει χρηστὸς ἦν. τοιοῦτον δ'
ἄρα τὸ παρ' ἀξίαν αὐτὸν καὶ παρ' ἐλπίδας εἰς
τιμὴν παρελθεῖν ἐποίησεν, ὡς δέον ᾧ τὴν τῆς
κτήσεως τῆς σῆς πίστιν καὶ τὴν οἰκονομίαν λαβεῖν
ἐξεγένετο καὶ τῶν πρεσβυτέρων οἰκετῶν προ-
τιμηθῆναι τούτῳ καὶ τῆς σῆς ψαύειν γυναικός."
58 παυσαμένη δὲ τῶν λόγων ἐπεδείκνυεν αὐτῷ τὸ
ἱμάτιον, ὡς ὅτ' ἐπεχείρει βιάσασθαι καταλιπόντος
αὐτό. Πεντεφρῆς δὲ μήτε δακρυούσῃ τῇ γυναικὶ
μήθ' οἷς ἔλεγε καὶ εἶδεν[1] ἀπιστεῖν ἔχων, τῷ τε
πρὸς αὐτὴν ἔρωτι πλέον νέμων, ἐπὶ μὲν τὴν τῆς
59 ἀληθείας ἐξέτασιν οὐκ ἐτρέπετο, δοὺς δὲ σωφρονεῖν
τῇ γυναικὶ πονηρὸν δ' εἶναι κατακρίνας τὸν
Ἰώσηπον τὸν μὲν εἰς τὴν τῶν κακούργων εἱρκτὴν

---

[1] + ipse Lat.: αὐτὸς has perhaps dropped out.

herself for so grievous a slight and of accusing him in advance seemed to her alike wise and womanly. So she sat with downcast eyes and in confusion, feigning in her wrath to attribute her grief at the disappointment of her lust to an attempt at violation; and when her husband arrived and, distressed at her appearance, asked her for the reason, she began her accusation of Joseph. "Mayest thou die, my husband," said she, "or else chastise this wicked slave who would fain have defiled thy bed. For neither the memory of what he was when he entered our house nor of the benefits which he has received of thy bounty has sufficed to chasten him; no, this fellow, who would have been ungrateful had he in any wise failed to show exemplary conduct towards us, has designed to abuse thy wedlock, and that on a festival, watching for thy absence. So, for all that seeming modesty in the past, it was fear of thee that restrained him and no virtuous disposition. To such a pass, it seems, has his unmerited and unlooked for promotion brought him, as to suppose that one who had succeeded in obtaining the charge and administration of thy estate and in being preferred to senior menials, had the right to lay hands even on thy wife." Having ceased speaking, she showed him the cloak, pretending that he had left it when he essayed to violate her. To Pentephres his wife's tears, her story, and what he saw himself left no room for incredulity, and unduly influenced by his love for her he was not careful to investigate the truth. Giving his wife the credit of innocence and condemning Joseph as a scoundrel, he cast him into

ἐνέβαλεν, ἐπὶ δὲ τῇ γυναικὶ καὶ μᾶλλον ἐφρόνει κοσμιότητα καὶ σωφροσύνην αὐτῇ μαρτυρῶν.

60 (v. 1) Ἰώσηπος μὲν οὖν πάντ' ἐπὶ τῷ θεῷ ποιησάμενος τὰ περὶ αὐτὸν οὐδ' εἰς ἀπολογίαν οὐδ' ἐπ' ἀκριβῆ τῶν γεγονότων δήλωσιν ἐτράπη, τὰ δεσμὰ δὲ καὶ τὴν ἀνάγκην σιγῶν ὑπῆλθεν, ἀμείνονα ἔσεσθαι τῶν δεδεκότων θαρρῶν τὸν τὴν αἰτίαν τῆς συμφορᾶς καὶ τὴν ἀλήθειαν εἰδότα θεόν,

61 οὗ πεῖραν τῆς προνοίας εὐθὺς ἐλάμβανεν· ὁ γὰρ δεσμοφύλαξ τήν τε ἐπιμέλειαν καὶ τὴν πίστιν αὐτοῦ κατανοήσας ἐν οἷς τάξειεν αὐτὸν καὶ τὸ ἀξίωμα τῆς μορφῆς ὑπανίει τε τῶν δεσμῶν καὶ τὸ δεινὸν ἐλαφρότερον αὐτῷ καὶ κοῦφον ἐποίει, διαίτῃ δὲ χρῆσθαι κρείττονι δεσμωτῶν ἐπέτρεπε.

62 τῶν δὲ ἐν τοῖς αὐτοῖς ὄντων εἴποτε παύσαιντο τῆς περὶ τὰ ἔργα ταλαιπωρίας εἰς ὁμιλίαν, οἷα φιλεῖ κατὰ κοινωνίαν τῆς ὁμοίας συμφορᾶς, τρεπομένων καὶ παρ' ἀλλήλων τὰς αἰτίας ἐφ' αἷς κατακριθεῖεν

63 ἀναπυνθανομένων, οἰνοχόος τοῦ βασιλέως καὶ σφόδρα δ' αὐτῷ τιμώμενος κατ' ὀργὴν δεδεμένος καὶ συνδιαφέρων τῷ Ἰωσήπῳ τὰς πέδας συνηθέστερος αὐτῷ μᾶλλον ἐγένετο καί, συνέσει γὰρ ἐδόκει αὐτὸν προύχειν, ὄναρ ἰδὼν ἐξέθετο παρακαλῶν δηλοῦν εἴ τι[1] σημαίνει, μεμφόμενος ὅτι τοῖς ἐκ τοῦ βασιλέως κακοῖς ἔτι τὸ θεῖον αὐτῷ καὶ τὰς ἐκ τῶν ὀνειράτων φροντίδας προστίθησιν.

64 (2) Ἔλεγε δ' οὖν ἰδεῖν κατὰ τοὺς ὕπνους τριῶν κλημάτων πεφυκυίας ἀμπέλου βότρυς ἐξ ἑκάστου

[1] εἴ τι] ὅ τι O (Lat. quid).

[a] The same phrase κοσμιότητα καὶ σωφροσύνην is used of Joseph in Philo, *De Jos.* 9 § 40.
[b] Amplification; *cf.* the *Roman* fashion of coupling a

the malefactors' prison, while of his wife he was yet prouder than before, testifying to her decorum and sobriety.[a]

(v. 1) Joseph, on his side, committing his cause entirely to God, sought neither to defend himself nor yet to render a strict account of what had passed, but silently underwent his bonds and confinement, confident that God, who knew the cause of his calamity and the truth, would prove stronger than those who had bound him; and of His providence he had proof forthwith. For the keeper of the prison, noting his diligence and fidelity in the tasks committed to him, along with the dignity of his features, gave him some relief from his chains and rendered his cruel fate lighter and more tolerable, allowing him moreover rations superior to prisoners' fare. Now his fellow-prisoners, during any cessation of their hard labours, used, as is the way with partners in misfortune, to fall into conversation and ask each other the reasons for their several condemnations. Among them was the king's cupbearer, once held by him in high esteem and then in a fit of anger imprisoned: this man, wearing the same fetters as Joseph,[b] became the more intimately acquainted with him, and, forming a high opinion of his sagacity, recounted to him a dream which he had seen and asked him to explain whatever meaning it had, complaining that to the injuries inflicted by the king the Deity added this further burden of vexatious dreams.

Joseph in prison.
Gen. xxxix. 21.

(2) He said that he had seen in his sleep a full-grown vine with three branches, from each of which

The butler's dream.
Gen. xl. 9

prisoner to his guard, *Δ.* xviii. 196 τὸν συνδεδεμένον αὐτῷ (Agrippa) στρατιώτην.

ἀποκρέμασθαι μεγάλους ἤδη καὶ πρὸς τρύγητον
ὡραίους, καὶ τούτους αὐτὸς ἀποθλίβειν εἰς φιάλην
ὑπέχοντος τοῦ βασιλέως διηθήσας τε τὸ γλεῦκος
δοῦναι τῷ βασιλεῖ πιεῖν, κἀκεῖνον δέξασθαι κεχαρι-
65 σμένως. τὸ μὲν οὖν ἑωραμένον ἐδήλου τοιοῦτον
ὄν, ἠξίου δ' εἴ τι μεμοίραται συνέσεως φράζειν
αὐτῷ τὴν πρόρρησιν τῆς ὄψεως. ὁ δὲ θαρρεῖν τε
παρεκάλει καὶ προσδοκᾶν ἐν τρισὶν ἡμέραις ἀπο-
λυθήσεσθαι τῶν δεσμῶν, τοῦ βασιλέως ποθήσαντος
αὐτοῦ τὴν διακονίαν καὶ πάλιν εἰς ταύτην αὐτὸν
66 ἐπανάξοντος· καρπὸν γὰρ ἐσήμαινεν ἀμπέλινον ἐπ'
ἀγαθῷ τὸν θεὸν ἀνθρώποις παρασχεῖν, ὃς αὐτῷ
τε ἐκείνῳ σπένδεται καὶ πίστιν ἀνθρώποις καὶ
φιλίαν ὁμηρεύει, διαλύων μὲν ἔχθρας τὰ πάθη δὲ
καὶ τὰς λύπας ἐξαιρῶν τοῖς προσφερομένοις αὐτὸν
67 καὶ πρὸς ἡδονὴν ὑποφέρων. " τοῦτον οὖν φῂς ἐκ
τριῶν ἀποθλιβέντα βοτρύων χερσὶ ταῖς σαῖς
προσέσθαι τὸν βασιλέα· καλὴν τοίνυν ἴσθι σοι τὴν
ὄψιν γεγενημένην καὶ προμηνύουσαν ἄφεσιν τῆς
παρούσης ἀνάγκης ἐν τοσαύταις ἡμέραις, ἐξ ὅσων
κλημάτων τὸν καρπὸν ἐτρύγησας κατὰ τοὺς
68 ὕπνους. μέμνησο μέντοι τούτων πειραθεὶς τοῦ
προκαταγγείλαντός σοι τὰ ἀγαθά, καὶ γενόμενος
ἐν ἐξουσίᾳ μὴ περιίδῃς ἡμᾶς ἐν οἷς καταλείψεις
πρὸς ἃ δεδηλώκαμεν ἀπερχόμενος· οὐδὲν γὰρ
69 ἐξαμαρτόντες ἐν δεσμοῖς γεγόναμεν, ἀλλ' ἀρετῆς
ἕνεκα καὶ σωφροσύνης τὰ τῶν κακούργων ὑπομένειν κατεκρίθημεν, οὐδέ γε μετ' οἰκείας ἡδονῆς
τὸν ταῦθ' ἡμᾶς ἐργασάμενον ὑβρίσαι θελήσαντες."
τῷ μὲν οὖν οἰνοχόῳ χαίρειν κατὰ τὸ εἰκὸς ἀκούσαντι τοιαύτης τῆς τοῦ ὀνείρατος ἐξηγήσεως

hung clusters of grapes, already large and ripe for the vintage, and that he had pressed these into a cup held out by the king, and having let the must run through he had given it to the king to drink and he had received it graciously. Such, he declared, was what he saw, and he desired Joseph, if he was gifted with any understanding, to tell him what the vision portended. And Joseph bade him be of good cheer and to expect within three days to be released from his bonds, since the king needed his service and would recall him to his office. For he explained how the fruit of the vine was given by God to men as a blessing, seeing that it is offered in libation to Himself and serves men as a pledge of fidelity and friendship, terminating feuds, banishing the sufferings and sorrows of those who take it to their lips, and wafting them down into delight.[a] "This juice, thou sayest, pressed from three clusters by thy hands, was accepted by the king. Well, it is a fine vision, be sure, that thou hast had, and one betokening release from thy present confinement within as many days as were the branches from which thou gatheredst the fruit in thy sleep. Howbeit, when these things befall thee, remember him who predicted thy felicity, and, once at liberty, do not neglect me in the state wherein thou wilt leave me when thou departest to that lot which I have foretold. For it was no crime that brought me into these bonds: nay, it was for virtue's sake and for sobriety that I was condemned to undergo a malefactor's fate, and because even the lure of my own pleasure would not induce me to dishonour him who has thus treated me." The butler, as may well be imagined, could but rejoice to hear such an inter-

[a] *Cf.* the praise of wine in 1 Esdras iii. 18 ff.

ὑπῆρχε καὶ περιμένειν τῶν δεδηλωμένων τὴν τελευτήν.

70 (3) Δοῦλος δέ τις ἐπὶ τῶν σιτοποιῶν τεταγμένος τοῦ βασιλέως συνδεδεμένος τῷ οἰνοχόῳ, τοιαύτην ποιησαμένου τοῦ Ἰωσήπου περὶ τῆς ὄψεως ἐκείνῳ τὴν ἀπόφασιν, εὔελπις ὤν, καὶ γὰρ καὐτὸς ὄναρ ἦν τεθεαμένος, ἠξίωσε τὸν Ἰώσηπον φράσαι, τί κἀκείνῳ δηλοῦν βούλεται τὰ διὰ τῆς παρελθούσης 71 νυκτὸς ὀφθέντα. ἦν δὲ τοιαῦτα· "τρία," φησί, "κανᾶ φέρειν ὑπὲρ τῆς κεφαλῆς ἔδοξα, δύο μὲν ἄρτων πλέα, τὸ δὲ τρίτον ὄψου τε καὶ ποικίλων βρωμάτων οἷα βασιλεῦσι σκευάζεται· καταπταμένους δ' οἰωνοὺς ἅπαντα δαπανῆσαι μηδένα λόγον 72 αὐτοῦ ποιουμένους ἀποσοβοῦντος." καὶ ὁ μὲν ὁμοίαν τὴν πρόρρησιν ἔσεσθαι τῇ τοῦ οἰνοχόοι προσεδόκα· ὁ δὲ Ἰώσηπος συλλαβὼν[1] τῷ λογισμῷ τὸ ὄναρ καὶ πρὸς αὐτὸν εἰπών, ὡς ἐβούλετ' ἂν ἀγαθῶν ἑρμηνευτὴς αὐτῷ γεγονέναι καὶ οὐχ οἵων τὸ ὄναρ αὐτῷ δηλοῖ, λέγει δύο τὰς πάσας ἔτι τοῦ ζῆν αὐτὸν ἔχειν ἡμέρας· τὰ γὰρ κανᾶ τοῦτο 73 σημαίνειν· τῇ τρίτῃ δ' αὐτὸν ἀνασταυρωθέντα βορὰν ἔσεσθαι πετεινοῖς οὐδὲν ἀμύνειν αὐτῷ δυνάμενον. καὶ δὴ ταῦτα τέλος ὅμοιον οἷς ὁ Ἰώσηπος εἶπεν ἀμφοτέροις ἔλαβε· τῇ γὰρ ἡμέρᾳ τῇ προειρημένῃ γενέθλιον τεθυκὼς ὁ βασιλεὺς τὸν μὲν ἐπὶ τῶν σιτοποιῶν ἀνεσταύρωσε, τὸν δὲ οἰνοχόον τῶν δεσμῶν ἀπολύσας ἐπὶ τῆς αὐτῆς ὑπηρεσίας κατέστησεν.

74 (4) Ἰώσηπον δὲ διετῆ χρόνον τοῖς δεσμοῖς

[1] RO Lat. (cf. ii. 15): συμβαλὼν rell.

[a] Philo has a similar preface, De Jos. 18 § 94 ἐβουλόμην

pretation of his dream and eagerly await the accomplishment of these disclosures.

(3) But another slave, once chief of the king's bakers and now imprisoned along with the butler, after Joseph had thus explained the other's vision, was full of hope—for he too had had a dream—and besought Joseph to tell him also what might be the signification of his visions of the night past. These were as follows : " Methought," said he, " that I was carrying three baskets upon my head, two filled with loaves, and the third with dainties and divers meats such as are prepared for kings, when birds flew down and devoured them all, heedless of my efforts to scare them away." He was expecting a prediction similar to that made to the butler ; but Joseph, grasping on reflexion the import of the dream, after assuring him that he could have wished to have good news to interpret to him [a] and not such as the dream disclosed to his mind, told him that he had in all but two days yet to live (the baskets indicated that), and that on the third day he would be crucified [b] and become food for the fowls, utterly powerless to defend himself. And in fact this all fell out just as Joseph had declared to both of them ; for on the day predicted the king, celebrating his birthday with a sacrifice, crucified the chief baker but released the butler from his bonds and restored him to his former office.

(4) Joseph, however, for two full years endured the

The baker's dream. Gen. xl. 16.

Joseph's liberation. Gen. xli. 1.

μὲν μὴ παραστῆναί σοι τὴν φαντασίαν . . . ὀκνῶ τε γάρ, εἰ καί τις ἄλλος, εἶναι κακῶν ἄγγελος.

[b] Or " impaled." Gen. xl. 19 (" lift thy head from off thee and hang thee on a tree ") implies decapitation and subsequent impalement of the corpse ; Josephus, omitting the former, appears to introduce the *Roman* penalty.

κακοπαθοῦντα καὶ μηδὲν ὑπὸ τοῦ οἰνοχόου κατὰ
μνήμην τῶν προειρημένων ὠφελούμενον ὁ θεὸς
ἀπέλυσε τῆς εἱρκτῆς τοιαύτην αὐτῷ τὴν ἀπαλ-
75 λαγὴν μηχανησάμενος· Φαραώθης ὁ βασιλεὺς ὑπὸ
τὴν αὐτὴν ἑσπέραν ὄψεις ἐνυπνίων θεασάμενος δύο
καὶ μετ' αὐτῶν τὴν ἑκατέρας ἐξήγησιν ταύτης μὲν
ἡμνημόνησε, τῶν δὲ ὀνειράτων κατέσχεν. ἀχθόμενος οὖν ἐπὶ τοῖς ἑωραμένοις, καὶ γὰρ ἐδόκει
σκυθρωπὰ ταῦτ' αὐτῷ, συνεκάλει μεθ' ἡμέραν
Αἰγυπτίων τοὺς λογιωτάτους χρῄζων μαθεῖν τῶν
76 ὀνειράτων τὴν κρίσιν. ἀπορούντων δ' ἐκείνων ἔτι
μᾶλλον ὁ βασιλεὺς ἐταράττετο. τὸν δὲ οἰνοχόον
ὁρῶντα τοῦ Φαραώθου τὴν σύγχυσιν ὑπέρχεται
μνήμη τοῦ Ἰωσήπου καὶ τῆς περὶ τῶν ὀνειράτων
77 συνέσεως, καὶ προσελθὼν ἐμήνυσεν αὐτῷ τὸν
Ἰώσηπον τήν τε ὄψιν, ἣν αὐτὸς εἶδεν ἐν τῇ εἱρκτῇ,
καὶ τὸ ἀποβὰν ἐκείνου φράσαντος, ὅτι τε σταυρω-
θείη κατὰ τὴν αὐτὴν ἡμέραν ὁ ἐπὶ τῶν σιτοποιῶν
κἀκείνῳ τοῦτο συμβαίη κατ' ἐξήγησιν ὀνείρατος
78 Ἰωσήπου προειπόντος. δεδέσθαι δὲ τοῦτον μὲν
ὑπὸ Πεντεφροῦ τοῦ ἐπὶ τῶν μαγείρων ὡς δοῦλον,
λέγειν δ' αὐτὸν Ἑβραίων ἐν ὀλίγοις εἶναι γένους
ἅμα καὶ τῆς τοῦ πατρὸς δόξης. "τοῦτον οὖν
μεταπεμψάμενος καὶ μὴ διὰ τὴν ἄρτι κακοπραγίαν
αὐτοῦ καταγνοὺς μαθήσῃ τὰ ὑπὸ τῶν ὀνειράτων
79 σοι δηλούμενα." κελεύσαντος οὖν τοῦ βασιλέως
εἰς ὄψιν αὐτοῦ τὸν Ἰώσηπον παραγαγεῖν τὸν μὲν
ἥκουσιν ἄγοντες οἱ κεκελευσμένοι τημελήσαντες
κατὰ πρόσταγμα τοῦ βασιλέως.
80 (5) Ὁ δὲ τῆς δεξιᾶς αὐτοῦ λαβόμενος "ὦ
νεανία," φησί, "σὺ γάρ μοι νῦν ἄριστος καὶ

JEWISH ANTIQUITIES, II. 74–80

miseries of bondage, without receiving any aid from the butler in memory of his predictions, until God released him from prison, devising the following means for his deliverance. King Pharaothes on one and the same evening saw in his dreams two visions together with the explanation of each of them [a]; he forgot the explanation, but retained the dreams. Oppressed by these sights, which to him seemed of evil aspect, he summoned on the morrow the sagest of the Egyptians, desiring to learn the interpretation of the dreams; and finding them baffled, the king was yet more disturbed. But into the mind of the butler, watching the monarch's perplexity, there stole the memory of Joseph and his skill in dreams; he approached, spoke to him of Joseph, recounted the vision which he himself had seen in prison and the issue as foretold by him, and how on the same day the chief baker had been crucified and how his fate too had befallen him in accordance with Joseph's prophetical interpretation of a dream. He added that the man had been imprisoned by Pentephres, the chief cook, as a slave, but that, according to his own account, he ranked, alike by birth and by his father's fame, among the foremost of the Hebrews. "Send then for him," he said, "nor spurn him for his present miserable state, and thou wilt learn the meaning of thy dreams." So the king commanded to bring Joseph into his presence, and the appointed officers returned bringing him with them, after giving him their attentions in accordance with the orders of royalty.

(5) The king took him by the hand and said: "Young man, forasmuch as thy excellence and ex-

Pharaoh's dreams. Gen. xli. 15.

[a] Amplification of Scripture.

σύνεσιν ἱκανώτατος ὑπὸ οἰκέτου τοὐμοῦ μεμαρ-
τύρησαι τῶν αὐτῶν ἀγαθῶν, ὧν καὶ τούτῳ μετ-
έδωκας, ἀξίωσον κἀμὲ φράσας ὅσα μοι κατὰ τοὺς
ὕπνους ὀνειράτων ὄψεις προδηλοῦσι· βούλομαι δέ
σε μηδὲν ὑποστελλόμενον φόβῳ κολακεῦσαι ψευδεῖ
λόγῳ καὶ τῷ πρὸς ἡδονήν, ἂν τἀληθὲς σκυθρω-
81 πότερον ᾖ. ἔδοξα γὰρ παρὰ ποταμὸν βαδίζων
βόας ἰδεῖν εὐτραφεῖς ἅμα καὶ μεγέθει διαφερούσας,
ἑπτὰ τὸν ἀριθμόν, ἀπὸ τοῦ νάματος χωρεῖν ἐπὶ τὸ
ἕλος, ἄλλας δὲ ταύταις τὸν ἀριθμὸν παραπλησίας
ἐκ τοῦ ἕλους ὑπαντῆσαι λίαν κατισχνωμένας καὶ
δεινὰς ὁραθῆναι, αἳ κατεσθίουσαι τὰς εὐτραφεῖς
καὶ μεγάλας οὐδὲν ὠφελοῦντο χαλεπῶς ὑπὸ τοῦ
82 λιμοῦ τετρυχωμέναι. μετὰ δὲ ταύτην τὴν ὄψιν
διεγερθεὶς ἐκ τοῦ ὕπνου καὶ τεταραγμένος[1] καὶ
τί ποτ' εἴη τὸ φάντασμα παρ' ἐμαυτῷ σκοπῶν
καταφέρομαι πάλιν εἰς ὕπνον καὶ δεύτερον ὄναρ
ὁρῶ πολὺ τοῦ προτέρου θαυμασιώτερον, ὃ με
83 καὶ μᾶλλον ἐκφοβεῖ καὶ ταράττει. στάχυας ἑπτὰ
ἑώρων ἀπὸ μιᾶς ῥίζης ἐκφύεντας καρηβαροῦντας
ἤδη καὶ κεκλιμένους ὑπὸ τοῦ καρποῦ καὶ τῆς πρὸς
ἄμητον ὥρας καὶ τούτοις ἑτέρους ἑπτὰ στάχυας
πλησίον λιφερνοῦντας καὶ ἀσθενεῖς ὑπὸ ἀδροσίας,
οἳ δαπανᾶν καὶ κατεσθίειν τοὺς ὡραίους τραπέντες
ἔκπληξίν μοι παρέσχον."

84 (6) Ἰώσηπος δὲ ὑπολαβών, "ὄνειρος μὲν οὗτος,"
εἶπεν, "ὦ βασιλεῦ, καίπερ ἐν δυσὶ μορφαῖς ὀφ-
θεὶς μίαν καὶ τὴν αὐτὴν ἀποσημαίνει τελευτὴν
τῶν ἐσομένων. τό τε γὰρ τὰς βοῦς ἰδεῖν, ζῷον
ἐπ' ἀρότρῳ πονεῖν γεγενημένον, ὑπὸ τῶν χειρόνων
85 κατεσθιομένας, καὶ οἱ στάχυες ὑπὸ τῶν ἐλαττόνων
δαπανώμενοι λιμὸν Αἰγύπτῳ καὶ ἀκαρπίαν ἐπὶ

treme sagacity have but now been attested to me by my servant, vouchsafe to me also the same good offices as thou hast rendered to him, by telling me what is foreshadowed by these dreams which I have seen in my sleep; and I would have thee suppress nothing through fear nor flatter me with lying speech designed to please, however grim the truth may be. Methought that, as I walked by the river, I saw kine well-fed and exceeding large, seven in number, faring from the stream to the marsh-land, and others of like number came from the marshes to meet them, sorely emaciated and fearful to behold, which devoured the fat and large kine but were nothing bettered, so grievously wasted were they with famine. After this vision I awoke from sleep and, being disquieted and pondering in my mind what this apparition might be, I sank once more asleep and saw a second dream far more wondrous than the first, which terrified and disquieted me yet more. I saw seven ears of corn, sprung from a single root, their heads already toppling and bent beneath the load of grain and its ripeness for harvest, and beside them seven other ears forlorn and weak from want of dew, which fell to consuming and devouring the ripe ears, causing me consternation."

(6) To this Joseph replied: "This dream, O king, albeit seen under two forms, denotes but one and the same event to come. For these kine, creatures born to labour at the plough, that thou sawest being devoured by those inferior to them, these ears of corn consumed by lesser ears, alike foretell for Egypt

Joseph's interpretation. Gen. xli. 25.

---

[1] + ὦν ROE.

τοσαῦτα προκαταγγέλλουσιν ἔτη τοῖς ἴσοις πρότερον εὐδαιμονησάσῃ, ὡς τὴν τούτων εὐφορίαν τῶν ἐτῶν ὑπὸ τῆς τῶν μετὰ τοσοῦτον ἀριθμὸν ἴσων ἀφορίας ὑπαναλωθῆναι. γενήσεται δ᾽ ἡ σπάνις τῶν ἀναγκαίων σφόδρα δυσκατόρθωτος.
86 σημεῖον δέ· αἱ γὰρ κατισχνωμέναι βόες δαπανήσασαι τὰς κρείττονας οὐκ ἴσχυσαν κορεσθῆναι. ὁ μέντοι θεὸς οὐκ ἐπὶ τῷ λυπεῖν τὰ μέλλοντα τοῖς ἀνθρώποις προδείκνυσιν, ἀλλ᾽ ὅπως προυγνωκότες κουφοτέρας συνέσει ποιῶνται τὰς πείρας τῶν κατηγγελμένων. σὺ τοίνυν ταμιευσάμενος τὰ γαθὰ τὰ κατὰ τὸν πρῶτον χρόνον γενησόμενα ποιήσεις ἀνεπαίσθητον Αἰγυπτίοις τὴν ἐπελευσομένην συμφοράν."

87 (7) Θαυμάσαντος δὲ τοῦ βασιλέως τὴν φρόνησιν καὶ τὴν σοφίαν τοῦ Ἰωσήπου καὶ πυθομένου, τίνα καὶ τρόπον ἂν προοικονομήσειεν ἐν τοῖς τῆς εὐετηρίας καιροῖς τὰ περὶ τῶν μετὰ ταύτην, ὡς ἂν
88 ἐλαφρότερα γένοιτο τὰ τῆς ἀφορίας, ὑπετίθετο καὶ συνεβούλευε φειδὼ [ποιεῖσθαι] τῶν ἀγαθῶν καὶ μὴ κατὰ περιουσίαν αὐτοῖς χρῆσθαι τοῖς Αἰγυπτίοις ἐπιτρέπειν, ἀλλ᾽ ὅσα ἂν κατὰ τρυφὴν ἀναλώσωσιν ἐκ περισσοῦ, ταῦτα τηρεῖν εἰς τὸν τῆς ἐνδείας καιρόν, ἀποτίθεσθαί τε παρῄνει λαμβάνοντα τὸν σῖτον παρὰ τῶν γεωργῶν τὰ διαρκῆ
89 μόνον εἰς διατροφὴν χορηγοῦντα. Φαραώθης δ᾽ ἀμφοτέρων θαυμάσας Ἰώσηπον, τῆς τε κρίσεως τοῦ ὀνείρατος καὶ τῆς συμβουλίας, αὐτῷ τὴν οἰκονομίαν παραδίδωσιν, ὥστε πράττειν ἃ καὶ τῷ πλήθει τῶν Αἰγυπτίων καὶ τῷ βασιλεῖ συμφέροντα ὑπολαμβάνει, τὸν ἐξευρόντα τὴν τοῦ πράγματος ὁδὸν καὶ προστάτην ἄριστον αὐτῆς ὑπο-

famine and dearth for as many years as the period of plenty preceding them, so that the fertility of the former years will be stealthily consumed by the sterility of those that follow in equal number. To provide relief for the dearth of provisions will, moreover, prove a task of exceeding difficulty : in token whereof the emaciated kine after devouring their betters could not be satisfied. Howbeit, it is not to distress men that God foreshows to them that which is to come, but that forewarned they may use their sagacity to alleviate the trials announced when they befall. Do thou then husband the bounties that the first period will bring, and thou wilt make the Egyptians unconscious of the ensuing disaster."

(7) Marvelling at the discernment and wisdom of Joseph, the king asked him how he should make provision beforehand during the seasons of plenty for those that were to follow, in order to render more tolerable the period of barrenness. In reply Joseph suggested and counselled him to be sparing of the gifts of earth and not to permit the Egyptians to use them extravagantly, but that all that surplus which they might expend on luxury should be reserved against the time of want. He further exhorted him to take the corn from the cultivators and store it, supplying them only with enough to suffice for their subsistence. Pharaothes, now doubly admiring Joseph, alike for the interpretation of the dream and for his counsel, entrusted the administration of this office to him, with power to act as he thought meet both for the people of Egypt and for their sovereign, deeming that he who had discovered the course to

Joseph as Pharaoh's minister.

Gen. xli. 39.

JOSEPHUS

90 λαβὼν γενήσεσθαι. ὁ δέ, ταύτης αὐτῷ τῆς ἐξουσίας ὑπὸ τοῦ βασιλέως δοθείσης σφραγῖδί τε χρῆσθαι τῇ αὐτοῦ καὶ πορφύραν ἐνδύσασθαι, διὰ τῆς γῆς ἁπάσης ἐλαύνων ἐφ' ἅρματος ἦγε τὸν σῖτον παρὰ τῶν γεωργῶν τὸν ἀρκοῦντα πρός τε σπόρον καὶ διατροφὴν ἑκάστοις ἀπομετρῶν, μηδενὶ σημαίνων τὴν αἰτίαν, ὑφ' ἧς ταῦτα ἔπραττε.

91 (vi. 1) Τριακοστὸν δ' ἔτος ἤδη τῆς ἡλικίας αὐτῷ διεληλύθει καὶ τιμῆς ἁπάσης ἀπέλαυε [παρὰ] τοῦ βασιλέως, καὶ προσηγόρευσεν αὐτὸν Ψονθομφάνηχον ἀπιδὼν αὐτοῦ πρὸς τὸ παράδοξον τῆς συνέσεως· σημαίνει γὰρ τὸ ὄνομα κρυπτῶν εὑρετήν. γαμεῖ δὲ καὶ γάμον ἀξιολογώτατον· ἄγεται γὰρ καὶ Πεντεφροῦ θυγατέρα τῶν ἐν Ἡλιουπόλει ἱερέων, συμπράξαντος αὐτῷ τοῦ βασιλέως, ἔτι

92 παρθένον Ἀσέννηθιν ὀνόματι. ἐκ ταύτης δὲ καὶ παῖδες αὐτῷ γίνονται πρὸ τῆς ἀκαρπίας, Μανασσῆς μὲν πρεσβύτερος, σημαίνει δ' ἐπίληθον, διὰ τὸ εὐδαιμονήσαντα λήθην εὑράσθαι τῶν ἀτυχημάτων, ὁ δὲ νεώτερος Ἐφραίμης,[1] ἀποδιδοὺς δὲ τοῦτο σημαίνει, διὰ τὸ ἀποδοθῆναι αὐτὸν τῇ ἐλευθερίᾳ τῶν

93 προγόνων. τῆς δ' Αἰγύπτου κατὰ τὴν Ἰωσήπου τῶν ὀνειράτων ἐξήγησιν μακαριστῶς ἔτη ἑπτὰ διαγαγούσης[2] ὁ λιμὸς ἥπτετο τῷ ὀγδόῳ ἔτει καὶ διὰ τὸ μὴ προησθημένοις ἐπιπεσεῖν τὸ κακὸν πονούμενοι χαλεπῶς ὑπ' αὐτοῦ πάντες ἐπὶ τὰς

---

[1] Ἐφράδης R, Εὐφράης M, Ἐφράνης Niese.
[2] διαγούσης codd.

---

[a] Gen. xli. 42 mentions only its frequent concomitant "fine linen."

[b] So LXX: Heb. Zaphenath-paneah. The interpretation here given of the *Hebrew* form of the name (the first half of which was connected with Heb. *záphan*, "to hide") recurs

pursue would also prove its best director. Empowered by the king with this authority and withal to use his seal and to be robed in purple,*a* Joseph now drove in a chariot throughout all the land, gathering in the corn from the farmers, meting out to each such as would suffice for sowing and sustenance, and revealing to none for what reason he so acted.

(vi. 1) He had now completed his thirtieth year and was in the enjoyment of every honour at the hand of the king, who called him Psonthomphanêch(os) *b* in view of his amazing intelligence, that name signifying " Discoverer of Secrets." He contracted moreover a most distinguished marriage, espousing in fact the daughter of Pentephres,*c* one of the priests of Heliopolis, the king assisting to bring about the match : she was yet a virgin and was named Asennêthis.*d* By her he had sons before the dearth : the elder Manasses, signifying " cause of forgetfulness," *e* because in his prosperity his father had found oblivion of his misfortunes, and the younger Ephraim, meaning " Restorer," *f* because he had been restored to the liberty of his forefathers. Now when Egypt, in accordance with Joseph's interpretation of the dreams, had passed seven years of blissful prosperity, in the eighth year the famine gripped it, and, since the blow had been unforeseen by those upon whom it fell, they felt it heavily and all flocked to the

Joseph's marriage and children. The famine. Gen. xli. 45 f.

xli. 51.

in the Syriac version and in the Targum of Onkelos. The meaning of the underlying Egyptian name is uncertain.

c Or Petephres : Heb. Potiphera.   *d* Heb. Asenath.
e The Biblical and correct interpretation.
f Here Josephus departs from the Biblical derivation from root *prh* (= " fruitful ") and apparently connects the name with the root *pr'*, with final guttural (= in Heb. " let loose," in Aramaic " repay ").

JOSEPHUS

94 [τοῦ] βασιλέως θύρας συνέρρεον. ὁ δὲ Ἰώσηπον ἐκάλει, κἀκεῖνος τὸν σῖτον αὐτοῖς ἀπεδίδοτο γεγενημένος σωτὴρ ὁμολογουμένως τοῦ πλήθους, καὶ τὴν ἀγορὰν οὐ τοῖς ἐγχωρίοις προυτίθει μόνον, ἀλλὰ καὶ τοῖς ξένοις ὠνεῖσθαι παρῆν πάντας ἀνθρώπους κατὰ συγγένειαν ἀξιοῦντος ἐπικουρίας τυγχάνειν Ἰωσήπου παρὰ τῶν εὐδαιμονίᾳ χρωμένων.

95 (2) Πέμπει δὲ καὶ Ἰάκωβος τῆς Χαναναίας δεινῶς ἐκτετρυχωμένης, πάσης γὰρ ἥψατο τῆς ἠπείρου τὸ δεινόν, τοὺς υἱοὺς ἅπαντας εἰς τὴν Αἴγυπτον ὠνησομένους σῖτον πεπυσμένος ἐφεῖσθαι τὴν ἀγορὰν καὶ ξένοις· μόνον δὲ κατέσχε Βενιαμεὶν ἐκ Ῥαχήλας αὐτῷ γεγονότα ὁμομήτριον δὲ

96 Ἰωσήπῳ. οἱ μὲν οὖν εἰς τὴν Αἴγυπτον ἐλθόντες ἐνετύγχανον τῷ Ἰωσήπῳ χρῄζοντες ἀγορᾶς· οὐδὲν γὰρ ἦν ὃ μὴ μετὰ γνώμης ἐπράττετο τῆς ἐκείνου· καὶ γὰρ τὸ θεραπεῦσαι τὸν βασιλέα τότε χρήσιμον ἐγίνετο τοῖς ἀνθρώποις, ὅτε καὶ τῆς Ἰωσήπου

97 τιμῆς ἐπιμεληθεῖεν. ὁ δὲ γνωρίσας τοὺς ἀδελφοὺς οὐδὲν ἐνθυμουμένους περὶ αὐτοῦ διὰ τὸ μειράκιον μὲν αὐτὸς ἀπαλλαγῆναι, εἰς τοῦτο δὲ προελθεῖν τῆς ἡλικίας, ὡς[1] τῶν χαρακτήρων ἐνηλλαγμένων[2] ἀγνώριστος αὐτοῖς εἶναι, τῷ δὲ μεγέθει τοῦ ἀξιώματος οὐδ᾽ εἰς ἐπίνοιαν ἐλθεῖν αὐτοῖς δυνάμενος[3] διεπείραζεν, ὡς ἔχοιεν γνώμης περὶ τῶν ὅλων.

98 τόν τε γὰρ σῖτον αὐτοῖς οὐκ ἀπεδίδοτο κατασκόπους τε τῶν βασιλέως πραγμάτων ἔλεγεν ἥκειν καὶ πολλαχόθεν μὲν αὐτοὺς συνεληλυθέναι, προφασίζεσθαι δὲ συγγένειαν· οὐ γὰρ εἶναι δυνατὸν ἀνδρὶ ἰδιώτῃ τοιούτους παῖδας καὶ τὰς μορφὰς οὕτως ἐπιφανεῖς ἐκτραφῆναι, δυσκόλου καὶ βασι-

99 λεῦσιν οὔσης [τῆς] τοιαύτης παιδοτροφίας. ὑπὲρ

king's gates. The king summoned Joseph, and he sold them corn, proving himself by common consent the saviour of the people. Nor did he open the market to the natives only: strangers also were permitted to buy, for Joseph held that all men, in virtue of their kinship, should receive succour from those in prosperity.

(2) And so, since Canaan was sorely wasted, the scourge having stricken the whole continent, Jacob too sent all his sons into Egypt to buy corn, having learnt that the market was open also to foreigners: he retained only Benjamin, his child by Rachel, born of the same mother as Joseph. The brethren, then, on reaching Egypt, waited upon Joseph desiring leave to buy; for nothing was done without his sanction, insomuch that to pay court to the king was profitable only to such as took heed to do homage likewise to Joseph. He recognized his brothers, but they had no thought of him, for he was but a lad when he parted from them and had reached an age when his features had so changed as to make him unrecognizable to them; moreover his exalted rank prevented any possibility of his even entering their minds. So he proceeded to test their feelings on affairs in general. Corn he would sell them none, declaring that it was to spy upon the king's realm that they were come, that they had banded together from various quarters, and that their kinship was but a feint; for it was impossible for any commoner to have reared such sons with figures so distinguished, when even kings found it hard to raise the like. It

_{Jacob's sons visit Egypt. Gen. xlii. 1.}

---

¹ Lat. (ut⟩: καί codd. ² ἠλλαγμένων ROE.
³ Niese: δυναμένοις codd.

δὲ τοῦ γνῶναι τὰ κατὰ τὸν πατέρα καὶ τὰ συμ-
βεβηκότα αὐτῷ μετὰ τὴν ἰδίαν ἀπαλλαγὴν ταῦτ'
ἔπραττε μαθεῖν τε βουλόμενος καὶ τὰ περὶ Βενιαμεὶν τὸν ἀδελφόν· ἐδεδίει γάρ, μὴ κἀκεῖνον ὁμοίως οἷς
εἰς αὐτὸν ἐτόλμησαν εἶεν ἀπεσκευασμένοι τοῦ γένους.
100 (3) Οἱ δ' ἦσαν ἐν ταραχῇ καὶ φόβῳ κίνδυνον τὸν
μέγιστον αὐτοῖς ἐπηρτῆσθαι νομίζοντες καὶ μηδὲν
περὶ τἀδελφοῦ κατὰ νοῦν λαμβάνοντες, καταστάντες τε πρὸς τὰς αἰτίας ἀπελογοῦντο Ῥουβήλου προηγοροῦντος, ὃς ἦν πρεσβύτατος αὐτῶν·
101 "ἡμεῖς," γὰρ εἶπεν, "οὐ κατ' ἀδικίαν δεῦρο ἤλ-
θομεν οὐδὲ κακουργήσοντες τὰ βασιλέως πράγματα, σωθῆναι δὲ ζητοῦντες[1] καὶ καταφυγὴν τῶν
ἐπεχόντων τὴν χώραν ἡμῶν κακῶν τὴν ὑμετέραν
φιλανθρωπίαν ὑπολαβόντες, οὓς οὐχὶ πολίταις
μόνοις τοῖς αὐτῶν ἀλλὰ καὶ ξένοις ἠκούομεν τὴν
ἀγορὰν τοῦ σίτου προτεθεικέναι, πᾶσι τὸ σώζε-
102 σθαι τοῖς δεομένοις παρέχειν διεγνωκότας. ὅτι δ'
ἐσμὲν ἀδελφοὶ καὶ κοινὸν ἡμῖν αἷμα, φανερὸν μὲν
καὶ τῆς μορφῆς τὸ οἰκεῖον καὶ μὴ πολὺ παρ-
ηλλαγμένον ποιεῖ, πατὴρ δ' ἐστὶν ἡμῖν Ἰάκωβος
ἀνὴρ Ἑβραῖος, ᾧ γινόμεθα δώδεκα παῖδες ἐκ
γυναικῶν τεσσάρων, ὧν πάντων περιόντων ἦμεν
103 εὐδαίμονες. ἀποθανόντος δὲ ἑνὸς τῶν ἀδελφῶν
Ἰωσήπου τὰ πράγματα ἡμῖν ἐπὶ τὸ χεῖρον μετ-
έβαλεν· ὅ τε γὰρ πατὴρ μακρὸν ἐπ' αὐτῷ πένθος
ἦρται[2] καὶ ἡμεῖς ὑπό τε τῆς ἐπὶ τῷ τεθνηκότι
συμφορᾶς καὶ τῆς τοῦ πρεσβύτου ταλαιπωρίας
104 κακοπαθοῦμεν. ἥκομέν τε νῦν ἐπ' ἀγορᾷ σίτου
τήν τε τοῦ πατρὸς ἐπιμέλειαν καὶ τὴν κατὰ τὸν
οἶκον πρόνοιαν Βενιαμεῖ τῷ νεωτάτῳ τῶν ἀδελφῶν

[1] χρήζοντες MSPL. [2] Ernesti: ἤρηται (ἤρκται) codd.

was but to discover news of his father and what had become of him after his own departure that he so acted; he moreover desired to learn the fate of his brother Benjamin, for he feared that, by such a ruse as they had practised on himself, they might have rid the family of him also.

(3) For their part, they were in trepidation and alarm, believing the gravest danger to be hanging over their heads and entertaining no thought whatever of their brother; and they set themselves to meet these charges with Rubel, as the eldest of them, for spokesman.[a] "We," said he, "are come hither with no nefarious intent nor to do mischief to the king's realm, but seeking to save our lives and in the belief that we should find a refuge from the ills that beset our country in your humanity, who, as we heard, had thrown open your corn-market not only to your fellow-citizens but also to foreigners, having resolved to provide the means of subsistence to all in need. That we are brethren and of one blood is evident from the marked features of each of us, differing but little; our father is Jacob, a Hebrew, and we, his twelve sons, were born to him by four wives. While we all lived, we were happy; but since the death of one brother, Joseph, our lot has changed for the worse, for our father has raised a long lamentation over him and we, alike from the misfortune of this death [b] and the old man's misery, are in evil case. And now we are come to buy corn, having entrusted the care of our father and the charge of the household to Benjamin, the youngest

Speech of Rubel. Cf. Gen. xlii. 10.

---

[a] Reuben is not mentioned here in Genesis.
[b] Or perhaps, "the ill fortune that followed his (Joseph's) death."

πεπιστευκότες· δύνασαι δὲ πέμψας εἰς τὸν ἡμέτερον οἶκον μαθεῖν, εἴ τι ψευδές ἐστι τῶν λεγομένων."

105 (4) Καὶ Ῥουβῆλος μὲν τοιούτοις ἐπειρᾶτο πείθειν τὸν Ἰώσηπον περὶ αὐτῶν τὰ ἀμείνω φρονῆσαι, ὁ δὲ τὸν Ἰάκωβον ζῶντα μαθὼν καὶ τὸν ἀδελφὸν οὐκ ἀπολωλότα τότε μὲν εἰς τὴν εἱρκτὴν αὐτοὺς ὡς ἐπὶ σχολῆς βασανίσων ἐνέβαλε, τῇ δὲ τρίτῃ
106 τῶν ἡμερῶν προαγαγὼν αὐτούς, "ἐπεί," φησί, "διισχυρίζεσθε μήτ' ἐπὶ κακουργίᾳ τῶν βασιλέως ἥκειν πραγμάτων εἶναί τε ἀδελφοὶ καὶ πατρὸς οὗ λέγετε, πείσαιτ' ἄν με ταῦθ' οὕτως ἔχειν, εἰ καταλίποιτε μὲν ἐξ αὑτῶν ἕνα παρ' ἐμοὶ μηδὲν ὑβριστικὸν πεισόμενον, ἀποκομίσαντες δὲ τὸν σῖτον πρὸς τὸν πατέρα πάλιν ἔλθοιτε πρὸς ἐμὲ τὸν ἀδελφόν, ὃν καταλιπεῖν ἐκεῖ φατέ, μεθ' ἑαυτῶν ἄγοντες· τοῦτο
107 γὰρ ἔσται πίστωμα τῆς ἀληθείας." οἱ δ' ἐν μείζοσι κακοῖς ἦσαν ἔκλαιόν τε καὶ συνεχῶς πρὸς ἀλλήλους ἀνωλοφύροντο τὴν Ἰωσήπου συμφοράν, ὡς διὰ τὰ κατ' ἐκείνου βουλευθέντα τιμωροῦντος αὐτοὺς τοῦ θεοῦ τούτοις περιπέσοιεν· Ῥουβῆλος δὲ πολὺς ἦν ἐπιπλήττων αὐτοῖς τῆς μετανοίας, ἐξ ἧς ὄφελος οὐδὲν Ἰωσήπῳ γίνεται, φέρειν δ' αὐτοὺς πᾶν ὅ τι καὶ πάθοιεν κατ' ἐκδικίαν ἐκείνου δρῶντος
108 αὐτὰ τοῦ θεοῦ καρτερῶς ἠξίου. ταῦτα δ' ἔλεγον πρὸς ἀλλήλους οὐχ ἡγούμενοι τὸν Ἰώσηπον γλώσσης τῆς αὐτῶν συνιέναι. κατήφεια δὲ πάντας εἶχε πρὸς τοὺς Ῥουβήλου λόγους καὶ τῶν πραγμάτων μετάμελος, ὥσπερ οὖν καὶ τῶν[1] ταῦτα

[1] ROE: ὥσπερ οὐκ αὐτῶν rell.

of us brothers. Thou hast but to send to our house to learn whether aught of these statements is false."

(4) Thus did Rubel essay to persuade Joseph to think better of them; but he, having learnt that Jacob was alive and that his brother had not perished, for the present cast them into prison as though to interrogate them at leisure. Then on the third day he brought them forth and said: "Seeing that ye asseverate that ye are come with no mischievous designs upon the king's realm, and that ye are brothers born of that father of whom ye speak, ye may convince me that it is even so by leaving with me one of your number, who shall undergo no violence, and, after carrying the corn to your father, returning to me, bringing with you the brother whom ye assert that ye left yonder; that shall serve as a guarantee of the truth." They, thus involved in yet greater troubles, wept and continued to deplore to each other the unfortunate fate of Joseph, saying that it was God's chastisement for their plots against him which had brought them to this pass. But Rubel roundly rebuked them for these regrets which could profit Joseph nothing, and strongly besought them to bear all that they might have to suffer, since it was God who inflicted it to avenge him. Thus they spoke with one another, never imagining that Joseph understood their language. But dejection now possessed them all at Rubel's words, and remorse for the deeds, aye and for the men who had decreed those deeds,[a] for which they

---

[a] Text and meaning uncertain. Other MSS. read ". . . for the deeds, as if they had not themselves decreed those deeds."

ψηφισαμένων, ἐφ' οἷς δίκαιον ἔκρινον τὸν θεὸν
109 κολαζόμενοι. βλέπων δ' οὕτως ἀμηχανοῦντας [αὐ-
τοὺς ὁ] Ἰώσηπος ὑπὸ τοῦ πάθους εἰς δάκρυα
προὐπιπτε καὶ μὴ βουλόμενος τοῖς ἀδελφοῖς γενέσθαι καταφανὴς ὑπεχώρει καὶ διαλιπὼν πάλιν ἧκε
110 πρὸς αὐτούς. καὶ Συμεῶνα κατασχὼν ὅμηρον
τῆς ἐπανόδου τῶν ἀδελφῶν γενησόμενον ἐκείνους
μεταλαβόντας τῆς ἀγορᾶς τοῦ σίτου προσέταξεν
ἀπιέναι, κελεύσας τῷ ὑπηρέτῃ τἀργύριον, ὃ πρὸς
τὴν ὠνὴν εἶεν τοῦ σίτου κεκομικότες, κρύφα τοῖς
φορτίοις ἐνθέντι ἀπολύειν κἀκεῖνο κομίζοντας. καὶ
ὁ μὲν τὰ ἐντεταλμένα ἔπραττεν.
111 (5) Οἱ δὲ Ἰακώβου παῖδες ἐλθόντες εἰς τὴν
Χαναναίαν ἀπήγγελλον τῷ πατρὶ τὰ κατὰ τὴν
Αἴγυπτον αὐτοῖς συμπεσόντα, καὶ ὅτι κατάσκοποι
δόξειαν ἀφῖχθαι τοῦ βασιλέως καὶ λέγοντες
ἀδελφοί τε εἶναι καὶ τὸν ἐνδέκατον οἴκοι καταλιπεῖν
παρὰ τῷ πατρὶ ἀπιστηθεῖεν, ὡς καταλίποιέν τε
Συμεῶνα παρὰ τῷ στρατηγῷ μέχρι Βενιαμεὶς
ὡς αὐτὸν ἀπιὼν πίστις αὐτοῖς τῶν εἰρημένων παρ'
112 αὑτῷ γένοιτο· ἠξίουν τε τὸν πατέρα μηδὲν φοβη-
θέντα πέμπειν σὺν αὐτοῖς τὸν νεανίσκον. Ἰακώβῳ
δ' οὐδὲν ἤρεσκε τῶν τοῖς υἱοῖς πεπραγμένων, καὶ
πρὸς τὴν Συμεῶνος δὲ κατοχὴν λυπηρῶς φέρων
ἀνόητον ἡγεῖτο προστιθέναι καὶ τὸν Βενιαμείν.
113 καὶ ὁ μὲν οὐδὲ Ῥουβήλου δεομένου καὶ τοὺς αὑτοῦ
παῖδας ἀντιδιδόντος, ἵνα εἴ τι πάθοι Βενιαμεὶς
κατὰ τὴν ἀποδημίαν ἀποκτείνειεν αὐτοὺς ὁ πάππος,
πείθεται τοῖς λόγοις. οἱ δ' ἠπόρουν ἐπὶ τοῖς
κακοῖς καὶ μᾶλλον αὐτοὺς ἐτάραττε τἀργύριον ἐν
τοῖς σακκίοις τοῦ σίτου κατακεκρυμμένον εὑρεθέν.
114 τοῦ δὲ σίτου τοῦ κομισθέντος ὑπ' αὐτῶν ἐπιλιπόν-

now judged that they were justly punished by God. Seeing them thus distraught, Joseph from emotion broke into tears, and not wishing to be visible to his brethren withdrew, and after a while came back to them again. Then, retaining Symeon as a hostage to ensure the return of his brethren, he bade them make their purchase of corn and be gone, having previously instructed the officer secretly to deposit in their packs the purchase-money which they had brought and to let them take it also along with them. These orders he duly executed.

(5) The sons of Jacob, on their return to Canaan, told their father what had befallen them in Egypt, how they were taken for persons come to spy upon the king, how when they said that they were brothers and had left the eleventh at home with their father, they were not believed, and how they had left Symeon behind with the governor until Benjamin should come to him to attest the truth of their statements; and they besought their father to have no fear and to send the youth along with them. But Jacob was in no wise pleased with his sons' doings, and, aggrieved at the detention of Symeon, he thought it folly to send Benjamin also to share his fate. Vainly did Rubel entreat him, offering his own sons in exchange, in order that, if any harm should befall Benjamin on the journey, their grandfather should put them to death: he remained unmoved by his words. In perplexity over their troubles, they were still more disquieted by the discovery of the money concealed in their sacks of corn. But when the corn which they had brought failed them and the

Second journey of the brothers to Egypt. Gen. xlii. 29.

xliii. 1.

τος καὶ τοῦ λιμοῦ μᾶλλον ἁπτομένου βιαζομένης
αὐτὸν τῆς ἀνάγκης ὁ Ἰάκωβος ἐκπέμπειν ἐγίνωσκε
115 τὸν Βενιαμεὶν μετὰ τῶν ἀδελφῶν· οὐ γὰρ ἦν αὐτοῖς
εἰς Αἴγυπτον ἀπελθεῖν μὴ μετὰ τῶν ἐπαγγελιῶν[1]
ἀπερχομένοις, καὶ τοῦ πάθους οὖν χείρονος καθ᾽
ἑκάστην ἡμέραν γινομένου καὶ τῶν υἱῶν δεομένων
116 οὐκ εἶχεν ὅ τι χρήσαιτο τοῖς παροῦσιν. Ἰούδα
δὲ τολμηροῦ τἆλλα τὴν φύσιν ἀνδρὸς χρησαμένου
πρὸς αὐτὸν παρρησίᾳ, ὡς οὐ προσῆκε μὲν αὐτὸν
περὶ τἀδελφοῦ δεδιέναι οὐδὲ τὰ μὴ δεινὰ δι᾽
ὑποψίας λαμβάνειν, πραχθήσεται γὰρ οὐδὲν τῶν[2]
περὶ τὸν ἀδελφόν, ᾧ μὴ παρέσται θεός, τοῦτο δὲ
συμβήσεσθαι πάντως καὶ παρ᾽ αὐτῷ μένοντι·
117 φανερὰν δ᾽ οὕτως αὐτῶν ἀπώλειαν μὴ καταδικάζειν
μηδὲ τὴν ἐκ Φαραώθου τῆς τροφῆς [αὐτῶν]
εὐπορίαν αὐτοὺς ἀφαιρεῖσθαι ἀλόγως περὶ τοῦ
παιδὸς δεδιότα, φροντίζειν δὲ καὶ τῆς Συμεῶνος
σωτηρίας, μὴ φειδοῖ τῆς Βενιαμεῖ ἀποδημίας
ἐκεῖνος ἀπόληται· πιστεῦσαι δὲ περὶ αὐτοῦ τῷ
θεῷ παραινοῦντος καὶ αὐτῷ, ὡς ἢ σῶον ἐπαν-
άξοντος αὐτῷ τὸν υἱὸν ἢ συγκαταστρέψοντος[3] ἅμα
118 ἐκείνῳ τὸν βίον, πεισθεὶς Ἰάκωβος παρεδίδου τὸν
Βενιαμεὶν καὶ τὴν τιμὴν τοῦ σίτου διπλασίονα τῶν
τε παρὰ τοῖς Χαναναίοις γεννωμένων τό τε τῆς
βαλάνου μύρον καὶ στακτὴν τερέβινθόν τε καὶ
μέλι δωρεὰς Ἰωσήπῳ κομίζειν. πολλὰ δὲ ἦν
παρὰ τοῦ πατρὸς ἐπὶ τῇ τῶν παίδων ἐξόδῳ δάκρυα
119 κἀκείνων αὐτῶν· ὁ μὲν γὰρ τοὺς υἱοὺς εἰ κομιεῖται
σώους ἐκ τῆς ἀποδημίας ἐφρόντιζεν, οἱ δ᾽ εἰ τὸν

---

[1] RO: ἐπηγγελμένων rell.
[2] Niese: αὐτῶν codd.
[3] ed. pr.: -στρέψαντος codd.

famine was tightening its grip, under pressure of necessity Jacob decided to send Benjamin away with his brethren; for it was impossible for them to return to Egypt if they left without fulfilling their promises, and, as the infliction daily grew worse and his sons persisted in their entreaties, he had no other course to take. Judas, ever of a hardy nature, frankly told him that he ought not to be alarmed for their brother nor harbour suspicions of dangers that did not exist, for nothing could be done to him save what God might send, and that was bound to befall even if he stayed with his father. Jacob should not then condemn them to manifest destruction nor deprive them of the abundance of provisions with which Pharaoh could furnish them through unreasonable fears for his child. Moreover, he should give some thought also to Symeon's safety, lest his hesitation to let Benjamin go should prove the other's ruin. As for Benjamin, he exhorted him to trust to God and to himself, for either he would bring his son back safe and sound or he would lay down his life along with him.[a] Thus persuaded, Jacob delivered Benjamin to them, together with double the price of the corn and some of the products of Canaan—balsam,[b] myrrh,[c] terebinth,[d] and honey—to take with them as presents for Joseph. Many were the tears shed by the father over his children's departure and by them also; he anxiously wondering whether his sons would be restored to him in safety after this journey, they whether they should find their father in

---

[a] Gen. xliii. 9, " If I bring him not unto thee . . . I shall have sinned against thee for ever."

[b] Meaning doubtful.   [c] Or " oil of cinnamon."

[d] Probably pistachio nuts.

πατέρα καταλάβοιεν ἐρρωμένον καὶ μηδὲν ὑπὸ τῆς ἐπ' αὐτοῖς λύπης κακωθέντα. ἡμερήσιον δὲ αὐτοῖς ἠνύσθη τὸ πένθος, καὶ ὁ μὲν πρεσβύτης κοπωθεὶς ὑπέμεινεν, οἱ δὲ ἐχώρουν εἰς Αἴγυπτον μετὰ κρείττονος ἐλπίδος τὴν ἐπὶ τοῖς παροῦσι λύπην ἰώμενοι.

120 (6) Ὡς δ' ἦλθον εἰς τὴν Αἴγυπτον κατάγονται μὲν παρὰ τὸν Ἰώσηπον, φόβος δὲ αὐτοὺς οὐχ ὁ τυχὼν διετάραττε, μὴ περὶ τῆς τοῦ σίτου τιμῆς ἐγκλήματα λάβωσιν ὡς αὐτοί τι κεκακουργηκότες, καὶ πρὸς τὸν ταμίαν τοῦ Ἰωσήπου πολλὴν ἀπολογίαν ἐποιοῦντο κατ' οἶκόν τε φάσκοντες εὑρεῖν ἐν τοῖς σάκκοις τὸ ἀργύριον καὶ νῦν ἥκειν ἐπαν-
121 άγοντες αὐτό. τοῦ δὲ μηδ' ὅ τι λέγουσιν εἰδέναι φήσαντος ἀνείθησαν τοῦ δέους. λύσας τε τὸν Συμεῶνα ἐτημέλει συνεσόμενον τοῖς ἀδελφοῖς.[1] ἐλθόντος δὲ ἐν τούτῳ καὶ Ἰωσήπου ἀπὸ τῆς θεραπείας τοῦ βασιλέως, τά τε δῶρα παρήγαγον[2] αὐτῷ καὶ πυθομένῳ περὶ τοῦ πατρὸς ἔλεγον ὅτι
122 καταλάβοιεν αὐτὸν ἐρρωμένον. ὁ δὲ μαθὼν περιόντα καὶ περὶ τοῦ Βενιαμεῖ εἰ οὗτος ὁ νεώτερος ἀδελφὸς εἴη, καὶ γὰρ ἦν αὐτὸν ἑωρακώς, ἀνέκρινε. τῶν δὲ φησάντων αὐτὸν εἶναι[3] θεὸν μὲν ἐπὶ πᾶσι
123 προστάτην εἶπεν, ὑπὸ δὲ τοῦ πάθους προαγόμενος εἰς δάκρυα μεθίστατο μὴ βουλόμενος καταφανὴς εἶναι τοῖς ἀδελφοῖς, ἐπὶ δεῖπνόν τε αὐτοὺς παραλαμβάνει καὶ κατακλίνονται οὕτως ὡς καὶ παρὰ τῷ πατρί. πάντας δὲ αὐτοὺς ὁ Ἰώσηπος δεξιούμενος

---

[1] λύσας τε . . . ἀδελφοῖς om. ROE.
[2] παρῆγον RO. [3] +οἰκέτην αὐτοῦ ROE.

health and in no wise stricken down by his sorrow on their behalf. A whole day was thus passed by them in mourning; then the old man was left broken-hearted behind, while they set forth for Egypt, healing their present grief with hopes of a better future.

(6) On reaching Egypt, they were conducted to Joseph's presence. But they were tormented with grave fear that they would be accused in the matter of the corn-money as guilty of some fraud, and they made profuse apology to Joseph's steward, assuring him that only on reaching home had they found the money in their sacks and that they were now come to bring it back. However, as he said that he had no idea what they meant, they were relieved from that alarm; moreover, he released Symeon and made him presentable [a] to rejoin his brothers. Meanwhile Joseph having come from his attendance upon the king, they offered him their gifts and when he asked them about their father they replied that they had found him in good health. Having learnt that he was still alive, he further inquired about Benjamin—for he had espied him—whether this was their younger brother; and when they replied that he was,[b] he exclaimed that God presided over all,[c] whereupon being reduced by his emotion to tears he withdrew, unwilling to betray himself to his brethren. He then invited them to supper, where couches were set for them in the same order as at their father's table. But Joseph, while entertaining them all with

Their reception by Joseph. Gen. xliii. 15.

[a] *Cf.* § 79 for similar attention to Joseph on release from prison.

[b] Or, as in other mss., "he was his (humble) servant."

[c] Gen. xliii. 29, "God be gracious unto thee, my son." It seems hardly possible to interpret the text as a similar blessing, "prayed God to be his constant protector."

219

διπλασίοσι μοίραις τῶν αὐτῷ παρακειμένων τὸν Βενιαμεὶν ἐτίμα.

124 (7) Ἐπεὶ δὲ μετὰ τὸ δεῖπνον εἰς ὕπνον ἐτράποντο, κελεύει τὸν ταμίαν[1] τόν τε σῖτον αὐτοῖς δοῦναι μεμετρημένον καὶ τὴν τιμὴν πάλιν ἐγκρύψαι τοῖς σακκίοις, εἰς δὲ τὸ τοῦ Βενιαμεῖ φορτίον καὶ σκύφον ἀργυροῦν, ᾧ πίνων ἔχαιρε, βαλόντα κατα-
125 λιπεῖν. ἐποίει δὲ ταῦτα διάπειραν βουλόμενος τῶν ἀδελφῶν λαβεῖν, πότερόν ποτε βοηθήσουσι τῷ Βενιαμεῖ κλοπῆς ἀγομένῳ καὶ δοκοῦντι κινδυνεύειν, ἢ καταλιπόντες ὡς οὐδὲν αὐτοὶ κεκακουρ-
126 γηκότες ἀπίασι πρὸς τὸν πατέρα. ποιήσαντος δὲ τοῦ οἰκέτου τὰ ἐντεταλμένα μεθ' ἡμέραν οὐδὲν τούτων εἰδότες οἱ τοῦ Ἰακώβου παῖδες ἀπῄεσαν, ἀπειληφότες τὸν Συμεῶνα καὶ διπλῆν χαρὰν χαίροντες ἐπί τε τούτῳ κἀπὶ τῷ Βενιαμεὶν ἀποκομίζειν τῷ πατρί, καθὼς ὑπέσχοντο. περιελαύνουσι δ' αὐτοὺς ἱππεῖς ἄγοντες τὸν οἰκέτην, ὃς ἐναπέθετο
127 τῷ τοῦ Βενιαμεῖ φορτίῳ τὸν σκύφον. ταραχθέντας δὲ ὑπὸ τῆς ἀδοκήτου τῶν ἱππέων ἐφόδου καὶ τὴν αἰτίαν πυθομένους δι' ἣν ἐπ' ἄνδρας ἐληλύθασιν,
128 οἳ μικρὸν ἔμπροσθεν τιμῆς καὶ ξενίας τετυχήκασιν αὐτῶν παρὰ τοῦ δεσπότου, κακίστους ἀπεκάλουν, οἳ μηδ' αὐτὸ τοῦτο τὴν ξενίαν καὶ τὴν φιλοφροσύνην τὴν Ἰωσήπου διὰ μνήμης λαβόντες οὐκ ὤκνησαν εἰς αὐτὸν ἄδικοι γενέσθαι, σκύφον δέ, ᾧ φιλοτησίας αὐτοῖς προὔπιεν, ἀράμενοι φέροιεν

[1] τῷ ταμίᾳ O.

---

[a] Gen. xliii. 34, "But Benjamin's mess was *five times* so much as any of theirs." The usual translation of Josephus,

cordiality, honoured Benjamin with double portions of the dishes before him.[a]

(7) But after the supper, when they had retired to rest, he ordered his steward to give them their measures of corn, and again to conceal the purchase-money in their sacks, but also to leave deposited in Benjamin's pack his own favourite silver drinking-cup. This he did to prove his brethren[b] and see whether they would assist Benjamin, when arrested for theft and in apparent danger, or would abandon him, assured of their own innocence, and return to their father. The servant executed his orders and, at daybreak, all unaware of these proceedings, the sons of Jacob departed along with Symeon, doubly delighted both at having recovered him and at bringing back Benjamin to their father in accordance with their promise. But suddenly they were surrounded by a troop of horsemen, bringing with them the servant who had deposited the cup in Benjamin's pack. Confounded by this unexpected attack of horse, they asked for what reason they assailed men who had but now enjoyed the honour and hospitality of their master. Their pursuers retorted by calling them scoundrels, who, unmindful of that very hospitality and benevolence of Joseph, had not scrupled to treat him ill, carrying off that loving-cup in which he had pledged their healths,[c] and setting more store

Discovery of Joseph's cup in Benjamin's sack. Gen. xliv. 1.

" with portions double *those of his neighbours* " would require παρακατακειμένων (not παρακειμένων).

[b] So Philo, *De Jos.* 39 § 232 (quoted by Weill) πάντα δ' ἦσαν ἀπόπειρα καὶ ταῦτα . . πῶς ἔχουσι . . εὐνοίας πρὸς τὸν ὁμομήτριον ἀδελφόν.

[c] So Philo, *De Jos.* 36 § 213 ἐν ᾧ προπόσεις προύπινεν ὑμῖν. The parallel in Gen. xliv. 5 has " whereby he indeed divineth."

κέρδους ἀδίκου τήν τε πρὸς Ἰώσηπον φιλίαν τόν τε ἑαυτῶν εἰ φωραθεῖεν κίνδυνον ἐν δευτέρῳ
129 θέμενοι· τιμωρίαν τε αὐτοῖς[1] ὑφέξειν ἠπείλουν οὐ λανθάνοντας τὸν θεὸν οὐδ᾽ ἀποδράντας μετὰ τῆς κλοπῆς, εἰ καὶ τὸν διακονούμενον οἰκέτην διέλαθον. πυνθάνεσθαί τε νῦν, τί παρόντες εἴημεν, ὡς οὐκ εἰδότας[2]· γνώσεσθαι μέντοι κολαζομένους αὐτίκα. καὶ ταῦτα καὶ πέρα τούτων ὁ οἰκέτης εἰς αὐτοὺς
130 λέγων ἐνύβριζεν. οἱ δὲ ὑπὸ ἀγνοίας τῶν περὶ αὐτοὺς ἐχλεύαζον ἐπὶ τοῖς λεγομένοις καὶ τῆς κουφολογίας τὸν οἰκέτην ἐθαύμαζον τολμῶντα αἰτίαν ἐπιφέρειν ἀνδράσιν, οἳ μηδὲ τὴν τοῦ σίτου τιμὴν ἐν τοῖς σακκίοις αὐτῶν εὑρεθεῖσαν κατέσχον, ἀλλ᾽ ἐκόμισαν μηδενὸς εἰδότος τὸ πραχθέν· τοσοῦ-
131 τον ἀποδεῖν τοῦ γνώμῃ κακουργῆσαι. τῆς μέντοι γε ἀρνήσεως ἀξιοπιστοτέραν ὑπολαβόντες τὴν ἔρευναν ἐκέλευον ταύτῃ χρῆσθαι, κἂν εὑρεθῇ τις ὑφῃρημένος ἅπαντας κολάζειν· οὐδὲν γὰρ αὑτοῖς συνειδότες ἦγον παρρησίαν, ὡς ἐδόκουν, ἀκίνδυνον. οἱ[3] δὲ τὴν ἔρευναν μὲν ἠξίωσαν ποιήσασθαι, τὴν μέντοι τιμωρίαν ἑνὸς ἔφασκον εἶναι τοῦ τὴν
132 κλοπὴν εὑρεθέντος πεποιημένου. τὴν δὲ ζήτησιν ποιούμενοι καὶ πάντας τοὺς ἄλλους ἐκπεριελθόντες κατὰ τὴν ἔρευναν ἐπὶ τὸν τελευταῖον Βενιαμεὶν ἧκον, οὐκ ἀγνοοῦντες ὅτι εἰς τὸ ἐκείνου σακκίον τὸν σκύφον εἶεν ἀποκεκρυφότες, ἀλλ᾽ ἀκριβῆ τὴν
133 ζήτησιν βουλόμενοι ποιεῖσθαι δοκεῖν. οἱ μὲν οὖν ἄλλοι τοῦ καθ᾽ αὑτοὺς ἀπηλλαγμένοι δέους ἐν τῇ περὶ τὸν Βενιαμεὶν φροντίδι τὸ λοιπὸν ἦσαν, ἐθάρρουν δ᾽ ὡς οὐδ᾽ ἐν ἐκείνῳ τῆς κακουργίας εὑρεθησομένης, ἐκάκιζόν τε τοὺς ἐπιδιώξαντας

[1] αὐτοὺς OE.   [2] εἰδότες codd.

on unrighteous gain than on the affection which they owed to Joseph and their own risk if detected; and they threatened them with instant penalty, for, notwithstanding their flight with the stolen property, they had not escaped the eye of God, even though they had eluded the ministering attendant. "And now you ask," they said, "why we are here, as though you did not know: well, chastisement will soon teach you." With such taunts and yet more did the servant too assail them. But they, ignorant how they stood, mocked at these speeches and expressed their astonishment at the levity with which this servant dared to bring an accusation against persons who had not kept the corn-money found in their sacks, but had brought it back, although no one knew anything of the affair: so far were they from committing a deliberate fraud. However, believing that a search would justify them better than denial, they bade them institute this and, were any individual convicted of pilfering, to punish them all; for, being conscious of no crime, they spoke boldly, supposing that they ran no risk. The Egyptians required search to be made, but declared that punishment should fall only on the individual convicted of the theft. So they proceeded to the investigation and, having passed all the others under review, came last of all to Benjamin; they knew well enough that it was in his sack that they had hidden the cup, but they wished to give their scrutiny a show of thoroughness. The rest, relieved from anxiety on their own account, were now only concerned with regard to Benjamin, but felt confident that he too would not be found in fault; and they abused their pursuers for

---

[3] ὁ ROE with sing. verbs following (ἠξίωσε, ἔφασκεν).

ὡς ἐμποδίσαντας αὐτοῖς τὴν ὁδὸν δυναμένοις ἤδη
134 προκεκοφέναι. ὡς δὲ τὸ τοῦ Βενιαμὶν φορτίον
ἐρευνῶντες λαμβάνουσι τὸν σκύφον εἰς οἰμωγὰς
καὶ θρήνους εὐθὺς ἐτράπησαν καὶ τὰς στολὰς
ἐπικαταρρήξαντες ἔκλαιόν τε τὸν ἀδελφὸν ἐπὶ τῇ
μελλούσῃ κολάσει τῆς κλοπῆς αὐτούς τε διαψευσο-
μένους[1] τὸν πατέρα περὶ τῆς Βενιαμὶν σωτηρίας.
135 ἐπέτεινε δὲ τὸ δεινὸν αὐτοῖς καὶ τὸ δόξαντας ἤδη
διαφυγεῖν τὰ σκυθρωπὰ διαφθονηθῆναι, τῶν δὲ
περὶ τὸν ἀδελφὸν κακῶν καὶ τῆς τοῦ πατρὸς ἐπ᾽
αὐτῷ λύπης ἐσομένους αὐτοὺς αἰτίους ἔλεγον
βιασαμένους ἄκοντα τὸν πατέρα συναποστεῖλαι.
136 (8) Οἱ μὲν οὖν ἱππεῖς παραλαβόντες τὸν Βενιαμὶν ἦγον πρὸς Ἰώσηπον καὶ τῶν ἀδελφῶν
ἑπομένων· ὁ δὲ τὸν μὲν ἰδὼν ἐν φυλακῇ, τοὺς
δ᾽ ἐν πενθίμοις σχήμασι, " τί δή," φησίν, " ὦ
κάκιστοι, φρονήσαντες ἢ περὶ τῆς ἐμῆς φιλανθρωπίας ἢ περὶ τοῦ θεοῦ τῆς προνοίας τοιαῦτα
πράττειν εἰς εὐεργέτην καὶ ξένον ἐτολμήσατε;"
137 τῶν δὲ παραδιδόντων αὑτοὺς εἰς κόλασιν ἐπὶ τῷ
σώζεσθαι Βενιαμὶν καὶ πάλιν ἀναμιμνησκομένων
τῶν εἰς Ἰώσηπον τετολμημένων κἀκεῖνον ἀπο-
καλούντων μακαριώτερον, εἰ μὲν τέθνηκεν ὅτι τῶν
κατὰ τὸν βίον ἀπήλλακται σκυθρωπῶν, εἰ δὲ
περίεστιν ὅτι τῆς παρὰ τοῦ θεοῦ κατ᾽ αὐτῶν
ἐκδικίας τυγχάνει, λεγόντων δ᾽ αὑτοὺς ἀλιτηρίους
τοῦ πατρός, ὅτι τῇ λύπῃ ἣν ἐπ᾽ ἐκείνῳ μέχρι νῦν
ἔχει καὶ τὴν ἐπὶ Βενιαμεῖ προσθήσουσι, πολὺς
ἦν κἀνταῦθ᾽ ὁ Ῥούβηλος αὐτῶν καθαπτόμενος.
138 Ἰωσήπου δὲ τοὺς μὲν ἀπολύοντος, οὐδὲν γὰρ
αὐτοὺς[2] ἀδικεῖν, ἀρκεῖσθαι δὲ μόνῃ τῇ τοῦ παιδὸς

---

[1] RO: διαψευσαμένους rell. [2] αὐτὸν RO Lat.

impeding their journey, on which they might by now have advanced far. But when Benjamin's pack was searched and the cup was found, they forthwith gave way to groans and lamentation and, rending their clothes, they mourned both for their brother and the impending punishment for his theft, and for themselves as like to prove deceivers of their father touching Benjamin's safety. What aggravated their misery was to find themselves baulked by jealous fortune just when they seemed to be quit of their tragedies; and alike for their brother's misfortunes and for the grief which it was to bring to their father they confessed themselves responsible, having constrained their father against his will to send him with them.

(8) So the horsemen arrested Benjamin and led him off to Joseph, the brothers following. But Joseph, seeing Benjamin in custody and his comrades in mourners' guise,[a] exclaimed, "What thought ye then, ye miscreants, of my generosity or of God's watchful eye, that ye dared thus to act towards your benefactor and host?" They, on their side, offered themselves for punishment to save Benjamin; and again they recalled that outrage upon Joseph, pronouncing him to be happier than they, for, if dead, he was released from the miseries of life, if living yet, God had now avenged him upon his persecutors; they denounced themselves as sinners against their father, for to that grief which he felt to this day for Joseph they would now add this sorrow for Benjamin; while Rubel, on this occasion also,[b] roundly rebuked them. But Joseph acquitted them, saying that they were guiltless and that he would be content merely

Arrest of Benjamin. Gen. xliv. 14.

---

[a] With clothes rent. [b] As before, § 107.

τιμωρίᾳ λέγοντος, οὔτε γὰρ τοῦτον ἀπολύειν διὰ τοὺς οὐδὲν ἐξαμαρτόντας σῶφρον ἔλεγεν οὔτε συγκολάζειν ἐκείνους τῷ τὴν κλοπὴν εἰργασμένῳ, βαδιοῦσι δὲ παρέξειν ἀσφάλειαν ἐπαγγελλομένου,
139 τοὺς μὲν ἄλλους ἔκπληξις ἔλαβε καὶ πρὸς τὸ πάθος ἀφωνία, Ἰούδας δὲ ὁ καὶ τὸν πατέρα πείσας ἐκπέμψαι τὸ μειράκιον καὶ τἆλλα δραστήριος ὢν ἀνὴρ ὑπὲρ τῆς τἀδελφοῦ σωτηρίας
140 ἔκρινε παραβάλλεσθαι, καὶ "δεινὰ μέν," εἶπεν, "ὦ στρατηγέ, τετολμήκαμεν εἰς σὲ καὶ τιμωρίας ἄξια καὶ τοῦ κόλασιν ὑποσχεῖν ἅπαντας ἡμᾶς δικαίως, εἰ καὶ τὸ ἀδίκημα μὴ ἄλλου τινός, ἀλλ' ἑνὸς τοῦ νεωτάτου γέγονεν. ὅμως δὲ ἀπεγνωκόσιν ἡμῖν τὴν δι' αὐτοῦ σωτηρίαν ἐλπὶς ὑπολέλειπται παρὰ τῆς σῆς χρηστότητος ἐγγυωμένη τὴν τοῦ
141 κινδύνου διαφυγήν. καὶ νῦν μὴ πρὸς τὸ ἡμέτερον ἀφορῶν μηδὲ τὸ κακούργημα σκοπῶν, ἀλλὰ πρὸς τὴν σαυτοῦ φύσιν, καὶ τὴν ἀρετὴν σύμβουλον ποιησάμενος ἀντὶ τῆς ὀργῆς, ἣν οἱ τἆλλα μικροὶ πρὸς ἰσχύος λαμβάνουσιν οὐκ ἐν τοῖς μεγάλοις μόνον ἀλλὰ καὶ ἐπὶ τοῖς τυχοῦσιν αὐτῇ χρώμενοι, γενοῦ πρὸς αὐτὴν μεγαλόφρων καὶ μὴ νικηθῇς ὑπ' αὐτῆς, ὥστε ἀποκτεῖναι τοὺς οὐδ' αὐτοὺς ὡς ἰδίας ἔτι τῆς σωτηρίας ἀντιποιουμένους, ἀλλὰ
142 παρὰ σοῦ λαβεῖν αὐτὴν ἀξιοῦντας. καὶ γὰρ οὐδὲ νῦν πρῶτον ἡμῖν αὐτὴν παρέξεις, ἀλλὰ [καὶ] τάχιον ἐλθοῦσιν ἐπὶ τὴν ἀγορὰν τοῦ σίτου καὶ τὴν εὐπορίαν τῆς τροφῆς ἐχαρίσω δοὺς ἀποκομίζειν καὶ τοῖς οἰκείοις ὅσα κινδυνεύοντας αὐτοὺς ὑπὸ τοῦ λιμοῦ
143 διαφθαρῆναι περιέσωσε. διαφέρει δ' οὐδὲν ἢ μὴ περιιδεῖν ἀπολλυμένους ὑπ' ἐνδείας τῶν ἀναγκαίων, ἢ μὴ κολάσαι δόξαντας ἁμαρτεῖν καὶ περὶ τὴν

to punish the child: it would be no more reasonable to release him for the sake of his innocent comrades than to make them share the penalty of the guilty thief: they could go and he promised them a safeguard. Thereat the rest were in consternation and speechless from emotion, but Judas, the one who had persuaded his father to send the lad and who was ever a man of energy, to save his brother resolved to brave the risk.

"Grave indeed, my lord governor," said he, "is this crime which we have perpetrated upon thee and deserving of a punishment, which it is but just that we should all undergo, even though the guilt rests with no other than one, the youngest of us. Nevertheless, though we despair of his salvation on his own merits, one hope is left to us in thy generosity, a hope that vouches for his escape from peril. And now look not at our position or the crime: look rather at thine own nature, make virtue thy counsellor in place of that wrath, which mean men take for strength, having recourse to it not in great matters only but in trivial: show thyself magnanimously its master and be not so far overcome by it as to slay such as make no claim on their own behalf, as though their lives were yet their own, but who crave them of thy hand. Ay, and it is not the first time that thou wilt have conferred this boon: already, when we came erstwhile to purchase corn, thou didst both graciously grant us abundance of provisions and permit us to carry to those of our households also the means of their salvation, when like to die of hunger. Yet the difference is naught between refusing to leave men to perish of starvation and refusing to punish apparent sinners who have been

Speech of Judah. Cf. Gen. xliv. 18-34.

εὐεργεσίαν τὴν ἀπὸ σοῦ λαμπρὰν γενομένην
φθονηθέντας, ἡ δ' αὐτὴ χάρις ἄλλῳ μέντοι τρόπῳ
144 διδομένη· σώσεις γὰρ οὓς εἰς τοῦτο καὶ ἔτρεφες
καὶ ψυχάς, ἃς ὑπὸ λιμοῦ καμεῖν οὐκ εἴασας, τηρή-
σεις ταῖς σαυτοῦ δωρεαῖς, ὡς θαυμαστὸν ἅμα καὶ
μέγα δοῦναί τε ψυχὰς ἡμῖν καὶ παρασχεῖν δι' ὧν
145 αὗται μενοῦσιν ἀπορουμένοις. οἶμαί τε τὸν θεόν,
αἰτίαν παρασκευάσαι βουλόμενον εἰς ἐπίδειξιν τοῦ
κατὰ τὴν ἀρετὴν περιόντος, ἡμᾶς εἰς τοῦτο περι-
στῆσαι συμφορᾶς, ἵνα καὶ τῶν εἰς αὐτὸν ἀδικη-
μάτων συγγινώσκων φανῇς τοῖς ἐπταικόσιν, ἀλλὰ
μὴ πρὸς μόνους τοὺς κατ' ἄλλην πρόφασιν δεο-
146 μένους ἐπικουρίας φιλάνθρωπος δοκοίης. ὡς μέγα
μὲν καὶ τὸ ποιῆσαί τινας εὖ καταστάντας εἰς
χρείαν, ἡγεμονικώτερον δὲ σῶσαι τοὺς ὑπὲρ τῶν
εἰς ἑαυτὸν τετολμημένων δίκην ὀφείλοντας· εἰ γὰρ
τὸ περὶ μικρῶν ζημιωμάτων ἀφεῖναι τοὺς πλημ-
μελήσαντας ἔπαινον ἤνεγκε τοῖς ὑπεριδοῦσι, τό γε
περὶ τούτων ἀόργητον, ὑπὲρ ὧν τὸ ζῆν ὑπεύθυνον
τῇ κολάσει γίνεται τῶν ἠδικηκότων, θεοῦ φύσει
147 προσετέθη. καὶ ἔγωγε, εἰ μὴ πατὴρ ἡμῖν ἦν
πῶς[1] ἐπὶ παίδων ἀποβολῇ ταλαιπωρεῖ διὰ τῆς ἐπὶ
Ἰωσήπῳ λύπης[2] ἐπιδεδειγμένος, οὐκ ἂν τοῦ γε
καθ' ἡμᾶς ἕνεκα περὶ τῆς σωτηρίας λόγους ἐποιη-
σάμην, εἰ μὴ ὅσον τῷ σῷ χαριζόμενος ἤθει σῴζειν
αὐτῷ καλῶς ἔχον,[3] καὶ τούτους οἳ λυπήσονται
τεθνηκότων οὐκ ἔχοντες παρείχομεν ἂν αὐτοὺς
148 πεισομένους ὅ τι καὶ θελήσειας· νῦν δ', οὐ γὰρ
αὐτοὺς ἐλεοῦντες, εἰ καὶ νέοι καὶ μήπω τῶν κατὰ
τὸν βίον ἀπολελαυκότες τεθνηξόμεθα, τὸ δὲ τοῦ

---

[1] M Lat.: ὃς rell.   [2] Dindorf: τελευτῆς codd.
[3] edd.: ἔχοντι codd.

grudged that splendid beneficence which thou hast shown them : it is but the same favour accorded in another fashion; for thou wilt be saving those whom thou hast nurtured to this end and preserving by thy bounties souls which thou wouldest not suffer to succumb to hunger, thus achieving the end, alike wonderful and great, of both giving us our lives and affording the means of their continuance in this our distress. Nay, I believe that it was God's good pleasure to provide occasion for a display of virtue in a surpassing form that has brought us to this depth of misery, that so it might be seen that thou pardonest offenders even the injuries done to thyself, and it might not be thought that thy humanity is reserved only for those who on other grounds stand in need of succour. For great though it be to benefit the needy, yet more princely is it to save those who have incurred righteous penalty for crimes perpetrated upon oneself; for if the pardoning of transgressors for light offences redounds to the credit of the indulgent judge, to refrain from wrath in the case of crimes which expose the culprit's life to his victim's vengeance is an attribute of the nature of God.

" For my own part, had not our father let us see by his grief for Joseph how deeply he feels the loss of children, I should never, on our own account, have made this plea for acquittal—save perchance to gratify thy natural and honourable instinct for clemency—and having none to mourn our loss we should have surrendered ourselves to suffer whatsoever penalty might seem good to thee. But now, it is from no pity for ourselves, young though we be and to die ere we have yet enjoyed what life has to

πατρὸς λογιζόμενοι καὶ τὸ γῆρας οἰκτείροντες τὸ
ἐκείνου ταύτας σοι τὰς δεήσεις προσφέρομεν καὶ
παραιτούμεθα ψυχὰς τὰς αὑτῶν, ἅς σοι τὸ ἡμέτερον κακούργημα πρὸς τιμωρίαν παρέδωκεν.
149 ὃς οὔτε πονηρὸς αὐτὸς οὔτε τοιούτους ἐσομένους
ἐγέννησεν, ἀλλὰ χρηστὸς ὢν καὶ πειραθῆναι
τοιούτων οὐχὶ δίκαιος καὶ νῦν μὲν ἀποδημούντων
ταῖς ὑπὲρ ἡμῶν φροντίσι κακοπαθεῖ, πυθόμενος
δὲ ἀπολωλότας καὶ τὴν αἰτίαν οὐχ ὑπομενεῖ ἀλλὰ
διὰ ταύτην πολὺ μᾶλλον τὸν βίον καταλείψει,[1]
150 καὶ τὸ ἄδοξον αὐτὸν τῆς ἡμετέρας καταστροφῆς
φθήσεται διαχρησάμενον καὶ κακὴν αὐτῷ ποιήσει
τὴν ἐκ τοῦ ζῆν ἀπαλλαγήν, πρὶν εἰς ἄλλους
φοιτῆσαι τὰ καθ' ἡμᾶς σπεύσαντος αὐτὸν εἰς
151 ἀναισθησίαν μεταγαγεῖν. γενόμενος οὖν ἐν τούτῳ
τὸν λογισμόν,[2] εἰ καὶ ἡ κακία σε παροξύνει νῦν
ἡ ἡμετέρα, τὸ κατ' αὐτῆς δίκαιον χάρισαι τῷ
πατρὶ καὶ δυνηθήτω πλέον ὁ πρὸς ἐκεῖνον ἔλεος
τῆς ἡμετέρας πονηρίας, καὶ γῆρας ἐν ἐρημίᾳ
βιωσόμενον καὶ τεθνηξόμενον ἡμῶν ἀπολομένων[3]
αἰδέσαι, τῷ πατέρων ὀνόματι ταύτην χαριζόμενος
152 τὴν δωρεάν. ἐν γὰρ τούτῳ καὶ τὸν σὲ φύσαντα
τιμᾷς καὶ σαυτῷ δίδως, ἀπολαύων μὲν ἤδη τῆς
προσηγορίας, ἀπαθὴς δ' ἐπ' αὐτῇ φυλαχθησόμενος
ὑπὸ τοῦ θεοῦ τοῦ πάντων πατρός, εἰς ὃν κατὰ
κοινωνίαν καὶ αὐτὸς τοῦ ὀνόματος εὐσεβεῖν δόξεις
τοῦ ἡμετέρου πατρὸς οἶκτον λαβὼν ἐφ' οἷς πείσεται
153 τῶν παίδων στερούμενος. σὸν οὖν, ἃ παρέσχεν
ἡμῖν ὁ θεὸς ταῦτ' ἔχοντ' ἐξουσίαν ἀφελέσθαι,
δοῦναι καὶ μηδὲν ἐκείνου διενεγκεῖν τῇ χάριτι·
τῆς γὰρ ἐπαμφότερον δυνάμεως τετυχηκότα καλὸν

---

[1] Lat.: καταλείπει, etc., codd.

give; it is from consideration for our father and compassion for his old age that we present this petition to thee and plead for our lives, which our misdeed has delivered into thine avenging hands. He is no knave, nor did he beget sons like to be knavish: no, he is an honest man, undeserving of such trials; at this moment in our absence he is tortured with anxiety for us, and if he learns of our ruin and the cause of it, he will endure no more: that news far more than all will speed his departure, the ignominy of our end will precipitate his own and make his exit from this world miserable, for ere our story reaches other ears he will have hastened to render himself insensible. Bear, then, these considerations in mind, and, however much *our* wrong-doing provokes thee now, graciously give up to our father that retribution which justice demands, and let pity for him outweigh our crime: respect the old age of one who must live and die in solitude in losing us, and grant this boon in the name of fatherhood. For in this name thou wilt alike be doing honour to thy sire and granting a favour to thyself, seeing that thou already rejoicest in that title and wilt be preserved in unimpaired possession of it by God, who is the Father of all; since, in virtue of that name that thou thyself sharest with Him, it will be deemed an act of piety towards *Him* to take pity on our father and the sufferings that he will endure if bereaved of his children. While, then, thou hast authority to take from us that which God has granted us, thy part rather is to give and in no whit to come behind Him in charity; for it beseems the possessor of such two-

---

[2] Lat. in hac ratione (=? ἐν τούτῳ τοῦ λογισμοῦ).
[3] edd.: ἀπολουμένων codd.

ταύτην ἐν τοῖς ἀγαθοῖς ἐπιδείκνυσθαι, καὶ παρὸν καὶ ἀπολλύειν τῆς μὲν κατὰ τοῦτο ἐξουσίας ὡς μηδ' ὑπαρχούσης ἐπιλανθάνεσθαι, μόνον δ' ἐπιτετράφθαι τὸ σώζειν ὑπολαμβάνειν, καὶ ὅσῳ τις πλείοσι τοῦτο παρέξει μᾶλλον αὐτῷ φαίνεσθαι 154 διδόντα. σὺ δὲ πάντας ἡμᾶς σώσεις τἀδελφῷ συγγνοὺς ὑπὲρ ὧν ἠτύχηκεν· οὐδὲ γὰρ ἡμῖν βιώσιμα τούτου κολασθέντος, οἷς γε πρὸς τὸν πατέρα μὴ ἔξεστιν ἀνασωθῆναι μόνοις, ἀλλ' ἐνθάδε δεῖ κοινωνῆσαι τούτῳ τῆς αὐτῆς καταστροφῆς 155 τοῦ βίου. καὶ δεησόμεθά σου, στρατηγέ, κατακρίναντος τὸν ἀδελφὸν ἡμῶν ἀποθανεῖν συγκολάσαι καὶ ἡμᾶς ὡς τοῦ ἀδικήματος κεκοινωνηκότας· οὐ γὰρ ἀξιώσομεν ἡμεῖς ὡς ἐπὶ λύπῃ τεθνηκότος αὐτοὺς ἀνελεῖν, ἀλλ' ὡς ὁμοίως αὐτῷ πονηροὶ 156 γεγονότες οὕτως ἀποθανεῖν. καὶ ὅτι μὲν καὶ νέος ὢν ἥμαρτε καὶ μήπω τὸ φρονεῖν ἐρηρεισμένος καὶ ὡς ἀνθρώπινον τοῖς τοιούτοις συγγνώμην νέμειν, σοὶ καταλιπὼν παύομαι περαιτέρω λέγειν, ἵν' εἰ μὲν κατακρίνειας ἡμῶν, τὰ μὴ λεχθέντα δόξῃ 157 βεβλαφέναι πρὸς τὸ σκυθρωπότερον ἡμᾶς, εἰ δ' ἀπολύσειας, κἀκεῖνα τῇ σαυτοῦ χρηστότητι συνιδὼν ἀπεψηφίσθαι νομισθῇς, οὐ σώσας μόνον ἡμᾶς ἀλλὰ καὶ δι' οὗ δικαιότεροι μᾶλλον φανούμεθα τυχεῖν χαριζόμενος καὶ πλέον ἡμῶν αὐτῶν ὑπὲρ τῆς 158 ἡμετέρας νοήσας σωτηρίας. εἴτ' οὖν κτείνειν αὐτὸν θέλεις, ἐμὲ τιμωρησάμενος ἀντὶ τούτου τῷ πατρὶ τοῦτον ἀπόπεμψον, εἴτε καὶ κατέχειν σοι δοκεῖ δοῦλον, ἐγὼ πρὸς τὰς χρείας σοι ὑπηρετικώτερος, ἀμείνων ὡς ὁρᾷς πρὸς ἑκάτερον τῶν 159 παθῶν ὑπάρχων." Ἰούδας μὲν οὖν πάντα ὑπομένειν ὑπὲρ τῆς τἀδελφοῦ σωτηρίας ἡδέως ἔχων ῥίπτει

fold power to display it in acts of generosity, and, though at liberty to destroy, to forget his rights in this regard as though they existed not, and to believe that he is only empowered to save, and that the more numerous the persons to whom he extends this favour the greater the distinction that he confers upon himself. But thou wilt be the saviour of us all in pardoning our brother his unfortunate error ; for life to us would be intolerable were he punished, since we cannot return in safety to our father alone, but must stay here to share his fate. And we shall entreat thee, my lord, shouldest thou condemn our brother to death, to punish us along with him as accomplices in the crime ; for we shall claim, not in grief for his death to make away with ourselves, but as equally guilty with him to die in like manner

" That the culprit is a youth whose judgment is not yet firm, and that it is human in such cases to accord indulgence, I leave it to thee and forbear to say more ; in order that, shouldest thou condemn us, it may be my omissions which may appear to have brought this severer injury upon us, and, shouldest thou absolve, our acquittal may be attributed to thy gracious and enlightened grasp of those further arguments ; for thou wilt not only have saved us, but have presented us with what will show us to have been even more deserving of success and taken more thought than ourselves for our salvation. If, then, thou wouldest slay him, punish me in his stead and send him back to his father, or, if it please thee to detain him as a slave, I am more serviceable for thy offices, being, as thou seest, better fitted for either fate."

Thereupon Judas, glad to endure anything to save his brother, flung himself at Joseph's feet, striving

πρὸ τῶν Ἰωσήπου ποδῶν ἑαυτόν, εἴ πως ἐκμαλάξειε
τὴν ὀργὴν αὐτοῦ καὶ καταπραΰνειεν ἀγωνιζόμενος,
προύπεσον δὲ καὶ οἱ ἀδελφοὶ πάντες δακρύοντες
καὶ παραδιδόντες ἑαυτοὺς ὑπὲρ τῆς Βενιαμὶν
ψυχῆς ἀπολουμένους.

160 (9) Ὁ δὲ Ἰώσηπος ἐλεγχόμενος ὑπὸ τοῦ πάθους
καὶ μηκέτι δυνάμενος τὴν τῆς ὀργῆς φέρειν
ὑπόκρισιν κελεύει μὲν ἀπελθεῖν τοὺς παρόντας,
ἵνα μόνοις αὐτὸν τοῖς ἀδελφοῖς ποιήσῃ φανερόν,
ἀναχωρησάντων δὲ ποιεῖ γνώριμον αὐτὸν τοῖς
161 ἀδελφοῖς καί φησι· " τῆς μὲν ἀρετῆς ὑμᾶς καὶ
τῆς εὐνοίας τῆς περὶ τὸν ἀδελφὸν ἡμῶν ἐπαινῶ
καὶ κρείττονας ἢ προσεδόκων ἐκ τῶν περὶ ἐμὲ
βεβουλευμένων εὑρίσκω, ταῦτα πάντα ποιήσας
ἐπὶ πείρᾳ τῆς ὑμετέρας φιλαδελφίας· φύσει δὲ
οὐδὲ περὶ ἐμὲ νομίζω πονηροὺς γεγονέναι, θεοῦ
δὲ¹ βουλήσει τήν τε νῦν πραγματευομένου τῶν
ἀγαθῶν ἀπόλαυσιν καὶ τὴν ἐς ὕστερον, ἂν εὐμενὴς
162 ἡμῖν παραμείνῃ. πατρός τε οὖν σωτηρίαν ἐγνωκὼς
οὐδ' ἐλπισθεῖσαν καὶ τοιούτους ὑμᾶς ὁρῶν περὶ
τὸν ἀδελφὸν οὐδ' ὧν εἰς ἐμὲ δοκεῖτε ἁμαρτεῖν ἔτι
μνημονεύω, παύσομαι δὲ τῆς ἐπ' αὐτοῖς μισο-
πονηρίας καὶ ὡς συναιτίοις τῶν τῷ θεῷ βεβουλευμένων εἰς τὰ παρόντα χάριν ἔχειν ὁμολογῶ.
163 ὑμᾶς τε βούλομαι καὶ αὐτοὺς λήθην ἐκείνων
λαβόντας ἥδεσθαι μᾶλλον, τῆς τότε ἀβουλίας εἰς
τοιοῦτον ἐπελθούσης τέλος, ἢ δυσφορεῖν αἰσχυνο-
μένους ἐπὶ τοῖς ἡμαρτημένοις. μὴ οὖν δόξῃ λυπεῖν
ὑμᾶς τὸ κατ' ἐμοῦ ψῆφον ἐνεγκεῖν πονηρὰν καὶ ἡ
ἐπ' αὐτῇ μετάνοια τῷ γε μὴ προχωρῆσαι τὰ
164 βεβουλευμένα. χαίροντες οὖν ἐπὶ τοῖς ἐκ θεοῦ
γεγενημένοις ἄπιτε ταῦτα δηλώσοντες τῷ πατρί,

by any means to mollify and appease his wrath; and all the brethren fell down before him, weeping and offering themselves as victims to save the life of Benjamin.

(9) Joseph, now betrayed by his emotion and unable longer to maintain that simulation of wrath, bade those present retire, in order to reveal himself to his brethren alone. Then, the rest having withdrawn, he made himself known to his brethren and said: " I commend you for your virtue and that affection for our brother and find you better men than I had expected from your plots against me; for all this that I have done was to test your brotherly love. Nor yet, I think, was it through your own nature that ye did me ill, but by the will of God, working out that happiness that we now enjoy and that shall be ours hereafter, if He continue to be gracious to us. Having, then, learnt beyond all hope that my father lives, and seeing you thus devoted to our brother, I remember no more those sins against me of which ye think yourselves guilty; I shall cease to bear you malice for them as the culprits; and as assistants in bringing God's purposes to the present issue I tender you my thanks. And for your part, I would have you too forget the past and rejoice that that old imprudence has resulted in such an end, rather than be afflicted with shame for your faults. Let it not appear, then, that ye are grieved by a wicked sentence passed upon me and by remorse thereat, seeing that your designs did not succeed. Go, therefore, rejoicing at what God has wrought, to tell these things to our father, lest haply

---

[1] SP: τε rell.

μὴ καὶ ταῖς ὑπὲρ ὑμῶν φροντίσιν ἀναλωθεὶς ζημιώσῃ μου τὸ κάλλιστον τῆς εὐδαιμονίας, πρὶν εἰς ὄψιν ἐλθεῖν τὴν ἐμὴν καὶ μεταλαβεῖν τῶν 165 παρόντων ἀποθανών. αὐτὸν δὲ τοῦτον καὶ γυναῖκας ὑμετέρας καὶ [τὰ] τέκνα καὶ πᾶσαν τὴν συγγένειαν ὑμῶν ἀναλαβόντες ἐνθάδε μετοικίζεσθε· οὐδὲ γὰρ ἀποδήμους εἶναι δεῖ τῶν ἀγαθῶν τῶν ἡμετέρων τοὺς ἐμοὶ φιλτάτους ἄλλως τε καὶ τοῦ λιμοῦ 166 λοιπὴν ἔτι πενταετίαν περιμενοῦντος." ταῦτ' εἰπὼν Ἰώσηπος περιβάλλει τοὺς ἀδελφούς· οἱ δ' ἐν δάκρυσιν ἦσαν καὶ λύπῃ τῶν ἐπ' αὐτῷ βεβουλευμένων τιμωρίας τ' οὐδὲν αὐτοῖς ἀπολιπεῖν ἐδόκει τεὔγνωμον τἀδελφοῦ. καὶ τότε μὲν ἦσαν 167 ἐν εὐωχίᾳ· βασιλεὺς δ' ἀκούσας ἥκοντας πρὸς τὸν Ἰώσηπον τοὺς ἀδελφοὺς ἥσθη τε μεγάλως καὶ ὡς ἐπ' οἰκείῳ διατεθεὶς ἀγαθῷ παρεῖχεν αὐτοῖς ἁμάξας σίτου πλήρεις καὶ χρυσὸν καὶ ἄργυρον ἀποκομίζειν τῷ πατρί. λαβόντες δὲ πλείω παρὰ τἀδελφοῦ τὰ μὲν τῷ πατρὶ φέρειν τὰ δὲ αὐτοὶ δωρεὰς ἔχειν ἕκαστος ἰδίας, πλειόνων ἠξιωμένου Βενιαμὶν παρ' αὐτούς, ἀπῄεσαν.

168 (vii. 1) Ὡς δ' ἀφικομένων τῶν παίδων Ἰάκωβος τὰ περὶ τὸν Ἰώσηπον ἔμαθεν, ὅτι μὴ μόνον εἴη τὸν θάνατον διαπεφευγὼς ἐφ' ᾧ πενθῶν διῆγεν, ἀλλὰ καὶ ζῇ μετὰ λαμπρᾶς εὐδαιμονίας βασιλεῖ συνδιέπων τὴν Αἴγυπτον καὶ τὴν ἅπασαν σχεδὸν 169 ἐγκεχειρισμένος αὐτῆς ἐπιμέλειαν, ἄπιστον μὲν οὐδὲν ἐδόκει τῶν ἠγγελμένων λογιζόμενος τοῦ θεοῦ τὴν μεγαλουργίαν καὶ τὴν πρὸς αὐτὸν εὔνοιαν, εἰ καὶ τῷ μεταξὺ χρόνῳ διέλιπεν, ὥρμητο δ' εὐθὺς πρὸς τὸν Ἰώσηπον.

he be consumed with brooding over you and rob me
of the best of my felicity, by dying ere he come into
my sight and partake of our present bliss. Do ye
bring him, him and your wives and children and all
your kinsfolk, and migrate hither; for those whom
I cherish most must not be exiled from the prosperity that is ours, above all when the famine has
still five years to continue." Having spoken thus
Joseph embraced his brethren. But they were
plunged in tears and grief for those designs upon
him and found no lack of chastisement in this forbearance of their brother. They then resorted to
festivity. But the king, hearing that Joseph's Gen. xlv. 16.
brethren were come to him, was highly delighted,
and, moved as though some fortune had befallen
himself, offered them wagons laden with corn, and
gold and silver, to carry to their father. Then, after
receiving further presents from their brother, some
to take to their father, others for each to keep as
his own, Benjamin being favoured with more than
the rest, they went on their way.

(vii. 1) Now when on the arrival of his sons Jacob Jacob
learnt the story of Joseph, how that he had not only departs
escaped that death which he had mourned so long, Ib. 25.
but was living in splendid fortune, sharing with the
king the government of Egypt and having well-nigh
the whole charge of it in his hands, he could deem
none of these reports incredible,[a] when he reflected
on God's mighty power and His benevolence towards
him, albeit for a while suspended; and he straight-
way sped forth to go to Joseph.

---

[a] Josephus omits, or deliberately contradicts, the mention
of his first incredulity: " his heart fainted, for he believed
them not," Gen. xlv. 26.

237

170 (2) Ὡς δὲ κατέσχεν ἐπὶ τὸ Ὅρκιον φρέαρ, θύσας αὐτόθι τῷ θεῷ καὶ φοβούμενος διὰ τὴν εὐδαιμονίαν τὴν ἐν Αἰγύπτῳ τῶν παίδων ἐμφιλοχωρησάντων τῇ οἰκήσει τῇ ἐν αὐτῇ, μὴ οὐκέτ' εἰς τὴν Χαναναίαν οἱ ἔγγονοι μετελθόντες κατά-
171 σχωσιν αὐτήν, ὡς ὁ θεὸς ἦν ὑπεσχημένος, ἅμα τε μὴ δίχα θεοῦ βουλήσεως γενομένης τῆς εἰς Αἴγυπτον ἀφόδου[1] διαφθαρῇ τὸ γένος αὐτοῦ, πρὸς δὲ τούτοις δεδιώς, μὴ προεξέλθῃ τοῦ βίου πρὶν εἰς ὄψιν Ἰωσήπου παραγενέσθαι, καταφέρεται στρέφων ἐν ἑαυτῷ τοῦτον τὸν λογισμὸν εἰς ὕπνον.
172 (3) Ἐπιστὰς δὲ ὁ θεὸς αὐτῷ καὶ δὶς ὀνομαστὶ καλέσας πυνθανομένῳ τίς ἐστιν," ἀλλ' οὐ δίκαιον," εἶπεν, " Ἰακώβῳ θεὸν ἀγνοεῖσθαι τὸν ἀεὶ παραστάτην καὶ βοηθὸν προγόνοις τε τοῖς σοῖς καὶ
173 μετ' αὐτοὺς σοὶ γενόμενον. στερουμένῳ τε γάρ σοι τῆς ἀρχῆς ὑπὸ τοῦ πατρὸς ταύτην ἐγὼ παρέσχον, καὶ κατ' ἐμὴν εὔνοιαν εἰς τὴν Μεσοποταμίαν μόνος σταλεὶς γάμων τε ἀγαθῶν ἔτυχες καὶ παίδων ἐπαγόμενος πλῆθος καὶ χρημάτων ἐνόστησας.
174 παρέμεινέ τέ σοι γενεὰ πᾶσα προνοίᾳ τῇ ἐμῇ, καὶ ὃν ἀπολωλέναι τῶν υἱῶν ἐδόκεις Ἰώσηπον [τοῦτον] εἰς ἀπόλαυσιν μειζόνων ἀγαθῶν ἤγαγον καὶ τῆς Αἰγύπτου κύριον, ὡς ὀλίγῳ διαφέρειν τοῦ βα-
175 σιλέως, ἐποίησα. ἥκω τε νῦν ὁδοῦ τε ταύτης ἡγεμὼν ἐσόμενος καὶ βίου σου τελευτὴν ἐν ταῖς Ἰωσήπου χερσὶ γενησομένην προδηλῶν καὶ μακρὸν αἰῶνα τῶν σῶν ἐγγόνων ἐν ἡγεμονίᾳ καὶ δόξῃ καταγγέλλων καταστήσων τε αὐτοὺς εἰς τὴν γῆν ἣν ὑπέσχημαι."

[1] ἐφόδου ROL (Lat. adventus).

(2) Halting at the Well of the Oath[a] he there offered sacrifice to God; and fearing that by reason of the prosperity prevalent in Egypt his sons would become so greatly enamoured of settling there, that their descendants would never more return to Canaan to take possession of it, as God had promised; and furthermore that having taken this departure into Egypt without God's sanction his race might be annihilated; yet terrified withal that he might quit this life before setting eyes on Joseph—these were the thoughts which he was revolving in his mind when he sank to sleep.

His vision at Beer-sheba.
Gen. xlvi. 1.

(3) Then God appeared to him and called him twice by name, and when Jacob asked who he was, "Nay," He said, "it were not right that Jacob should be ignorant of God, who has ever been a protector and helper alike to thy forefathers and afterward to thee. For when thou wast like to be deprived of the princedom by thy father, it was I who gave it thee; through my favour was it that, when sent all alone to Mesopotamia, thou wast blessed in wedlock and brought with thee an abundance of children and of riches on thy return. And if that progeny has all been preserved to thee, it is through my providence: ay, that son of thine whom thou thoughtest to have lost, even Joseph, him have I led to yet greater felicity, and made him lord of Egypt, hardly differing from its king. And now am I come to be thy guide upon this journey and to foreshew to thee that thou wilt end thy days in Joseph's arms, to announce a long era of dominion and glory for thy posterity, and that I will establish them in the land which I have promised."

[a] Beer-sheba.

176 (4) Τούτῳ θαρρήσας τῷ ὀνείρατι προθυμότερον εἰς τὴν Αἴγυπτον σὺν τοῖς υἱοῖς καὶ παισὶν τοῖς τούτων ἀπηλλάττετο. ἦσαν δ' οἱ πάντες[1] ἑβδομήκοντα. τὰ μὲν οὖν ὀνόματα δηλῶσαι τούτων οὐκ ἐδοκίμαζον καὶ μάλιστα διὰ τὴν δυσκολίαν
177 αὐτῶν· ἵνα μέντοι παραστήσω τοῖς οὐχ ὑπολαμβάνουσιν ἡμᾶς ἐκ τῆς Μεσοποταμίας ἀλλ' Αἰγυπτίους εἶναι, ἀναγκαῖον ἡγησάμην μνησθῆναι τῶν ὀνομάτων. Ἰακώβου μὲν οὖν παῖδες ἦσαν δώδεκα· τούτων Ἰώσηπος ἤδη προαφῖκτο· τοὺς οὖν μετ' αὐτὸν καὶ τοὺς ἐκ τούτων γεγονότας δηλώσομεν.
178 Ῥουβήλου μὲν ἦσαν παῖδες τέσσαρες, Ἀνώχης Φαλοὺς Ἐσσαρῶν Χάρμισος· Συμεῶνος δ' ἕξ, Ἰούμηλος Ἰάμεινος Πούθοδος Ἰαχῖνος Σόαρος Σααρᾶς· τρεῖς δὲ Λευὶ γεγόνασιν υἱοί, Γολγόμης Κάαθος Μάραιρος· Ἰούδᾳ δὲ παῖδες ἦσαν τρεῖς, Σάλας Φάρεσος Ἐζελεός, υἱωνοὶ δὲ δύο γεγονότες ἐκ Φαρέσου, Ἐσρὼν καὶ Ἄμουρος. Ἰσακχάρου δὲ τέσσαρες, Θούλας Φρουρᾶς Ἰωβος Σαμάρων.
179 τρεῖς δὲ Ζαβουλὼν ἦγεν υἱούς, Σάραδον Ἤλωνα Ἰάνηλον. τοῦτο μὲν τὸ ἐκ Λείας γένος· καὶ αὐτῇ συνανῄει καὶ θυγάτηρ αὐτῆς Δεῖνα. τρεῖς οὗτοι
180 καὶ τριάκοντα. Ῥαχήλας δὲ παῖδες ἦσαν δύο· τούτων Ἰωσήπῳ μὲν γεγόνεισαν υἱοὶ Μανασσῆς καὶ Ἐφραίμης. Βενιαμεῖ δὲ τῷ ἑτέρῳ δέκα,

---

[1] + πέντε καὶ RO (after LXX).

[a] So the Hebrew text of Genesis: LXX, including further descendants born in Egypt, raises the total to 75.

[b] Josephus, like Strabo and other Hellenistic writers, commonly omits lists of uncouth names contained in his sources: see Cadbury, *Making of Luke-Acts*, p. 124 with note.

[c] So LXX (some MSS.): Heb. Pallu.

[d] Bibl. Hezron (Ἀσρών).   [e] Carmi.   [f] Jemuel.

JEWISH ANTIQUITIES, II. 176-180

(4) Encouraged by this dream, Jacob with greater ardour departed for Egypt along with his sons and his sons' children: there were in all seventy *a* of them. I was inclined not to recount their names, mainly on account of their difficulty; however, to confute those persons who imagine us to be not of Mesopotamian origin but Egyptians, I have thought it necessary to mention them.*b* Well, Jacob had twelve sons, of whom Joseph had already departed in advance: we proceed, then, to enumerate those who followed him and their descendants. Rubel had four sons, Anoch(es), Phalus,*c* Essaron,*d* Charmis(os)*e*; Symeon six, Jumel(os),*f* Jamin(os), Pouthod(os),*g* Jachin(os), Soar(os),*h* Saar(as)*i*; Levi had three sons, Golgom(es),*j* Kaath(os),*k* Marair(os)*l*; Judas three sons, Salas,*m* Phares(os),*n* Ezele(os),*o* and two grandsons, born of Phares, Esron*p* and Amour(os)*q*; Issachar had four, Thoulas,*r* Phrouras,*s* Job(os), Samaron*t* while Zabulon brought with him three, Sarad(os),*u* Elon, Janel(os).*v* Such was the progeny of Leah, who was also accompanied by her daughter Dinah — in all thirty-three souls. Rachel had two sons: to the one, Joseph, were born Manasses and Ephraim; to the other, Benjamin, ten sons, Bol(os),*w*

The seventy descendants of Jacob.
Gen. xlvi. 8.

---

g Ohad ('Αώδ).
h Zohar (Σαάρ).
i Shaul.
j Gershon.
k So LXX Καάθ: Heb. Kohath.
l Merari.
m Shelah (Σηλώμ).
n So LXX: Heb. Perez.
o Zerah (Ζαρά); Josephus here properly omits the two sons, Er and Onan, who died in Canaan (Gen. xlvi. 12).
p Hezron.
q Hamul ('Ιεμουήλ).
r Tola (Θωλά).
s Puvah (Φουά).
t Shimron (Ζαμβράν).
u Sered.
v Jahleel ('Αλοήλ or 'Ιαήλ).
w Bela (Βαλά)

JOSEPHUS

Βόλος Βάκχαρις Ἀσαβῆλος Γήλας Νεεμάνης Ἴης Ἄρως Νομφθὴς Ὀππαῖς Ἄροδος.¹ οὗτοι τέσσαρες καὶ δέκα πρὸς τοῖς πρότερον κατειλεγμένοις εἰς ἑπτὰ καὶ τεσσαράκοντα γίνονται τὸν 181 ἀριθμόν. καὶ τὸ μὲν γνήσιον γένος τῷ Ἰακώβῳ τοῦτο ἦν, ἐκ Βάλλας δὲ αὐτῷ γίνονται τῆς Ῥαχήλας θεραπαινίδος Δάνος καὶ Νεφθαλίς, ᾧ τέσσαρες εἵποντο παῖδες, Ἐλίηλος Γοῦνις Σάρης τε καὶ Σέλλιμος, Δάνῳ δὲ μονογενὲς ἦν παιδίον 182 Οὖσις. τούτων προσγινομένων τοῖς προειρημένοις πεντήκοντα καὶ τεσσάρων πληροῦσιν ἀριθμόν. Γάδης δὲ καὶ Ἄσηρος ἐκ Ζελφᾶς μὲν ἦσαν, ἣν Λείας δὲ αὕτη θεραπαινίς, παῖδας δ' ἐπήγοντο Γάδης μὲν ἑπτά, Ζοφωνίαν Οὔγιν Σοῦνιν Ζάβρωνα 183 Εἰρήνην Ἐρωίδην Ἀριήλην, Ἀσήρῳ δὲ ἦν θυγάτηρ καὶ ἄρσενες ἀριθμὸν ἕξ, οἷς ὀνόματα Ἰώμνης Ἰσούσιος Ἠιούβης Βάρης Ἀβαρός τε καὶ Μελχίηλος. τούτων ἑκκαίδεκα ὄντων καὶ προστιθεμένων τοῖς πεντήκοντα τέσσαρσιν ὁ προειρημένος ἀριθμὸς πληροῦται μὴ συγκαταλεγέντος αὐτοῖς Ἰακώβου.

184 (5) Μαθὼν δὲ Ἰώσηπος παραγινόμενον² τὸν πατέρα, καὶ γὰρ προλαβὼν Ἰούδας ὁ ἀδελφὸς ἐδήλωσεν αὐτῷ τὴν ἄφιξιν, ἀπαντησόμενος ἔξεισι καὶ καθ' Ἡρώων πόλιν αὐτῷ συνέβαλεν. ὁ δ'

¹ Σάροδος codd. ² RO : παραγενόμενον rell.

[a] Becher (Βοχώρ with variants). [b] Ashbel.
[c] Gera ; Josephus follows the Hebrew in reckoning him and the five following persons as sons (not, as in LXX, grandsons) of Benjamin.
[d] So LXX (some MSS.) : Heb. Naaman. [e] Ehi (Ἀγχεὶς).
[f] Rosh. [g] Muppim (Μαμφείν). [h] Huppim (Ὀφιμίν).
[i] Ard (Ἀράδ) ; LXX makes him a great-grandson of Benjamin. [j] Jahzeel (Ἰασιὴλ with variants).

Bacchar(is),*a* Asabel(os),*b* Gêlas,*c* Neeman(es),*d* Iês,*e* Arôs,*f* Nomphthes,*g* Oppais,*h* Arod(os).*i* These fourteen, added to the previous list, amount to a total of forty-seven. Such was the offspring of Jacob born in wedlock. He had moreover by Balla, the handmaid of Rachel, Dan and Nephthali(s): the latter was accompanied by four children, Eliêl(os),*j* Gounis, Sares,*k* and Sellim(os)*l*; Dan had but one infant, Ousis.*m* These, added to the foregoing, make up a total of fifty-four. Gad and Asêr were sons of Zelpha, the handmaid of Leah: Gad brought with him seven sons, Zophônias,*n* Ougis,*o* Sounis,*p* Zabron,*q* Irênês, Erôidês, Arieles*r*; Asêr had one daughter*s* and six sons, whose names were Jômnes,*t* Isousi(os),*u* Êioubes,*v* Bares,*w* Abar(os),*x* and Melchiêl(os).*y* Adding these sixteen to the fifty-four, we obtain the sum total afore-mentioned, Jacob not being included.

Gen. xlvi. 21.

Ib. 16.

(5) Joseph had learnt of the approach of his father, for his brother Judas had gone on before to announce his coming; and he went out to meet him and joined him at Heroopolis.*z* Jacob from joy, so unlooked-for

Jacob in Egypt. *Ib.* 28.

---

k Jezer (Ἰ(σ)σαάρ).
m Hushim (Ἀσόμ).
o Haggi (Ἀγγείς).
q Ezbon (Θασοβάν).
s Named Serah in Genesis.
u Ishvah.   *v* Ishvi (Ἰεούλ).
x Heber (Χοβώρ); he and the next are in Genesis grandsons of Aser.
l Shillem (Σελλήμ some mss. of LXX).
n Ziphion (Σαφών).
p Shuni (Σαυνίς).
r Eri, Arodi, Areli.
t Imnah (Ἰεμνά).
w Beriah (Βαριά).
y So LXX: Heb. Malchiel.

z Josephus takes over this name from the LXX: the Hebrew text mentions "the land of Goshen." Heroopolis has been identified as the Egyptian Pithom (Ex. i. 11), and Goshen, in which it lay, as the region extending from the eastern arm of the Delta to the Valley of Suez and the Salt Lakes.

JOSEPHUS

ὑπὸ τῆς χαρᾶς ἀπροσδοκήτου τε καὶ μεγάλης γενομένης μικροῦ δεῖν ἐξέλιπεν, ἀλλ' ἀνεζωπύρησεν αὐτὸν Ἰώσηπος οὐδ' αὐτὸς μὲν κρατῆσαι δυνηθεὶς ὡς μὴ ταὐτὸ παθεῖν ὑφ' ἡδονῆς, οὐ μέντοι τὸν αὐτὸν τρόπον τῷ πατρὶ γενόμενος ἥττων τοῦ
185 πάθους. ἔπειτα τὸν μὲν ἠρέμα κελεύσας ὁδεύειν αὐτὸς δὲ παραλαβὼν πέντε τῶν ἀδελφῶν ἠπείγετο πρὸς τὸν βασιλέα φράσων αὐτῷ παραγενόμενον μετὰ τοῦ γένους τὸν Ἰάκωβον. ὁ δὲ τοῦτο χαίρων ἤκουσε καὶ τὸν Ἰώσηπον ἐκέλευσεν αὐτῷ λέγειν τίνι βίῳ τερπόμενοι διατελοῦσιν, ὡς αὐτοῖς τοῦτον
186 ἐπιτρέψειε διάγειν. ὁ δὲ ποιμένας αὐτοὺς ἀγαθοὺς ἔλεγε καὶ μηδενὶ τῶν ἄλλων ἢ τούτῳ μόνῳ προσανέχειν, τοῦ τε μὴ διαζευγνυμένους ἀλλ' ἐν ταὐτῷ τυγχάνοντας ἐπιμελεῖσθαι τοῦ πατρὸς προνοούμενος τοῦ τε τοῖς Αἰγυπτίοις εἶναι προσφιλεῖς μηδὲν πράττοντας τῶν αὐτῶν ἐκείνοις· Αἰγυπτίοις γὰρ ἀπειρημένον ἦν περὶ νομὰς ἀναστρέφεσθαι.
187 (6) Τοῦ δ' Ἰακώβου παραγενομένου πρὸς τὸν βασιλέα καὶ ἀσπαζομένου τε καὶ κατευχομένου περὶ τῆς βασιλείας αὐτῷ ὁ Φαραώθης ἐπυνθάνετο,
188 πόσον ἤδη βεβιωκὼς εἴη χρόνον. τοῦ δ' ἑκατὸν ἔτη καὶ τριάκοντα γεγονέναι φήσαντος ἐθαύμασε τοῦ μήκους τῆς ζωῆς τὸν Ἰάκωβον. εἰπόντος δ' ὡς ἥττονα τῶν προγόνων εἴη βεβιωκὼς ἔτη συνεχώρησεν αὐτῷ ζῆν μετὰ τῶν τέκνων ἐν Ἡλίου πόλει· ἐν ἐκείνῃ γὰρ καὶ οἱ ποιμένες αὐτοῦ τὰς νομὰς εἶχον.

---

[a] After Gen. xlvi. 34 "for every shepherd is an abomination unto the Egyptians." "While there ⸺ that

and so great, was like to die, but Joseph revived him; he too was not master enough of himself to resist the same emotion of delight, but was not, like his father, overcome by it. Then, bidding his father journey gently on, he with five of his brethren sped to the king to tell him of Jacob's arrival with his family. The king rejoiced at the news and bade Joseph tell him what kind of life it was their pleasure to pursue, so that he might permit them to follow the same. Joseph replied that they were good shepherds and devoted themselves to no other calling save that, being anxious both that they should not be separated but, living together, should look after their father, and also that they should ingratiate themselves with the Egyptians by not following any of their pursuits, for the Egyptians were forbidden to occupy themselves with pasture.[a]

(6) When Jacob came into the king's presence and had saluted him and offered his felicitations for his reign,[b] Pharaothes asked him how long he had lived. He replied that he was one hundred and thirty years old, whereat the king marvelled at his great age. To that he answered that his years were fewer than those of his forefathers; the king then permitted him to live with his children in Heliopolis,[c] for it was there that his own shepherds had their pasturage.[d]

Jacob before Pharaoh. Gen. xlvii. 7.

swine-herds and cow-herds were looked down on by the Egyptians, the statement that shepherds were held in special abhorrence has not been confirmed " (Skinner).

[b] Or " realm."

[c] Gen. xlvii. 11, " in the land of Rameses ": Heliopolis or On lay near the south end of the Delta, east of the Pelusiac branch of the Nile.

[d] This addition of Josephus appears, as it stands, a little inconsistent with the last words of the previous paragraph.

189 (7) Ὁ δὲ λιμὸς τοῖς Αἰγυπτίοις ἐπετείνετο καὶ τὸ δεινὸν ἀπορώτερον ἔτι καὶ μᾶλλον αὐτοῖς ἐγίνετο μήτε τοῦ ποταμοῦ [τὴν γῆν] ἐπάρδοντος, οὐ γὰρ ηὔξανε, μήτε ὕοντος τοῦ θεοῦ πρόνοιάν τε μηδεμίαν αὐτῶν ὑπ' ἀγνοίας πεποιημένων. καὶ τοῦ Ἰωσήπου τὸν σῖτον ἐπὶ χρήμασιν αὐτοῖς διδόντος, ὡς¹ ταῦτ' αὐτοῖς ἐπέλιπε, τῶν βοσκημάτων
190 ἐωνοῦντο τὸν σῖτον καὶ τῶν ἀνδραπόδων· οἷς δὲ καὶ γῆς τις ἦν μοῖρα ταύτην² παρεχώρουν ἐπὶ τιμῇ τροφῆς. οὕτως τε τοῦ βασιλέως πάσης αὐτῶν τῆς περιουσίας κυρίου γεγενημένου, μετῳκίσθησαν ἄλλος ἀλλαχοῦ,³ ὅπως βεβαία γένηται τῷ βασιλεῖ τῆς χώρας τούτων ἡ κτῆσις, πλὴν τῶν
191 ἱερέων· τούτοις γὰρ ἔμενεν ἡ χώρα αὐτῶν. ἐδούλου τ' αὐτῶν οὐ τὰ σώματα μόνον τὸ δεινὸν ἀλλὰ καὶ τὰς διανοίας, καὶ τὸ λοιπὸν εἰς ἀσχήμονα τῆς τροφῆς εὐπορίαν αὐτοὺς κατηνάγκαζε. λωφήσαντος δὲ τοῦ κακοῦ καὶ τοῦ τε ποταμοῦ τῆς γῆς ἐπιβάντος καὶ ταύτης τοὺς καρποὺς ἀφθόνως
192 ἐκφερούσης, ὁ Ἰώσηπος εἰς ἑκάστην παραγενόμενος πόλιν καὶ συλλέγων ἐν αὐταῖς τὸ πλῆθος τήν τε γῆν αὐτοῖς, ἣν ἐκείνων παραχωρούντων βασιλεὺς ἔχειν ἠδύνατο καὶ καρποῦσθαι μόνος, εἰς ἅπαν ἐχαρίζετο καὶ κτῆμα ἴδιον ἡγουμένους φιλεργεῖν παρεκάλει τὴν πέμπτην τῶν καρπῶν τῷ βασιλεῖ τελοῦντας ὑπὲρ τῆς χώρας, ἣν δίδωσιν
193 αὐτοῖς οὖσαν αὐτοῦ. τοὺς δὲ παρ' ἐλπίδας κυρίους τῆς γῆς καθισταμένους χαρά τε ἐλάμβανε καὶ ὑφίσταντο τὰ προστάγματα. καὶ τούτῳ τῷ τρόπῳ τό τε ἀξίωμα παρὰ τοῖς Αἰγυπτίοις αὐτοῦ μεῖζον

¹ So Lat.: + δὲ codd.   ² ταύτης E Zon.
³ RO: ἀλλαχόσε rell.

(7) But the famine was now tightening its hold upon the Egyptians and the scourge reducing them to ever increasing straits: the river no more watered the land, for it had ceased to rise, nor did God send rain,[a] and they in their ignorance had taken no precautions. Joseph still granted them corn for their money, and, when money failed, they bought the corn with their flocks and their slaves; any who moreover had a parcel of ground surrendered it to purchase food. And thus it befell that the king became owner of all their substance, and they were transported from place to place, in order to assure to the king the possession of their territory, save only the priests, for these kept their domains. Furthermore, this scourge enslaved not only their bodies but their minds [b] and drove them thereafter to degrading means of subsistence. But when the evil abated and the river overflowed the land and the land yielded its fruits in abundance, Joseph repaired to each city and, convening the inhabitants, bestowed upon them in perpetuity the land which they had ceded to the king and which he might have held and reserved for his sole benefit; this he exhorted them to regard as their own property and to cultivate assiduously, while paying the fifth of the produce to the king in return for the ground which he had given them, being really his. And they, thus unexpectedly become proprietors of the soil, were delighted and undertook to comply with these injunctions. By these means Joseph increased at once his own reputation

New law of land tenure in Egypt. Gen. xlvii. 13.

[a] This remark, as Reland observed, ignores the fact that Egypt is practically a rainless country.

[b] Based on Thuc. ii. 61 δουλοῖ γὰρ φρόνημα τὸ αἰφνίδιον κτλ. (Pericles on the plague of Athens); 'a favourite phrase of Josephus or his assistant; *cf.* iii. 56, xix. 42.

JOSEPHUS

Ἰώσηπος ἀπεργάζεται¹ πλείω τε τὴν εὔνοιαν τῷ βασιλεῖ παρ' αὐτῶν, ὅ τε τοῦ τελεῖν τὴν πέμπτην τῶν καρπῶν νόμος ἔμεινε καὶ μέχρι τῶν ὕστερον βασιλέων.

194 (viii. 1) Ἰάκωβος δὲ ἑπτακαιδέκατον ἔτος ἐν Αἰγύπτῳ διατρίψας καὶ νόσῳ χρησάμενος παρόντων αὐτῷ τῶν υἱῶν ἀπέθανεν, ἐπευξάμενος τοῖς μὲν κτῆσιν ἀγαθῶν καὶ προειπὼν αὐτοῖς κατὰ προφητείαν, πῶς μέλλει τῶν ἐκ τῆς γενεᾶς αὐτῶν ἕκαστος κατοικεῖν τὴν Χαναναίαν, ὃ² δὴ καὶ πολ-
195 λοῖς ὕστερον χρόνοις ἐγένετο, Ἰωσήπου δ' ἐγκώμιον διεξελθών, ὅτι μὴ μνησικακήσειε τοῖς ἀδελφοῖς, ἀλλὰ καὶ τούτου πλέον χρηστὸς εἰς αὐτοὺς ἐγένετο δωρησάμενος αὐτοὺς ἀγαθοῖς, οἷς οὐδὲ εὐεργέτας τινὲς ἠμείψαντο, προσέταξε τοῖς ἰδίοις παισίν, ἵνα τοὺς Ἰωσήπου παῖδας Ἐφραίμην καὶ Μανασσῆν εἰς τὸν αὑτῶν ἀριθμὸν προσῶνται διαιρούμενοι μετ' αὐτῶν τὴν Χαναναίαν, περὶ ὧν
196 ὕστερον ἐροῦμεν. ἠξίου μέντοι καὶ ταφῆς ἐν Νεβρῶνι τυγχάνειν· τελευτᾷ δὲ βιοὺς ἔτη τὰ πάντα τριῶν δέοντα πεντήκοντα καὶ ἑκατόν, μηδενὸς μὲν τῶν προγόνων ἀπολειφθεὶς ἐπ' εὐσεβείᾳ τοῦ θεοῦ, τυχὼν δὲ ἀμοιβῆς ἧς δίκαιον ἦν τοὺς οὕτως ἀγαθοὺς γεγονότας. Ἰώσηπος δὲ συγχωρήσαντος αὐτῷ τοῦ βασιλέως τὸν τοῦ πατρὸς νεκρὸν εἰς
197 Νεβρῶνα κομίσας ἐκεῖ θάπτει πολυτελῶς. τῶν δ' ἀδελφῶν οὐ βουλομένων αὐτῷ συνυποστρέφειν, δέος γὰρ αὐτοὺς εἶχε μὴ τεθνηκότος αὐτοῖς τοῦ πατρὸς τιμωρήσαιτο τῆς εἰς αὐτὸν ἐπιβουλῆς, οὐκέτ' ὄντος ᾧ χαρίζοιτο τὴν πρὸς αὐτοὺς μετριότητα, πείθει μηδὲν ὑφορᾶσθαι μηδ' ἔχειν αὐτὸν δι' ὑποψίας, ἀγαγὼν δὲ μεθ' αὑτοῦ κτῆσιν πολλὴν

with the Egyptians and their loyalty to the king. The law imposing payment of the fifth of the produce remained in force under the later kings. *Gen. xlvii. 26.*

(viii. 1) After passing seventeen years in Egypt, Jacob fell sick and died. His sons were present at his end, and he offered prayers that they might attain to felicity and foretold to them in prophetic words how each of their descendants was destined to find a habitation in Canaan, as in fact long after came to pass. Upon Joseph he lavished praises, for that he had borne no malice against his brethren, nay, more than that, had been generous to them in loading them with presents such as some would not have given even to requite their benefactors; and he charged his own sons to reckon among their number Joseph's sons, Ephraim and Manasses, and to let them share in the division of Canaan—of which events we shall speak hereafter. Furthermore he desired to be buried at Hebron. So he died, having lived in all but three years short of one hundred and fifty, having come behind none of his forefathers in piety towards God and having met with the recompense which such virtue deserved. Joseph, with the sanction of the king, conveyed his father's corpse to Hebron and there gave it sumptuous burial. His brethren thereafter were loth to return with him, fearing that, now their father was dead, he would avenge himself for that plot upon his life, seeing that there was no longer any to thank him for showing forbearance towards them; but he persuaded them to have no misgivings nor to regard him with suspicion, and, taking them with him, he granted them

Death and burial of Jacob. Ib. 28, xlviii. 1, xlix. 1.

Ib. xlvii. 28.

Ib. l. 4.

---

¹ + καὶ codd.
² Lat.· τοῦτο codd.

ἐχαρίσατο καὶ πάσῃ περὶ αὐτοὺς σπουδῇ χρώμενος οὐκ ἀπέλιπε.

198 (2) Τελευτᾷ δὲ καὶ οὗτος ἔτη βιώσας ἑκατὸν καὶ δέκα θαυμάσιος τὴν ἀρετὴν γενόμενος καὶ λογισμῷ πάντα διοικῶν καὶ τὴν ἐξουσίαν ταμιευόμενος, ὃ δὴ καὶ τῆς τοιαύτης εὐδαιμονίας αἴτιον αὐτῷ παρὰ τοῖς Αἰγυπτίοις ἀλλαχόθεν ἥκοντι καὶ μετὰ τοιαύτης κακοπραγίας, μεθ' ἧς προειρήκαμεν,
199 ὑπῆρχε. τελευτῶσι δ' αὐτοῦ καὶ οἱ ἀδελφοὶ ζήσαντες εὐδαιμόνως ἐπὶ τῆς Αἰγύπτου. καὶ τούτων μὲν τὰ σώματα κομίσαντες μετὰ χρόνον οἱ ἀπόγονοι [καὶ οἱ παῖδες]¹ ἔθαψαν ἐν Νεβρῶνι,
200 τὰ δὲ Ἰωσήπου ὀστᾶ ὕστερον, ὅτε μετανέστησαν ἐκ τῆς Αἰγύπτου οἱ Ἑβραῖοι, εἰς τὴν Χαναναίαν ἐκόμισαν· οὕτως γὰρ αὐτοὺς ὁ Ἰώσηπος ἐξώρκισε. τούτων οὖν ἕκαστος ὡς ἔσχε καὶ τίσι πόνοις ἐκράτησαν τῆς Χαναναίας σημανῶ προδιηγησάμενος τὴν αἰτίαν δι' ἣν τὴν Αἴγυπτον ἐξέλιπον.

201 (ix. 1) Αἰγυπτίοις τρυφεροῖς καὶ ῥᾳθύμοις πρὸς πόνους οὖσι καὶ τῶν τε ἄλλων ἡδονῶν ἥττοσι καὶ δὴ καὶ τῆς κατὰ φιλοκέρδειαν συνέβη δεινῶς πρὸς τοὺς Ἑβραίους διατεθῆναι κατὰ φθόνον τῆς εὐ
202 δαιμονίας. ὁρῶντες γὰρ τὸ τῶν Ἰσραηλιτῶν γένος ἀκμάζον καὶ δι' ἀρετὴν καὶ τὴν πρὸς τὸ πονεῖν εὐφυΐαν πλήθει χρημάτων ἤδη λαμπρούς, καθ' αὑτῶν αὔξεσθαι τούτους ὑπελάμβανον, ὧν τ' ἦσαν [εὖ] ὑπὸ Ἰωσήπου τετυχηκότες διὰ χρόνου μῆκος λήθην λαβόντες καὶ τῆς βασιλείας εἰς ἄλλον οἶκον

¹ om. E Lat.

great possessions and never ceased to hold them in highest regard.

(2) Then he too died, at the age of one hundred and ten years, a man of admirable virtue, who directed all affairs by the dictates of reason and made but sparing use of his authority; to which fact he owed that great prosperity of his among the Egyptians, albeit he had come as a stranger and in such pitiful circumstances as we have previously described. His brethren also died after sojourning happily in Egypt. Their bodies were carried some time afterwards by their descendants [and their sons] to Hebron and buried there.[a] But as for Joseph's bones, it was only later, when the Hebrews migrated from Egypt, that they conveyed them to Canaan, in accordance with the oath which Joseph had laid upon them. How it fared with each of them and by what efforts they conquered Canaan I shall recount, after first relating the reason for which they left Egypt.

(ix. 1) The Egyptians, being a voluptuous people and slack to labour, slaves to pleasure in general and to a love of lucre in particular, eventually became bitterly disposed towards the Hebrews through envy of their prosperity. For seeing the race of the Israelites flourishing and that their virtues and aptitude for labour had already gained them the distinction of abundant wealth, they believed that their growth in power was to their own detriment. Those benefits which they had received from Joseph being through lapse of time forgotten, and the kingdom having now passed to another dynasty,

---

[a] Not mentioned in the Old Testament narrative, but *cf* Acts vii. 16.

μετεληλυθυίας δεινῶς ἐνύβριζόν τε τοῖς Ἰσραηλίταις
203 καὶ ταλαιπωρίας αὐτοῖς ποικίλας ἐπενόουν. τόν
τε γὰρ ποταμὸν εἰς διώρυχας αὐτοῖς πολλὰς προσ-
έταξαν διατεμεῖν τείχη τε οἰκοδομῆσαι ταῖς πόλεσι
καὶ χώματα, ὅπως ἂν εἴργοι τὸν ποταμὸν μὴ
λιμνάζειν [ἕως ἐκείνων]¹ ἐπεκβαίνοντα, πυραμίδας
τε ἀνοικοδομοῦντες ἐξετρύχουν ἡμῶν τὸ γένος, ὡς
τέχνας τε παντοίας ἀναδιδάσκεσθαι καὶ τοῖς πόνοις
204 γενέσθαι συνήθεις. καὶ τετρακοσίων μὲν ἐτῶν
χρόνον διήνυσαν ταῖς ταλαιπωρίαις· ἀντεφιλονίκουν
γὰρ οἱ μὲν Αἰγύπτιοι τοῖς πόνοις ἐξαπολέσαι τοὺς
Ἰσραηλίτας θέλοντες, οἱ δ᾽ ἀεὶ κρείττους φαίνεσθαι
τῶν ἐπιταγμάτων.

205 (2) Ἐν τούτοις δ᾽ ὄντων αὐτῶν τοῖς πράγμασιν
αἰτία τοῦ μᾶλλον σπουδάσαι περὶ τὸν ἀφανισμὸν
τοῦ γένους ἡμῶν τοῖς Αἰγυπτίοις προσεγένετο
τοιαύτη· τῶν ἱερογραμματέων τις, καὶ γάρ εἰσι
δεινοὶ περὶ τῶν μελλόντων τὴν ἀλήθειαν εἰπεῖν,
ἀγγέλλει τῷ βασιλεῖ τεχθήσεσθαί τινα κατ᾽
ἐκεῖνον τὸν καιρὸν τοῖς Ἰσραηλίταις, ὃς ταπεινώσει
μὲν τὴν Αἰγυπτίων ἡγεμονίαν, αὐξήσει δὲ τοὺς
Ἰσραηλίτας τραφεὶς ἀρετῇ τε πάντας ὑπερβαλεῖ
206 καὶ δόξαν ἀείμνηστον κτήσεται. δείσας δ᾽ ὁ
βασιλεὺς κατὰ γνώμην τὴν ἐκείνου κελεύει πᾶν
τὸ γεννηθὲν ἄρσεν ὑπὸ τῶν Ἰσραηλιτῶν εἰς τὸν
ποταμὸν ῥιπτοῦντας διαφθείρειν, παραφυλάσσειν
τε τὰς ὠδῖνας τῶν Ἑβραίων γυναικῶν καὶ τοὺς
τοκετοὺς αὐτῶν παρατηρεῖν τὰς Αἰγυπτίων μαίας·

¹ om. ROE Lat.

[a] Amplification of Scripture, which specifies only the building of " store cities, Pithom and Raamses," Ex. i. 11.

[b] A round number, found also in Gen. xv. 13, but inconsistent with other statements of Josephus. In Ex. xii. 40,

they grossly maltreated the Israelites and devised for them all manner of hardships. Thus they ordered them to divide the river into numerous canals, to build ramparts for the cities and dikes to hold the waters of the river and to prevent them from forming marshes when they overflowed its banks; and with the rearing of pyramid after pyramid they exhausted our race,[a] which was thus apprenticed to all manner of crafts and became inured to toil. For full four hundred years [b] they endured these hardships: it was indeed a contest between them, the Egyptians striving to kill off the Israelites with drudgery, and these ever to show themselves superior to their tasks.

(2) While they were in this plight, a further incident had the effect of stimulating the Egyptians yet more to exterminate our race. One of the sacred scribes [c]—persons with considerable skill in accurately predicting the future—announced to the king that there would be born to the Israelites at that time one who would abase the sovereignty of the Egyptians and exalt the Israelites, were he reared to manhood, and would surpass all men in virtue and win everlasting renown. Alarmed thereat, the king, on this sage's advice, ordered that every male child born to the Israelites should be destroyed by being cast into the river, and that the labours of Hebrew women with child should be observed and watch kept for their delivery by the Egyptian midwives:

Egyptian prediction of birth of Moses: orders to destroy the Israelite infants. Cf. Ex. i. 15.

where the sojourn in Egypt is reckoned as 430 years, Josephus, following the LXX, includes in that period the previous sojourn in Canaan and reduces the stay in Egypt by one-half (to 215 years).

[c] Egyptian priests, keepers and interpreters of the sacred records. A Rabbinic allusion to a similar prediction of the Egyptian astrologers is quoted by Weill.

JOSEPHUS

207 ὑπὸ γὰρ τούτων αὐτὰς ἐκέλευε μαιοῦσθαι, αἳ διὰ συγγένειαν ἔμελλον μὴ παραβήσεσθαι τὴν τοῦ βασιλέως βούλησιν· τοὺς μέντοι καταφρονήσαντας τοῦ προστάγματος καὶ σώζειν λάθρα τολμήσαντας τὸ τεχθὲν αὐτοῖς ἀναιρεῖσθαι σὺν τῇ γενεᾷ προσ-
208 έταξεν. δεινὸν οὖν τοῖς ὑπομένουσι τὸ πάθος, οὔ[1] καθὸ παίδων ἀπεστεροῦντο καὶ γονεῖς ὄντες αὐτοὶ πρὸς τὴν ἀπώλειαν ὑπούργουν τῶν γεννωμένων, ἀλλὰ καὶ ἡ ἐπίνοια τῆς τοῦ γένους αὐτῶν ἐπιλείψεως, φθειρομένων μὲν τῶν τικτομένων, αὐτῶν δὲ διαλυθησομένων, χαλεπὴν αὐτοῖς καὶ
209 δυσπαραμύθητον ἐποίει τὴν συμφοράν. καὶ οἱ μὲν ἦσαν ἐν τούτῳ τῷ κακῷ· κρατήσειε δ' ἂν οὐδεὶς τῆς τοῦ θεοῦ γνώμης οὐδὲ μυρίας τέχνας ἐπὶ τούτῳ μηχανησάμενος· ὅ τε γὰρ παῖς, ὃν προεῖπεν ὁ ἱερογραμματεύς, τρέφεται λαθὼν τὴν τοῦ βασιλέως φυλακὴν καὶ ἀληθὴς ἐπὶ τοῖς ἐξ αὐτοῦ γενησομένοις ὁ προειπὼν εὑρέθη. γίνεται δ' οὕτως.

210 (3) Ἀμαράμης τῶν εὖ γεγονότων παρὰ τοῖς Ἑβραίοις, ὡς δεδιὼς ὑπὲρ τοῦ παντὸς ἔθνους, μὴ σπάνει τῆς ἐπιτραφησομένης νεότητος ἐπιλείπῃ, καὶ χαλεπῶς ἐφ' αὑτῷ φέρων, ἐκύει γὰρ αὐτῷ τὸ
211 γύναιον, ἐν ἀμηχάνοις ἦν, καὶ πρὸς ἱκετείαν τοῦ θεοῦ τρέπεται παρακαλῶν οἶκτον ἤδη τινὰ λαβεῖν αὐτὸν ἀνθρώπων μηδὲν τῆς εἰς αὐτὸν θρησκείας παραβεβηκότων δοῦναί τ' ἀπαλλαγὴν αὐτοῖς ὧν παρ' ἐκεῖνον ἐκακοπάθουν τὸν καιρὸν καὶ τῆς ἐπ'
212 ἀπωλείᾳ τοῦ γένους αὐτῶν ἐλπίδος. ὁ δὲ θεὸς ἐλεήσας αὐτὸν καὶ πρὸς τὴν ἱκεσίαν ἐπικλασθεὶς

[1] non tantum Lat.

for this office was, by his orders, to be performed by women who, as compatriots of the king, were not likely to transgress his will [a]: those who notwithstanding defied this decree and ventured stealthily to save their offspring he ordered to be put to death along with their progeny. Terrible then was the calamity confronting the victims: not only were they to be bereft of their children, not only must the parents themselves be accessories to the destruction of their offspring, but the design of extinguishing their race by the massacre of the infants and their own approaching dissolution rendered their lot cruel and inconsolable. Such was their miserable situation; but no man can defeat the will of God, whatever countless devices he may contrive to that end. For this child, whose birth the sacred scribe had foretold, was reared, eluding the king's vigilance, and the prophet's words concerning all that was to be wrought through him proved true; and this is how it happened.

(3) Amaram(es),[b] a Hebrew of noble birth, fearing that the whole race would be extinguished through lack of the succeeding generation, and seriously anxious on his own account because his wife was with child, was in grievous perplexity. He accordingly had recourse to prayer to God, beseeching Him to take some pity at length on men who had in no wise transgressed in their worship of Him, and to grant them deliverance from the tribulations of the present time and from the prospect of the extermination of their race. And God had compassion on him and, moved by his supplication, appeared to him in his

God's prediction to Amram.

[a] Contrary to Ex. i. 15 ff., which states that the orders were given to the Hebrew midwives.

[b] The name Amram, omitted in Ex. ii. 1, is mentioned later (vi. 20).

ἐφίσταται κατὰ τοὺς ὕπνους αὐτῷ καὶ μήτε ἀπογινώσκειν αὐτὸν περὶ τῶν μελλόντων παρεκάλει τήν τε εὐσέβειαν αὐτῶν ἔλεγε διὰ μνήμης ἔχειν καὶ τὴν ὑπὲρ αὐτῆς ἀμοιβὴν ἀεὶ παρέξειν, ἤδη μὲν καὶ τοῖς προγόνοις αὐτῶν δωρησάμενος τὸ γενέσθαι τοσοῦτον πλῆθος αὐτοὺς ἐξ ὀλίγων·
213 καὶ Ἄβραμον μὲν μόνον ἐκ τῆς Μεσοποταμίας εἰς τὴν Χαναναίαν παραγενόμενον εὐδαιμονῆσαι τά τε ἄλλα καὶ τῆς γυναικὸς αὐτῷ πρὸς γονὴν ἀκάρπως ἐχούσης πρότερον, ἔπειτα κατὰ τὴν αὐτοῦ βούλησιν ἀγαθῆς πρὸς τοῦτο γενομένης, τεκνῶσαι παῖδας καὶ καταλιπεῖν μὲν Ἰσμαήλῳ καὶ τοῖς ἐξ αὐτοῦ τὴν Ἀράβων χώραν, τοῖς δ' ἐκ Κατούρας τὴν Τρωγλοδῦτιν, Ἰσάκῳ δὲ τὴν
214 Χαναναίαν. "ὅσα τε πολεμῶν κατὰ τὴν ἐμήν," φησί, "συμμαχίαν ἠνδραγάθησε κἂν ἀσεβεῖς εἶναι δόξαιτε[1] μὴ διὰ μνήμης ἔχοντες. Ἰάκωβον δὲ καὶ τοῖς οὐχ ὁμοφύλοις γνώριμον εἶναι συμβέβηκεν ἐπί τε μεγέθει τῆς εὐδαιμονίας μεθ' ἧς ἐβίωσε καὶ παισὶ τοῖς αὐτοῦ κατέλιπεν, οὗ μετὰ ἑβδομήκοντα τῶν πάντων εἰς Αἴγυπτον ἀφικομένου ὑπὲρ ἑξήκοντά που μυριάδες[2] ἤδη γεγόνατε.
215 νῦν δ' ἐμὲ τοῦ κοινῇ συμφέροντος ὑμῶν ἴστε προνοούμενον καὶ τῆς σῆς εὐκλείας· ὁ παῖς γὰρ οὗτος, οὗ τὴν γένεσιν Αἰγύπτιοι δεδιότες κατέκριναν ἀπολλύναι τὰ ἐξ Ἰσραηλιτῶν τικτόμενα, σὸς ἔσται, καὶ λήσεται μὲν τοὺς ἐπ' ὀλέθρῳ παρα-
216 φυλάσσοντας, τραφεὶς δὲ παραδόξως τὸ μὲν Ἑβραίων γένος τῆς παρ' Αἰγυπτίοις ἀνάγκης ἀπολύσει, μνήμης δὲ ἐφ' ὅσον μενεῖ χρόνον τὰ

---

[1] edd.: δόξητε καὶ codd.
[2] μυριάδας Ε.

sleep,[a] exhorted him not to despair of the future, and told him that He had their piety in remembrance and would ever give them its due recompense, even as He had already granted their forefathers to grow from a few souls into so great a multitude. He recalled how Abraham, departing alone from Mesopotamia on his journey to Canaan, had in every way been blessed and above all how his wife, once barren, had thereafter, thanks to His will, been rendered fertile; how he had begotten sons and had bequeathed to Ishmael and his descendants the land of Arabia, to his children by Katura Troglodytis,[b] to Isaac Canaan. "Aye," He said, "and all that prowess that he displayed in war under my auspices,[c] ye would indeed be deemed impious not to hold in remembrance. Jacob too became famous even among an alien people for the height of that prosperity to which he attained in his lifetime and which he left to his children; with but seventy souls in all he arrived in Egypt, and already ye are become upwards of six hundred thousand.[d] And now be it known to you that I am watching over the common welfare of you all and thine own renown. This child, whose birth has filled the Egyptians with such dread that they have condemned to destruction all the offspring of the Israelites, shall indeed be thine; he shall escape those who are watching to destroy him, and, reared in marvellous wise, he shall deliver the Hebrew race from their bondage in Egypt, and be remem-

[a] Amram's dream, an amplification of the Biblical narrative, is mentioned in the oldest Rabbinic commentary on Exodus, known as *Mechilta* (Weill).
[b] i. 238 f.   [c] In the rescue of Lot.
[d] The traditional exaggerated figure of the adult males who left Egypt (Ex. xii. 37, Numb. xi. 21).

σύμπαντα τεύξεται παρ' ἀνθρώποις οὐχ Ἑβραίοις μόνον ἀλλὰ καὶ παρὰ τοῖς ἀλλοφύλοις, ἐμοῦ τοῦτο χαριζομένου σοί τε καὶ τοῖς ἐκ σοῦ γενησομένοις. ἔσται δ' αὐτῷ καὶ ὁ ἀδελφὸς τοιοῦτος, ὥστε τὴν ἐμὴν ἕξειν ἱερωσύνην αὐτόν τε καὶ τοὺς ἐγγόνους αὐτοῦ διὰ παντὸς τοῦ χρόνου."

217 (4) Ταῦτα τῆς ὄψεως αὐτῷ δηλωσάσης περιεγερθείς[1] ὁ Ἀμαράμης ἐδήλου τῇ Ἰωχαβέλῃ, γυνὴ δ' ἦν αὐτοῦ, καὶ τὸ δέος ἔτι μεῖζον διὰ τὴν τοῦ ὀνείρου πρόρρησιν αὐτοῖς συνίστατο· οὐ γὰρ ὡς περὶ παιδὸς μόνον εὐλαβεῖς ἦσαν, ἀλλὰ καὶ ὡς
218 ἐπὶ μεγέθει τοσαύτης εὐδαιμονίας ἐσομένου. τοῖς μέντοι προκατηγγελμένοις ὑπὸ τοῦ θεοῦ πίστιν ὁ τοκετὸς τῆς γυναικὸς παρεῖχε λαθούσης τοὺς φύλακας διὰ τὴν τῶν ὠδίνων ἐπιείκειαν καὶ τῷ μὴ βιαίας αὐτῇ προσπεσεῖν τὰς ἀλγηδόνας. καὶ τρεῖς μὲν μῆνας παρ' αὐτοῖς τρέφουσι λανθάνοντες·
219 ἔπειτα δὲ δείσας Ἀμαράμης, μὴ κατάφωρος γένηται καὶ πεσὼν ὑπὸ τὴν τοῦ βασιλέως ὀργὴν αὐτός τε ἀπόληται[2] μετὰ τοῦ παιδίου καὶ τοῦ θεοῦ τὴν ἐπαγγελίαν ἀφανίσειεν, ἔγνω μᾶλλον ἐπὶ τούτῳ ποιήσασθαι τὴν τοῦ παιδὸς σωτηρίαν καὶ πρόνοιαν ἢ τῷ λήσεσθαι πεπιστευκώς, τοῦτο δ' ἦν ἄδηλον, ἐναποκινδυνεύειν οὐ τῷ παιδὶ μόνον
220 κρυφαίως τρεφομένῳ ἀλλὰ καὶ αὐτῷ· τὸν δὲ θεὸν ἡγεῖτο πᾶσαν ἐκποριεῖν ἀσφάλειαν ὑπὲρ τοῦ μηδὲν ψευδὲς γενέσθαι τῶν εἰρημένων. ταῦτα κρίναντες μηχανῶνται πλέγμα βίβλινον, ἐμφερὲς τῇ κατὰ σκευῇ κοιτίδι, μεγέθους αὐτὸ ποιήσαντες αὐτάρκους εἰς τὸ μετ' εὐρυχωρίας ἐναποκεῖσθαι τὸ

---

[1] περιχαρὴς ἐγερθεὶς RO.
[2] ἀπολεῖται codd.

JEWISH ANTIQUITIES, II. 216–220

bered, so long as the universe shall endure, not by Hebrews alone but even by alien nations; that favour do I bestow upon thee and upon thy posterity. Furthermore, he shall have a brother so blessed as to hold my priesthood, he and his descendants, throughout all ages."

(4) These things revealed to him in vision, Amaram on awaking disclosed to Jochabel(e),[a] his wife; and their fears were only the more intensified by the prediction in the dream. For it was not merely for a child that they were anxious, but for that high felicity for which he was destined. However, their belief in the promises of God was confirmed by the manner of the woman's delivery, since she escaped the vigilance of the watch, thanks to the gentleness of her travail, which spared her any violent throes.[b] For three months they reared the child in secret; and then Amaram, fearing that he would be detected and, incurring the king's wrath, would perish himself along with the young child and thus bring God's promise to nought, resolved to commit the salvation and protection of the child to Him, rather than to trust to the uncertain chance of concealment and thereby endanger not only the child, clandestinely reared, but himself also; assured that God would provide complete security that nothing should be falsified of that which He had spoken. Having so determined, they constructed a basket of papyrus reeds, fashioned in the form of a cradle, spacious enough to give the infant ample room for repose;

Birth of Moses: his exposure on the Nile.

Ex. ii. 2.

---

[a] Bibl. Jochebed (LXX Ἰωχαβέδ) Ex. vi. 20: the final consonant in the form above comes from confusion of the Greek letters Δ and Λ and is perhaps attributable to later scribes.

[b] Amplification, with Rabbinic parallel (Weill).

221 βρέφος, ἔπειτα χρίσαντες ἀσφάλτῳ, τῷ γὰρ
ὕδατι τὴν διὰ τῶν πλεγμάτων ἀποφράττειν εἴσοδον
ἡ ἄσφαλτος πέφυκεν, ἐντιθέασι τὸ παιδίον καὶ
κατὰ τοῦ ποταμοῦ βαλόντες εἴασαν ἐπὶ τῷ θεῷ
τὴν σωτηρίαν αὐτοῦ. καὶ τὸ μὲν ὁ ποταμὸς
παραλαβὼν ἔφερε, Μαριάμη δὲ τοῦ παιδὸς ἀδελφὴ
κελευσθεῖσα ὑπὸ τῆς μητρὸς ἀντιπαρεξῄει φερό-
222 μενον ὅποι χωρήσει ὀψομένη τὸ πλέγμα. ἔνθα
καὶ διέδειξεν ὁ θεὸς μηδὲν μὲν τὴν ἀνθρωπίνην
σύνεσιν, πᾶν δ᾽ ὅ τι καὶ βουληθείη πράττειν αὐτὸ[1]
τέλους ἀγαθοῦ τυγχάνον, καὶ διαμαρτάνοντας μὲν
τοὺς ὑπὲρ οἰκείας ἀσφαλείας ἄλλων κατακρίνοντας
ὄλεθρον καὶ πολλῇ περὶ τοῦτο[2] χρησαμένους
223 σπουδῇ, σῳζομένους δ᾽ ἐκ παραδόξου καὶ σχεδὸν
ἐκ μέσου τῶν κακῶν εὑρισκομένους τὴν εὐπραγίαν
τοὺς κινδυνεύοντας τῇ τοῦ θεοῦ γνώμῃ. τοιοῦτον
δέ τι καὶ περὶ τὸν παῖδα τοῦτον γενόμενον ἐμφανίζει
τὴν ἰσχὺν τοῦ θεοῦ.

224 (5) Θέρμουθις ἦν θυγάτηρ τοῦ βασιλέως. αὕτη
παίζουσα παρὰ τὰς ἠόνας τοῦ ποταμοῦ καὶ φερό-
μενον ὑπὸ τοῦ ῥεύματος θεασαμένη τὸ πλέγμα
κολυμβητὰς ἐπιπέμπει κελεύσασα τὴν κοιτίδα
πρὸς αὑτὴν ἐκκομίσαι. παραγενομένων δὲ τῶν
ἐπὶ τούτῳ σταλέντων μετὰ τῆς κοιτίδος ἰδοῦσα
τὸ παιδίον ὑπερηγάπησε μεγέθους τε ἕνεκα καὶ
225 κάλλους· τοσαύτῃ γὰρ ὁ θεὸς περὶ Μωυσῆν ἐχρήσατο σπουδῇ, ὡς ὑπ᾽ αὐτῶν τῶν ψηφισαμένων διὰ
τὴν αὐτοῦ γένεσιν καὶ τῶν ἄλλων τῶν ἐκ τοῦ
Ἑβραίων γένους ἀπώλειαν ποιῆσαι τροφῆς καὶ

---

[1] αὐτὸς (ipse) Lat.
[2] Bekker: τούτου (τούτους) codd.

[a] Miriam (LXX Μαριάμ) Ex. xv. 20.

JEWISH ANTIQUITIES, II. 221–225

then, having daubed it with bitumen, that substance serving to prevent the water from penetrating through the wicker-work, they placed the young child within and, launching it on the river, committed his salvation to God. The river received its charge and bore it on, while Mariam(e),[a] the sister of the child, at her mother's bidding, kept pace with it along the bank to see whither the basket would go. Then once again did God plainly show that human intelligence is nothing worth, but that all that He wills to accomplish reaches its perfect end, and that they who, to save themselves, condemn others to destruction utterly fail, whatever diligence they may employ, while those are saved by a miracle and attain success almost from the very jaws of disaster, who hazard all by divine decree. Even so did the fate that befell this child display the power of God.

(5) The king had a daughter, Thermuthis.[b] Playing by the river bank and spying the basket being borne down the stream, she sent off some swimmers [c] with orders to bring that cot to her. When these returned from their errand with the cot, she, at sight of the little child, was enchanted at its size and beauty; for such was the tender care which God showed for Moses, that the very persons who by reason of his birth had decreed the destruction of all children of Hebrew parentage were made to con-

His rescue by the princess. Cf. **Ex. ii. 5.**

---

[b] Unnamed in Scripture, this princess bore various names in tradition. That in the text recurs in the *Book of Jubilees* (xlvii. 5, "Tharmuth"), a Jewish work of c. 100 B.C. with which Josephus elsewhere agrees. Syncellus (i. 227, quoted by Charles) adds a second, Θέρμουθις ἡ καὶ Φαρίη (*alias* Isis). Artapanus (2nd cent. B.C., *ap.* Eus. *Praep. Ev.* ix. 27) calls her Merris; the Talmud, after 1 Chron. iv. 18, Bithiah.

[c] Ex. ii. 5 "her handmaid" (LXX τὴν ἅβραν).

261

JOSEPHUS

ἐπιμελείας ἀξιωθῆναι. κελεύει τε γύναιον ἡ Θέρ
226 μουθις ἀχθῆναι παρέξον θηλὴν τῷ παιδίῳ. μὴ
προσεμένου δὲ αὐτοῦ τὴν θηλὴν ἀλλ' ἀποστρα
φέντος καὶ τοῦτ' ἐπὶ πολλῶν ποιήσαντος γυναικῶν,
ἡ Μαριάμη παρατυγχάνουσα τοῖς γινομένοις οὐχ
ὥστε ἐκ παρασκευῆς δοκεῖν ἀλλὰ κατὰ θεωρίαν,
" μάτην," εἶπεν, " ὦ βασίλισσα, ταύτας ἐπὶ
τροφῇ τοῦ παιδὸς μετακαλῇ τὰς γυναῖκας, αἳ
μηδὲν πρὸς αὐτὸ συγγενὲς ἔχουσιν. εἰ μέντοι
τινὰ τῶν Ἑβραΐδων γυναικῶν ἀχθῆναι ποιήσειας,
227 τάχα ἂν προσοῖτο θηλὴν ὁμοφύλου." δόξασαν δὲ
λέγειν εὖ κελεύει τοῦτ' αὐτὴν ἐκπορίσαι καὶ τῶν
γαλουχουσῶν τινα μεταθεῖν.¹ ἡ δὲ τοιαύτης ἐξ
ουσίας λαβομένη παρῆν ἄγουσα τὴν μητέρα μηδενὶ
γινωσκομένην. καὶ τὸ παιδίον ἀσμενίσαν πως
προσφύεται τῇ θηλῇ, καὶ δεηθείσης τε τῆς βασι
λίδος πιστεύεται τὴν τροφὴν τοῦ παιδίου πρὸς τὸ
πᾶν.²

228 (6) Κἀπ' αὐτῶν τὴν ἐπίκλησιν ταύτην τῶν συμ
βεβηκότων ἔθετο εἰς τὸν ποταμὸν ἐμπεσόντι· τὸ
γὰρ ὕδωρ μῶυ Αἰγύπτιοι καλοῦσιν, ἐσῆς δὲ τοὺς³
σωθέντας· συνθέντες οὖν ἐξ ἀμφοτέρων τὴν προσ
229 ηγορίαν αὐτῷ ταύτην τίθενται. καὶ ἦν ὁμολογου
μένως κατὰ τὴν τοῦ θεοῦ πρόρρησιν φρονήματός
τε μεγέθει καὶ πόνων καταφρονήσει Ἑβραίων
ἄριστος. Ἅβραμος γὰρ αὐτῷ πατὴρ ἕβδομος·
Ἀμαράμου γὰρ αὐτὸς ἦν παῖς τοῦ Καάθου,
Καάθου δὲ πατὴρ Λευὶς ὁ τοῦ Ἰακώβου, ὃς

¹ RO: μετελθεῖν rell.
² Niese suspects a lacuna.
³ Lat., Eustath.: + ἐξ ὕδατος codd.

---

[a] Josephus rejects the Biblical *Hebrew* etymology (Ex. ii.

JEWISH ANTIQUITIES, II. 225-229

descend to nourish and tend him. And so Thermuthis ordered a woman to be brought to suckle the infant. But when, instead of taking the breast, it spurned it, and then repeated this action with several women, Mariam, who had come upon the scene, apparently without design and from mere curiosity, said, " It is lost labour, my royal lady, to summon to feed the child these women who have no ties of kinship with it. Wert thou now to have one of the Hebrew women fetched, maybe it would take the breast of one of its own race." Her advice seemed sound, and the princess bade her do this service herself and run for a foster-mother. Availing herself of such permission, the girl returned bringing the mother, whom no one knew. Thereupon the infant, gleefully as it were, fastened upon the breast, and, by request of the princess, the mother was permanently entrusted with its nurture.

(6) It was indeed from this very incident that the princess gave him the name recalling his immersion in the river, for the Egyptians call water *môu* and those who are saved *esês*[a]; so they conferred on him this name compounded of both words. And all agree that, in accordance with the prediction of God, for grandeur of intellect and contempt of toils he was the noblest Hebrew of them all. [He was the seventh from Abraham, being the son of Amaram, who was the son of Caath, whose father was Levi,

His name and beauty. *Cf.* Ex. ii. 10.

10, " because I *drew* him *out* of the water," Heb. *mashah*, " draw out ") for one professedly Egyptian. The first half of his interpretation recurs in *Ap.* i. 286, and in Philo, *De vit. Mos.* i. 4, § 17 τὸ γὰρ ὕδωρ μῶυ ὀνομάζουσιν Αἰγύπτιοι. But " the Coptic etymology, *mo* ' water ' and *uše* ' rescued,' " " which for a time obtained general currency," is now in turn abandoned (*Enc. Bibl.* art. Moses).

263

ἦν Ἰσάκῳ γενόμενος, Ἀβράμου δὲ οὗτος ἦν. 230 σύνεσις δὲ οὐ κατὰ τὴν ἡλικίαν ἐφύετ᾽ αὐτῷ τοῦ δὲ ταύτης μέτρου πολὺ κρείττων, καὶ πρεσβυτέραν διεδείκνυεν ταύτης τὴν περιουσίαν ἐν¹ ταῖς παιδιαῖς, καὶ μειζόνων τῶν ὑπ᾽ ἀνδρὸς γενησομένων ἐπαγγελίαν εἶχε τὰ τότε πραττόμενα. καὶ τριετεῖ μὲν αὐτῷ γεγενημένῳ θαυμαστὸν ὁ θεὸς τὸ τῆς 231 ἡλικίας ἐξῆρεν ἀνάστημα, πρὸς δὲ κάλλος οὐδεὶς ἀφιλότιμος ἦν οὕτως, ὡς Μωυσῆν θεασάμενος μὴ ἐκπλαγῆναι τῆς εὐμορφίας, πολλοῖς τε συνέβαινε καθ᾽ ὁδὸν φερομένῳ συντυγχάνουσιν ἐπιστρέφεσθαι μὲν ὑπὸ τῆς ὄψεως τοῦ παιδός, ἀφιέναι δὲ τὰ σπουδαζόμενα καὶ τῇ θεωρίᾳ προσευσχολεῖν αὐτοῦ· καὶ γὰρ ἡ χάρις ἡ παιδικὴ πολλὴ καὶ ἄκρατος περὶ αὐτὸν οὖσα κατεῖχε τοὺς ὁρῶντας.

232 (7) Ὄντα δ᾽ αὐτὸν τοιοῦτον ἡ Θέρμουθις παῖδα ποιεῖται γονῆς γνησίας οὐ μεμοιραμένη, καί ποτε κομίσασα τὸν Μωυσῆν πρὸς τὸν πατέρα ἐπεδείκνυε τοῦτον καὶ ὡς φροντίσειε διαδοχῆς, εἰ καὶ βουλήσει θεοῦ μὴ τύχοι παιδὸς γνησίου, πρὸς αὐτὸν² ἔλεγεν, ἀναθρεψαμένη παῖδα μορφῇ τε θεῖον καὶ φρονήματι γενναῖον, θαυμασίως δὲ αὐτὸν καὶ παρὰ τῆς τοῦ ποταμοῦ λαβοῦσα χάριτος " ἐμαυτῆς μὲν ἡγησάμην παῖδα ποιήσασθαι, τῆς δὲ σῆς βασιλείας 233 διάδοχον." ταῦτα λέγουσα ταῖς τοῦ πατρὸς χερσὶν

¹ Read perhaps κἀν.   ² + τε codd.

ᵃ The sentence, condemned by some editors as an interruption of the narrative, may be a postscript of the author. The statement, in accordance with Scripture, that Moses was in the fourth generation from Jacob, conflicts with the 400 years' stay in Egypt (§ 204).

ᵇ Or " age "; cf. and contrast Lk. ii. 52.

the son of Jacob, who was the son of Isaac, the son of Abraham.]*a* His growth in understanding was not in line with his growth in stature,*b* but far outran the measure of his years: its maturer excellence was displayed in his very games, and his actions then gave promise of the greater deeds to be wrought by him on reaching manhood. When he was three years old, God gave wondrous increase to his stature; and none was so indifferent to beauty as not, on seeing Moses, to be amazed at his comeliness. And it often happened that persons meeting him as he was borne along the highway turned, attracted by the child's appearance, and neglected their serious affairs to gaze at leisure upon him: indeed childish charm so perfect and pure as his held the beholders spellbound.*c*

(7) Such was the child whom Thermuthis adopted as her son,*d* being blessed with no offspring of her own. Now one day she brought Moses to her father and showed him to him, and told him how she had been mindful for the succession, were it God's will to grant her no child of her own, by bringing up a boy of divine beauty and generous spirit, and by what a miracle she had received him of the river's bounty, " and methought," she said, " to make him my child and heir to thy kingdom." With these words she

The infant Moses and Pharaoh.

---

c S. Stephen's phrase, ἦν ἀστεῖος τῷ θεῷ (Acts vii. 20), is the only Biblical allusion to the child's beauty, attested by Rabbinical tradition. *Cf.* the Midrash on Ex. ii. 10 (ed. Wünsche), " Pharaoh's daughter . . . let him no more leave the king's palace; because he was beautiful all wished to see him, and whoever saw him could not turn away from him."

d Ex. ii. 10; the rest of this section and the chapter following it are amplification of the Scripture narrative.

ἐντίθησι τὸ βρέφος, ὁ δὲ λαβὼν καὶ προσστερνισάμενος κατὰ φιλοφρόνησιν χάριν τῆς θυγατρὸς ἐπιτίθησιν αὐτῷ τὸ διάδημα· καταφέρει δ' ὁ Μωυσῆς εἰς τὴν γῆν περιελόμενος αὐτὸ κατὰ
234 νηπιότητα δῆθεν ἐπέβαινέ τε αὐτῷ τοῖς ποσί. καὶ τοῦτο ἔδοξεν οἰωνὸν ἐπὶ τῇ βασιλείᾳ φέρειν. θεασάμενος δ' ὁ ἱερογραμματεὺς ὁ καὶ τὴν γένεσιν αὐτοῦ προειπὼν ἐπὶ ταπεινώσει τῆς Αἰγυπτίων ἀρχῆς ἐσομένην ὥρμησεν ἀποκτεῖναι, καὶ δεινὸν
235 ἀνακραγών, "οὗτος," εἶπε, "βασιλεῦ, ὁ παῖς ἐκεῖνος, ὃν κτείνασιν ἡμῖν ἐδήλωσεν ὁ θεὸς ἀφόβοις εἶναι, μαρτυρεῖ τῇ προαγορεύσει ⟨διὰ⟩[1] τοῦ γεγονότος ἐπιβεβηκὼς ἡγεμονίᾳ τῇ σῇ καὶ πατῶν τὸ διάδημα. τοῦτον οὖν ἀνελὼν Αἰγυπτίοις μὲν τὸ ἀπ' αὐτοῦ δέος ἄνες, Ἑβραίοις δὲ τὴν ἐλπίδα τοῦ
236 δι' αὐτὸν θάρσους ἀφελοῦ." φθάνει δ' αὐτὸν ἡ Θέρμουθις ἐξαρπάσασα, καὶ πρὸς τὸν φόνον ὀκνηρὸς ἦν ὁ βασιλεύς, τοιοῦτον αὐτὸν τοῦ θεοῦ παρασκευάσαντος, ᾧ πρόνοια τῆς Μωυσέος σωτηρίας ἦν. ἐτρέφετο οὖν πολλῆς ἐπιμελείας τυγχάνων, καὶ τοῖς μὲν Ἑβραίοις ἐπ' αὐτῷ παρῆν ἐλπὶς[2] περὶ
237 τῶν ὅλων, δι' ὑποψίας δ' εἶχον Αἰγύπτιοι τὴν ἀνατροφὴν αὐτοῦ· μηδενὸς δ' ὄντος φανεροῦ, δι' ὃν[3] κἂν ἀπέκτεινεν αὐτὸν ὁ βασιλεὺς [μηδὲν ὄντα][4] ἢ συγγενοῦς[5] διὰ τῆς εἰσποιήσεως ἢ τῶν ἄλλων τινός,[6] ᾧ πλέον ὑπὲρ ὠφελείας τῆς Αἰγυπτίων ἐκ

[1] ins. Ernesti.   [2] ROE: εὐέλπισιν εἶναι rell.
[3] RO: δ rell.
[4] μηδὲ ὄντος O: the words have perhaps come in from the previous line.
[5] μηδὲν ... συγγενοῦς] v.l. ἢ μηδὲν ὄντα καὶ συγγενῆ.
[6] v.l. τις.

laid the babe in her father's arms; and he took and clasped him affectionately to his breast and, to please his daughter, placed his diadem upon his head. But Moses tore it off and flung it to the ground, in mere childishness, and trampled it underfoot[a]; and this was taken as an omen of evil import to the kingdom. At that spectacle the sacred scribe who had foretold that this child's birth would lead to the abasement of the Egyptian empire rushed forward to kill him with a fearful shout: "This," he cried, "O king, this is that child whom God declared that we must kill to allay our terrors; he bears out the prediction by that act of insulting thy dominion and trampling the diadem under foot. Kill him then and at one stroke relieve the Egyptians of their fear of him and deprive the Hebrews of the courageous hopes that he inspires." But Thermuthis was too quick for him and snatched the child away; the king too delayed to slay him, from a hesitation induced by God, whose providence watched over Moses' life. He was accordingly educated with the utmost care, the Hebrews resting the highest hopes upon him for their future, while the Egyptians viewed his upbringing with misgiving. However, since even if the king slew him, there was no one else in sight, whether relative by adoption or any other, in whom they could put more confidence to act in the interest

[a] The Midrash on Ex. ii. 10 already quoted gives the legend in another form, "Pharaoh kissed and embraced him and took him to his breast, and he [Moses] took the crown from Pharaoh's head and set it upon his own, as he was once to do, when grown to manhood." Another Midrash, *Tanchuma* quoted by Weill, agrees with Josephus, except that the child seizes the crown from the king's head.

JOSEPHUS

τοῦ προειδέναι τὰ μέλλοντα θαρρεῖν παρῆν, ἀπείχοντο τῆς ἀναιρέσεως αὐτοῦ.

238 (x. 1) Μωυσῆς μὲν [οὖν] τῷ προειρημένῳ τρόπῳ γεννηθείς τε καὶ τραφεὶς καὶ παρελθὼν εἰς ἡλικίαν φανερὰν τοῖς Αἰγυπτίοις τὴν ἀρετὴν ἐποίησε καὶ τὸ ἐπὶ ταπεινώσει μὲν τῇ ἐκείνων, ἐπ' αὐξήσει δὲ τῶν Ἑβραίων γεγονέναι τοιαύτης ἀφορμῆς λαβό-
239 μενος· Αἰθίοπες, πρόσοικοι δ' εἰσὶ τοῖς Αἰγυπτίοις, ἐμβαλόντες εἰς χώραν αὐτῶν ἔφερον καὶ ἦγον τὰ τῶν Αἰγυπτίων. οἱ δ' ὑπ' ὀργῆς στρατεύουσιν ἐπ' αὐτοὺς ἀμυνούμενοι[1] τῆς καταφρονήσεως, καὶ τῇ μάχῃ κρατηθέντες οἱ μὲν αὐτῶν ἔπεσον οἱ δ' αἰσχρῶς εἰς τὴν οἰκείαν διεσώθησαν φυγόντες.
240 ἐπηκολούθησαν δὲ διώκοντες Αἰθίοπες καί, μαλακίας ὑπολαβόντες τὸ μὴ κρατεῖν ἁπάσης τῆς Αἰγύπτου, τῆς χώρας ἐπὶ πλεῖον ἥπτοντο καὶ γευσάμενοι τῶν ἀγαθῶν οὐκέτ' αὐτῶν ἀπείχοντο· ὡς δὲ τὰ γειτνιῶντα μέρη πρῶτον αὐτοῖς ἐπερχομένων οὐκ ἐτόλμων ἀντιστρατεύειν, προὔβησαν ἄχρι Μέμφεως καὶ τῆς θαλάσσης οὐδεμιᾶς τῶν
241 πόλεων ἀντισχεῖν δυνηθείσης. τῷ δὲ κακῷ πιεζόμενοι πρὸς χρησμοὺς Αἰγύπτιοι καὶ μαντείας τρέπονται· συμβουλεύσαντος δ' αὐτοῖς τοῦ θεοῦ συμμάχῳ χρήσασθαι τῷ Ἑβραίῳ κελεύει ὁ βασιλεὺς τὴν θυγατέρα παρασχεῖν τὸν Μωυσῆν στρα-
242 τηγὸν αὐτῷ γενησόμενον. ἡ δὲ ὅρκους ποιησα-

[1] Lat.: ἀμυνόμενοι codd.

[a] Text corrupt and meaning obscure. I take it to mean that there was no other heir apparent. With the reading δι' ὅ (for δι' ὅν) and other changes found in the "inferior" type of MSS., we might translate (with Weill) "But since there was no apparent motive why he should be killed

of the Egyptians through his foreknowledge of the future,[a] they refrained from slaying him.

(x. 1) Moses then, born and brought up in the manner already described, on coming of age gave the Egyptians signal proof of his merits and that he was born for their humiliation and for the advancement of the Hebrews; here is the occasion which he seized.[b] The Ethiopians, who are neighbours of the Egyptians, invaded their territory and pillaged their possessions; the Egyptians in indignation made a campaign against them to avenge the affront and, being beaten in battle, some fell and the rest ingloriously escaped to their own land by flight. But the Ethiopians followed in hot pursuit, and, deeming it feebleness not to subdue the whole of Egypt, they assailed the country far and wide and, having tasted of its riches, refused to relinquish their hold; and, since the neighbouring districts exposed to their first incursions did not venture to oppose them, they advanced as far as Memphis and to the sea, none of the cities being able to withstand them. Oppressed by this calamity, the Egyptians had recourse to oracles and divinations; and when counsel came to them from God to take the Hebrew for their ally, the king bade his daughter give up Moses to serve as his general. And she, after her father had sworn

Ethiopian invasion of Egypt: Moses selected as general of Egyptian army.

whether by the king, whose relative he was by adoption, or by any other who had greater hardihood in the interests," etc.
  [b] The following legend, an invention of the Jewish colony at Alexandria, doubtless grew out of the obscure allusion in Numb. xii. 1 to the " Cushite woman " whom Moses " had married " ; the existence of this Ethiopian wife called for explanation. A collateral form of the legend appears in Artapanus (2nd cent. B.C., *ap.* Eus. *Praep. Ev.* ix. 27. 432 d) ; the narrative of Josephus is more detailed and cannot be derived directly from Artapanus.

μένῳ, ὥστε μηδὲν διαθεῖναι κακόν, παραδιδῶσιν ἀντὶ μεγάλης μὲν εὐεργεσίας κρίνουσα τὴν συμμαχίαν, κακίζουσα δὲ τοὺς ἱερέας, εἰ κτεῖναι προαγορεύσαντες αὐτὸν ὡς πολέμιον οὐκ ᾐδοῦντο νῦν χρῄζοντες αὐτοῦ τῆς ἐπικουρίας.

243 (2) Μωυσῆς δὲ ὑπό τε τῆς Θερμούθιδος παρακληθεὶς καὶ ὑπὸ τοῦ βασιλέως ἡδέως προσδέχεται τὸ ἔργον· ἔχαιρον δ' οἱ ἱερογραμματεῖς ἀμφοτέρων τῶν ἐθνῶν, Αἰγυπτίων μὲν ὡς τούς τε πολεμίους τῇ ἐκείνου κρατήσοντες ἀρετῇ καὶ τὸν Μωυσῆν [ἐν]¹ ταὐτῷ δόλῳ κατεργασόμενοι, οἱ δὲ τῶν Ἑβραίων ὡς φυγεῖν αὐτοῖς ἐσομένου τοὺς Αἰγυ-
244 πτίους διὰ τὸ Μωυσῆν αὐτοῖς στρατηγεῖν. ὁ δὲ φθάσας πρὶν ἢ καὶ πυθέσθαι τοὺς πολεμίους τὴν ἔφοδον αὐτοῦ τὸν στρατὸν ἀναλαβὼν ἦγεν, οὐ διὰ τοῦ ποταμοῦ ποιησάμενος τὴν ἐλασίαν ἀλλὰ διὰ γῆς. ἔνθα τῆς αὐτοῦ συνέσεως θαυμαστὴν ἐπίδειξιν
245 ἐποιήσατο· τῆς γὰρ γῆς οὔσης χαλεπῆς ὁδευθῆναι διὰ πλῆθος ἑρπετῶν, παμφορωτάτη γάρ ἐστι τούτων, ὡς καὶ τὰ παρ' ἄλλοις οὐκ ὄντα μόνη τρέφειν δυνάμει τε καὶ κακίᾳ καὶ τῷ τῆς ὄψεως ἀσυνήθει διαφέροντα, τινὰ δ' αὐτῶν ἐστι καὶ πετεινὰ ὡς λανθάνοντα μὲν ἀπὸ γῆς κακουργεῖν καὶ μὴ προϊδομένους ἀδικεῖν ὑπερπετῆ γενόμενα, νοεῖ πρὸς ἀσφάλειαν καὶ ἀβλαβῆ πορείαν τοῦ στρατεύματος
246 στρατήγημα θαυμαστόν· πλέγματα γὰρ ἐμφερῆ κιβωτοῖς ἐκ βίβλου² κατασκευάσας καὶ πληρώσας ἴβεων ἐκόμιζε. πολεμιώτατον δ' ἐστὶν ὄφεσι τοῦτο τὸ ζῷον· φεύγουσί τε γὰρ ἐπερχομένας καὶ ἀφιστάμενοι καθάπερ ὑπ' ἐλάφων ἁρπαζόμενοι κατα-

¹ RO: om. rell.   ² βύβλου Dindorf.

to do him no injury, surrendered him, judging that great benefit would come of such an alliance, while reproaching the knavish priests who, after having spoken of putting him to death as an enemy, were now not ashamed to crave his succour.

(2) Moses, thus summoned both by Thermuthis and by the king,[a] gladly accepted the task, to the delight of the sacred scribes of both nations; for the Egyptians hoped through his valour both to defeat their foes and at the same time to make away with Moses by guile, while the Hebrew hierarchy foresaw the possibility of escape from the Egyptians with Moses as their general. He thereupon, to surprise the enemy before they had even learnt of his approach, mustered and marched off his army, taking the route not by way of the river but through the interior. There he gave a wonderful proof of his sagacity. For the route is rendered difficult for a march by reason of a multitude of serpents, which the region produces in abundant varieties, insomuch that there are some found nowhere else and bred here alone, remarkable for their power, their malignity, and their strange aspect; and among them are some which are actually winged, so that they can attack one from their hiding-place in the ground or inflict unforeseen injury by rising into the air. Moses, then, to provide security and an innocuous passage for his troops, devised a marvellous stratagem: he had baskets, resembling chests,[b] made of the bark of papyrus, and took these with him full of ibises. Now this animal is the serpents' deadliest enemy: they flee before its onset and in making off are caught, just as they are by

His victorious campaign.

Desert march and circumvention of the serpents.

---

[a] Called Chenephres by Artapanus.   [b] Or "arks."

πίνονται· χειροήθεις δ' εἰσὶν αἱ ἴβεις καὶ πρὸς μόνον
247 τὸ τῶν ὄφεων γένος ἄγριοι. καὶ περὶ μὲν τούτων
παρίημι νῦν γράφειν οὐκ ἀγνοούντων τῶν Ἑλλήνων τῆς ἴβιδος τὸ εἶδος. ὡς οὖν εἰς τὴν γῆν
ἐνέβαλε τὴν θηριοτρόφον, ταύταις ἀπεμάχετο τὴν
τῶν ἑρπετῶν φύσιν ἐπαφεὶς αὐτοῖς καὶ προ-
πολεμούσαις χρώμενος. τοῦτον οὖν ὁδεύσας τὸν
248 τρόπον οὐδὲ προμαθοῦσι παρῆν τοῖς Αἰθίοψι, καὶ
συμβαλὼν αὐτοῖς κρατεῖ τῇ μάχῃ καὶ τῶν ἐλπίδων,
ἃς εἶχον ἐπὶ τοὺς Αἰγυπτίους, ἀφαιρεῖται τάς τε
πόλεις αὐτῶν ἐπῄει καταστρεφόμενος, καὶ φόνος
πολὺς τῶν Αἰθιόπων ἐπράττετο. καὶ τῆς διὰ
Μωυσῆν εὐπραγίας γευσάμενον τὸ τῶν Αἰγυπτίων
στράτευμα πονεῖν οὐκ ἔκαμνεν, ὡς περὶ ἀνδρα-
ποδισμοῦ καὶ παντελοῦς ἀναστάσεως τὸν κίνδυνον
249 εἶναι τοῖς Αἰθίοψι· καὶ τέλος συνελαθέντες εἰς
Σαβὰν πόλιν βασίλειον οὖσαν τῆς Αἰθιοπίας, ἣν
ὕστερον Καμβύσης Μερόην ἐπωνόμασεν ἀδελφῆς
ἰδίας τοῦτο καλουμένης, ἐπολιορκοῦντο. ἦν δὲ
δυσπολιόρκητον σφόδρα τὸ χωρίον τοῦ τε Νείλου
περιέχοντος αὐτὴν καὶ κυκλουμένου ποταμῶν τε
ἄλλων Ἀστάπου καὶ Ἀσταβόρα δύσμαχον τοῖς
250 πειρωμένοις διαβαίνειν τὸ ῥεῦμα ποιούντων· ἡ
γὰρ πόλις ἐντὸς οὖσα ὡς νῆσος οἰκεῖται τείχους
τε αὐτῇ καρτεροῦ περιηγμένου καὶ πρὸς μὲν

---

[a] I was tempted to read ὑπ᾽ ἐλαφ⟨ροτέρ⟩ων "by their nimbler adversaries": but no emendation is needed. Bochart, *Hierozoicon*, i. 885 f. (1675), quotes an array of classical allusions to serpent-eating stags, who, according to one scholiast, derived their very name ἔλαφος from the habit: εἴρηται δὲ παρὰ τὸ ἐλεῖν τὰς ὄφεις, οἱονεὶ ἐλοφίς τις ὤν! See Mair's Oppian (L.C.L.), ad *Cyn*. ii. 233, *Hal*. ii. 289.

[b] All that Artapanus tells us is that the war lasted ten years and that on account of the size of his army Moses

JEWISH ANTIQUITIES, II. 246–250

stags,[a] and swallowed up. The ibis is otherwise a tame creature and ferocious only to the serpent tribe; but I refrain from further words on this subject, for Greeks are not unacquainted with the nature of the ibis. When, therefore, he entered the infested region, he by means of these birds beat off the vermin, letting them loose upon them and using these auxiliaries to clear the ground.[b] Having thus accomplished the march, he came wholly unexpected upon the Ethiopians, joined battle with them and defeated them, crushing their cherished hopes of mastering the Egyptians, and then proceeded to attack and overthrow their cities, great carnage of the Ethiopians ensuing. After tasting of this success which Moses had brought them, the Egyptian army showed such indefatigable energy that the Ethiopians were menaced with servitude and complete extirpation. In the end they were all driven into Saba, the capital of the Ethiopian realm, which Cambyses later called Meroe after the name of his sister,[c] and were there besieged. But the place offered extreme obstacles to a besieger, for the Nile enclosed it in a circle and other rivers, the Astapus[d] and the Astabaras,[e] added to the difficulty of the attack for any who attempted to cross the current. The city which lies within in fact resembles an island: strong walls encompass it and as a bulwark against its enemies

built a city, called Hermopolis, in which he consecrated the ibis because it slays the creatures that injure men (καὶ τὴν ἶβιν ἐν αὐτῇ καθιερῶσαι διὰ τὸ ταύτην τὰ βλάπτοντα ζῷα τοὺς ἀνθρώπους ἀναιρεῖν).

[c] Who died there: according to another account, she was his wife (Strabo, xvii. 5. 790).

[d] The *Bahr-el-Azrek* or Blue Nile.

[e] A minor tributary; *Tacazzé* is the name given to it in Smith's *Dict. of Greek and Roman Geography*.

τοὺς πολεμίους πρόβλημα τοὺς ποταμοὺς ἔχουσα χώματά τε μεγάλα μεταξὺ τοῦ τείχους, ὥστε ἀνεπίκλυστον εἶναι βιαιότερον ὑπὸ πληθώρας[1] φερομένων, ἅπερ καὶ τοῖς περαιωσαμένοις τοὺς ποταμοὺς ἄπορον ἐποίει τῆς πόλεως τὴν ἅλωσιν.
251 φέροντι τοίνυν ἀηδῶς τῷ Μωυσεῖ τὴν τοῦ στρατεύματος ἀργίαν, εἰς χεῖρας γὰρ οὐκ ἐτόλμων ἀπαντᾶν
252 οἱ πολέμιοι, συνέτυχέ τι τοιοῦτον. Θάρβις θυγάτηρ ἦν τοῦ Αἰθιόπων βασιλέως. αὕτη τὸν Μωυσῆν πλησίον τοῖς τείχεσι προσάγοντα τὴν στρατιὰν καὶ μαχόμενον γενναίως ἀποσκοποῦσα καὶ τῆς ἐπινοίας τῶν ἐγχειρήσεων θαυμάζουσα, καὶ τοῖς τε Αἰγυπτίοις αἴτιον ἀπεγνωκόσιν ἤδη τὴν ἐλευθερίαν τῆς εὐπραγίας ὑπολαμβάνουσα καὶ τοῖς Αἰθίοψιν αὐχοῦσιν ἐπὶ τοῖς κατ' αὐτῶν κατωρθωμένοις τοῦ περὶ τῶν ἐσχάτων κινδύνου, εἰς ἔρωτα δεινὸν ὤλισθεν αὐτοῦ καὶ περιόντος τοῦ πάθους πέμπει πρὸς αὐτὸν τῶν οἰκετῶν τοὺς πιστοτάτους δια-
253 λεγομένη περὶ γάμου. προσδεξαμένου δὲ τὸν λόγον ἐπὶ τῷ παραδοῦναι τὴν πόλιν καὶ ποιησαμένου πίστεις ἐνόρκους ἦ μὴν ἄξεσθαι γυναῖκα καὶ κρατήσαντα τῆς πόλεως μὴ παραβήσεσθαι τὰς συνθήκας, φθάνει τὸ ἔργον τοὺς λόγους. καὶ μετὰ τὴν ἀναίρεσιν τῶν Αἰθιόπων εὐχαριστήσας τῷ θεῷ συνετέλει τὸν γάμον Μωυσῆς καὶ τοὺς Αἰγυπτίους ἀπήγαγεν εἰς τὴν ἑαυτῶν.
254 (xi. 1) Οἱ δ' ἐξ ὧν ἐσώζοντο ὑπὸ Μωυσέος μῖσος ἐκ τούτων πρὸς αὐτὸν ἀνελάμβανον καὶ θερμότερον ἅπτεσθαι τῶν κατ' αὐτοῦ βουλευμάτων ἠξίουν, ὑπονοοῦντες μὲν μὴ διὰ τὴν εὐπραγίαν νεωτερίσειε κατὰ τὴν Αἴγυπτον, διδάσκοντες δὲ
255 τὸν βασιλέα περὶ τῆς σφαγῆς. ὁ δὲ καὶ καθ'

it has the rivers, besides great dikes within the ramparts to protect it from inundation when the force of the swollen streams is unusually violent; and it is these which made the capture of the town so difficult even to those who had crossed the rivers. Moses, then, was chafing at the inaction of his army, for the enemy would not venture upon an engagement, when he met with the following adventure. Tharbis, the daughter of the king of the Ethiopians, watching Moses bringing his troops close beneath the ramparts and fighting valiantly, marvelled at the ingenuity of his manœuvres and, understanding that it was to him that the Egyptians, who but now despaired of their independence, owed all their success, and through him that the Ethiopians, so boastful of their feats against them, were reduced to the last straits, fell madly in love with him; and under the mastery of this passion she sent to him the most trusty of her menials to make him an offer of marriage. He accepted the proposal on condition that she would surrender the town, pledged himself by oath verily to take her to wife and, once master of the town, not to violate the pact, whereupon action outstripped parley. After chastisement of the Ethiopians, Moses rendered thanks to God, celebrated the nuptials, and led the Egyptians back to their own land.

Moses marries the Ethiopian princess.

(xi. 1) But the Egyptians, thus saved by Moses, conceived from their very deliverance a hatred for him and thought good to pursue with greater ardour their plots upon his life, suspecting that he would take advantage of his success to revolutionize Egypt, and suggesting to the king that he should be put to death. He on his own part was harbouring thoughts

Flight of Moses to Madian. Cf. Ex. ii. 15.

---

¹ ROE: πλημμύρας rell.

JOSEPHUS

αὐτὸν μὲν εἶχε τὴν τοῦ πράγματος ἐπίνοιαν ὑπό τε φθόνου τῆς Μωυσέος στρατηγίας καὶ ὑπὸ δέους ταπεινώσεως, ἐπειχθεὶς δ' ὑπὸ τῶν ἱερογραμματέων οἷός τε ἦν ἐγχειρεῖν τῇ Μωυσέος ἀναιρέσει.
256 φθάσας δὲ τὴν ἐπιβουλὴν καταμαθεῖν λαθὼν ὑπέξεισι· καὶ τῶν ὁδῶν φυλαττομένων ποιεῖται διὰ τῆς ἐρήμου τὸν δρασμὸν καὶ ὅθεν ἦν ὑπόνοια μὴ λαβεῖν τοὺς ἐχθρούς,[1] ἄπορός τε ὢν τροφῆς
257 ἀπηλλάττετο τῇ καρτερίᾳ καταφρονῶν, εἴς τε πόλιν Μαδιανὴν ἀφικόμενος πρὸς μὲν τῇ Ἐρυθρᾷ θαλάσσῃ κειμένην ἐπώνυμον δ' ἑνὸς τῶν Ἀβράμῳ γενομένων ἐκ Κατούρας υἱῶν, καθεσθεὶς ἐπί τινος φρέατος ἐκ τοῦ κόπου καὶ τῆς ταλαιπωρίας ἠρέμει μεσημβρίας οὔσης οὐ πόρρω τῆς πόλεως. ἐνταῦθ' αὐτῷ συνέβη καὶ πρᾶξις ἐκ διαίτης τῶν αὐτόθι συστήσασα τὴν ἀρετὴν αὐτοῦ καὶ πρὸς τὸ κρεῖττον ἀφορμὴν παρασχοῦσα.

258 (2) Τῶν γὰρ χωρίων δυσύδρων ὄντων προκατελάμβανον οἱ ποιμένες τὰ φρέατα, ὅπως μὴ προεξαναλωμένου τοῦ ὕδατος ὑπὸ τῶν ἄλλων σπανίζοι ποτοῦ τὰ θρέμματα. παραγίνονται οὖν ἐπὶ τὸ φρέαρ ἑπτὰ παρθένοι ἀδελφαί, Ῥαγουήλου θυγατέρες ἱερέως καὶ πολλῆς ἠξιωμένου τιμῆς παρὰ τοῖς
259 ἐπιχωρίοις, αἳ τῶν τοῦ πατρὸς ποιμνίων ἐπιμελούμεναι, διὰ τὸ ταύτην ὑπουργίαν εἶναι καὶ γυναιξὶν ἐπιχώριον παρὰ τοῖς Τρωγλοδύταις, φθάσασαι τὸ αὔταρκες ἐκ τοῦ φρέατος ἀνέσπασαν ὕδωρ

[1] καὶ ὅθεν . . ἐχθρούς om. Lat.

[a] Josephus omits the Biblical motive for Pharaoh's wrath, viz. the murder of an Egyptian by Moses.
[b] Such seems to be the meaning: ὅθεν = ἐκεῖσε ὅθεν.
[c] Ex. ii. 15, "the land of Midian" (LXX Μαδιάμ). Ptolemy and Arabic geographers mention a place Μοδίανα, Madyan,

of so doing, alike from envy of Moses' generalship and from fear of seeing himself abased, and so, when instigated by the hierarchy, was prepared to lend a hand in the murder of Moses.[a] Their victim, however, informed betimes of the plot, secretly escaped, and, since the roads were guarded, directed his flight across the desert and to where he had no fear of being caught by his foes[b]; he left without provisions, proudly confident of his powers of endurance. On reaching the town of Madian(e),[c] situated by the Red Sea and named after one of Abraham's sons by Katura,[d] he sat down on the brink of a well and there rested after his toil and hardships, at midday, not far from the town. Here he was destined to play a part, arising out of the customs of the inhabitants, which exhibited his merits and proved the opening of better fortune.

(2) For, those regions being scant of water, the shepherds used to make a first claim on the wells, for fear that, the water being exhausted by others beforehand, there should be nothing for their flocks to drink. Now there came to this well seven sisters, virgin daughters of Raguel,[e] a priest held in high veneration by the people of the country; they were in charge of their father's flocks, for this function is customarily undertaken by women also among the Troglodytes,[f] and, arriving first, they drew from the

Moses at the well. Ex. ii. 16

on the *east* of the Gulf of Akabah, opposite the southern extremity of the Sinaitic peninsula (Driver *in loc.*); but, if the traditional identification of Sinai is correct, the context requires a place on the west of the gulf.

[d] Gen. xxv. 2.

[e] So LXX (Ex. ii. 18), Heb. Reuel, alias Jethro.

[f] " Cave-dwellers " inhabiting the region on either shore of the Red Sea (*A.* i. 239, ii. 213).

τοῖς ποιμνίοις εἰς δεξαμενάς, αἳ πρὸς ἐκδοχὴν τοῦ
ὕδατος ἐγεγόνεισαν. ἐπιστάντων δὲ ποιμένων ταῖς
παρθένοις, ὥστ' αὐτοὶ τοῦ ὕδατος κρατεῖν, Μωυσῆς δεινὸν ἡγησάμενος εἶναι περιιδεῖν ἀδικου-
μένας τὰς κόρας καὶ τὴν βίαν τὴν τῶν ἀνδρῶν ἐᾶσαι κρείττονα γενέσθαι τοῦ τῶν παρθένων
δικαίου, τοὺς μὲν εἶρξε πλεονεκτεῖν ἐθέλοντας,
ταῖς δὲ παρέσχε τὴν πρέπουσαν[1] βοήθειαν. αἱ δ'
εὐεργετηθεῖσαι παρῆσαν πρὸς τὸν πατέρα τήν τε
ὕβριν τῶν ποιμένων αὐτῷ διηγούμεναι καὶ τὴν
ἐπικουρίαν τοῦ ξένου, παρεκάλουν τε μὴ ματαίαν
αὐτῷ γενέσθαι τὴν εὐποιίαν μηδ' ἀμοιβῆς ὑστεροῦσαν. ὁ δὲ τάς τε παῖδας ἀπεδέξατο τῆς περὶ τὸν
εὐεργετηκότα σπουδῆς καὶ τὸν Μωυσῆν εἰς ὄψιν
ἐκέλευεν ἄγειν αὐτῷ τευξόμενον χάριτος δικαίας.
ὡς δ' ἧκε, τήν τε τῶν θυγατέρων αὐτῷ ἀπεσήμαινε μαρτυρίαν ἐπὶ τῇ βοηθείᾳ καὶ τῆς ἀρετῆς
αὐτὸν θαυμάζων οὐκ εἰς ἀναισθήτους εὐεργεσιῶν
καταθέσθαι τὴν ἐπικουρίαν ἔλεγεν, ἀλλ' ἱκανοὺς
ἐκτῖσαι χάριν καὶ τῷ μεγέθει τῆς ἀμοιβῆς ὑπερ-
βαλεῖν τὸ μέτρον τῆς εὐποιίας. ποιεῖται δ' αὐτὸν
υἱὸν καὶ μίαν τῶν θυγατέρων πρὸς γάμον δίδωσι
τῶν τε θρεμμάτων, ἐν τούτοις γὰρ ἡ πᾶσα κτῆσις
τὸ παλαιὸν ἦν τοῖς βαρβάροις, ἀποδείκνυσιν
ἐπιμελητὴν καὶ δεσπότην.

(xii. 1) Καὶ Μωυσῆς μὲν τοιούτων τυχὼν τῶν
παρὰ τοῦ Ἰεθεγλαίου,[2] τοῦτο γὰρ ἦν ἐπίκλημα τῷ
Ῥαγουήλῳ, διῆγεν αὐτόθι ποιμαίνων τὰ βοσκήματα. χρόνῳ δ' ὕστερον νέμων ἐπὶ τὸ Σιναῖον

[1] ROE: δέουσαν rell.
[2] RM: Ἰοθογλαίου O: Getheglech Lat.: Ἰεθόρου (Ἰοθόρου) rell.

well sufficient water for their flocks into troughs constructed to receive it. But when shepherds appearing set upon the young women, in order to appropriate the water for themselves, Moses, deeming it monstrous to overlook this injury to the girls and to suffer these men's violence to triumph over the maidens' rights, beat off the arrogant intruders, and afforded the others opportune aid. And they, after this beneficent act, went to their father, and, recounting the shepherds' insolence and the succour which the stranger had lent them, besought him not to let such charity go for nought or unrewarded. The father commended his children for their zeal for their benefactor and bade them bring Moses to his presence to receive the gratitude that was his due. On his arrival, he told him of his daughters' testimony to the help which he had rendered, and, expressing admiration for his gallantry, added that he had not bestowed this service upon those who had no sense of gratitude, but on persons well able to requite a favour, indeed to outdo by the amplitude of the reward the measure of the benefit. He therewith adopted him as his son, gave him one of his daughters in marriage, and appointed him keeper and master of his flocks, for in those consisted of yore all the wealth of the barbarian races.

(xii. 1) So Moses, having received these benefits from Ietheglaeus [a]—such was the surname of Raguel—abode there feeding the cattle. And some while afterward he led the flocks to graze on the mount called Sinai; it is the highest of the mountains

---

[a] So the MSS. followed by Niese; but the form may be a mere conglomerate of the names Ἰόθορος and Ῥαγούηλος.

265 καλούμενον ὄρος ἄγει τὰ ποίμνια· τοῦτο δ' ἐστὶν ὑψηλότατον τῶν ταύτῃ ὀρῶν καὶ πρὸς νομὰς ἄριστον, ἀγαθῆς φυομένης πόας καὶ διὰ τὸ δόξαν ἔχειν ἐνδιατρίβειν αὐτῷ τὸν θεὸν οὐ κατανεμηθείσης πρότερον, οὐ τολμώντων ἐμβατεύειν εἰς αὐτὸ τῶν ποιμένων· ἔνθα δὴ καὶ τέρας αὐτῷ
266 συντυγχάνει θαυμάσιον. πῦρ γὰρ θάμνου βάτον νεμόμενον τὴν περὶ αὐτὸν χλόην τό τε ἄνθος αὐτοῦ παρῆλθεν ἀβλαβὲς καὶ τῶν ἐγκάρπων κλάδων οὐδὲν ἠφάνισε καὶ ταῦτα τῆς φλογὸς πολλῆς καὶ
267 ὀξυτάτης ὑπαρχούσης. ὁ δὲ καὶ αὐτὴν μὲν ἔδεισε τὴν ὄψιν παράδοξον γενομένην, κατεπλάγη δ' ἔτι μᾶλλον φωνὴν τοῦ πυρὸς ἀφέντος καὶ ὀνομαστὶ καλέσαντος αὐτὸν καὶ ποιησαμένου λόγους, οἷς τό τε θάρσος αὐτοῦ τολμήσαντος παρελθεῖν εἰς χωρίον, εἰς ὃ μηδεὶς ἀνθρώπων πρότερον ἀφῖκτο διὰ τὸ εἶναι θεῖον, ἐσήμαινε καὶ συνεβούλευε τῆς φλογὸς[1] πορρωτάτω χωρεῖν καὶ ἀρκεῖσθαι μὲν οἷς ἑώρακεν ἀγαθὸν ὄντα καὶ μεγάλων ἀνδρῶν ἔγγονον,
268 πολυπραγμονεῖν δὲ μηδέν· τούτοις περισσότερον προηγόρευέν τε τὴν ἐσομένην αὐτῷ δόξαν καὶ τιμὴν παρ' ἀνθρώπων τοῦ θεοῦ συμπαρόντος, καὶ θαρροῦντα ἐκέλευεν εἰς τὴν Αἴγυπτον ἀπιέναι στρατηγὸν καὶ ἡγεμόνα τῆς Ἑβραίων πληθύος ἐσόμενον καὶ τῆς ὕβρεως τῆς ἐκεῖ τοὺς συγγενεῖς
269 ἀπαλλάξοντα· " καὶ γὰρ γῆν οἰκήσουσι," φησί, " ταύτην εὐδαίμονα, ἣν Ἄβραμος ᾤκησεν ὁ ὑμέτερος πρόγονος καὶ τῶν πάντων ἀπολαύσουσιν ἀγαθῶν, εἰς ταῦτα σοῦ καὶ τῆς σῆς συνέσεως αὐτοῖς ἡγουμένης." ἐξαγαγόντα μέντοι τοὺς Ἑβραίους ἐκ τῆς Αἰγύπτου θυσίας ἐκέλευε χαριστηρίους

[1] + ὡς SP.

in this region and the best for pasturage, for it produces excellent turf and, owing to a belief that the Deity sojourned there, had not hitherto been cropped, the shepherds not venturing to invade it. Here it was that he witnessed an amazing prodigy: a fire was ablaze on a bramble-bush, yet had left its vesture of green and its bloom intact, nor had one of its fruit-laden branches been consumed, albeit the flame was great and exceeding fierce. Moses was terrified at this strange spectacle, but was amazed yet more when this fire found a tongue, called him by name, and communed with him, signifying to him his hardihood in venturing to approach a spot whither no man had penetrated before by reason of its divinity, and admonishing him to withdraw as far as might be from the flame, to be content with what he, as a man of virtue sprung from illustrious ancestors, had seen, but to pry no further. The voice furthermore predicted the glory and honour that he would win from men, under God's auspices, and bade him courageously return to Egypt, to act as commander and leader of the Hebrew hosts, and to deliver his kinsmen from the outrage that they there endured. " For indeed," continued the voice, " they shall inhabit this favoured land wherein Abraham dwelt, the forefather of your race, and shall enjoy all its blessings, and it is thou, aye and thy sagacity, that shall conduct them thither." Howbeit He charged him, after he had brought the Hebrews out of Egypt, to come to that

ἀφικόμενον εἰς ἐκεῖνον ἐκτελέσαι τὸν τόπον. τοσαῦτα μὲν ἐκ τοῦ πυρὸς θεοκλυτεῖται.

270 (2) Μωυσῆς δ' ἐκπεπληγμένος οἷς τ' εἶδε καὶ πολὺ μᾶλλον οἷς ἤκουσε, " δυνάμει μὲν ἀπιστεῖν," ἔφη, " τῇ σῇ, δέσποτα, ἣν αὐτός τε θρησκεύω καὶ προγόνοις οἶδα φανερὰν γενομένην, μανιωδέστερον 271 ἢ κατὰ τὴν ἐμαυτοῦ φρόνησιν ἡγοῦμαι. πλὴν ἀπορῶ, πῶς ἂν ἰδιώτης ἀνὴρ καὶ μηδεμιᾶς ἰσχύος εὐπορῶν ἢ πείσω λόγοις τοὺς οἰκείους ἀφέντας ἣν ἄρτι κατοικοῦσι γῆν ἕπεσθαί μοι πρὸς ἣν αὐτὸς ἡγοῦμαι, ἢ κἂν ἐκεῖνοι πεισθῶσι, πῶς ἂν βιασαίμην Φαραώθην ἐπιτρέψαι τὴν ἔξοδον τούτοις, ὧν τοῖς πόνοις καὶ τοῖς ἔργοις τὴν οἰκείαν αὔξουσιν εὐδαιμονίαν."

272 (3) Ὁ δὲ θεὸς αὐτῷ περὶ πάντων συνεβούλευε θαρρεῖν ὑπισχνούμενος αὐτὸς παρέσεσθαι καὶ οὗ μὲν ἂν δέῃ λόγων, πειθὼ παρέξειν, οὗ δ' ἂν ἔργων, ἰσχὺν χορηγήσειν, ἐκέλευέ τε τὴν βακτηρίαν ἐπὶ τὴν γῆν ἀφέντα πίστιν ὧν ὑπισχνεῖται λαμβάνειν. καὶ ποιήσαντος δράκων εἷρπε καὶ συνειλούμενος σπειρηδὸν ὡς διώκουσιν ἐπ' ἀμύνῃ τὴν κεφαλὴν 273 ἐπανέτεινεν· εἶτα πάλιν βάκτρον ἦν. μετὰ τοῦτο δὲ καθεῖναι τὴν δεξιὰν εἰς τὸν κόλπον προσέταξεν· ὑπακούσας δὲ λευκὴν καὶ τιτάνῳ τὴν χρόαν ὁμοίαν προεκόμισεν· εἶτ' εἰς τὸ σύνηθες κατέστη. κελευσθεὶς δὲ καὶ τοῦ πλησίον ὕδατος λαβὼν ἐπὶ τὴν γῆν 274 ἐκχέαι ὁρᾷ τὴν χρόαν αἱματώδη γενομένην. θαυμάζοντα δ' ἐπὶ τούτοις θαρρεῖν παρεκελεύετο καὶ βοηθὸν εἰδέναι μέγιστον αὐτῷ συνεσόμενον καὶ σημείοις πρὸς τὸ πιστεύεσθαι παρὰ πᾶσι χρῆσθαι, " ὅτι πεμφθεὶς ὑπ' ἐμοῦ πάντα κατὰ τὰς ἐμὰς

---

[a] Ex. iv. 6, " leprous, as (white as) snow."

spot and there offer sacrifices of thanksgiving. Such were the divine oracles that issued from the fire.

(2) Moses, in consternation at that which he had seen and much more at that which he had heard, replied : " To mistrust, O Lord, thy power, which I venerate myself and know to have been manifested to my forefathers, were madness too gross, I trow, for my mind to conceive. Yet am I at a loss to know how I, a mere commoner, blest with no strength, could either find words to persuade my people to quit that land that they now inhabit and follow me to that whereunto I would lead them, or even should they be persuaded, how I should constrain Pharaothes to permit the exodus of those to whose toils and tasks his subjects look to swell their own prosperity." *He shrinks from his commission, Ex. iii. 11 (cf. iv. 10),*

(3) But God exhorted him to have perfect confidence, promising Himself to assist him and, when words were needed, to lend persuasion, when action was called for, to furnish strength ; and He bade him cast his staff to the ground and to have faith in His promises. Moses did so, and, lo, there was a serpent crawling and coiling itself in spiral fashion and rearing its head as in defence against assailants ; then once more it became a stick. Next He bade him put his right hand into his bosom : he obeyed and drew it forth white, of a colour resembling chalk [a] ; then it resumed its ordinary aspect. Receiving a further command to take of the water of a neighbouring brook and pour it on the ground, he beheld it turned to the colour of blood. And while he marvelled at these wonders, God exhorted him to be of good courage, to be assured that His mighty aid would be ever with him, and to use miracles to convince all men (said He) " that thou art sent by me and doest all at *but is reassured by miracles. Ex. iv. 1.*

ἐντολὰς ποιεῖς. κελεύω δὲ μηδὲν ἔτι μελλήσαντα σπεύδειν εἰς τὴν Αἴγυπτον καὶ νυκτὸς καὶ ἡμέρας ἐπειγόμενον καὶ μὴ τρίβοντα τὸν χρόνον πλείω ποιεῖν τοῦτον Ἑβραίοις ἐν δουλείᾳ κακοπαθοῦσι."

275 (4) Μωυσῆς δ' οὐκ ἔχων ἀπιστεῖν οἷς ἐπηγγέλλετο τὸ θεῖον θεατής γε τοιούτων βεβαιωμάτων καὶ ἀκροατὴς γενόμενος, εὐξάμενος αὐτῷ καὶ πειραθῆναι ταύτης τῆς δυνάμεως ἐν Αἰγύπτῳ δεηθεὶς[1] ἠντιβόλει μηδὲ ὀνόματος αὐτῷ γνῶσιν τοῦ ἰδίου φθονῆσαι, φωνῆς δ' αὐτῷ μετεσχηκότι καὶ ὄψεως ἔτι καὶ τὴν προσηγορίαν εἰπεῖν, ἵνα θύων ἐξ ὀνόματος αὐτὸν παρεῖναι τοῖς ἱεροῖς[2] παρακαλῇ.

276 καὶ ὁ θεὸς αὐτῷ σημαίνει τὴν αὐτοῦ προσηγορίαν οὐ πρότερον εἰς ἀνθρώπους παρελθοῦσαν, περὶ ἧς οὔ μοι θεμιτὸν εἰπεῖν. Μωυσεῖ μέντοι τὰ σημεῖα ταῦτα οὐ τότε μόνον, διὰ παντὸς δὲ ὁπότε δεηθείη συνετύγχανεν· ἐξ ὧν ἁπάντων πλέον περὶ τῆς ἀληθείας τῷ πυρὶ νέμων καὶ τὸν θεὸν εὐμενῆ παραστάτην ἕξειν πιστεύων τούς τε οἰκείους σώσειν[3] ἤλπιζε καὶ τοὺς Αἰγυπτίους κακοῖς περιβαλεῖν.

277 (xiii. 1) Καὶ πυθόμενος τὸν τῶν Αἰγυπτίων τεθνάναι βασιλέα Φαραώθην, ἐφ' οὕπερ αὐτὸς ἔφυγε, δεῖται Ῥαγουήλου συγχωρῆσαι κατὰ ὠφέλειαν αὐτῷ τῶν συγγενῶν εἰς Αἴγυπτον ἐλθεῖν, καὶ παραλαβὼν τὴν Σαπφώραν ἣν ἐγεγαμήκει, τοῦ Ῥαγουήλου θυγατέρα, καὶ τοὺς ἐξ αὐτῆς παῖδας

---

[1] δοθείσης SPLA. [2] ΜΕ: ἱερείοις rell. [3] σώζειν codd.

---

[a] The ineffable tetragrammaton, viz. the four consonants JHVH, which only the high priest was permitted to pronounce. To safeguard and hallow the Name, the surrogate

my command. And I bid thee without more delay make speed to Egypt, pressing forward by night and day, and by no dallying to prolong the time for the Hebrews, now suffering in servitude."

(4) Moses, unable to doubt the promises of the Deity, after having seen and heard such confirmation of them, prayed and entreated that he might be vouchsafed this power in Egypt; he also besought Him not to deny him the knowledge of His name, but, since he had been granted speech with Him and vision of Him, further to tell him how He should be addressed, so that, when sacrificing, he might invoke Him by name to be present at the sacred rites. Then God revealed to him His name, which ere then had not come to men's ears, and of which I am forbidden to speak.[a] Moreover, Moses found those miracles at his service not on that occasion only but at all times whensoever there was need of them; from all which tokens he came to trust more firmly in the oracle from the fire, to believe that God would be his gracious protector, and to hope to be able to deliver his people and to bring disaster upon the Egyptians.

Revelation of the divine name Ex. iii. 13.

(xiii. 1) Accordingly, on learning that the king of Egypt, the Pharaothes under whom he had fled the country, was dead, he besought Raguel to permit him for the welfare of his countrymen to go to Egypt; and, taking with him Sapphora,[b] his wife, daughter of Raguel, and the children whom he had by her, Gêrsos

Moses returns to Egypt. Ex. iv. 18.

Ădonai (LXX Κύριος) was employed, and JHVH in Hebrew MSS. was written with the vowels of the latter, to indicate "Read Adonai"; hence, through later neglect of the intention of the scribes, arose the form Jehovah, which has acquired a sacredness of its own, but in its origin is a hybrid.

[b] Bibl. Zipporah (LXX Σεπφώρα).

Γῆρσον καὶ Ἐλεάζαρον ὥρμησεν εἰς τὴν Αἴγυπτον·
278 τῶν δ' ὀνομάτων τούτων Γῆρσος μὲν σημαίνει κατὰ Ἑβραίων διάλεκτον, ὅτι εἰς ξένην γῆν, Ἐλεάζαρος δὲ συμμάχῳ τῷ πατρῴῳ θεῷ χρησά-
279 μενον αὐτὸν Αἰγυπτίους διαφυγεῖν. γενομένῳ δ' αὐτῷ πλησίον τῶν ὅρων ὁ ἀδελφὸς Ἀαρὼν ὑπήντησε τοῦ θεοῦ κελεύσαντος, πρὸς ὃν ἀποσημαίνει τὰ ἐν τῷ ὄρει συντυχόντα καὶ τοῦ θεοῦ τὰς ἐντολάς. προϊοῦσι δ' αὐτοῖς ὑπηντίαζον Ἑβραίων οἱ ἀξιολογώτατοι τὴν παρουσίαν αὐτοῦ
280 μεμαθηκότες, οἷς Μωυσῆς τὰ σημεῖα διηγούμενος ἐπεὶ πιθανὸς οὐκ ἦν παρέσχεν αὐτῶν τὴν ὄψιν. οἱ δ' ὑπ' ἐκπλήξεως τῶν παρὰ δόξαν αὐτοῖς ὁρωμένων ἀνεθάρσουν καὶ περὶ τῶν ὅλων ἦσαν εὐέλπιδες, ὡς θεοῦ προνοουμένου τῆς ἀσφαλείας αὐτῶν.

281 (2) Ἐπεὶ δὲ καταπειθεῖς εἶχεν ἤδη τοὺς Ἑβραίους [ὁ] Μωυσῆς καὶ οἷς ἂν κελεύσῃ τούτοις ἀκολουθήσειν ὁμολογοῦντας καὶ τῆς ἐλευθερίας ἐρῶντας, παραγίνεται πρὸς τὸν βασιλέα τὴν ἡγεμονίαν
282 νεωστὶ παρειληφότα, καὶ ὅσα τε ὠφελήσειεν Αἰγυπτίους ὑπὸ Αἰθιόπων καταφρονουμένους καὶ διαρπαζομένης αὐτῶν τῆς χώρας ἐδήλου, στρατηγίᾳ καὶ πόνοις χρησάμενος ὡς περὶ οἰκείων, ὅτι δὲ[1] κινδυνεύσειεν ἐπὶ τούτοις ὑπ' αὐτῶν ἀμοιβὰς οὐ
283 δικαίας κομιζόμενος ἀνεδίδασκεν, τά τε κατὰ τὸ

---

[1] v.ll. ὅτι δή, ὅτι τε: should perhaps be transposed before στρατηγίᾳ with Lat. "et quia militia."

[a] Bibl. Gershom (Γηρσάμ).
[b] Josephus takes over this etymology from Ex. ii. 22 (xviii. 3), "For he said, I have been a sojourner (Heb. *gêr*) in a strange land." The Biblical writer interpreted the name

and Eleazar, he hastened thither. Of these two names, the one, Gêrsos,[a] means in the Hebrew tongue that he had come to "a foreign land"[b]; the other, Eleazar,[c] that it was with the assistance of the God of his fathers that he had escaped from the Egyptians. On approaching the frontier he was met, at God's bidding, by his brother Aaron, to whom he revealed what had befallen him on the mount and the commandments of God. And they, as they proceeded on their way, were met by the most distinguished of the Hebrews, who had learnt of his coming[d]: Moses, failing to convince these by a mere description of the miracles, performed them before their eyes. Amazed at this astonishing spectacle, they took courage and were in hopes that all would go well, since God was caring for their safety.

(2) Now that he was assured of the allegiance of the Hebrews, of their agreement to follow his orders, and of their love of liberty, Moses betook himself to the king, recently promoted to the throne, and represented to him what services he had rendered to the Egyptians, when they were humiliated and their country was ravaged by the Ethiopians, giving him to know how he had commanded and laboured and imperilled himself for the troops, as for his own people, and how for these services he had received from them no due reward. Furthermore, what had befallen him

---

as *gêr shām*, "a sojourner there"; according to a sounder etymology (from the verb *gārash*) it would mean "expulsion" (Driver).

[c] Bibl. Eliezer (so LXX), from *El* (God) and *ezer* (help): Ex. xviii. 4, "For (he said) the God of my father was my help and delivered me from the sword of Pharaoh."

[d] In Ex. iv. 29 the elders of Israel are called together by Moses and Aaron.

JOSEPHUS

Σιναῖον ὄρος αὐτῷ συντυχόντα καὶ τὰς τοῦ θεοῦ φωνὰς καὶ τὰ πρὸς πίστιν ὧν οὗτος αὐτῷ προστάξειεν ὑπ' αὐτοῦ δειχθέντα σημεῖα καθ' ἕκαστον ἐξετίθετο, παρεκάλει τε μὴ ἀπιστοῦντα τούτοις ἐμποδὼν ἵστασθαι τῇ τοῦ θεοῦ γνώμῃ.

284 (3) Χλευάσαντος δὲ τοῦ βασιλέως Μωυσῆς ἔργῳ παρεῖχεν αὐτῷ βλέπειν τὰ σημεῖα τὰ κατὰ τὸ Σιναῖον ὄρος γενόμενα· ὁ δ' ἀγανακτήσας πονηρὸν μὲν αὐτὸν ἀπεκάλει καὶ πρότερον φυγόντα τὴν παρ' Αἰγυπτίοις δουλείαν καὶ νῦν ἐξ ἀπάτης αὐτοῦ τὴν ἄφιξιν πεποιημένον καὶ τερατουργίαις καὶ
285 μαγείαις καταπλῆξαι[1] ἐπικεχειρηκότα. καὶ ταῦθ' ἅμα λέγων κελεύει τοὺς ἱερεῖς τὰς αὐτὰς ὄψεις αὐτῷ παρασχεῖν ὁρᾶν, ὡς Αἰγυπτίων σοφῶν ὄντων καὶ περὶ τὴν τούτων ἐπιστήμην, καὶ ὅτι μὴ μόνος αὐτὸς ἔμπειρος ὢν εἰς θεὸν δύναται τὸ ἐν αὐτῇ παράδοξον ἀναφέρων πιθανὸς ὡς παρ'[2] ἀπαιδεύτοις ὑπάρχειν. καὶ μεθεμένων ἐκείνων τὰς
286 βακτηρίας δράκοντες ἦσαν. Μωυσῆς δ' οὐ καταπλαγείς, "οὐδ' αὐτὸς μέν," εἶπεν, "ὦ βασιλεῦ, τῆς Αἰγυπτίων σοφίας καταφρονῶ, τοσῷδε μέντοι κρείττονα τὰ ὑπ' ἐμοῦ πραττόμενα τῆς τούτων μαγείας καὶ τέχνης φημί, ὅσῳ τὰ θεῖα τῶν ἀνθρωπίνων διαφέρει. δείξω δὲ οὐ κατὰ γοητείαν καὶ πλάνην τῆς ἀληθοῦς δόξης τἀμά, κατὰ δὲ θεοῦ
287 πρόνοιαν καὶ δύναμιν φαινόμενα." καὶ ταῦτ' εἰπὼν μεθίησιν ἐπὶ τῆς γῆς τὴν βακτηρίαν κελεύσας αὐτὴν εἰς ὄφιν μεταβαλεῖν· ἡ δ' ἐπείθετο καὶ τὰς τῶν Αἰγυπτίων βακτηρίας, αἳ δράκοντες ἐδόκουν,

---

[1] καταπλήξειν codd.   [2] ὡς παρ'] ὥσπερ RO.

[a] The "magicians" or rather "sacred scribes" of Ex. vii. 11.

on Mount Sinai, the utterances of God and the miraculous signs which He had shown him to inspire confidence in His injunctions, all this he rehearsed in detail and besought him by no incredulity to obstruct God's purpose.

(3) When the king mocked, Moses caused him to see with his own eyes the signs that had been wrought on the mount of Sinai. But the king was wroth and dubbed him a criminal, who had once escaped from servitude in Egypt and had now effected his return by fraud and was trying to impose on him by juggleries and magic. With these words he ordered the priests[a] to give him an exhibition of the same spectacles, and show that the Egyptians were skilled in these arts also, and that Moses could not, by posing as the only expert and pretending that he owed his marvellous gifts to God, expect them, as simpletons, to believe him.[b] The priests thereupon dropped their staves, which became pythons. But Moses, nothing daunted, said, "Indeed, O king, I too disdain not the cunning of the Egyptians, but I assert that the deeds wrought by me so far surpass their magic and their art as things divine are remote from what is human. And I will show that it is from no witchcraft or deception of true judgement, but from God's providence and power that my miracles proceed." With that he dropped his staff to earth, bidding it be transformed into a serpent. It obeyed and, making the circuit of the Egyptians' staves, which looked like pythons, de-

Moses and the magicians. Ex. vii. 10.

[b] There seems no reason, with Reinach and Dindorf, to reject this clause (beginning " and that Moses . . ."), though the text may be a little confused: the language betrays the hand of an assistant.

περιιοῦσα κατήσθιε μέχρι πάσας ἀνήλωσεν· εἶτ' εἰς τὸ αὑτῆς σχῆμα μεταπεσοῦσαν κομίζεται Μωυσῆς.

288 (2) Ὁ δὲ βασιλεὺς οὐδὲν τούτῳ μᾶλλον πραχθέντι καταπλήττεται, προσοργισθεὶς δὲ καὶ μηδὲν αὐτῷ προχωρήσειν εἰπὼν ἐκ τῆς κατ' Αἰγυπτίων σοφίας καὶ δεινότητος κελεύει τὸν ἐπὶ τῶν Ἑβραίων τεταγμένον μηδεμίαν αὐτοῖς ἄνεσιν παρέχειν τοῦ πονεῖν, ἀλλὰ πλείοσι τῶν πρότερον κακοῖς αὐτοὺς 289 καταναγκάζειν. ὁ δὲ ἄχυρον αὐτοῖς παρέχων εἰς τὴν πλινθείαν πρότερον οὐκέτι παρεῖχεν, ἀλλ' ἡμέρας μὲν ἐπὶ τοῖς ἔργοις ταλαιπωρεῖν ἐποίει, νυκτὸς δὲ συνάγειν τὸ ἄχυρον. καὶ τοῦ δεινοῦ διπλασίονος ὄντος αὐτοῖς ἐν αἰτίαις Μωυσῆν εἶχον, ὡς τῶν ἔργων αὐτοῖς καὶ τῆς ταλαιπωρίας δι' 290 ἐκεῖνον χαλεπωτέρας γεγενημένης. ὁ δ' οὔτε πρὸς τὰς τοῦ βασιλέως ἀπειλὰς ἔκαμνεν οὔτε πρὸς τὰς τῶν Ἑβραίων μέμψεις ἐνεδίδου, τήν τε ψυχὴν παραστησάμενος πρὸς ἑκάτερον ἐπὶ τῷ πονεῖν καὶ τοῖς οἰκείοις ἐκπορίζειν τὴν ἐλευθερίαν ὑπῆρχε.

291 καὶ παραγενόμενος πρὸς τὸν βασιλέα ἔπειθεν αὐτὸν ἀπολύειν τοὺς Ἑβραίους ἐπὶ τὸ Σιναῖον ὄρος ἐκεῖ θύσοντας τῷ θεῷ, τοῦτο γὰρ αὐτὸν κεκελευκέναι, καὶ μηδὲν ἀντιπράττειν οἷς ἐκεῖνος βούλεται, τὴν δ' εὐμένειαν αὐτοῦ περὶ παντὸς ποιούμενον συγχωρεῖν αὐτοῖς τὴν ἔξοδον, μὴ καὶ λάθῃ τούτων κωλυτὴς γενόμενος αὐτὸν αἰτιάσασθαι πάσχων ὅσα παθεῖν εἰκὸς τὸν ἀντιπράττοντα θεοῦ προστάγμασι·

292 τοῖς γὰρ χόλον ἐπ' αὐτοὺς κινήσασι θεῖον ἐξ ἁπάντων φύεσθαι τὰ δεινὰ καὶ οὔτε γῆ τούτοις οὔτε ἀὴρ φίλος οὔτε γοναὶ τέκνων κατὰ φύσιν, ἀλλ' ἐχθρὰ πάντα καὶ πολέμια. πειραθήσεσθαί

voured them until it had consumed them all; then it reverted to its own shape and was recovered by Moses.

(4) Howbeit the king was no more dumbfounded by this performance, but only indignant thereat, and, telling Moses that it would profit him nothing to practise his cunning and craft upon the Egyptians, he ordered the overseer of the Hebrews to grant them no relaxation from their labours, but to subject them to hardships yet more oppressive than before. Accordingly that officer, who had heretofore provided them with straw for their brick-making, provided it no more, but constrained them in the daytime to toil at their tasks and at night to collect the straw. Their affliction being thus doubled, they held Moses to account for this increased severity of their labours and pains. But he, neither wavering before the king's threats, nor yielding to the recriminations of the Hebrews, steeled his soul against both and devoted all his efforts to procuring his people's liberty. So he went to the king and urged him to let the Hebrews go to Mount Sinai to sacrifice there to God, for so He had commanded, and in no wise to oppose His will, but to esteem His gracious favour above all else and permit them exit; lest haply, in hindering them, he should unwittingly have but himself to blame for suffering such a fate as was like to befall him who opposed the commands of God; for to them that rouse the divine ire dread calamities arise from all around them: to them neither earth nor air is friendly, to them no progeny is born after nature's laws, but all things are hostile and at enmity; and

τε τούτων Αἰγυπτίους ἔφασκε μετὰ καὶ τοῦ τὸν Ἑβραίων λαὸν ἀπελθεῖν ἐκ τῆς χώρας αὐτῶν ἀκόντων ἐκείνων.

293 (xiv. 1) Τοῦ δὲ βασιλέως ἐκφαυλίζοντος τοὺς Μωυσέος λόγους καὶ μηδεμίαν ἐπιστροφὴν ἔτι ποιουμένου πάθη δεινὰ τοὺς Αἰγυπτίους κατελάμβανεν, ὧν ἕκαστον ἐκθήσομαι διά τε τὸ μὴ πρότερόν τισι συμβάντα τότε [τοῖς] Αἰγυπτίοις εἰς πεῖραν ἐλθεῖν καὶ διὰ τὸ βούλεσθαι Μωυσῆν μηδὲν ὧν προεῖπεν αὐτοῖς ψευσάμενον ἐπιδεῖξαι, καὶ ὅτι συμφέρει τοῖς ἀνθρώποις μαθοῦσι φυλάττεσθαι ταῦτα ποιεῖν, ἐφ' οἷς μὴ δυσαρεστήσει¹ τὸ θεῖον μηδ' εἰς ὀργὴν τραπὲν² ἀμυνεῖται³ τῆς ἀδικίας
294 αὐτούς. ὁ γὰρ ποταμὸς αὐτοῖς αἱματώδης θεοῦ κελεύσαντος ἐρρύη πίνεσθαι μὴ δυνάμενος, καὶ πηγὴν ἑτέραν ὑδάτων οὐκ ἔχουσιν οὐχὶ τὴν χρόαν μόνον ἦν τοιοῦτος, ἀλλὰ καὶ τοῖς πειρωμένοις
295 ἀλγήματα καὶ πικρὰν ὀδύνην προσέφερεν. ἦν δὲ τοιοῦτος μὲν Αἰγυπτίοις, Ἑβραίοις δὲ γλυκὺς καὶ πότιμος καὶ μηδὲν τοῦ κατὰ φύσιν παρηλλαγμένος. πρὸς οὖν τὸ παράδοξον ἀμηχανήσας ὁ βασιλεὺς καὶ δείσας περὶ τῶν Αἰγυπτίων συνεχώρει τοῖς Ἑβραίοις ἀπιέναι· καὶ τοῦ κακοῦ λωφήσαντος πάλιν τὴν γνώμην μετέβαλεν οὐκ ἐπιτρέπων τὴν ἄφοδον αὐτοῖς.

296 (2) Ὁ θεὸς δὲ ἀγνωμονοῦντος καὶ μετὰ τὴν ἀπαλλαγὴν τῆς συμφορᾶς οὐκέτι σωφρονεῖν ἐθέλοντος ἄλλην τοῖς Αἰγυπτίοις ἐπιφέρει πληγήν· βατράχων πλῆθος ἄπειρον τὴν γῆν αὐτῶν ἐπεβόσκετο, μεστὸς δὲ τούτων καὶ ὁ ποταμὸς ἦν,

¹ O: δυσαρεστήσῃ rell.　　² ROE: περιτραπὲν rell.
³ ἀμύνηται codd.

such trials, he affirmed, would the Egyptians undergo and withal would see the people of the Hebrews quit their country despite their will.

(xiv. 1). But, since the king disdained these words of Moses and paid no more heed to them, dire plagues descended upon the Egyptians. I shall recount them all,[a] first because no such plagues as the Egyptians then experienced ever befell any nation before, next from a desire to show that Moses in not one of his predictions to them was mistaken, and further because it behoves mankind to learn to restrict themselves to such action as shall not offend the Deity nor provoke Him in wrath to punish them for their iniquities.

The plagues of Egypt, why narrated in full.

To begin with, their river, at God's command, ran with a blood-red stream, impossible to drink: other source of water they had none, nor was it only the colour which rendered it so repugnant, but whoever sought to drink of it was seized with tortures and excruciating pain. Such were its effects upon the Egyptians, but for the Hebrews it remained sweet and drinkable and suffered no change from its natural state. Perplexed, therefore, at this prodigy and apprehensive for the Egyptians, the king permitted the Hebrews to depart; and then, when the plague abated, he again changed his mind and denied them exit.

The blood-red Nile. Cf. Ex. vii. 15.

(2) But God, seeing that the graceless king after deliverance from this calamity was no longer willing to be wise, brought another plague upon the Egyptians. An endless multitude of frogs now devoured their land, while the river was full of them,

The frogs. Ex. viii. 1.

---

[a] He omits one, the fifth.

ὡς διαμωμένους τὸ ποτὸν τῷ τῶν ζῴων ἰχῶρι κεκακωμένον λαμβάνειν ἐναποθνῃσκόντων καὶ συν-
297 διαφθειρομένων τῷ ὕδατι, ἥ τε χώρα μεστὴ κακῆς ἦν ἰλύος γεννωμένων τε καὶ ἀποθνῃσκόντων, τάς τε κατ' οἶκον αὐτῶν διαίτας ἠφάνιζον ἐν βρωτοῖς εὑρισκόμενοι καὶ ποτοῖς καὶ ταῖς εὐναῖς αὐτῶν ἐπιπολάζοντες, ὀσμή τε χαλεπὴ ἦν καὶ δυσώδης ἀποθνῃσκόντων τῶν βατράχων καὶ ζών-
298 των καὶ διεφθαρμένων. ὑπὸ δὲ τούτων τῶν κακῶν ἐλαυνομένων τῶν Αἰγυπτίων τὸν Μωυσῆν ἐκέλευσεν ὁ βασιλεὺς οἴχεσθαι τοὺς Ἑβραίους λαβόντα, καὶ παραχρῆμα τοῦτ' εἰπόντος ἠφάνιστο τῶν βατράχων τὸ πλῆθος καὶ ἥ τε γῆ καὶ ὁ
299 ποταμὸς εἰς τὴν ἰδίαν φύσιν κατέστησαν. Φαραώθης δὲ ἅμα τοῦ τε πάθους ἀπήλλακτο [ἡ γῆ]¹ καὶ τῆς αἰτίας ἐπελέληστο καὶ τοὺς Ἑβραίους κατεῖχε, καὶ ὥσπερ πλειόνων παθημάτων φύσεις βουλόμενος μαθεῖν οὐκέτ' ἠφίει τοῖς περὶ τὸν Μωυσῆν ἐξιέναι, φόβῳ μᾶλλον ἢ φρονήσει ταύτην αὐτοῖς ἐπιτρέπων.

300 (3) Πάλιν οὖν ἄλλου κακοῦ προσβολῇ μετῄει τὸ θεῖον αὐτοῦ τὴν ἀπάτην· φθειρῶν γὰρ τοῖς Αἰγυπτίοις ἐξήνθησεν ἄπειρόν τι πλῆθος ἔνδοθεν ἀναδιδομένων, ὑφ' ὧν κακοὶ κακῶς ἀπώλλυντο μήτε λουτροῖς μήτε χρίσεσι φαρμάκων διαφθεῖραι τὸ
301 γένος αὐτῶν δυνάμενοι. καὶ πρὸς τοῦτο τὸ δεινὸν ὁ τῶν Αἰγυπτίων βασιλεὺς ταραχθεὶς καὶ δείσας ὁμοῦ τὸν ὄλεθρον τοῦ λαοῦ καὶ τὴν αἰσχύνην δὲ τῆς ἀπωλείας λογισάμενος ἐξ ἡμίσους ὑπὸ φαυλό-

¹ Probably a gloss.

[a] Or "scraped (the soil)," cf. iii. 10 διαμωμένοις τὴν ψάμμον. The word is drawn from Thuc. iv. 26, "the soldiers were in

insomuch that when they delved *a* they found their drinking-water befouled with the juices of these creatures dying and putrefying in it: the country was saturated with their horrible slime as they bred and died: all articles *b* of the household they ruined, being found in their meat and drink and swarming over their beds: a stench, intolerable and foul, was everywhere, of frogs dying, living, and dead. Seeing the Egyptians harassed by these pests, the king bade Moses be gone and the Hebrews with him, and no sooner had he said this than the mass of frogs disappeared and land and river returned to their natural state. But Pharaothes, on the instant that he was quit of this plague, forgot the reason of it and retained the Hebrews; and, as though desirous to learn the nature of further inflictions, withdrew that permission to the followers of Moses to depart, which fear rather than wisdom had extorted from him.

(3) Again therefore the Deity sent a fresh plague to punish him for his deceit. A vast multitude of lice *c* broke out on the persons of the Egyptians, issuing from their bodies, whereby the miserable wretches miserably perished, neither lotions nor unguents availing them to destroy these vermin. Confounded by this scourge, dreading the destruction of his people, and withal reflecting on the ignominy of such an end, the king of Egypt was forced to listen to reason, though, in his depravity, still only in half

The lice. Ex. viii. 16.

the habit of scraping away the shingle ($διαμώμενοι τὸν κάχληκα$) and drinking any water which they could get " (Jowett); the detail is taken over from the Biblical account of the *first* plague, Ex. vii. 24, " And all the Egyptians digged round about the river for water to drink."

b Or " stores," " comforts," including food and dress.

c LXX reads $σκνῖφες$ (= " gnats," rather than " fleas").

JOSEPHUS

302 τητος ἠναγκάζετο σωφρονεῖν· τοῖς μὲν γὰρ Ἑβραίοις αὐτοῖς ἐδίδου τὴν ἄφοδον, καὶ πρὸς τοῦτο λωφήσαντος τέκνα καὶ γυναῖκας ὅμηρα τῆς ὑποστροφῆς αὐτῶν καταλιπεῖν αὐτοὺς ἠξίου. προσεξαγριαίνει δὴ τὸν θεὸν νομίσας ἀπατήσειν αὐτοῦ τὴν πρόνοιαν, ὥσπερ Μωυσέος ἀλλ' οὐκ ἐκείνου τιμωροῦντος τὴν Αἴγυπτον ὑπὲρ τῶν Ἑβραίων·

303 θηρίων γὰρ παντοίων καὶ πολυτρόπων, ὧν εἰς ὄψιν οὐδεὶς ἀπηντήκει πρότερον, τὴν χώραν αὐτῶν ἐγέμισεν, ὑφ' ὧν αὐτοί τε ἀπώλλυντο καὶ ἡ γῆ τῆς ἐπιμελείας τῆς παρὰ τῶν γεωργῶν ἀπεστερεῖτο, εἰ δέ τι καὶ διέφυγε τὴν ὑπ' ἐκείνοις ἀπώλειαν, νόσῳ τοῦτο καὶ τῶν ἀνθρώπων ὑπομενόντων ἐδαπανᾶτο.

304 (4) Τοῦ δὲ Φαραώθου μηδ' οὕτως εἴκοντος τοῖς τοῦ θεοῦ βουλήμασιν, ἀλλὰ τὰς μὲν γυναῖκας συναπαίρειν τοῖς ἀνδράσιν ἀξιοῦντος καταλείπεσθαι δὲ τοὺς παῖδας, οὐκ ἠπόρει τὸ θεῖον τὴν πονηρίαν αὐτοῦ ποικίλοις κακοῖς καὶ μείζοσι τῶν προενδεδημηκότων μετερχόμενον βασανίσαι· ἀλλὰ γὰρ δεινῶς αὐτοῖς ἐξηλκοῦτο τὰ σώματα τῶν ἐντὸς διαφθειρομένων, καὶ τὸ πολὺ τῶν Αἰγυπτίων

305 οὕτως ἀπώλλυτο. μηδ' ὑπὸ ταύτης δὲ τῆς πληγῆς σωφρονιζομένου τοῦ βασιλέως χάλαζα, μήτε πρότερον τοῦ κατ' Αἴγυπτον ἀέρος τοῦτο πεπονθότος μήθ' ὁμοία τῇ παρ' ἄλλοις ὥρᾳ χειμῶνος κατιούσῃ, μείζων δὲ τῆς παρὰ τοῖς τὰ βόρεια καὶ τὴν ἄρκτον

---

[a] Detail attached in Ex. x. 10 f. to a later plague.

[b] These " beasts of every sort and kind " are the equivalent of the fourth plague in the Biblical narrative, the " swarms of flies " (LXX the " dog-fly," κυνόμυια) of Ex. viii. 21. The single Heb. word translated " swarms-of-flies," viz. 'ārōb,

measure; for he offered egress to the Hebrews themselves, and when thereupon the plague ceased he required them to leave their wives and children behind as hostages for their return.[a] Thus he did but exasperate God the more, in thinking to impose upon His providence, as though it were Moses and not He who was punishing Egypt on the Hebrews' behalf; for He now sent wild beasts[b] of every species and kind, the like of which no man had ever encountered before, to infest their country, whereby the people perished and the land was deprived of the care of its labourers, while all that escaped their ravages was wasted by disease even though the men stood their ground.[c]

Wild beasts. Cf. Ex. viii. 21.

(4) Yet since even so Pharaothes would not yield to the will of God, but, while permitting the wives to accompany their husbands, required the children to be left behind,[d] the Deity lacked not the means to pursue and torment the sinner with divers chastisements yet mightier than those prevalent heretofore; for now their bodies were smitten with horrible ulcers and their intestines wasted away, and the greater part of the Egyptians perished thus. But when even this plague failed to sober the king, hail, till then unknown to the climate of Egypt, nor yet like that which in other countries falls in winter, but hail larger than that known to the dwellers in northern, polar

Ulcers. Ex. ix. 8.

Hail. Ex. ix. 18.

might mean a "*mixture*" and is actually so rendered in the Syriac and later Greek versions. Hence this menagerie of Josephus. The fifth plague, the murrain on cattle (Ex. ix. 1), he omits altogether.

[c] *i.e.* the labourers in the fields. But the meaning is doubtful: perhaps "even though the population survived it."

[d] Detail not in Scripture; in Ex. x. 10 f. wives and children are to remain.

νεμομένοις, ἔαρος ἀκμάζοντος κατενεχθεῖσα τοὺς
306 καρποὺς αὐτῶν κατέκλασεν. ἔπειτα φῦλον ἀκρί-
δων ἐπινέμεται τὴν ὑπὸ τῆς χαλάζης μὴ κατα-
βλαβεῖσαν σποράν, ὥστε πρὸς τἀκριβὲς[1] πάσας
τοῖς Αἰγυπτίοις τὰς ἀπὸ τῆς γῆς τῶν καρπῶν
ἐλπίδας διολέσαι.

307 (5) Ἤρκει μὲν οὖν τὸν δίχα πονηρίας ἀνόητον
καὶ τὰ προειρημένα τῶν κακῶν εἰς σύνεσιν καὶ τοῦ
συμφέροντος τὴν ἐπίνοιαν ὠφελῆσαι, Φαραώθης
δὲ οὐ τοσοῦτον ὑπὸ ἀφροσύνης ὅσον ὑπὸ κακίας
ὅμως αἰσθόμενος[2] τῆς αἰτίας ἀντεφιλονίκει τῷ
θεῷ καὶ τοῦ κρείττονος ἑκὼν προδότης ἐγένετο,
καὶ κελεύει μὲν τὸν Μωυσῆν μετά τε γυναικῶν
καὶ παίδων ἀπάγειν τοὺς Ἑβραίους, τὴν δὲ λείαν
αὐτοῖς καταλιπεῖν ἐφθαρμένης αὐτοῖς τῆς οἰκείας.
308 τοῦ δὲ Μωυσέος οὐχὶ δίκαια φήσαντος αὐτὸν
ἀξιοῦν, δεῖν γὰρ αὐτοὺς τῷ θεῷ τὰς θυσίας ἐκ τῆς
λείας ἐπενεγκεῖν, καὶ τριβομένου διὰ ταύτην τὴν
αἰτίαν τοῦ χρόνου σκότος βαθὺ καὶ φέγγους
ἄμοιρον περιχεῖται τοῖς Αἰγυπτίοις, ὑφ' οὗ τάς
τε ὄψεις ἀποκλειομένοις καὶ τὰς ἀναπνοὰς ἐμφραττ-
τομένοις ὑπὸ παχύτητος οἰκτρῶς τε ἀποθνήσκειν
συνέβαινε καὶ δεδιέναι μὴ καταποθῶσιν ὑπὸ τοῦ
309 νέφους. εἶτα τούτου διασκεδασθέντος μετὰ τρεῖς
ἡμέρας καὶ τοσαύτας νύκτας, ὡς οὐ μετενόει πρὸς
τὴν ἔξοδον τῶν Ἑβραίων ὁ Φαραώθης, προσελθὼν
ὁ Μωυσῆς φησιν "ἄχρι πότε ἀπειθεῖς τῇ τοῦ
θεοῦ γνώμῃ; κελεύει γὰρ οὗτος ἀπολύειν τοὺς
Ἑβραίους, καὶ οὐκ ἔστιν ἑτέρως ἀπαλλαγῆναι τῶν
310 κακῶν ὑμᾶς μὴ ταῦτα ποιήσαντας." ὁ δὲ βασιλεὺς
ὀργισθεὶς ἐπὶ τοῖς εἰρημένοις ἠπείλησεν αὐτοῦ τὴν

[1] Niese: ἀκριβὲς codd.

regions, descended when spring was at its prime and beat down their crops. Thereafter a horde of locusts devoured whatever seed had not been ruined by the hail, thus literally destroying all hopes that the Egyptians may have cherished of a harvest from the soil.

(5) The calamities already named might indeed have sufficed to recall to reason and a sense of his own interests a mere imbecile devoid of malice. But Pharaothes, less fool than knave, though alive to the cause of it all, was matching himself against God as a deliberate traitor to the cause of virtue; and now[a] he ordered Moses to take off the Hebrews, women and children included, but to leave their live stock[b] to the Egyptians, who had lost their own. Moses replied that this demand was inequitable, since they needed their cattle to offer sacrifices to God, and while time in consequence dragged on, dense darkness, without a particle of light, enveloped the Egyptians—darkness so thick that their eyes were blinded by it and their breath choked, and they either met with a miserable end or lived in terror of being swallowed up by the fog. This dispersed after three days and as many nights and then, since Pharaothes was still impenitent regarding the departure of the Hebrews, Moses went to him and said: "How long wilt thou disobey the will of God? For the command is His, to let the Hebrews go; and by no other means can thy people be quit of these ills save by acting thus." Infuriated by this speech, the king threatened

---

[a] In Exodus these orders *follow* the plague of darkness.
[b] λεία, constantly used of cattle.

---

² Lat., ed. pr.: + γὰρ codd.

κεφαλὴν ἀποτεμεῖν, εἰ πάλιν περὶ τούτων ἐνοχλῶν αὐτῷ προσέλθοι. Μωυσῆς δὲ αὐτὸς οὐκέτι ποιήσεσθαι περὶ τούτων λόγους ἔφησεν, αὐτὸν δὲ ἐκεῖνον σὺν καὶ τοῖς πρώτοις τῶν Αἰγυπτίων παρακαλέσειν τοὺς Ἑβραίους ἀπελθεῖν. καὶ ὁ μὲν ταῦτ᾿ εἰπὼν ἀπαλλάσσεται.

311 (6) Ὁ δὲ θεὸς δηλώσας ἔτι μιᾷ πληγῇ τοὺς Αἰγυπτίους καταναγκάσειν ἀπολῦσαι τοὺς Ἑραίους ἐκέλευσε[1] Μωυσῆν παραγγεῖλαι τῷ λαῷ θυσίαν ἑτοίμην ἔχειν, παρασκευασαμένους τῇ δεκάτῃ[2] τοῦ Ξανθικοῦ μηνὸς εἰς τὴν τεσσαρεσκαιδεκάτην, ὃς παρὰ μὲν Αἰγυπτίοις Φαρμουθὶ καλεῖται, Νισὰν δὲ παρ᾿ Ἑβραίοις, Μακεδόνες δ᾿ αὐτὸν Ξανθικὸν προσαγορεύουσιν, ἀπάγειν τε τοὺς Ἑβραίους

312 πάντα ἐπικομιζομένους. καὶ ὁ μὲν ἑτοίμους ἔχων ἤδη τοὺς Ἑβραίους πρὸς τὴν ἔξοδον καὶ διατάξας εἰς φατρίας ἐν ταὐτῷ συνεῖχεν, ἐνστάσης δὲ τῆς τεσσαρεσκαιδεκάτης πάντες πρὸς ἄφοδον ἔχοντες ἔθυον καὶ τῷ αἵματι τὰς οἰκίας ἥγνιζον ὑσσώπου κόμαις ἀναλαβόντες, καὶ δειπνήσαντες τὰ λοιπὰ τῶν κρεῶν ἔκαυσαν ὡς ἐξελευ-

313 σόμενοι. ὅθεν νῦν ἔτι κατὰ τὸ ἔθος οὕτως θύομεν τὴν ἑορτὴν πάσχα καλοῦντες, σημαίνει δ᾿ ὑπερβάσια, διότι κατ᾿ ἐκείνην τὴν ἡμέραν ὁ θεὸς αὐτῶν ὑπερβὰς Αἰγυπτίοις ἐναπέσκηψε τὴν νόσον. ἡ γὰρ φθορὰ τῶν πρωτοτόκων κατ᾿ ἐκείνην ἔπεισι τὴν νύκτα τοῖς Αἰγυπτίοις, ὡς συνελθόντας πολλοὺς

[1] ἐκέλευε RO. [2] τρισκαιδεκάτῃ ME.

[a] Not tribes; the Attic φ(ρ)ατρία was a subdivision of the φυλή, and the use of the word in *B.J.* vi. 423 (*cf. A.* iii. 248) with reference to contemporary Passover practice shows that little companies of between ten and twenty persons are intended.

to behead him, should he ever again come and pester him on this matter. Moses replied that for his part he would speak thereon no more, but that it was the king himself, along with the chief of the Egyptians, who would implore the Hebrews to depart. And with those words he left him.

(6) God, having revealed that by yet one more plague he would constrain the Egyptians to release the Hebrews, now bade Moses instruct the people to have ready a sacrifice, making preparations on the tenth of the month Xanthicus over against the fourteenth day (this is the month called by the Egyptians Pharmuthi, by the Hebrews Nisan, and by the Macedonians termed Xanthicus) and then to lead off the Hebrews, taking all their possessions with them. He accordingly had the Hebrews ready betimes for departure, and ranging them in fraternities[a] kept them assembled together; then when the fourteenth day was come the whole body, in readiness to start, sacrificed, purified the houses with the blood, using bunches of hyssop to sprinkle it,[b] and after the repast burnt the remnants of the meat as persons on the eve of departure. Hence comes it that to this day we keep this sacrifice in the same customary manner, calling the feast *Pascha*, which signifies " passing over," because on that day God passed over our people when he smote the Egyptians with plague.[c] For on that selfsame night destruction visited the firstborn of Egypt, insomuch that multitudes of

The Passover. Death of the firstborn.
Ex. xi. 1.
xii. 3.

xii. 27.

---

[b] Literally " refreshing them (the houses) with bunches of hyssop ": ἀναλαμβάνειν, elsewhere = " refresh," " recover " (*e.g. A.* xv. 312), is here synonymous with ἁγνίζειν, " purify."

[c] ἐναπέσκηψε τὴν νόσον (" launched the plague upon ") after Thuc. ii. 47 (of the plague of Athens).

τῶν περὶ τὸ βασίλειον διαιτωμένων τῷ Φαραώθῃ
συμβουλεύειν ἀπολύειν τοὺς Ἑβραίους. καὶ Μωυσῆν καλέσας ἐκεῖνος ἀπιέναι προσέταξεν, εἰ τῆς χώρας ἐξέλθοιεν παύσεσθαι¹ τὴν Αἴγυπτον κακοπαθοῦσαν ὑπολαβών, δώροις τε τοὺς Ἑβραίους ἐτίμων, οἱ μὲν ὑπὲρ τοῦ τάχιον ἐξελθεῖν, οἱ δὲ καὶ κατὰ γειτνιακὴν πρὸς αὐτοὺς συνήθειαν.

(xv. 1) Καὶ οἱ μὲν ἐξῄεσαν κλαιόντων καὶ μετανοούντων ὅτι χρήσαιντο χαλεπῶς αὐτοῖς τῶν Αἰγυπτίων, τὴν δὲ πορείαν ἐποιοῦντο κατὰ Λητοῦς πόλιν ἔρημον οὖσαν ἐν τοῖς τότε· Βαβυλὼν γὰρ ὕστερον ἐκεῖ κτίζεται Καμβύσου καταστρεφομένου τὴν Αἴγυπτον. συντόμως δὲ ποιούμενοι τὴν ἄφοδον εἰς Βεελσεφῶντα χωρίον τριταῖοι παραγίνονται τῆς Ἐρυθρᾶς θαλάσσης. μηδενὸς δὲ τῶν ἀπὸ τῆς γῆς εὐποροῦντες διὰ τὴν ἐρημίαν πεφυραμένοις τοῖς ἀλεύροις καὶ πεπηγόσι μόνον ὑπὸ βραχείας θερμότητος τοῖς ἀπ' αὐτῶν ἄρτοις διετρέφοντο, καὶ τούτοις ἐπὶ τριάκονθ' ἡμέρας ἐχρήσαντο· πρὸς πλείονα γὰρ οὐκ ἐξήρκεσε χρόνον αὐτοῖς ὅσα ἐκ τῆς Αἰγύπτου ἐπεφέροντο, καὶ ταῦτα τὴν τροφὴν ταμιευομένοις καὶ πρὸς ἀνάγκην ἀλλὰ μὴ πρὸς κόρον αὐτῇ χρωμένοις· ὅθεν εἰς μνήμην τῆς τότε

¹ παύσασθαι codd.

---

[a] In the year 525 B.C. Strabo (xvii. 807) mentions the Egyptian Babylon as a strong fortress, in or near " the Letopolite nome," founded by certain Babylonian emigrants and in his day the camp of one of the three Roman legions in Egypt. Modern explorers have identified the two places

those whose dwellings surrounded the palace trooped to Pharaothes to urge him to let the Hebrews go. And he, summoning Moses, ordered him to depart, supposing that, once his people were quit of the country, Egypt's sufferings would cease. They even honoured the Hebrews with gifts, some to speed their departure, others from neighbourly feelings towards old acquaintances.

(xv. 1) So they departed, amid the lamentation and regrets of the Egyptians for having treated them so badly. They took the road for Letopolis, at that time desert, afterwards the site of Babylon, founded by Cambyses when he subjugated Egypt.[a] Quitting the country by the shortest route they arrived on the third day at Beelsephon,[b] a place beside the Red Sea. Being bereft of any sustenance from the barren soil, they kneaded flour, baked it with merely a slight heating, and subsisted on the bread so made; on this they lived for thirty days,[c] for they could make what they had brought from Egypt last no longer, notwithstanding that they rationed the food, limiting the portions to bare needs without eating to satiety. Hence it is that, in memory of that time of scarcity,

xii. 35 f.

The exodus.
Ex. xii. 37.

xiv. 2.

xii. 39.

---

named, Babylon (*Fostat*) near Old Cairo, and Letopolis (*Usim*) some ten miles north of it, on the opposite (western) bank of the Nile. On the other hand, the Biblical "Succoth" (Ex. xii. 37), has been identified as the *Thukke* of Egyptian inscriptions, and the "Pithom" of Ex. i. 11, lying far to the N.E. of Babylon on the eastern confines of "the land of Goshen." Josephus thus indicates a more southerly desert route as the "shortest route" to the Red Sea.

[b] Bibl. Baal-zephon, not identified.

[c] Inferred from Ex. xvi. 1, where we read that the Israelites reached the wilderness of Sin "on the 15th day of the second month," *i.e.* a month after leaving Egypt on the 15th Nisan, and there first began to eat manna.

303

ἐνδείας ἑορτὴν ἄγομεν ἐφ' ἡμέρας ὀκτὼ τὴν τῶν
ἀζύμων λεγομένην. τὸ μὲν οὖν πᾶν πλῆθος τῶν
μετανισταμένων γυναιξὶν ἅμα καὶ τέκνοις σκο-
ποῦσιν οὐκ εὐαρίθμητον ἦν, οἱ δὲ στρατεύσιμον
ἔχοντες τὴν ἡλικίαν περὶ ἑξήκοντα μυριάδες ἦσαν.

318 (2) Κατέλιπον δὲ τὴν Αἴγυπτον μηνὶ Ξανθικῷ
πεντεκαιδεκάτῃ κατὰ σελήνην μετὰ ἔτη τριάκοντα
καὶ τετρακόσια ἢ τὸν πρόγονον ἡμῶν Ἄβραμον
εἰς τὴν Χαναναίαν ἐλθεῖν, τῆς δὲ Ἰακώβου μετ-
αναστάσεως εἰς τὴν Αἴγυπτον γενομένης διακοσίοις
319 πρὸς τοῖς δεκαπέντε ἐνιαυτοῖς ὕστερον. Μωυσῆς[1]
δ' ἐγεγόνει μὲν ἔτος ὀγδοηκοστὸν ἤδη, ὁ δὲ
ἀδελφὸς αὐτοῦ Ἀαρὼν τρισὶ πλείοσιν.[2] ἐπεκομί-
ζοντο δὲ καὶ τὰ τοῦ Ἰωσήπου ὀστᾶ, ταῦτ' ἐκείνου
τοῖς υἱοῖς αὐτοῦ κελεύσαντος.

320 (3) Αἰγύπτιοι δ' ἐπὶ τοῖς Ἑβραίοις ἐξελθοῦσι
μετενόουν καὶ τοῦ βασιλέως δεινῶς φέροντος ὡς
κατὰ γοητείαν τὴν Μωυσέος τούτων γεγονότων
ἐπ' αὐτοὺς ἐγνώκεσαν ἀπιέναι. καὶ λαβόντες
ὅπλα καὶ παρασκευὴν ἐδίωκον ὡς ἐπανάξοντες
αὐτοὺς εἰ καταλάβοιεν· καὶ γὰρ οὐκέτ' αὐτοὺς
ἐνέχεσθαι[3] τῷ θεῷ· τὴν γὰρ ἔξοδον αὐτοῖς γε-
321 γονέναι· κρατήσειν δὲ ῥᾳδίως αὐτῶν ὑπέλαβον
ἀνόπλων τε ὄντων καὶ ὑπὸ τῆς ὁδοιπορίας κεκο-

[1] RO: Μωυσῆ (-σει) rell.   [2] πλεῖον Niese.
[3] ROE: ἐντεύξεσθαι rell.

---

[a] Originally seven days, Nisan 15-21 (Lev. xxiii. 6, *cf.*
Ex. xii. 18 f., and so Josephus himself *A.* iii. 249), "but
from time immemorial the Jews outside of Palestine have
added a day to their principal festivals" (Oesterley-Box,
Religion and Worship of Synagogue, ed. 2, 385).

[b] The Macedonian month (approximately April) equated
by Josephus with the Hebrew Nisan.

[c] These dates conflict with other statements in Josephus (*e.g.*

we keep for eight*a* days a feast called the feast of unleavened bread. To estimate the total number of emigrants, including women and children, were no easy task, but those of military age numbered about six hundred thousand.

(2) They left Egypt in the month of Xanthicus,*b* on the fifteenth by lunar reckoning, 430 years after the coming of our forefather Abraham to Canaan, Jacob's migration to Egypt having taken place 215 years later.*c* Moses had already reached his eightieth year; his brother Aaron was three years older. They were bringing with them the bones of Joseph in accordance with that patriarch's injunctions to his sons.

(3) But the Egyptians repented of having let the Hebrews go and, their king being mortified at the thought that it was the jugglery of Moses that had brought this about, they resolved to set out after them. So with arms and full equipment they started in pursuit, determined to bring them back could they overtake them; for no longer (they deemed) were they accountable to God, now that these people had had their exodus, and they looked for an easy victory over unarmed*d* folk, exhausted by their march. Inquiring,

ii. 204 note). The figure 430 comes from Exodus: the other figure (dividing the whole period from Abraham's migration to Canaan to the emigration from Egypt into two equal parts) is perhaps taken over from the Jewish historian Demetrius (Freudenthal, *Hellenistische Studien*, 49 note, quoted by Weill).

d Opposed to Ex. xiii. 18 Heb. " went up *armed* out of Egypt " (a rare verb misinterpreted by LXX). Weill appositely quotes the extract, apparently from Demetrius, in Euseb. *Praep. Ev.* ix. 29 fin.: ἐπιζητεῖν δέ τινα πῶς οἱ Ἰσραηλῖται ὅπλα ἔσχον, ἄνοπλοι ἐξελθόντες . . . φαίνεται οὖν τοὺς μὴ κατακλυσθέντας τοῖς ἐκείνων ὅπλοις χρήσασθαι (precisely as stated by Josephus below, § 349).

305

πωμένων. παρ' ἑκάστων τε ἀναπυνθανόμενοι ᾗ χωρήσειαν ἐπέσπευδον τὴν δίωξιν, καίτοι χαλεπῆς οὔσης ὁδευθῆναι τῆς γῆς οὐ στρατοπέδοις μόνον 322 ἀλλὰ καὶ καθ' ἕνα. Μωυσῆς δὲ ταύτῃ τοὺς Ἑβραίους ἀπήγαγεν, ἵν' εἰ μετανοήσαντες οἱ Αἰγύπτιοι διώκειν ἐθέλοιεν τιμωρίαν τῆς πονηρίας καὶ παραβάσεως τῶν ὡμολογημένων ὑπόσχοιεν, καὶ διὰ Παλαιστίνους, ⟨οὓς⟩[1] δυσμενῶς ἔχοντας κατὰ παλαιὰν ἀπέχθειαν οὖσαν ὁπωσοῦν ἐβούλετο[2] λανθάνειν ἀπερχόμενος· ὅμορος γάρ ἐστι τῇ τῶν 323 Αἰγυπτίων χώρᾳ· καὶ διὰ τοῦτο τὴν μὲν ἄγουσαν εἰς τὴν Παλαιστίνην οὐκ ἀνήγαγε τὸν λαόν, ἀλλὰ διὰ τῆς ἐρήμου πολλὴν ἀνύσας ὁδὸν καὶ κακοπαθήσας ἠθέλησεν ἐμβαλεῖν εἰς τὴν Χαναναίαν· ἔτι τε καὶ διὰ τὰς ἐντολὰς τοῦ θεοῦ κελεύσαντος ἄγειν τὸν λαὸν εἰς τὸ Σιναῖον ὄρος ἐκεῖ ποιήσοντας 324 τὰς θυσίας. καταλαβόντες δὲ τοὺς Ἑβραίους οἱ Αἰγύπτιοι εἰς μάχην παρεσκευάζοντο καὶ συνελαύνουσιν αὐτοὺς ὑπὸ πολυχειρίας εἰς ὀλίγον χωρίον· ἑξακόσια γὰρ αὐτοῖς ἅρματα εἵπετο σὺν ἱππεῦσι πεντακισμυρίοις καὶ ὁπλιτῶν μυριάδες ἦσαν εἴκοσι. τὰς δὲ ὁδοὺς ἀπεφράγνυσαν, αἷς φεύξεσθαι τοὺς Ἑβραίους ὑπελάμβανον, μεταξὺ κρημνῶν αὐτοὺς ἀπροσβάτων καὶ τῆς θαλάττης 325 ἀπολαμβάνοντες· τελευτᾷ γὰρ εἰς αὐτὴν ὄρος ὑπὸ τραχύτητος ὁδῶν ἄπορον καὶ φυγῆς ἀπολαμβανο-

[1] ins. Niese.   [2] LE Lat.: ἐβουλεύετο rell.

[a] Ex. "For God said, Lest peradventure the people repent when they see war, and they return to Egypt."
[b] Josephus is replying to anti-Semite objections raised at

therefore, on all hands which route the fugitives had taken, they vigorously pushed the pursuit, albeit the ground was difficult to traverse not only for great armies but even for a solitary traveller. Now Moses had led the Hebrews out by this route in order that, if the Egyptians changed their minds and wished to pursue them, they should be punished for this malicious breach of the pact ; partly also on account of the Philistines, a people hostile in virtue of an ancient feud, from whom he wished at all costs to conceal his departure, for their country was coterminous with that of the Egyptians.[a] That was why [b] he did not conduct his people by the direct route to Palestine, but chose to accomplish a long and arduous march through the desert in order to invade Canaan. Furthermore he was influenced by the behests of God, who had commanded him to lead His people to Mount Sinai, there to do Him sacrifice. However the Egyptians, having overtaken the Hebrews, prepared for battle and, thanks to their multitudinous forces, cooped them into a narrow space : they were, in fact, being pursued by 600 chariots along with 50,000 horsemen and heavy infantry to the number of 200,000.[c] Barring all routes by which they expected the Hebrews to attempt escape,[d] they confined them between inaccessible cliffs and the sea ; for it was the sea in which terminated a mountain whose rugged face was destitute of tracks[e] and prohibitive for retreat.

Three reasons for the route taken by Moses.

Ex. xiii. 17.

xiv. 9.

xiv. 7

Alexandria: Why this route ? Whence did they get their arms ? etc.

[c] The 600 chariots are Biblical, the other figures imaginary.

[d] The retreat from Syracuse is in mind : τάς τε ὁδοὺς τὰς κατὰ τὴν χώραν, ᾗ εἰκὸς ἦν τοὺς Ἀθηναίους ἰέναι, ἀπεφράγνυσαν Thuc. vii. 74.

[e] Or perhaps "whose rugged tracks made it impracticable."

μενον. τοιγαροῦν ἐν τῇ εἰσβολῇ[1] τῇ πρὸς θάλατταν τοῦ ὄρους τοὺς Ἑβραίους ἀπέφραττον τῷ στρατοπέδῳ κατὰ στόμα τοῦτο ἱδρυσάμενοι, ὅπως τὴν εἰς τὸ πεδίον ἔξοδον ὦσιν αὐτοὺς ἀφῃρημένοι.

326 (4) Μήτ' οὖν ὑπομένειν πολιορκουμένων τρόπῳ διὰ τὴν ἔνδειαν τῶν ἐπιτηδείων δυνάμενοι μήτε φυγῆς εὐπορίαν ὁρῶντες, ὅπλων τε σπανίζοντες εἰ καὶ μάχεσθαι δόξειεν αὐτοῖς, ἐν ἐλπίδι τοῦ πάντως ἀπολεῖσθαι[2] καθειστήκεσαν, εἰ μὴ παραδώσουσιν ἑαυτοὺς τοῖς Αἰγυπτίοις ἐθελουσίως.
327 καὶ τὸν Μωυσῆν ᾐτιῶντο πάντων ἐπιλελησμένοι τῶν ἐκ θεοῦ πρὸς τὴν ἐλευθερίαν αὐτοῖς σημείων γεγονότων, ὡς καὶ τὸν προφήτην παρορμῶντα καὶ τὴν σωτηρίαν αὐτοῖς ἐπαγγελλόμενον ὑπὸ ἀπιστίας λίθοις ἐθελῆσαι βαλεῖν παραδιδόναι τε
328 σφᾶς τοῖς Αἰγυπτίοις διεγνωκέναι. πένθος τε ἦν καὶ ὀδυρμοὶ γυναικῶν καὶ παίδων πρὸ ὀφθαλμῶν ἐχόντων τὸν ὄλεθρον, ὄρεσι καὶ θαλάττῃ περικεκλεισμένων καὶ πολεμίοις καὶ φυγὴν οὐδαμόθεν ἐκ τούτων ἐπινοούντων.

329 (5) Μωυσῆς δὲ καίπερ ἀγριαίνοντος πρὸς αὐτὸν τοῦ πλήθους οὔτ' αὐτὸς ἐνέκαμνε τῇ περὶ αὐτοὺς προνοίᾳ καὶ τῷ θεῷ κατεφρόνει, τά τε ἄλλα πρὸς τὴν ἐλευθερίαν αὐτοῖς ὅσα προεῖπε παρεσχηκότος καὶ μηδὲ τότ' αὐτοὺς ἐάσοντος ὑπὸ τοῖς ἐχθροῖς
330 γενομένους ἢ δουλεύειν ἢ ἀπολέσθαι, καὶ στὰς ἐν μέσοις "οὐδὲ ἀνθρώποις," εἶπε, "καλῶς τὰ παρόντα πεπολιτευμένοις πρὸς ὑμᾶς[3] δίκαιον ἦν ἀπιστεῖν ὡς οὐχ ὁμοίοις ἐσομένοις πρὸς τὰ μέλλοντα, τῆς δὲ τοῦ θεοῦ νῦν ἀπογινώσκειν ὑμᾶς

---
[1] ROE: προσβολῇ M: συμβολῇ rell.
[2] Niese: ἀπολέσθαι codd. [3] Niese: ἡμᾶς codd.

Accordingly, occupying the pass where the mountain abuts upon the sea, they blocked the passage of the Hebrews, pitching their camp at its mouth, to prevent their escape to the plain.^a

(4) Thus, unable, for lack of supplies, to hold out in the manner of the beleaguered, seeing no opportunity for flight, and destitute of arms even should they decide to give battle, the Hebrews were left with no prospect but that of utter destruction, failing deliberate surrender to the Egyptians. And now they turned to accusing Moses, forgetful of all those miracles wrought by God in token of their liberation, insomuch that the words of the prophet, who cheered them and promised them salvation, were met with incredulity and they wished to stone him and resolved to give themselves up to the Egyptians. Then there were the wailings and lamentations of women and children, with death before their eyes, hemmed in by mountains, sea, and enemy, and seeing nowhere from these any imaginable escape. *The Hebrews distress. Cf. Ex. xiv. 10.*

(5) But Moses, for all that enragement of the multitude against him, relaxed not his forethought on their behalf, and proudly trusted in God, who, having done all that He had promised towards their deliverance, would not now suffer them to fall into their enemies' hands whether for servitude or destruction. Standing up, then, in their midst, he said: "Were they but men who till now have happily directed your affairs, it were an injustice to doubt that even they would prove themselves alike in future; but to despair at this moment of the providence of God were an act of madness, seeing that from Him *Exhortation of Moses. Cf. Ex. xiv. 13.*

^a Or "table-land."

331 προνοίας μανίας ἔργον ἂν εἴη, παρ' οὗ πάνθ' ὑμῖν ἀπήντηκεν ὅσα δι' ἐμοῦ πρὸς σωτηρίαν καὶ τὴν ἀπαλλαγὴν τῆς δουλείας οὐδὲ προσδοκῶσιν ὑπέσχετο. μᾶλλον δ' ἐχρῆν ἀπόρους,[1] ὡς δοκεῖτε, γεγενημένους βοηθὸν ἐλπίζειν τὸν θεόν, οὗ καὶ τὸ νῦν εἰς ταύτην ὑμᾶς περικεκλεῖσθαι 332 τὴν δυσχωρίαν ἔργον, ἵν' ἐξ ἀμηχάνων ὅθεν οὔτ' αὐτοὶ νομίζετε σωτηρίαν ἕξειν οὔθ' οἱ πολέμιοι, ἐκ τούτων ῥυσάμενος τήν τε ἰσχὺν ἐπιδείξηται τὴν ἑαυτοῦ καὶ τὴν περὶ ὑμᾶς πρόνοιαν. οὐ γὰρ ἐπὶ μικροῖς τὸ θεῖον τὴν ἑαυτοῦ συμμαχίαν οἷς ἂν εὔνουν ᾖ δίδωσιν, ἀλλ' ἐφ' οἷς[2] ἀνθρωπίνην ἐλπίδα μὴ βλέποι πρὸς τὸ κρεῖττον παροῦσαν. 333 ὅθεν τοιούτῳ βοηθῷ πεπιστευκότες, ᾧ δύναμις καὶ τὰ μικρὰ ποιῆσαι μεγάλα καὶ τῶν τηλικούτων ἀσθένειαν καταψηφίσασθαι, μὴ καταπέπληχθε τὴν Αἰγυπτίων παρασκευήν, μηδ' ὅτι θάλασσα καὶ κατόπιν ὑμῖν ὄρη φυγῆς ὁδὸν οὐ παρέχοντα διὰ τοῦτ' ἀπογινώσκετε τὴν σωτηρίαν· γένοιτο γὰρ ἂν καὶ ταῦθ' ὑμῖν πεδία τοῦ θεοῦ θελήσαντος καὶ γῆ τὸ πέλαγος."

334 (xvi. 1) Τοσαῦτα εἰπὼν ἦγεν αὐτοὺς ἐπὶ τὴν θάλασσαν τῶν Αἰγυπτίων ὁρώντων· ἐν ὄψει γὰρ ἦσαν καὶ τῷ πόνῳ τεταλαιπωρημένοι τῆς διώξεως εἰς τὴν ὑστεραίαν τὴν μάχην ὑπερβαλέσθαι καλῶς ἔχειν ὑπελάμβανον. ἐπειδὴ δὲ πρὸς τῷ αἰγιαλῷ Μωυσῆς ἐγεγόνει, λαβὼν τὴν βακτηρίαν τὸν θεὸν ἱκέτευε καὶ σύμμαχον καὶ βοηθὸν ἐκάλει λέγων· 335 "οὐδ' αὐτὸς μὲν ἀγνοεῖς, ὅτι φυγεῖν ἡμῖν ἐκ τῶν παρόντων οὔτε κατὰ ῥώμην οὔτε κατ' ἐπίνοιάν ἐστιν ἀνθρωπίνην, ἀλλ' εἰ δή τι πάντως σωτήριον στρατῷ τῷ κατὰ τὴν σὴν βούλησιν ἀφέντι τὴν

there has come to you everything that He promised to perform through me for your salvation and deliverance from bondage, though far beyond your expectations. Rather ought ye, in straits such as ye deem hopeless, to expect help from God, who has even now caused you to be compassed about on this difficult ground, to the end that, in extricating you from extremities, whence neither ye nor the enemy think ye can escape, He may display both His own power and His tender care for you. For it is not in trivial circumstances that the Deity lends His own aid to whom He favours, but where He sees men have lost all hope of ameliorating their lot. Wherefore, have faith in such a defender, who has power alike to make the little great and to sentence such mighty hosts as these to impotence. Be not dismayed at the Egyptians' array, nor, because yonder sea and the mountains behind you offer no means of escape, for that reason despair of your salvation; for ye may see these hills levelled to a plain, should God so will, or land emerge from the deep."

(xvi. 1) Having spoken thus far, he led them towards the sea under the eyes of the Egyptians; for these were in view but, exhausted with the fatigue of the pursuit, judged it well to defer battle until the morrow. Then, when he reached the shore, Moses took his staff and made supplication to God, invoking His alliance and aid in these words: "Thou thyself knowest full well that escape from our present plight passes alike the might and the wit of man; nay, if there be any means of salvation at all for this host which at thy will has left Egypt, thine it is to

Prayer of Moses.

---

[1] ROE: ἐν ἀπόροις rell.   [2] + ἂν Bekker.

336 Αἴγυπτον, σόν ἐστιν ἐκπορίζειν. ἡμεῖς τε ἄλλην ἀπεγνωκότες ἐλπίδα καὶ μηχανὴν εἰς τὴν ἀπὸ σοῦ μόνου καταφεύγομεν, καὶ εἴ τι παρὰ τῆς σῆς ἔλθοι προνοίας ἐξαρπάσαι τῆς Αἰγυπτίων ὀργῆς ἡμᾶς δυνάμενον ἀφορῶμεν. ἀφίκοιτο δὲ τοῦτο ταχέως τὴν σὴν ἐμφανίσον ἡμῖν δύναμιν καὶ τὸν λαὸν ὑπὸ ἀνελπιστίας καταπεπτωκότα πρὸς τὸ χεῖρον ἀνάστησον εἰς εὐθυμίαν καὶ τὸ περὶ τῆς
337 σωτηρίας θάρσος. ἐν οὐκ ἀλλοτρίοις δ' ἐσμὲν τοῖς ἀπόροις, ἀλλὰ σὴ μὲν ἡ θάλασσα, σὸν δὲ τὸ περικλεῖον ἡμᾶς ὄρος, ὡς ἀνοιγῆναι μὲν τοῦτο σοῦ κελεύσαντος, ἠπειρωθῆναι δὲ καὶ τὸ πέλαγος, εἶναι δὲ ἡμῖν ἀποδρᾶναι καὶ δι' ἀέρος δόξαν ἰσχύι τῇ σῇ τοῦτον ἡμᾶς σώζεσθαι τὸν τρόπον."

338 (2) Τοσαῦτα ἐπιθειάσας τύπτει τῇ βακτηρίᾳ τὴν θάλατταν. ἡ δ' ὑπὸ τῆς πληγῆς ἀνεκόπη καὶ εἰς αὑτὴν ὑποχωρήσασα γυμνὴν ἀφίησι τὴν
339 γῆν ὁδὸν Ἑβραίοις εἶναι καὶ φυγήν. Μωυσῆς δὲ ὁρῶν τὴν ἐπιφάνειαν τοῦ θεοῦ καὶ τὸ πέλαγος ἐκκεχωρηκὸς αὐτοῖς τῆς ἰδίας ἠπείρου πρῶτος ἐνέβαινεν αὐτῇ καὶ τοὺς Ἑβραίους ἐκέλευεν ἕπεσθαι διὰ θείας ὁδοῦ ποιουμένους τὴν πορείαν καὶ τῷ κινδύνῳ τῶν παρόντων πολεμίων ἡδομένους καὶ χάριν ἔχοντας διὰ τὴν παράλογον οὕτως ἐξ αὐτοῦ σωτηρίαν ἀναφανεῖσαν.

340 (3) Τῶν δ' οὐκέτ' ὀκνούντων, ἀλλ' ἱεμένων μετὰ σπουδῆς ὡς συμπαρόντος αὐτοῖς τοῦ θεοῦ, μαίνεσθαι μὲν αὐτοὺς τὸ πρῶτον Αἰγύπτιοι ἐδόκουν ὡς ἐπὶ πρόδηλον ὄλεθρον ὁρμωμένους, ἐπεὶ δὲ ἑώρων ἀβλαβεῖς ἐπὶ τὸ πολὺ προκεκοφότας καὶ μηδὲν αὐτοῖς ἐμπόδιον μηδὲ δυσχερὲς ἀπαντῆσαν, διώκειν ὡρμήκεσαν αὐτοὺς ὡς κἀκείνοις ἠρεμήσοντος τοῦ

provide it. For our part, despairing of other hope or resource, we fling ourselves upon thy protection alone, and expectantly, if aught be forthcoming from thy providence of might to snatch us from the wrath of the Egyptians, we look to thee. May it come quickly, this aid that shall manifest to us thy power; raise the hearts of this people, whom hopelessness has sunk into the depths of woe, to serenity and confidence of salvation. Nor are these straits in which we find ourselves without thy domain; nay, thine is the sea, thine the mountain that encompasseth us: this then can open at thy command, or the deep become dry land, or we might e'en find escape through the air, should it please thine almighty power that after this manner we should be saved."

(2) After this solemn appeal to God, he smote the sea with his staff. And at that stroke it recoiled and, retreating into itself, left bare the soil, affording passage and flight for the Hebrews. Moses, beholding this clear manifestation of God and the sea withdrawn from its own bed to give them place, set the first foot upon it and bade the Hebrews follow him and pursue their way by this God-sent road, rejoicing at the peril awaiting their advancing foes and rendering thanks to God for the salvation thus miraculously brought by Him to light. *Miraculous passage of the Red Sea. Ex. xiv. 21.*

(3) They, without more ado, sped forth with zest, assured of God's attendant presence; whereupon the Egyptians at first deemed them mad, thus rushing to a certain death, but when they saw them far advanced unscathed, unchecked by obstacle or discomfiture, they made speed to pursue them, imagining that the sea would remain motionless for them also, and with *Destruction of the Egyptians. Ex. xiv. 23.*

πελάγους, καὶ προτάξαντες τὴν ἵππον κατέβαινον.
341 Ἑβραῖοι δὲ καθοπλιζομένους καὶ τὸν χρόνον εἰς τοῦτο τρίβοντας ἔφθασαν ἐπὶ[1] τὴν ἀντιπέραν γῆν ἀπαθεῖς ἐκφυγόντες, ὅθεν καὶ θαρσαλεωτέροις συνέβαινε πρὸς τὴν δίωξιν ὡς οὐδὲν οὐδ᾽ αὐτῶν
342 πεισομένων εἶναι. Αἰγύπτιοι δ᾽ ἐλάνθανον ἰδίαν ὁδὸν Ἑβραίοις γεγενημένην, ἀλλ᾽ οὐχὶ κοινὴν ἐπεμβαίνοντες καὶ μέχρι σωτηρίας τῶν κεκινδυνευκότων πεποιημένην, ἀλλ᾽ οὐχὶ καὶ τοῖς ἐπ᾽ ἀπωλείᾳ τῇ τούτων ὡρμημένοις χρῆσθαι θέλουσιν.
343 ὡς οὖν ὁ τῶν Αἰγυπτίων στρατὸς ἅπας ἐντὸς ἦν, ἐπιχεῖται πάλιν ἡ θάλασσα καὶ περικαταλαμβάνει ῥοώδης ὑπὸ πνευμάτων κατιοῦσα τοὺς Αἰγυπτίους, ὄμβροι τ᾽ ἀπ᾽ οὐρανοῦ κατέβαινον καὶ βρονταὶ σκληραὶ προσεξαπτομένης ἀστραπῆς καὶ
344 κεραυνοὶ δὲ κατηνέχθησαν. ὅλως δ᾽ οὐδὲν ἦν τῶν ἐπ᾽ ἀπωλείᾳ κατὰ μῆνιν θεοῦ συμπιπτόντων ἀνθρώποις, ὃ μὴ τότε συνῆλθε· καὶ γὰρ νὺξ αὐτοὺς ζοφώδης καὶ σκοτεινὴ κατέλαβε. καὶ οἱ μὲν οὕτως ἀπώλοντο πάντες, ὡς μηδ᾽ ἄγγελον τῆς συμφορᾶς τοῖς ὑπολελειμμένοις ὑποστρέψαι.
345 (4) Τοὺς δ᾽ Ἑβραίους οὐδὲ κατασχεῖν ἦν ἐπὶ τῇ χαρᾷ τῆς παραδόξου σωτηρίας καὶ τῇ τῶν πολεμίων ἀπωλείᾳ, βεβαίως νομίζοντας ἠλευθερῶσθαι τῶν ἀναγκαζόντων δουλεύειν διεφθαρμένων καὶ τὸν θεὸν οὕτως ἐναργῶς ἔχοντας βοη-
346 θοῦντα. καὶ οἱ μὲν αὐτοί τε τὸν κίνδυνον οὕτως ἐκφυγόντες καὶ προσέτι τοὺς ἐχθροὺς ἐπιδόντες κεκολασμένους, ὡς οὐκ ἄλλοι τινὲς μνημονεύονται

[1] εἰς R.

the cavalry leading they proceeded to descend. But the Hebrews, while their enemies were arming and wasting time over that, had outstripped them and emerged unharmed on the opposite shore; this, however, but stimulated the ardour of the Egyptians for the pursuit, in the belief that they too would suffer nothing. Little dreamed they that it was a road reserved for the Hebrews, no public highway, whereon they were setting foot, a road created solely for the salvation of those in jeopardy, not for the use of them that were bent upon their destruction. When, therefore, the entire army of the Egyptians was once within it, back poured the sea, enveloping and with swelling wind-swept billows descending upon the Egyptians: rain fell in torrents from heaven, crashing thunder accompanied the flash of lightning, aye and thunderbolts were hurled.[a] In short, there was not one of those destructive forces which in token of God's wrath combine to smite mankind that failed to assemble then; for withal a night of gloom and darkness overwhelmed them. Thus perished they to a man, without a single one remaining to return with tidings of the disaster to those whom they had left at home.

(4) As for the Hebrews, they could scarce contain themselves for joy at this miraculous deliverance and the destruction of their foes, believing themselves assuredly at liberty, now that the tyrants that would have enslaved them had perished and that God had so manifestly befriended them. After having themselves thus escaped from peril and furthermore beheld their enemies punished in such wise as within

Exultation of the Hebrews and the song of Moses. Ex. xv. 1-21.

[a] For these added details *cf.* Ps. lxxvii. 16-20 ("The waters saw thee," etc., quoted by Weill).

τῶν πρόσθεν ἀνθρώπων, ἐν ὕμνοις ἦσαν καὶ παιδιαῖς ὅλην τὴν νύκτα, καὶ Μωυσῆς ᾠδὴν εἰς τὸν θεὸν ἐγκώμιόν τε καὶ τῆς εὐμενείας εὐχαριστίαν περιέχουσαν ἐν ἑξαμέτρῳ τόνῳ συντίθησιν.

347 (5) Ἐγὼ μὲν οὖν ὡς εὗρον ἐν ταῖς ἱεραῖς βίβλοις οὕτως ἕκαστον τούτων παραδέδωκα· θαυμάσῃ δὲ μηδεὶς τοῦ λόγου τὸ παράδοξον, εἰ ἀρχαίοις ἀνθρώποις καὶ πονηρίας ἀπείροις εὑρέθη σωτηρίας ὁδὸς καὶ διὰ θαλάσσης εἴτε κατὰ
348 βούλησιν θεοῦ εἴτε κατὰ ταὐτόματον, ὁπότε καὶ τοῖς περὶ τὸν Ἀλέξανδρον τὸν βασιλέα τῆς Μακεδονίας χθὲς καὶ πρώην γεγονόσιν ὑπεχώρησε τὸ Παμφύλιον πέλαγος καὶ ὁδὸν ἄλλην οὐκ ἔχουσι παρέσχε τὴν δι' αὐτοῦ, καταλῦσαι τὴν Περσῶν ἡγεμονίαν τοῦ θεοῦ θελήσαντος, καὶ τοῦτο πάντες ὁμολογοῦσιν οἱ τὰς Ἀλεξάνδρου πράξεις συγγραψάμενοι. περὶ μὲν οὖν τούτων ὡς ἑκάστῳ δοκεῖ διαλαμβανέτω.

349 (6) Τῇ δ' ὑστεραίᾳ τὰ ὅπλα τῶν Αἰγυπτίων προσενεχθέντα τῷ στρατοπέδῳ τῶν Ἑβραίων ὑπὸ τοῦ ῥοῦ καὶ τῆς βίας τοῦ πνεύματος ἐπ' ἐκεῖνο ἐκδιδούσης[1] ὁ Μωυσῆς καὶ τοῦτο εἰκάσας τῇ τοῦ

[1] ΜΕ: εἰσδιδούσης rell.

---

[a] A classical metre, to which there is no known analogy in Hebrew poetry: *cf. Ant.* iv. 303, where another ποίησις ἑξάμετρος is attributed to Moses.

men's memory no others had ever been before, they passed that whole night in melody and mirth, Moses himself composing in hexameter verse [a] a song to God to enshrine His praises and their thankfulness for His gracious favour.

(5) For my part, I have recounted each detail here told just as I found it in the sacred books. Nor let anyone marvel at the astonishing nature of the narrative or doubt that it was given to men of old, innocent of crime, to find a road of salvation through the sea itself, whether by the will of God or maybe by accident, seeing that the hosts of Alexander king of Macedon, men born but the other day, beheld the Pamphylian Sea retire before them and, when other road there was none, offer a passage through itself, what time it pleased God to overthrow the Persian empire; and on that all are agreed who have recorded Alexander's exploits.[b] However on these matters everyone is welcome to his own opinion.[c]

Parallel event in the history of Alexander the Great.

(6) On the morrow, the arms of the Egyptians having been carried up to the Hebrews' camp by the tide and the force of the wind setting in that direction, Moses, surmising that this too was due to the providence of God, to ensure that even in weapons they

How the Hebrews got their arms.

---

[b] The story is told by Arrian i. 26 (αὐτὸς δὲ παρὰ τὴν θάλασσαν διὰ τοῦ αἰγιαλοῦ ἦγε τοὺς ἀμφ' αὑτόν. ἔστι δὲ ταύτῃ ἡ ὁδὸς οὐκ ἄλλως, ὅτι μὴ τῶν ἀπ' ἄρκτου ἀνέμων πνεόντων ... τότε δ' ἐκ νότων σκληρῶν βορέαι ἐπιπνεύσαντες οὐκ ἄνευ τοῦ θείου, ὡς αὐτός τε καὶ οἱ ἀμφ' αὑτὸν ἐξηγοῦντο, εὐμαρῆ καὶ ταχεῖαν τὴν πάροδον παρέσχον), by Strabo xiv. 666 f. (who says that Alexander trusted mainly to luck and that the troops were immersed μέχρι ὀμφαλοῦ) and by others. The scene was near Phaselis, on the confines of Lycia and Pamphylia.

[c] For this formula see i. 108 note.

θεοῦ προνοίᾳ γεγονέναι, ὅπως μηδὲ ὅπλων ὦσιν ἄποροι, συναγαγὼν καὶ τούτοις σκεπάσας τοὺς Ἑβραίους ἦγεν ἐπὶ τὸ Σιναῖον ὄρος θύσων ἐκεῖ τῷ θεῷ καὶ τὰ σῶστρα τῆς πληθύος ἀποδώσων, καθὼς αὐτῷ καὶ προείρητο.

---

[a] For these added details, perhaps derived from Demetrius, see § 321 note.

should not be wanting, collected them and, having accoutred the Hebrews therein,[a] led them forward for Mount Sinai, with intent there to sacrifice to God and to render to Him the thank-offerings of the people for their deliverance, even as he had received commandment.[b]

[b] § 269.

ΒΙΒΛΙΟΝ Γ

(i. 1) Παραδόξου δὲ τῆς σωτηρίας τοῖς Ἑβραίοις οὕτως γενομένης δεινῶς ἐλύπει πάλιν αὐτοὺς ἀγομένους ἐπὶ τὸ Σιναῖον ὄρος ἡ χώρα τελέως οὖσα ἔρημος καὶ τῶν τε πρὸς τροφὴν αὐτοῖς ἄπορος, σπανίζουσα δὲ καὶ ὕδατος εἰς τὸ ἔσχατον, καὶ μὴ μόνον ἀνθρώποις τι παρασχεῖν ἐνδεής, ἀλλὰ καὶ μηδ' ἄλλο τι τῶν ζώων ἱκανὴ βόσκειν· ψαφαρὰ γάρ ἐστι καὶ νοτερὸν ἐξ αὐτῆς οὐδὲν ὅ τι καὶ φῦσαι καρπὸν δύναιτο. τοιαύτην δὲ οὖσαν τὴν χώραν ἐξ ἀνάγκης ὥδευον ἑτέραν 2 ἀπελθεῖν οὐκ ἔχοντες. ἐπεφέροντο δ' ἐκ τῆς προωδοιπορημένης ὕδωρ τοῦ στρατηγοῦ κεκελευκότος, καὶ τούτου δαπανηθέντος ἐκ φρεάτων ἐποιοῦντο τὴν ὑδρείαν ἐπιπόνως διὰ σκληρότητα τῆς γῆς, καὶ τὸ εὑρισκόμενον δὲ πικρὸν ἀλλ' οὐ 3 πότιμον ἦν, καὶ τοῦτο δὲ σπάνιον. ἀφικνοῦνται δὲ τοῦτον ὁδεύοντες τὸν τρόπον περὶ δείλην ὀψίαν εἰς Μὰρ τόπον οὕτως διὰ τὴν τοῦ ὕδατος κακίαν ὀνομάσαντες· μὰρ γὰρ ἡ πικρία λέγεται. καὶ αὐτόθι τεταλαιπωρημένοι τῷ τε συνεχεῖ τῆς ὁδοιπορίας καὶ τῇ τῆς τροφῆς ἀπορίᾳ, καὶ γὰρ τότ' αὐτοὺς τελείως ἐπιλελοίπει, κατάγονται· 4 φρέαρ γὰρ ἦν, διὸ καὶ μᾶλλον ἔμειναν, οὐδ' αὐτὸ μὲν ἐξαρκεῖν δυνάμενον τοσούτῳ στρατῷ, βραχεῖαν

BOOK III

(i. 1) The Hebrews, thus miraculously saved, were again in sore distress when led onward to Mount Sinai. The country was absolute desert, devoid of anything for their sustenance, while the scarcity of water was extreme; not only could the soil furnish nothing for man but it was even incapable of supporting any species of beast, being in fact sandy and without a particle of moisture propitious to vegetation. Such was the country which they were constrained to travel, no other route being open to them. They had brought with them some water from the district already traversed, by order of their chief, and when this was exhausted [a] they sought to draw more from wells: it was a laborious task owing to the hardness of the soil, and what they found was bitter, undrinkable, and withal scanty. Journeying thus, they arrived towards evening at Mar,[b] a place which they so named from the vileness of its water, *mar* meaning "bitterness"; and there, worn out with ceaseless marching and lack of food, which had now completely failed them, they halted. There was a well—a further reason for stopping there—doubtless by itself insufficient for so large an army, yet a source

<small>Sufferings on march through the desert. Ex. xv. 22.</small>

<small>The waters of Mar. Ex. xv. 23.</small>

---

[a] Amplification of Biblical narrative.

[b] Bibl. Marah, LXX Μερρά translated, as by Josephus, πικρία: Heb. *Mar* = "bitter" or "bitterness."

μέντοι παρέχον αὐτοῖς εὐθυμίαν ἐν ἐκείνοις εὑρεθὲν τοῖς χωρίοις· καὶ γὰρ ἤκουον παρὰ τῶν ἐξερευνώντων μηδὲν ἔμπροσθεν βαδίζουσιν εἶναι. πικρὸν δὲ ἐκεῖνο τὸ ὕδωρ καὶ ἄποτον ἦν, οὐκ ἀνθρώποις μόνον ἀλλὰ καὶ τοῖς ὑποζυγίοις ἀφόρητον.

5 (2) Ὁρῶν δ' ὁ Μωυσῆς ἀθύμως διακειμένους καὶ τοῦ πράγματος τὸ ἀναντίλεκτον, οὐ γὰρ καθαρὸς ἦν στρατὸς ὥστε τῷ βιαζομένῳ τῆς ἀνάγκης ἀντιτάξαι τὸ ἀνδρεῖον, ἀλλὰ διέφθειρε τὸ κατ' ἐκείνους γενναῖον παίδων[1] τε καὶ γυναικῶν ὄχλος ἀσθενέστερος τῆς ἐκ λόγων ⟨ὢν⟩[2] διδασκαλίας, ἐν χαλεπωτέροις ἦν τὴν συμφορὰν τὴν ἁπάν-
6 των ἰδίαν αὐτοῦ ποιούμενος· καὶ γὰρ οὐδ' ἐπ' ἄλλον τινὰ συνέτρεχον ἀλλ' ἐπ' αὐτόν, ἀντιβολοῦντες γύναια μὲν ὑπὲρ νηπίων οἱ δ' ἄνδρες ὑπὲρ ἐκείνων μὴ περιορᾶν, ἀλλ' ἐκπορίζειν αὐτοῖς ἀφορμήν τινα σωτηρίας. ἱκετεύειν οὖν τρέπεται τὸν θεὸν μεταβαλεῖν τὸ ὕδωρ ἐκ τῆς παρούσης
7 κακίας καὶ πότιμον αὐτοῖς παρασχεῖν. καὶ κατανεύσαντος τοῦ θεοῦ τὴν χάριν λαβὼν ἀποτομάδος[3] τὸ ἄκρον ἐν ποσὶν ἐρριμμένης διαιρεῖ μέσην καὶ κατὰ [τὸ] μῆκος τὴν τομὴν ποιησάμενος, ἔπειτα μεθεὶς εἰς τὸ φρέαρ ἔπειθε τοὺς Ἑβραίους τὸν θεὸν ἐπήκοον αὐτοῦ τῶν εὐχῶν γεγονέναι καὶ ὑπεσχῆσθαι τὸ ὕδωρ αὐτοῖς παρέξειν οἷον ἐπιθυμοῦσιν, ἂν πρὸς τὰ ὑπ' αὐτοῦ κελευόμενα μὴ
8 ὀκνηρῶς ἀλλὰ προθύμως ὑπουργῶσιν. ἐρομένων δ' αὐτῶν, τί καὶ ποιούντων ἂν μεταβάλοι τὸ ὕδωρ

[1] Lat. (infantum): παῖδες codd.
[2] ins. Niese.   [3] τομάδος RO.

of slight encouragement to them when found in those regions; for they had heard from their scouts that none was to be had by proceeding further. That water, however, proved bitter, and not only could the men not drink it, but even the beasts of burden found it intolerable.

(2) Moses, seeing their despondency and the indisputable gravity of the case—for this was no sound army, capable of meeting the stress of necessity with manly fortitude, but one whose nobler instincts were vitiated by a rabble of women and children, too feeble to respond to oral admonition—Moses, I say, was in yet more serious straits, in that he made the sufferings of all his own. For it was to no other than to him that they all flocked, imploring him, wives for their infants, husbands for their wives, not to neglect them, but to procure them some means of salvation. He therefore betook himself to prayer, entreating God to change that present evil property of the water and to render it drinkable. And, God having consented to grant that favour, he picked up the end of a stick that lay at his feet, cleft it in twain, lengthwise,[a] and then, flinging it into the well, impressed upon the Hebrews that God had lent an ear to his prayers and had promised to render the water such as they desired, provided that they executed His orders with no remissness, but with alacrity.[b] On their asking what they must do to procure the

Cf. Ex. xv. 25.

---

[a] These details, with the sequel, have no parallel in Exodus, which merely states that " the Lord shewed him a tree, and he cast it into the waters, and the waters were made sweet."

[b] Ex. xv. 26 appends to the miracle a " proviso " of another character, viz. that Israel would be spared the plagues of Egypt " if thou wilt diligently hearken," etc.

JOSEPHUS

ἐπὶ τὸ κρεῖττον, κελεύει τοὺς ἐν ἀκμῇ περιστάντας ἐξαντλεῖν λέγων τὸ ὑπολειπόμενον ἔσεσθαι πότιμον αὐτοῖς προεκκενωθέντος τοῦ πλείονος. καὶ οἱ μὲν ἐπόνουν, τὸ δ' ὑπὸ τῶν συνεχῶν πληγῶν γεγυμνασμένον καὶ κεκαθαρμένον ἤδη πότιμον ἦν.

9 (3) Ἄραντες δ' ἐκεῖθεν εἰς ʰἮλιν ἀφικνοῦνται πόρρωθεν μὲν ἀγαθὴν ὁραθῆναι, καὶ γὰρ φοινικόφυτος ἦν, πλησιάζουσα¹ δ' ἀπηλέγχετο πονηρά· καὶ γὰρ οἱ φοίνικες ὄντες οὐ πλείους ἑβδομήκοντα δυσαυξεῖς τε ἦσαν καὶ χαμαίζηλοι δι' ὕδατος 10 ἀπορίαν ψαφαροῦ τοῦ παντὸς ὄντος χωρίου· οὔτε γὰρ ἐκ τῶν πηγῶν, δώδεκα οὐσῶν τὸν ἀριθμόν, νοτερόν τι καὶ πρὸς ἄρδευσιν² αὐτοῖς διεπίδα³ χρήσιμον, ἀλλὰ μὴ δυναμένων ἐκβλύσαι μηδ' ἀνασχεῖν ἰκμάδες ἦσαν ὀλίγαι, καὶ διαμωμένοις τὴν ψάμμον οὐδὲν ἀπήντα, κἂν εἴ τι δὲ στάζον ἔλαβον εἰς χεῖρας, ἄχρηστον ηὕρισκον ὑπὸ τοῦ 11 θολερὸν εἶναι· καρπόν τε φέρειν ἦν ἀσθενῆ τὰ δένδρα διὰ σπάνιν τῆς ἐξ ὕδατος εἰς τοῦτο ἀφορμῆς καὶ παρακλήσεως. εἶχον οὖν ἐν αἰτίᾳ τὸν στρατηγὸν καὶ κατεβόων αὐτοῦ τὴν ταλαιπωρίαν καὶ τὴν πεῖραν τῶν κακῶν δι' αὐτὸν πάσχειν λέγοντες· τριακοστὴν γὰρ ἐκείνην ὁδεύοντες ἡμέραν ὅσα μὲν ἐπεφέροντο πάντ' ἦσαν ἀναλωκότες, μηδενὶ δὲ περιτυγχάνοντες δυσέλπιδες ἦσαν περὶ 12 τῶν ὅλων. πρὸς δὲ τῷ παρόντι κακῷ τὴν διά-

¹ *v.l.* πλησιάζουσι.
² καὶ πρὸς ἄρδ.] προσαρδεῦον RO.
³ conj. after Dindorf (διεπήδα) : δι' ἐλπίδα codd.

ᵃ A rationalistic explanation of the miracle : *cf. B.J.* iv. 8. 3 (quoted by Weill).
ᵇ Bibl. Elim, LXX Αἰλείμ.
ᶜ After Thuc. iv. 26 (Pylos) : *cf. Ant.* ii. 296.

JEWISH ANTIQUITIES, III. 8–12

amelioration of the water, he bade those in the prime of life stand in a ring and draw, declaring that what remained, after they had drained off the larger part, would be drinkable. So they set to work, and the water, belaboured and purified by these incessant blows, at length became good to drink.[a]

(3) Departing thence, they reached Elis,[b] a spot which from a distance made a good show, being planted with palm-trees, but on approach proved bad; for the palms, numbering no more than seventy, were dwarfed and stunted through lack of water, the whole place being sandy. For from the springs which existed, to the number of twelve, there oozed no liquid sufficient to water them: impotent to gush forth or rise to the surface these yielded but a few drops; and persons scraping the sand [c] encountered nothing, even such driblets as they received into their hands being found useless, so foul their nature. And the trees were too feeble to bear fruit for lack of water to give them the needful stimulus and encouragement. So they fell to accusing and denouncing their general, declaring that this misery and experience of woe which they were undergoing were all due to him. For it was now their thirtieth day on the march,[d] the provisions which they had brought with them were all exhausted,[e] and, lighting upon nothing whatever, they were in utter despair. With minds obsessed with their present woes, precluding

The climax at Elim.
Ex. xv. 27.

---

[d] *Cf.* Ex. xvi. 1, which states that the Israelites left Elim "on the 15th day of the second month," reckoning from the exodus, which had taken place on the 15th of the first month (*cf.* Ex. xii. 18).

[e] So the Palestinian Targum on Ex. xvi. 2: "On that day the bread which they had brought out of Egypt was finished" (Weill).

νοιαν ὄντες καὶ ἐν μνήμῃ εἶναι τῶν ὑπηργμένων
αὐτοῖς ἔκ τε τοῦ θεοῦ καὶ τῆς Μωυσέος ἀρετῆς καὶ
συνέσεως κωλυόμενοι, δι' ὀργῆς τὸν στρατηγὸν
εἶχον καὶ βάλλειν αὐτὸν ὡρμήκεσαν ὡς αἰτιώτατον
τῆς ἐν ποσὶ συμφορᾶς.

13 (4) Ὁ δ' οὕτως ἀνηρεθισμένου τοῦ πλήθους καὶ
πικρῶς ἐπ' αὐτὸν κεκινημένου, τῷ θεῷ θαρρῶν
καὶ τῷ συνειδότι τῆς περὶ τοὺς ὁμοφύλους προνοίας, πάρεισιν εἰς μέσους καὶ καταβοώντων καὶ
κατὰ χεῖρας ἔτι τοὺς λίθους ἐχόντων, ὀραθῆναί
τε κεχαρισμένος ὢν καὶ πλήθεσιν ὁμιλεῖν πιθα-
14 νώτατος, καταπαύειν ἤρξατο τῆς ὀργῆς, μὴ τῶν
παρόντων αὐτοὺς δυσκόλων μεμνημένους λήθην
ἔχειν τῶν ἔμπροσθεν εὐεργεσιῶν παρακαλῶν, μηδ'
ὅτι νῦν πονοῦσι τῆς διανοίας ἐκβάλλειν τὰς τοῦ
θεοῦ χάριτας καὶ δωρεάς, ὧν μεγάλων καὶ ἐκ
παραδόξου ἔτυχον γενομένων, προσδοκᾶν δὲ καὶ
15 τῆς παρούσης ἀπαλλαγὴν[1] ἀμηχανίας ἐκ τῆς τοῦ
θεοῦ κηδεμονίας, ὃν εἰκὸς δοκιμάζοντα τὴν ἀρετὴν
αὐτῶν πῶς τε καρτερίας ἔχουσι καὶ μνήμης τῶν
προϋπηργμένων, εἰ μὴ πρὸς ἐκεῖνα γίγνοιντο διὰ
τὰ ἐν ποσὶ κακά, γυμνάζειν αὐτοὺς τοῖς ἄρτι
16 χαλεποῖς. ἐλέγχεσθαι δὲ αὐτοὺς οὐκ ἀγαθοὺς
οὔτε περὶ τὴν ὑπομονὴν οὔτε περὶ τὴν μνήμην
τῶν εὖ γεγονότων, οὕτως μὲν τοῦ θεοῦ καὶ τῆς
ἐκείνου γνώμης καθ' ἣν ἐκλελοίπασι τὴν Αἴγυπτον
καταφρονοῦντας, οὕτως δὲ πρὸς αὐτὸν τὸν ὑπηρέ-
την αὐτοῦ διατεθέντας, καὶ ταῦτα μηδὲν αὐτοὺς
διαψευσάμενον περὶ ὧν εἴποι τε καὶ πράττειν κατ'

[1] ἀπαλλαγὴν edd.: ἀπαλλαγῆναι codd.

---

[a] In Exodus the murmuring against Moses begins *after*

all memory of past blessings which they owed to God on the one hand, to the virtue and sagacity of Moses on the other, they viewed their general with indignation and were eager to stone him, as the man most answerable for their instant distress.[a]

(4) But he, before this mob so excited and embittered against him, confident in God and in the consciousness of his own care for his countrymen, advanced into their midst and, as they clamoured upon him and still held the stones in their hands, he, with that winning presence of his and that extraordinary influence in addressing a crowd, began to pacify their wrath. He exhorted them not, with present discomforts engrossing all their thoughts, to forget the benefits of the past, nor because they suffered now to banish from their minds the favours and bounties, so great and unlooked for, which they had received from God. Rather ought they to expect relief also from their present straits to come from God's solicitude, for it was probably to test their manhood, to see what fortitude they possessed, what memory of past services, and whether their thoughts would not revert to those services because of the troubles now in their path, that He was exercising them with these trials of the moment. But now they were convicted of failure, both in endurance and in recollection of benefits received, by showing at once such contempt of God and of His purpose, in accordance with which they had left Egypt, and such demeanour towards himself, God's minister, albeit he had never proved false to them in aught that he had said or in any order that he had given them at

Moses calms the angry mob.

the departure from Elim (xvi. 2) and the allusion to stoning comes still later, at Rephidim (xvii. 4).

17 ἐντολὴν τοῦ θεοῦ κελεύσειε. κατηρίθμει τε πάντα, πῶς τε φθαρεῖεν Αἰγύπτιοι κατέχειν αὐτοὺς παρὰ τὴν τοῦ θεοῦ γνώμην βιαζόμενοι, καὶ τίνα τρόπον ὁ αὐτὸς ποταμὸς ἐκείνοις μὲν αἷμα ἦν καὶ ἄποτος
18 αὐτοῖς δὲ πότιμος καὶ γλυκύς, πῶς τε διὰ τῆς θαλάσσης ἀναφυγούσης αὐτοῖς[1] πορρωτάτω καινὴν ὁδὸν ἀπελθόντες αὐτῇ ταύτῃ σωθεῖησαν μὲν αὐτοί, τοὺς δὲ ἐχθροὺς ἐπίδοιεν ἀπολωλότας, ὅτι τε σπανίζοντας ὅπλων εἰς εὐπορίαν ὁ θεὸς καὶ τούτων καταστήσειε, τά τε ἄλλα ὅσα πρὸς αὐτῷ τῷ διαφθαρήσεσθαι δόξαντας γεγονέναι καὶ σώσειεν
19 ὁ θεὸς ἐκ παραλόγου καὶ ὡς δύναμις αὐτῷ· μὴ ἀπογινώσκειν δὲ μηδὲ νῦν αὐτοῦ τὴν πρόνοιαν, ἀλλ᾿ ἀοργήτως περιμένειν λογιζομένους μὲν τὴν ἐπικουρίαν μηδὲ βραδεῖαν γίνεσθαι, εἰ μὴ παραυτίκα καὶ εἰ μὴ πρίν τινος πειραθῆναι δυσκόλου πάρεστιν, ἡγουμένους δὲ οὐ κατὰ ὀλιγωρίαν μέλλειν τὸν θεόν, ἀλλ᾿ ἐπὶ πείρᾳ τῆς ἀνδρείας αὐτῶν
20 καὶ τῆς περὶ τὴν ἐλευθερίαν ἡδονῆς, ἵνα μάθοι πότερόν ποτε καὶ τροφῆς ἀπορίαν καὶ σπάνιν ὕδατος ὑπὲρ αὐτῆς ἐστ᾿ ἐνεγκεῖν γενναῖοι, ἢ δουλεύειν μᾶλλον ἀγαπᾶτε καθάπερ τὰ βοσκήματα τοῖς κρατοῦσι καὶ τοῖς πρὸς τὰς ἐκείνων ὑπηρεσίας
21 ἀφθόνως τρεφομένοις· δεδιέναι δ᾿ εἰπὼν οὐχ οὕτως ὑπὲρ τῆς ἑαυτοῦ σωτηρίας, πείσεσθαι γὰρ οὐδὲν κακὸν ἀδίκως ἀποθανών, ἀλλ᾿ ὑπὲρ αὐτῶν, μὴ δι᾿ ὧνπερ αὐτὸν βάλλουσι λίθων τοῦ θεοῦ κατακρίνειν
22 νομισθῶσιν, (5) ἐπράυνεν αὐτοὺς καὶ τῆς μὲν τοῦ βάλλειν ὁρμῆς ἐπέσχε καὶ εἰς μετάνοιαν ὧν ἔμελλον δρᾶν ἔτρεψε. παθεῖν δ᾿ οὐκ ἀλόγως αὐτοὺς

[1] ML: αὐτῆς rell.

God's command. He then enumerated everything, how the Egyptians had been destroyed in attempting to detain them by force in opposition to the will of God, how the selfsame river had for those become bloody and undrinkable while remaining for themselves drinkable and sweet, how through the waters of the sea retiring far before them they had departed by a new road, finding therein salvation for themselves while seeing their enemies perish, how, when they lacked arms, God had abundantly provided them even with these; further recounting all the other occasions on which, when they seemed on the verge of destruction, God had delivered them by ways unlooked for, such as lay within His power. So they should not despair even now of His providence, but should await it without anger, not deeming His succour tardy, even if it came not forthwith and before they had had some experience of discomfort, but rather believing that it was not from negligence that God thus tarried, but to test their manhood and their delight in liberty, " that He may learn (said he) whether for once ye have the spirit to endure for its sake both deprivation of food and lack of water, or prefer slavery, like the beasts which slave for the masters who feed them lavishly in view of their services." He added that, if he feared anything, it was not so much for his own safety—for it would be no misfortune to him to be unjustly done to death— as for them, lest in flinging those stones at him they should be thought to be pronouncing sentence upon God.

(5) Thus he calmed them, restraining that impulse to stone him and moving them to repent of their intended action. But, holding those feelings

Miraculous gift of quails.

JOSEPHUS

διὰ τὴν ἀνάγκην τοῦτο νομίσας ἔγνω δεῖν ἐφ' ἱκετείαν τοῦ θεοῦ καὶ παράκλησιν ἐλθεῖν, καὶ ἀναβὰς ἐπί τινα σκοπὴν ᾔτει πόρον τινὰ τῷ λαῷ 23 καὶ τῆς ἐνδείας ἀπαλλαγήν· ἐν αὐτῷ γὰρ εἶναι τὴν σωτηρίαν αὐτοῦ καὶ οὐκ ἐν ἄλλῳ· συγγινώσκειν δὲ τοῖς νῦν ὑπὸ τῆς ἀνάγκης ὑπὸ τοῦ λαοῦ πραττομένοις, φύσει δυσαρέστου καὶ φιλαιτίου τοῦ τῶν ἀνθρώπων ἐν οἷς ἂν ἀτυχῇ γένους ὄντος. ὁ θεὸς δὲ προνοήσειν τε ἐπαγγέλλεται καὶ παρέξειν 24 ἀφορμὴν ἣν ποθοῦσι. Μωυσῆς δὲ τοῦ θεοῦ ταῦτ' ἀκούσας καταβαίνει πρὸς τὸ πλῆθος· οἱ δ' ὡς ἑώρων καὶ ταῖς ἐπαγγελίαις ταῖς παρὰ τοῦ θεοῦ γεγηθότα μετέβαλον ἐκ τῆς κατηφείας πρὸς τὸ ἱλαρώτερον, καὶ στὰς ἐκεῖνος ἐν μέσοις ἥκειν ἔλεγε φέρων αὐτοῖς παρὰ τοῦ θεοῦ τὴν [περὶ] τῶν 25 ἐνεστηκότων ἀπόρων ἀπαλλαγήν. καὶ μετ' ὀλίγον ὀρτύγων πλῆθος, τρέφει δὲ τοῦτο τὸ ὄρνεον ὡς οὐδὲν ἕτερον ὁ Ἀράβιος κόλπος, ἐφίπταται τὴν μεταξὺ θάλατταν ὑπερελθὸν καὶ ὑπὸ κόπου τε ἅμα τῆς πτήσεως καὶ πρόσγαιον μᾶλλον τῶν ἄλλων ὂν καταφέρεται εἰς τοὺς Ἑβραίους· οἱ δὲ συλλαμβάνοντες ὡς τροφὴν αὐτοῖς τοῦ θεοῦ ταύτην μηχανησαμένου τὴν ἔνδειαν ἰῶνται, καὶ Μωυσῆς ἐπ' εὐχὰς τρέπεται τοῦ θεοῦ ταχεῖαν καὶ παρὰ τὴν ὑπόσχεσιν ποιησαμένου τὴν ἐπικουρίαν.

26 (6) Εὐθὺς δὲ μετὰ τὴν πρώτην ἀφορμὴν τῆς τροφῆς καὶ δευτέραν αὐτοῖς κατέπεμπεν ὁ θεός· ἀνέχοντος γὰρ τοῦ Μωυσέος τὰς χεῖρας ἐπὶ ταῖς εὐχαῖς δρόσος κατηνέχθη, καὶ περιπηγνυμένης ταῖς

---

[a] Josephus, *more suo*, explains the miracle by natural causes; *cf.* § 8.

of theirs induced by stress to be not unreasonable, he concluded that he ought to approach God with supplication and entreaty; and, mounting a certain eminence, he besought Him to grant some succour to His people and relief from their distress—for it was upon Him and on no other that their lives depended—and to pardon the people what they would but now have done under stress of necessity, seeing that the race of men was by nature morose and censorious in misfortune. God thereon promised to take care of them and to provide the resources which they craved. Having received this response from God, Moses descended to the multitude; and they, on seeing him all radiant at the divine promises, passed from dejection into a gayer mood, while he, standing in their midst, told them that he had come to bring them from God deliverance from their present straits. And, not long after, a flock of quails—a species of bird abundant, above all others, in the Arabian gulf—came flying over this stretch of sea, and, alike wearied by their flight and withal accustomed more than other birds to skim the ground,[a] settled in the Hebrews' camp. And they, collecting them as the food devised for them by God, assuaged their hunger; while Moses addressed his thankful prayers to God for sending succour so prompt and in keeping with [b] His promise.

Cf. Ex. xvi. 11 f.

Ib. 13.

(6) Immediately after this first supply of food God sent down to them a second. For, while Moses raised his hands in prayer, a dew descended, and, as this congealed about his hands,[c] Moses, surmising

The manna. *Ib.* 13 ff.

---

[b] Or, possibly, "even beyond (even prompter than) His promise."

[c] Midrashic addition to the Biblical narrative.

χερσὶ Μωυσῆς ὑπονοήσας καὶ ταύτην εἰς τροφὴν ἥκειν αὐτοῖς παρὰ τοῦ θεοῦ γεύεταί τε καὶ ἡσθείς,
27 τοῦ πλήθους ἀγνοοῦντος καὶ νομίζοντος νίφεσθαι καὶ τῆς ὥρας εἶναι τοῦ ἔτους¹ τὸ γινόμενον, ἀνεδίδασκεν οὐ κατὰ τὴν ἐκείνων ὑπόληψιν ἀπ' οὐρανοῦ καταφέρεσθαι τὴν δρόσον, ἀλλ' ἐπὶ σωτηρίᾳ τῇ αὐτῶν καὶ διατροφῇ, καὶ γευόμενος² τοῦτο αὐτοῖς
28 παρεῖχε πιστεύειν. οἱ δὲ μιμούμενοι τὸν στρατηγὸν ἥδοντο τῷ βρώματι· μέλιτι γὰρ ἦν τὴν γλυκύτητα καὶ τὴν ἡδονὴν ἐμφερές, ὅμοιον δὲ τῇ τῶν ἀρωμάτων βδέλλῃ, τὸ δὲ μέγεθος τῷ κοριάννου σπέρματι· καὶ περὶ συλλογὴν λίαν αὐτοῦ
29 ἐσπουδάκεσαν. παρηγγέλλετο δ' ἐξ ἴσου πᾶσιν ἀσσαρῶνα, τοῦτο δ' ἐστὶ μέτρον, εἰς ἑκάστην ἡμέραν συλλέγειν ὡς οὐκ ἐπιλείψοντος αὐτοῖς τοῦ βρώματος, ἵνα μὴ τοῖς ἀδυνάτοις ἄπορον ᾖ τὸ λαμβάνειν δι' ἀλκὴν τῶν δυνατωτέρων πλεονεκ-
30 τούντων περὶ τὴν ἀναίρεσιν. οἱ μέντοι πλέον τοῦ προστεταγμένου μέτρου συναγαγόντες οὐδὲν περισσότερον εἶχον τοῦ κακοπαθῆσαι, ἀσσαρῶνος γὰρ οὐδὲν πλέον εὕρισκον, τοῦ δ' ὑπολειφθέντος εἰς τὴν ἐπιοῦσαν ὄνησις οὐδ' ἥτις ἦν διεφθαρμένου ὑπό τε σκωλήκων καὶ πικρίας· οὕτω θεῖον ἦν τὸ
31 βρῶμα καὶ παράδοξον. ἀμύνει δὲ τοῖς ταύτην νεμομένοις τὴν ἐκ τῶν ἄλλων ἀπορίαν, ἔτι δὲ

¹ ME: ὑετοῦ rell.
² γενομένοις ROE (perhaps rightly).

---

[a] Exodus (xvi. 14) merely speaks of the manna as " small as the hoar frost on the ground " ; the comparison to snow, as M. Weill points out, occurs already in Artapanus (*c.*

JEWISH ANTIQUITIES, III. 26–31

that this too was a nutriment come to them from God, tasted it and was delighted; and, whereas the multitude in their ignorance took this for snow [a] and attributed the phenomenon to the season of the year, he instructed them that this heaven-descending dew was not as they supposed, but was sent for their salvation and sustenance, and, tasting it, he bade them thus too to convince themselves. They then, imitating their leader, were delighted with what they ate, for it had the sweet and delicious taste of honey and resembled the spicy herb called *bdellium*, its size being that of a coriander seed; and they fell to collecting it with the keenest ardour. Orders, however, were issued to all alike to collect each day but an *assarôn* [b] (that being the name of a measure), since this food would never fail them; this was to ensure that the weak should not be prevented from obtaining anything, should their stronger brethren avail themselves of their vigour to amass a larger harvest. Those who nevertheless collected more than the prescribed measure reaped therefrom nothing further than their pains, for they found no more than an *assarôn*; while anything left over for the morrow was of no service whatever, being polluted by worms and bitterness, so divine nad miraculous was this food. It is a mains ay to dwellers in these parts against their dearth of other

Ex. xvi. 31; Numb. xi. 7.

Ex. xvi. 16.

---

100 B.C.), χιόνι παραπλήσιον τὴν χρόαν (*ap.* Eusebius, *Praep. Ev.* ix. 436 c). "The season of the year" was apparently the spring (§ 11); and snow at any season in the Arabian desert is practically unknown.

[b] In Exodus an *ômer* (LXX γόμορ). Josephus substitutes for this, here and elsewhere, the word *assarôn*, a Hellenized form of the Hebrew '*issarôn*, meaning "a tenth part" *sc.* of an *ephah*, in other words an *omer* (Ex. xvi. 36).

καὶ νῦν ὕεται πᾶς ἐκεῖνος ὁ τόπος, καθάπερ καὶ τότε Μωυσεῖ χαριζόμενον τὸ θεῖον κατέπεμψε τὴν 32 διατροφήν. καλοῦσι δὲ Ἑβραῖοι τὸ βρῶμα τοῦτο μάννα· τὸ γὰρ μάν ἐπερώτησις κατὰ τὴν ἡμετέραν διάλεκτον τί τοῦτ' ἔστιν ἀνακρίνουσα. καὶ οἱ μὲν χαίροντες ἐπὶ τοῖς ἀπ' οὐρανοῦ καταπεμφθεῖσιν αὐτοῖς διετέλουν, τῇ δὲ τροφῇ ταύτῃ τεσσαράκοντα ἔτεσιν ἐχρήσαντο ἐφ' ὅσον χρόνον ἦσαν ἐν τῇ ἐρήμῳ.

33 (7) Ὡς δ' ἐκεῖθεν ἄραντες εἰς Ῥαφιδεὶν ἧκον, ταλαιπωρηθέντες ὑπὸ δίψους εἰς ἔσχατον, ἔν τε ταῖς πρότερον ἡμέραις πίδαξιν ὀλίγαις ἐντυγχάνοντες καὶ τότε παντάπασιν ἄνυδρον εὑρόντες τὴν γῆν, ἐν κακοῖς ἦσαν καὶ πάλιν δι' ὀργῆς τὸν 34 Μωυσῆν ἐποιοῦντο. ὁ δὲ τὴν ὁρμὴν τοῦ πλήθους πρὸς μικρὸν ἐκκλίνας ἐπὶ λιτὰς τρέπεται τοῦ θεοῦ, παρακαλῶν ὡς τροφὴν ἔδωκεν ἀπορουμένοις οὕτως καὶ ποτὸν παρασχεῖν, διαφθειρομένης καὶ τῆς ἐπὶ 35 τροφῇ χάριτος ποτοῦ μὴ παρόντος. ὁ δ' οὐκ εἰς μακρὰν τὴν δωρεὰν ἀνεβάλλετο, τῷ δὲ Μωυσεῖ παρέξειν ὑπισχνεῖται πηγὴν καὶ πλῆθος ὕδατος ὅθεν οὐ προσδοκήσειαν, καὶ κελεύει τῷ βάκτρῳ πλήξαντα τὴν πέτραν, ἣν ἑώρων αὐτόθι παρα-

---

[a] I hesitate to depart from the rendering of all previous translators from Hudson, " *Qui vero eo vescebantur* alio non egebant victu " to M. Weill, " Il remplaçait *pour ceux qui en mangeaient* tous les autres aliments absents " ; the latter traces here an allusion to the widespread Rabbinical tradition, found already in the Book of Wisdom (xvi. 20 f.), that the manna assumed the taste that was most pleasant to the eater. But (1) νέμεσθαι in Josephus usually means " inhabit " (*A.* v. 262 etc.), or occasionally " graze " (of cattle), but never " eat " (of men) ; (2) the fem. ταύτην cannot refer to the neuter word for food, βρῶμα, whereas the ellipse of γῆν is

provisions,[a] and to this very day[b] all that region is watered by a rain like to that which then, as a favour to Moses, the Deity sent down for men's sustenance. The Hebrews call this food *manna*[c]; for the word *man* is an interrogative in our language, asking the question "What is this?"[d] So they continued to rejoice in their heaven-sent gift, living on this food for forty years, all the time that they were in the desert.

Ex. xvi. 15.

(7) When, departing thence, they reached Raphidin,[e] in extreme agony from thirst—for having on the earlier days lit upon some scanty springs, they then found themselves in an absolutely waterless region—they were in sore distress and again vented their wrath on Moses. But he, shunning for a while the onset of the crowd, had recourse to prayer, beseeching God, as He had given meat to them in their need, so now to afford them drink, for their gratitude for the meat would perish were drink withheld. Nor did God long defer this boon, but promised Moses that He would provide a spring with abundance of water whence they looked not for it; He then bade him strike with his staff the rock which stood there

Water from the rock. *Ib.* xvii. 1.

---

frequent: (3) the second half of the sentence ("all that region") supports the rendering above. There *may* be an allusion to the Rabbinical tradition, but, did we not know of that tradition from other sources, it would hardly have been discovered from the present passage.

[b] Travellers in Arabia have identified the manna as an exudation of a species of the tamarisk-tree; "a fresh supply appears each night during its season (June and July)," *Encycl. Bibl. s.v.*

[c] Heb. *mân*, LXX μάν or μάννα.

[d] The same popular etymology appears in the Heb. and LXX.

[e] Bibl. Rephidim, LXX (like Jos.) Ῥαφιδείν.

κειμένην, παρ' αὐτῆς λαμβάνειν τὴν εὐπορίαν ὧν δέονται· φροντίζειν[1] γὰρ καὶ τοῦ μὴ σὺν πόνῳ μηδ'
36 ἐργασίᾳ τὸ ποτὸν αὐτοῖς φανῆναι. καὶ Μωυσῆς ταῦτα λαβὼν παρὰ τοῦ θεοῦ παραγίνεται πρὸς τὸν λαὸν περιμένοντα καὶ εἰς αὐτὸν ἀφορῶντα· καὶ γὰρ ἤδη καθεώρων αὐτὸν ἀπὸ τῆς σκοπῆς ὁρμώμενον. ὡς δ' ἧκεν, ἀπολύειν αὐτοὺς καὶ ταύτης τῆς ἀνάγκης τὸν θεὸν ἔλεγε καὶ κεχαρίσθαι[2] σωτηρίαν οὐδ' ἐλπισθεῖσαν ἐκ τῆς πέτρας ποταμὸν
37 αὐτοῖς ῥυήσεσθαι λέγων. τῶν δὲ πρὸς τὴν ἀκοὴν καταπλαγέντων, εἰ ὑπό τε τοῦ δίψους καὶ τῆς ὁδοιπορίας τεταλαιπωρημένοις ἀνάγκη γένοιτο κόπτειν τὴν πέτραν, ὁ Μωυσῆς πλήττει τῇ βακτηρίᾳ, καὶ χανούσης ἐξέβλυσεν ὕδωρ πολὺ καὶ δι-
38 αυγέστατον. οἱ δὲ τῷ παραδόξῳ τοῦ γεγονότος κατεπλάγησαν, καὶ πρὸς τὴν ὄψιν αὐτοῖς ἤδη τὸ δίψος ἔληγε, καὶ πίνουσιν ἡδὺ καὶ γλυκὺ τὸ νᾶμα καὶ οἷον ἂν εἴη θεοῦ τὸ δῶρον δόντος ἐφαίνετο· τόν τε οὖν Μωυσῆν ἐθαύμαζον οὕτως ὑπὸ τοῦ θεοῦ τετιμημένον, καὶ θυσίαις ἠμείβοντο τὴν τοῦ θεοῦ περὶ αὐτοὺς πρόνοιαν. δηλοῖ δὲ ἐν τῷ ἱερῷ ἀνακειμένη γραφὴ τὸν θεὸν προειπεῖν Μωυσεῖ οὕτως ἐκ τῆς πέτρας ἀναδοθήσεσθαι ὕδωρ.
39 (ii. 1) Τοῦ δὲ [τῶν] Ἑβραίων ὀνόματος ἤδη πολλοῦ κατὰ πάντας διαβοωμένου καὶ τοῦ περὶ αὐτῶν λόγου φοιτῶντος ἐν φόβῳ συνέβαινεν οὐ μικρῷ τοὺς ἐπιχωρίους εἶναι, καὶ πρεσβευόμενοι

[1] MSP: φροντίζει rell.   [2] χαρίσασθαι RO.

[a] Cf. other allusions to " writings deposited in the temple " in A. iv. 303 (the song of Moses), v. 61 (Joshua's staying of the sun). I believe that these refer not to the Scriptures

before their eyes, and from it accept a plenteous draught of what they needed; for He would moreover see to it that this water should appear for them without toil or travail. Moses, having received this response from God, now approached the people, who were expectant and had their eyes fixed upon him, having already observed him hastening from the hill. When he arrived, he told them that God would deliver them from this distress also and had even vouchsafed to save them in unexpected wise: a river was to flow for them out of the rock. And while they at this news were aghast at the thought of being forced, all spent as they were with thirst and travel, to cleave the rock, Moses struck it with his staff, whereupon it opened and there gushed out a copious stream of most pellucid water. Amazed at this marvellous prodigy, the mere sight of which already slaked their thirst, they drank and found the current sweet and delicious and all that was to be looked for in a gift from God. Therefrom too they conceived an admiration for Moses, so high in God's esteem, and they offered sacrifices in return for God's care for their welfare. A writing deposited in the temple attests that God foretold to Moses that water would thus spring forth from the rock.[a]

(ii. 1) The fame of the Hebrews being now mightily noised abroad and talk of them being current everywhere, the inhabitants of the country came to be not a little afraid; and sending embassies to and fro

The Amalekites prepare for war. Ex. xvii. 8.

generally but to a separate collection of chants made for the use of the temple singers, and that the allusion here is to the little song to the well in Numb. xxi. 16 ff., with the introductory promise "Gather the people together and I will give them water." See my *Josephus the Man and the Historian* (New York, 1929), p. 90.

πρὸς ἀλλήλους παρεκάλουν ἀμύνειν καὶ πειρᾶσθαι
40 τοὺς ἄνδρας διαφθείρειν. ἐτύγχανον δὲ [οἱ] πρὸς
τοῦτο ἐνάγοντες οἵ τε τὴν Γοβολῖτιν καὶ τὴν
Πέτραν κατοικοῦντες, οἳ καλοῦνται μὲν 'Αμαληκῖ-
ται, μαχιμώτατοι δὲ τῶν ἐκεῖσε ἐθνῶν ὑπῆρχον·
ὧν πέμποντες οἱ βασιλεῖς ἀλλήλους τε καὶ τοὺς
περιοίκους ἐπὶ τὸν πρὸς Ἑβραίους πόλεμον παρεκάλουν, στρατὸν ἀλλότριον καὶ τῆς Αἰγυπτίων
ἀποδράντα δουλείας ἐφεδρεύειν αὑτοῖς λέγοντες,
41 ὃν οὐ καλῶς ἔχει περιορᾶν, ἀλλὰ πρὶν ἢ λαβεῖν
ἰσχὺν καὶ παρελθεῖν εἰς εὐπορίαν καὶ αὐτὸν τῆς
πρὸς ἡμᾶς κατάρξαι μάχης θαρρήσαντας τῷ μηδὲν
αὐτοῖς παρ' ἡμῶν ἀπαντᾶν καταλύειν ἀσφαλὲς καὶ
σῶφρον, δίκην αὐτοὺς καὶ περὶ τῆς ἐρήμου[1] καὶ
τῶν ἐν αὐτῇ πραχθέντων ἀπαιτοῦντας, ἀλλ' οὐχ
ὅταν ταῖς πόλεσιν ἡμῶν καὶ τοῖς ἀγαθοῖς ἐπιβάλωσι
42 τὰς χεῖρας. οἱ δὲ ἀρχομένην δύναμιν ἐχθρῶν πει-
ρώμενοι καταλύειν ἀγαθοὶ συνεῖναι μᾶλλον ἢ οἱ προ-
κόψασαν μείζω κωλύοντες γενέσθαι· οἱ μὲν γὰρ τοῦ
περισσοῦ δοκοῦσι νεμεσᾶν, οἱ δ' οὐδεμίαν αὑτοῖς
ἀφορμὴν καθ' αὑτῶν ἐῶσι γενέσθαι. τοιαῦτα τοῖς τε
πλησιοχώροις καὶ πρὸς ἀλλήλους πρεσβευόμενοι
χωρεῖν τοῖς Ἑβραίοις ἐγνώκεσαν εἰς μάχην.
43 (2) Μωυσεῖ δ' οὐδὲν προσδοκῶντι πολέμιον
ἀπορίαν καὶ ταραχὴν ἐνεποίει τὰ τῶν ἐπιχωρίων,
καὶ παρόντων ἐπὶ τὴν μάχην ἤδη καὶ κινδυνεύειν
δέον ἐθορύβει χαλεπῶς τὸ τῶν Ἑβραίων πλῆθος
ἐν ἀπορίᾳ μὲν ὂν ἁπάντων, μέλλον δὲ πολεμεῖν

[1] Text doubtful: Reinach's conj. ἐφόδου does not satisfactorily account for αὐτῇ.

[a] Mentioned, in conjunction with Amalek, in A. ii. 6

they exhorted each other to repel and endeavour to destroy these upstarts. The instigators of this movement were those inhabitants of Gobolitis[a] and Petra[b] who are called Amalekites and were the most warlike of the peoples in those parts. It was their kings who sent messages exhorting one another and the neighbouring peoples to make war on the Hebrews.[c] "An army of aliens," they said, "has escaped from bondage in Egypt and is lying in wait to attack us. It behoves us not to disregard them; no, before they gain strength and obtain resources and themselves open battle upon us, emboldened by meeting with no opposition on our part, it were safer and prudent to crush them, exacting retribution for [their incursion into] the wilderness and for what they have done there, instead of waiting until they have laid hands on our cities and our goods. Those who essay to crush an enemy's power at the outset show greater sagacity than they who, when it is already far advanced, would prevent its extension; for these seem but resentful of its superabundant strength, whereas those never give it any handle against them." Addressing such messages by embassies to the neighbouring districts and to one another, they decided to engage the Hebrews in battle.

(2) To Moses, expectant of no hostility, this rising of the natives was a source of perplexity and trouble; while, since they were already advancing to battle and the peril had to be faced, there was grave agitation in the Hebrews' host, destitute of everything,

Moses encourages the Hebrews.

(*cf.* ix. 188), and doubtless identical with the "Gebal" (also linked with Amalek) of Ps. lxxxiii. 7.

[b] Future capital of the Nabataeans; Josephus uses the names of a later age.

[c] Weill quotes a Rabbinical parallel for this invitation.

πρὸς ἀνθρώπους τοῖς πᾶσι καλῶς ἐξηρτυμένους.[1]
44 παραμυθίας οὖν ὁ Μωυσῆς ἤρχετο καὶ θαρρεῖν παρεκάλει τῇ τοῦ θεοῦ ψήφῳ πεπιστευκότας, ὑφ' ἧς εἰς τὴν ἐλευθερίαν ἠρμένοι κατανικήσειαν τοὺς
45 περὶ αὐτῆς εἰς μάχην αὐτοῖς καθισταμένους, ὑπολαμβάνειν δὲ τὸ μὲν αὐτῶν εἶναι στράτευμα πολὺ καὶ πάντων ἀπροσδεές, ὅπλων χρημάτων τροφῆς τῶν ἄλλων, ὧν παρόντων ἐκ πεποιθήσεως πολεμοῦσιν ἄνθρωποι, κρίνοντας ἐν τῇ παρὰ τοῦ θεοῦ συμμαχίᾳ ταῦτα αὐτοῖς παρεῖναι, τὸ δὲ τῶν ἐναντίων ὀλίγον ἄνοπλον ἀσθενές, οἷον καὶ μὴ ὑπὸ τοιούτων, οἷοις αὐτοῖς σύνοιδεν οὖσιν, νικᾶσθαι
46 βουλομένου τοῦ θεοῦ. εἰδέναι δ' οἷος οὗτος ἐπίκουρος ἐκ πολλῶν πεπειραμένους καὶ δεινοτέρων τοῦ πολέμου· τοῦτον μὲν γὰρ εἶναι πρὸς ἀνθρώπους, ἃ δ' ἦν αὐτοῖς πρὸς λιμὸν καὶ δίψος ἄπορα καὶ πρὸς ὄρη καὶ θάλασσαν ὁδὸν οὐκ ἔχουσι φυγῆς, ταῦτ' αὐτοῖς διὰ τὴν εὐμένειαν τὴν παρὰ τοῦ θεοῦ νενικῆσθαι. νῦν δὲ γίνεσθαι παρεκάλει προθυμοτάτους, ὡς τῆς ἁπάντων εὐπορίας αὐτοῖς ἐν τῷ κρατῆσαι τῶν ἐχθρῶν κειμένης.
47 (3) Καὶ Μωυσῆς μὲν τοιούτοις παρεθάρσυνε τὸ πλῆθος λόγοις, συγκαλῶν ⟨τε⟩[2] τούς τε φυλάρχους καὶ τῶν ἐν τέλει καθ' ἑκάστους τε καὶ σὺν ἀλλήλοις τοὺς μὲν νεωτέρους παρεκάλει πείθεσθαι τοῖς πρεσβυτέροις, τοὺς δὲ ἀκροᾶσθαι τοῦ στρατηγοῦ·
48 οἱ δ' ἦσαν ἐπὶ τὸν κίνδυνον τὰς ψυχὰς ἠρμένοι καὶ πρὸς τὸ δεινὸν ἑτοίμως ἔχοντες ἤλπιζον ἀπαλλαγήσεσθαί ποτε τῶν κακῶν, καὶ τὸν Μωυσῆν ἐκέλευον ἄγειν αὐτοὺς ἐπὶ τοὺς πολεμίους ἤδη καὶ μὴ μέλλειν, ὡς τῆς ἀναβολῆς ἐμποδιζούσης

[1] Niese: ἐξηρτυσμένους RO: ἐξηρτισμένους (-ημένους) rell.

yet destined to contend with men at all points perfectly equipped. Moses accordingly proceeded to console them. He bade them take courage, trusting in God's decree, through which they had been promoted to liberty and triumphed over such as set themselves in battle against them to dispute it. They should regard their own army as great and lacking in nought—arms, money, provisions, all those things on the possession of which men rely in going to war—deeming that in having God as their ally they possessed them all; while that of their adversaries should appear as puny, unarmed, weak, such a force that by men so mean, as He knew them to be, God would not will to be defeated. They knew what a protector they had in Him from many experiences even more awful than war; for war was waged against men, but those hopeless straits with which they had contended were hunger and thirst, mountains and sea when they had no means of flight, and yet these through the gracious mercy of God had by them been overcome. So now he bade them show the keenest ardour, since affluence in everything would be their reward in defeating their foes.

(3) With such words did Moses embolden the multitude, and, calling up the heads of the tribes and the other officers singly and all together, he exhorted the juniors to obey their elders and these to hearken to their general. And they, with hearts elated at the peril, were ready to face the horror of it, hoping ere long to be quit of their miseries, and they urged Moses to lead them instantly and without procrastination against the enemy, since delay might damp

He puts Joshua in command.
Ex. xvii. 9.

---

^a ins. Niese.

49 τὴν προθυμίαν αὐτῶν. ὁ δὲ τῆς πληθύος ἀποκρίνας πᾶν τὸ μάχιμον Ἰησοῦν ἐφίστησιν αὐτῷ, Ναύηκου μὲν υἱὸν φυλῆς τῆς Ἐφραιμίτιδος, ἀνδρειότατον δὲ καὶ πόνους ὑποστῆναι γενναῖον[1] καὶ νοῆσαί τε καὶ εἰπεῖν ἱκανώτατον καὶ θρησκεύοντα τὸν θεὸν ἐκπρεπῶς καὶ Μωυσῆν διδάσκαλον τῆς πρὸς αὐτὸν εὐσεβείας πεποιημένον τιμώμενόν τε παρὰ τοῖς
50 Ἑβραίοις. βραχὺ δέ τι περὶ τὸ ὕδωρ ἔταξε τῶν ὁπλιτῶν ἐπὶ φυλακῇ παίδων καὶ γυναικῶν τοῦ τε παντὸς[2] στρατοπέδου. καὶ νύκτα μὲν πᾶσαν ἐν παρασκευαῖς ἦσαν τῶν τε ὅπλων εἴ τι πεπονηκὸς ἦν ἀναλαμβάνοντες καὶ τοῖς στρατηγοῖς προσέχοντες, ὡς ὁρμήσοντες ἐπὶ τὴν μάχην ὁπότε κελεύσειεν αὐτοὺς Μωυσῆς. διηγρύπνει δὲ καὶ Μωυσῆς ἀναδιδάσκων τὸν Ἰησοῦν ὃν τρόπον ἐκτάξειε τὸ
51 στρατόπεδον. ἠργμένης δὲ ὑποφαίνειν τῆς ἡμέρας αὖθις τόν τε Ἰησοῦν παρεκάλει μηδὲν χείρονα φανῆναι κατὰ τὸ ἔργον τῆς οὔσης περὶ αὐτὸν ἐλπίδος δόξαν τε διὰ τῆς παρούσης κτήσασθαι στρατηγίας παρὰ τοῖς ἀρχομένοις ἐπὶ τοῖς γεγενημένοις, τῶν τε Ἑβραίων τοὺς ἀξιολογωτάτους ἰδίᾳ παρεκάλει καὶ σύμπαν ἤδη τὸ πλῆθος ὡπλι-
52 σμένον παρώρμα. καὶ ὁ μὲν οὕτως παραστησάμενος τὸν στρατὸν τοῖς τε λόγοις καὶ τῇ διὰ τῶν ἔργων παρασκευῇ ἀνεχώρει πρὸς τὸ ὄρος θεῷ τε καὶ Ἰησοῦ παραδιδοὺς τὸ στράτευμα.
53 (4) Προσέμισγον δὲ οἱ πολέμιοι κἂν χερσὶν ἦν ἡ μάχη· προθυμίᾳ τε[3] καὶ διακελευσμῷ τὰ πρὸς

[1] RO: γεννικὸν rell.
[2] πρὸς παντὸς ML, whence πρόπαντος Dindorf.
[3] δὲ RO.

their ardour. Moses then, having selected from the crowd all of military efficiency, put at their head Joshua,[a] son of Nauêkos,[b] of the tribe of Ephraim,[c] a man of extreme courage, valiant in endurance of toil, highly gifted in intellect and speech, and withal one who worshipped God with a singular piety which he had learnt from Moses, and who was held in esteem by the Hebrews. He also posted a small force of armed men around the water as a protection for the children and women and for the camp in general. All that night they passed in preparations, repairing any damaged arms and attentive to their generals, ready to plunge into the fray so soon as Moses gave them the order. Moses too passed a wakeful night, instructing Joshua how to marshal his forces. At the first streak of dawn he once more exhorted Joshua to prove himself in action no whit inferior to the hopes that were built upon him and to win through this command a reputation with his troops for his achievements; he next exhorted the most notable of the Hebrews one by one, and finally addressed stirring words to the whole host assembled in arms. For himself, having thus animated the forces by his words and by all these active preparations, he withdrew to the mountain, consigning the campaign to God and to Joshua.

(4) The adversaries met and a hand-to-hand contest ensued, fought with great spirit and with mutual

Victory of the Hebrews: the spoils. Ex. xvii. 11.

[a] Greek "Jesus."
[b] The Hellenized form of Ναυή, the LXX equivalent for the Hebrew "Nun."
[c] Derived from Numb. xiii. 8.

ἀλλήλους χρωμένων μέχρι μὲν . . .¹ οὖν Μωυσῆς
αὖθις² ἀνίσχει τὰς χεῖρας, καὶ τοὺς Ἀμαληκίτας
κατεπόνουν οἱ Ἑβραῖοι. τὸν οὖν πόνον τῆς ἀνα-
τάσεως τῶν χειρῶν ὁ Μωυσῆς οὐχ ὑπομένων, ὁσάκις
γὰρ³ αὐτὰς καθίει τοσαυτάκις ἐλαττοῦσθαι τοὺς
54 οἰκείους αὐτοῦ συνέβαινε, κελεύει τόν τε ἀδελφὸν
Ἀαρῶνα καὶ τῆς ἀδελφῆς Μαριάμμης τὸν ἄνδρα
Οὖρον ὄνομα στάντας ἑκατέρωθεν αὐτοῦ δια-
κρατεῖν τὰς χεῖρας καὶ μὴ ἐπιτρέπειν κάμνειν
βοηθοῦντας.⁴ καὶ τούτου γενομένου κατὰ κράτος
ἐνίκων τοὺς Ἀμαληκίτας οἱ Ἑβραῖοι, καὶ πάντες
ἂν ἀπωλώλεισαν, εἰ μὴ νυκτὸς ἐπιγενομένης ἀπ-
55 έσχοντο τοῦ κτείνειν. νίκην καλλίστην καὶ καιριωτά-
την ⟨ταύτην⟩⁵ νικῶσιν ἡμῶν οἱ πρόγονοι· καὶ γὰρ
τῶν ἐπιστρατευσάντων ἐκράτησαν καὶ τοὺς περιοίκους ἐφόβησαν, μεγάλων τε καὶ λαμπρῶν ἐκ τοῦ
πονεῖν ἐπέτυχον ἀγαθῶν ἑλόντες τὸ στρατόπεδον
τῶν πολεμίων, πλούτους τε μεγάλους δημοσίᾳ καὶ
κατ' ἰδίαν ἔσχον οὐδὲ τῆς ἀναγκαίας⁶ τροφῆς
56 πρότερον εὐπορούντες. ὑπῆρξε δ' αὐτοῖς οὐκ εἰς
τὸ παρὸν μόνον ἀλλὰ καὶ εἰς τὸν αὖθις αἰῶνα τῶν
ἀγαθῶν αἰτία κατορθωθεῖσα ἡ προειρημένη μάχη·
οὐ γὰρ τὰ σώματα μόνον τῶν ἐπιστρατευσάντων
ἐδούλωσαν ἀλλὰ καὶ τὰ φρονήματα, καὶ τοῖς περι-
οίκοις ἅπασι μετὰ τὴν ἐκείνων ἧτταν ἐγένοντο
φοβεροί, αὐτοί τε πλούτου μεγάλου δύναμιν προσ-
57 έλαβον· πολὺς γὰρ ὁ ἄργυρός τε καὶ χρυσὸς
ἐγκατελήφθη⁷ ἐν τῷ στρατοπέδῳ καὶ σκεύη χαλκᾶ,

¹ ? lacuna (Niese).   ³ ὀρθὰς conj. Cocceii.
² Niese: ἂν RO, γὰρ ἂν rell.   ⁴ βοηθοῦντα Dindorf.
⁵ ins. Niese.   ⁶ ἀναγκαίου R.

shouts of encouragement.[a] So long as Moses held his hands erect, the Amalekites were discomfited by the Hebrews. Moses, therefore, unequal to the strain of this extension of his arms, and seeing that as often as he dropped them so often were his men worsted, bade his brother Aaron and his sister Mariamme's husband, by name Ur,[b] stand on either side of him to support his hands and by their aid not suffer them to flag. That done, the Hebrews inflicted a crushing defeat on the Amalekites, who would all have perished, had not night supervened to stay the carnage. A most noble victory and most timely was this that our forefathers won; for they defeated their assailants, terrified the neighbouring nations, and withal acquired by their efforts great and magnificent riches, having captured their enemy's camp and thereby obtained stores of wealth both for public and private use, they who but now had lacked even the necessaries of life. Nor was it only for the present, but also for the age to come, that their success in this battle proved productive of blessings; for they enslaved not the persons only of their assailants but also their spirit, and became to all the neighbouring races, after the defeat of those first adversaries, a source of terror, while they themselves amassed a great quantity of wealth. For abundant silver and gold was captured in the camp, as also vessels of

---

[a] With this description of the battle a new hand appears, that of the "Thucydidean" assistant (see Introduction): κἂν χερσὶν ἦν ἡ μάχη comes from Thuc. iv. 43, προθυμίᾳ καὶ διακελευσμῷ χρωμένων from iv. 11 (with vii. 71).

[b] Bibl. Hur, LXX Ὤρ. Scripture mentions no relationship between him and Moses: Rabbinical tradition represents him as not the husband, but the son, of Miriam (see Weill's note).

---

⁷ ἐγκατελείφθη most MSS.

JOSEPHUS

οἷς ἐχρῶντο περὶ τὴν δίαιταν, πολὺ δὲ ἐπίσημον πλῆθος ἑκατέρων ὅσα τε ὑφαντὰ καὶ κόσμοι περὶ τὰς ὁπλίσεις ἥ τε ἄλλη θεραπεία καὶ κατασκευὴ ἐκείνων λεία τε παντοία κτηνῶν καὶ ὅσα φιλεῖ 58 στρατοπέδοις ἐξωδευκόσιν ἕπεσθαι. φρονήματός τε ὑπεπλήσθησαν ἐπ' ἀνδρείᾳ Ἑβραῖοι καὶ πολλὴ μεταποίησις ἦν ἀρετῆς αὐτοῖς, πρός τε τῷ πονεῖν ἦσαν ἀεὶ τούτῳ πάντα ληπτὰ νομίζοντες εἶναι. καὶ ταύτης μὲν τῆς μάχης τοῦτο τὸ πέρας.

59 (5) Τῇ δ' ὑστεραίᾳ Μωυσῆς νεκρούς τε ἐσκύλευε τῶν πολεμίων καὶ τὰς παντευχίας τῶν φυγόντων συνέλεγεν ἀριστεῦσί τε τιμὰς ἐδίδου καὶ τὸν στρατηγὸν Ἰησοῦν ἐνεκωμίαζε μαρτυρούμενον ἐφ' οἷς ἔπραξεν ὑπὸ παντὸς τοῦ στρατοῦ. ἀπέθανεν δὲ Ἑβραίων μὲν οὐδείς, τῶν δὲ πολεμίων ὅσους 60 οὐδ' ἀριθμῷ γνῶναι δυνατὸν ἦν. θύσας δὲ χαριστήρια βωμὸν ἱδρύεται, νικαῖον ὀνομάσας τὸν θεόν, προεφήτευέ τε πανωλεθρίᾳ τοὺς Ἀμαληκίτας ἀπολουμένους καὶ μηδένα αὐτῶν ὑπολειφθησόμενον εἰς αὖθις διὰ τὸ Ἑβραίοις ἐπιστρατεύσασθαι καὶ ταῦτα ἐν ἐρήμῳ τε γῇ καὶ ταλαιπωρουμένοις, τόν 61 τε στρατὸν εὐωχίαις ἀνελάμβανε. καὶ ταύτην μὲν τὴν μάχην πρώτην μαχεσάμενοι πρὸς τοὺς κατατολμήσαντας αὐτῶν μετὰ τὴν ἐξ Αἰγύπτου γενομένην ἔξοδον οὕτως ἐπολέμησαν· ἐπεὶ δὲ τὴν τῶν ἐπινικίων ἑορτὴν ἤγαγον, ὁ Μωυσῆς ἀνα-

---

[a] All this description of the spoil is unscriptural, but, as M. Weill suggests, may be based on tradition: it was necessary to explain how the Hebrews obtained the rich materials for the making of the tabernacle. A certain duplication in the narrative here (the double mention of the capture of the camp and its riches) and below may be due to the employment at this point of *two* assistants.

brass, which served for their meals, a mass of coins of both metals, all manner of woven fabrics, decorations for armour, with all the accompanying trappings and apparatus, spoils of all sorts of beasts of burden, and everything that is wont to accompany armies into the field.[a] The Hebrews now too began to plume themselves on their valour and to have high aspirations to heroism,[b] while they became assiduous in toil, convinced that by it all things are attainable. Such was the issue of this battle.

(5) On the morrow Moses had the corpses of the enemy stripped and all the armour shed by the fugitives collected; he presented rewards to the valiant and eulogized their general Joshua, whose exploits were attested by the whole army. Indeed of the Hebrews not a man had perished, while the enemy's dead were past numbering. Offering sacrifices of thanksgiving, he erected an altar, calling God by the name of " Giver of victory "[c]; and he predicted that the Amalekites were to be utterly exterminated and not one of them should survive to after ages, because they had set upon the Hebrews at a time when they were in desert country and in sore distress.[d] He then regaled the troops with festivity.

Such was the issue of this fight, the first that they fought with daring aggressors after their exodus from Egypt. When the festival in honour of the victory had been celebrated, Moses, having rested the

Celebration of the victory, and arrival at Mount Sinai.

Ex. xvii. 15.

xvii. 14.

[b] πολλὴ μεταποίησις ἦν ἀρετῆς after Thuc. ii. 51 οἱ ἀρετῆς τι μεταποιούμενοι (" those who aspired to heroism," Jowett), a phrase frequently echoed by this " Thucydidean " συνεργός.

[c] Bibl. Jehovah-nissi (" J. is my banner "), LXX Κύριος καταφυγή μου; in Exodus the name is given not to God but to the altar.

[d] *Cf. A.* iv. 304 (with Deut. xxv. 17 ff. " Remember what Amalek did ").

παύσας ἐπ᾿ ὀλίγας ἡμέρας τοὺς Ἑβραίους μετὰ
62 τὴν μάχην προῆγε συντεταγμένους· πολὺ δ᾿ ἦν ἤδη
τὸ ὁπλιτικὸν αὐτοῖς· καὶ προϊὼν κατ᾿ ὀλίγον ἐν
τριμήνῳ μετὰ τὴν ἐξ Αἰγύπτου κίνησιν παρῆν ἐπὶ
τὸ Σιναῖον ὄρος, ἐν ᾧ τά τε περὶ τὸν θάμνον αὐτῷ
καὶ τὰ λοιπὰ φαντάσματα συντυχεῖν προειρήκαμεν.
63 (iii) Καὶ Ῥαγούηλος ὁ πενθερὸς τὴν αὐτοῦ
πυνθανόμενος εὐπραξίαν ἀσμένως ἀπήντα, τόν τε
Μωυσῆν καὶ τὴν Σαπφώραν δεχόμενος καὶ τοὺς
παῖδας αὐτῶν. ἥδεται δὲ Μωυσῆς ἐπὶ τῇ τοῦ
πενθεροῦ ἀφίξει καὶ θύσας εὐωχεῖ τὸ πλῆθος τοῦ
θάμνου πλησίον, ὃς διαπεφεύγει τοῦ πυρὸς τὴν
64 φλόγωσιν· καὶ τὸ μὲν πλῆθος κατὰ συγγενείας[1]
ὡς ἕκαστοι τῆς εὐωχίας μετελάμβανον, Ἀαρὼν
δὲ σὺν τοῖς παροῦσι Ῥαγούηλον προσλαβόμενος
ὕμνους τε ᾖδον εἰς τὸν θεὸν ὡς τῆς σωτηρίας
αὐτοῖς καὶ τῆς ἐλευθερίας αἴτιον καὶ ποριστὴν
65 γεγενημένον, καὶ τὸν στρατηγὸν εὐφήμουν ὡς
κατὰ ἀρετὴν ἐκείνου πάντων αὐτοῖς κατὰ νοῦν
ἀπηντηκότων. καὶ Ῥαγούηλος πολλὰ μὲν ἐγ-
κώμια τοῦ πλήθους ἐπὶ τῇ πρὸς τὸν Μωυσῆν εὐ-
χαριστίᾳ διεξῄει, ἐθαύμαζε δὲ καὶ τὸν Μωυσῆν
τῆς ἐπὶ σωτηρίᾳ τῶν φίλων ἀνδραγαθίας.
66 (iv. 1) Τῇ δ᾿ ὑστεραίᾳ θεασάμενος ὁ Ῥαγούηλος

[1] συγγένειαν RO.

---

[a] Josephus transposes the Biblical order of events, placing the arrival at Sinai (Ex. xix. 1) *before* the visit of Jethro (Ex. xviii). But as the Bible itself represents this visit as made when Moses " was encamped at the mount of God " (Ex. xviii. 5), it is highly probable that Josephus has only reverted to what was the original arrangement of the narrative (Driver's *Exodus, Camb. Bible*).

[b] *A.* ii. 264 ff.

JEWISH ANTIQUITIES, III. 61-66

Hebrews for a few days after the battle, led them forward in ordered ranks; a considerable body of them was by now armed. Advancing by short stages, within three months after the departure from Egypt, he reached Mount Sinai,[a] where he had met with the miracle of the bush and the other visions which we have already related.[b]

Ex. xix. 1.

(iii.) And now Raguel,[c] his father-in-law, hearing of his success, went with gladness to meet him, warmly welcoming Moses and Sapphora[d] and their children. Moses rejoiced at this visit of his father-in-law and, having offered sacrifice, made a feast for the people,[e] hard by the bush which had escaped combustion in the fire. The whole multitude, ranged in family groups, partook of the banquet; while Aaron with his company, joined by Raguel, chanted hymns to God, as the author and dispenser of their salvation and their liberty. They sung too the praises of their general, to whose merit it was due that all had befallen to their hearts' content. And Raguel was profuse in eulogies of the people for their gratitude to Moses, while he admired Moses for the gallantry which he had devoted to the salvation of his friends.

Visit of Raguel. *Ib.* xviii. 1.

Cf. ib. 12.

(iv. 1) On the morrow Raguel watched Moses

[c] Bibl. Jethro, *alias* Re'uel (LXX Ῥαγουήλ), as he is called in the first passage where he is mentioned (Ex. ii. 18); Josephus uses the latter name (*A.* ii. 258), except in *A.* ii. 264, v. 127.

[d] Bibl. Zipporah. In the Biblical account Jethro *brings back* Zipporah and the children to Moses, after a temporary separation; in Josephus the family had never been parted (*cf.* Ex. iv. 20).

[e] In Exodus Jethro offers sacrifices, and Aaron and the elders of Israel join him in the sacred meal: nothing is said about a public feast given by Moses.

τὸν Μωυσῆν ἐν ὄχλῳ πραγμάτων ὄντα· διέλυε γὰρ
τὰς δίκας τοῖς δεομένοις, πάντων ἐπ' αὐτὸν βα-
διζόντων καὶ μόνως ἂν τοῦ δικαίου τυχεῖν ἡγου-
67 μένων, εἰ διαιτητὴς αὐτοῖς οὗτος γένοιτο· καὶ γὰρ
τοῖς ἡττωμένοις κοῦφον ἐδόκει τὸ λείπεσθαι, κατὰ
δικαιοσύνην οὐ κατὰ πλεονεξίαν αὐτὸ πάσχειν
νομίζουσι· τότε μὲν ἡσυχίαν ἦγε μὴ βουλόμενος
ἐμποδίζειν τοῖς ἀρετῇ χρῆσθαι τοῦ στρατηγοῦ
θέλουσι, παυσάμενον δὲ τοῦ θορύβου παραλαβὼν
68 καὶ συμμονωθεὶς ἀνεδίδασκεν ἃ δεῖ ποιεῖν. καὶ
συνεβούλευε τῆς μὲν ἐπὶ τοῖς ἥττοσι ταλαιπωρίας
ἑτέροις ἐκστῆναι, περὶ δὲ τῶν μειζόνων καὶ τῆς
σωτηρίας τοῦ πλήθους ἔχειν τὴν πρόνοιαν αὐτόν·
δικάσαι μὲν γὰρ ἀγαθοὺς κἂν ἄλλους Ἑβραίων
εὑρεθῆναι, φροντίσαι δὲ τοσούτων μυριάδων σωτηρίας οὐκ ἄλλον τινὰ δύνασθαι μὴ Μωυσῆν γε-
69 νόμενον. " αἰσθανόμενος οὖν τῆς ἀρετῆς," φησί,
" σαυτοῦ καὶ οἷος γέγονας ἐπὶ τῷ τὸν λαὸν
ὑπουργῶν τῷ θεῷ σώζειν, τὴν μὲν τῶν ἐγκλημάτων
δίαιταν ἐπίτρεψον αὐτοῖς ποιεῖσθαι καὶ ἐπ' ἄλλων,
σὺ δὲ πρὸς μόνῃ τῇ τοῦ θεοῦ θεραπείᾳ κατέχων
σεαυτὸν διατέλει ζητῶν οἷς ἂν τὸ πλῆθος ἀπ-
70 αλλάξειας τῆς νῦν ἀπορίας. ὑποθήκαις δὲ ταῖς
ἐμαῖς περὶ τῶν ἀνθρωπίνων χρησάμενος τὸν στρατὸν ἐξετάσεις ἀκριβῶς καὶ κατὰ μυρίους τούτων
κεκριμένους ἄρχοντας ἀποδείξεις, εἶτα κατὰ χιλίους,
διαιρήσεις δὲ μετ' αὐτοὺς εἰς πεντακοσίους, καὶ
71 πάλιν εἰς ἑκατόν, εἶτ' εἰς πεντήκοντα. ἄρχοντάς
τε ἐπὶ τούτοις τάξεις, οἳ κατὰ τριάκοντα μερι-
σθέντας διακοσμήσουσι καὶ κατὰ εἴκοσι καὶ κατὰ

immersed in the turmoil of affairs. For he used to decide the disputes of those who sought his aid, and all came to him, thinking that only so would they obtain justice, if they had him for their arbitrator; even the unsuccessful made light of failure, convinced that it was justice and not cupidity that determined their fate. At the moment Raguel held his peace, loth to hinder any who would avail themselves of the talents of their chief; but, once quit of the tumult, he took him aside and, closeted with him, instructed him what he ought to do. He advised him to depute to others the tedium of the petty cases and to reserve his own oversight to the more important and to the welfare of the community; for other capable Hebrews could be found to sit in judgement, but to watch over the welfare of such myriads was a task which no other could perform save a Moses. "Conscious, then, of thine own merits," said he, "and what a part thou hast to play in the salvation of the people by ministering to God, suffer them to commit to others the arbitration of disputes; and do thou devote thyself solely and continuously to attendance upon God, searching by what means thou mayest deliver the people from their present straits. Follow but my advice on mundane matters, and thou wilt review thy army diligently and divide it into groups of ten thousand men, over whom thou wilt appoint selected chiefs, then into thousands; next thou wilt proceed to divide these into groups of five hundred, and these again into hundreds and fifties.[a] [Thou wilt moreover appoint officers over these to marshal them in sections of thirty, of twenty,

[a] In Ex. xviii. 21 the division is into groups of 1000, 100, 50, and 10.

δέκα συναριθμουμένους, ἔστω δέ τις ἐπὶ τούτοις
εἷς τὴν προσηγορίαν ἀπὸ τοῦ τῶν ἀρχομένων
ἀριθμοῦ λαμβάνων, δοκιμασθέντες ὑπὸ τοῦ πλή-
72 θους παντὸς εἶναι ἀγαθοὶ καὶ δίκαιοι, οἳ περί τε
τῶν διαφόρων[1] αὐτοῖς κρινοῦσι κἂν ᾖ τι μεῖζον
ἐπὶ τοὺς ἐν ἀξιώματι τὴν περὶ τούτου διάγνωσιν
ἐπανοίσουσιν· ἂν δὲ κἀκείνους διαφύγῃ τὸ περὶ
τοῦ πράγματος δύσκολον, ἐπὶ σὲ τοῦτο ἀνα-
πέμψουσιν. ἔσται γὰρ οὕτως ἀμφότερα· καὶ
τῶν δικαίων Ἑβραῖοι τεύξονται καὶ σὺ τῷ θεῷ
προσεδρεύων εὐμενέστερον ἂν ποιήσειας αὐτὸν τῷ
στρατῷ."

73 (2) Ταῦτα Ῥαγουήλου παραινέσαντος Μωυσῆς
ἀσμένως προσήκατο τὴν συμβουλίαν καὶ ποιεῖ
κατὰ τὴν ὑποθήκην τὴν ἐκείνου, τοῦ τρόπου τὴν
ἐπίνοιαν οὐκ ἀποκρυψάμενος οὐδὲ σφετερισάμενος
αὐτήν, ἀλλὰ ποιήσας φανερὸν τὸν ἐξευρηκότα τῷ
74 πλήθει. κἂν τοῖς βιβλίοις δὲ Ῥαγουῆλον ἔγραψεν
ὡς εὑρηκότα τὴν διάταξιν τὴν προειρημένην, καλῶς ἔχειν ἡγούμενος τἀληθῆ μαρτυρεῖν τοῖς ἀξίοις,
εἰ καὶ δόξαν ἔμελλε φέρειν ἐπιγραφομένῳ τὰ ὑπὸ
ἄλλων εὑρημένα, ὥστε τὴν Μωυσέος ἀρετὴν κἀκ
τούτου καταμαθεῖν. ἀλλὰ περὶ μὲν ταύτης εὐ-
καίρως ἐν ἄλλοις τῆς γραφῆς δηλώσομεν.

75 (v. 1) Μωυσῆς δὲ συγκαλέσας τὴν πληθὺν αὐτὸς
μὲν εἰς τὸ ὄρος ἀπέρχεσθαι τὸ Σιναῖον ἔλεγεν ὡς
συνεσόμενος τῷ θεῷ καί τι λαβὼν παρ' αὐτοῦ
χρήσιμον[2] ἐπανήξων πρὸς αὐτούς, ἐκείνους δ'

[1] ML: διαφορῶν rell.
[2] καί τινα λαβὼν . . χρησμὸν SP.

---

[a] This sentence is excluded from the text by M. Weill. As he remarks, it is difficult to reconcile the groups of 30 and

and of ten all told.]*a* Let each group have its own chief, taking his title from the number of men under his command; let them be approved by the whole multitude as upright and just persons, who are to sit in judgement on their differences, and in graver cases are to refer the decision to the higher officials. Then, if these too are baffled by the difficulty of the case, they shall send it up to thee. This will secure two things: the Hebrews will obtain justice, and thou, by assiduous attendance upon God, wilt belike render Him more propitious to the army."

(2) Raguel having tendered this advice, Moses gladly accepted it and acted in accordance with his suggestion, neither concealing the origin of the practice nor claiming it as his own, but openly avowing the inventor to the multitude. Nay, in the books too he recorded the name of Raguel, as inventor of the aforesaid system, deeming it meet to bear faithful witness to merit, whatever glory might be won by taking credit for the inventions of others. Thus even herefrom may one learn the integrity of Moses *b*; but of that we shall have abundant occasion to speak in other parts of this work.

Moses frankly adopts it. Ex. xviii. 24.

(v. 1) Moses now, having convoked the assembly, told them that he himself was departing to Mount Sinai, intending to commune with God and, after receiving from Him somewhat of profit,*c* to return

Moses ascends Mount Sinai. Ib. xix. 2 f.

20 with those of 50, unless we may suppose that each 50 was subdivided into smaller groups of 30 and 20. The groups of 10 alone have warrant in Scripture.

b Rabbinical tradition pays a similar tribute to Moses (*Sifré* quoted by Weill). *Cf.* a similar commendation on his integrity in recording, without appropriating, the prophecies of Balaam, *A.* iv. 157 f.

c Or, with the other reading, "some oracle."

ἐκέλευσε πλησίον μετασκηνῶσαι τῷ ὄρει τὴν
76 γειτνίασιν τοῦ θεοῦ προτιμήσαντας. ταῦτ' εἰπὼν
ἀνῄει[1] πρὸς τὸ Σιναῖον, ὑψηλότατον τῶν ἐν ἐκείνοις τοῖς χωρίοις ὀρῶν τυγχάνον καὶ διὰ τὴν
ὑπερβολὴν τοῦ μεγέθους καὶ τῶν κρημνῶν τὸ
ἀπότομον ἀνθρώποις οὐ μόνον οὐκ ἀναβατὸν ἀλλ'
οὐδὲ ὁραθῆναι δίχα πόνου τῆς ὄψεως δυνάμενον,
ἄλλως τε διὰ τὸ λόγον εἶναι περὶ τοῦ τὸν θεὸν ἐν
77 αὐτῷ διατρίβειν φοβερὸν καὶ ἀπρόσιτον. Ἑβραῖοι δὲ κατὰ τὰς Μωυσέος ἐντολὰς μετεσκήνουν
καὶ τὰς ὑπωρείας τοῦ ὄρους κατελαμβάνοντο,
ἠρμένοι ταῖς διανοίαις ὡς μετὰ τῆς ἐπαγγελίας
τῶν ἀγαθῶν, ἣν προύτεινεν αὐτοῖς, ἐπανήξοντος
78 Μωυσέος παρὰ τοῦ θεοῦ. ἑορτάζοντες δὲ τὸν
στρατηγὸν περιέμενον ἁγνεύοντες τήν τε ἄλλην
ἁγνείαν καὶ ἀπὸ συνουσίας τῆς γυναικῶν ἡμέρας
τρεῖς, καθὼς ἐκεῖνος αὐτοῖς προεῖπε, καὶ παρα-
καλοῦντες τὸν θεὸν εὐμενῆ συμβάλλοντα Μωυσεῖ
δοῦναι δωρεάν, ὑφ' ἧς εὖ βιώσονται. ταῖς τ' οὖν
διαίταις ἐχρῶντο πολυτελεστέραις καὶ τῷ κόσμῳ
γυναιξὶν ὁμοῦ καὶ τέκνοις ἐκπρεπῶς[2] ἤσκηντο.

79 (2) Ἐπὶ δύο μὲν οὖν ἡμέρας εὐωχούμενοι διῆγον,
τῇ τρίτῃ δὲ πρὶν ἢ τὸν ἥλιον ἀνασχεῖν νεφέλη τε
ὑπερίζανε[3] τοῦ παντὸς στρατοπέδου τῶν Ἑβραίων, οὐ πρότερον τοῦτο ἰδόντων γενομένου, καὶ
τὸ χωρίον οὗ τὰς σκηνὰς ἦσαν πεποιημένοι περι-
80 έγραφε, καὶ τοῦ λοιποῦ παντὸς ἐν αἰθρίᾳ τυγχάνοντος ἄνεμοί τε σφοδροὶ λάβρον κινοῦντες
ὑετὸν κατήγιζον, ἀστραπαί τε ἦσαν φοβεραὶ τοῖς
ὁρῶσι, καὶ κεραυνοὶ κατενεχθέντες ἐδήλουν τὴν

[1] ἄνεισι SP.   [2] RME: εὐπρεπῶς rell.
[3] ὑπεράνω ἀνέσχε RO.

JEWISH ANTIQUITIES, III. 75-80

to them; for their part, he bade them transfer their camp close to the mount, in honour preferring the neighbourhood of God. Having spoken thus, he went up to Sinai, which was the highest of the mountains in those regions, having proportions so massive and cliffs so precipitous as put it not only beyond men's power to scale but even to contemplate without tiring the eye; still more did the rumour of God's sojourning thereon render it awful and unapproachable. However the Hebrews, in compliance with the behests of Moses, shifted their camp and occupied the foot of the mountain, exulting in the thought that Moses would return from God's presence with that promise of blessings which he had led them to expect. In festal fashion they awaited their leader,[a] practising purity in general and abstaining in particular from union with their wives for three days, as he had enjoined upon them, while beseeching God to be gracious in His converse with Moses and to grant him a gift which would promote their happiness. Withal they partook of more sumptuous fare and arrayed themselves, along with their wives and children, in splendid attire. *Cf.* Ex. xix. 17.

Cf. ib. 14 f.

(2) So for two days they continued in festivity. But on the third, before the sun arose, a cloud settled down over the whole camp of the Hebrews, who had seen not the like before, enveloping the spot whereon they had pitched their tents; and, while all the rest of heaven remained serene, blustering winds, bringing tempestuous rain, came sweeping down, lightning terrified the beholders, and thunderbolts hurled from The thunders of Sinai. *Ib.* 16.

---

[a] In Exodus Moses descends from the mount to give instructions for this "sanctification" of the people.

παρουσίαν τοῦ θεοῦ οἷς Μωυσῆς ἤθελεν[1] εὐμενοῦς
81 παρατυχόντος. καὶ περὶ μὲν τούτων ὡς βούλεται
φρονείτω ἕκαστος τῶν ἐντευξομένων, ἐμοὶ δὲ
ἀνάγκη ταῦτα ἱστορεῖν καθάπερ ἐν ταῖς ἱεραῖς
βίβλοις ἀναγέγραπται. τούς γε μὴν[2] Ἑβραίους τά
τε ὁρώμενα καὶ ὁ ταῖς ἀκοαῖς προσβάλλων ψόφος
82 δεινῶς ἐτάραττεν, ἀήθεις τε γὰρ ἦσαν αὐτῶν, καὶ
ὁ περὶ τοῦ ὄρους διαπεφοιτηκὼς λόγος ὡς εἰς
αὐτὸ τοῦτο φοιτῶντος τοῦ θεοῦ σφόδρα τὴν διά
νοιαν αὐτῶν ἐξέπληττε. κατεῖχον δ' αὐτοὺς πρὸς
ταῖς σκηναῖς ἀχθόμενοι καὶ τόν τε Μωυσῆν ἀπ
ολωλέναι νομίζοντες ὑπ' ὀργῆς τοῦ θεοῦ καὶ περὶ
αὑτῶν ὅμοια προσδοκῶντες.

83 (3) Οὕτως δ' αὐτῶν διακειμένων ἐπιφαίνεται
Μωυσῆς γαῦρός τε καὶ μέγα φρονῶν. ὀφθείς τε
οὖν αὐτὸς ἀπαλλάσσει τοῦ δέους αὐτοὺς καὶ περὶ
τῶν μελλόντων κρείττονας ὑπετίθετο τὰς ἐλπίδας,
αἴθριός τε καὶ καθαρὸς ὁ ἀὴρ τῶν πρὸ ὀλίγου
84 παθῶν ἦν Μωυσέος παραγεγονότος. ἐπὶ τούτοις
οὖν συγκαλεῖ τὸ πλῆθος εἰς ἐκκλησίαν ἀκουσόμε
νον ὧν ὁ θεὸς εἴποι πρὸς αὐτόν, καὶ συναθροισθέν
των στὰς ἐπὶ ὑψηλοῦ τινος, ὅθεν ἔμελλον πάντες
ἀκούσεσθαι, "ὁ μὲν θεός," εἶπεν, "ὦ Ἑβραῖοι,
καθάπερ καὶ πρότερον εὐμενὴς προσεδέξατό με
καὶ βίον τε ὑμῖν εὐδαίμονα καὶ πολιτείας κόσμον
ὑπαγορεύσας πάρεστι καὶ αὐτὸς εἰς τὸ στρατό
85 πεδον. πρὸς γοῦν αὐτοῦ καὶ τῶν ἔργων, ἃ δι'
ἐκεῖνον ἡμῖν ἤδη πέπρακται, μὴ καταφρονήσητε
τῶν λεγομένων εἰς ἐμὲ τὸν λέγοντα ἀφορῶντες
μηδ' ὅτι γλῶττα [ταῦτα] ἀνθρωπίνη πρὸς ὑμᾶς
λέγει, τὴν δ' ἀρετὴν αὐτῶν κατανοήσαντες ἐπι-

[1] ἔχαιρεν RO.   [2] γε μὴν E: τε (γε, δὲ) rell.

aloft signified the advent of God propitious to the desires of Moses. Of these happenings each of my readers may think as he will [a]; for my part, I am constrained to relate them as they are recorded in the sacred books. As for the Hebrews, the sights that they saw and the din that struck their ears sorely disquieted them, for they were unaccustomed thereto and the rumour current concerning this mountain, that here was the very resort of God, deeply dismayed their minds. They kept to their tents, dispirited, imagining that Moses had perished beneath the wrath of God and expecting a like fate for themselves.

(3) Such was their mood when suddenly Moses appeared, radiant and high-hearted. The mere sight of him rid them of their terrors and prompted brighter hopes for the future; the air too became serene and purged of its recent disturbances on the arrival of Moses. Thereupon he summoned the people to assembly to hear what God had said to him, and, when all were collected, he stood on an eminence whence all might hear him and "Hebrews," said he, "God, as of yore, has received me graciously and, having dictated for you rules for a blissful life and an ordered government, is coming Himself into the camp. In His name, then, and in the name of all that through Him has already been wrought for us, scorn not the words now to be spoken, through looking only on me, the speaker, or by reason that it is a human tongue that addresses you. Nay, mark but their excellence and ye will discern the

Return of Moses, and his address to the people.[b]

[a] *Cf. A.* i. 108 note.   [b] No parallel in Scripture.

γνώσεσθε καὶ τὸ μέγεθος τοῦ νενοηκότος καὶ ἐπὶ συμφέροντι τῷ ὑμετέρῳ πρὸς ἐμὲ μὴ φθονήσαντος 86 εἰπεῖν. οὐ γὰρ Μωυσῆς ὁ Ἀμαράμου καὶ Ἰωχαβάδης¹ υἱός, ἀλλ' ὁ τὸν Νεῖλον ἀναγκάσας ᾑματωμένον ὑπὲρ ὑμῶν ῥυῆναι καὶ ποικίλοις δαμάσας κακοῖς τὸ τῶν Αἰγυπτίων φρόνημα, ὁ διὰ θαλάσσης ὁδὸν ὑμῖν² παρασχών, ὁ καὶ τροφὴν ἐξ οὐρανοῦ μηχανησάμενος ἐλθεῖν ἀπορουμένοις, ὁ 87 ποτὸν ἐκ πέτρας ἀναβλύσας σπανίζουσι, δι' ὃν Ἄδαμος τῶν ἀπὸ γῆς τε καρπῶν καὶ θαλάσσης μεταλαμβάνει, δι' ὃν Νῶχος ἐκ τῆς ἐπομβρίας διέφυγε, δι' ὃν Ἄβραμος ὁ ἡμέτερος πρόγονος ἐξ ἀλήτου τὴν Χαναναίαν κατέσχε γῆν, δι' ὃν Ἴσακος γηραιοῖς ἐτέχθη γονεῦσι, δι' ὃν Ἰάκωβος δώδεκα παίδων ἀρεταῖς ἐκοσμήθη, δι' ὃν Ἰώσηπος ἐδεσπότευσε τῆς Αἰγυπτίων δυνάμεως, οὗτος ὑμῖν τούτους χαρίζεται τοὺς λόγους δι' ἑρμηνέως ἐμοῦ. 88 σεβάσμιοι δ' ὑμῖν γενέσθωσαν καὶ παίδων περιμαχητότεροι καὶ γυναικῶν· εὐδαίμονα γὰρ διάξετε βίον τούτοις ἑπόμενοι καὶ γῆς ἀπολαύοντες καρπίμου καὶ θαλάσσης ἀχειμάστου καὶ τέκνων γονῆς κατὰ φύσιν τικτομένων καὶ πολεμίοις ἔσεσθε φοβεροί· τῷ θεῷ γὰρ εἰς ὄψιν ἐλθὼν ἀκροατὴς ἀφθάρτου φωνῆς ἐγενόμην· οὕτως ἐκείνῳ τοῦ γένους ἡμῶν καὶ τῆς τούτου μέλει διαμονῆς."

89 (4) Ταῦτ' εἰπὼν προάγει τὸν λαὸν γυναιξὶν ὁμοῦ καὶ τέκνοις, ὡς ἀκούσαιεν τοῦ θεοῦ διαλεγομένου πρὸς αὐτοὺς περὶ τῶν πρακτέων, ἵνα μὴ βλαβείη τῶν λεγομένων ἡ ἀρετὴ ὑπὸ ἀνθρωπίνης γλώττης ἀσθενῶς εἰς γνῶσιν αὐτοῖς παρα- 90 διδομένη. πάντες τε ἤκουον φωνῆς ὑψόθεν παραγενομένης³ εἰς ἅπαντας, ὡς διαφυγεῖν μηδένα τῶν

majesty of Him who conceived them and, for your profit, disdained not to speak them to me. For it is not Moses, son of Amaram and Jochabad,[1] but He who constrained the Nile to flow for your sake a blood-red stream and tamed with divers plagues the pride of the Egyptians, He who opened for you a path through the sea, He who caused meat to descend from heaven when ye were destitute, water to gush from the rock when ye lacked it, He thanks to whom Adam partook of the produce of land and sea, Noah escaped the deluge, Abraham our forefather passed from wandering to settle in the land of Canaan, He who caused Isaac to be born of aged parents, Jacob to be graced by the virtues of twelve sons, Joseph to become lord of the Egyptians' might—He it is who favours you with these commandments, using me for interpreter. Let them be had by you in veneration: battle for them more jealously than for children and wives. For blissful will be your life, do ye but follow these: ye will enjoy a fruitful earth, a sea unvext by tempest, a breed of children born in nature's way, and ye will be redoubtable to your foes. For I have been admitted to a sight of God, I have listened to an immortal voice: such care hath He for our[2] race and for its perpetuation."

(4) That said, he made the people advance with their wives and children, to hear God speak to them of their duties, to the end that the excellence of the spoken words might not be impaired by human tongue in being feebly transmitted[3] to their knowledge. And all heard a voice which came from on high to the ears of all, in such wise that not one of those ten words

Delivery of the Decalogue.
Ex. xix. 17, xx. 1.

---

[1] Ἰωχαβέλης SPL (Lat. Iochobel).
[2] Bekker: ἡμῖν codd. [3] παραγινομένης E.

δέκα¹ λόγων οὓς Μωυσῆς ἐν ταῖς δύο πλαξὶ γεγραμμένους κατέλιπεν· οὓς οὐ θεμιτόν ἐστιν ἡμῖν λέγειν φανερῶς πρὸς λέξιν, τὰς δὲ δυνάμεις αὐτῶν δηλώσομεν.

91 (5) Διδάσκει μὲν οὖν ἡμᾶς ὁ πρῶτος λόγος, ὅτι θεός ἐστιν εἷς καὶ τοῦτον δεῖ σέβεσθαι μόνον· ὁ δὲ δεύτερος κελεύει μηδενὸς εἰκόνα ζῴου ποιήσαντας προσκυνεῖν· ὁ τρίτος δὲ ἐπὶ μηδενὶ φαύλῳ τὸν θεὸν ὀμνύναι· ὁ δὲ τέταρτος παρατηρεῖν τὰς 92 ἑβδομάδας ἀναπαυομένους ἀπὸ παντὸς ἔργου· ὁ δὲ πέμπτος γονεῖς τιμᾶν· ὁ δὲ ἕκτος ἀπέχεσθαι φόνου· ὁ δὲ ἕβδομος μὴ μοιχεύειν· ὁ δὲ ὄγδοος μὴ κλοπὴν δρᾶν· ὁ δὲ ἔνατος μὴ ψευδομαρτυρεῖν· ὁ δὲ δέκατος μηδενὸς ἀλλοτρίου ἐπιθυμίαν λαμβάνειν.

93 (6) Καὶ τὸ μὲν πλῆθος [ὡς] ἀκροασάμενον αὐτοῦ τοῦ θεοῦ περὶ ὧν Μωυσῆς διελέχθη χαῖρον ἐπὶ τοῖς προειρημένοις τοῦ συλλόγου διελύθη, ταῖς δ' ἐφεξῆς² φοιτῶντες ἐπὶ τὴν σκηνὴν ἠξίουν αὐτὸν 94 καὶ νόμους αὐτοῖς παρὰ τοῦ θεοῦ κομίζειν. ὁ δὲ τούτους τε τίθεται καὶ περὶ τῶν ὅλων ὃν ἂν πραχθείη τρόπον ἐν τοῖς αὖθις ἀπεσήμαινε χρόνοις, ὧν μνησθήσομαι κατὰ καιρὸν οἰκεῖον. τοὺς δὲ πλείονας τῶν νόμων εἰς ἑτέραν ἀνατίθεμαι γραφήν, ἰδίαν περὶ αὐτῶν ποιησόμενος ἀφήγησιν.

95 (7) Οὕτω δὲ τῶν πραγμάτων αὐτοῖς ἐχόντων ὁ Μωυσῆς πάλιν εἰς τὸ Σιναῖον ὄρος ἀνῄει προειπὼν

¹ τῶν δέκα conj. Niese : καὶ codd. (probably through misreading of τῶν ί).
² RO : ἑξῆς rell.

ᵃ Rabbinical literature is said to furnish no parallel for this scruple (Weill).
ᵇ The introductory verse of Exodus (xx. 2, " I am the

escaped them which Moses has left inscribed on the two tables. These words it is not permitted us to state explicitly, to the letter,[a] but we will indicate their purport.

(5) The first word teaches us that God is one [b] and that He only must be worshipped. The second commands us to make no image of any living creature for adoration, the third not to swear by God on any frivolous matter, the fourth to keep every seventh day by resting from all work, the fifth to honour our parents, the sixth to refrain from murder, the seventh not to commit adultery, the eighth not to steal, the ninth not to bear false witness, the tenth to covet nothing that belongs to another.

Summary of the Decalogue.

(6) The people, having thus heard from the very mouth of God that of which Moses had told them, rejoicing in these commandments dispersed from the assembly. But on the following days, resorting oft to their leader's tent, they besought him to bring them laws also from God.[c] And he both established these laws and in after times indicated how they should act in all circumstances. Of these ordinances I shall make mention in due time ; the major portion of the laws, however, I reserve for another work, intending to make them the subject of a special treatise.[d]

The Hebrews ask for a code.

(7) Such was the position of affairs when Moses again went up into Mount Sinai, after forewarning

LORD thy God. . . .") is treated as part of the first commandment : *cf.* our Prayer-book version.

[c] This seems to correspond to Ex. xx. 19, " And they said unto Moses, Speak thou with us and we will hear : but let not God speak with us, lest we die." The verb " *bring* (them laws) " is thus emphatic.

[d] *Cf. A.* i. 25 note.

JOSEPHUS

τοῖς Ἑβραίοις, βλεπόντων δ' αὐτῶν ἐποιεῖτο τὴν ἄνοδον. καὶ χρόνου τριβομένου, τεσσαράκοντα γὰρ ἡμέρας διήγαγεν ἀπ' αὐτῶν, δέος εἶχε τοὺς Ἑβραίους, μή τι Μωυσῆς πάθοι, καὶ τῶν συντυχόντων δεινῶν οὐκ ἔστιν ὃ οὕτως ἐλύπησεν αὐτούς, ὡς τὸ
96 νομίζειν Μωυσῆν ἀπολωλέναι. ἦν γὰρ τοῖς ἀνθρώποις ἔρις, τῶν μὲν ἀπολωλέναι λεγόντων θηρίοις περιπεσόντα, καὶ μάλιστα ὅσοι πρὸς αὐτὸν ἀπεχθῶς ἦσαν διακείμενοι ταύτην τὴν ψῆφον ἔφερον,
97 τῶν δὲ πρὸς τὸ θεῖον ἀνακεχωρηκέναι· τοὺς δὲ σώφρονας καὶ μηδέτερον τῶν λεγομένων εἰς ἡδονὴν λαμβάνοντας ἰδίαν, καὶ τὸ θηρίοις περιπεσόντα ἀποθανεῖν ἀνθρώπινον ἡγουμένους καὶ τὸ ὑπὸ τοῦ θεοῦ πρὸς αὐτὸν μεταστῆναι διὰ τὴν προσοῦσαν ἀρετὴν εἰκὸς νομίζοντας, πράως ἔχειν οὗτος
98 ὁ λογισμὸς ἐποίει. προστάτου δὲ ἠρημῶσθαι καὶ κηδεμόνος ὑπολαμβάνοντες, οἵου τυχεῖν οὐκ ἂν ἄλλου δύναιντο, σφόδρα λυπούμενοι διετέλουν καὶ οὔτε πενθεῖν¹ αὐτοὺς εἴα τὸ προσδοκᾶν τι χρηστὸν περὶ τἀνδρὸς οὔτε μὴ λυπεῖσθαι καὶ κατηφεῖν ἠδύναντο. τὸ δὲ στρατόπεδον οὐκ ἐθάρρουν μετάγειν Μωυσέος αὐτοὺς ἐκεῖ παραμένειν προειρηκότος.

99 (8) Ἤδη δὲ τεσσαράκοντα ἡμερῶν διεληλυθυιῶν καὶ τοσούτων νυκτῶν παρῆν οὐδενὸς σιτίου τῶν τοῖς ἀνθρώποις νενομισμένων γεγευμένος. χαρᾶς δ' ἐνέπλησε τὴν στρατιὰν ἐπιφανείς, καὶ

¹ edd.: ὑπονοεῖν codd.

ᵃ Cf. A. iv. 326.
ᵇ Or (with the mss.) "suspect (any harm)."
ᶜ Ex. xxxiv. 28, "He did neither eat bread nor drink water." Josephus combines the *two* periods of forty days on the mount and deliberately omits the episode of the

the Hebrews, before whose eyes he made the ascent. Then, as time dragged on—for he was full forty days parted from them—a fear seized the Hebrews that something had befallen Moses, and of all the horrors that they had encountered none so deeply distressed them as the thought that Moses had perished. There was a conflict of opinions : some said that he had fallen a victim to wild beasts—it was principally those who were ill disposed towards him who voted for that view—others that he had been taken back to the divinity.[a] But the sober-minded, who found no private satisfaction in either statement—who held that to die under the fangs of beasts was a human accident, and that he should be translated by God to Himself by reason of his inherent virtue was likely enough—were moved by these reflections to retain their composure. Imagining themselves, however, to have been bereft of a patron and protector, the like of whom they could never meet again, they continued in the deepest distress ; and while their earnest expectation of some good news of their hero would not permit them to mourn,[b] so neither could they restrain their grief and dejection. Nor durst they break up the camp, Moses having charged them to abide there.

Moses' second absence for forty days creates rumours of his death. Cf. Ex. xxxii. 1.

(8) At length, when forty days had passed and as many nights, he came, having tasted of no food of such sort as is customary with men.[c] His appearance filled the army with joy ; and he proceeded to dis-

Moses returns with the tables of the Law. Ib. 15.

golden calf (Ex. xxxii) with the sequel, in order to avoid giving any handle to the malicious fables about the Jews current in his day (their alleged cult of an ass, etc., *contra Apionem, passim*). He has promised to omit nothing (*A.* i. 17) and, as a rule, includes the discreditable incidents in his nation's history : this is the most glaring exception.

τὴν τοῦ θεοῦ πρόνοιαν ἣν εἶχε περὶ αὐτῶν ἀπεδή-
λου, τόν τε τρόπον καθ᾽ ὃν εὐδαιμονήσουσι πολι-
τευόμενοι λέγων αὐτῷ κατὰ ταύτας ὑποθέσθαι τὰs
100 ἡμέρας, καὶ σκηνὴν ὅτι βούλεται γενέσθαι αὐτῷ,
εἰς ἣν κάτεισι πρὸς αὐτοὺς παραγινόμενος, "ὅπως
καὶ μεταβαίνοντες ἀλλαχοῦ ταύτην ἐπαγώμεθα καὶ
μηκέτι δεώμεθα τῆς ἐπὶ τὸ Σιναῖον ἀνόδου, ἀλλ᾽
αὐτὸς ἐπιφοιτῶν τῇ σκηνῇ παρατυγχάνῃ ταῖς
101 ἡμετέραις εὐχαῖς. γενήσεται δὲ ἡ σκηνὴ μέτροις
τε καὶ κατασκευῇ οἷς αὐτὸς ὑπέδειξεν ὑμῶν
ἀόκνως ἐχόντων πρὸς τὸ ἔργον." ταῦτ᾽ εἰπὼν
δύο πλάκας αὐτοῖς ἐπιδείκνυσιν ἐγγεγραμμένους
ἐχούσας τοὺς δέκα λόγους, ἐν ἑκατέρᾳ πέντε.
καὶ χεὶρ ἦν ἐπὶ τῇ γραφῇ τοῦ θεοῦ.

102 (vi. 1) Οἱ δὲ χαίροντες οἷς τε ἑώρων καὶ οἷς
ἤκουον τοῦ στρατηγοῦ τῆς κατὰ δύναμιν αὐτῶν
σπουδῆς οὐκ ἀπελείποντο, ἀλλ᾽ εἰσέφερον ἄργυρόν
τε καὶ χρυσὸν καὶ χαλκόν, ξύλα τε τῆς καλλίστης
ὕλης καὶ μηδὲν ὑπὸ τῆς σήψεως παθεῖν δυνάμενα,
αἰγείους τε τρίχας καὶ δορὰς προβάτων τὰς μὲν
ὑακίνθῳ βεβαμμένας τὰς δὲ φοίνικι· αἱ δὲ πορφύρας ἄνθος, ἕτεραι δὲ λευκὴν παρεῖχον τὴν χρόαν·
103 ἔριά τε τοῖς προειρημένοις ἄνθεσι μεμολυσμένα
καὶ λίνου βύσσον λίθους τε τούτοις ἐνδεδεμένους,
οὓς χρυσίῳ καθειργνύντες ἄνθρωποι κόσμῳ χρῶνται πολυτελεῖ, θυμιαμάτων τε πλῆθος συνέφερον·

---

[a] Not stated in Scripture. For the conflicting Rabbinical traditions on the subject of the arrangement of the ten commandments on the two tables see M. Weill's note: the view

close the care which God had for them, telling them that He had during these days shown him that manner of government which would promote their happiness, and that He desired that a tabernacle should be made for Him, whither He would descend whensoever He came among them, " to the intent," said he, " that when we move elsewhere we may take this with us and have no more need to ascend to Sinai, but that He himself, frequenting the tabernacle, may be present at our prayers. This tabernacle shall be fashioned of the dimensions and with the equipment which He himself has indicated, and ye are diligently to apply yourselves to the task." Having so said, he showed them two tables on which were graven the ten words, five on either of them[a]; and the writing thereon was from the hand of God.

Ex. xxv. 8 f.

Cf. ib. xxxi. 18, xxxii. 15 f.

(vi. 1) And they, rejoicing alike at what they had seen and at what they had heard from their general, failed not to show all the zeal of which they were capable. They brought their silver and gold and bronze, timber of the finest quality liable to no injury from rot,[b] goats' hair and sheepskins, some dyed blue, others crimson,[c] some displaying the sheen of purple, others of a pure white hue. They brought moreover wool dyed with the selfsame colours and fine linen cloth, with precious stones worked into the fabrics, such as men set in gold and use as ornaments of costly price, along with a mass of spices.

The TABERNACLE: its materials. *Ib.* xxxv. 5 (with xxv. 2).

expressed by Josephus was shared by R. Ḥanina (early 2nd cent.). For a further detail added by Josephus see § 138.

[b] Ex. xxv. 5, " acacia wood " (Heb. *shittim*): Josephus follows the interpretation of the LXX (ξύλα ἄσηπτα).

[c] In Exodus " scarlet."

ἐκ γὰρ τοιαύτης ὕλης κατεσκεύασε τὴν σκηνήν.
ἡ δ' οὐδὲν μεταφερομένου καὶ συμπερινοστοῦντος
104 ναοῦ διέφερε. τούτων οὖν κατὰ σπουδὴν συγκομισθέντων, ἑκάστου καὶ παρὰ δύναμιν φιλοτιμησαμένου, ἀρχιτέκτονας τοῖς ἔργοις ἐφίστησι κατ'
ἐντολὴν τοῦ θεοῦ οὓς καὶ τὸ πλῆθος ἂν ἐπελέξατο
105 τῆς ἐξουσίας ἐπ' αὐτῷ γενομένης. τὰ δὲ ὀνόματα
αὐτῶν, καὶ γὰρ ἐν ταῖς ἱεραῖς βίβλοις ἀναγέγραπται, ταῦτ' ἦν· Βασάηλος [μὲν] Οὐρὶ παῖς τῆς Ἰούδα
φυλῆς υἱωνὸς[1] δὲ Μαριάμμης τῆς ἀδελφῆς τοῦ
στρατηγοῦ, Ἐλίβαζος δὲ Ἰσαμάχου Δάνιδος φυλῆς.
106 τὸ δὲ πλῆθος οὕτως ὑπὸ προθυμίας τοῖς ἐγχειρουμένοις ἐπῆλθεν, ὥστε Μωυσῆς ἀνεῖρξεν αὐτοὺς
ὑποκηρυξάμενος ἀρκεῖν τοὺς ὄντας· τοῦτο γὰρ οἱ
δημιουργοὶ προειρήκεσαν· ἐχώρουν οὖν ἐπὶ τὴν τῆς
107 σκηνῆς κατασκευήν, καὶ Μωυσῆς αὐτοὺς ἕκαστα
περὶ τῶν μέτρων κατὰ τὴν ὑποθήκην τοῦ θεοῦ
καὶ τοῦ μεγέθους ὅσα τε δεῖ σκεύη χωρεῖν αὐτὴν
ἀνεδίδασκε πρὸς τὰς θυσίας ὑπηρετήσοντα. ἐφιλοτιμοῦντο δὲ καὶ γυναῖκες περί τε στολὰς ἱερατικὰς
καὶ περὶ τὰ ἄλλα ὅσων ἔχρῃζε τὸ ἔργον κόσμου τε
καὶ λειτουργίας ἕνεκα τοῦ θεοῦ.
108 (2) Πάντων δ' ἐν ἑτοίμῳ γεγενημένων χρυσίου
τε [καὶ ἀργύρου][2] καὶ χαλκοῦ καὶ τῶν ὑφαντῶν,
προειπὼν ἑορτὴν Μωυσῆς καὶ θυσίας κατὰ τὴν
ἑκάστου δύναμιν ἵστη τὴν σκηνήν, πρῶτον μὲν
αἴθριον διαμετρησάμενος τὸ μὲν εὖρος πεντήκοντα

[1] Bernard: υἱὸς codd.   [2] ins. Lat.: om. codd.

---

[a] Bibl. Bezalel.

[b] mss. erroneously "son." Exodus mentions his grandfather Hur, and Hur according to Josephus was the husband of Miriam (§ 54).

[c] Bibl. Oholiab (lxx Ἐλιάβ), son of Ahisamach.

JEWISH ANTIQUITIES, III. 103-108

For of such materials did Moses construct the tabernacle, which indeed was no other than a portable and itinerant temple. These objects, then, being promptly assembled, each having emulously contributed what he could and more, he appointed architects for the works, in accordance with the commandment of God, yet those whom the people too would have chosen had they been empowered to do so. Their names—for these are recorded also in the holy books— were Basael,[a] son of Uri, of the tribe of Judah, grandson [b] of Mariamme, the sister of the chief, and Elibaz, son of Isamach,[c] of the tribe of Dan. The people, for their part, showed such ardour in volunteering for the task in hand, that Moses restrained them, having proclamation made that there were enough[d] already, for so had the craftsmen told him. They proceeded then to construct the tabernacle, while Moses, in accordance with the prompting of God, instructed them on every detail concerning its measurements, its compass, and what objects it must contain for the service of the sacrifices. Women themselves vied with one another in providing priestly vestments and all else that the work demanded for its adornment and for the ministry of God.

(2) When all was in readiness—gold, silver, bronze, and fabrics—Moses, having first given orders for a feast and sacrifices according to every man's ability, proceeded to set up the tabernacle. He began by measuring out a court, in breadth fifty cubits and in

Ex. xxxi. 2.

Ib. xxxvi. 5.

Ib. xxxv. 25.

The court enclosing the tabernacle. *Ib.* xl. 17.

Ib. xxvii. 9.

---

[d] In Exodus the reference is to the superabundant offerings, in Josephus to the surplus of volunteers for the work (τοὺς ὄντας): the old Latin version of Josephus conforms to the Hebrew, "ea quae data fuissent."

367

109 πηχῶν ἑκατὸν δὲ τὸ μῆκος. κάμακας δὲ ἔστησε χαλκέας πενταπήχεις τὸ ὕψος καθ' ἑκατέραν πλευρὰν εἴκοσι τῶν ἐπιμηκεστέρων, δέκα δὲ τῶν ἐν πλάτει κειμένων τῆς κατόπιν, κρίκοι δὲ τῶν καμάκων ἑκάστῃ προσῆσαν· ... κιονόκρανα μὲν ἀργύρεα, βάσεις δὲ χρυσαῖ[1] σαυρωτῆρσιν ἐμφερεῖς,
110 χαλκαῖ δὲ ἦσαν, ἐπὶ τῆς γῆς ἐρηρεισμέναι. ἐξήπτετο δὲ τῶν κρίκων καλώδια τὴν ἀρχὴν ἥλων χαλκέων πηχυαίων τὸ μέγεθος ἐκδεδεμένα, οἳ καθ' ἑκάστην κάμακα παρέντες κατὰ τοῦ ἐδάφους ἀκίνητον ὑπὸ βίας ἀνέμων τὴν σκηνὴν ἔμελλον παρέξειν. σινδὼν δ' ἐκ βύσσου ποικιλωτάτη[2] διὰ πασῶν ἐπῄει, ἀπὸ τοῦ κιονοκράνου κατιοῦσα μέχρι τῆς βάσεως πολλὴ κεχυμένη, περιφράττουσα ἅπαν ἐν κύκλῳ τὸ χωρίον, ὡς μηδὲν δοκεῖν τείχους
111 διαφέρειν. καὶ οὕτως μὲν εἶχον αἱ τρεῖς πλευραὶ τοῦ περιβόλου· τῆς δὲ τετάρτης πλευρᾶς, πεντήκοντα γὰρ οὖσα πήχεων ἡ ἑτέρα μέτωπον τοῦ παντὸς ἦν, εἴκοσι μὲν πήχεις ἀνεῴγεσαν κατὰ πύλας, ἐν αἷς ἀνὰ δύο κάμακες εἱστήκεσαν κατὰ
112 μίμησιν πυλώνων. ὅλαις δ' αὐταῖς ἄργυρος ἦν ἐπικεχαλκευμένος[3] πάρεξ τῶν βάσεων· χαλκαῖ γὰρ ἦσαν. ἑκατέρωθεν δὲ τοῦ πυλῶνος τρεῖς κάμακες ἦσαν ἑστῶσαι, αἳ τοῖς πυλούχοις ἐμβεβήκεσαν ἐρηρεισμέναι, καὶ κατ' αὐτῶν δὲ βύσσινον ὕφος
113 σινδόνος ἦν περιηγμένον. τὸ δὲ κατὰ τὰς πύλας, μῆκος μὲν ὂν πήχεων εἴκοσι πέντε δὲ βάθος,[4] ὕψος ἦν πορφύρας φοίνικος σὺν ὑακίνθῳ καὶ βύσσῳ πεποιημένον πολλῶν αὐτῷ συνανθούντων καὶ

---

[1] (?) χρυσοῖς (cf. Hdt. vii. 41).
[2] μαλακωτάτη MSP Lat.   [3] ἐπικεχαλκωμένος codd.
[4] Niese: μήκους μὲν ὄντος ... βάθους codd.

JEWISH ANTIQUITIES, III. 109–113

length a hundred. Then he erected shafts of bronze fifty cubits high, twenty on each of the two longer sides, and ten broadwise on the rearward side, rings being attached to every shaft. Their capitals were of silver, their sockets, gilded and resembling the spikes[a] of lances, were of bronze and firmly planted in the soil. To the rings were attached cords, whose other end was made fast to pegs of bronze, a cubit long, which were driven into the ground over against each shaft, to render the tabernacle motionless under the pressure of the winds. A cloth of fine linen of most intricate texture[b] crowned all these shafts, depending from capital to base with ample sweep, compassing the whole place about in such wise that it seemed no other than a wall. Such was the aspect of the three sides of the enclosure. On the fourth side—this last, of fifty cubits length, formed the front of the whole structure—there was an opening of twenty cubits gatewise, where on the one side and on the other stood two shafts in imitation of pylons[c]; these shafts were entirely overlaid with silver except their bases, which were of bronze. On either side of this porch stood three shafts, which were attached[d] to the uprights supporting the gates and firmly secured ; and from these too hung a curtain woven of fine linen wrapping them about. But before the gates, extending to a length of twenty cubits and a height of five, was a tapestry of purple and crimson, interwoven with blue and fine linen, and beautified with

Ex. xxvii. 16.

[a] Or, with emended text, " resembling the gilded spikes."
[b] The Biblical " fine *twined* linen," *i.e.* " made from yarn of which each thread was composed of many delicate strands " (Driver on Ex. xxv. 4).   [c] *i.e.* (?) " gate-pillars."
[d] (?) by transverse beams : Greek " passed into."

369

ποικίλων, ὁπόσα μὴ ζῴων ἐξετυποῦντο μορφάς.
114 ἐντὸς δὲ τῶν πυλῶν περιρραντήριον ἦν χάλκεον ὁμοίαν αὐτῷ καὶ τὴν κρηπῖδα παρεχόμενον, ἐξ οὗ τοῖς ἱερεῦσι τὰς χεῖρας ἀποπλύνειν καὶ τῶν ποδῶν καταχεῖν παρῆν. καὶ ὁ μὲν τοῦ αἰθρίου περίβολος τοῦτον τὸν τρόπον ἦν διακεκοσμημένος.
115 (3) Τὴν δὲ σκηνὴν ἵστησιν αὐτοῦ κατὰ μέσον τετραμμένην πρὸς τὰς ἀνατολάς, ἵνα πρῶτον ὁ ἥλιος ἐπ' αὐτὴν ἀνιὼν ἀφίῃ τὰς ἀκτῖνας. καὶ τὸ μὲν μῆκος αὐτῆς ἐπὶ πήχεις ἐγήγερτο τριάκοντα τὸ δὲ εὖρος ἐπὶ δέκα διειστήκει, καὶ ὁ μὲν ἕτερος τῶν τοίχων νότιος ἦν, ὁ δὲ ἕτερος κατὰ βορέαν ἐτέτραπτο, κατόπιν δ' αὐτῆς ἡ δύσις κατελείπετο.
116 ἀνίστασθαι δ' αὐτὴν ἐχρῆν ἐφ' ὅσον προβαίνοι τὸ εὖρος. κίονες δ' ἦσαν ξύλου πεποιημένοι κατὰ πλευρὰν ἑκατέραν εἴκοσι, τετράγωνοι μὲν τὸ σχῆμα εἰργασμένοι, εἰς δὲ πλάτος διεστῶτες πήχεώς τε καὶ ἡμίσους, τὸ δὲ βάθος δακτύλων
117 τεσσάρων. λεπίδες δ' αὐτοῖς ἦσαν ἐπικεχαλκευμέναι πανταχόθεν χρυσαῖ διά τε τῶν ἔνδοθεν καὶ τῶν ἐκτὸς μερῶν. δύο δ' αὐτῶν ἑκάστῳ προσῆσαν στρόφιγγες ἐλαυνόμενοι κατὰ δύο βάσεων· αὗται δ' ἀργυραῖ μὲν ἦσαν, πυλὶς δ' ἑκατέρᾳ τούτων
118 προσῆν δεχομένη τὴν στρόφιγγα. τοῦ δὲ κατὰ δύσιν τοίχου κίονες μὲν ἓξ ἦσαν, συνῄεσαν δ' ἀλλήλοις ἀκριβῶς ἅπαντες, ὥστε μεμυκότων τῶν ἁρμῶν ὡς ἕνα δοκεῖν εἶναι τοῖχον αὐτῶν τὴν συνέλευσιν, χρύσειον τά τε ἔνδοθεν καὶ τὰ ἐκτός.
119 ἀνηλόγει γὰρ ὁ τῶν κιόνων ἀριθμός· εἴκοσι γὰρ

---

[a] Added detail, not in the Bible: cf. § 126.
[b] Or "in the eastern portion" (not directly in the centre).
[c] Jos. κίονες: Bibl. ḳerashim, LXX στύλοι, R.V. "boards,"

JEWISH ANTIQUITIES, III. 113–119

many and divers designs, but with nothing representing the forms of animals.[a] Within the gates stood a laver of bronze, on a base of the same material, where the priests could wash their hands and sprinkle water on their feet. Such was the arrangement of the precincts of the outer court.

Ex. xxx. 18.

(3) The tabernacle Moses set in the centre of this, facing eastward,[b] in order that the sun, at its rising, should shed its first rays upon it. Its length extended to thirty cubits and its breadth to ten; one of its walls was to the south, the other to the north, and in its rear lay the west. Its height had to be made equal to its breadth. Each of the two sides consisted of twenty pillars[c] of wood, wrought in rectangular form, of the breadth of a cubit and a half and a thickness of four fingers.[d] These were completely coated with plates of gold, on the interior as well as the exterior surfaces. Each of them was provided with two pivots fitting into two sockets; these last were of silver and had each its aperture to admit the pivot.[e] The western wall had six pillars, and all so perfectly united to each other that, the joints being closed up, they seemed to coalesce into a single wall, gilded both within and without. For the number of the pillars was in due proportion.[f] [On the long sides] there were twenty of them, each having a

The tabernacle itself: the exterior.

Ib. xxvi. 15; xxxvi. 20.

now explained as open *frames* with two uprights and crossrails (A. R. S. Kennedy, art. Tabernacle in Hastings, *D.B.* iv. 660 with illustration).

[d] Thickness not stated in Scripture.

[e] These sockets or bases may be regarded " as square plinths . . . forming a continuous foundation wall round the dwelling " (Kennedy).

[f] *i.e.* proportionate to the length of the sides. The Greek text is defective at this point.

ἦσαν καὶ παρεῖχε πλάτος * * *[1] τρίτον σπιθαμῆς
ἕκαστος αὐτῶν, ὥστε συμπληροῦσθαι τοὺς τριάκοντα πήχεις ὑπ' αὐτῶν· κατὰ δὲ τὸν ὄπισθεν
τοῖχον, ἐννέα γὰρ πήχεις οἱ ἓξ κίονες παρέχονται
συνελθόντες, δυ' ἑτέρους ποιοῦνται κίονας ἐκ
πήχεως[2] τετμημένους, οὓς ἐγγωνίους ἔθεσαν ἐπ'
120 ἴσης τοῖς μείζοσιν ἠσκημένους. ἕκαστος δὲ τῶν
κιόνων κρίκους εἶχε χρυσέους κατὰ τὸ ἔξω μέτωπον προσφυεῖς ὥσπερ ῥίζαις τισὶν ἐμπεπλεγ-
μένους κατὰ στίχον πρὸς ἀλλήλους τετραμμένους[3]
τὴν περιφέρειαν, καὶ δι' αὐτῶν ἐπίχρυσοι σκυταλίδες ἐλαυνόμεναι πέντε πήχεων ἑκάστη τὸ μέγεθος
σύνδεσμος ἦσαν τῶν κιόνων, ἐμβαινούσης κατὰ
κεφαλὴν σκυταλίδος ἑκάστης τῇ ἑτέρᾳ τεχνητῷ
121 στρόφιγγι κοχλίου τρόπον δεδημιουργημένῳ. κατὰ
δὲ τὸν ὄπισθεν τοῖχον μία φάλαγξ ἦν διὰ πάντων
ἰοῦσα τῶν κιόνων, εἰς ἣν ἐνέβαινον πλάγιαι αἱ
τελευταῖαι τῶν σκυταλίδων ἐξ ἑκατέρου τοίχου
τῶν ἐπιμηκεστέρων καὶ κρατεῖσθαι συνέβαινεν
αὐταῖς γιγλύμοις τῷ θήλει τοῦ ἄρρενος συνελ-
θόντος. τοῦτο μέντοι πρὸς τὸ μήθ' ὑπὸ ἀνέμων
κραδαίνεσθαι μήτ' ἄλλης αἰτίας τὴν σκηνὴν
συνεῖχεν, ἀλλ' ἀκίνητον αὐτὴν ἐν ἠρεμίᾳ πολλῇ
διαφυλάξειν ἔμελλεν.
122 (4.) Ἐντὸς δὲ διελὼν τὸ μῆκος αὐτῆς εἰς τρία
μέρη μετὰ δέκα πήχεας ἡρμοσμένους ἐκ τοῦ μυχοῦ

---

[1] mensuram unius et dimidii cubiti, altitudo Lat.: lacuna in Greek text.
[2] medio cubito Lat.: read perhaps ἐκ πήχεως ⟨β'⟩ τετμημένους; cf. Plato, Symp. 191 D τετμημένος ἐξ ἑνὸς δύο.
[3] Text as emended by Bernard after Lat.: κρίκον . . . χρύσεον . . . προσφυὴς . . . ἐμπεπλεγμένος . . . τετραμμένοι codd.

breadth [of one and a half cubits and a thickness] of a third of a span,[a] so that they filled the whole length of thirty cubits. But on the rear wall, where the six pillars conjoined covered but nine cubits, they made two extra pillars, each of half a cubit,[b] which they placed at the angles and adorned in the same fashion as the larger pillars.[c] All these pillars had rings of gold attached to their outer face, fixed to them as it were by roots, and forming a row of parallel circles; and through these passed gilt rods, five cubits long, which served to bind the pillars together, each rod at its extremity entering the next through a nut cunningly wrought in the form of a shell. The rear wall had but a single bar which passed right across all the pillars, and into which were inserted laterally the last of the rods on either of the two long walls and there held fast by screws,[d] the "male" piece fitting into the "female."[e] This secured the tabernacle against agitation by the winds or by other cause and was calculated to keep it unmoved in perfect stability.

(4) Internally, dividing its length into three portions,[f] at a measured distance of ten cubits from the

Ex. **xxvi.** 22.

Cf. ib xxvi. 26.

The interior

---

[a] *i.e.* the four finger-breadths of § 116.

[b] Literally "of a cubit cut (in two)."

[c] The object of these two extra pillars or frames is obscure. "Apparently they are intended to strengthen the two corners . . . the second frame forming a buttress" (Driver on Ex. xxvi. 24).

[d] Something in the nature of a pivot working in a socket is indicated.

[e] Many of these details lack Scriptural authority.

[f] *i.e.* dividing the 30 cubits into three equal portions and assigning one portion or 10 cubits to the sanctuary and two portions or 20 cubits to the rest: there was but the one *partition*.

τέσσαρας ἵστησι κίονας, ὁμοίως τοῖς ἄλλοις εἰργασμένους καὶ βάσεσιν ὁμοίαις ἐπικειμένους, διαλείποντας ἀλλήλων κατ' ὀλίγον. τὸ δ' ἐνδοτέρωθεν¹ αὐτῶν ἄδυτον ἦν, τὸ δὲ λοιπὸν ἡ σκηνὴ 123 τοῖς ἱερεῦσιν ἀνεῖτο. τὴν μέντοι διαμέτρησιν τὴν τοιαύτην τῆς σκηνῆς καὶ μίμησιν τῆς τῶν ὅλων φύσεως συνέβαινεν εἶναι· τὸ μὲν γὰρ τρίτον αὐτῆς μέρος τὸ ἐντὸς τῶν τεσσάρων κιόνων, ὃ τοῖς ἱερεῦσιν ἦν ἄβατον, ὡς οὐρανὸς ἀνεῖτο τῷ θεῷ, οἱ δ' εἴκοσι πήχεις, ὥσπερ γῆ καὶ θάλασσα βάσιμος ἀνθρώποις, οὕτως τοῖς ἱερεῦσι μόνοις ἐπετέτραπτο. 124 κατὰ μέτωπον δέ, ἐξ οὗ τὴν εἴσοδον ἦσαν πεποιημένοι, κίονες ἕστασαν χρύσεοι χαλκείαις βάσεσιν ἐφεστῶτες τὸν ἀριθμὸν πέντε. κατεπετάννυσαν δὲ τὴν σκηνὴν ὕφεσι βύσσου καὶ πορφύρας ὑακίνθου καὶ φοίνικος βαφῆς συγκεκραμένης.² 125 καὶ πρῶτον μὲν ἦν³ πήχεων δέκα πανταχόθεν, ᾧ κατεπετάννυσαν τοὺς κίονας, οἳ διαιροῦντες τὸν νεὼν τὸ ἄδυτον ἔνδον αὐτῶν ἀπελάμβανον· καὶ τοῦτο ἦν τὸ ποιοῦν αὐτὸ μηδενὶ κάτοπτον. καὶ ὁ μὲν πᾶς ναὸς ἅγιον ἐκαλεῖτο, τὸ δ' ἄβατον τὸ ἐντὸς τῶν τεσσάρων κιόνων τοῦ ἁγίου τὸ ἅγιον. 126 ὡραῖον δὲ τὸ φάρσος ἄνθεσι παντοίοις, ὅσα γῆθεν ἀνέρχεται, διαπεποικιλμένον τοῖς τε ἄλλοις ἅπασιν ἐνυφασμένον, ὅσα κόσμον οἴσειν ἔμελλε, πλὴν

¹ ἐνδοτέρω P: ἐνδότερον RO.
Niese: συγκεκραμένοις (-μένοι RO) codd.
³ + ἐκ RO: + ἐν SPL.

[a] The "inmost part," *i.e.* the east wall.
[b] *Cf.* §§ 180 ff., where this idea is expanded.
[c] Or (as in Exodus) "scarlet." Part was pure *byssus* or fine linen (undyed): other parts were dyed.
[d] Greek "Holy of Holy": the plural is used in Exodus (Heb. and LXX).

farther end *a* he set up four pillars, constructed like the rest and resting upon similar sockets, but placed slightly apart. The area within these pillars was the sanctuary; the rest of the tabernacle was open to the priests. Now this partitionment of the tabernacle was withal an imitation of universal nature *b*; for the third part of it, that within the four pillars, which was inaccessible to the priests, was like heaven devoted to God, while the twenty cubits' space, even as earth and sea are accessible to men, was in like manner assigned to the priests alone. But on the front, by which they entered, stood pillars of gold, resting on sockets of bronze, to the number of five. Ex. xxvi. 37.

The tabernacle was covered with curtains woven of fine linen, in which the hues of purple and blue and crimson *c* were blended. Of these the first measured ten cubits either way and was spread over the pillars which divided the temple and screened off the sanctuary; this it was which rendered the latter invisible to the eyes of any. The whole temple was called "Holy (Place)," its inaccessible shrine within the four pillars the "Holy of Holies." *d* This curtain was of great beauty, being decked with every manner of flower that earth produces and interwoven with all other designs that could lend to its adornment, save only the forms of living creatures.*e* The curtains. *Ib.* 31. *Ib.* xxvi. 33.

e It is remarkable that Josephus, while introducing floral and other decorations, ignores or rather excludes the only ornament of the veil of the temple mentioned in Scripture, viz. the "cherubim." He is concerned, as apologist, to give no handle to current slanders about the Jewish worship of animals (*cf.* §§ 99 note and 113); and when later (§ 137) he cannot avoid a mention of cherubim, he is careful to note that they are unlike any creatures that man's eyes have seen.

JOSEPHUS

127 ζώων μορφῆς. ἕτερον δὲ τούτῳ καὶ τῷ μεγέθει καὶ τῇ ὑφῇ καὶ τῇ χρόᾳ παραπλήσιον τοὺς ἐπὶ ταῖς εἰσόδοις πέντε κίονας περιέβαλλε, κατὰ γωνίαν ἑκάστου κίονος κρίκου κατέχοντος αὐτό, ἀπὸ κορυφῆς ἄχρι ἡμίσους τοῦ κίονος. τὸ δὲ λοιπὸν
128 εἴσοδος ἀνεῖτο τοῖς ἱερεῦσιν ὑποδυομένοις. ὑπὲρ δὲ τούτου λίνεον ἦν ἰσομέγεθες φάρσος ἐφελκόμενον ἀπὸ κάλων ἐπὶ θάτερα, τῶν κρίκων τῷ τε ὕφει καὶ τῷ κάλῳ διακονούντων πρός τε τὸ ἐκπετάννυσθαι καὶ συνελκόμενον ἵστασθαι κατὰ γωνίαν, ἐμποδὼν οὐκ ἐσόμενον πρὸς τὸ κατοπτεύεσθαι καὶ μάλιστα ἐν ταῖς ἐπισήμοις ἡμέραις.
129 κατὰ δὲ τὰς λοιπὰς καὶ μάλισθ' ὅταν ᾖ νιφετώδης προπετανννύμενον στεγανὸν ἐποίει τὸ ἐκ τῶν βαμμάτων ὕφος· ὅθεν δὴ παρέμεινε τὸ ἔθος καὶ τὸν ναὸν οἰκοδομησαμένων ἡμῶν, ὥστε τὴν σινδόνα
130 τοιουτότροπον περικεῖσθαι ταῖς εἰσόδοις. δέκα[1] δὲ ἄλλα φάρση πηχῶν τὸ πλάτος τεσσάρων τὸ δὲ μῆκος ὀκτὼ καὶ εἴκοσι, χρυσείους ἔχοντα γιγλύμους ἐπὶ συναφῇ θηλείας τε καὶ ἄρρενος συνείλεκτο, ὡς ἓν εἶναι δοκεῖν, εἶτα ὑπερτεινόμενα τοῦ ναοῦ τό τ' ἐφύπερθεν ἐσκίαζε καὶ τῶν τοίχων τοὺς κατὰ πλευρὰν καὶ κατόπιν ἑστῶτας ἀπὸ τῆς γῆς
131 ὅσον πῆχυν ἀνέχοντα. ἴσαι δὲ τῷ πλάτει καὶ ἄλλαι σινδόνες, μιᾷ πλείους τὸν ἀριθμὸν τὸ δὲ μῆκος ὑπερβάλλουσαι, τριακονταπήχεις γὰρ ἦσαν, ὑφασμέναι δ' ἐκ τριχῶν ὁμοίως κατὰ λεπτουργίαν ταῖς ἐκ τῶν ἐρίων πεποιημέναι[2] ἐτέταντο μέχρι

---

[1] RO: δώδεκα rell.   [2] Lat.: πεποιημέναις codd.

---

[a] Being the " work of the embroiderer " (Ex. xxvi. 36),

JEWISH ANTIQUITIES, III. 127–131

A second, corresponding to the first in dimensions, texture, and hue,[a] enveloped the five pillars that stood at the entrance; supported by rings at the corner of each pillar, it hung from the top to the middle of the pillar; the rest of the space was left as a passage for the priests entering beneath it. Above this was another covering of linen, of the same dimensions, which was drawn by cords to either side, the rings serving alike for curtain and cord, so that it could either be outspread or rolled together and stowed into a corner, in order that it should not intercept the view, above all on the great days. On other days, and in particular when snow was in the air, it was unfolded and served to protect the curtain of divers colours; hence the custom, which continued even after we had built the temple, of extending a similar linen curtain before the entrance. Ten further curtains, four cubits broad and twenty-eight cubits long, provided with golden couplings fitting mutually into each other,[b] were so joined as to appear like a single piece[c]; being then extended over the sacred building, they completely covered the top, as also the side walls and the wall in rear to a distance of a cubit from the ground. Then there were other hangings, of equal breadth with the last, but one more in number and of more considerable length, measuring thirty cubits; woven of hair,[d] but with the same fine craftsmanship as those of wool, these

Ex. xxvi. 36 f.; xxxvi. 37 f.

Ib. xxvi. 1.

Ib. xxvi. 7.

not of the "designer" or pattern-weaver, this screen lacked the cherubim.

[b] Literally "screws for the union of 'female' and 'male' pieces" (cf. § 121). Exodus mentions fifty "loops" of violet tape and fifty golden "clasps" (xxvi. 4-6).

[c] Ex. xxvi. 3 speaks of *two* sets of five curtains each.

[d] Bibl. "of goats' hair."

τῆς γῆς κεχυμέναι ⟨καὶ⟩¹ κατὰ θύρας ἀετώματι
παραπλήσιον καὶ παστάδι² παρεῖχον, τοῦ ἑνδε-
132 κάτου φάρσους εἰς τοῦτο παρειλημμένου. ἄλλαι
δ' ἐπάνω τούτων ἐκ διφθερῶν κατεσκευασμέναι
ὑπερῄεσαν σκέπη καὶ βοήθεια ταῖς ὑφανταῖς ἔν τε
τοῖς καύμασι καὶ ὁπότε ὑετὸς εἴη γεγενημέναι.
πολλὴ δ' ἔκπληξις ἐλάμβανε τοὺς πόρρωθεν θεω-
μένους· τὴν γὰρ χρόαν τοῖς κατὰ τὸν οὐρανὸν συμ-
βαίνουσιν οὐδὲν ἐδόκουν διαφέρειν. αἱ δ' ἐκ τῆς
133 τριχὸς καὶ τῶν διφθερῶν πεποιημέναι κατῄεσαν
ὁμοίως τῷ περὶ τὰς πύλας ὑφάσματι τό τε καῦμα
καὶ τὴν ἀπὸ τῶν ὄμβρων ὕβριν ἀπομαχόμεναι.
καὶ ἡ μὲν σκηνὴ τοῦτον πήγνυται τὸν τρόπον.

134 (5) Γίνεται δὲ καὶ κιβωτὸς τῷ θεῷ ξύλων
ἰσχυρῶν τὴν φύσιν καὶ σῆψιν παθεῖν οὐ δυναμένων·
ἡ δ' ἐρῶν μὲν καλεῖται κατὰ τὴν ἡμετέραν γλῶτ-
135 ταν, ἡ δὲ κατασκευὴ τοιαύτη τις ἦν· μῆκος μὲν
ἦν αὐτῇ πέντε σπιθαμῶν, τὸ δ' εὖρος καὶ τὸ
βάθος τριῶν σπιθαμῶν εἰς ἑκάτερον· χρυσῷ δὲ
τά τ' ἐντὸς καὶ τὰ ἔξωθεν περιελήλαστο³ πᾶσα,
ὡς ἀποκεκρύφθαι τὴν ξύλωσιν, στρόφιγξί τε
χρυσέοις τὸ ἐπίθεμα προσηνωμένον εἶχε θαυμαστῶς,
ὃ πανταχόθεν ἴσον ἦν κατ' οὐδέτερον μέρος
136 ἐξοχαῖς τὴν εὐαρμοστίαν λυμαινόμενον. καὶ καθ'
ἑκάτερον δὲ τοῖχον τῶν ἐπιμηκεστέρων κρίκοι
προσῆσαν⁴ χρύσεοι δύο τοῦ παντὸς διήκοντες
ξύλου, καὶ δι' αὐτῶν ἔνετοι σκυταλίδες ἐπίχρυσοι καθ' ἑκάτερον τοῖχον, ὡς ἂν ὑπ' αὐτῶν
ὁπότε δεήσειεν ἄγοιτο κινουμένη· οὐ γὰρ ἐπὶ
ζεύγους ἐκομίζετο, ἀλλ' ὑπὸ τῶν ἱερέων ἐφέρετο.

---

¹ ins. Dindorf. ² παραστάδι RO. ³ περιελήλατο LE.
⁴ Niese: προσῆεσαν (προῄεσαν) codd.

extended freely to the ground, and at the doorway they presented the appearance of a pediment and porch, the eleventh piece being put to this use.[a] Yet others, formed of skins, surmounted these, serving as shelter and protection for the textiles against both the scorching heat and occasional rain. Profound amazement struck all who beheld these from afar, their colours seeming so exactly to resemble those that meet the eye in the heavens. The coverings of hair and of skins descended likewise over the veil at the doorway, to defend it from the heat and from the havoc of beating rain. In such manner was the tabernacle constructed.

(5) Furthermore there was made for God an ark of stout timber of a nature that could not rot; the ark is called *erôn*[b] in our tongue, and its construction was on this wise. It had a length of five spans, and a breadth and height of three spans alike; both within and without it was all encased in gold, so as to conceal the woodwork, and it had a cover united to it by golden pivots[c] with marvellous art, so even was the surface at every point, with no protuberance anywhere to mar the perfect adjustment. To each of its longer sides were affixed two golden rings, penetrating the wood, and through these were passed gilt rods on either side, by means of which it might, when necessary, be carried on the march; for it was not drawn by a yoke of beasts, but was borne

The ark. Ex. xxv. 10; xxxvii. 1.

---

[a] Ex. xxvi. 9 "thou ... shalt double over the sixth curtain in the forefront of the tent"; this is now interpreted to refer not to a kind of portal *above* the entrance, but to the doubling of the curtain "*in front of* the Dwelling, so as to hang down there for two cubits, forming a kind of valance" (Driver).   [b] Heb. *arôn*.

[c] Or "hinges"; a detail peculiar to Josephus.

JOSEPHUS

137 τῷ δὲ ἐπιθέματι αὐτῆς ἦσαν πρόστυποι δύο, Χερουβεῖς[1] μὲν αὐτοὺς Ἑβραῖοι καλοῦσι, ζῷα δέ ἐστι πετεινὰ μορφὴν δ' οὐδενὶ τῶν ὑπ' ἀνθρώπων ἑωραμένων παραπλήσια, Μωυσῆς δέ φησι 138 τῷ θρόνῳ τοῦ θεοῦ προστυπεῖς ἑωρακέναι. ταύτῃ τὰς δύο πλάκας, ἐν αἷς τοὺς δέκα λόγους συγγεγράφθαι συμβεβήκει, ἀνὰ πέντε μὲν εἰς ἑκατέραν ἀνὰ δύο δὲ καὶ ἥμισυ κατὰ μέτωπον, ἐγκατέθετο. καὶ ταύτην ⟨μὲν⟩[2] ἐν τῷ ἀδύτῳ κατατίθησιν.

139 (6) Ἐν δὲ τῷ ναῷ τράπεζαν ἱδρύεται Δελφικαῖς παραπλησίαν, τὸ μῆκος μὲν δύο πηχῶν, τὸ δὲ πλάτος ἑνὸς πήχεως καὶ σπιθαμῶν τριῶν τὸ ὕψος. ἦσαν δ' αὐτῇ πόδες τὰ μὲν ἐξ ἡμίσους ἕως τῶν κάτω τελέως ἐξηρτισμένοι, οἷς Δωριεῖς προστιθέασι ταῖς κλίναις ἐμφερεῖς, τὸ δὲ πρὸς 140 αὐτὴν ἀνατεῖνον τετράγωνοι τῇ ἐργασίᾳ. κοιλαίνεται δὲ καθ' ἕκαστον πλευρὸν κοιλαίνουσά πως κατὰ παλαιστὴν τὸ ἔδαφος, ἕλικος περιθεούσης τό τε ἄνω καὶ τὸ κάτω μέρος τοῦ σώματος, καθ' ἕκαστον δὲ τῶν ποδῶν καὶ ταύτῃ ἐλήλατο κρίκος οὐκ ἄπωθεν τοῦ ἐπιθέματος, δι' ὧν ᾖσαν στελεοὶ χρύσεοι ξύλου τἄνερθεν ὄντες,

---

[1] χερουβὶμ ROE Lat.   [2] ins. Niese.

[a] Not in the Pentateuch, nor apparently (to judge from M. Weill's silence) in any known Rabbinical tradition. Perhaps, as suggested by M. Weill, a reminiscence of Ezekiel's vision, in which cherubim uphold the firmament which supports God's throne (Ezek. x. 1).

[b] The tables being regarded as ὀπισθόγραφα. For this last detail no parallel has been found in Rabbinical tradition; for "five on each" *cf.* § 101 note.   M. Weill, however, renders "deux et demie par *colonne.*"

by the priests. To the cover were affixed two figures, Ex. xxv. 18.
"cherubs" as the Hebrews call them—winged
creatures these, but in form unlike to any that man's
eyes have seen, and Moses says that he saw them
sculptured upon the throne of God.[a] Within this
ark he deposited the two tables, whereon had been
recorded the ten commandments, five on each of
them, and two and a half on either face.[b] The
ark itself he laid up in the sanctuary.

(6) Within the temple he installed a table, like Table of shewbread.
to those at Delphi, in length two cubits, in breadth Ib. xxv. 23;
a cubit, and of a height of three spans.[c] It had legs[d] xxxvii. 10.
which in their lower half were exquisitely finished,
resembling those which the Dorians affix to their
couches; in the upper portion reaching to the board
they were of quadrangular make. It was hollowed Cf. ib. xxv.
out on each side to a depth of about three inches,[e] 24 f.
a spiral border running round the upper and the
lower portion of the body of the table. Each of
the legs, here again,[f] had attached to it a ring, not
far from the board, and through these passed golden
staves, internally of wood, and not removable.[g]

[c] "Three spans" = Bibl. "a cubit and a half"; the cubit
(18 in.) being equivalent to two spans.
[d] Details not in Scripture.
[e] Literally "it is hollowed out on each side, hollowing out
the surface for about a palm" (four finger-breadths). This
appears to mean that the *edge* of the four sides of the table
took the form of four sunk panels (there are traces of this
in the representation on the Arch of Titus), with a spiral
moulding above and below. See Driver on Exodus *loc. cit.*
[f] καὶ ταύτῃ, like the sides of the ark (§ 136).
[g] There is no need to omit the negative with Weill ("qu'on
pouvait retirer facilement"). *Cf.* Ex. xxv. 15 (of the ark)
"The staves shall be in the rings of the ark: *they shall not
be taken from it*" (LXX ἀκίνητοι).

141 οὐκ ἐξαίρετοι· κοῖλον γὰρ εἶχεν ἐπ' αὐτοῖς τὸ κατὰ τοὺς κρίκους κοινωθέντας[1] οὐδὲ γάρ εἰσι διηνεκεῖς, ἀλλὰ πρὶν συνελθεῖν εἰς τὸ ἄπειρον εἰς περονίδας τὴν ἀρχὴν τελευτῶντες, ὧν ἡ μὲν εἰς τὸ προανέχον ἐμβαίνει τῆς τραπέζης, ἡ δὲ εἰς τὸν πόδα· καὶ τούτοις κατὰ τὰς ὁδοὺς ἐκομίζετο.

142 ἐπὶ ταύτης, ἐτίθετο γὰρ ἐν τῷ ναῷ τετραμμένῃ πρὸς ἄρκτον οὐ πόρρω τοῦ μυχοῦ, διετίθεσαν ἄρτους τε δώδεκα ἀζύμους κατὰ ἓξ ἐπαλλήλους [κειμένους] καθαροῦ πάνυ τοῦ ἀλεύρου ἐκ δύο ἀσσαρώνων,[2] ὃ μέτρον Ἑβραίων ἑπτὰ κοτύλας

143 Ἀττικὰς ἔχει. ὑπὲρ δὲ τῶν ἄρτων ἐτίθεντο φιάλαι δύο χρύσεαι λιβάνου πλήρεις, μετὰ δὲ ἡμέρας ἑπτὰ πάλιν ἄλλοι ἐκομίζοντο [ἄρτοι] ἐν τῷ καλουμένῳ ὑφ' ἡμῶν σαββάτῳ· τὴν γὰρ ἑβδόμην ἡμέραν σάββατα καλοῦμεν· τὴν δ' αἰτίαν ἐξ ἧς ταῦτα ἐπενοήθησαν ἐν ἑτέροις ἐροῦμεν.

144 (7) Κατὰ πρόσωπον δὲ τῆς τραπέζης τῷ πρὸς μεσημβρίαν τετραμμένῳ τοίχῳ πλησίον ἵσταται λυχνία ἐκ χρυσοῦ κεχωνευμένη διάκενος σταθμὸν ἔχουσα μνᾶς ἑκατόν· Ἑβραῖοι μὲν καλοῦσι κίγχαρες, εἰς δὲ τὴν Ἑλληνικὴν μεταβαλλόμενον

145 γλῶτταν σημαίνει τάλαντον. πεποίηται δὲ σφαιρία καὶ κρίνα σὺν ῥοΐσκοις καὶ κρατηριδίοις, ἑβδομήκοντα δ' ἦν τὰ πάντα, ἐξ ὧν ἀπὸ μιᾶς βάσεως

---

[1] κοινωθὲν Bernard.   [2] ἀσσάρων codd.

---

[a] *i.e.* the outer court or Holy Place (as opposed to the Holy of Holies).

[b] Greek " recess."

[c] For *assarôn* = " tenth part " (of an ephah) = *omer* see iii. 29 note : it is the word used in Lev. *loc. cit.*, " two tenth parts (of an ephah) shall be in one cake."

JEWISH ANTIQUITIES, III. 141-145

For the portion of the leg where the rings were attached was hollowed out to receive them; nor were the rings themselves continuous, but before completing the circle terminated in pins, of which one was inserted into the projecting edge of the table and the other into the leg. By these staves it was carried on the march. On this table, which was placed in the temple [a] on the northern side not far from the sanctuary,[b] they set out twelve loaves of unleavened bread, in two opposite rows of six, made of perfectly pure flour of the amount of two *assarôns*,[c] that being a Hebrew measure equivalent to seven Attic *cotylae*.[d] Above these loaves were set two cups [e] of gold filled with incense. After seven days the loaves were replaced by others on the day which we call Sabbath, that being our name for the seventh day. Of the reason which led them to devise all this we shall speak elsewhere.[f]

Lev. xxiv. 5.
(Ex. xxv. 30.)

(7) Facing the table, near the south wall, stood a candelabrum of cast gold, hollow, and of the weight of a hundred minae; this (weight) the Hebrews call *kinchares*,[g] a word which, translated into Greek, denotes a talent. It was made up of globules [h] and lilies, along with pomegranates and little bowls, numbering seventy in all; of these it was composed

The candelabrum.
Ex. xxv. 31.

---

[d] There is an apparent error of about one half in this estimate. In terms of pints, an *assarôn* or *omer* = c. 6½ pints (arts. on Weights and Measures in Hastings *B.D.* and *Encycl. Bibl.*); an Attic *cotyla* = nearly ½ pint, 7 *cotylae* = c. 3¼ pints.

[e] The representation on the Arch of Titus shows two cups resting on the table.

[f] In the projected work on "Customs and Causes" (i. 25).

[g] Heb. *kikkar*, Ex. xxv. 39 (LXX τάλαντον). The Greek talent = 60 minas, not 100, as is here implied.

[h] "Knops" in the English version of Exodus.

383

συνετέθη πρὸς ὕψος, ποιήσαντος αὐτὴν συγκειμένην εἰς μοίρας εἰς ὅσας τοὺς πλανήτας καὶ 146 τὸν ἥλιον κατανέμουσιν. ἀπαρτίζεται δὲ εἰς ἑπτὰ κεφαλὰς καταλλήλας ἐν στίχῳ διακειμένας. λύχνοι δ᾽ ἐπιφέρονται αὐταῖς ἑπτὰ κατὰ μίαν, τῶν πλανητῶν τὸν ἀριθμὸν μεμιμημένοι, ὁρῶσι δὲ εἴς τε τὴν ἀνατολὴν καὶ τὴν μεσημβρίαν λοξῶς αὐτῆς κειμένης.

147 (8) Μεταξὺ δ᾽ αὐτῆς καὶ τῆς τραπέζης ἔνδον, ὡς προεῖπον, θυμιατήριον ξύλινον μέν, ἐξ οὗ καὶ τὰ πρότερα ἦν σκεύη μὴ σηπόμενα,[1] στερεὰ δὲ περιελήλατ᾽ αὐτῷ λεπίς, πηχυαῖον μὲν κατὰ πλευρὰν ἑκάστην τὸ πλάτος ὕψος δὲ διπλάσιον.
148 ἐπῆν τε ἐσχάρα χρυσεία ὑπερανεστῶσα ἔχουσα κατὰ γωνίαν ἑκάστην στέφανον καὶ τοῦτον δ᾽ ἐκπεριοδεύοντα χρύσεον, ᾗ καὶ κρίκοι καὶ σκυταλίδες προσῆσαν,[2] αἷς κατὰ τὰς ὁδοὺς ὑπὸ τῶν
149 ἱερέων ἐφέρετο. ἵδρυτο δὲ καὶ πρὸ τῆς σκηνῆς βωμὸς χάλκεος, ὑπόξυλος καὶ αὐτός, ἑκάστην πλευρὰν πέντε πήχεσιν ἐκμεμετρημένος, τὸ δὲ ὕψος τρίπηχυς, ὁμοίως τῷ χρυσῷ κεκοσμημένος, χαλκείαις λεπίσιν ἐξησκημένος, δικτύῳ τὴν ἐσχάραν ἐμφερής· ἐξεδέχετο γὰρ ἡ γῆ τὸ ἀπὸ τῆς ἐσχάρας πῦρ καταφερόμενον τῆς βάσεως διὰ παν-
150 τὸς οὐχ ὑποκειμένης. ἀντικρὺ δ᾽ ἐτίθεντο τοῦ †χρυσέου[3] οἰνοχόαι τε καὶ φιάλαι σὺν θυΐσκαις καὶ

[1] σηπόμενον Bernard.   [2] προσῆεσαν codd.
[3] τοῦ χρυσ.] τοῦ βωμοῦ E: om. Lat.

---

[a] See § 182 for the ten degrees assigned to each of the seven planets.   [b] Greek "heads."

[c] § 139 ; as opposed to the altar of burnt-offering (below), which stood in the court outside.

[d] Meaning a little uncertain. The Bible speaks of *horns*

from its single base right up to the top, having been made to consist of as many portions as are assigned to the planets with the sun.[a] It terminated in seven branches[b] regularly disposed in a row. Each branch bore one lamp, recalling the number of the planets; the seven lamps faced south-east, the candelabrum being placed cross-wise.

(8) Between this last and the table, within the building as I have already said,[c] stood an incense-altar of wood, of the same imperishable material as the previous utensils, but completely encased in a massive sheet of metal; the breadth of each side was a cubit and its height two. Superimposed upon this was a brazier of gold, furnished at each corner with a crown, forming a circle likewise of gold[d]; here also rings and rods were attached, by which it was borne by the priests on the march. There was erected moreover in front of the tabernacle an altar of bronze, this too having a wooden interior; each side measured five cubits and it was three cubits high; while likewise adorned with gold, it was plated with sheets of bronze and had a brazier[e] resembling network; the ground was, in fact, the receptacle for all burning fuel that fell from the brazier, the base not extending beneath the whole of its surface. Over against the altar were set wine-cans and cups, along with censers and bowls; these were (of gold), and

Altar of incense.
Ex. xxx. 1.

Altar of burnt-offering.
Ib. xxvii. 1.

at the corners and " a crown " (*i.e.* " rim " or " moulding ") " round about " it.

[e] So (ἐσχάρα) the LXX; but the Hebrew *mikbar* is generally taken to be a " grating " (so A.V.) rising *vertically* from the ground as a support for the " ledge round the altar," on which the priests presumably stood. Josephus strangely ignores the sacrosanct " horns " of this altar.

385

JOSEPHUS

κρατῆρσιν †ἦσαν†[1] ὅσα τε ἄλλα [σκεύη] πρὸς τὰς ἱερουργίας πεποίητο χρύσεα[2] πάντα ὑπῆρχε. καὶ ἡ μὲν σκηνὴ τοιαύτη τε ἦν καὶ τὰ περὶ αὐτὴν σκεύη.

151 (vii. 1) Γίνονται δὲ καὶ τοῖς ἱερεῦσι στολαὶ πᾶσί τε τοῖς ἄλλοις, οὓς χααναίας[3] καλοῦσι, καὶ δὴ καὶ τῷ ἀρχιερεῖ, ὃν ἀναραβάχην[4] προσαγορεύουσι· σημαίνει δὲ ἀρχιερέα. τὴν μὲν οὖν τῶν
152 ἄλλων στολὴν τοιαύτην εἶναι συμβέβηκεν. ὅταν δὲ προσίῃ ταῖς ἱερουργίαις ὁ ἱερεὺς ἡγνευκὼς ἦν ὁ νόμος ἁγνείαν προαγορεύει,[5] πρῶτον μὲν περιτίθεται τὸν μαχανάσην[6] λεγόμενον· βούλεται δὲ τοῦτο συνακτῆρα μὲν δηλοῦν, διάζωμα δ' ἐστὶ περὶ τὰ αἰδοῖα ῥαπτὸν ἐκ βύσσου κλωστῆς εἰργασμένον[7] ἐμβαινόντων εἰς αὐτὸ τῶν ποδῶν ὥσπερ εἰς ἀναξυρίδας, ἀποτέμνεται δὲ ὑπὲρ ἥμισυ καὶ τελευτῆσαν ἄχρι τῆς λαγόνος περὶ αὐτὴν ἀποσφίγγεται.

153 (2) Ἐπὶ δὲ τούτῳ λίνεον ἔνδυμα διπλῆς φορεῖ

---

[1] ἦσαν] om E Lat.: ἐκ χρυσοῦ Bernard.
[2] aerea aurea Lat.: χάλκεα Bernard.
[3] Bernard: χαναίας ed. pr.: χαναναίας codd.
[4] ME (-ήχην SP): ἀραβάχην rell.: ἀραβάρχην (ex Lat.) Niese.
[5] Niese: προαγορεύει codd.
[6] Bernard: μαναχάσην codd.
[7] ROE: εἰργνύμενον rell.

---

[a] The list of vessels differs from that in the parallel passage in Ex. xxvii. 3, but the LXX has one item (the φιάλαι, " cups " or " pans ") in common with Josephus. There is a further difference as regards their material; according to Exodus " all the vessels thereof thou shalt make *of brass*," but

386

JEWISH ANTIQUITIES, III. 150-153

whatsoever other objects were made for the sacred services were all of gold.[a] Such was the tabernacle with all its appurtenances.

(vii. 1) Moreover, vestments were made for the priests, both for the general body, whom they call *chaanaeae*,[b] and in particular for the high-priest, whom they entitle *anarabaches*,[c] signifying "high-priest." Now the vestments of the priests in general were as follows.[d] When the priest is proceeding to perform his sacred ministrations, after undergoing the purification which the law prescribes, first of all he puts on what is called the *machanases*.[e] The word denotes a "binder," in other words drawers covering the loins, stitched of fine spun linen, into which the legs are inserted as into breeches; this garment is cut short above the waist and terminates at the thighs, around which it is drawn tight.

(2) Over this he wears a linen robe, of a double

Vestments of the priests.
Ex. xxviii.

The breeches.
Ib. 42.

The tunic.
Ib. (4) 39.

Josephus has the support of the Old Latin version of the LXX ("aurea" for χαλκᾶ) and the text may therefore stand.

[b] Hellenized form of the Aramaic *kahanya*, "priests" (Hebr. *kohanim*).

[c] Hellenization of Aramaic *kahana rabba*, "high priest," with omission (or transposition) of the initial *k*.

[d] This sentence is suspect, because, as Reinach justly remarks, it is couched in a form which in good Greek is applicable only to a description already given: "Such then were the vestments" etc. He would therefore regard it as a misplaced "doublet" to the last clause of § 158; while Niese indicates a lacuna preceding it. But there are indications that Josephus, as distinct from his assistants, was not familiar with the word τοιόσδε, "as follows," and used τοιοῦτος instead; a parallel occurs later in this book (iii. 273 end).

[e] Heb. *miknesaim* (dual); Josephus, by his translation συνακτήρ ("binder"), clearly derives the word from the verb *kanas* ("gather," "collect").

σινδόνος βυσσίνης, χεθομένη μὲν καλεῖται, λίνεον δὲ τοῦτο σημαίνει· χέθον γὰρ τὸ λίνον ἡμεῖς καλοῦμεν. ἔστι δὲ τοῦτο τὸ ἔνδυμα ποδήρης χιτὼν περιγεγραμμένος τῷ σώματι καὶ τὰς χειρῖ-
154 δας περὶ τοῖς βραχίοσιν κατεσφιγμένος, ὃν ἐπιζώννυνται κατὰ στῆθος ὀλίγον τῆς μασχάλης ὑπεράνω τὴν ζώνην περιάγοντες, πλατεῖαν μὲν ὡς εἰς τέσσαρας δακτύλους, διακένως δ' ὑφασμένην ὥστε λεβηρίδα δοκεῖν ὄφεως· ἄνθη δ' εἰς αὐτὴν ἐνύφανται φοίνικι¹ καὶ πορφύρᾳ μετὰ ὑακίνθου καὶ βύσσου πεποικιλμένα, στήμων δ' ἐστὶ μόνη βύσ-
155 σος. καὶ λαβοῦσα τὴν ἀρχὴν τῆς ἑλίξεως κατὰ στέρνον καὶ περιελθοῦσα πάλιν δεῖται, καὶ κέχυται μὲν πολλὴ μέχρι καὶ τῶν σφυρῶν ἕως οὗ μηδὲν ὁ ἱερεὺς ἐνεργεῖ, πρὸς γὰρ εὐπρέπειαν οὕτως ἔχει τοῖς ὁρῶσι καλῶς, ὅταν δὲ σπουδάζειν περὶ τὰς θυσίας δέῃ καὶ διακονεῖν, ὅπως μὴ κινουμένης ἐμποδίζηται πρὸς τὸ ἔργον, ἀναβαλόμενος ἐπὶ
156 τὸν λαιὸν ὦμον φέρει. Μωυσῆς μὲν οὖν ἀβανήθ² αὐτὴν ἐκάλεσεν, ἡμεῖς δὲ παρὰ Βαβυλωνίων μεμαθηκότες ἐμίαν αὐτὴν καλοῦμεν· οὕτως γὰρ προσαγορεύεται παρ' αὐτοῖς. οὗτος ὁ χιτὼν κολποῦται μὲν οὐδαμόθεν, λαγαρὸν δὲ παρέχων τὸν βροχωτῆρα τοῦ αὐχένος ἁρπεδόσιν ἐκ τῆς ὤας

¹ ed. pr.: φοίνιξι codd.   ² ἀβαῖθ RO.

---

[a] M. Weill adduces *Yoma* 71 b for the tradition that "in the texture of the priestly vestments each thread was doubled several times."

[b] Heb. *ketôneth* (Aramaic *kituna*) = "tunic": Aramaic *kitan* = "linen" (no Heb. equivalent). Josephus takes his terms from the Aramaic, Hellenizes them, and perhaps traces a connexion with the Greek χιτών used below.

[c] The sash is wound *twice* round the body (§ 155), at the

texture [a] of fine *byssus*; it is called *chethomenê*, that is to say " of linen," *chethon* being our name for linen.[b] This robe is a tunic descending to the ankles, enveloping the body and with long sleeves tightly laced round the arms; they gird it at the breast, winding to a little above the armpits [c] the sash, which is of a breadth of about four fingers and has an open texture [d] giving it the appearance of a serpent's skin. Therein are interwoven flowers of divers hues, of crimson [e] and purple, blue and fine linen, but the warp is purely of fine linen. Wound a first time at the breast, after passing round it once again, it is tied and then hangs at length,[f] sweeping to the ankles, that is so long as the priest has no task in hand, for so its beauty is displayed to the beholders' advantage; but when it behoves him to attend to the sacrifices and perform his ministry, in order that the movements of the sash may not impede his actions, he throws it back over his left shoulder. Moses gave it the name of *abanêth*,[g] but we have learnt from the Babylonians to call it *hemian*,[h] for so is it designated among them. This tunic is nowhere folded, but has a loose opening at the neck, and by means of strings fastened to the

The sash.

breast and above; at the second winding it is carried up in front, where it is tied, almost to the neck. Such seems to be the meaning.

[d] This is perhaps to be connected with the " chequer work " of Scripture (*tashbēz*, " something of the nature of a 'check,' obtained by the weaver alternating threads of different colours in warp and woof," Driver), though that word is applied to the tunic and not to the sash. Of the sash the Bible gives no description. [e] Or " scarlet."

[f] According to the Talmud it was 32 cubits (48 feet) long!

[g] Heb. *'abnēt* (Ex. xxviii. 39).

[h] The Aramaic equivalent used in the Targum, and said to be of Persian origin.

JOSEPHUS

καὶ τῶν κατὰ στέρνον καὶ μετάφρενον ἠρτημέναις ἀναδεῖται ὑπὲρ ἑκατέραν κατακλεῖδα· μασσαβαζάνης καλεῖται.

157 (3) Ὑπὲρ δὲ τῆς κεφαλῆς φορεῖ πῖλον ἄκωνον οὐ δικνούμενον εἰς πᾶσαν αὐτὴν ἀλλ' ἐπ' ὀλίγον ὑπερβεβηκότα μέσης· καλεῖται μὲν μασναεφθῆς, τῇ δὲ κατασκευῇ τοιοῦτός ἐστιν ὡς στεφάνη δοκεῖν ἐξ ὑφάσματος λινέου ταινία πεποιημένη παχεῖα· καὶ γὰρ ἐπιπτυσσόμενον ῥάπτεται πολλάκις.

158 ἔπειτα σινδὼν ἄνωθεν αὐτὸν ἐκπεριέρχεται διήκουσα μέχρι μετώπων, τήν τε ῥαφὴν τῆς ταινίας καὶ τὸ ἀπ' αὐτῆς ἀπρεπὲς καλύπτουσα καὶ ὅλῳ¹ δὲ τῷ κρανίῳ γιγνομένη ἐπίπεδον· ἥρμοσται δὲ ἀκριβῶς, ὡς ἂν μὴ περιρρυείη πονοῦντος περὶ τὴν ἱερουργίαν. καὶ ὁποία μέν ἐστιν ἡ τῶν πολλῶν ἱερέων στολὴ δεδηλώκαμεν.

159 (4) Ὁ δὲ ἀρχιερεὺς κοσμεῖται μὲν καὶ ταύτῃ παραλιπὼν οὐδὲν τῶν προειρημένων, ἐπενδυσάμενος δ' ἐξ ὑακίνθου πεποιημένον χιτῶνα, ποδήρης δ' ἐστὶ καὶ οὗτος, μεεὶρ καλεῖται κατὰ τὴν ἡμετέραν γλῶσσαν, ζώνῃ περισφίγγεται βάμμασιν οἷς ἡ πρότερον ἤνθει διαπεποικιλμένη χρυσοῦ συν-

160 υφασμένου· κατὰ πέζαν δ' αὐτῷ προσερραμμένοι θύσανοι ῥοῶν τρόπον ἐκ βαφῆς μεμιμημένοι ἀπήρτηντο καὶ κώδωνες χρύσεοι κατὰ πολλὴν ἐπι-

¹ ὅλη RO.

---

^a Heb. *mishbezeth* = " chequer-work "; the tunic is not so named in Exodus, but cognate words are used of it in xxviii. 4 " a tunic of chequer work " and 39 " thou shalt chequer the tunic."

^b Heb. *miznepheth* (Ex. xxviii. 4, 39). In Exodus this is the name given to the turban of the high-priest; those of the ordinary priests are there called *migbā'oth* (Ex. xxviii. 40)

border at the breast and at the back is supported on each shoulder. It is called *massabazanes*.[a]

(3) Upon his head he wears a cap without a peak, not covering the whole head but extending slightly beyond the middle of it. It is called *masnaephthes*,[b] and is so fashioned as to resemble a coronet, consisting of a band of woven linen thickly compressed ; for it is wound round and round and stitched repeatedly. This is then enveloped by a muslin veil descending from above to the forehead, thus concealing the stitches of the head-band with their unsightly appearance and presenting to the skull a completely even surface. This head-gear is adjusted with care so as not to slip off while the priest is busy with his sacred ministry. We have now described the nature of the vestments of the ordinary priests.

The turban

(4) The high-priest is arrayed in like manner, omitting none of the things already mentioned, but over and above these he puts on a tunic of blue [d] material. This too reaches to the feet, and is called in our tongue *meeir* [e] ; it is girt about him with a sash decked with the same gay hues as adorned the first, with gold interwoven into its texture. To its lower edge were stitched depending tassels, coloured to represent pomegranates, along with bells of gold,

Vestments of the high-priest [c] *: the tunic. Ex. xxviii. 31.*

and, to judge from the etymology of that word, were apparently *convex*, like the ordinary Greek πῖλος, " in shape resembling a half-egg " (Driver *in loc.*). Josephus, in speaking of a πῖλος ἄκωνος and in assimilating the turbans of the two orders of priests (*cf.* § 172), directly contradicts this : his account with its precise details, not derived from Scripture, is doubtless drawn from personal recollection and accurately represents the customs and terminology of his time.

[c] *Cf. B.J.* v. 231-6.
[d] Or " violet."
[e] Heb. *me'îl*.

τήδευσιν τῆς εὐπρεπείας, ὥστε μέσον ἀπολαμβάνεσθαι δυοῖν τε κωδώνοιν ῥοΐσκον, καὶ ῥοῶν
161 κωδώνιον. ἔστι δ' ὁ χιτὼν οὗτος οὐκ ἐκ δυοῖν περιτμημάτων, ὥστε ῥαπτὸς ἐπὶ τῶν ὤμων εἶναι καὶ τῶν παρὰ πλευράν, φάρσος δ' ἓν ἐπίμηκες ὑφασμένον σχιστὸν ἔχει βροχωτῆρα ⟨οὐ⟩¹ πλάγιον, ἀλλὰ κατὰ μῆκος ἐρρωγότα πρός τε τὸ στέρνον καὶ μέσον τὸ μετάφρενον· πέζα δ' αὐτῷ προσέρραπται ὑπὲρ τοῦ μὴ διελέγχεσθαι τῆς τομῆς τὴν δυσπρέπειαν· ὁμοίως δὲ καὶ ὅθεν αἱ χεῖρες διείργονται σχιστός ἐστιν.

162 (5) Ἐπὶ δὲ τούτοις τρίτον ἐνδύεται τὸν λεγόμενον μὲν ἐφώδην, Ἑλληνικῇ δ' ἐπωμίδι προσεοικότα· γίνεται γὰρ τοῦτον τὸν τρόπον. ὑφανθεὶς ἐπὶ βάθος πηχυαῖον ἔκ τε χρωμάτων παντοίων καὶ χρυσοῦ συμπεποικιλμένος ἀπερίπτυκτον τοῦ στέρνου τὸ μέσον καταλιμπάνει, χειρῖσί τε ἠσκημένος καὶ τῷ παντὶ σχήματι χιτὼν εἶναι
163 πεποιημένος. τῷ δὲ διακένῳ τοῦ ἐνδύματος σύνεισι περίτμημα σπιθαμῆς τὸ μέγεθος χρυσῷ τε καὶ τοῖς αὐτοῖς τῷ ἐφώδῃ βάμμασι διηνθισμένον· ἐσσὴν μὲν καλεῖται, σημαίνει δὲ τοῦτο κατὰ τὴν

¹ ins. (ex Lat.) Bernard.

---

^a As, we must infer, was the under tunic already described.
^b Cf. John xix. 23 f. ἦν δὲ ὁ χιτὼν ἄραφος, ἐκ τῶν ἄνωθεν ὑφαντὸς δι' ὅλου : though this is considered to be " only a verbal coincidence : the idea of a high-priestly robe does not enter here " (Bernard *in loc.*).
^c It was this slit which the high-priest prolonged by tearing it further down the front when he " rent his tunics " in token of horror or grief (Mk. xiv. 63).

JEWISH ANTIQUITIES, III. 160-163

disposed with a keen regard for beauty, so that between each pair of bells there hung a pomegranate and between the pomegranates a little bell. But this tunic is not composed of two pieces,[a] to be stitched at the shoulders and at the sides : it is one long woven cloth,[b] with a slit for the neck, parted not crosswise but lengthwise from the breast to a point in the middle of the back.[c] A border is stitched thereto to hide from the eye the unsightliness of the cut. There are similar slits through which the hands are passed.

(5) Above these vestments he puts on yet a third, which is called an *ephod* and resembles the Grecian *epômis*,[d] being made in the following fashion. A woven fabric of the length of a cubit, of all manner of colours along with gold embroidery, it leaves the middle of the breast uncovered, is provided with sleeves,[e] and in general presents the appearance of a tunic. But into the gap in this vestment is inserted a piece of the dimensions [f] of a span, variegated with gold and with the same colours as the ephod; it is called *essên*,[g] a word signifying in Greek speech

The *ephod*. Ex. xxviii. 6.

The *essen* (or 'breastplate'). *Ib.* 15.

---

[d] Ἐπωμίς is the LXX version of the Heb. *ephod*. The *epômis* was the upper part (in modern language " bodice ") of a woman's tunic, fastened on the shoulder by brooches. The *ephod* was a kind of waistcoat having, like the *epômis*, shoulder-straps, on which were sardonyxes.

[e] Sleeves are not mentioned in Scripture or (according to M. Weill) in tradition.

[f] It was " foursquare," of equal length and breadth (Ex. xxviii. 16).

[g] Heb. *ḥōshen*, English Bible " breastplate," more correctly " pouch " (Driver). It was " doubled " (Ex. *loc. cit.*) to form a bag or pouch, in which the Urim and Thummim were kept. The form ἐσσήν is attributed also to the unknown " Hebrew " (ὁ Ἑβραῖος) in MSS. of the LXX (Ex. xxviii. 22).

164 Ἑλλήνων γλῶτταν λόγιον[1]· πληροῖ δὲ ἀκριβῶς τοῦ ἐφόδου ὅπερ ὑφαίνοντες κατὰ στῆθος ἐξέλιπον, ἐνοῦται δ' ὑπὸ κρίκων χρυσέων αὐτῷ τε κατὰ γωνίαν ἑκάστην κἀκείνῳ τῶν ἴσων προσκεκοινω-μένων, ῥάμματος ὑακίνθου παραληφθέντος εἰς τὴν
165 πρὸς ἀλλήλους κατάδεσιν τοῖς κρίκοις. πρὸς δὲ τὸ μὴ χαλαρὸν εἶναι τὸ ἐν μέσῳ τῶν κρίκων καταλιμπανόμενον ῥαφὴν αὐτοῦ νήμασιν ὑακινθί-νοις ἐπενόησαν. πορποῦσι δὲ τὴν ἐπωμίδα σαρ-δόνυχες δύο κατὰ τῶν ὤμων, ἑκάτερον τέλος ἐπ' αὐτοὺς ἐπιθέον χρύσεον ἔχοντες, πρὸς τὸ ταῖς
166 περονίσιν ἐπιτήδειον εἶναι. ἐγγέγραπται δὲ τού-τοις τῶν Ἰακώβου παίδων τὰ ὀνόματα γράμμασιν ἐπιχωρίοις γλώσσῃ τῇ ἡμετέρᾳ κατὰ ἓξ τῶν λίθων ἑκατέρῳ, οἱ πρεσβύτεροι δ' εἰσὶ κατὰ ὦμον τὸν δεξιόν. ἐπίασι δὲ καὶ τὸν ἐσσῆνα λίθοι δώ-δεκα μεγέθει καὶ κάλλει διαφέροντες, οὐ κτητὸς ἀνθρώποις κόσμος διὰ τιμῆς ὑπερβολὴν ὄντες·
167 οὗτοι μέντοι κατὰ στίχον τρεῖς ἐπὶ τεσσάρων διακείμενοι γραμμῶν ἐνήσκηνται τῷ ὕφει, χρυσὸς δ' αὐτοὺς ἐκπεριέρχεται τὰς ἕλικας ἐντιθεὶς τῷ
168 ὕφει πρὸς τὸ μὴ διαρρεῖν οὕτως πεποιημένος. καὶ ἡ μὲν πρώτη τριάς ἐστι σαρδόνυξ τόπαζος σμά-ραγδος, ἡ δευτέρα δὲ ἄνθρακα παρέχεται καὶ ἴασπιν καὶ σάπφειρον, τῆς δὲ τρίτης λίγυρος μὲν

[1] λογεῖον SPL.

---

[a] λόγιον is the LXX version, from which Josephus again borrows: Philo similarly uses λογεῖον (*De vita Mos.* ii. 13, 154 M.). Josephus attributes the oracular properties of the *essēn* to the precious stones on its surface (iii. 215 ff.), not to the Urim and Thummim beneath; on these last mysterious objects he is silent.

logion ("oracle").[a] This exactly fills the space in the fabric which was left vacant at the breast, and is united by gold rings at each of its angles to corresponding rings attached to the ephod,[b] a blue thread being passed through the rings to bind them together. Furthermore, to prevent any sagging of the middle portion between the rings, they devised the plan of stitching it with blue thread. The *epômis* is buckled on to the shoulders by two sardonyxes,[c] fitted on this side and that with golden extremities[d] extending over the shoulders and serving to hold the pins. On these stones are graven the names of the sons of Jacob in our tongue and in the native characters, six on each stone, those of the elder sons being on the right shoulder.[e] On the *essên* also there are stones, twelve in number, of extraordinary size and beauty—ornament not procurable by man by reason of its surpassing value. Now these stones are ranged three in a row, in four lines, and worked into the fabric, being enclasped in gold wire whose coils are so inserted into the fabric as to prevent them from slipping out. The first triad comprises sardonyx,[f] topaz, emerald; the second exhibits carbuncle, jasper, sapphire; the third begins with jacinth,[g]

<small>The two sardonyx stones on the shoulders. Ex. xxviii. 9.</small>

<small>The twelve stones on the *essen*. Ib. 17.</small>

---

[b] I give the general sense: the exact meaning of προσκεκοινωμένων is doubtful.

[c] Heb. *shōham*, E.V. "onyx" (margin "beryl"), LXX σμάραγδος ("emerald").

[d] *i.e.* "enclosed in filigree settings (or "rosettes," E.V. "ouches") of gold" (Driver).

[e] Ex. xxviii. 10 says merely "according to their birth" (*i.e.* "according to their ages").

[f] "Sardius" in Exodus (LXX and E.V.), as also in the parallel passage in *B.J.* v. 234.

[g] Or "amber"; the Heb. word in Exodus perhaps means "cairngorm."

ἄρχει εἶτα ἀμέθυσος ἀχάτης δὲ τρίτος, ἔνατος ὢν τοῖς πᾶσι, τετάρτου δὲ στίχου χρυσόλιθος μὲν πρόκειται μετὰ δὲ αὐτὸν ὄνυξ εἶτα βήρυλλος τελευταῖος οὗτος. γράμματα δὲ ἐπετέτμητο πᾶσι τῶν Ἰακώβου υἱῶν, οὓς καὶ φυλάρχους νομίζομεν, ἑκάστου τῶν λίθων ὀνόματι τετιμημένου κατὰ τάξιν ἣν ἕκαστον αὐτῶν γενέσθαι συμβέβηκε. τῶν οὖν κρίκων ἀσθενῶν ὄντων καθ' αὑτοὺς ἐνεγκεῖν τὸ βάρος τῶν λίθων ἑτέρους δύο κρίκους μείζονας τῇ πέζῃ τοῦ ἐσσήνου, ᾗπερ ἀνήκει πρὸς τὸν τράχηλον, ἐμβεβηκότας τῷ ὑφάσματι ποιοῦσι, δεξομένους ἁλύσεις εἰργασμένας, αἳ συνῇσαν¹ κατ' ἄκρον τῶν ὤμων σειραῖς ἐκ χρυσοῦ πεπλεγμέναις συνάπτουσαι, ὧν τὸ ἄκρον ἀνεστραμμένον ἐνέβαινε κρίκῳ προέχοντι τῆς νωτιαίας πέζης τοῦ ἐφόδου· καὶ τοῦτο ἦν ἀσφάλεια τῷ ἐσσήνῃ πρὸς τὸ μὴ περιρρεῖν. ζώνη δὲ τῷ ἐσσήνῃ προσέρραπτο βάμμασιν οἷς προεῖπον μετὰ χρυσίου προσφερής, ἣ περιοδεύσασα δεῖται πάλιν ἐπὶ τῇ ῥαφῇ καὶ κατακρεμνᾶται· τοὺς δὲ θυσάνους χρύσεαι σύριγγες καθ' ἑκατέραν ἄκραν ἐκλαβοῦσαι πάντας ἐμπεριέχουσιν [αὗται].

¹ συνῄεσαν R²O.

---

[a] In emphasizing the order in the last two rows Josephus is deliberately correcting that which he has given in his earlier work, *B.J.* v. 234. The order in the respective texts is as follows:

then comes amethyst, and in the third place stands agate, ninth in the whole series; the fourth row is headed by chrysolite, next onyx, and then beryl, last of the series.[a] All the stones have letters graven upon them, forming the names of the sons of Jacob, whom we esteem withal as our tribal chiefs, each stone being honoured with one name, according to the order in which each of them was born. And since the rings were too feeble by themselves to support the weight of the gems, they made two other larger rings and inserted them into the fabric at the border of the *essên* nearest to the neck; these were designed to receive wrought chains, which on the top of the shoulders joined and were linked to cords of golden twine, whose extremity in the reverse direction passed through a ring projecting from the border at the back of the ephod. This secured the *essên* against any slip. The *essên* more- Ex. xxviii. 8. over had stitched to it a band, of the like hues of which I have spoken, along with gold; this after passing round the body was then tied at the seam [b] and hung down. The tassels at either extremity of this band were caught into golden sheaths which embraced them all.[c]

	Exodus.	Josephus, *B.J.*	Josephus, *Ant.*
Row 3	jacinth, agate, amethyst	agate, amethyst, jacinth	jacinth, amethyst, agate
Row 4	beryl, onyx, jasper	onyx, beryl, chrysolite	chrysolite, onyx, beryl

[b] *i.e.* at the point where the *essên* was stitched to the *ephod*.
[c] This detail, among others, is peculiar to Josephus.

JOSEPHUS

172 (6) Πῖλος[1] δὲ ἦν μὲν ὁ καὶ πρότερον αὐτῷ παραπλησίως εἰργασμένος τοῖς πᾶσιν ἱερεῦσιν, ὑπὲρ[2] αὐτὸν δὲ συνερραμμένος ἕτερος ἐξ ὑακίνθου πεποικιλμένος, περιέρχεται δὲ[3] στέφανος χρύσεος ἐπὶ τριστιχίαν κεχαλκευμένος. θάλλει δ' ἐπ' αὐτῷ κάλυξ χρύσεος τῇ σακχάρῳ βοτάνῃ παρ' ἡμῖν λεγομένῃ ἀπομεμιμημένος, ὑὸς δὲ κύαμον Ἑλλήνων οἱ περὶ τομὰς ῥιζῶν ἐμπείρως ἔχοντες προσαγορεύουσιν.
173 εἰ δέ τις ἢ[4] θεασάμενος τὴν βοτάνην ἀμαθίᾳ τούτου ἀγνοεῖ τὴν φύσιν αὐτῆς ἢ τὴν κλῆσιν ἐπιστάμενος οὐκ ἰδὼν δ' ἂν γνωρίσειε, τοῖς οὕτω
174 δὴ ἔχουσι σημανῶ τὸν τρόπον· βοτάνη μέν ἐστιν ὑπὲρ τρεῖς σπιθαμὰς πολλάκις αὐξανομένη τὸ ὕψος, τὴν δὲ ῥίζαν ἐμφερὴς βουνιάδι, ταύτῃ γὰρ οὐκ ἂν ἁμάρτοι τις εἰκάζων αὐτήν, τὰ δὲ φύλλα τοῖς εὐζώμοις· ἐκ μέντοι τῶν κλάδων ἀνίησι

[1] πῖλον RO.   [2] ed. pr.: ὑπ' codd.
[3] δὲ ins. Lat., ed. pr.: om. codd.   [4] v.ll. μὴ, ἢ μὴ.

---

[a] This paragraph on the head-dress is, apart from the allusion to the plate of gold at the close, peculiar to Josephus: the Scriptural description is confined to a few verses, Ex. xxviii. 36-39 (with the parallel passage xxxix. 30 f.). Very curious is the botanical lore displayed, no less than seven plants being named. A simpler and rather different description appears in *B.J.* v. 235. See the full discussion in *Encyl. Bibl. s.v.* "Mitre."

[b] Or perhaps "that already (described)."

[c] Or "violet."

[d] Exodus knows of no "crown," but only of the "plate of gold" mentioned below; with Josephus *cf.* Ecclesiasticus xlv. 12 "a crown of gold upon the mitre."

[e] Aramaic *shakruna* (connected with Heb. *shākar* = "be intoxicated"). See Löw, *Aramäische Pflanzennamen,* Leipzig, 1881, p. 381 (quoted by Weill).

JEWISH ANTIQUITIES, III. 172–174

(6) For head-dress^a the high-priest had first ^b a cap made in the same fashion as that of all the priests; but over this was stitched a second of blue^c embroidery, which was encircled by a crown of gold ^d wrought in three tiers, and sprouting above this was a golden calyx recalling the plant which with us is called *saccharon*,^e but which Greeks expert in the cutting of simples term henbane.^f In case there are any who, having seen the plant, never learnt its name and are ignorant of its nature, or, though knowing the name, would not recognize it if they saw it, for the benefit of such I proceed to describe it. It is a plant which often grows to a height of above three spans, with a root resembling a turnip ^g—one may not incorrectly draw this comparison—and leaves like those of the rocket.^h Now out of its branches it

The turban and crown of gold.

^f *Hyoscyamus niger.* I am indebted for the following to Mr. F. Howarth, B.Sc., Lecturer in Botany in the Imperial College of Science and Technology.

"Botanically there would appear to be a slight confusion in the description. The 'husk which detaches itself' is, no doubt, the corolla, which is shed—but which does not envelope the calyx but the ovary, which later becomes the fruit. The mistake probably arises from the fact that, before the corolla is shed, the calyx is small and inconspicuous, but becomes large and prominent afterwards, *i.e.* as the fruit develops. The lid mentioned is not on the calyx but on the fruit (matured ovary); the fruit and calyx are quite distinct throughout, though the fruit is enveloped in the spiky calyx. The fruit dehisces by throwing off the cap, splitting at the well-marked rim at X."

^g *Brassica rapa.*   ^h *Brassica eruca.*

κάλυκα προσεχῆ τῷ κλωνί, περίεισι δ' αὐτὴν ἔλυτρον, ὅπερ ἀποκρίνεται καθ' αὑτὸ πρὸς τὸν καρπὸν μεταβαλεῖν ἠργμένης· ὁ δὲ κάλυξ μεγέθους ἐστὶ σκυταλίδος τοῦ μικροῦ δακτύλου, κρατῆρι δ' ἐμφερὴς τὴν περιγραφήν. σημανῶ δὲ καὶ τοῦτο
175 τοῖς οὐ μεμαθηκόσι· σφαιρίδος εἰς δύο τετμημένης περὶ τῷ πυθμένι τὴν ἑτέραν τομὴν ἔχει φυόμενος ἀπὸ ῥίζης περιφερής· εἶτα συνιὼν κατ' ὀλίγον ὑποκοιλαινούσης εὐπρεπῶς τῆς ὑποχωρήσεως ἀνευρύνεται πάλιν ἠρέμα κατὰ χεῖλος,
176 ὁμοίως ὀμφαλῷ ῥοιᾶς τετμημένος. ἐπίθεμα δ' αὐτῷ ἡμισφαίριον προσπέφυκεν ἀκριβῶς ⟨ὡς⟩[1] ἂν εἴποι τις τετορνευμένον, ὑπερανεστώσας ἔχον τὰς ἐντομάς, ἃς εἶπον τῇ ῥοιᾷ παραπλησίως βλαστάνειν, ἀκανθώδεις καὶ εἰς ὀξὺ παντελῶς
177 ἀποληγούσας τὸ ἄκρον. φυλάττει δ' †ὑπὸ[2] τῷ ἐπιθέματι τὸν καρπὸν διὰ παντὸς τοῦ κάλυκος, ὄντα βοτάνης σπέρματι τῆς σιδηρίτιδος ὅμοιον, ἀφίησι δ' ἄνθος τῷ τῆς μήκωνος πλαταγωνίῳ
178 δυνάμενον δοκεῖν ἐμφερὲς εἶναι. ἐκ τούτου μὲν στέφανος ἐκκεχάλκευται ὅσον ἀπὸ τοῦ ἰνίου πρὸς ἑκάτερον τῶν κροτάφων. τὸ δὲ μέτωπον ἡ μὲν ἐφιελὶς οὐκ ἔπεισι, λεγέσθω γὰρ οὕτως ὁ κάλυξ, τελαμὼν δ' ἐστὶ χρύσεος, ὃς ἱεροῖς γράμμασι τοῦ

---

[1] ins. Niese.   [2] ἐπὶ codd.

[a] Or "projecting top."
[b] The mss. have "on."
[c] (?) *Verbena*.
[d] Meaning unknown.

JEWISH ANTIQUITIES, III. 174-178

puts forth a calyx closely adhering to the twig, and enveloped in a husk which detaches itself automatically when it begins to turn into fruit; this calyx is as big as a joint of the little finger and resembles a bowl in contour. This too I will describe for those unfamiliar with it. Imagine a ball cut in two: the calyx at the stem presents the lower half of this, emerging from its base in rounded form; then gradually converging with a graceful re-entrant curve, it broadens out again gently near the rim, where it is indented like the navel [a] of a pomegranate. Its hemispherical lid adheres closely to it, turned (as one might say) to a nicety, and is surmounted by those jagged spikes whose growth I compared to that on the pomegranate, prickly and terminating in quite a sharp point. Beneath [b] this lid the plant preserves its fruit which fills the whole of the calyx and resembles the seed of the herb *sideritis* [c]; while the flower which it produces may be thought comparable to the broad petals of a poppy. It was, then, on the model of this plant that was wrought the crown extending from the nape of the neck to the two temples; the forehead, however, was not covered by the *ephielis* [d] (for so we may call the calyx), but had a plate [e] of gold, bearing graven in sacred [f] Ex. xxviii. 36 f., xxxix. 30 f.

[e] Or "band" (Gr. τελαμών): Heb. ẓiẓ, LXX πέταλον ("leaf"), E.V. "plate." The Heb. ẓiẓ (normally = "flower") has here been variously interpreted as (1) a burnished plate (the commonly accepted view), (2) a flower-like ornamentation, (3) a garland or fillet. One may suspect that the foregoing elaborate description of a portion of the head-dress in *botanical* terms—though referring not to the "plate" but to the "calyx"—has been evolved out of interpretation (2).

[f] *i.e.* the older Hebrew characters found on inscriptions, as opposed to the later "square" characters: *cf.* Aristeas § 98 γράμμασιν ἁγίοις.

401

θεοῦ τὴν προσηγορίαν ἐπιτετμημένος ἐστί. καὶ τοιοῦτος μὲν ὁ τοῦ ἀρχιερέως κόσμος ἐστί.

179 (7) Θαυμάσειε δ' ἄν τις τῶν ἀνθρώπων τὴν πρὸς ἡμᾶς ἀπέχθειαν, ἣν ὡς ἐκφαυλιζόντων ἡμῶν τὸ θεῖον ὅπερ αὐτοὶ σέβειν προῄρηνται διατετελέ-
180 κασιν ἐσχηκότες. εἰ γάρ τις τῆς σκηνῆς κατανοήσειε τὴν πῆξιν καὶ τοῦ ἱερέως ἴδοι τὴν στολὴν τά τε σκεύη, οἷς περὶ τὴν ἱερουργίαν χρώμεθα, τόν τε νομοθέτην εὑρήσει θεῖον ἄνδρα καὶ ματαίως ἡμᾶς ὑπὸ τῶν ἄλλων τὰς βλασφημίας ἀκούοντας· ἕκαστα γὰρ τούτων εἰς ἀπομίμησιν καὶ διατύπωσιν τῶν ὅλων, εἴ τις ἀφθόνως ἐθέλοι καὶ μετὰ συνέσεως σκοπεῖν, εὑρήσει γεγονότα.
181 τήν τε γὰρ σκηνὴν τριάκοντα πηχῶν οὖσαν νείμας εἰς τρία καὶ δύο μέρη πᾶσιν ἀνεὶς τοῖς ἱερεῦσιν ὥσπερ βέβηλόν τινα καὶ κοινὸν τόπον, τὴν γῆν καὶ τὴν θάλασσαν ἀποσημαίνει· καὶ γὰρ ταῦτα πᾶσίν ἐστιν ἐπίβατα· τὴν δὲ τρίτην μοῖραν μόνῳ περιέγραψε τῷ θεῷ διὰ τὸ καὶ τὸν οὐρανὸν ἀνεπί-
182 βατον εἶναι ἀνθρώποις. ἐπί τε τῇ τραπέζῃ τοὺς δώδεκα θεὶς[1] ἄρτους ἀποσημαίνει τὸν ἐνιαυτὸν εἰς τοσούτους μῆνας διῃρημένον. τὴν δὲ λυχνίαν ἐξ ἑβδομήκοντα μορίων ποιήσας συγκειμένην τὰς τῶν

[1] τιθείς RO.

---

[a] The tetragrammaton ΥΗΥΗ (Anglice 'Jehovah'): so B.J. v. 235 (note) and Aristeas § 98, rather than as in Exodus " Holy (or " Holiness ") to ΥΗΥΗ."

characters the name of God.[a] Such is the apparel of the high-priest.

(7) But one may well be astonished at the hatred which men have for us and which they have so persistently maintained, from an idea that we slight the divinity whom they themselves profess to venerate. For if one reflects on the construction of the tabernacle and looks at the vestments of the priest and the vessels which we use for the sacred ministry, he will discover that our lawgiver was a man of God and that these blasphemous charges brought against us by the rest of men are idle. In fact, every one of these objects is intended to recall and represent the universe, as he will find if he will but consent to examine them without prejudice and with understanding.[b] Thus, to take the tabernacle, thirty cubits long, by dividing this into three parts and giving up two of them to the priests, as a place approachable and open to all, Moses signifies the earth and the sea, since these too are accessible to all; but the third portion he reserved for God alone, because heaven also is inaccessible to men. Again, by placing upon the table the twelve loaves, he signifies that the year is divided into as many months. By making the candelabrum to consist of seventy portions,[c] he

Symbolism of the tabernacle and the vestments.

[b] Josephus has already touched on this allegorical interpretation above (§ 123 μίμησιν τῆς τῶν ὅλων φύσεως) and in his earlier work (*B.J.* v. 212 f. εἰκόνα τῶν ὅλων). Philo gives a similar explanation, *De vita Mos.* ii. 6 (88) and 12 (117 ff.), which indeed appears to have been fairly widespread; Weill quotes parallels from the Midrashim and even from the Samaritan liturgy.

[c] § 145. But the component portions enumerated in Ex. xxv. 33 ff. seem to amount to 69 only (see *Encycl. Bibl.* i. 645 n. 3).

πλανητῶν δεκαμοιρίας[1] ᾐνίξατο, καὶ λύχνους ὑπὲρ αὐτῆς ἑπτὰ τῶν πλανητῶν τὴν φοράν· τοσοῦτοι 183 γάρ εἰσι τὸν ἀριθμόν. τά τε φάρση ἐκ τεσσάρων ὑφανθέντα τὴν τῶν στοιχείων φύσιν δηλοῖ· ἥ τε γὰρ βύσσος τὴν γῆν ἀποσημαίνειν ἔοικε διὰ τὸ ἐξ αὐτῆς ἀνεῖσθαι τὸ λίνον, ἥ τε πορφύρα τὴν θάλασσαν τῷ πεφοινῖχθαι τῶν ἰχθύων τῷ αἵματι, τὸν δὲ ἀέρα βούλεται δηλοῦν ὁ ὑάκινθος, καὶ ὁ 184 φοῖνιξ δ' ἂν εἴη τεκμήριον τοῦ πυρός. ἀποσημαίνει δὲ καὶ ὁ τοῦ ἀρχιερέως χιτὼν τὴν γῆν λίνεος ὤν, ὁ δὲ ὑάκινθος τὸν πόλον, ἀστραπαῖς μὲν κατὰ τοὺς ῥοΐσκους ἀπεικασμένος βρονταῖς δὲ κατὰ τὸν τῶν κωδώνων ψόφον. καὶ τὴν ἐφαπτίδα τοῦ παντὸς τὴν φύσιν ἐκ τεσσάρων δοχθεῖσαν γενέσθαι[2] τῷ θεῷ, χρυσῷ συνυφασμένην κατ' 185 ἐπίνοιαν οἶμαι τῆς προσούσης ἅπασιν αὐγῆς. καὶ τὸν ἐσσῆνα μέσον ὄντα τῆς ἐφαπτίδος ἐν τρόπῳ γῆς ἔταξε· καὶ γὰρ αὕτη τὸν μεσαίτατον τόπον ἔχει· ζώνῃ τε περιοδεύσας τὸν ὠκεανὸν ἀποσημαίνει· καὶ γὰρ οὗτος ἐμπεριείληφε τὰ πάντα. δηλοῖ δὲ καὶ τὸν ἥλιον καὶ τὴν σελήνην τῶν σαρ-

---

[1] ex Lat. Bernard: δωδεκαμοιρίας (δώδεκα μοίρας) codd.
[2] δοχθ. γεν. RO: γενέσθαι δειχθεῖσαν rell.

---

[a] The reading of the old Latin version, *decamoriae*, must on arithmetical grounds (70 = 7 × 10) be preferred to the text of the Greek mss. indicating a *twelve*-fold division. Δεκαμοιρία is a synonym for δεκανός, the vulgar term used by ancient astronomers to denote a portion of the heavens occupying 10 degrees of the Zodiac or a power presiding over those 10 degrees. "Astrologers for the most part allot [these divisions of 10°] to the seven planets," Housman, *Manilii Astronomicon* lib. iv. p. vii. But it must be noted that the Zodiac, with its 360°, comprises 36 'decans' in all; of this Josephus says nothing. Prof. Housman has kindly

hinted at the ten degree provinces *a* of the planets, and by the seven lamps thereon the course of the planets themselves, for such is their number.*b* The tapestries woven of four materials denote the natural elements: thus the fine linen appears to typify the earth, because from it springs up the flax, and the purple the sea, since it is incarnadined with the blood of fish; the air must be indicated by the blue, and the crimson *c* will be the symbol of fire. The highpriest's tunic likewise signifies the earth, being of linen, and its blue the arch of heaven, while it recalls the lightnings by its pomegranates, the thunder by the sound of its bells. His upper garment,*d* too, denotes universal nature, which it pleased God to make of four elements; being further interwoven with gold in token, I imagine, of the all-pervading sunlight. The *essên*, again, he set in the midst of this garment, after the manner of the earth, which occupies the midmost place *e*; and by the girdle *f* wherewith he encompassed it he signified the ocean, which holds the whole in its embrace. Sun and moon are indicated by the two sardonyxes wherewith he

---

confirmed this interpretation and referred me for another instance of δεκαμοιρία = δεκανός to an anonymous treatise printed in Wachsmuth's Lydus, *De ostentis*, ed. 2 p. 174, lines 8 and 10.

b viz. Saturn, Jupiter, Mars, Venus, Mercury, with Sun and Moon; *cf.* Philo, *De vita Mos.* ii. 9 (102) τὴν λυχνίαν δι' ἧς αἰνίττεται τὰς τῶν φωσφόρων κινήσεις ἀστέρων. In *B.J.* vii. 149 the seven lamps "indicate the honour paid to that number (or perhaps " to the week," τῆς ἑβδομάδος) by the Jews."

c Or "scarlet= κόκκος, the word used in Exodus (LXX) and in the parallel passage in *B.J.* v. 213.

d *Ephaptis*, another term for what has previously been called the *ephod* or *epômis* (§ 162).

e In the universe.   *f* Or "sash."

δονύχων ἑκάτερος, οἷς ἐνεπόρπωσε τὸν ἀρχιερέα. 186 τήν τε δωδεκάδα τῶν λίθων εἴτε τοὺς μῆνάς τις θέλοι νοεῖν, εἴτε τὸν οὕτως ἀριθμὸν τῶν ἀστέρων, ὃν ζωδιακὸν κύκλον Ἕλληνες καλοῦσι, τῆς κατ' ἐκεῖνον γνώμης οὐκ ἂν ἁμάρτοι· καὶ ὁ πῖλος δέ μοι δοκεῖ τὸν οὐρανὸν τεκμηριοῦν ὑακίνθινος πε- 187 ποιημένος, οὐ γὰρ ἂν ἄλλως ὑπερανετίθετο αὐτῷ τὸ ὄνομα τοῦ θεοῦ τῇ στεφάνῃ ἠγλαϊσμένον καὶ ταύτῃ χρυσέᾳ,[1] διὰ τὴν αὐγήν, ᾗ μάλιστα χαίρει τὸ θεῖον. καὶ ταῦτα μὲν ἐπὶ τοσοῦτόν μοι δεδηλώσθω πολλάκις τε καὶ ἐν πολλοῖς τὴν ἀρετὴν τοῦ νομοθέτου παρεξόντων ἡμῖν διελθεῖν τῶν πραγμάτων.

188 (viii. 1) Ὡς δὲ τὸ προειρημένον πέρας εἶχε, τῶν ἀναθημάτων μήπω καθιερωμένων ἐπιστὰς ὁ θεὸς Μωυσεῖ τὴν ἱερωσύνην Ἀαρῶνι τἀδελφῷ προσέταξε δοῦναι ὡς ἁπάντων δι' ἀρετὴν τῆς τιμῆς δικαιοτέρῳ τυχεῖν. καὶ συναγαγὼν εἰς ἐκκλησίαν τὸ πλῆθος τήν τε ἀρετὴν αὐτοῦ καὶ τὴν εὔνοιαν διεξῄει καὶ τοὺς κινδύνους οὓς ὑπομείνειεν ὑπὲρ 189 αὐτῶν. μαρτυρούντων δ' ἐφ' ἅπασιν αὐτῷ καὶ τὸ περὶ αὐτὸν πρόθυμον ἐνδεικνυμένων, " ἄνδρες," εἶπεν, " Ἰσραηλῖται, τὸ μὲν ἔργον ἤδη τέλος ἔχει οἷον αὐτῷ τε τῷ θεῷ ἥδιστον ἦν καὶ δυνατὸν ἡμῖν, ἐπεὶ δὲ δεῖ τοῦτον τῇ σκηνῇ καταδέχεσθαι, δεῖ πρῶτον ἡμῖν[2] τοῦ ἱερατευσομένου καὶ ὑπηρετήσοντος ταῖς θυσίαις καὶ ταῖς ὑπὲρ ἡμῶν εὐχαῖς.

[1] χρυσείᾳ SP.   [2] ὑμῖν ROSP : om. Lat.

[a] § 165. So Clement of Alexandria, *Strom.* v. 668 P. οἱ δύο ἄνθρακες διά τε τὸν Κρόνον καὶ τὴν Σελήνην; Philo mentions this explanation but prefers another, *De vita Mos.* ii. 12 (122).

pinned the high-priest's robe.[a] As for the twelve stones, whether one would prefer to read in them the months or the constellations of like number, which the Greeks call the circle of the zodiac, he will not mistake the lawgiver's intention. Furthermore, the head-dress appears to me to symbolize heaven, being blue ; else it would not have borne upon it the name of God, blazoned upon the crown—a crown, moreover, of gold by reason of that sheen in which the Deity most delights.[b] Let it suffice me to have pursued this topic thus far, since my subject will afford me frequent and ample occasion to discourse upon the merits of the lawgiver.

(viii. 1) Now when the work of which I have spoken was complete but the offerings had not yet been consecrated, God appeared to Moses and charged him to confer the priesthood upon Aaron his brother, as the man whose virtues rendered him more deserving than all to obtain this dignity. So, convening the people in assembly, he recounted his own merits, his benevolence, and the perils which he had sustained on their behalf. And when they attested that all his words were true and displayed their devotion to him, " Men of Israel," said he, " the work has now reached its end, as was best pleasing to God himself and as we had power to accomplish it ; but since it behoves us to receive Him into the tabernacle, we need first of all one to discharge the office of priest and minister for the sacrifices and for the intercessions on our behalf.

Aaron appointed high-priest. Ex. xxviii. 1 ; Lev. viii. 1.

---

[b] *Cf.* § 184; and Milton, *Par. Lost* iii. 3 "since God is light, And never but in unapproachèd light Dwelt from eternity."

JOSEPHUS

190 καὶ ἔγωγε ταύτης ἐμοὶ τῆς σκέψεως ἐπιτραπείσης ἐμαυτὸν ἂν τῆς τιμῆς ἄξιον ἔκρινα, διά τε τὸ φύσει πάντας εἶναι φιλαύτους καὶ ὅτι πολλὰ ἐμαυτῷ καμόντι περὶ σωτηρίας τῆς ὑμετέρας σύνοιδα· νῦν δ' αὐτὸς ὁ θεὸς Ἀαρῶνα τῆς τιμῆς [ταύτης]¹ ἄξιον ἔκρινε καὶ τοῦτον ᾕρηται ἱερέα,
191 τὸν δικαιότερον ἡμῶν² μᾶλλον εἰδώς, ὡς οὗτος ἐνδύσεται στολὴν τῷ θεῷ καθωσιωμένην καὶ βωμῶν ἐπιμέλειαν ἕξει καὶ πρόνοιαν ἱερείων καὶ τὰς ὑπὲρ ἡμῶν εὐχὰς ποιήσεται πρὸς τὸν θεὸν ἡδέως ἀκουσόμενον, ὅτι τε κήδεται γένους τοῦ ἡμετέρου καὶ παρ' ἀνδρὸς ὃν αὐτὸς ἐπελέξατο
192 γινομένας προσδέχεται ταύτας." Ἑβραῖοι δὲ ἠρέσκοντο τοῖς λεγομένοις καὶ συνῄνουν τῇ τοῦ θεοῦ χειροτονίᾳ· ἦν γὰρ Ἀαρὼν διά τε τὸ γένος καὶ τὴν προφητείαν καὶ τὴν ἀρετὴν τἀδελφοῦ πρὸς [τὴν]³ τιμὴν ἁπάντων ἀξιολογώτερος. ἦσαν δ' αὐτῷ καὶ παῖδες κατ' ἐκεῖνον τὸν χρόνον τέσσαρες Νάβαδος Ἀβιοῦς Ἐλεάζαρος Ἰθάμαρος.

193 (2) Ὅσα δὲ τῶν πρὸς τὴν τῆς σκηνῆς κατασκευὴν παρεσκευασμένων ἦν περιττά, ταῦτ' ἐκέλευσεν εἰς φάρση σκεπαστήρια τῆς τε σκηνῆς αὐτῆς καὶ τῆς λυχνίας καὶ τοῦ θυμιατηρίου καὶ τῶν ἄλλων σκευῶν ἀναλῶσαι, ὅπως κατὰ τὴν ὁδοιπορίαν ταῦτα μήτ' ἐξ ὑετοῦ μηδὲν μήτ' ἐκ
194 κονιορτοῦ βλάπτηται. τό τε πλῆθος ἀθροίσας

---

¹ om. RO. ² ex Lat.: ὑμῶν codd.
³ ins. MSL (Lat.): om. rell.

ᵃ So the Jewish Midrash on Lev. viii. 1 (quoted by Weill).
ᵇ Or " the more deserving of us (twain) " ; or possibly " knowing better than ourselves who is the more worthy to don " etc.

JEWISH ANTIQUITIES, III. 190-194

For my part, had the weighing of this matter been entrusted to me, I should have adjudged myself worthy of the dignity,[a] alike from that self-love that is innate in all, as also because I am conscious of having laboured abundantly for your salvation. But now God himself has judged Aaron worthy of this honour and has chosen him to be priest, knowing him to be the most deserving among us.[b] So it is he who will don the vestments consecrated to God, have charge of the altars, attend to the sacrifices, and offer the prayers on our behalf to God, who will gladly hear them, both from the care that He has for our race, and because, coming from a man of His own choosing, He cannot but accept them." The Hebrews were pleased with this speech and acquiesced in the divine election; for Aaron, by reason of his birth, his prophetical gift, and his brother's virtues, was more highly qualified than all for the dignity. He had at that time four sons: Nabad,[c] Abihu, Eleazar, and Ithamar.

(2) As for the surplus[d] of the materials provided for the furniture of the tabernacle, all these Moses ordered to be devoted to making protective coverings for the tabernacle itself, for the candelabrum, for the altar of incense, and for the other vessels, in order that these should suffer no injury on the march, whether from rain or dust. Then, assembling the

Coverings for the tabernacle.

---

[c] So, with transposition of consonants in a few LXX MSS., as opposed to the ordinary form "Nadab" (Ex. xxviii. 1).

[d] This sentence finds no parallel in Scripture. Weill suggests that "surplus" comes from Josephus having read the obscure word *serād*, rendered "finely wrought (garments)" in Ex. xxxi. 10 etc., as *sarid* "remaining over"; but the context of Exodus has nothing about protective coverings.

πάλιν εἰσφορὰν αὐτῷ προσέταξεν εἰσφέρειν σίκλου
195 τὸ ἥμισυ καθ' ἕκαστον, ὁ δὲ σίκλος νόμισμα
Ἑβραίων ὢν Ἀττικὰς δέχεται δραχμὰς τέσσαρας·
196 οἱ δ' ἑτοίμως ὑπήκουον οἷς ἐκέλευσε Μωυσῆς καὶ
τὸ πλῆθος τῶν εἰσφερόντων ἦν ἑξήκοντα μυριάδες
καὶ πεντακισχίλιοι καὶ πεντακόσιοι καὶ πεντήκοντα. ἔφερον δὲ τὸ ἀργύριον τῶν ἐλευθέρων οἱ
ἀπὸ εἴκοσι ἐτῶν ἄχρι πεντήκοντα γεγονότες. τὸ
δὲ συγκομισθὲν εἰς τὰς περὶ τὴν σκηνὴν χρείας
ἀναλοῦτο.
197 (3) Ἥγνιζε δὲ καὶ τὴν σκηνὴν καὶ τοὺς ἱερέας
τρόπῳ τοιούτῳ ποιούμενος αὐτῶν τὴν κάθαρσιν.
σμύρνης ἐπιλέκτου σίκλους πεντακοσίους καὶ ἴρεως
ἴσους, κινναμώμου δὲ καὶ καλάμου, ἔστι δὲ καὶ
τοῦτο εἶδος θυμιάματος, ἡμίσειαν τῶν πρότερον
ὁλκὴν κεκομμένα δεύειν ἐκέλευσεν, ἐλαίου τε
ἐλαΐνου εἶν, μέτρον δ' ἐστὶ τοῦτο ἐπιχώριον δύο
χόας Ἀττικοὺς δεχόμενον, ἀναμίξαντας καὶ καθ-
εψήσαντας σκευάσαι τέχνῃ μυρεψῶν χρῖσμα εὐ-
198 ωδέστατον. κἄπειτα τοῦτο λαβὼν αὐτούς τε τοὺς
ἱερέας καὶ πᾶσαν τὴν σκηνὴν χρίων κεκάθαρκε,
τά τε θυμιώμενα, πολλὰ δ' ἐστὶ ταῦτα καὶ ποικίλα,
κατὰ τὴν σκηνὴν ἐπὶ τοῦ χρυσοῦ θυμιατηρίου
μεγάλης πάνυ τιμῆς ὄντα συνεφέρετο, ὧν παρα-
λείπω τὴν φύσιν ἐκδιηγεῖσθαι, μὴ δι' ὄχλου
199 γένηται τοῖς ἐντυγχάνουσι. δὶς δὲ τῆς ἡμέρας
πρίν τε ἀνασχεῖν τὸν ἥλιον καὶ πρὸς δυσμαῖς
θυμιᾶν ἐχρῆν ἔλαιόν τε ἁγνίσαντας φυλάσσειν εἰς
τοὺς λύχνους, ὧν τοὺς μὲν τρεῖς ἐπὶ τῇ ἱερᾷ

[a] The annual poll-tax imposed on Jews for the upkeep of

people again, he imposed on them a contribution of half a shekel *a* for each man, the shekel being a Hebrew coin equivalent to four Attic drachms.*b* They promptly obeyed this behest of Moses and the number of contributors amounted to 605,550,*c* the money being brought by all free men aged from twenty years up to fifty. The sum thus collected was expended upon the needs of the tabernacle.

The half-shekel contribution.
Ex. xxx. 11 ff.

(3) Furthermore he sanctified both the tabernacle and the priests, proceeding on this wise to their purification. Five hundred shekels of choice myrrh, an equal quantity of iris, with half that weight of cinnamon and calamus *d* (another species of perfume) were, by his orders, to be pounded and soaked; a *hin* of olive oil (the *hin* being a native measure equivalent to two Attic *choes*) was to be mixed therewith and the whole concocted and boiled down by the perfumer's art into an ointment of sweetest fragrance. Then, taking this, he anointed both the priests themselves and all the tabernacle, thus purifying all. Also the perfumes, of which there were many of divers kinds, were all assembled in the tabernacle on the golden altar of incense, being of exceeding value; their nature I forbear to describe from fear of wearying my readers. But twice each day, before sunrise and at sunset, it was requisite to burn incense and to sanctify oil in reservation for the lamps, three of

The anointing oil and perfumes of purification.
Ib. 22.

Cf. 2 Chron. xiii. 11.

the temple up to its destruction in A.D. 70, when the tax was confiscated by the Romans (*B.J.* vii. 218).

b Reinach disputes this computation; but at least it accords with the use of δίδραχμον for the half-shekel tax, which is found not only in Josephus (*A.* xviii. 312, *cf. B.J. loc. cit.*) but in Matt. xvii. 24.

c Heb. and LXX "603,550" (Ex. xxxviii. 26).

d The Greek names for these perfumes are those used in LXX.

λυχνία φέγγειν ἔδει τῷ θεῷ κατὰ πᾶσαν ἡμέραν, τοὺς δὲ λοιποὺς περὶ τὴν ἑσπέραν ἅπτοντας.

200 (4) Ἁπάντων δ' ἤδη πέρας εἰληφότων ἔδοξαν ἄριστοι τῶν δημιουργῶν Βεσελέηλος[1] καὶ Ἐλίαβος, τῶν γὰρ ἐξευρημένων τοῖς προτέροις αὐτοὶ προεθυμήθησαν ἀμείνονα προσεξεργάσασθαι, λαβεῖν τε ἐπίνοιαν ὧν πρότερον ἠγνόουν τὴν κατασκευὴν ἱκανώτατοι· τούτων μέντοι Βεσελέηλον συνέβη 201 κριθῆναι τὸν κράτιστον. ὁ δὲ πᾶς χρόνος εἰς τὸ ἔργον διῆλθε μηνῶν ἑπτὰ καὶ μετὰ τοῦτο ἀφ' οὗ τὴν Αἴγυπτον ἐξέλιπον ἐνιαυτὸς αὐτοῖς πρῶτος ἐτελειοῦτο. ἀρχομένου δὲ τοῦ δευτέρου ἔτους, μηνὶ Ξανθικῷ κατὰ Μακεδόνας Νισὰν δὲ κατὰ Ἑβραίους, νουμηνίᾳ τὴν σκηνὴν ἀφιεροῦσι καὶ πάνθ' ὅσα περὶ αὐτὴν σκεύη μοι δεδήλωται.

202 (5) Ἐπέδειξε δὲ ὁ θεὸς αὐτὸν ἡσθέντα τῷ ἔργῳ τῶν Ἑβραίων καὶ μὴ μάτην αὐτοὺς πονήσαντας ὑπερηφανίᾳ τῆς χρήσεως, ἀλλ' ἐπεξενώθη καὶ κατεσκήνωσε⟨ν ἐν⟩ τῷ ναῷ τούτῳ. τὴν δὲ παρ- 203 ουσίαν οὕτως ἐποίησεν· ὁ μὲν οὐρανὸς καθαρὸς ἦν, ὑπὲρ δὲ τὴν σκηνὴν μόνην ἤχλυσεν οὔτε βαθεῖ πάνυ νέφει καὶ πυκνῷ περιλαβὼν αὐτήν, ὥστ' εἶναι δόξαι χειμέριον, οὔτε μὴν λεπτὸν οὕτως, ὥστε τὴν ὄψιν ἰσχῦσαί τι δι' αὐτοῦ κατανοῆσαι· ἡδεῖα δὲ ἀπ' αὐτοῦ δρόσος ἔρρει καὶ θεοῦ δηλοῦσα παρουσίαν τοῖς τοῦτο καὶ βουλομένοις καὶ πεπιστευκόσι.

[1] Βεσέβηλος RM; *sic infra* Βεσέβηλον M; *cf.* § 105.

[a] From the Bible it appears that the lamps were lit only at even (Ex. xxx. 8, 1 Sam. iii. 3), but ambiguous phrases in other passages gave rise to conflicting traditions. That given by Josephus is said to have the support of the oldest

which had to be kept burning on the holy candelabrum in God's honour throughout the day, the rest being lit at even.[a]

(4) Everything having now been completed, the craftsmen who were pronounced the most excellent were Beseleêl and Eliab, for to the inventions of their predecessors they were zealous to add others yet better and were most capable in contriving objects the fabrication of which was till then unknown; but of the two Beseleêl was adjudged the best. The whole time occupied upon the work was seven months,[b] at the close of which was completed their first year since their departure from Egypt. It was at the beginning of the second year, in the month of Xanthicus according to the Macedonians and of Nisan according to the Hebrews, on the new moon, that they consecrated the tabernacle with all the vessels pertaining thereto which I have described.

The craftsmen.

The consecration of the tabernacle. Ex. xl. 17.

(5) Then did God manifest that He was well pleased with the work of the Hebrews and, far from rendering their labour vain by disdaining to make use of it,[c] He came as their guest and took up His abode in this sanctuary. And it was on this wise that He made his entry. While the heaven was serene, over the tabernacle alone darkness descended, enveloping it in a cloud not so profound and dense as might be attributed to winter storm, nor yet so tenuous that the eye could perceive a thing through it; but a delicious dew[d] was distilled therefrom, revealing God's presence to those who both desired it and believed in it.

Manifestation of God's presence. Ib. 34.

Rabbinical commentary on Numbers and Deuteronomy (*Sifré*, p. 16 a, quoted by Weill).
[b] Reckoning not in Scripture.
[c] Text doubtful.   [d] Not in Scripture.

204 (6) Μωυσῆς δὲ τοὺς τέκτονας οἵαις εἰκὸς ἦν δωρεαῖς τοὺς τοιαῦτα ἐργασαμένους τιμήσας ἔθυεν ἐν τῷ τῆς σκηνῆς αἰθρίῳ κατὰ προσταγὴν τοῦ θεοῦ ταῦρον καὶ κριὸν καὶ ἔριφον ὑπὲρ ἁμαρτάδων,
205 καὶ δή, λέγειν γὰρ ἐν τοῖς περὶ θυσιῶν μέλλω τὰ πρασσόμενα περὶ τὰς ἱερουργίας ἐν ἐκείνοις δηλώσων περί τε ὧν ὁλοκαυτεῖν κελεύει καὶ ὧν μεταλαμβάνειν τῆς βρώσεως ἐφίησιν ὁ νόμος, κἀκ τοῦ αἵματος τῶν τεθυμένων τήν τε στολὴν τοῦ Ἀαρῶνος καὶ αὐτὸν σὺν τοῖς παισὶν ἔρραινεν ἀφαγνίσας πηγαίοις τε ὕδασι καὶ μύρῳ, ἵνα τοῦ θεοῦ γί-
206 γνοιντο. ἐπὶ μὲν οὖν ἡμέρας ἑπτὰ τοῦτον τὸν τρόπον αὐτούς τε καὶ τὰς στολὰς ἐθεράπευε τήν τε σκηνὴν καὶ τὰ περὶ αὐτὴν σκεύη ἐλαίῳ τε προθυμιωμένῳ,[1] καθὼς εἶπον, καὶ τῷ αἵματι τῶν ταύρων καὶ κριῶν σφαγέντων καθ' ἑκάστην ἡμέραν ἑνὸς κατὰ γένος, τῇ δὲ ὀγδόῃ κατήγγειλεν ἑορτὴν
207 τῷ λαῷ καὶ θύειν προσέταξε κατὰ δύναμιν. οἱ δ' ἀλλήλοις ἁμιλλώμενοι καὶ ὑπερβάλλειν φιλοτιμούμενοι τὰς θυσίας, ἃς ἕκαστος ἐπιφέροι, τοῖς λεγομένοις ὑπήκουον. ἐπικειμένων δὲ τῶν ἱερῶν[2] τῷ βωμῷ αἰφνίδιον ἐξ αὐτῶν[3] πῦρ ἀνήφθη αὐτόματον, καὶ ὅμοιον ἀστραπῆς λαμπηδόνι ὁρώμενον τῇ φλογὶ πάντα ἐδαπάνα τὰ ἐπὶ τοῦ βωμοῦ.
208 (7) Συνέβη δὲ καὶ Ἀαρῶνι συμφορά τις ἐκ τού-

[1] ML: προθυομένῳ SPE: προχριομένων(ν) O(R).
[2] ἱερείων SPL. [3] αὐτοῦ RO.

[a] The projected work on "Customs and Causes" often mentioned already: not, I think, "when I come to speak of the sacrifices later on": §§ 224 ff. do not contain the detailed information here promised. The text here (a parenthesis, perhaps a P.S.) and below (§§ 213 f., 218, 223 f.)

JEWISH ANTIQUITIES, III. 204-208

(6) Moses, after recompensing with fitting bounties the craftsmen who had executed works so excellent, sacrificed in the outer court of the tabernacle, as enjoined by God, a bull, a ram, and a kid as atonement for sins. (I propose in my treatise on sacrifices [a] to speak of the ritual of these sacred ceremonies, and to indicate there in which cases the law ordains a holocaust of the victim, and in which it permits a portion to be used for consumption.) Then, with the blood of the victims, he sprinkled Aaron's vestments and Aaron himself, together with his sons, purging them with water from the spring and with sweet oil, in order to devote them to God. So for seven days he continued this process, purifying both them and their vestments, as also the tabernacle and its vessels, both with oil that had been previously fumigated, as I have said,[b] and with the blood of bulls and of goats, of which they slaughtered every day one of each sort; then on the eighth day he announced a feast for the people and bade them offer sacrifices, each according to his means. They thereupon, vying with and striving to surpass one another in their respective offerings, obeyed these behests. And when the victims were laid upon the altar, of a sudden a fire blazed up therefrom spontaneously, and, like a flash of lightning before their eyes, consumed everything upon the altar in flame.

Inaugural ceremonies. Ex. xxix. 1; Lev. viii. 1.

Ib. ix. 24.

(7) But this fire was also the cause of a misfortune

betrays signs of rewriting. The author seems to be in doubt how much to include in the present work on the sacrifices, how much to reserve for a separate treatise, and breaks off more than once from the subject. Probably, when the projected treatise was finally abandoned, he incorporated much more of its intended contents in later editions of the *Antiquities*.   [b] § 199.

JOSEPHUS

του λογιζομένῳ ὡς ἐπ' ἀνθρώπῳ καὶ πατρί, γενναίως δ' ὑπ' αὐτοῦ καρτερηθεῖσα, ὅτι καὶ τὴν ψυχὴν πρὸς τὰ συμπίπτοντα στερρὸς ἦν καὶ κατὰ 209 βούλησιν τοῦ θεοῦ ἡγεῖτο τὸ πάθος γεγονέναι· τῶν γὰρ υἱῶν αὐτοῦ τεσσάρων ὄντων, ὡς προεῖπον, δύο οἱ πρεσβύτεροι Νάβαδος καὶ Ἀβιοῦς κομίσαντες ἐπὶ τὸν βωμὸν οὐχ ὧν προεῖπε Μωυσῆς θυμιαμάτων,[1] ἀλλ' οἷς ἐχρῶντο πρότερον, κατεκαύθησαν τοῦ πυρὸς ἐπ' αὐτοὺς τὴν ὁρμὴν βαλόντος καὶ τὰ στέρνα καὶ τὰ πρόσωπα φλέγειν αὐτῶν 210 ἀρξαμένου καὶ σβέσαι μηδενὸς δυναμένου. καὶ οἱ μὲν οὕτως ἀπέθανον, Μωυσῆς δὲ κελεύει τὸν πατέρα αὐτῶν καὶ τοὺς ἀδελφοὺς βαστάξαντας τὰ σώματα καὶ κομίσαντας τῆς παρεμβολῆς ἔξω θάψαι μεγαλοπρεπῶς. πενθεῖ δὲ αὐτοὺς τὸ πλῆθος χαλεπῶς ἐπὶ τῷ θανάτῳ παρὰ δόξαν οὕτω γεγενη- 211 μένῳ διατεθέν. μόνους δὲ Μωυσῆς τοὺς ἀδελφοὺς αὐτῶν καὶ τὸν πατέρα μὴ φροντίζειν τῆς ἐπ' αὐτοῖς λύπης ἠξίωσε, προκρίναντας τὴν εἰς τὸν θεὸν τιμὴν τοῦ περὶ αὐτοὺς σκυθρωποῦ· ἤδη γὰρ Ἀαρὼν καὶ τὴν στολὴν τὴν ἱερὰν ἠμφίεστο.

212 (8) Μωυσῆς δὲ πᾶσαν τιμὴν παραιτησάμενος, ἣν ἑώρα τὸ πλῆθος αὐτῷ παρασχεῖν ἕτοιμον, πρὸς μόνῃ τῇ τοῦ θεοῦ θεραπείᾳ διετέλει. καὶ τῶν μὲν εἰς τὸ Σιναῖον ἀνόδων ἀπείχετο, εἰς δὲ τὴν σκηνὴν εἰσιὼν ἐχρηματίζετο περὶ ὧν ἐδεῖτο παρὰ τοῦ θεοῦ, ἰδιωτεύων καὶ τῇ στολῇ καὶ πᾶσι τοῖς ἄλλοις ἄγων ἑαυτὸν δημοτικώτερον καὶ μηδὲν βουλόμενος τῶν πολλῶν διαφέρειν δοκεῖν ἢ μόνῳ 213 τῷ προνοούμενος αὐτῶν βλέπεσθαι. ἔτι δὲ τὴν

[1] O: θυμάτων rell.

[a] § 192.   [b] Bibl. Nadab (§ 192 note).

for Aaron, if regarded as a man and a father, albeit the blow was valiantly borne by him, because he had a soul steeled against accidents and believed that it was by God's will that the tragedy befell. For he had four sons, as I have already mentioned,[a] and of these the two eldest, Nabad[b] and Abihu, having brought to the altar, not the incense which Moses had prescribed, but such as they had used aforetime, were burnt to death, the fire darting out upon them and beginning to consume their breasts and faces while none could extinguish it. Thus they died; and Moses bade their father and their brethren[c] take up their corpses, convey them without the camp, and give them lordly burial. They were mourned by the multitude, who were grievously affected by the death which had so unexpectedly befallen them; their brethren and their father alone did Moses require to refrain from any thoughts of grief for them, putting the homage due to God above any frowning over their loss. For Aaron had already been invested with the priestly robes.

(8) Moses, for his part, having declined every honour which he saw that the people were ready to confer on him, devoted himself solely to the service of God. Desisting from further ascents of Sinai, he now entered the tabernacle and there received responses on all that he besought from God; dressed like any ordinary person, in all else he bore himself as a simple commoner, who desired in nothing to appear different from the crowd, save only in being seen to have their interests at heart. Furthermore,

---

[c] In Lev. x. 4 it is "Mishael and Elzaphan, the sons of Uzziel the uncle of Aaron" who are instructed to remove the corpses.

JOSEPHUS

πολιτείαν καὶ νόμους [αὐτῶν]¹ ἔγραφε, καθ' οὓς κεχαρισμένως τῷ θεῷ βιώσονται μηδὲν ἀλλήλοις ἐγκαλεῖν ἔχοντες· ταῦτα μέντοι κατὰ τὴν ὑπαγόρευσιν τοῦ θεοῦ συνετάττετο. διέξειμι μὲν οὖν περὶ τῆς πολιτείας καὶ τῶν νόμων.

214 (9) Ὃ μέντοι περὶ τῆς τοῦ ἀρχιερέως στολῆς παρέλιπον διελθεῖν βούλομαι· οὐδαμόθεν γὰρ προφητῶν² κακουργίαις κατέλιπεν ἀφορμήν, εἰ καὶ³ τινες τοιοῦτοι γένοιντο παρεγχειρεῖν τῷ τοῦ θεοῦ ἀξιώματι, αὐτοκράτορα δ' εἶναι τὸν θεὸν παρατυγχάνειν τοῖς ἱεροῖς κατέλιπεν ὁπότε θελήσειε καὶ μὴ παρεῖναι, καὶ τοῦτ' οὐχ Ἑβραίοις δῆλον εἶναι μόνον ἠθέλησεν, ἀλλὰ καὶ τῶν ξένων τοῖς παρα-
215 τυγχάνουσι. τῶν γὰρ λίθων, οὓς ἐπὶ τοῖς ὤμοις φέρειν τὸν ἀρχιερέα προεῖπον, σαρδόνυχες δὲ ἦσαν καὶ σημαίνειν αὐτῶν τὴν φύσιν ἡγοῦμαι περισσὸν πᾶσιν εἰς γνῶσιν ἀφιγμένων, συνέβαινε λάμπειν, ὁπότε ταῖς ἱερουργίαις ὁ θεὸς παρείη, τὸν ἕτερον τὸν ἐπὶ τῷ δεξιῷ τῶν ὤμων πεπορπημένον αὐγῆς ἀποπηδώσης καὶ τοῖς πορρωτάτω φαινομένης, οὐ
216 πρότερον ταύτης ὑπαρχούσης τῷ λίθῳ. θαυμαστὸν μὲν οὖν καὶ τοῦτο τοῖς μὴ τὴν σοφίαν ἐπ' ἐκ-

¹ ins. RO: om. rell.
² συκοφαντῶν SPL. ³ O: δέ rell.

---

^a In fact we have a little below chapters on the sacrifices and laws of purity connected therewith (§§ 224-273), followed by marriage and other laws (§§ 274-286); the summary of the "constitution" or Mosaic code as a whole is postponed to the next book (iv. 196 ff.). See notes on § 205 and § 222.
^b § 165.
^c What follows is the author's interpretation of the mysterious Urim and Thummim (words meaning "Lights and Per-

he was committing to writing their constitution and laws, in accordance with which they would live a life well-pleasing to God, without any cause for mutual reproach; all this, however, he drew up under the inspiration of God. I will proceed, then, to dilate on the constitution and the laws.*a*

(9) However, I would here record a detail which I omitted concerning the vestments of the high-priest. For Moses left no possible opening for the malpractices of prophets, should there in fact be any capable of abusing the divine prerogative, but left to God supreme authority whether to attend the sacred rites, when it so pleased Him, or to absent himself; and this he wished to be made manifest not to Hebrews only but also to any strangers who chanced to be present. Well, of those stones which, as I said before,*b* the high-priest wore upon his shoulders—they were sardonyxes, and I deem it superfluous to indicate the nature of jewels familiar to all—it came about, whenever God assisted at the sacred ceremonies, that the one that was buckled on the right shoulder began to shine,*c* a light glancing from it, visible to the most distant, of which the stone had before betrayed no trace. That alone should be marvel enough for such as have not culti-

Oracular flashing of the stones on the high-priest's robes.

fections "), and an erroneous one. All that can be said with certainty about these primitive objects of divination is that they were something distinct from the stones on shoulder and breastplate and were kept *within* the latter: "And thou shalt put *in* the breastplate (or "pouch") of judgement the Urim and the Thummim" (Ex. xxviii. 30). The LXX rendering of that passage, καὶ ἐπιθήσεις ἐπὶ (*on*) τὸ λόγιον τῆς κρίσεως τὴν δήλωσιν καὶ τὴν ἀλήθειαν, and its rendering elsewhere (Numb. xxvii. 21) of Urim by δῆλοι (*sc.* λίθοι, "conspicuous stones") seems to have led to the interpretation in the text. See Hastings, *D.B. s.v.*

JOSEPHUS

φαυλισμῷ τῶν θείων ἠσκηκόσιν, ὃ δ' ἐστὶ τούτου
θαυμασιώτερον ἐρῶ· διὰ γὰρ τῶν δώδεκα λίθων,
οὓς κατὰ στέρνον ὁ ἀρχιερεὺς ἐνερραμμένους τῷ
ἐσσῆνι φορεῖ, νίκην μέλλουσι πολεμεῖν προεμήνυεν
217 ὁ θεός· τοσαύτη γὰρ ἀπήστραπτεν ἀπ' αὐτῶν αὐγὴ
μήπω στρατιᾶς κεκινημένης, ὡς τῷ πλήθει
παντὶ γνώριμον εἶναι τὸ παρεῖναι τὸν θεὸν εἰς
τὴν ἐπικουρίαν, ὅθεν Ἕλληνες οἱ τὰ ἡμέτερα
τιμῶντες ἔθη διὰ τὸ μηδὲν ἀντιλέγειν δύνασθαι
218 τούτοις τὸν ἐσσῆνα λόγιον καλοῦσιν. ἐπαύσατο
μὲν οὖν ὅ τε ἐσσὴν καὶ ὁ σαρδόνυξ τοῦ λάμπειν
ἔτεσι διακοσίοις πρότερον ἢ ταύτην ἐμὲ συνθεῖναι
τὴν γραφήν, τοῦ θεοῦ δυσχεράναντος ἐπὶ τῇ
παραβάσει τῶν νόμων, περὶ ὧν ἐροῦμεν εὐκαιρό-
τερον. τρέψομαι δὲ νῦν ἐπὶ τὸν ἑξῆς λόγον.

219 (10) Καθιερωμένης γὰρ ἤδη[1] τῆς σκηνῆς καὶ
διακεκοσμημένων τῶν περὶ τοὺς ἱερέας τό τε
πλῆθος ὁμόσκηνον αὐτῷ τὸν θεὸν ἔκρινεν εἶναι
καὶ τρέπεται πρὸς θυσίας τε καὶ ἀνέσεις[2] ὡς
ἅπασαν ἤδη κακοῦ προσδοκίαν ἀπεωσμένον, καὶ
περὶ τῶν μελλόντων ὡς ἀμεινόνων εὐθυμοῦντες[3]
δωρεάς τε τῷ θεῷ τὰς μὲν κοινῇ τὰς δὲ [καὶ][4]
220 κατ' ἰδίαν ἀνετίθεσαν κατὰ φυλάς. οἵ τε γὰρ
φύλαρχοι κατὰ δύο συνελθόντες ἅμαξαν καὶ δύο
βόας προσκομίζουσιν· ἓξ μὲν οὖν ἦσαν αὗται καὶ

---

[1] δὴ RO. [2] ex Lat. requiem: αἰνέσεις codd.
[3] conj. Cocceii: ἐπιθυμοῦντες codd. [4] om. RO.

---

[a] λόγιον is the LXX version of the Heb. word rendered in the E.V. "breastplate," Ex. xxviii. 15 etc.
[b] The work was completed in A.D. 93–94 (xx. 267) and was probably 15 or more years in the making. The 200 years

JEWISH ANTIQUITIES, III. 216-220

vated a superior wisdom to disparage all religious things; but I have yet a greater marvel to record. By means of the twelve stones, which the high-priest wore upon his breast stitched into the *essên*, God foreshowed victory to those on the eve of battle. For so brilliant a light flashed out from them, ere the army was yet in motion, that it was evident to the whole host that God had come to their aid. Hence it is that those Greeks who revere our practices, because they can in no way gainsay them, call the *essên logion* ("oracle").*a* Howbeit, *essên* and sardonyx alike ceased to shine two hundred years before I composed this work,*b* because of God's displeasure at the transgression of the laws. But of them we shall have a better opportunity to speak; for the present I will revert to the course of my narrative.

(10) The tabernacle having now been consecrated and all arrangements made relating to the priests, the people, assured of God's fellowship with them in the tent, gave themselves up to the offering of sacrifices and to relaxation,*c* believing themselves at last to have banished all prospect of ill and in cheerful confidence that the future had better things in store; and, tribe by tribe, they offered gifts, whether public or private, to God. Thus the tribal leaders came two and two, each pair bringing a wagon and two oxen, there being six such wagons

Offerings of the tribal chiefs.
Numb. vii. 1.

take us back to the close of the theocracy at the death of John Hyrcanus (135-105 B.C.), the prophet who "was so closely in touch with the Deity that he was never ignorant of the future" (*B.J.* i. 69). But the statement is unsupported. According to Palestinian tradition the oracle of Urim and Thummim ceased earlier, "at the death of the first prophets" after the return from captivity (*Sota* ix. 14, quoted by Weill).

c Or, with another reading, "praises."

421

τὴν σκηνὴν ἐν ταῖς ὁδοιπορίαις παρεκόμιζον. πρὸς τούτοις ἕκαστος φιάλην τε κομίζει καὶ τρύβλιον καὶ θυΐσκην, τὴν μὲν δαρεικοὺς δέκα δυναμένην 221 καὶ πλήρη θυμιαμάτων· τὸ δὲ τρύβλιον καὶ ἡ φιάλη, ἀργυρᾶ δὲ ἦν, σίκλους μὲν αἱ δύο διακοσίους εἷλκον, εἰς δὲ τὴν φιάλην ἑβδομήκοντα μόνοι δεδαπάνηντο, πλήρεις δὲ ἦσαν ἀλεύρων ἐλαίῳ πεφυραμένων, οἷς ἐπὶ τῷ βωμῷ χρῶνται πρὸς τὰς ἱερουργίας· μόσχον τε καὶ κριὸν σὺν ἀρνίῳ τῶν ἐτησίων[1] ὁλομελῆ καυθησόμενα καὶ σὺν αὐτοῖς 222 χίμαρον ἐπὶ παραιτήσει ἁμαρτημάτων. προσῆγε δὲ τῶν ἀρχόντων ἕκαστος καὶ ἑτέρας θυσίας σωτηρίους λεγομένας καθ' ἑκάστην ἡμέραν δύο βόας καὶ πέντε κριοὺς σὺν ἀρνάσιν ἐτείοις καὶ ἐρίφοις. οὗτοι μὲν δὴ θύουσιν ἐπὶ ἡμέρας δώδεκα κατὰ πᾶσαν ἡμέραν εἷς· Μωυσῆς δὲ οὐκέτ' ἀναβαίνων ἐπὶ τὸ Σιναῖον ἀλλ' εἰς τὴν σκηνὴν εἰσιὼν ἀνεμάνθανε παρὰ θεοῦ περί τε τῶν πρακτέων καὶ 223 τῶν νόμων τῆς συντάξεως· οὓς κρείττονας ἢ κατὰ σύνεσιν ἀνθρωπίνην ὄντας εἰς τὸν ἅπαντα βεβαίως αἰῶνα συνέβη φυλαχθῆναι, δωρεὰν εἶναι δόξαντας τοῦ θεοῦ, ὡς μήτ' ἐν εἰρήνῃ ὑπὸ τρυφῆς μήτ' ἐν πολέμῳ κατ' ἀνάγκην Ἑβραίους παραβῆναί τινα τῶν νόμων. ἀλλὰ περὶ μὲν τούτων παύομαι

[1] τῶν ἐτ.] ἐτείῳ RO.

---

[a] Or "platter"; the Greek terms used for the three articles are those employed by the LXX (Numb. vii. 13 f., E.V. "charger ... bowl ... spoon").

JEWISH ANTIQUITIES, III. 220-223

which transported the tabernacle on the march. Furthermore, each of them brought a salver,[a] a bowl, and a censer, this last being of the value of ten darics [b] and filled with materials for incense. As for the bowl and the salver, which were of silver, the two together weighed 200 shekels, but to the salver were devoted but seventy; these were full of flour of wheat saturated in oil, such as they use on the altar for the sacrifices. They brought too a calf and a ram, with a lamb of a year old, all these to be burnt whole, along with a kid to make intercession for sins. Each of the chiefs brought moreover other sacrifices called those " of salvation," [c] each day two oxen, five rams, with as many lambs of a year old and kids. These chiefs thus continued to sacrifice for twelve days, one on each day.

Meanwhile Moses,[d] no longer ascending Mount Sinai but entering into the tabernacle, was there diligently seeking instruction from God on duties to be done and on the compilation of the laws. Those laws, excellent beyond the standard of human wisdom, have, so it has come to pass, been in every age rigidly observed, because they are believed to be a gift of God, insomuch that neither in peace, through luxury, nor in war, under constraint, have Hebrews transgressed any one of them. But I for-

Numb. vii. 89.

---

[b] A Persian gold coin; Heb. and LXX (Numb. vii. 14) name no coin; E.V. "ten *shekels.*"

[c] Or " deliverance " " welfare," after LXX: Heb. *shelāmim,* E.V. "peace-offerings." They are referred to below as "thank-offerings" ($\dot{\eta}$ χαριστήριος § 225).

[d] This sentence is a repetition of part of §§ 212 f.; the "doublet" again suggests (*cf.* § 205 note) that the text has been worked over without being thoroughly revised. For "doublets" as indicating interpolation see Laqueur, *Der jüd. Historiker Fl. Josephus,* pp. 65, 88 etc.

JOSEPHUS

λέγων γραφὴν ἑτέραν ἠξιωκὼς συνθεῖναι περὶ τῶν νόμων.

224 (ix. 1) Νυνὶ δ' ὀλίγων τινῶν ἐπιμνησθήσομαι τῶν ἐφ' ἁγνείαις καὶ ἱερουργίαις κειμένων· καὶ γὰρ τὸν λόγον μοι περὶ τῶν θυσιῶν ἐνεστάναι συμβέβηκε. δύο μὲν γάρ εἰσιν ἱερουργίαι, τούτων δ' ἡ μὲν ὑπὸ τῶν ἰδιωτῶν ἑτέρα δ' ὑπὸ τοῦ δήμου 225 συντελούμεναι κατὰ δύο γίνονται τρόπους· τῆς μὲν ὁλοκαυτεῖται πᾶν τὸ θυόμενον καὶ διὰ τοῦτο καὶ τὴν προσηγορίαν τοιαύτην ἔλαβεν, ἡ δὲ χαριστήριός τέ ἐστι καὶ κατ' εὐωχίαν δρᾶται τῶν 226 τεθυκότων· ἐρῶ δὲ περὶ τῆς προτέρας. ἀνὴρ ἰδιώτης ὁλοκαυτῶν θύει μὲν βοῦν καὶ ἀρνίον καὶ ἔριφον· ταῦτα μὲν ἐπέτεια, τοὺς δὲ βοῦς ἐφεῖται θύειν καὶ προήκοντας· ἄρρενα δὲ ὁλοκαυτεῖται τὰ πάντα. σφαγέντων δὲ τούτων τὸν κύκλον τῷ 227 αἵματι δεύουσι τοῦ βωμοῦ οἱ ἱερεῖς, εἶτα καθαρὰ ποιήσαντες διαμελίζουσι καὶ πάσαντες ἁλσὶν ἐπὶ τὸν βωμὸν ἀνατιθέασι σχιζῶν ἤδη πεπληρωμένον

---

^a i.e. in the projected " Customs and Causes " (§ 205 note). This raises a doubt whether in the parallel passage (§ 213) he refers to the projected or to the present work.

^b Or " purity laws," referring to cap. xi. §§ 258 ff. (see § 273 in particular).

^c Philo draws the same distinction, τῶν θυσιῶν αἱ μέν εἰσιν ὑπὲρ ἅπαντος τοῦ ἔθνους . . . αἱ δ' ὑπὲρ ἑκάστου (*De Victimis* 3, § 168, quoted by Weill).

^d The meaning " holocaust " (LXX ὁλοκαύτωμα or -καύτωσις E.V. " burnt-offering ") is not inherent in the Hebrew *'ōlāh*, which strictly = " that which goes up " to heaven.

^e Details not in Scripture. Throughout these chapters on ritual Josephus borrows to some extent from tradition ; for the full Rabbinical parallels the reader should consult the invaluable commentary of M. Weill (in the French trans-

JEWISH ANTIQUITIES, III. 223-227

bear to say more about them, having resolved to compose another treatise upon these laws.[a]

(ix. 1) Here I will but mention some few of the regulations concerning purifications [b] and the ritual of sacrifice, since I have been led to speak of the sacrifices. There are two kinds of sacrifice—one offered by individuals, the other by the community [c] —taking two distinct forms. In the first, the whole of the sacrificial victim is burnt entire, whence the sacrifice derives its corresponding name [d]; the other is of the nature of a thank-offering and performed with the intention of providing a feast for those who have offered it. I will begin by speaking of the first type. An individual who offers a holocaust kills an ox, a lamb, and a kid, these last being a year old; the slain oxen may be older than this [e]; but all victims for these holocausts must be males.[f] The beasts being slaughtered, the priests drench with the blood the circuit [g] of the altar, and then, after cleansing them,[h] dismember them, sprinkle them with salt,[i] and lay them upon the altar, already laden

SACRIFICES of various kinds. Whole burnt-offerings. Lev. i. 1.

i. 3, 10.

i. 5, 11.

---

lation, ed. T. Reinach), to which the present writer is deeply indebted. See also G. F. Moore's art. "Sacrifice" in *Encycl. Bibl.* According to tradition (*Para* i. 3) lambs and kids, as well as oxen, might be over a year old.

[f] All quadrupeds (Lev. i. 3, 10); for birds, not mentioned by Josephus, Leviticus (i. 14) laid down no similar restriction and tradition permitted the use of females.

[g] So Lev. i. 5: traditionally only the N.E. and S.W. corners.

[h] Lev. specifies only the washing of inwards and legs, mentioned below; but 2 Chron. iv. 6 suggests complete cleansing.

[i] The regulation of Lev. ii. 13, though there confined to the "meal offering," was taken to apply to all sacrifices.

425

καὶ πυρὸς φλεγομένου. τοὺς δὲ πόδας τῶν ἱερείων καὶ τὰ κατὰ νηδὺν ἐκκαθάραντες ἀκριβῶς τοῖς ἄλλοις καθαγνισθησόμενα προσεπιφέρουσι, τὰς δορὰς τῶν ἱερέων λαμβανόντων. καὶ ὁ μὲν τῆς ὁλοκαυτώσεως τρόπος ἐστὶν οὗτος.

228 (2) Τὰς δὲ χαριστηρίους θυσίας ἐπιτελοῦντες ταὐτὰ μὲν ζῷα θύουσιν, ὁλόκληρα δὲ ταῦτα καὶ τῶν ἐπετείων πρεσβύτερα, ἄρρενα μέντοι θήλεσι συνδυαζόμενα. θύσαντες δὲ ταῦτα φοινίσσουσι μὲν αἵματι τὸν βωμόν, τοὺς δὲ νεφροὺς καὶ τὸν ἐπίπλουν καὶ πάντα τὰ πιμελῆ σὺν τῷ λοβῷ τοῦ ἥπατος καὶ σὺν αὐτοῖς τὴν οὐρὰν τοῦ ἀρνὸς
229 ἐπιφέρουσι τῷ βωμῷ. τὸ δὲ στῆθος καὶ τὴν κνήμην τὴν δεξιὰν τοῖς ἱερεῦσι παρασχόντες ἐπὶ δύο ἡμέρας εὐωχοῦνται τοῖς καταλειπομένοις τῶν κρεῶν, ἃ δ' ἂν περισσεύσῃ κατακαίουσι.

230 (3) Θύουσι δὲ καὶ ὑπὲρ ἁμαρτάδων[1] καὶ ὁμοίως τῷ προειρημένῳ τὸ περὶ τῶν ἁμαρτάδων τῆς ἱερουργίας τρόπῳ γίνεται. οἱ δὲ ἀδύνατοι πορίζειν τὰ τέλεια θύματα περιστερὰς ἢ τρυγόνας δύο, ὧν τὸ μὲν ὁλοκαυτεῖται τῷ θεῷ, τὸ δὲ τοῖς ἱερεῦσιν εἰς βρῶσιν διδόασιν. ἀκριβέστερον δὲ περὶ τῆς θυσίας τῶνδε τῶν ζῴων ἐν τοῖς περὶ θυσιῶν
231 ἐροῦμεν. ὁ μὲν γὰρ κατὰ ἄγνοιαν εἰς τοῦτο προπεσὼν ἄρνα καὶ ἔριφον θήλειαν τῶν αὐτοετῶν προσφέρει, καὶ τῷ μὲν αἵματι δεύει τὸν βωμὸν ὁ ἱερεύς, οὐχ ὡς τὸ πρῶτον ἀλλὰ τῶν γωνιῶν τὰς

[1] χαριστηρίων SPL.

---

[a] Lev. i. 6 mentions the flaying of the larger animal only.
[b] Heb. *shelāmim*, E.V. "peace - offerings" (margin "thank-offerings"), LXX θυσία σωτηρίου; "peace-offering" connects the word with *shalom* "peace," "thank-offering"

JEWISH ANTIQUITIES, III. 227-231

with wood and alight. The feet and the inwards of Lev. i. 9, 13. the victims are carefully cleansed before being placed with the other portions for consecration in the flames; the skins are taken by the priests.[a] Such is the manner of the whole burnt-offering.

(2) In the performance of sacrifices of thank-offering,[b] the same beasts are offered, but these must be without blemish, and may be upwards of a year old,[c] and males or females indifferently. Having slain these, they stain the altar with their blood; the kidneys, the caul, all the fat along with the lobe of the liver, as also the lamb's tail, they then lay upon the altar. But the breast and the right leg are offered to the priests, and for two days they feast upon the remainder of the flesh, all that is left over being burnt up. *Thank-offerings. Ib. iii. 1.*

(3) They offer sacrifices also for sins, the ritual for these being similar to that just described. But those who are unable to afford the full sacrifices[d] bring two pigeons or two turtle-doves, of which one is burnt as a holocaust to God, and the other is given to the priests to be eaten. I shall, however, speak more precisely on the offering of these creatures in my treatise on the sacrifices.[e] A person who through ignorance has fallen into sin brings a lamb and a female kid[f] of a year old,[g] and with the blood the priest sprinkles the altar, not, however, as before, *Sin-offerings: ib. v. 7. (i) for sins of ignorance. Ib. iv. 27, 32.*

with the cognate verb *shillam* "repay" (as a return to God for benefits received).

[c] Leviticus specifies no age.
[d] *i.e.* the larger victim: "if his means suffice not for a lamb" (Lev. v. 7). [e] The projected work (i. 25 note).
[f] In Lev. lamb and kid are alternatives.
[g] I follow Whiston: αὐτοετής must here, I think, mean "just a year," not (as Hudson and Weill render) "of the same year" (*cf*. § 237). This detail comes from Numb. xv. 27.

ἐξοχάς, καὶ τούς τε νεφροὺς καὶ τὴν ἄλλην πιμελὴν
σὺν τῷ λοβῷ τοῦ ἥπατος ἐπιφέρουσι τῷ βωμῷ,
οἱ δὲ ἱερεῖς τάς τε δορὰς ἀποφέρονται καὶ τὰ κρέα
ἐπ' ἐκείνης δαπανήσοντες¹ τῆς ἡμέρας ἐν τῷ
ἱερῷ· ὁ γὰρ νόμος εἰς τὴν αὔριον ἀπολιπεῖν οὐκ
232 ἐᾷ. ὁ δὲ ἁμαρτὼν μὲν αὑτῷ δὲ συνειδὼς καὶ
μηδένα ἔχων τὸν ἐξελέγχοντα κριὸν θύει, τοῦ
νόμου τοῦτο κελεύοντος, οὗ τὰ κρέα κατὰ τὸ
ἱερὸν ὁμοίως οἱ ἱερεῖς αὐθημερὸν σιτοῦνται. οἱ
δὲ ἄρχοντες ἐφ' οἷς ἡμάρτανον ἐκθυόμενοι ταὐτὰ
μὲν κομίζουσι τοῖς ἰδιώταις, διαλλάσσουσι δὲ τῷ
προσάγειν θύματα ταῦρον ἔριφον ἄρσενας.
233 (4) Νόμος δὲ ταῖς ἰδιωτικαῖς καὶ ταῖς δημοσίαις
θυσίαις καὶ ἄλευρον ἐπιφέρεσθαι καθαρώτατον,
ἀρνὶ μὲν ἀσσαρῶνος μέτρον κριῷ δὲ δυοῖν ταύρῳ
δὲ τριῶν. τοῦτο καθαγνίζουσιν² ἐπὶ τῷ βωμῷ
234 μεμαγμένον ἐλαίῳ· κομίζεται γὰρ δὴ καὶ ἔλαιον
ὑπὸ τῶν τεθυκότων, ἐπὶ μὲν βοῒ εἰνὸς ἥμισυ, ἐπὶ
δὲ κριῷ μέρος τούτου τρίτον τοῦ μέτρου, καὶ
τετάρτη μερὶς ἐπ' ἀρνί· ὁ δ' εἶν μέτρον ἀρχαῖον
Ἑβραίων ⟨ὢν⟩³ δύναται δύο χόας Ἀττικούς. τὸ
δ' αὐτὸ μέτρον τῷ ἐλαίῳ καὶ οἴνου παρῆγον,
235 σπένδουσι δὲ περὶ τὸν βωμὸν τὸν οἶνον. εἰ δέ τις
θυσίαν οὐκ ἐπιτελῶν ἐπήνεγκε κατ' εὐχὴν σεμίδαλιν,
ταύτης ἀπαρχὴν μίαν ἐπιβάλλει τῷ βωμῷ δράκα,
τὴν δὲ λοιπὴν οἱ ἱερεῖς πρὸς τροφὴν λαμβάνουσιν

¹ Niese ex Lat.: δαπανήσαντες codd.
² RO: καθαγιάζουσιν rell.   ³ ins. Niese.

[a] *i.e.* " the horns of the altar " (Lev. iv. 30-34).
[b] Reference unverifiable.
[c] " Ils offrent *en plus* " (Weill). This makes intelligible sense, but the meaning can hardly be extracted from προσάγειν.

but only the projecting corners*a*; the kidneys, along with the fat and the lobe of the liver, are laid upon the altar; but the priests carry off the skins and also the flesh, which they will consume that same day in the temple, for the law*b* does not permit it to be left until the morrow. On the other hand, the sinner who is conscious of sin, but has none to convict him of it, sacrifices a ram (so the law ordains), whose flesh is likewise consumed in the temple by the priests on the selfsame day. The rulers, when making sacrifices of atonement for their sins, bring the same things as private individuals, with the difference that they offer*c* males, a bull and a kid.*d*

Lev. iv. 9.
(ii.) for wilful sins. Ib. vi. 2. (= v. 21 Hebr.).
iv. 22 f.

(4) A further law ordains that for all sacrifices, private and public, there should be offered also wheat flour, perfectly pure, of the measure of an *assarôn*[e] for a lamb, of two for a ram, and of three for a bullock. This they devote to the flames on the altar, kneaded in oil; for those offering sacrifice bring oil as well, for an ox half a *hin*, for a ram the third part of this measure, for a lamb a quarter—the *hin* being an ancient Hebrew measure, equivalent to two Attic *choes*.[f] They brought moreover the same measure of wine as of oil, pouring the wine as a libation around the altar. But if anyone, without performing sacrifice, offered fine flour in fulfilment of a vow, he took a handful of this and flung it as first-fruits upon the altar; the rest was appropriated by the priests for consumption, whether boiled (for

Offerings of meal, oil, and wine.
Numb. xv. 4-10.
Lev. ii. 1, vi. 14 (7 Hebr.).

---

d Lev. (iv. 23) names only "a goat, a male without blemish" as the offering of a "ruler"; a bullock is the sin-offering of the high-priest and of the whole congregation (iv. 3, 14).

e = "a tenth part (of an *ephah*)," Numb. xv. 4, otherwise an *omer*: see § 29 note.   *f Cf.* § 197.

JOSEPHUS

ἢ ἑψηθεῖσαν, ἐλαίῳ γὰρ συμπεφύραται, ἢ γενομένων ἄρτων. ἱερέως δὲ κομίσαντος καὶ ὁποσονοῦν 236 ὁλοκαυτεῖν ἀναγκαῖον. κωλύει δὲ ὁ νόμος θύειν ζῷον αὐθημερὸν[1] μετὰ τοῦ γεγεννηκότος ἐπὶ ταὐτό, οὐδ᾽ ἄλλως δὲ πρὶν ὀγδόην ἡμέραν γεννηθέντι διελθεῖν. γίνονται δὲ ἄλλαι θυσίαι ὑπὲρ τοῦ τὰς νόσους διαφυγεῖν ἢ κατ᾽ ἄλλας αἰτίας, εἰς ἃς πέμματα σὺν ἱερείοις ἀναλίσκεται, ὧν εἰς τὴν ὑστεραίαν[2] οὐδὲν ὑπολιπεῖν ἐστι νόμιμον, τῶν ἱερέων μέρος ἴδιον λαβόντων.

237 (x. 1) Ἐκ δὲ τοῦ δημοσίου ἀναλώματος νόμος ἐστὶν ἄρνα καθ᾽ ἑκάστην ἡμέραν σφάζεσθαι τῶν αὐτοετῶν ἀρχομένης τε ἡμέρας καὶ ληγούσης, κατὰ δὲ ἑβδόμην ἡμέραν, ἥτις σάββατα καλεῖται, δύο σφάττουσι τὸν αὐτὸν τρόπον ἱερουργοῦντες.
238 τῇ δὲ νουμηνίᾳ τάς τε καθημερινὰς θυσίας ἐπιτελοῦσι καὶ δύο βόας σὺν ἀρνάσιν ἐνιαυσιαίοις ἑπτὰ καὶ κριόν, ἔριφον δὲ ἐπὶ παραιτήσεσιν[3] ἁμαρτάδων, εἴ τι κατὰ λήθην γένοιτο.

239 (2) Τῷ δ᾽ ἑβδόμῳ μηνί, ὃν Μακεδόνες Ὑπερβερεταῖον καλοῦσι, προσθέντες τοῖς εἰρημένοις ταῦρον καὶ κριὸν καὶ ἄρνας ἑπτὰ θύουσι καὶ ἔριφον ὑπὲρ ἁμαρτάδων.

[1] RO: αὐθημερινὸν rell.
[2] Niese: ὑστέραν (ἑτέραν RO) codd.
[3] παραιτήσει Niese (cf. xviii. 117).

[a] Perhaps referring to the "sacrifice of thanksgiving" (χαρμοσύνης LXX) in the verses of Leviticus immediately following (xxii. 29 f.) though neither "sickness" nor "sweetmeats" are there specified.

[b] Cf. Ap. ii. 77. This was the view of the Pharisees, based on the use of the plural in Numb. xxviii. 2, "shall ye observe," as opposed to that of the Sadducees who, on the strength of the singular in v. 4, "shalt *thou* offer," main-

it had been soaked in oil) or in the form of bread. But if offered, in whatever quantity, by a priest, it had to be burnt entire.

Lev. vi. 23 (16).

The law further forbids us to sacrifice any animal on the same day and in the same place as its parent, and in no case before eight days have elapsed since its birth. There are also other sacrifices *a* offered for escape from sickness or for other reasons; upon these, along with the victims, sweetmeats are expended, of which nothing may be left over for the morrow, the priests receiving a special portion.

Further sacrificial regulations. *Ib.* xxii. 27 f.

(x. 1) The law ordains that at the public expense *b* a lamb of a year old *c* shall be slain daily, both at the opening and at the close *d* of the day; but on the seventh day, which is called the sabbath, they slay two (on each occasion), the ritual being otherwise the same. On the new moon, besides the daily sacrifices, they offer two oxen, together with seven yearling lambs and a ram, as also a kid in expiation for any sins which may have been committed through forgetfulness.

Daily sacrifices: sabbaths and new moons. Numb. xxviii. 3-15: Ex. xxix. 38 ff.

(2) In the seventh month, which the Macedonians call Hyperberetaeus,*e* in addition to the aforesaid victims, they sacrifice a bull, a ram, seven lambs, and a kid as sin-offering.

Sacrifices of the 7th month: 1st day. Numb. xxix. 1.

tained that the *Tamid* (" continuous " daily sacrifice) could be offered and paid for by individuals (Weill, quoting references).

c § 231 note : Bibl. " of the first year " (LXX ἐνιαυσίους).

d According to Ex. xxix. 39 " between the two evenings " (at twilight); actually in the Herodian temple between 3 and 4 o'clock, *A.* xiv. 65 περὶ ἐνάτην ὥραν, Mishna *Pesaḥim* v. 1.

e *i.e.* in Hebrew terminology, on the 1st of *Tishri*, otherwise *Rosh Ha-shanah* (" head of the year "), the autumnal New Year's Day (September-October) or " F. of Trumpets." The words " on the new moon " have either dropped out of the text or are to be supplied from the previous sentence.

JOSEPHUS

240 (3) Δεκάτῃ δὲ τοῦ αὐτοῦ μηνὸς κατὰ σελήνην διανηστεύοντες ἕως ἑσπέρας θύουσιν[1] ἐν ταύτῃ τῇ ἡμέρᾳ ταῦρόν τε καὶ κριοὺς δύο καὶ ἄρνας
241 ἑπτὰ καὶ ὑπὲρ ἁμαρτάδων ἔριφον. προσάγουσι δὲ δύο πρὸς τούτοις ἐρίφους, ὧν ὁ μὲν ζῶν εἰς τὴν ὑπερόριον ἐρημίαν πέμπεται ἀποτροπιασμὸς καὶ παραίτησις τοῦ πλήθους παντὸς ὑπὲρ ἁμαρτημάτων ἐσόμενος, τὸν δ' ἐν τοῖς προαστείοις εἰς καθαρώτατον ἄγοντες χωρίον αὐτόθι σὺν αὐτῇ καί-
242 ουσι τῇ δορᾷ μηδὲν ὅλως καθάραντες. συγκατακαίεται δὲ ταῦρος οὐχ ὑπὸ τοῦ δήμου προσαχθείς, ἀλλ' ἐκ τῶν ἰδίων ἀναλωμάτων τοῦ ἀρχιερέως παρασχόντος· οὗ δὴ σφαγέντος εἰσκομίσας εἰς τὸν ναὸν τοῦ αἵματος ἅμα καὶ τοῦ ἐρίφου ῥαίνει τῷ
243 δακτύλῳ τὸν ὄροφον ἑπτάκις, τοῦ δ' αὐτοῦ καὶ τὸ ἔδαφος καὶ τοσαυτάκις εἰς τὸν ναὸν καὶ περὶ τὸν χρύσεον βωμὸν καὶ τὸ λοιπὸν περὶ τῷ μείζονι κομίσας εἰς τὸ αἴθριον· πρὸς τούτοις τὰς ἐξοχὰς καὶ τοὺς νεφροὺς καὶ τὴν πιμελὴν σὺν τῷ λοβῷ τοῦ ἥπατος ἐπιφέρουσι τῷ βωμῷ. παρέχεται δὲ καὶ κριὸν ὁ ἀρχιερεὺς ὁλοκαύτωσιν τῷ θεῷ.
244 (4) Τῇ δὲ πέμπτῃ τοῦ αὐτοῦ μηνὸς καὶ δεκάτῃ,

---

[1] Dindorf: θύουσι δ' codd. (which Niese retains, indicating a lacuna before it).

---

[a] 10th *Tishri*, *Yom Kippur* or "Day of Atonement," the most solemn fast in the Jewish calendar.

[b] "*One* ram" Numb. xxix. 8, "one ram" Lev. xvi. 5; Josephus appears to adopt the view held by some Rabbis that the two passages refer to different sacrifices (see Weill).

[c] Josephus here distantly alludes to the mysterious figure, taken over from primitive pagan belief, of *Azazel* (prob. = "entire removal," LXX ἀποπομπαῖος), the wilderness spirit or *jinn* to whom the scapegoat was sent, Lev. xvi. 8 ff.

(3) On the tenth of the same lunar month [a] they fast until evening; on this day they sacrifice a bull, two rams,[b] seven lambs, and a kid as sin-offering. But besides these they offer two kids, of which one is sent alive into the wilderness beyond the frontiers, being intended to avert [c] and serve as an expiation for the sins of the whole people; while the other they conduct to the suburbs [d] to a spot that is perfectly pure, and there burn it, skin and all, without any cleansing whatsoever. Along with it is burnt a bullock, which is not offered by the community but is provided at his own expense [e] by the high-priest. So soon as this bullock has been slain, he brings into the sanctuary some of its blood, as also of the blood of the kid, and with his finger sprinkles it toward the ceiling seven times, and likewise on the floor,[f] and as many times over the sanctuary itself and around the golden altar [g]; the rest he carries into the outer court and sprinkles about the larger altar.[h] Furthermore, they lay upon the altar the extremities, the kidneys, and the fat with the lobe of the liver.[i] The high-priest also provides on his own account a ram for a burnt-offering to God.

(4) On the fifteenth of this same month, at which

10th day (Day of Atonement). Numb. xxix. 7. The scapegoat and other ceremonies. Lev. xvi. 5 ff.

xvi. 14.

xvi. 18.

xvi. 25.

xvi. 3.

15th day: F. of Tabernacles

---

[d] "Without the camp," Lev. xvi. 27.

[e] So the Talmud interpreted the repeated phrase "the bullock which is for himself," Lev. xvi. 6, 11.

[f] Details not in Scripture; according to tradition once upwards, seven times on the floor (*Yoma* v. 4, 5, *ap.* Weill).

[g] The altar of incense, § 147.

[h] The brazen altar, § 149. Leviticus mentions one altar only, "He shall go out unto the altar that is before the Lord," clearly (it would seem) meaning the brazen altar, though interpreted by the Mishna as the golden altar (*Yoma* v. 5).

[i] Added details: Lev. mentions only the burning of the fat.

τρεπομένου τὸ λοιπὸν τοῦ καιροῦ πρὸς τὴν χειμερινὴν[1] ὥραν, σκηνὰς πήγνυσθαι κελεύει κατ' οἰκίαν ἕκαστον, τό[2] κρύος ὑφορωμένους ἐπὶ 245 φυλακῇ τοῦ ἔτους, ὅταν τε[3] πατρίδων ἐπιτύχοιεν, παραγινομένους εἰς ἐκείνην τὴν πόλιν, ἣν διὰ τὸν ναὸν μητρόπολιν ἕξουσιν, ἐφ' ἡμέρας ὀκτὼ ἑορτὴν ἄγοντας ὁλοκαυτεῖν τε καὶ θύειν τῷ θεῷ τότε χαριστήρια, φέροντας ἐν ταῖς χερσὶν εἰρεσιώνην μυρσίνης καὶ ἰτέας σὺν κράδῃ φοίνικος πεποιημένην τοῦ μήλου τοῦ τῆς περσέας προσόντος. 246 εἶναι δὲ τῇ πρώτῃ τῶν ἡμερῶν τὴν τῆς ὁλοκαυτώσεως θυσίαν ἐκ τριῶν καὶ δέκα βοῶν καὶ ἀρνῶν ἑνὶ πλειόνων καὶ κριῶν δύο, κατὰ παραίτησιν ἁμαρτιῶν ἐρίφου προστιθεμένου. ταῖς δ' ἑξῆς ἡμέραις ὁ μὲν αὐτὸς ἀριθμὸς τῶν ἀρνῶν καὶ τῶν κριῶν σὺν τῷ ἐρίφῳ θύεται, ὑφαιροῦντες δὲ ἑκάστης ἡμέρας ἕνα τῶν βοῶν εἰς ἑπτὰ[4] καταν-
247 τῶσιν. ἀνίενται δὲ ἀπὸ παντὸς ἔργου κατὰ τὴν ὀγδόην ἡμέραν καὶ τῷ θεῷ, καθὰ προειρήκαμεν,[5]

[1] RO; χειμέριον rell.   [2] Lat., ed. pr.: τό τε codd.
[3] ὅταν τε Lat. (dumque), ed. pr.: ὅταν codd.
[4] πέντε RO.   [5] καθάπερ εἰρήκαμεν ROM.

---

[a] The F. of *Sukkoth* ("Tabernacles" or "Booths," Gr. σκηνοπηγία) synchronized with the autumnal equinox, Philo, *De Spec. Leg.* ii. 24, § 204 καιρὸν ἔχουσα τὸν μετοπωρινῆς ἰσημερίας, or in Rabbinical terminology the *Teḳuphah*, the "circuit" or revolution of the year (Ex. xxxiv. 22).

[b] Literally "for protection against the year," or possibly "in observance of (the season of) the year." This curious statement, suggestive not of a special festival, but of a practice to be continued throughout the winter, seems to stand alone. The nearest parallel is one of two alternative suggestions of Philo (*loc. cit.*), viz. that the dwelling in tents during the period of the feast indicated a return to a more sheltered

the turning-point to the winter season is now reached,[a] Moses bids each family to fix up tents, apprehensive of the cold and as a protection against the year's inclemency.[b] Moreover, when they should have won their fatherland,[c] they were to repair to that city which they would in honour of the temple regard as their metropolis, and there for eight days keep festival: they were to offer burnt-offerings and sacrifices of thanksgiving to God in those days, bearing in their hands a bouquet composed of myrtle[d] and willow with a branch of palm,[e] along with fruit of the persea.[f] On the first of those days their burnt sacrifice should consist of thirteen oxen, as many lambs and one over, two rams, and a kid to boot in propitiation for sins. On the following days the same number of lambs and of rams is sacrificed, together with the kid, but they reduce that of the oxen by one daily until they reach seven.[g] They abstain from all work on the eighth day[h] and, as we have said,[i] sacrifice to God a calf, a ram, seven

Numb. xxix. 12: Lev. xxiii. 34.

Lev. xxiii. 40.

Numb. xxix. 13.

Ib. 35.

---

existence (στεγανωτέρας διαίτης) after the open-air life during the harvest, with its exposure to cold (κρυμός) and heat. He adds the Biblical interpretation (Lev. xxiii. 42 f.), viz. that it commemorates the dwelling in huts during the wanderings in the wilderness. *Sukkah* is Isaiah's word for "a booth in a vineyard," and *Sukkoth*, the vintage festival, is now thought to derive its name from the improvised shelters of the grape-gatherers.

[c] The Greek has the plural, "native cities" (or "estates").

[d] In Lev. "boughs of thick trees," traditionally interpreted as myrtle (Onkelos etc.).

[e] Known as the *lulab*.

[f] Lev. (vaguely) "fruit of goodly trees"; the fruit actually carried, known as the *ethrog*, was a kind of citron (*A.* xiii. 372 κιτρίοις αὐτὸν ἔβαλλον).   [g] *i.e.* on the seventh day.

[h] Kept as a "closing festival" (Heb. *'aẓereth*).

[i] Reference unverifiable.

μόσχον τε θύουσι¹ καὶ κριὸν καὶ ἄρνας ἑπτά, ὑπὲρ δὲ ἁμαρτημάτων παραιτήσεως ἔριφον. καὶ ταῦτα μὲν Ἑβραίοις τὰς σκηνὰς πηγνύουσιν ἐπιτελεῖν ἐστι πάτριον.

248 (5) Τῷ δὲ μηνὶ τῷ Ξανθικῷ, ὃς Νισὰν παρ' ἡμῖν καλεῖται καὶ τοῦ ἔτους ἐστὶν ἀρχή, τεσσαρεσκαιδεκάτῃ κατὰ σελήνην ἐν κριῷ τοῦ ἡλίου καθεστῶτος, τούτῳ γὰρ τῷ μηνὶ τῆς ὑπ' Αἰγυπτίους δουλείας ἠλευθερώθημεν, καὶ τὴν θυσίαν, ἣν τότ' ἐξιόντας ἀπ' Αἰγύπτου θῦσαι προεῖπον ἡμᾶς πάσχα λεγομένην, δι' ἔτους ἑκάστου θύειν ἐνόμισεν, καὶ δὴ τελοῦμεν αὐτὴν κατὰ φατρίας μηδενὸς τῶν τεθυ-
249 μένων εἰς τὴν ἐπιοῦσαν τηρουμένου. πέμπτῃ δὲ καὶ δεκάτῃ διαδέχεται τὴν πάσχα ἡ τῶν ἀζύμων ἑορτὴ ἑπτὰ ἡμέρας οὖσα, καθ' ἣν ἀζύμοις τρέφονται καὶ καθ' ἑκάστην ἡμέραν ταῦροι σφάζονται δύο καὶ κριὸς μὲν εἷς ἑπτὰ δὲ ἄρνες. καὶ ταῦτα μὲν ὁλοκαυτεῖται προστιθεμένου τοῖς πᾶσι καὶ ἐρίφου ὑπὲρ ἁμαρτάδων εἰς εὐωχίαν κατὰ ἡμέραν ἑκάστην
250 τοῖς ἱερεῦσιν. τῇ δὲ δευτέρᾳ τῶν ἀζύμων ἡμέρᾳ, ἕκτη δ' ἐστὶν αὕτη καὶ δεκάτη, τῶν καρπῶν οὓς ἐθέρισαν, οὐ γὰρ ἥψαντο πρότερον αὐτῶν, μεταλαμβάνουσι καὶ τὸν θεὸν ἡγούμενοι τιμᾶν δίκαιον εἶναι πρῶτον, παρ' οὗ τῆς εὐπορίας τούτων ἔτυχον, τὰς ἀπαρχὰς αὐτῷ τῆς κριθῆς ἐπιφέρουσι τρόπον

---

¹ θύομεν R (θυόμενον O).

---

[a] The ecclesiastical year, beginning in the spring; A. i. 81 note.
[b] ii. 311 ff.
[c] Or "companies," ii. 312 note.
[d] Reckoned as "eight" in ii. 317 (with note).
[e] "On the morrow of the sabbath" Lev. xxiii. 11 and 15, an ambiguous and disputed phrase, on the interpretation of

JEWISH ANTIQUITIES, III. 247-250

lambs, and a kid in propitiation for sins. Such are the rites, handed down from their forefathers, which the Hebrews observe when they erect their tabernacles.

(5) In the month of Xanthicus, which with us is called Nisan and begins the year,[a] on the fourteenth day by lunar reckoning, the sun being then in Aries, our lawgiver, seeing that in this month we were delivered from bondage to the Egyptians, ordained that we should year by year offer the same sacrifice which, as I have already said,[b] we offered then on departure from Egypt—the sacrifice called *Pascha*. And so in fact we celebrate it by fraternities,[c] nothing of the sacrificial victims being kept for the morrow. On the fifteenth the Passover is followed up by the Feast of Unleavened bread, lasting seven[d] days, during which our people subsist on unleavened loaves and each day there are slaughtered two bulls, a ram, and seven lambs. These are all used for burnt-offerings, a kid being further added as sin-offering, which serves each day to regale the priests. On the second day of unleavened bread,[e] that is to say the sixteenth,[f] our people partake of the crops which they have reaped and which have not been touched till then, and esteeming it right first to do homage to God, to whom they owe the abundance of these gifts, they offer to Him the first-fruits of the barley

F. of Passover and of Unleavened Bread.
Lev. xxiii. 5.

Ib. 6, Numb. xxviii. 17.

Lev. xxiii. 11.

---

which the date of Pentecost depended (§ 252). Josephus follows the orthodox Pharisaic view that "the sabbath" meant the first day of the F. of Unleavened Bread; so too the LXX (τῇ ἐπαύριον τῆς πρώτης) and Philo (ἑορτὴ ἐν ἑορτῇ ἡ μετὰ τὴν πρώτην εὐθὺς ἡμέραν, *De Spec. Leg.* ii. 20, § 162). The Sadducees (and in later days the Karaites) identified it with the ordinary sabbath falling within the festal week.

[f] Of Nisan.

JOSEPHUS

251 τοιοῦτον. φρύξαντες τῶν ἀσταχύων τὸ δράγμα καὶ πτίσαντες καὶ καθαρὰς πρὸς ἄλεστον τὰς κριθὰς ποιήσαντες τῷ βωμῷ ἀσσαρῶνα προσφέρουσι τῷ θεῷ, καὶ μίαν ἐξ αὐτοῦ δράκα ἐπιβαλόντες τὸ λοιπὸν ἀφιᾶσιν εἰς χρῆσιν τοῖς ἱερεῦσι· καὶ τότε λοιπὸν δημοσίᾳ ἔξεστι πᾶσι καὶ ἰδίᾳ θερίζειν. θύουσι δ' ἐπὶ ταῖς ἀπαρχαῖς τῶν καρπῶν ἀρνίον εἰς ὁλοκάρπωσιν[1] τῷ θεῷ.

252 (6) Ἑβδόμης ἑβδομάδος διαγεγενημένης μετὰ ταύτην τὴν θυσίαν, αὗται δ' εἰσὶν αἱ τῶν ἑβδομάδων ἡμέραι τεσσαράκοντα καὶ ἐννέα, τῇ πεντηκοστῇ, ἣν Ἑβραῖοι ἀσαρθὰ καλοῦσι, σημαίνει δὲ τοῦτο πεντηκοστήν, [καθ' ἣν][2] προσάγουσι τῷ θεῷ ἄρτον[3] ἀλφίτων μὲν πυρίνων ἀσσαρῶνας δύο μετὰ

253 ζύμης γεγονότων, θυμάτων δὲ ἄρνας δύο· ταῦτα μὲν γὰρ τῷ θεῷ προσάγειν νόμιμον,[4] εἰς δὲ δεῖπνον τοῖς ἱερεῦσι σκευάζεται καὶ καταλιπεῖν οὐδέν ἐστιν ἐξ αὐτῶν εἰς τὴν ἐπιοῦσαν συγκεχωρημένον· ὁλοκαυτωθησομένους μόσχους τε θύουσι τρεῖς καὶ κριοὺς δύο καὶ ἄρνας τεσσαρεσκαίδεκα,

---

[1] ὁλοκαύτωσιν RO.   [2] om. ed. pr.
[3] L : ἄρτων (panes Lat.) rell.
[4] Niese: νόμιμον μόνον RO : μόνον rell.

---

[a] In Leviticus the ceremony consists of the bringing of the first sheaf (*ómer*, δράγμα) straight from the harvest-field to the priest, who " waves " it before the Lord ; there is a mere gesture of presentation. The sheaf, according to Philo (*loc. cit.*), gave its name (δράγμα) to the feast. On the other hand, the preparation of the barley and the throwing of a handful on the altar, as described by Josephus, rest on later tradition ; for the processes of preparation (here not very intelligibly expressed) Weill refers to the Mishna (*Menaḥoth* vi. 4).

in the following wise. After parching and crushing the little sheaf of ears and purifying the barley for grinding,[a] they bring to the altar an *assarôn*[b] for God, and, having flung a handful thereof on the altar, they leave the rest for the use of the priests. Thereafter all are permitted, publicly or individually, to begin harvest. Moreover, besides the first-fruits of the crops, they offer a young lamb as a burnt-offering to God.

Lev. xxiii. 12.

(6) When the seventh week following this sacrifice has elapsed—these are the forty-nine days of the (so-called) "Weeks"[c]—on the fiftieth day, which the Hebrews call *Asartha*, the word denoting "fiftieth,"[d] they present to God a loaf[e] of two *assarôns* of flour of wheat made with leaven and, as sacrifice, two lambs. These are by ordinance to be offered to God,[f] but are made up into a repast for the priests, and it is not permitted to leave any portion of them over for the morrow.[g] As whole burnt-offerings they further sacrifice three calves, two rams, four-

F. of Pentecost. Lev. xxiii. 15.

Ib. 18 f.; Numb. xxviii. 27 ff.

[b] Or '*ômer* (§ 233); Hebrew uses the same word for this *measure* and for "sheaf," a fact which may have assisted the change of practice (previous note).

[c] The seven weeks, reckoned from the "waving" of the barley-sheaf (Lev. xxiii. 15) or from the time of first putting the sickle to the corn (Deut. xvi. 9), which gave to the F. of wheat-harvest its name "Feast of Weeks" (*Shābu'oth*).

[d] Not "Pentecost," which would be equally unintelligible to Greeks and would require the article. This is one of the author's loose etymological statements. '*Azartha* is the Aramaic equivalent of the Heb. '*azereth*, the post-Biblical name for the F. of Weeks or Pentecost, and probably means "closing (festival)," as occurring at the close of the seven weeks.

[e] "*Two* wave loaves," Lev. xxiii. 17.

[f] Some MSS. add "alone."

[g] Weill quotes the Mishna, *Menaḥoth* xi. 9, for an extension of the time, under certain circumstances, to three days.

254 ἐρίφους δὲ δύο ὑπὲρ ἁμαρτημάτων. ἔστι δ' οὐδεμία τῶν ἑορτῶν, καθ' ἣν οὐχ ὁλοκαυτοῦσιν οὐδὲ τῶν πόνων τῶν ἐπὶ τοῖς ἔργοις ἄνεσιν οὐ διδόασιν, ἀλλ' ἐν πάσαις νόμιμον τό τε τῆς θυσίας εἶδος καὶ τὸ τῆς ἀργίας ἀταλαίπωρον καὶ πρὸς εὐωχίας[1] εἰσὶ τεθυκότες.

255 (7) Ἐκ μέντοι τοῦ κοινοῦ σῖτος ὀπτὸς ζύμης ἄμοιρος, ἀσσαρῶνες δ' εἴκοσι καὶ τέσσαρες εἰς τοῦτο ἀναλοῦνται. ὀπτῶνται δὲ ἀνὰ δύο διαιρεθέντες μὲν τῇ πρὸ τοῦ σαββάτου, τῷ δὲ σαββάτῳ πρωῒ κομισθέντες ἐπὶ τῆς ἱερᾶς τραπέζης τίθενται 256 κατὰ ἓξ εἰς ἀλλήλους τετραμμένοι. δύο δὲ χρυσέων ὑπερκειμένων πινάκων λιβανωτοῦ γεμόντων διαμένουσιν ἕως τοῦ ἑτέρου σαββάτου· καὶ τότε μὲν ἀντ' ἐκείνων ἄλλοι κομίζονται, οἱ δὲ τοῖς ἱερεῦσι πρὸς τροφὴν δίδονται, καὶ τοῦ λιβανωτοῦ θυμιωμένου ἐπὶ τῷ ἱερῷ πυρί, ἐφ' ᾧ καὶ ὁλοκαυτοῦσι τὰ πάντα, λιβανωτὸς[2] ὑπὲρ ἐκείνου ἄλλος ὑπὲρ 257 τῶν ἄρτων προτίθεται.[3] θύει δ' ὁ ἱερεὺς ἐκ τῶν ἰδίων ἀναλωμάτων, καὶ δὶς ἑκάστης ἡμέρας τοῦτο ποιεῖ, ἄλευρον ἐλαίῳ μεμαγμένον[4] καὶ πεπηγὸς ὀπτήσει βραχείᾳ, καὶ εἷς μέν ἐστιν ἀσσαρὼν τοῦ ἀλεύρου, τούτου δὲ τὸ μὲν ἥμισυ[5] πρωΐ, τὸ δ' ἕτερον δείλης ἐπιφέρει τῷ πυρί. τὸν μὲν οὖν περὶ

---

[1] εὐωχίαις Niese.   [2] RO: +δὲ rell.
[3] Niese: προστίθεται codd.
[4] μεμιγμένον ROM Lat.   [5] +τὸ RO.

teen lambs, with two kids in atonement for sins.[a] There is, in fact, no festival whereon they do not offer burnt-offerings or fail to grant relaxation from the toils of labour: for each is prescribed the class of sacrifice and the period of untroubled repose, and it is with a feast in view that their sacrifices have been offered.

(7) At the public expense is provided bread baked without leaven,[b] twenty-four *assarôns* being employed for the purpose.[c] The loaves are baked two and two separately on the eve of the sabbath; then on the sabbath morn they are brought in and laid on the holy table in two opposite rows of six each. Two golden platters [d] laden with frankincense are placed over them, and so they remain until the following sabbath. Then others are brought in their stead, the former loaves are given to the priests for food, while the incense is burnt on the same holy fire whereon they consume all the burnt-offerings, and other incense to replace it is laid out above the loaves. The priest at his own expense, and that twice a day, offers meal soaked in oil and hardened by a little cooking; the amount is an *assarôn* of meal, of which one half is put by him on the fire in the morning and the other towards evening. The explanation of

The shewbread.
Lev. xxiv. 5.

Oblations of the priest.
Ib. vi. 20 (13 Heb.).

---

[a] The figures for these animals differ in the two Biblical lists. Josephus adds the two lists together (except in the case of the rams, of which Lev. names two and Numbers one). In thus treating the lists as independent and complementary, he agrees with R. Akiba (*Menaḥoth* 45 b, quoted by Weill).

[b] So § 142 (not in Leviticus); the previous mention of these loaves accounts for some abruptness here.

[c] "Two tenth parts of an ephah," *i.e.* two *assarôns* going to each of the twelve cakes (Lev. *loc. cit.*).

[d] Two *cups* are shown on the table as depicted on the Arch of Titus; *cf.* § 143, where they are called φιάλαι.

JOSEPHUS

τούτων λόγον ἀκριβέστερον αὖθις δηλώσομεν, ἱκανὰ δέ μοι δοκεῖ καὶ νῦν περὶ αὐτῶν προειρῆσθαι.

258 (xi. 1) Μωυσῆς δὲ τὴν Λευῖτιν φυλὴν τῆς πρὸς τὸν λαὸν κοινωνίας ὑπεξελόμενος ἱερὰν ἐσομένην ἥγνιζε πηγαίοις ὕδασι καὶ ἀενάοις καὶ θυσίαις, ἃς ἐπὶ τοῖς τοιούτοις νομίμους παρέχονται τῷ θεῷ, τήν τε σκηνὴν αὐτοῖς καὶ τὰ σκεύη τὰ ἱερὰ καὶ τὰ ἄλλ' ὅσα πρὸς σκέπην τῆς σκηνῆς ἐπεποίητο παρέδωκεν, ὅπως ὑφηγουμένων τῶν ἱερέων ὑπηρετήσωσιν· ἤδη γὰρ τῷ θεῷ καθιέρωντο.[1]

259 (2) Καὶ περὶ τῶν ζῴων δὲ διέκρινεν ἕκαστον, ὅ τι[2] τρέφοιντο καὶ οὗ πάλιν ἀπεχόμενοι διατελοῖεν, περὶ ὧν ἐν οἷς ἂν ἡμῖν ἀφορμὴ τῆς γραφῆς γένηται διελευσόμεθα τὰς αἰτίας προστιθέντες, ἀφ'[3] ὧν κινηθεὶς τὰ μὲν αὐτῶν βρωτὰ[4] ἡμῖν ἐκέλευσεν

260 εἶναι, τῶν δὲ προσέταξεν ἀπέχεσθαι. αἵματος μέντοι παντὸς εἰς τροφὴν ἀπηγόρευσε τὴν χρῆσιν ψυχὴν αὐτὸ καὶ πνεῦμα νομίζων, καὶ κρέως τοῦ τεθνηκότος αὐτομάτως ζῴου τὴν βρῶσιν διεκώλυσεν, ἐπίπλου τε καὶ στέατος αἰγείου καὶ προβατείου καὶ τοῦ τῶν βοῶν ἀπέχεσθαι προεῖπεν.

261 (3) Ἀπήλασε δὲ τῆς πόλεως καὶ τοὺς λέπρᾳ τὰ σώματα κακωθέντας καὶ τοὺς περὶ τὴν γονὴν ῥεομένους· καὶ τὰς γυναῖκας δ' αἷς ἡ τῶν κατὰ

---

[1] SP(L): καθιέρωτο rell.
[2] ὅτι codd.: ᾧ τε has been suggested.
[3] ὑφ' Niese.   [4] R: βρώματα rell.

---

[a] In the projected "Customs and Causes," i. 25.
[b] The priests (§ 198); or, with the other reading "it" (the tabernacle, *ibid.*).
[c] In the projected work.

these matters will be given in greater detail hereafter[a]; for the present I think that what I have said already about them will suffice.

(xi. 1) Now Moses, having segregated the tribe of Levi from the general community, to make of it a holy tribe, purified it with the waters of perennial springs and with the sacrifices which on such occasions they offer to God as by law ordained; and to them he committed the tabernacle and the sacred vessels and everything that had been made for the covering of the tabernacle, to the end that they should act as ministers under the direction of the priests. For they[b] had already been consecrated to God. PURITY LAWS. Consecration of the Levites. Numb. iii. 5

(2) Moreover, as concerning animals, he distinguished in detail those which might be eaten and those on the contrary from which one must perpetually abstain. On these, whenever the occasion may come for treating of them, we shall discourse at length,[c] supplying the reasons which influenced him in ruling that some of them were eatable and in enjoining us to abstain from others. Howsoever, blood of any description he has forbidden to be used for food, regarding it as the soul and spirit; he has prohibited the eating of the flesh of an animal dying a natural death; and he has further required us to abstain from the caul[d] and from the fat of goats, sheep, and oxen. Food laws. Lev. xvii. 10 f. xi. 39. vii. 23.

(3) He banished from the city[e] alike those whose bodies were afflicted with leprosy and those with contagious disease.[f] Women too, when beset by Concerning lepers and the unclean; Ib. xiii.-xv.

[d] Not mentioned in Lev. *loc. cit.*
[e] " Without the camp " Lev. xiii. 46 (of the leper).
[f] Gonorrhoea; expulsion from " camp " or " city " is not specified in Leviticus in this instance.

443

φύσιν ἔκκρισις ἐπίοι¹ μετέστησε πρὸς ἡμέραν ἑβδόμην, μεθ' ἣν ὡς ἤδη καθαραῖς ἐνδημεῖν ἐφίησιν.
262 ὁμοίως δὲ καὶ τοῖς κηδεύσασι νεκρὸν μετὰ τοσαύτας ἡμέρας νόμιμον τὸ ἐνδημεῖν· τὸν δ' ὑπὲρ τὸν ἀριθμὸν τούτων τῶν ἡμερῶν ἐνεχόμενον ἐν τῷ μιάσματι θύειν νόμιμον ἀμνάδας δύο, ὧν τὴν μὲν ἑτέραν καθαγνίζειν δεῖ, τὴν δ' ἑτέραν οἱ ἱερεῖς
263 λαμβάνουσιν. ὁμοίως δὲ θύουσι καὶ περὶ τοῦ τὴν γονὴν ῥεομένου· ὃς δ' ἂν κατὰ τοὺς ὕπνους ἀποκρίνῃ γονήν, καθεὶς αὑτὸν εἰς ὕδωρ ψυχρὸν ὁμοίως τοῖς κατὰ νόμον γυναικὶ πλησιάζουσιν
264 ἐξουσίαν ἔχει. τοὺς δὲ λεπροὺς εἰς τὸ παντελὲς ἐξήλασε τῆς πόλεως μηδενὶ συνδιαιτωμένους καὶ νεκροῦ μηδὲν διαφέροντας· ἂν δέ τις ἐξικετεύσας τὸν θεὸν ἀπολυθῇ τῆς νόσου καὶ τὴν ἐρρωμένην κομίσηται χρόαν, ὁ δὴ τοιοῦτος ποικίλαις ἀμείβεται θυσίαις τὸν θεόν, περὶ ὧν ὕστερον ἐροῦμεν.

265 (4) Ὅθεν καὶ καταγελάσειεν ἄν τις τῶν λεγόντων Μωυσῆν λέπρᾳ κεκακωμένον αὐτόν τε ἀπ' Αἰγύπτου φυγεῖν καὶ τῶν ἐκπεσόντων διὰ ταύτην τὴν αἰτίαν ἡγησάμενον εἰς τὴν Χαναναίαν ἀγαγεῖν
266 αὐτούς. εἰ γὰρ τοῦτ' ἦν ἀληθές, οὐκ ἂν ἐπὶ τῇ αὑτοῦ Μωυσῆς ἀτιμίᾳ τοιαῦτ' ἐνομοθέτησεν, οἷς εὔλογον ἦν αὐτὸν καὶ ἑτέρων εἰσηγουμένων ἀντειρηκέναι, καὶ ταῦτα παρὰ πολλοῖς οὖσι λεπρῶν ἔθνεσι καὶ τιμῆς ἀπολαυόντων, οὐ μόνον ὕβρεως καὶ φυγῆς ἀπηλλαγμένων, ἀλλὰ καὶ τὰς

¹ ἔπεισι RO.

---

[a] Cf. *Ap.* ii. 205 for purification of house and inmates after a funeral. [b] No Scriptural parallel.
[c] Weill compares Numb. xii. 12 "as one dead" (of Miriam smitten with leprosy).

their natural secretions, he secluded until the seventh day, after which they were permitted, as now pure, to return to society. A like rule applies to those who have paid the last rites to the dead: after the same number of days they may rejoin their fellows.[a] But a person who exceeds this number of days in a state of defilement is required to sacrifice two lambs, of which one must be devoted to the flames and the other is taken by the priests.[b] The same sacrifices are offered in a case of contagious disease; but he who has an issue in his sleep will, by plunging into cold water, exonerate himself, like those who lawfully cohabit with their wives. Lepers, on the other hand, he banished outright from the city, to have intercourse with no man and as in no way differing from a corpse.[c] But if any by supplication to God obtains release from this disease and recovers a healthy skin, such an one returns thanks to God by divers sacrifices of which we shall speak hereafter.[d]

Lev. xv. 19.
Numb. xix. 11; xxxi. 19.
Lev. xv. 16.

(4) From all this one can but regard as ridiculous those [e] who assert that Moses, being struck with leprosy, was himself forced to flee from Egypt and, taking command of all who had been expelled for the same reason, conducted them to Canaan. For, were this true, Moses would never have issued to his own humiliation statutes such as these, against which in all likelihood he would have himself protested had others introduced them, more especially since among many nations there are lepers in the enjoyment of honours, who, far from undergoing contumely and exile, conduct the most brilliant

Absurdity of legends about the leprosy of Moses and his followers.

[d] In the projected work.
[e] Like Manetho, whose scurrilous charges are confuted at length in the *contra Apionem*; see in particular *Ap.* i. chap. 31, §§ 279 ff.

ἐπισημοτάτας στρατείας στρατευομένων καὶ τὰς πολιτικὰς ἀρχὰς πιστευομένων καὶ εἰς ἱερὰ καὶ
267 ναοὺς ἐχόντων ἐξουσίαν εἰσιέναι· ὥστ᾽ οὐδὲν ἐκώλυε καὶ Μωυσῆν, εἰ τοιούτῳ τινὶ συμπτώματι περὶ τὴν χρόαν ᾖ[1] τὸ σὺν αὐτῷ πλῆθος ἠλάττωτο, νομοθετῆσαι περὶ αὐτῶν τὰ κάλλιστα καὶ μηδεμίαν
268 τοιαύτην ὁρίσαι ζημίαν. ἀλλὰ δῆλον μέν, ὡς ταῦτα περὶ ἡμῶν λέγουσιν ὑπὸ βασκανίας προαγόμενοι, Μωυσῆς δὲ τούτων καθαρὸς ὢν ἐν καθαροῖς τοῖς ὁμοφύλοις περὶ τῶν νενοσηκότων ἐνομοθέτει κατὰ τιμὴν τοῦ θεοῦ τοῦτο ποιῶν. ἀλλὰ περὶ μὲν τούτων ἕκαστος ὡς αὐτῷ δοκεῖ σκοπείτω.

269 (5) Τὰς δὲ γυναῖκας ἐπειδὰν τέκωσιν εἰς τὸ ἱερὸν εἰσιέναι κεκώλυκε καὶ θυσιῶν ἅπτεσθαι μέχρι τεσσαράκοντα ἡμερῶν, ἂν ἄρρεν τὸ τεχθὲν ᾖ· διπλασίονας γὰρ εἶναι τὰς ἡμέρας ἐπὶ θηλυτοκίαις συμβέβηκεν. εἰσιοῦσαι μέντοι μετὰ τὴν προειρημένην προθεσμίαν θυσίας ἐπιτελοῦσιν, ἃς οἱ ἱερεῖς πρὸς τὸν θεὸν διανέμονται.

270 (6) Ἂν δ᾽ ὑπονοήσῃ μεμοιχεῦσθαί τις αὐτῷ τὴν γυναῖκα, κομίζει κριθῆς ἀληλεσμένης ἀσσαρῶνα, καὶ μίαν αὐτῆς δράκα ἐπιβαλόντες τῷ θεῷ τὸ λοιπὸν τοῖς ἱερεῦσι διδόασιν εἰς τροφήν. τὴν δὲ γυναῖκα στήσας τις τῶν ἱερέων κατὰ τὰς πύλας, αἱ δ᾽ εἰσὶ τετραμμέναι πρὸς τὸν νεών, καὶ τῆς

[1] ipse aut Lat. = ⟨ἢ αὐτὸς⟩ ἢ Bernard.

---

[a] With obvious reference to Naaman, captain of the host of the king of Syria, who leaned on this leper's hand in the house of Rimmon (2 Kings v. 1, 18).

[b] Notwithstanding their calumnies, the Egyptians "wish to claim Moses as one of themselves" (*Ap.* i. 279).

[c] On this formula, usually relating to incidents of a miraculous or quasi-mythical nature, see i. 108 note.

campaigns, are entrusted with offices of state, and have the right of entry to sacred courts and temples.[a] Consequently there was nothing to prevent Moses, had he or the host that accompanied him been marred by any such accident to the skin, from laying down laws concerning lepers of the most favourable character, instead of imposing any penalty of this nature. No; it is clear that in making these statements about us they are instigated by jealousy,[b] and that Moses was immune from all that, and, living among countrymen equally immune, that he legislated concerning those so diseased, and that it was in God's honour that he thus acted. However, on these matters let everyone judge as seems good to him.[c]

(5) Women after childbirth are forbidden by him to enter the temple or to touch the sacrifices[d] until forty days have elapsed, if it is a male infant; double that number is prescribed for the birth of a female. But they enter at the end of the aforesaid term to offer sacrifices, which the priests apportion to God.

Impurity of women in childbirth. Lev. xii. 2.

(6) If[e] a man suspects his wife of having committed adultery, he brings an *assarôn* of ground barley, of which a handful is devoted[f] to God and the rest is given to the priests for consumption. As for the woman, one of the priests stations her at the gates which face the temple[g] and, after removing

Ordeal of suspected adulteress. Numb. v. 12.

---

[d] " She shall touch no hallowed thing," Lev. xii. 4.

[e] A whole tractate of the Mishnah (*Sôṭah*) is devoted to this subject; see also Philo, *De spec. leg.* iii. 10, §§ 52 ff.

[f] Literally " they throw upon (the altar)."

[g] " Shall set her before the Lord," Numb. v. 16. " In later times, according to *Sôṭah* i. 5, the accused were brought to the Nicanor or eastern gate of the temple," G. B. Gray, *Int. Crit. Comm. in loc.*

447

κεφαλῆς τὸ ἱμάτιον ἀφελὼν ἐπιγράφει μὲν τοῦ
271 θεοῦ τὴν προσηγορίαν διφθέρα, κελεύει δὲ ὀμνύειν
μηδὲν ἠδικηκέναι τὸν ἄνδρα, παραβᾶσαν δὲ τὸ
σῶφρον τοῦ δεξιοῦ σκέλους ἔξαρθρον γενέσθαι καὶ
τὴν γαστέρα πρησθεῖσαν οὕτως ἀποθανεῖν· ἂν δ'
ὑπὸ πολλοῦ τοῦ ἔρωτος καὶ τῆς διὰ τοῦτον ζηλο-
τυπίας προπετῶς ὁ ἀνὴρ διὰ τὴν ὑπόνοιαν εἴη
κεκινημένος, μηνὶ δεκάτῳ γενέσθαι παιδίον ἄρρεν
272 αὐτῇ. τῶν δ' ὅρκων τελειωθέντων τῆς διφθέρας
ἀπαλείψας τοὔνομα εἰς φιάλην ἐκπιέζει, προκομίσας τε ἐκ τοῦ ἱεροῦ γῆς εἴ τι προστύχοι καὶ
καταπάσας ἐκπιεῖν δίδωσιν· ἡ δ' εἰ μὲν ἀδίκως
ἐνεκλήθη, ἐγκύμων τε γίνεται καὶ τελεσφορεῖται
273 κατὰ τὴν γαστέρα· ψευσαμένη δὲ τὸν ἄνδρα ἐπὶ
τοῖς γάμοις καὶ τὸν θεὸν ἐπὶ τοῖς ὅρκοις μετ'
αἰσχύνης καταστρέφει τὸν βίον, τοῦ τε σκέλους
ἐκπεσόντος αὐτῇ καὶ τὴν κοιλίαν ὑδέρου καταλαβόντος. καὶ περὶ μὲν τῶν θυσιῶν καὶ τῆς ἁγνείας
τῆς ἐπ' αὐταῖς ταῦτα Μωυσῆς τοῖς ὁμοφύλοις
προενόησε, νόμους δὲ αὐτοῖς τοιούτους ἔθετο.

274 (xii. 1) Μοιχείαν μὲν εἰς τὸ παντελὲς ἀπεῖπε
νομίσας εὔδαιμον τὸ περὶ τοὺς γάμους ὑγιαίνειν τοὺς

---

[a] According to Scripture (Numb. v. 23) and tradition, the words of the imprecation.

[b] According to Sōṭah ii. 4 a roll of parchment (*megillah*), the use of διφθέρα (the rougher unprepared skin) being expressly forbidden; Numb. "a book," Philo χαρτίδιον.

[c] Numb. v. 28 says merely that the woman, if innocent, "shall conceive seed." M. Weill quotes a discussion (*Sifré in loc.*) between R. Akiba and R. Ishmael on the interpretation of the phrase; according to the latter if she had hitherto had daughters only, she would henceforth have sons.

[d] *i.e.* the impression. "Potions into which written words

JEWISH ANTIQUITIES, III. 270-274

the veil from her head, inscribes the name of God *a* upon a skin *b*; he then bids her declare upon oath that she had done her husband no wrong, and that if she had violated decency then might her right leg be put out of joint, her belly swell and so might she die; but if, through excess of love and ensuing jealousy her husband had been precipitately moved to suspect her, then might she give birth in the tenth month to a male child.*c* These oaths being completed, the priest expunges from the skin the Name thereon and wrings it *d* into a bowl; then picking up any morsels of the temple soil that may come to hand he sprinkles them in and gives her to drink. And she, if she has been unjustly accused, becomes pregnant and brings the fruit of her womb to maturity; but if she has proved false to her husband in wedlock and to God by her oaths, she comes to an ignominious end, her leg falling away and dropsy attacking her belly.*e* Such were the provisions concerning sacrifices and the purification relating thereto that Moses made for his countrymen; and here are the further laws *f* which he drew up for them.

(xii. 1) Adultery he absolutely prohibited, deeming it blessed that men should be sane-minded con-

VARIOUS LAWS. Forbidden marriages. Lev. xx. 10.

have been washed off are widely credited with particular virtues" (G. B. Gray, quoting parallels from Tibet and Mahommedan Egypt).

e Numb. v. 27, "her belly shall swell and her thigh shall fall away." It has been suggested that in the primitive rite the meaning may have been that though the woman grows great with child ("the swelling belly") the birth would be abortive; "thigh" is probably euphemistic (Gray, *op. cit.* p. 48).

f Here, as in § 151 (note), I take τοιούτους (which in class. Greek is retrospective) to be used for τοιούσδε "as follows." *Iosephus ipse scripsit.*

449

JOSEPHUS

ἄνδρας, καὶ ταῖς τε πόλεσι καὶ τοῖς οἴκοις συμφέρειν τὸ τοὺς παῖδας εἶναι γνησίους. καὶ τὸ μίσγεσθαι δὲ μητράσιν ὡς[1] κακὸν μέγιστον ὁ νόμος ἀπεῖπεν, ὁμοίως δὲ καὶ πατρὸς συνεῖναι γαμετῇ καὶ τηθίσι καὶ ἀδελφαῖς καὶ παίδων γυναιξὶν ὡς ἔκφυλον ἔχον τὴν ἀδικίαν μεμίσηκεν. ἐκώλυσε δὲ
275 καὶ γυναικὶ μεμιασμένῃ τοῖς κατὰ φύσιν πλησιάζειν μηδὲ κτήνεσιν εἰς συνουσίαν φοιτᾶν μηδὲ τὴν πρὸς τὰ ἄρρενα μῖξιν τιμᾶν διὰ τὴν ἐπ' αὐτοῖς ὥραν ἡδονὴν θηρωμένους παράνομον. κατὰ δὲ τῶν εἰς ταῦτ' ἐξυβρισάντων θάνατον ὥρισε τὴν τιμωρίαν.
276 (2) Τῶν δ' ἱερέων καὶ διπλασίονα τὴν ἁγνείαν ἐποίησε· τούτων τε γὰρ αὐτοὺς ὁμοίως τοῖς ἄλλοις εἶργει καὶ προσέτι γαμεῖν τὰς ἡταιρηκυίας ἐκώλυσε, μήτε δούλην μήτ' αἰχμάλωτον γαμεῖν αὐτοὺς κεκώλυκε[2] καὶ τὰς ἐκ καπηλείας καὶ τοῦ πανδοκεύειν πεπορισμένας τὸν βίον μηδὲ τὰς τῶν προτέρων ἀνδρῶν ἐφ' αἰσδηποτοῦν αἰτίαις ἀπηλλαγ-
277 μένας. τὸν ἀρχιερέα μέντοι οὐδὲ τεθνηκότος

[1] Lat., ed. pr.: om. codd.   [2] Text a little doubtful.

^a So *Yebamoth* 61 a (Weill). In *A.* iv. 244 f. the prohibition to marry a slave (or a harlot) applies to the laity also.

^b Leviticus *loc. cit.* names three classes of women whom the priest is forbidden to marry: (1) harlot, (2) "polluted," (3) divorced. Josephus mentions the first and the third, but seems to replace the second by two (or more) other classes. His first category, τὰς ἡταιρηκυίας, corresponds to the first (not, as Weill suggests, to the second) in Lev.: ἡταιρημένη (ἐταιριζομένη) is his normal euphemism for πόρνη, *A.* iv. 206, 245, v. 306, viii. 417. "Slave or prisoner of war" seems to be his interpretation of "polluted": for this prohibition *cf. Ap.* i. 30 ff. on the strict scrutiny of priestly marriages, especially after war, in particular § 35 "they disallow marriage with any who have been taken captive, suspecting them of having had frequent intercourse with

cerning wedlock and that it was to the interest alike of the state and the family that children should be legitimate. Again, to have intercourse with one's mother is condemned by the law as grossest of sins; likewise union with a stepmother, an aunt, a sister, or the wife of one's child is viewed with abhorrence as an outrageous crime. He moreover forbade cohabitation with a menstruous woman, mating with a beast, or the toleration of the practice of sodomy in the pursuit of lawless pleasure. For those guilty of such outrages he decreed the penalty of death.

Lev. xx. 18, 15, 13.

(2) From the priests he exacted a double degree of purity. For not only did he debar them, in common with all others, from the aforesaid practices, but he further forbade them to wed a harlot, he forbids them to wed a slave *a* or a prisoner of war, aye or such women as gain their livelihood by hawking or innkeeping or who have for whatsoever reasons been separated from their former husbands.*b* As for the

Special laws for the priests.

Ib. xxi. 7.

foreigners " (*i.e.* been " polluted "): Weill quotes *Kethuboth* ii. 9 to similar effect, *cf.* also *Ant.* xiii. 292 (an alleged instance of such disqualification). Then follows the strange addition " hawkers or innkeepers " (a single class, for κάπηλος Lat. *caupo* also = tavern-keeper). With this must be connected the fact that the Targum commonly translates the Heb. *zonah* " harlot " by the word *pundokita* (derived from the verb πανδοκεύειν, " keep an inn," here used by Josephus), *e.g.* in Joshua ii. 1, Jd. xi. 1, *cf.* 1 K. iii. 16; while Josephus himself speaks of the house of Rahab (Bibl. " the harlot ") as a " hostelry " (καταγώγιον), *A.* v. 7. Whether this translation arose merely from the ill-fame of inns and innkeepers (see '*Aboda zara* ii. 1 with Elmslie's note in *Texts and Studies* viii. 2) or has other etymological explanation behind it (Weill sees in it a supposed connexion of *zonah* with the vb. *zun* " to feed ") is uncertain; anyhow the " innkeeper " of Josephus has been evolved out of the " harlot " of the Bible through the medium of current Aramaic exegesis.

ἀνδρὸς ἠξίωσε γυναῖκα, τοῦτο τοῖς ἄλλοις ἱερεῦσι συγχωρῶν, μόνην δ' αὐτῷ [δέδωκε] γαμεῖν παρθένον καὶ ταύτην φυλέτην[1]· ὅθεν οὐδὲ νεκρῷ πρόσεισιν ὁ ἀρχιερεὺς τῶν λοιπῶν οὐ κεκωλυμένων ἀδελφοῖς καὶ γονεῦσι καὶ παισὶ τοῖς αὐτῶν προσ-
278 ιέναι μεταστᾶσιν. ἀφελεῖς δὲ εἶναι πᾶσαν ἀφέλειαν· τὸν δὲ μὴ ὁλόκληρον τῶν ἱερέων νέμεσθαι πρὸς τοὺς ἱερεῖς ἐκέλευσε τὰ γέρα, ἀναβαίνειν δὲ ἐπὶ τὸν βωμὸν καὶ εἰσιέναι εἰς τὸν ναὸν ἐκώλυσε· μὴ μόνον δὲ περὶ τὰς ἱερουργίας καθαροὺς εἶναι, σπουδάζειν δὲ καὶ περὶ τὴν αὐτῶν δίαιταν, ὥστ' αὐτὴν ἄμεμ-
279 πτον εἶναι. καὶ διὰ ταύτην τὴν αἰτίαν οἱ τὴν ἱερατικὴν στολὴν φοροῦντες ἄμωμοί τέ εἰσι καὶ περὶ πάντα καθαροὶ καὶ νηφάλιοι, πίνειν οἶνον ἕως οὗ τὴν στολὴν ἔχουσι κεκωλυμένοι· ἔτι δὲ καὶ τὰ ἱερεῖα θύουσιν ὁλόκληρα καὶ κατὰ μηδὲν λελωβημένα.

280 (3) Ταῦτα μὲν οὖν ἤδη καὶ κατὰ τὸν ζωῆς χρόνον τῆς αὐτοῦ γινόμενα παρέδωκε Μωυσῆς, τῶν δὲ αὖθις καίπερ ἐπὶ τῆς ἐρημίας διαιτώμενος προενόησεν, ὅπως ἐπειδὰν τὴν Χαναναίαν λάβωσι
281 τάδε ποιῶσι· δι' ἑβδόμου ἔτους ἄνεσιν δίδωσι τῇ γῇ ἀπό τε ἀρότρου καὶ φυτείας, ὥσπερ καὶ αὐτοῖς δι' ἑβδόμης ἡμέρας τὴν ἀπὸ τῶν ἔργων προεῖπεν ἀνάπαυσιν. καὶ τῶν αὐτομάτως ἀναδοθέντων ἀπὸ

[1] conj. Mangey (*ap.* Weill): φυλάττειν codd.

---

[a] The acute emendation φυλέτην (for φυλάττειν), quoted by Weill from Mangey on Philo ii. 229 M., is certainly right: for φυλέτης *cf. Ant.* iv. 14 f., 20 etc.: Philo's expression is μὴ παρθένον μόνον ἀλλὰ καὶ ἱέρειαν ἐξ ἱερέων. On the other hand, the Biblical restriction is less rigid, " a virgin *of his own people* " Lev. *loc. cit.* (*cf.* Ezek. xliv. 22), and so elsewhere Josephus himself, *Ap.* i. 31 ἐξ ὁμοεθνοῦς γυναικὸς παιδοποιεῖσθαι; tradition also (*ap.* Weill) admitted the laxer rule.

JEWISH ANTIQUITIES, III. 277–281

high-priest, he would not suffer him to take even a woman whose husband was dead, though he concedes this to the other priests: none but a virgin may he wed and withal one of his own tribe.[a] From like motives the high-priest never approaches a corpse, whereas the other priests are not forbidden to approach a brother, a parent or a child of their own when deceased. They must be exempt from all physical blemish. A priest who is not wholly free of such defect he authorized to partake with the other priests of their perquisites,[b] but to ascend to the altar or to enter the sacred building is forbidden him. Nor is it only during the sacred ministrations that purity is essential: they must see to it also that their private life be beyond reproach. That is why wearers of the priestly robes are spotless, immaculately pure, and sober, for wine is forbidden them so long as they wear the robe.[c] Furthermore, the very victims which they sacrifice are entirely perfect and free from all mutilation.

Lev. xxi. 14.
xxi. 11.
xxi. 1 ff.
xxi. 17.
xxi. 21 ff.
x. 9 (Ezek. xliv. 21).
xxii. 19 ff.

(3) Such, then, are the laws, already in operation during his lifetime, which Moses has transmitted to us; but there were others for after times which, albeit sojourning in the wilderness, he devised beforehand, to the end that they should practise them after the conquest of Canaan. Thus every seventh year he grants the land repose from ploughing and planting, even as he had prescribed to the people rest from their labours every seventh day; as for the spontaneous products of the soil, the

The sabbatical year.
Lev. xxv. 1.

---

[b] " He shall eat the bread (LXX τὰ δῶρα) of his God," Lev. xxi. 22.

[c] *i.e.* when on duty: " when ye go into the tent of meeting," Lev. *loc. cit.* Tradition (*ap.* Weill) did not regard this as an absolute prohibition. *Cf. Ap.* i. 199, ii. 108.

453

τῆς γῆς κοινὴν εἶναι τοῖς θέλουσι τὴν χρῆσιν, τῶν τε ὁμοφύλων καὶ τῶν ἀλλοτριοχώρων, μηδὲν ἐξ αὑτῶν φυλάττοντας· ποιεῖν δὲ τοῦτο καὶ μεθ᾽ 282 ἑβδόμην ἐτῶν ἑβδομάδα. ταῦτα πεντήκοντα μέν ἐστιν ἔτη τὰ πάντα, καλεῖται δὲ ὑπὸ Ἑβραίων ὁ πεντηκοστὸς ἐνιαυτὸς ἰώβηλος, ἐν ᾧ οἵ τε χρεῶσται τῶν δανείων ἀπολύονται καὶ οἱ δουλεύοντες ἐλεύθεροι ἀφίενται, οὓς ὄντας ὁμοφύλους καὶ παραβάντας τι τῶν νομίμων τῷ σχήματι τῆς δουλείας ἐκόλασε θάνατον οὐκ ἐκδεχομένους. 283 ἀποδίδωσι δὲ καὶ τοὺς ἀγροὺς τοῖς ἀρχῆθεν αὐτῶν δεσπόταις τοῦτον τὸν τρόπον· ἐνστάντος τοῦ ἰωβήλου, ἐλευθερίαν δὲ σημαίνει τοὔνομα, συνέρχονται ὅ τε ἀποδόμενος τὸ χωρίον καὶ ὁ πριάμενος, καὶ λογισάμενοι τοὺς καρποὺς καὶ τὰς εἰς τὸ χωρίον δαπάνας γεγενημένας τῶν μὲν καρπῶν πλεονάζειν εὑρεθέντων προσδέχεται τὸν ἀγρὸν ὁ 284 ἀποδόμενος, τοῦ δ᾽ ἀναλώματος ὑπερβάλλοντος

---

^a See note *d* below.

^b Josephus is here in error or at least at variance with Scripture. The "release" from debts applied not to the year of jubilee, but to the seventh or sabbatical year (Deut. xv. 1 ff.); it is uncertain whether it " was an actual remission of loans, or merely the suspension, for one year, of the creditor's right to demand payment" (Driver *in loc.*). In any case the law, which led to abuses, had early in the first century A.D. been virtually abrogated by a so-called *prosbol* (προσβολή) of Hillel.

^c Scripture does not speak of punishment but of voluntary servitude resulting from poverty. " And if thy brother be waxen poor with thee, and sell himself unto thee, thou shalt not make him to serve as a bondservant: as an hired servant and as a sojourner he shall be with thee " etc., Lev. *loc. cit.*; this explains the σχῆμα δουλείας in the text. *Cf. A.* iv. 273 for further details.

enjoyment of these was to be open to all desirous of them, whether countryman or alien, none of them being kept back. This practice was also to be observed at the end of the seventh week of years. This is the period amounting to fifty years in all, of which the fiftieth year is called by the Hebrews *Jôbêl*[a]; at that season debtors are absolved from their debts[b] and slaves are set at liberty, that is to say those who are members of the race and having transgressed some requirement of the law have by it been punished[c] by reduction to a servile condition, without being condemned to death. Now too he restores estates to their original owners after the following fashion. When the *Jôbêl* comes round—the name denotes " liberty "[d]—the vendor and the purchaser of the site meet together and reckon up the products of the site and the outgoings expended upon it.[e] Then if the proceeds are found to exceed the outgoings, the vendor recovers the estate; but if the

The year of jubilee. Lev. xxv. 8.

Lev. xxv. 39.

Cf. xxv. 13-16.

Cf. xxv. 27.

---

[d] One of the author's loose etymological statements (*cf. A.* v. 34). The traditional, and doubtless correct, meaning of *jôbêl* is " ram," an abbreviation for " ram's horn," " cornet," by the sounding of which the " jubilee " was proclaimed. For *jôbêl* (Lev. xxv. 10) LXX writes ἐνιαυτὸς ἀφέσεως σημασία; here σημασία (" signalling ") is the translation of *jôbêl*, while ἄφεσις = Heb. *deror*, " liberty," as the context shows. Josephus has erroneously equated *jôbêl* = ἄφεσις = ἐλευθερία.

[e] Leviticus says nothing about a reckoning up *at the jubilee* or the three cases mentioned in the next sentence. All that it implies is that the leasehold alone could be sold and that the price was to be based on the number of crops intervening between the date of sale and the jubilee (*vv.* 15 f.): this price was apparently to be estimated at the time of the sale: the land could at any time be redeemed on payment of the value of the crops between the date of redemption and the next jubilee (*v.* 27).

ὑπὲρ τοῦ λείποντος ⟨μὴ⟩[1] καταβαλὼν τὸ ἱκνού-
μενον ἐξίσταται[2] τῆς κτήσεως, ἴσων δὲ συναριθμου-
μένων τῶν τε καρπῶν καὶ τῶν ἀναλωμάτων
285 ἀποδίδωσι τοῖς καὶ πρότερον νεμηθεῖσι. τὸ αὐτὸ
δὲ καὶ ἐπὶ ταῖς οἰκίαις νόμιμον ἰσχύειν ἠθέλησε
ταῖς κατὰ κώμας πεπραμέναις· περὶ γὰρ τῶν ἐν
τῇ πόλει πεπραμένων ἔγνωκεν ἑτέρως· εἰ μὲν γὰρ
πρὸ τοῦ τελειωθῆναι τὸν ἐνιαυτὸν καταβάλοι τὸ
ἀργύριον, ἀναγκάζει τὸν πριάμενον ἀποδοῦναι, εἰ
δὲ πλῆρες γένοιτο τὸ ἔτος, βεβαιοῖ τὴν κτῆσιν τῷ
286 πριαμένῳ. ταύτην Μωυσῆς τὴν διάταξιν τῶν
νόμων, ὅθ᾽ ὑπὸ τὸ Σιναῖον καθιδρύκει τὴν στρατιάν,
ἐξέμαθε παρὰ τοῦ θεοῦ καὶ τοῖς Ἑβραίοις γεγραμ-
μένην παραδίδωσιν.

287 (4) Ἐπειδὴ δὲ καλῶς αὐτῷ τὰ περὶ τὴν νομο-
θεσίαν ἔχειν ἐδόκει, πρὸς ἐξέτασιν τοῦ στρατοῦ τὸ
λοιπὸν ἐτράπη τῶν πολεμικῶν ἤδη κατὰ νοῦν
ἔχων ἅπτεσθαι, προστάσσει τε τοῖς φυλάρχοις
πλὴν τῆς Λευίτιδος φυλῆς ἀκριβῶς τὸν ἀριθμὸν
ἐκμαθεῖν τῶν στρατεύεσθαι δυναμένων· ἱεροὶ γὰρ
288 ἦσαν οἱ Λευῖται καὶ πάντων ἀτελεῖς. γενομένης
δὲ τῆς ἐξετάσεως εὑρέθησαν μυριάδες ἑξήκοντα
τῶν ὁπλιτεύειν δυναμένων, ὄντων ἀπὸ εἴκοσι ἐτῶν
ἕως πεντήκοντα, καὶ τρισχίλιοι πρὸς ἑξακοσίοις

[1] ins. Herwerden.   [2] ἐξέρχεται R: ἐξέχεται OM.

---

[a] Text emended, with Herwerden and Weill, by insertion of a negative. The MSS. have " he pays ... *and* forfeits the property." [b] Greek " he."
[c] We have a similar transition from civil to military matters in iv. 292. In both cases the hand of the " Thucydidean " assistant who was later to take a large share in the

expenditure preponderates, he must pay a sufficient sum to cover the deficit or forfeit the property [a]; if, lastly, the figures for revenue and expenditure are equal, the legislator [b] restores the land to its former possessors. In the case of houses, Moses desired the same regulation to apply to the sale of those situated in villages. For the sale of town houses he decreed otherwise: in those cases, if before the expiry of the year the price was paid, he compels the purchaser to surrender the house; but if a full year has elapsed, he confirms to the purchaser his right of possession. Such was the code of laws which Moses, while keeping his army encamped beneath Mount Sinai, learnt from the mouth of God and transmitted in writing to the Hebrews.

Lev. xxv. 31.

xxv. 29.

(4) And now that all matters of legislation seemed to him in good order, he next turned his attention to an inspection of his army, already contemplating the prosecution of affairs of war.[c] He accordingly gave orders to the tribal leaders, with the exception of the tribe of Levi, to ascertain the exact number of those capable of military service, the Levites being a holy tribe and exempt from all claims. The inspection having duly been held, there were found to be 603,650 [d] men capable of bearing arms,[e] from twenty

Numbering of the army. Numb. i. 1.

i. 45 f.

work (*A*. xvii-xix), here makes its appearance, as it has done already in the account of the battle with Amalek (iii. 53 ff.). In these earlier books he is employed as a sort of "war correspondent." The phrase πολεμικῶν ἅπτεσθαι is based on Thuc. v. 61 ἅπτεσθαι πολέμου (*cf. A*. xviii. 278).

[d] Heb. and LXX "603,550"; but the additional century in Josephus has the support of the Armenian version. *Cf.* iii. 196 for a similar difference of figures.

[e] ὁπλιτεύειν is Thucydidean and in Josephus recurs only in *A*. xix. 243.

καὶ πεντήκοντα. ἀντὶ δὲ Λευὶ κατέλεξεν εἰς τοὺς φυλάρχους Μανασσῆν τὸν Ἰωσήπου παῖδα καὶ Ἐφραίμην¹ ἀντὶ τοῦ Ἰωσήπου· δέησις δὲ ἦν αὕτη Ἰακώβου πρὸς Ἰώσηπον ποιητοὺς αὐτῷ παρασχεῖν τοὺς παῖδας, ὡς καὶ προεῖπον.

289 (5) Πηγνύντες δὲ τὴν σκηνὴν μέσην ἀπελάμβανον τριῶν φυλῶν κατὰ πλευρὰν ἑκάστην παρασκηνουμένων· ὁδοὶ δὲ διὰ μέσων ἐτέτμηντο, καὶ κόσμος ἦν ἀγορᾶς, καὶ τῶν πωλουμένων ἕκαστον ἐν τάξει διέκειτο, καὶ δημιουργοὶ τέχνης ἁπάσης ἐν τοῖς ἐργαστηρίοις ἦσαν, οὐδενί τε ἄλλῳ ἢ πόλει μετ-
290 ανισταμένῃ καὶ καθιδρυμένῃ ἐῴκει. τὰ δὲ περὶ τὴν σκηνὴν πρῶτοι μὲν οἱ ἱερεῖς κατεῖχον, ἔπειτα δὲ οἱ Λευῖται πάντες ὄντες τὸ πλῆθος, ἐξητάσθησαν γὰρ καὶ αὐτοὶ τοῦ μὲν ἄρρενος ὅσον τριακοστὴν εἶχεν ἡμέραν γενόμενον, δισμύριοι καὶ δισχίλιοι² πρὸς τοῖς ὀκτακοσίοις ὀγδοήκοντα. καὶ ἐφ᾽ ὅσον μὲν ὑπὲρ τὴν σκηνὴν συνέβαινεν ἑστάναι τὴν νεφέλην, μένειν αὐτοῖς ὡς ἐπιδημοῦντος ἐδόκει τοῦ θεοῦ, τρεπομένης δὲ ταύτης μετανίστασθαι.

291 (6) Εὗρε δὲ καὶ βυκάνης τρόπον ἐξ ἀργύρου ποιησάμενος, ἔστι δὲ τοιαύτη· μῆκος μὲν ἔχει πηχυαῖον ὀλίγῳ λεῖπον, στενὴ δ᾽ ἐστὶ σύριγξ

¹ SPE: Ἐφράην M, Ἐφράθην RO, Εὐφράνην L.
² τρισχίλιοι MLEZon.

---

[a] Numb. "from twenty years old and upward"; cf. A. iii. 196.   [b] Cf. ii. 195.

JEWISH ANTIQUITIES, III. 288-291

to fifty *a* years of age. In place of Levi he enrolled among the tribal leaders Manasseh, son of Joseph, and Ephraim in the stead of Joseph, in accordance with the request which Jacob had made to Joseph to give up his children to be adopted by their grandsire, as I have already related.*b*

(5) In the pitching of their camp the tabernacle was given a central isolated position, three tribes being encamped along each side, with roads laid out between them. Here too was an orderly market-place, articles of merchandise lay ranged each in its place, and artisans of every craft had their workshops: in short it was like nothing so much as a city ever shifting and settling down.*c* The region directly surrounding the tabernacle was occupied by the priests,*d* after whom came the Levites, amounting in all—for the numbering included these also, that is to say all males upwards of thirty days old—to 22,880 *e* souls. And so long as the cloud was found stationary above the tabernacle, they thought good to tarry, believing that God was sojourning among them, but, when it removed, then to break their camp.

(6) Moses further invented a kind of clarion, which he had made for him in silver, on this wise. In length a little short of a cubit, it is a narrow tube,

Arrangement of the camp.
Numb. ii. 1.

Cf. i. 53.

Cf. iii. 39.

ix. 18.

The silver trumpets and their signals.
Numb. x. 1.

---

c The Hebrew camp is modelled on that of the Romans, which also is compared to an improvised city (*B.J.* iii. 82 f.), the tabernacle here replacing the *praetorium*. The last phrase is a combination of Thuc. vii. 75 οὐδὲν γὰρ ἄλλο ἢ πόλει ... ἐῴκεσαν ὑποφευγούσῃ with i. 12 ἡ Ἑλλὰς ἔτι μετανίστατό τε καὶ κατῳκίζετο.

d Not mentioned in Numb. *loc. cit.*: "the Levites shall pitch round about the tabernacle."

e Some MSS. read 23,880. Both figures differ from the Biblical round number of 22,000 (Numb. iii. 39 Heb. and LXX).

459

αὐλοῦ βραχεῖ παχυτέρα, παρέχουσα δὲ εὖρος ἀρκοῦν ἐπὶ τῷ στόματι πρὸς ὑποδοχὴν πνεύματος εἰς κώδωνα ταῖς σάλπιγξι παραπλησίως τελοῦν[1]· ἀσώσρα καλεῖται κατὰ τὴν Ἑβραίων γλῶσσαν.
292 γίνονται δὲ δύο, καὶ τῇ μὲν ἑτέρᾳ πρὸς παρακέλευσιν καὶ συλλογὴν ἐχρῶντο τοῦ πλήθους εἰς τὰς ἐκκλησίας· καὶ μιᾷ μὲν ἀποσημήναντος ἔδει τὰς ἀρχὰς συνελθεῖν σκεψομένας περὶ τῶν οἰκείων,
293 ἀμφοτέραις δὲ συνῆγε τὸ πλῆθος. τῆς δὲ σκηνῆς μετακινουμένης ταῦτα ἐγίνετο· ἀποσημήναντος γὰρ τὸ πρῶτον οἱ παρὰ ταῖς ἀνατολαῖς ἐσκηνωκότες ἀνίσταντο, καὶ πρὸς τὴν δευτέραν οἱ πρὸς τὸν νότον αὖθις[2] καθεστῶτες. εἶθ᾽ ἡ σκηνὴ λυομένη μέση τῶν προϊουσῶν ἐξ φυλῶν ἐκομίζετο καὶ τῶν ἑπομένων ἕξ, Λευῖται δὲ περὶ τὴν σκηνὴν πάντες
294 ἦσαν. τρίτον δὲ σημήναντος τὸ κατὰ λίβα τετραμμένον τῶν ἐσκηνωκότων μέρος ἐκινεῖτο,[3] καὶ τέταρτον τὸ κατὰ βορρᾶν. ταῖς δὲ βυκάναις ἐχρῶντο καὶ ἐπὶ ταῖς ἱερουργίαις προσάγοντες τὰς θυσίας καὶ τοῖς σαββάτοις καὶ ταῖς λοιπαῖς ἡμέραις. θύει δὲ τότε πρῶτον μετὰ τὴν ἀναχώρησιν τὴν ἐξ Αἰγύπτου τὴν πάσχα[4] λεγομένην ἐπὶ τῆς ἐρήμου.

295 (xiii) Καὶ βραχὺ διαλιπὼν ἀπανίσταται τοῦ Σιναίου ὄρους καὶ τόπους τινὰς ἀμείψας, περὶ ὧν

---

[1] ed. pr.: τελοῦντα codd.   [2] RO: αὐτῆς rell.
[3] ed. pr.: ἐνέκειτο codd.   [4] φάσκα RO.

---

[a] Ḥaẓoẓerah, the straight trumpet depicted on the Arch of Titus; as opposed to the *shophar* or curved horn, used mainly for secular purposes.

[b] Greek "he" (*i.e.* Moses had the people convened).

slightly thicker than a flute, with a mouthpiece wide enough to admit the breath and a bell-shaped extremity such as trumpets have. It is called *asôsra* [a] in the Hebrew tongue. Two such instruments were made, one being reserved for summoning and collecting the people to the assemblies: if only one sounded, it behoved the chiefs to meet for deliberation on their own affairs; with the two together they [b] convened the people. When the tabernacle was to be moved, this was the procedure: at the first signal those who were encamped on the east arose, at the second it was the turn for those stationed to the south. Then the tabernacle, being taken to pieces, was carried in the centre, between the six tribes in front and the six which followed it, the Levites being all grouped around it. At the third signal the western section of the camp moved off, at the fourth the northern contingent.[c] These clarions they used also for their sacrificial ceremonies, when bringing the victims to the altar, both on the sabbath and on the other (festal) days.[d] And now it was that Moses, for the first time since their departure from Egypt, kept the sacrifice called *Pascha* in the wilderness.

Numb. x. 5.

Cf. ii. 17.

x. 10.

Keeping of Passover. *Ib.* ix. 1.

(xiii) After a brief interval he broke up his camp at Mount Sinai, and, passing certain localities of

Departure from Sinai: renewed murmurings. *Ib.* xi. 1.

[c] The third and fourth signals are mentioned here (Numb. x. 6) by the LXX only (not in the Hebrew text); but this order of movement has already been stated in Numb. ii. 18 ff.

[d] Numb. *loc. cit.* mentions three occasions for their use: "the day (LXX "days") of your gladness" (*i.e.* extraordinary public festivals), fixed feasts, and new moons. The sabbath is not specified, but according to tradition (*Sifré*, cited by Weill) it was indicated by the first two phrases.

δηλώσομεν, εἴς τι χωρίον Ἐσερμὼθ λεγόμενον παρῆν, κἀκεῖ τὸ πλῆθος πάλιν στασιάζειν ἄρχεται, καὶ τὸν Μωυσῆν αἰτιᾶσθαι τῶν τε κατὰ τὴν 296 ἀποδημίαν αὐτῷ πεπειραμένων, καὶ ὅτι γῆς αὐτοὺς ἀγαθῆς πείσαντος ἀπαναστῆναι τὴν μὲν ἀπολέσειαν, ἀντὶ δὲ ἧς ὑπέσχετο παρέξειν εὐδαιμονίας ἐν ταύταις ἀλῶνται ταῖς ταλαιπωρίαις, ὕδατος μὲν σπανίζοντες, εἰ δὲ καὶ τὴν μάνναν ἐπιλιπεῖν συμ- 297 βαίη τέλεον ἀπολούμενοι. πολλὰ δὲ εἰς τὸν ἄνδρα καὶ δεινὰ λεγόντων, εἷς δέ τις αὐτοῖς παρῄνει, μήτε Μωυσέος καὶ τῶν πεπονημένων αὐτῷ περὶ τῆς κοινῆς σωτηρίας ἀμνημονεῖν μήτ' ἀπογινώσκειν τῆς ἐκ τοῦ θεοῦ βοηθείας. τὸ δὲ πλῆθος πρὸς τοῦτο μᾶλλον ἐκινήθη καὶ θορυβῆσαν ἔτι μᾶλλον 298 πρὸς τὸν Μωυσῆν ἐπετείνετο. Μωυσῆς δὲ παραθαρσύνων αὐτοὺς οὕτως ἀπεγνωκότας ὑπέσχετο, καίπερ αἰσχρῶς ὑπ' αὐτῶν περιυβρισμένος, πλῆθος αὐτοῖς παρέξειν κρεῶν οὐκ εἰς μίαν ἡμέραν ἀλλ' εἰς πλείονας. ἀπιστούντων δ' ἐπὶ τούτῳ καί τινος ἐρομένου, πόθεν ἂν τοσαύταις εὐπορήσειε μυριάσι τῶν προειρημένων, "ὁ θεός," εἶπε, "κἀγὼ καίτοι κακῶς ἀκούοντες πρὸς ὑμῶν οὐκ ἂν ἀποσταίημεν κάμνοντες ὑπὲρ ὑμῶν, καὶ ταῦτα οὐκ εἰς μακρὰν 299 ἔσται." ἅμα ταῦτ' ἔλεγε καὶ πίμπλαται τὸ στρατόπεδον ὀρτύγων ἅπαν καὶ ἤθροιζον αὐτοὺς περι-

---

[a] He does not revert to these; possibly he refers to his projected work, or, as has been suggested, a negative may have dropped out. The stages named in Numb. xi are Taberah (v. 3), Kibroth-hattaavah and Hazeroth (34 f.); Josephus omits the first and reverses the order of the second and third.

[b] Bibl. Hazeroth (Ἀσηρώθ), Numb. xi. 35. But, as Weill suggests, the form Ἐσερμὼθ in Josephus recalls rather the

which we shall speak,*a* came to a place called Esermoth.*b* There the multitude began to revolt once more and to reproach Moses for the trials which they had undergone on these peregrinations: that good land which he had persuaded them to quit was now lost to them, but, instead of the felicity which he had promised to procure, here they were wandering in these miseries, lacking water and, should the manna happen to fail, doomed to utter destruction. Amid this torrent of abuse showered upon the hero, there was yet one *c* who admonished them not to be unmindful of Moses and what he had suffered for the salvation of all, nor to despair of God's aid. But at that the multitude was only roused the more and uproariously and yet more fiercely inveighed against Moses. He, however, to embolden them in their deep despair, promised, albeit so shamefully outraged by them, to procure for them meat in abundance, not for one day only but for many more. But since they put no faith in that and someone asked whence could he get for such myriads those predicted supplies,*d* "God," said he, "and I, though vilified by you, will never cease our efforts on your behalf; they will come at no distant date." Even as he spake, the camp was filled with quails on every side, and they gathered round them and collected them.

Numb. xi. 4.

Miraculous gift of quails. *Cf.* xi. 19.

xi. 31.

Semite patriarch Hazarmaveth (Ἀσαρμώθ) in Gen. x. 26, who gave his name to a district on the south coast of Arabia, the modern *Hadramaut* (Driver).

c Unscriptural addition: possibly to be connected with the story of Eldad and Medad, who "prophesied in the camp," Numb. xi. 26.

d In Scripture it is God who makes the promise to Moses, and Moses himself who is sceptical (Numb. xi. 21 f.); Josephus throws the odium of this disbelief upon another.

463

στάντες. ὁ μέντοι θεὸς οὐκ εἰς μακρὰν μετέρχεται τοὺς Ἑβραίους τῆς εἰς αὐτὸν θρασύτητος καὶ λοιδορίας· ἀπέθανε γὰρ οὐκ ὀλίγον πλῆθος αὐτῶν, καὶ νῦν ἔτι κατ' ἐπωνυμίαν ὁ χῶρος ὀνομάζεται Καβρωθαβά, ἐπιθυμίας μνημεῖα λέγοιτο ⟨ἄν⟩.[1]

300 (xiv. 1) Ἀναγαγὼν δὲ αὐτοὺς ἐκεῖθεν ὁ Μωυσῆς εἰς τὴν καλουμένην Φάραγγα πλησίον οὖσαν τοῖς Χαναναίων ὁρίοις[2] καὶ χαλεπὴν ἐνδιαιτᾶσθαι εἰς ἐκκλησίαν ἀθροίζει τὸ πλῆθος καὶ καταστάς, " δύο," φησί, " τοῦ θεοῦ κρίναντος ὑμῖν παρασχεῖν ἀγαθά, ἐλευθερίαν καὶ γῆς κτῆσιν εὐδαίμονος, τὴν μὲν ἤδη δόντος ἔχετε, τὴν δὲ ἤδη λήψεσθε.
301 Χαναναίων γὰρ ἐπὶ τοῖς ὅροις καθήμεθα, καὶ κωλύσει τὸ λοιπὸν ἐπιόντας οὐ μόνον οὐ βασιλεὺς οὐ πόλις ἡμᾶς, ἀλλ' οὐδὲ τὸ πᾶν ἀθροισθὲν αὐτῶν[3] ἔθνος. παρασκευαζώμεθα οὖν πρὸς τὸ ἔργον· οὐ γὰρ ἀμαχητὶ παραχωρήσουσιν ἡμῖν τῆς γῆς, ἀλλὰ
302 μεγάλοις αὐτὴν ἀγῶσιν ἀφαιρεθέντες. πέμψωμεν δὲ κατασκόπους, οἳ τῆς τε[4] γῆς ἀρετὴν κατανοήσουσι καὶ πόση δύναμις αὐτοῖς. πρὸ δὲ πάντων ὁμονοῶμεν καὶ τὸν θεόν, ὅς ἐστιν ἐπὶ πᾶσιν ἡμῖν βοηθὸς καὶ σύμμαχος, διὰ τιμῆς ἔχωμεν."

303 (2) Μωυσέος δὲ ταῦτ' εἰπόντος τὸ πλῆθος αὐτὸν τιμαῖς ἀμείβεται, καὶ κατασκόπους αἱρεῖται δώδεκα τῶν γνωριμωτάτων, ἐξ ἑκάστης φυλῆς ἕνα, οἳ διεξελθόντες ἀπὸ τῶν πρὸς Αἰγύπτῳ τὴν Χαναναίαν

---

[1] ins. Niese.   [2] ed. pr., Lat.: ὅροις L: χωρίοις rell.
[3] ἀθροισθέντων RO.
[4] τῆς τε ed. pr.: τῆσδε τῆς (or τῆς δὲ) codd.

---

[a] Heb. Kibroth-hattaavah; Josephus takes over the correct Greek translation, ἐπιθυμίας μνημεῖα, from the LXX.
[b] Josephus significantly omits Numb. xii, the narrative

However God, not long after, chastised the Hebrews for their abusive insolence towards Him: in fact no small number of them perished. And to this day, that spot still bears the surname of Kabrothaba,[a] that is to say, "graves of lust." [Numb. xi. 34.]

(xiv. 1) Thence[b] Moses led them up into the so-called Ravine,[c] nigh to the Canaanite frontier and grievous for habitation. There he collected the people in assembly and standing before them said: "Of the two blessings which God has resolved to grant you, liberty and the possession of a favoured land, the first through His gift ye already have, and the second ye are forthwith to receive. For we are seated on the frontiers of the Canaanites, and henceforth our advance shall be stayed not only by neither king nor city, nay not even by their whole united nation. Prepare we then for the task; for it is not without a combat that they will cede to us their territory, but only when after mighty struggles they are dispossessed of it. Let us then send scouts to mark the richness of the land and the strength of its people's forces. But, before all, let us be of one mind and hold God, who is ever our helper and ally, in lasting honour." [Speech of Moses on the borders of Canaan. xiii. 1.]

(2) These words of Moses were rewarded by the respectful attention of the people, and they selected twelve scouts from their most notable men, one from each tribe. These, starting from the Egyptian frontier, traversed Canaan from end to end, reached [Mission and report of the spies. xiii. 3.]

of the slanders brought against Moses by Miriam and Aaron; he has already, in Book ii, explained how Moses came to marry a "Cushite woman."

[c] Gr. "Pharanx," a Hellenization of the Heb. Paran (LXX Φαράν), Numb. xii. 16. The "wilderness of Paran" lay north of Sinai, south of Kadesh, and west of Edom.

ἅπασαν ἐπί τε Ἀμάθην πόλιν καὶ Λίβανον ἀφικνοῦνται τὸ ὄρος, καὶ τήν τε τῆς γῆς φύσιν καὶ τὴν τῶν ἐνοικούντων ἀνθρώπων ἐξιστορήσαντες παρῆσαν τεσσαράκοντα ἡμέραις εἰς πᾶν καταχρησάμενοι
304 τὸ ἔργον, ἔτι τε καρποὺς ὧν ἔφερεν ἡ γῆ κομίζοντες, τῇ τε τούτων εὐπρεπείᾳ καὶ τῷ πλήθει τῶν ἀγαθῶν, ἃ τὴν γῆν ἔχειν διηγοῦντο, πολεμεῖν ἐπαίροντες τὸ πλῆθος, φοβοῦντες δὲ πάλιν αὐτὸ τῷ τῆς κτήσεως ἀπόρῳ, ποταμούς τε διαβῆναι λέγοντες ἀδυνάτους ὑπὸ μεγέθους ἅμα καὶ βάθους καὶ ὄρη ἀμήχανα τοῖς ὁδεύουσι καὶ πόλεις καρ-
305 τερὰς τείχεσι καὶ περιβόλων ὀχυρότητι· ἐν δ' Ἑβρῶνι καὶ τῶν γιγάντων ἔφασκον τοὺς ἀπογόνους καταλαβεῖν. καὶ οἱ μὲν κατάσκοποι τεθεαμένοι πάντων οἷς μετὰ τὴν ἔξοδον τὴν ἀπ' Αἰγύπτου ἐνέτυχον μείζω τὰ κατὰ τὴν Χαναναίαν αὐτοί τε κατεπλάγησαν[1] καὶ τὸ πλῆθος οὕτως ἔχειν[2] ἐπειρῶντο.

306 (3) Οἱ δὲ ἄπορον ἐξ ὧν ἠκροάσαντο τὴν κτῆσιν τῆς γῆς ὑπελάμβανον καὶ διαλυθέντες ἐκ τῆς ἐκκλησίας σὺν γυναιξὶ καὶ παισὶν ὀλοφυρόμενοι διῆγον, ὡς οὐδὲν ἔργῳ τοῦ θεοῦ βοηθοῦντος λόγῳ
307 δὲ μόνον ὑπισχνουμένου. καὶ τὸν Μωυσῆν πάλιν ᾐτιῶντο καὶ κατεβόων αὐτοῦ καὶ τοῦ ἀδελφοῦ Ἀαρῶνος τοῦ ἀρχιερέως. καὶ πονηρὰν μὲν καὶ μετὰ τῶν εἰς τοὺς ἄνδρας βλασφημιῶν διάγουσι τὴν νύκτα, πρωῒ δ' εἰς τὴν ἐκκλησίαν συντρέχουσι,

[1] κατεπεπληγέσαν L (καταπεπληγέσαν M).
[2] +⟨πείθειν⟩ Niese.

---

[a] Hamath on the Orontes in north Syria. The Biblical

the city of Amathe *a* and Mount Libanus, and after fully exploring the nature of the country and of its inhabitants returned, having spent but forty days over the whole task. They moreover brought with them some of the produce of the country. By the beauty of these fruits and by the abundance of good things which, according to their report, the land contained, they roused the military ardour of the people; but they terrified them, on the other hand, by the difficulties of conquest, declaring that there were rivers impossible to cross, so broad and deep withal were they, mountains impracticable for passage, cities fortified by ramparts and solid ring-walls, while in Hebron they asserted that they had lit upon the descendants of the giants. Thus the scouts, having seen that the things of Canaan surpassed in magnitude all that they had encountered since the exodus from Egypt, were not only themselves panic-stricken, but sought to reduce the people to the same condition.

(3) And they, after what they had heard, deemed the conquest of the country impracticable and, when dismissed from the assembly, gave themselves up to lamentation with their wives and children, as though God tendered them no actual aid, but only verbal promises. Once more they blamed Moses and loaded him with abuse, him and his brother Aaron, the high-priest. In this sorry condition, then, amid vituperations upon the two of them, did they pass the night; and next morning they rushed together

Numb. xiii. 25.

xiii. 22, 33.

Dejection and revolt of the Hebrews. xiv. 1.

phrase (Numb. xiii. 21) "the entering in of (entrance to) Hamath," elsewhere named as the northern boundary of Canaan, means a region far to the south of the city itself, perhaps the depression between Lebanon and Hermon.

δι' ἐννοίας ἔχοντες καταλεύσαντες τόν τε Μωυσῆν καὶ τὸν Ἀαρῶνα ἐπὶ τὴν Αἴγυπτον ὑποστρέφειν.

308 (4) Τῶν δὲ κατασκόπων Ἰησοῦς τε ὁ Ναυήχου παῖς φυλῆς Ἐφραιμίτιδος καὶ Χάλεβος τῆς Ἰούδα φυλῆς φοβηθέντες χωροῦσιν εἰς μέσους καὶ τὸ πλῆθος κατεῖχον, θαρσεῖν δεόμενοι καὶ μήτε ψευδολογίαν κατακρίνειν τοῦ θεοῦ μήτε πιστεύειν τοῖς ἐκ τοῦ μὴ τἀληθῆ περὶ τῶν Χαναναίων εἰρηκέναι καταπληξαμένοις, ἀλλὰ τοῖς ἐπὶ τὴν εὐδαιμονίαν καὶ τὴν κτῆσιν αὐτοὺς τῶν ἀγαθῶν
309 παρορμῶσιν· οὔτε γὰρ τῶν ὀρῶν τὸ μέγεθος οὔτε τῶν ποταμῶν τὸ βάθος τοῖς ἀρετὴν ἠσκηκόσιν ἐμποδὼν στήσεσθαι πρὸς τὰ ἔργα, καὶ ταῦτα τοῦ θεοῦ συμπροθυμουμένου καὶ ὑπερμαχοῦντος αὐτῶν. "ἴωμεν οὖν," ἔφασαν, "ἐπὶ τοὺς πολεμίους μηδὲν ἔχοντες δι' ὑποψίας ἡγεμόνι τε τῷ θεῷ πεπιστευκότες καὶ ὁδηγοῦσιν ἡμῖν ἑπόμενοι."
310 καὶ οἱ μὲν ταῦτα λέγοντες ἐπεχείρουν τὴν ὀργὴν καταπραΰνειν τοῦ πλήθους, Μωυσῆς δὲ καὶ Ἀαρὼν πεσόντες ἐπὶ τὴν γῆν τὸν θεὸν ἱκέτευον οὐχ ὑπὲρ τῆς ἑαυτῶν σωτηρίας, ἀλλ' ὅπως τῆς ἀμαθίας παύσῃ τὸ πλῆθος καὶ καταστήσῃ τὴν διάνοιαν αὐτῶν ὑπὸ τῆς ἀμηχανίας τοῦ παραστάντος αὐτοῖς πάθους τεταραγμένην· παρῆν δ' ἡ νεφέλη καὶ στᾶσα ὑπὲρ τὴν σκηνὴν ἐσήμαινε τὴν ἐπιφάνειαν τοῦ θεοῦ.

311 (xv. 1) Μωυσῆς δὲ θαρσήσας πάρεισιν εἰς τὸ πλῆθος καὶ τὸν θεὸν ἐδήλου κινηθέντα ὑπὸ τῆς ὕβρεως αὐτῶν[1] λήψεσθαι τιμωρίαν, οὐκ ἀξίαν μὲν τῶν ἁμαρτημάτων,[2] οἵαν δὲ οἱ πατέρες ἐπὶ νου-
312 θεσίᾳ τοῖς τέκνοις ἐπιφέρουσι. παρελθόντι γὰρ εἰς

[1] αὐτῷ RO: αὐτῷ Niese. [2] RO: ἐξημαρτημένων rell.

to the assembly, with intent to stone Moses and Aaron and to return to Egypt.

(4) But two of the scouts, Jesus, son of Nauechos[a] of the tribe of Ephraim and Caleb of the tribe of Judah, in horror made their way into the midst and sought to restrain the crowd, entreating them to be courageous and neither to accuse God of untruthfulness nor to put faith in those who had terrified them by false statements concerning the Canaanites, but rather to trust those who exhorted them to proceed to prosperity and the acquisition of those good things. For neither the height of the mountains nor the depth of the rivers would prove obstacles to the activities of men of tried valour, above all when God was seconding their ardour and championing their cause. "Go we then forward," said they, "against the foe, with no lurking misgivings; trust in our leader, God, and follow us who will show you the way!" By these words did they endeavour to allay the passion of the multitude. Meanwhile, Moses and Aaron, prostrated to earth, were supplicating God, not for their own salvation, but that He would rid the people of their ignorance and calm their spirits, disordered by the helplessness of their present plight. Then there appeared the cloud which, resting above the tabernacle, signalized the presence of God.

(xv. 1) Moses, emboldened, now approached the people and announced that God, moved by their insolence, would exact retribution, not indeed proportionate to their errors, but such as fathers inflict upon their children for their admonition. For, so he

[a] Joshua son of Nun (iii. 49 note).

JOSEPHUS

τὴν σκηνὴν αὐτῷ καὶ περὶ τῆς μελλούσης ὑπ' αὐτῶν ἀπωλείας ἀποκλαιομένῳ τὸν θεὸν ὑπομνῆσαι μέν, ὅσα παθόντες ἐξ αὐτοῦ καὶ πηλίκων εὐεργεσιῶν μεταλαβόντες ἀχάριστοι πρὸς αὐτὸν γένοιντο, ὅτι τε τῇ νῦν τῶν κατασκόπων ὑπαχθέντες δειλίᾳ τοὺς ἐκείνων λόγους ἀληθεστέρους
313 τῆς ὑποσχέσεως ἡγήσαντο τῆς αὐτοῦ. καὶ διὰ ταυτην τὴν αἰτίαν οὐκ ἀπολεῖ μὲν ἅπαντας οὐδ' ἐξαφανίσει τὸ γένος αὐτῶν, ὃ πάντων μᾶλλον ἀνθρώπων ἔσχε διὰ τιμῆς, τὴν μέντοι Χαναναίαν οὐ παρέξειν γῆν αὐτοῖς λαβεῖν οὐδὲ τὴν ἀπ' αὐτῆς
314 εὐδαιμονίαν, ἀνεστίους δὲ ποιήσειν καὶ ἀπόλιδας ἐπὶ τῆς ἐρημίας ἐπ' ἔτη τεσσαράκοντα καταβιῶναι, τῆς παρανομίας ποινὴν ταύτην ἐκτίνοντας. "παισὶ μέντοι τοῖς ὑμετέροις παραδώσειν τὴν γῆν ὑπέσχετο κἀκείνους τῶν ἀγαθῶν, ὧν ἑαυτοῖς ὑπὸ ἀκρασίας ἐφθονήσατε μετασχεῖν, ποιήσειν δεσπότας."

315 (2) Ταῦτα δὲ Μωυσέος κατὰ τὴν τοῦ θεοῦ γνώμην διαλεχθέντος ἐν λύπῃ καὶ συμφορᾷ τὸ πλῆθος ἐγένετο, καὶ τὸν Μωυσῆν παρεκάλει καταλλάκτην αὐτῶν γενέσθαι πρὸς τὸν θεὸν καὶ τῆς ἄλης τῆς κατὰ τὴν ἐρημίαν ἀπαλλάξαντα πόλεις αὐτοῖς παρασχεῖν. ὁ δ' οὐκ ἔφασκε τὸν θεὸν τοιαύτην πεῖραν προσήσεσθαι,[1] μὴ γὰρ κατὰ κουφότητα προαχθῆναι τὸν θεὸν ἀνθρωπίνην εἰς τὴν ὀργὴν τὴν πρὸς αὐτοὺς ἀλλὰ γνώμῃ καταψηφισά-
316 μενον αὐτῶν. οὐ δεῖ δὲ ἀπιστεῖν, εἰ Μωυσῆς εἷς ἀνὴρ ὢν τοσαύτας μυριάδας ὀργιζομένας ἐπράυνε καὶ μετήγαγεν εἰς τὸ ἡμερώτερον·[2] ὁ γὰρ θεὸς αὐτῷ συμπαρὼν ἡττᾶσθαι τοῖς λόγοις αὐτοῦ τὸ

---

[1] Dindorf: προσοίσεσθαι codd.
[2] μετήγαγε πρὸς τὸ ἥμερον RO.

told them, when he entered the tabernacle and was deploring his destined destruction at their hands, God had recalled to him how, after all that He had done for them, after all those benefits received, they had proved ungrateful to Him, and how even now, seduced by their spies' faintheartedness, they had reckoned their reports more faithful to the truth than His own promise. And that was why, though He would not consign all to destruction nor exterminate their race, which He esteemed above all mankind, He would yet not suffer them to occupy the land of Canaan or to enjoy its prosperity. Homeless and citiless, he would cause them for forty years to eke out life in the wilderness : this was the penalty that they must pay for their transgression. "Howbeit," he added, "to your children has He promised to give this land and to make them masters of those good things, in which ye through lack of self-control have yourselves declined to share." *Numb. xiv. 31.*

(2) When Moses in accordance with God's purpose had thus addressed them, the people were plunged in grief and affliction, and they besought Moses to intercede for them with God and to spare them that wandering in the wilderness and to give them cities. But he declared that God would admit of no such attempt [a]; for it was not with the lightness of men that God had been brought to this indignation against them, but He had deliberately passed sentence upon them. Nor need one refuse to believe that Moses, by himself alone, calmed such myriads of angry men and brought them back to a gentler mood, for God was present with him, preparing the *Their vain supplications and submission.*

---

[a] No premature attempt at conquest, such as is described at the opening of Book iv.

πλῆθος παρεσκεύαζε, καὶ πολλάκις παρακούσαντες ἀσύμφορον αὑτοῖς τὴν ἀπείθειαν ἐπέγνωσαν ἐκ τοῦ συμφορᾷ περιπεσεῖν.

317 (3) Θαυμαστὸς δὲ τῆς ἀρετῆς ὁ ἀνὴρ καὶ τῆς ἰσχύος τῆς τοῦ πιστεύεσθαι περὶ ὧν ἂν εἴπειεν[1] οὐ παρ' ὃν ἔζη χρόνον ὑπῆρξε μόνον, ἀλλὰ καὶ νῦν· ἔστι γοῦν οὐδεὶς Ἑβραίων, ὃς οὐχὶ καθάπερ παρόντος αὐτοῦ καὶ κολάσοντος ἂν ἀκοσμῇ πειθαρχεῖ τοῖς ὑπ' αὐτοῦ νομοθετηθεῖσι, κἂν 318 λαθεῖν δύνηται. καὶ πολλὰ μὲν καὶ ἄλλα τεκμήρια τῆς ὑπὲρ ἄνθρωπόν ἐστι δυνάμεως αὐτοῦ, ἤδη δέ τινες καὶ τῶν ὑπὲρ Εὐφράτην μηνῶν ὁδὸν τεσσάρων ἐλθόντες κατὰ τιμὴν τοῦ παρ' ἡμῖν ἱεροῦ μετὰ πολλῶν κινδύνων καὶ ἀναλωμάτων καὶ θύσαντες οὐκ ἴσχυσαν τῶν ἱερείων μεταλαβεῖν, Μωυσέος ἀπηγορευκότος ἐπί τινι τῶν οὐ νομιζομένων οὐδ' 319 ἐκ τῶν πατρίων ἡμῖν αὐτοῖς συντυχόντων. καὶ οἱ μὲν μηδὲ θύσαντες, οἱ δὲ ἡμιέργους τὰς θυσίας καταλιπόντες, πολλοὶ δ' οὐδ' ἀρχὴν εἰσελθεῖν εἰς τὸ ἱερὸν δυνηθέντες ἀπίασιν, ὑπακούειν τοῖς Μωυσέος προστάγμασι μᾶλλον ἢ ποιεῖν τὰ κατὰ βούλησιν τὴν ἑαυτῶν προτιμῶντες, καὶ τὸν ἐλέγξοντα περὶ τούτων αὐτοὺς οὐ δεδιότες, ἀλλὰ μόνον 320 τὸ συνειδὸς ὑφορώμενοι. οὕτως ἡ νομοθεσία τοῦ θεοῦ δοκοῦσα τὸν ἄνδρα πεποίηκε τῆς αὐτοῦ φύσεως κρείττονα νομίζεσθαι. οὐ μὴν ἀλλὰ καὶ τοῦδε τοῦ πολέμου μικρὸν ἔμπροσθεν, Κλαυδίου

[1] Dindorf: εἴποιεν (εἴποι) codd.

hearts of the people to yield to his words; moreover, having often disregarded him, they had learnt the unprofitableness of disobedience from the calamities into which they had fallen.

(3) But the admiration in which that hero was held for his virtues and his marvellous power of inspiring faith in all his utterances were not confined to his lifetime: they are alive to-day. Certainly there is not a Hebrew who does not, just as if he were still there and ready to punish him for any breach of discipline, obey the laws laid down by Moses, even though in violating them he could escape detection. Many other proofs of that superhuman power of his might be adduced; and only recently certain persons from beyond the Euphrates, after a journey of four months, undertaken from veneration of our temple and involving great perils and expense, having offered sacrifices, could not partake of the victims, because Moses had forbidden this to any of those not governed by our laws nor affiliated through the customs of their fathers to ourselves. Accordingly, some without sacrificing at all, others leaving their sacrifices half completed, many of them unable so much as to gain entrance to the temple, they went their way, preferring to conform to the injunctions of Moses rather than to act in accordance with their own will, and that from no fear of being reproved in this matter but solely through misgivings of conscience. So surely has that legislation, being believed to come from God, caused this man to be ranked higher than his own (human) nature. But yet again: shortly before the recent war, Claudius

The abiding authority of Moses: two recent instances.

JOSEPHUS

'Ρωμαίων ἄρχοντος Ἰσμαήλου δὲ παρ' ἡμῖν
ἀρχιερέως ὄντος, καὶ λιμοῦ τὴν χώραν ἡμῶν καταλαβόντος, ὡς τεσσάρων δραχμῶν πωλεῖσθαι τὸν
321 ἀσσαρῶνα, κομισθέντος ἀλεύρου κατὰ τὴν ἑορτὴν
τῶν ἀζύμων εἰς κόρους ἑβδομήκοντα, μέδιμνοι
δὲ οὗτοι Σικελοὶ μέν εἰσιν εἷς καὶ τριάκοντα[1]
Ἀττικοὶ δὲ τεσσαράκοντα εἷς, οὐδεὶς ἐτόλμησε
τῶν ἱερέων κρίμνον ἐμφαγεῖν[2] τοσαύτης ἀπορίας
τὴν γῆν κατεχούσης, δεδιὼς τὸν νόμον καὶ τὴν
ὀργήν, ἣν καὶ ἐπὶ ἀνεξελέγκτοις ἀεὶ τὸ θεῖον τοῖς
322 ἀδικήμασιν ἔχει. ὥστ' οὐ δεῖ θαυμάζειν περὶ
τῶν τότε πεπραγμένων, ὁπότε καὶ μέχρι τοῦ νῦν
τὰ καταλειφθέντα ὑπὸ Μωυσέος γράμματα τηλικαύτην ἰσχὺν ἔχει, ὥστε καὶ τοὺς μισοῦντας
ἡμᾶς ὁμολογεῖν, ὅτι[3] τὴν πολιτείαν ἡμῖν ὁ κατα-
στησάμενός ἐστι θεὸς διὰ Μωυσέος καὶ τῆς ἀρετῆς
τῆς ἐκείνου. ἀλλὰ περὶ μὲν τούτων ὡς αὐτῷ
τινι δοκεῖ διαλήψεται.

---

[1] ed. pr., Lat.: τριακόσιοι codd.
[2] ἐμφαγεῖν] ἐν φαγεῖν L Exc. ed. pr. (perhaps rightly).
[3] + καὶ RO.

---

[a] Ishmael ben Phiabi, who was high priest c. A.D. 59–61, when *Nero* was emperor (*A.* xx. 179, 194: Schürer, *G.J.V.*[3] ii. 219). The mention of Claudius (who died in 54 A.D.) is a slip. The house of Phiabi provided other high-priests—a Jesus under Herod the Great (*A.* xv. 322), and another Ishmael under Tiberius (xviii. 34); but there is no record

being ruler of the Romans and Ishmael *a* our high-priest, when our country was in the grip of a famine so severe that an *assarôn* *b* was sold for four drachms, and when there had been brought in during the Feast of Unleavened bread no less than seventy *cors* of flour—equivalent to thirty-one Sicilian or forty-one Attic *medimni* *c*—not one of the priests ventured to consume a crumb,*d* albeit such dearth prevailed throughout the country, from fear of the law and of the wrath wherewith the Deity ever regards even crimes which elude detection. Wherefore one need not marvel at what happened then, seeing that to this very day the writings left by Moses have such authority that even our enemies admit that our constitution was established by God himself, through the agency of Moses and of his merits. But on this subject everyone will form his own opinion.

of an Ishmael under Claudius, and the words "shortly before the war" (which broke out in 66) confirm the reference to the Neronian dignitary.

b Otherwise an *ômer* or "tenth part" of an ephah (iii. 29, 142).

c In such statements Josephus is usually untrustworthy and in this instance inconsistent: in *A*. xv. 314 he gives the equation, 1 *cor* = 10 Attic *medimni*. The Attic *medimnus* was about a bushel and a half.

d Or "a loaf." We must apparently assume that the "flour" was brought in the form of *leavened* loaves, which might not be eaten at that season.

APPENDIX

AN ANCIENT TABLE OF CONTENTS

There has come down to us, prefixed to each book of the *Jewish Antiquities*, and introduced by the words " These are the things contained in the . . . book of the histories of Josephus of the *Jewish Archaeology*," a rough table of contents, together with a statement of the number of years covered by each book. The " titles " of the several sections are numbered in Books I-X, but not in the later books. Since these headings stand not only in the oldest mss but already in the Latin version made in the fifth or sixth century, they possess an interest on the score of antiquity, by whomsoever compiled, and are accordingly (for Books I-III) reproduced below. How much earlier than the date of the Latin version they may be is unknown. The reference to Eusebius in the chronological statement at the end of the heading to Book I betrays a date not earlier than the fourth century ; but that these chronological statements are later than the summaries of contents is indicated by their varying position (before or after the summary) and by their absence, in the earlier books, from the Latin version. In his *Jewish War* Josephus himself incorporated a rough summary of the whole in his proem (i. 19-29) ; and, though it is

ANCIENT TABLE OF CONTENTS

improbable that these more elaborate chapter headings are the production of his pen, they may well be not far removed from him in date. They are ostensibly written by a Jew (I. vii " our forefather Abraham "), and the phraseology occasionally suggests the hand of one of the author's assistants. References to the smaller sections and pages of the present edition are appended.

ΒΙΒΛΙΟΝ Α

Προοίμιον περὶ τῆς ὅλης πραγματείας.[1]

αʹ. Ἡ τοῦ κόσμου σύστασις καὶ διάταξις τῶν στοιχείων.

βʹ. Περὶ τοῦ γένους Ἀδάμου καὶ τῶν ἀπ' αὐτοῦ δέκα γενεῶν τῶν μέχρι τοῦ κατακλυσμοῦ.

γʹ. Ὡς ὁ κατακλυσμὸς ἐγένετο καὶ ὃν τρόπον Νῶχος σωθεὶς ἐν λάρνακι μετὰ τῶν συγγενῶν κατῴκησεν ἐν τῷ Σινάρῳ πεδίῳ.

δʹ. Ὡς πύργον[2] οἱ παῖδες αὐτοῦ ἐφ' ὕβρει τοῦ θεοῦ ᾠκοδόμησαν,[3] καὶ ὡς τὰς φωνὰς αὐτῶν μετέβαλε καὶ ὁ τόπος, ἐν ᾧ τοῦτο γέγονε, Βαβυλὼν ἐκλήθη.

εʹ. Ὡς οἱ Νώχου ἔγγονοι πᾶσαν τὴν οἰκουμένην ἐπῴκησαν.

ϛʹ. Ὅτι τῶν ἐθνῶν ἕκαστον ἀπὸ τῶν οἰκισάντων[4] προσηγορεύθη.

ζʹ. Ὅπως Ἄβραμος ὁ πρόγονος ἡμῶν ἐξελθὼν ἐκ τῆς Χαλδαίων γῆς κατέσχε τὴν τότε μὲν Χαναναίαν νῦν δὲ Ἰουδαίαν λεγομένην.

---

[1] om. Lat. (in which the table of contents stands after the Proem).
[2] πύργον Niese: πύργος ὃν codd.
[3] + κατέπεσεν ed. pr.
[4] Niese: οἰκησάντων codd.

BOOK I

	In this edition SECTION	PAGE
Preface concerning the whole work .	1	2
(i) The construction of the world and disposition of the elements . .	27	14
(ii) Concerning the race of Adam and the ten generations from him up to the flood	34	16
(iii) How the flood came and how Noah, being saved in an ark with his family, settled in the plain of Sinar .	72	32
(iv) How his sons built a tower, in God's despite, and how He confounded [a] their languages and the place wherein this was done was called Babylon	113	54
(v) How the descendants of Noah colonized all the habitable earth .	120	58
(vi) How that each of the nations was named after its founder . .	122	58
(vii) How Abraham, our forefather, quitting the land of the Chaldaeans, occupied that which was then called Canaan and now Judaea . . .	154	76

[a] Gr. "changed."

η'. Ὅτι λιμοῦ τὴν Χαναναίαν καταλαβόντος εἰς Αἴγυπτον ἀπῆρε καὶ διατρίψας ἐν αὐτῇ τινα χρόνον ὑπέστρεψεν ὀπίσω.

θ'. Ἧττα Σοδομιτῶν Ἀσσυρίων αὐτοῖς ἐπιστρατευσάντων.

ι'. Ὡς Ἄβραμος ἐπὶ τοὺς Ἀσσυρίους ἐκστρατεύσας ἐνίκησε καὶ τοὺς αἰχμαλώτους τῶν Σοδομιτῶν ἔσωσε καὶ τὴν λείαν ἣν ἔλαβον ἀφείλετο.

ια'. Πῶς τὸ Σοδομιτῶν ἔθνος θεὸς κατεστρέψατο χολωθεὶς αὐτοῖς ἐφ' οἷς ἡμάρτανον.

ιβ'. Περὶ Ἰσμαήλου τοῦ Ἀβράμου καὶ τῶν ἐγγόνων αὐτοῦ Ἀράβων.

ιγ'. Περὶ Ἰσάκου, ὃς ἦν γνήσιος παῖς Ἀβράμου.

ιδ'. Περὶ Σάρρας τῆς Ἀβράμου γυναικός, καὶ πῶς τὸν βίον κατέστρεψεν.

ιε'. Ὡς ἐκ Κατούρης Ἀβράμῳ γαμηθείσης τὸ τῶν Τρωγλοδυτῶν Ἀράβων[1] ἔθνος ἐγεννήθη.

ις'. Περὶ τῆς Ἀβράμου τελευτῆς.

ιζ'. Περὶ τῆς Ἰσάκου παίδων Ἡσαῦ καὶ Ἰακώβου γενέσεως καὶ διατροφῆς.

ιη'. Ἰακώβου φυγὴ εἰς τὴν Μεσοποταμίαν διὰ τὸν ἐκ τἀδελφοῦ φόβον, καὶ ὡς γήμας ἐκεῖ καὶ δώδεκα γεννήσας παῖδας πάλιν εἰς τὴν Χαναναίαν ἐπανῆλθεν.

[1] om. Lat.

ANCIENT TABLE OF CONTENTS

	SECTION	PAGE
(viii) How that, a famine prevailing in Canaan, he removed to Egypt and, having abode there some time, returned back again.	161	80
(ix) Defeat of the Sodomites, attacked by the Assyrians	171	84
(x) How Abraham marched against the Assyrians and overcame them, delivered the Sodomite prisoners and recovered the booty which the enemy had taken	176	86
(xi) How God exterminated the race of the Sodomites, being incensed with them for their sins	194	94
(xii) Concerning Ishmael, son of Abraham, and his descendants, the Arabs	[186 214	92] 106
(xiii) Concerning Isaac, the legitimate son of Abraham	222	108
(xiv) Concerning Sarra, wife of Abraham, and how she died	237	116
(xv) How from Katura's marriage with Abraham sprang the race of the Troglodyte Arabs	238	116
(xvi) Concerning the death of Abraham	256	126
(xvii) Concerning the birth and upbringing of Isaac's sons, Esau and Jacob	257	126
(xviii) Jacob's flight to Mesopotamia from fear of his brother, and how, having married there and begotten twelve sons, he returned again to Canaan	278	134

ιθ′. Ὡς Ἴσακος τελευτήσας ἐτάφη ἐν Νεβρῶνι.
Περιέχει ἡ βίβλος χρόνον ἐτῶν ὡς Ἰώσηπος ‚γη΄,
Ἑβραῖοι ‚αωοβ΄, Εὐσέβιος ‚γυνθ΄.[1]

ΒΙΒΛΙΟΝ Β

α′. Ὡς Ἡσαῦς καὶ Ἰάκωβος Ἰσάκου παῖδες ὄντες διείλοντο τὴν οἴκησιν καὶ Ἡσαῦς μὲν τὴν Ἰδουμαίαν κατέσχεν, Ἰάκωβος δὲ τὴν Χαναναίαν.

β′. Ὡς Ἰώσηπος ὁ νεώτατος τῶν Ἰακώβου παίδων ὀνειράτων αὐτῷ προδεικνύντων τὴν μέλλουσαν εὐδαιμονίαν ὑπὸ τῶν ἀδελφῶν ἐφθονήθη.

γ′. Ὡς αὐτὸς οὗτος εἰς Αἴγυπτον πραθεὶς ὑπὸ τῶν ἀδελφῶν διὰ τὸ πρὸς αὐτὸν μῖσος καὶ γενόμενος ἐπίσημος ἐκεῖ καὶ λαμπρὸς[2] τοὺς ἀδελφοὺς ἔσχεν ὑποχειρίους.

[δ′. Ἡ τοῦ πατρὸς αὐτοῦ μετὰ τῆς γενεᾶς πάσης πρὸς αὐτὸν μετάβασις διὰ τὸν γενόμενον λιμόν.

ε′. Ὅσα τοῖς Ἑβραίοις ἐν Αἰγύπτῳ συνέβη κακοπαθοῦσιν ἐπ᾽ ἔτη τετρακόσια.

ϛ′. Ὡς Μωσέως ἡγουμένου τὴν Αἴγυπτον ἐξέλιπον.

ζ′. Ἡ Μωσέως γένεσις καὶ ἀνατροφή.

---

[1] περιέχει ... γυνθ′] om. SL Lat.: περιέχει ἡ βίβλος χρόνον ἐτῶν ‚γωλγ΄ P (the opening words of this MS).
[2] λαμπρότατος RO.

[a] So the Latin version: the Greek MSS have "Nebron" (i. 170 note).

ANCIENT TABLE OF CONTENTS

	SECTION	PAGE
(xix) How Isaac died and was buried at Hebron [a]	345	164

The book covers a period of 3008 years according to Josephus, of 1872 according to the Hebrews, of 3459 according to Eusebius.

BOOK II

	SECTION	PAGE
(i) How Esau and Jacob, sons of Isaac, divided the territory, Esau occupying Idumaea and Jacob Canaan	1	168
(ii) How Joseph, the youngest of Jacob's sons, by his dreams foreshowing his future fortune, excited the envy of his brethren	9	172
(iii) How the same, being sold into Egypt by his brethren because of the hate that they bore him, and there becoming great and illustrious, had his brethren at his mercy	20	176
[(iv) The migration of his father with all his family to join him because of the famine	168	236
(v) What befell the Hebrews in Egypt, suffering affliction for 400 years	201	250
(vi) How, under the leadership of Moses, they left Egypt	[315	302]
(vii) Birth and education of Moses	205	252

483

η'. Ὡς ἡ θάλασσα τοῖς Ἑβραίοις διωκομένοις ὑπὸ τῶν Αἰγυπτίων ἀνακοπεῖσα φυγὴν δι' αὐτῆς παρέσχεν.

Περιέχει δὲ ἡ βίβλος ἔτη διακόσια εἴκοσι.][1]

ΒΙΒΛΙΟΝ Γ[2]

α'. Ὡς Μωυσῆς τὸν λαὸν ἀπ' Αἰγύπτου ἀναλαβὼν ἤγαγεν ἐπὶ τὸ Σιναῖον ὄρος πολλὰ ταλαιπωρήσαντα ἐν τῇ ὁδοιπορίᾳ.

β'. Ὡς πολεμήσαντες Ἑβραίοις Ἀμαληκῖται καὶ οἱ πέριξ ἡττήθησαν καὶ πολλὴν τῆς στρατιᾶς ἀπέβαλον.[3]

γ'. Ὅτι τὸν πενθερὸν αὐτοῦ Ἰεθὴρ Μωυσῆς παραγενόμενον πρὸς αὐτὸν εἰς τὸ Σιναῖον ἀσμένως ὑπεδέξατο.

δ'. Ὡς ὑπέθετο διατάξαι τὸν λαὸν αὐτῷ κατὰ χιλιάρχους καὶ ἑκατοντάρχους ἄτακτον ὄντα τὸ πρῶτον, καὶ ὡς[4] ἕκαστα τούτων ἐποίησε Μωυσῆς κατὰ τὴν τοῦ πενθεροῦ παραίνεσιν.

[1] The bracketed portion (in MSP) is omitted by ROL Lat.; in place of it cod. O has ὡς Ἑβραῖοι ἐδούλευσαν τοῖς Αἰγυπτίοις | ὡς Μωϋσῆς τραφεὶς ὑπὸ τῆς Φαραώθου παιδὸς καὶ μέγας γενόμενος πληγὰς προσῆξε τοῖς Αἰγυπτίοις ὑπὲρ τοῦ λαοῦ | ὡς λαβὼν τὸν λαὸν καὶ διελὼν τὴν ἐρυθρὰν αὐτοὺς διεπέρασεν.

[2] List of contents in ROSP Lat.: om. ML.

[3] Section omitted by O, with corresponding alteration of the subsequent figures: καὶ πολλὴν . . . ἀπέβαλον] et Israhelitae praedam hostium perceperunt Lat.; πολλὴν] τὴν πολλὴν SP.

[4] καὶ ὡς] quomodo Lat., beginning a new section (v), with alteration of subsequent figures.

ANCIENT TABLE OF CONTENTS

	SECTION	PAGE
(viii) How, when the Hebrews were pursued by the Egyptians, the sea recoiled and afforded them flight through itself	320	304

And the book covers 220 years.][a]

BOOK III

	SECTION	PAGE
(i) How Moses, having rescued the people from Egypt, led them to Mount Sinai, after enduring many hardships on the journey	1	320
(ii) How the Amalekites and neighbouring peoples, having made war on the Hebrews, were defeated and lost a large part of their army.	39	336
(iii) How that his father-in-law Jether[b] having come to join him at Sinai, Moses gladly received him	63	348
(iv) How he suggested to him to draw up the people, that had not been marshalled aforetime, under captains of thousands and of hundreds, and how Moses did all this in accordance with the counsel of his father-in-law	66	348

[a] The principal ancient authorities omit these last five sections. The older division, three sections only, seems to have stopped midway through the book, and to have been supplemented later; another set of "titles" for the latter half appears in one MS, as shown opposite.

[b] Jethro: Raguel in the text of *A*. iii. 63.

JEWISH ANTIQUITIES, III

ε΄. Ὡς ἀναβὰς Μωυσῆς ἐπὶ τὸ Σιναῖον ὄρος καὶ λαβὼν παρὰ τοῦ θεοῦ τοὺς νόμους τοῖς Ἑβραίοις ἔδωκεν.

ϛ΄. Περὶ τῆς σκηνῆς ἣν κατεσκεύασε Μωυσῆς ἐν τῇ ἐρημίᾳ εἰς τιμὴν τοῦ θεοῦ, ὥστε ναὸν εἶναι δοκεῖν.

ζ΄. Τίνες τε τοῖς ἱερεῦσίν εἰσιν αἱ στολαὶ καὶ ἡ τοῦ ἀρχιερέως· καὶ τῶν ἁγνειῶν οἱ τρόποι καὶ περὶ τῶν ἑορτῶν καὶ ὡς ἑκάστη τῶν ἑορτῶν[1] διατέτακται.[2]

η΄. Ὡς ἐκεῖθεν ἄρας Μωυσῆς ἤγαγε τὸν λαὸν εἰς τοὺς ὅρους τῶν Χαναναίων καὶ τοὺς κατοψομένους αὐτῶν τὴν χώραν καὶ τῶν πόλεων τὸ μέγεθος[3] ἐξαπέστειλεν.

θ΄. Ὅτι τῶν πεμφθέντων μετὰ τεσσαρακοστὴν ὑποστρεψάντων ἡμέραν καὶ λεγόντων οὐκ ἀξιομάχους αὐτοὺς ἀλλὰ τὴν τῶν Χαναναίων ὑπεξαιρόντων δύναμιν, τὸ πλῆθος ταραχθὲν καὶ πεσὸν εἰς ἀπόγνωσιν ὥρμησεν ὥστε καταλεῦσαι παρὰ μικρὸν[4] τὸν Μωυσῆν καὶ πάλιν εἰς τὴν Αἴγυπτον ὑποστρέψαι δουλεύειν διεγνωκότες.

ι΄. Καὶ ὡς ἐπὶ τούτῳ Μωυσῆς διαγανακτήσας τὸν θεὸν αὐτοῖς ἐπὶ ἔτη τεσσαράκοντα τὴν ἐπὶ τῆς ἐρημίας διατριβὴν προεῖπεν[5] ὠργίσθαι,[6] καὶ μήτ'

---

[1] ἑορτῶν] ἡμερῶν SP.
[2] καὶ τῶν ... διατέτακται] et quae purificationes et quemadmodum de festiuitatibus et singulis diebus fuerit constitutum Lat.
[3] τὸ μέγ.] magnitudines Lat.
[4] παρὰ μικρὸν om. SP.
[5] SP Lat.: προειπεῖν rell.
[6] text doubtful (iratum Lat.).

ANCIENT TABLE OF CONTENTS

	SECTION	PAGE
(v) How Moses, having gone up to Mount Sinai and received the laws from God, gave them to the Hebrews .	75	352
(vi) Concerning the tabernacle which Moses constructed in the wilderness to the honour of God, in semblance of a temple	102	364
(vii) What are the vestments of the priests and of the high priest : and the various forms of purification : and concerning the festivals and how each of the festivals [a] is ordered . . .	151 224 237	386 424 430
(viii) How Moses, removing thence, led the people to the confines of the Canaanites and sent out men to explore their country and the extent of their cities	295	460
(ix) How that the envoys returning after forty days and declaring that they were no match for the enemy and exaggerating the strength of the Canaanites, the multitude, confounded and driven to despair, set upon Moses, so that he was well-nigh stoned, having withal determined to return to Egypt to servitude	303	464
(x) And how, indignant thereat, Moses announced that God had in wrath decreed [b] for them a sojourn for forty years in the wilderness, and		

[a] Or, according to another reading, "days."
[b] Text doubtful.

εἰς Αἴγυπτον ὑποστρέφειν μήτε λαβεῖν τὴν Χαναναίαν.

Περιέχει ἡ βίβλος χρόνον ἐτῶν δύο.[1]

[1] μήτε λαβεῖν . . . δύο om. Lat.

ANCIENT TABLE OF CONTENTS

	SECTION	PAGE
that they would neither return to Egypt nor conquer Canaan	311	468

The book covers a period of two years.